KT-166-894

BRYN THOMAS was born in Zimbabwe where he grew up on a farm. Since graduating from Durham University with a degree in anthropology, travel on five continents has included a Saharan journey in a home-built kit-car, a solo 2500km cycle ride through the Andes, eight Himalayan treks and 40,000km of rail travel.

The first edition of this book, shortlisted for the Thomas Cook Travel and Guide Book Awards, was the result of several trips on the Trans-Siberian and six months in the Reading Room of the British Library. Subsequent publications have included *Trekking in the Annapurna Region*, also published by Trailblazer, and guides to India, Goa and Britain which he co-authored for Lonely Planet. In 1991 he set up Trailblazer, to produce the series of route guides for adventurous travellers that has now grown to almost 40 titles.

NICK HILL updated the Siberian section of this sixth edition of the *Trans-Siberian Handbook*. After completing a design degree at university, Nick headed off into Asia for a short trip; several fascinating years later he had crossed the continent overland four times.

Russia has long intrigued Nick and in the several trips he has now made it has proved to be among the most interesting and thought-provoking places he has visited – and the people the most friendly. He currently lives in Bangkok.

JOHN KING updated the first three sections of this book and co-ordinated the project. John grew up in the USA and was a physics teacher and an environmental consultant before hitting the road. After a three-month journey across China and Pakistan in 1987 he wrote his first guidebook: to the Karakoram Highway. Next came a two-year odyssey through the USSR resulting in the publication of a guidebook which coincided neatly with the collapse of the Union. John has also co-authored guides to Central Asia, Pakistan, the Czech & Slovak republics, Portugal and south-west France. He lives with his wife and children in south-west England.

Trans-Siberian Handbook
First edition 1988; this sixth edition November 2003, reprinted with amendments 2004

Publisher
Trailblazer Publications
The Old Manse, Tower Rd, Hindhead, Surrey, GU26 6SU, UK
Fax (+44) 01428-607571
Email: info@trailblazer-guides.com
www.trailblazer-guides.com

British Library Cataloguing in Publication Data
A catalogue record for this book is available from the British Library

ISBN 1-873756-70-4

© Ron Ziel 2003
Cover photograph

© Tatyana Pozar-Burgar 2003
Photographs opposite: pp80-1

© Nick Hill 2003
Photographs opposite: p80; p176, pp272-3, pp432-3, illustrations

© Bryn Thomas 2003
Text, maps and all other photographs

The right of Bryn Thomas to be identified as the author of this work has been asserted by him in accordance with the Copyright, Designs and Patents Act 1988

Series editor: Patricia Major
Editor: John King
Cartography: Nick Hill
Typesetting and layout: Anna Jacomb-Hood
Illustrations: Nick Hill
Index: Jane Thomas

All rights reserved. Other than brief extracts for the purposes of review no part of this publication may be produced in any form without the written consent of the publisher and copyright owner.

Important note
Every effort has been made by the author and publisher to ensure that the information contained herein is as accurate and up to date as possible. However, they are unable to accept responsibility for any inconvenience, loss or injury sustained by anyone as a result of the advice and information given in this guide.

Printed on chlorine-free paper by
D2Print (☎ +65-6295 5598), Singapore

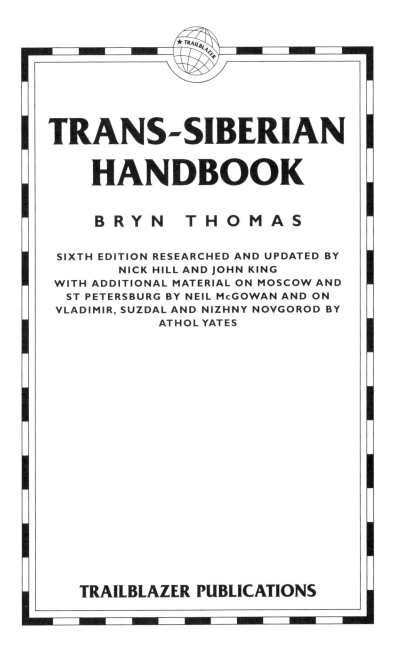

TRANS-SIBERIAN HANDBOOK

BRYN THOMAS

SIXTH EDITION RESEARCHED AND UPDATED BY
NICK HILL AND JOHN KING
WITH ADDITIONAL MATERIAL ON MOSCOW AND
ST PETERSBURG BY NEIL McGOWAN AND ON
VLADIMIR, SUZDAL AND NIZHNY NOVGOROD BY
ATHOL YATES

TRAILBLAZER PUBLICATIONS

For our long-suffering Series Editor

Acknowledgements

From Nick: Thanks to Bill and Jenny Hill and Ms Nun for their continual support and interest. I must also thank Bata, Yvgeny, Provodnik 87, Sergei in Tomsk, the administrator in Novosibirsk railway station, Lena Davigova from Kazan, Vadim and Julia, Oleg 'small drink' Yelokhin, Marina and Nara (again), Provodnitsa 250, the *militsia* in Chita, Maxim's brother from Belogorsk, Luda and Lena from Spassk, Duncan Taylor, Provodnik 185 and to the countless number of people who went out of their way to help me but whose names I never knew. Thanks also to Bryn and John.

From John: My thanks to Moscow resident Neil McGowan for generously sharing a broad knowledge of his adopted city. Another invaluable Moscow helper was Olga Belnik of Galileo-Rus. Out of Beijing came ready help on a great many occasions from Andy Jones of Monkey Business. Thanks also to Jan Wigsten of Eco Tours in Ulan Bator for the answers to Mongolia questions, and to Jim Gill of Travel Directors in Perth. Finally, my hat is off to mapmaker/researcher Nick Hill for his patience, cheer and skill.

From Bryn: I am greatly indebted to the numerous people who have helped me with the research of this project since the publication in 1988 of what was the first book I had ever written. I should like to thank Jane Thomas not only for the current comprehensive index but also for her extensive work in compiling the original strip maps and town plans. Nick Hill has built on her foundations with consummate skill; I'm grateful to him for the digitized maps, his excellent line drawings and also for all his work as researcher and updater of the Siberia section. Thanks also to John King for returning to Russia to update the first three sections of the book and for his thorough and perceptive editing of the text – Patricia Major is a hard act to follow.

Thanks to Neil McGowan for researching and updating the Moscow and St Petersburg sections; Tatyana Pozar-Burgar for photographs; Athol Yates for Vladimir, Suzdal and Nizhny Novgorod, the accompanying railway text, the carriage plan and all his and Tatyana's work on the fourth edition of the book; Athol Yates and Nicholas Zvegintzov for the railway dictionary, Dominic Streatfeild-James who updated the third edition (and whose wry comments survive); Doug Streatfeild-James for the Chinese words and phrases section; Neil Taylor (Regent Holidays) for general tips and advice; Ron Ziel for the cover photograph; and Corinne Sinclair for Chinese language skills. I am particularly grateful to Anna Jacomb-Hood for researching and updating Part 6, for typesetting and laydown and for so much help in other ways with the production of the book.

Among the readers who wrote: thanks to Jay Gary Finkelstein (USA), Reijo Härkönen (Finland), James Boyd (Ireland), Jakub Pilch (Poland), Ian Whitby (UK), Oded Paporisch (Israel), Felicity Wilcox (UK), Glenn Harvey (Australia), Elizabeth Watson (UK), Matz Lonnedal Risberg (Norway), Edward Wilson (UK), Yiannis Gikas (Greece), Andrew Wingham (UK), Terry Nakazono (USA), Dominic Streatfeild-James (UK), Dr Malcolm Hannan (UK), Dmitri Gorokhov (Russia), Stephen McLaughlin (UK), Laura Hamelen (UK), Angela Hollingsworth (UK), Howard Dymock (UK), John Gothard (UK), Walter Spoerle (Germany), Will Harrison-Cripps (UK), Gordon Gill (USA), Claudia Gamperle (Switzerland), Katya Voronicheva (Russia), Alexander Hartig, Andrea Marcialis (Italy), Diana Valia Chen and Andrew van der Westhuyzen (Australia), Dr Mark Krebs, Emmanuel du Teilhet (France), Benedikt Jaeger (Germany), Marcus Patzig (Germany), Valeria Kuteeva (Russia), Col Francis and Christine Emmorey (UK), Lawrence Cotter (USA), Emmy Gengler (USA), Helen Revell, Karin MacArthur (Australia), Mark Taylor (UK), Philip Robinson (UK, for the aside on Siberian post past), Heather Oxley (UK), Asger Christiansen (Denmark), Laurens den Dulk (Netherlands), Nancy Scarth (Canada), Phil Davies (UK), Malcolm Carroll (UK), Andrew Young (UK).

Quotations used in Part 5 are from the *Guide to the Great Siberian Railway 1900*. Background information for Vladimir, Suzdal and Nizhny Novogorod was written by Athol Yates and updated from material originally published in *Russia by Rail* (Bradt Travel Guides).

A note on prices and a request

In this guide most prices are given in dollars since their value appears to remain reliably constant from year to year: convert at the current exchange rate for the rouble price. Note that although US$ are shown here only roubles are accepted in Russia.

The author and publisher have tried to ensure that this guide is as accurate and up to date as possible but things change quickly in Russia. If you notice any changes or omissions please write to Bryn Thomas at Trailblazer (address on p2) or email him (bryn.thomas @trailblazer-guides.com). A free copy of the next edition will be sent to persons making a significant contribution.

Cover photograph: A rare picture, taken in the early 1970s, of the Trans-Siberian being hauled by a steam engine (© Ron Ziel 2003).

CONTENTS

PART 4: CITY GUIDES AND PLANS

PART 5: ROUTE GUIDES AND MAPS

PART 6: DESTINATIONS AND DEPARTURES

APPENDICES

INDEX

INTRODUCTION

There can be few people who have not, at some time in their lives, wondered what it must be like to travel on the Trans-Siberian Railway – to cross Russia and the wild forests and steppes of Siberia on the world's longest railway journey. The distances spanned by this famous line are immense: almost 6000 miles (a seven-day journey) between Moscow and the Pacific port of Vladivostok (for boat connections to Japan) and just under 5000 miles (five days) between Moscow and Beijing.

Ever since a rail service linking Europe with the Far East was established at the turn of the century, foreign travellers and adventurers have been drawn to this great journey. Most of the early travellers crossed Siberia in the comfort of the carriages of the Belgian Wagon Lits company, which were as luxurious as those of the Venice-Simplon Orient Express of today. Things changed somewhat after the Russian Revolution in 1917 and it became increasingly difficult for foreigners to obtain permits for Siberia. It was not until the 1960s that the situation improved and Westerners began to use the railway again for getting to Japan, taking the boat from Nakhodka (it now leaves from Vladivostok) for the last part of the journey. In the early 1980s, travel restrictions for foreigners visiting China were eased and since then many people have found the Trans-Siberian a cheap and interesting way to get to or from both the Middle Kingdom and Mongolia.

In this jet age, the great advantage of going by rail is that it allows passengers to absorb something of the ethos of the country through which they are travelling: on a journey on this train you are guaranteed to meet local people for this is no 'tourist special' but a working service; you may find yourself draining a bottle of vodka with a Russian soldier, discussing politics with a Chinese academic or drinking Russian champagne with a Mongolian trader.

Now a democracy with a market economy, Russia is undergoing phenomenal changes after decades of stagnation. While the ending of the Cold War may have removed some of the mystique of travelling in the former USSR, the fact that Russia is now much more accessible means that there are new travel opportunities right across the country. With foreigners no longer obliged to stay in overpriced Intourist hotels, visiting the country is cheaper now than ever before.

Although travel in Siberia today presents few of the dangers and difficulties that it did earlier this century, a journey on the Trans-Siberian still demands a considerable amount of planning and preparation. The aim of this guide is to help you cut through the red tape when arranging the trip, to give background information on Russia and Siberia and to provide a kilometre-by-kilometre guide to the entire route of the greatest rail adventure – the Trans-Siberian.

Routes and costs

'Best of all, he would tell me of the great train that ran across half the world ... He held me enthralled then, and today, a life-time later, the spell still holds. He told me the train's history, its beginnings ... how a Tzar had said, 'Let the Railway be built!' And it was ... For me, nothing was ever the same again. I had fallen in love with the Traveller's travels. Gradually, I became possessed by love of a horizon and a train which would take me there ...'

Lesley Blanch *Journey into the Mind's Eye*

ROUTE OPTIONS

Travellers crossing Siberia have a choice of three main routes: the Trans-Siberian, Trans-Manchurian and Trans-Mongolian. The Trans-Siberian is the most expensive route as it crosses the entire length of Siberia to the Pacific terminus at Vladivostok. The Trans-Manchurian travels through most of Siberia before turning south through Manchuria and ending in Beijing. The Trans-Mongolian also terminates in Beijing but travels via Mongolia which gives you the chance to stop off in Ulan Bator.

> ❏ **The Longest Journey**
> If it's a long-distance rail-travel record you're after, begin your journey in Vila Real de Santo António in southern Portugal, cross Europe to Moscow, take the Trans-Mongolian route from there to Beijing and continue to Ho Chi Minh City (Saigon) in Vietnam – a journey of 17,852km (11,155 miles).

If you want to travel on to Japan after your trip you have several options. From Vladivostok there are ferries (mid-June to December) and flights. There are also cheaper ferry services from various Chinese ports including Shanghai, Tianjin and Qingdao, all of them within easy reach of Beijing.

Trans-Manchurian and Trans-Mongolian travellers can continue from Beijing by train round China, which has an extensive rail system and also direct rail links into Vietnam.

COSTS

Overall costs

How much you pay for a trip on the world's longest railway line depends on the level of comfort you demand, the number of stops you wish to make along the way and the amount of time you're prepared to put into getting hold of a budget ticket.

Although the cheapest tickets for rail travel between Moscow and Beijing (and purchased in these cities) currently cost around US$220 (£175), this does not reflect what you'll end up paying for your trip. Among other big costs to factor in are transport to your departure point, transport back at the end of your journey, accommodation in Moscow, Beijing and any stopover towns, and of course food. If you want to buy your own tickets en route you must budget for the extra time that this will take. In this light the independent package deals offered by many travel agents can be better value than they might appear. Packages on the Trans-Siberian between Moscow and Beijing, including transfers and one night's accommodation in Moscow, start at about £400/US$650.

Single flights from London cost around £150 to Moscow or £230 to Beijing. The cheapest fully inclusive Trans-Siberian holidays cost from around £1300 including flights to and from London.

From New York, one-way flights cost around US$500-700 to Moscow or US$500-800 to Beijing, depending on the season. The cheapest fully inclusive Trans-Siberian holidays cost from around US$2200 per person in high season, including flights to and from New York.

From Australia, single flights cost around A$1200 to Beijing or A$1900-2400 to Moscow, depending on the season. The cheapest fully-inclusive Trans-Manchurian trip costs around A$3040 per person including two nights in Moscow. A 10-day Vladivostok to Moscow budget package costs from about A$3220 with flights.

If a two-week guided rail tour from Moscow to Vladivostok with comfortable accommodation in private saloon cars pulled partly by old steam locomotives is more your idea of travelling then be prepared to part with around US$5000 (see Trans-Siberian Express Company, p25).

Travel in Russia – better value, fewer restrictions

Travel in Russia is much better value and far less restricted than it was in the communist era. It is now easier to get a visa (see p19) and relatively easy to travel independently. You are no longer obliged to deal with Intourist and you needn't pre-book hotel rooms. Train tickets are easy to buy although long-distance tickets can still be problematic in the summer season.

Not the Trans-Siberian Express!

Travel writers often wax lyrical about the fabled 'Trans-Siberian Express' but in fact no regular train service of that name exists. While the British generally refer to their trains by a time (eg, 'the 10.35 to Clapham'), the Russians and Chinese identify theirs by a number (eg, 'Train No 3' from Beijing to Moscow). As in other countries a few crack services have been singled out and given names, but 'Trans-Siberian Express' is not among them. 'Trans-Siberian', 'Trans-Mongolian' and 'Trans-Manchurian' are, however, common terms for the main **routes** across Siberia and between Moscow and Beijing.

The train which runs all the way from Moscow to Vladivostok is the No 2, and going in the other direction it's the No 1; both services are also called the 'Rossiya'. The No 20 covers the full Trans-Manchurian route from Moscow to Beijing, while in the other direction it's the No 19; these are both called the 'Vostok'. Trains on the Trans-Mongolian route between Moscow and Beijing, and most other long-distance services, are identified only by number.

In Soviet times all travel arrangements for foreigners were handled by the monolithic organizations of Intourist (general travel), Sputnik (youth travel) and CCTE (business travel). All charged monopoly prices, and travellers' options were restricted. These organizations have now been broken up and the travel market has opened up. You'll still see plenty of Intourist hotels and Intourist travel desks, but the hotels are gradually being displaced, at least at the upper end, by foreign-run establishments, and the travel desks by lean young Russian and foreign travel agencies.

Accommodation costs

The price and value of accommodation in Russia varies wildly. A few hotels continue to charge foreign visitors more than they charge Russians, so that what may be excellent value to a local is absurdly bad value for you. This book notes 'foreigner' prices wherever this is the case, though you may be able to do better on the spot. You will almost certainly be offered the most expensive room first, so get in the habit of asking for something cheaper.

Moscow and St Petersburg are the only places with genuinely five-star hotels (US$350/£220 or more per night) although a number of Trans-Siberian

---

What if I don't want to do it all by train?
Of course you needn't sit in a train for a week to see Siberia or Mongolia. It's quite feasible to fly to or from an intermediate point and travel only part of the way by rail. During the 2003 SARS outbreak in China (see p50), for example, some east-bound travellers took Trans-Siberian services only as far as Ulan Bator, then flew on to Beijing and directly out of China.

Major airports along the Trans-Siberian which have nonstop air connections with Moscow, Beijing or other international hubs include **Yekaterinburg** (Moscow daily from US$120, Frankfurt three times weekly, Prague and Cologne weekly), **Novosibirsk** (Moscow daily from US$140, Frankfurt and Hanover almost daily in summer from US$440, Beijing via Shenyang three times weekly from US$370, Seoul weekly from US$500), **Irkutsk** (Moscow daily from US$270, Niigata weekly from US$480) and **Ulan Bator** (Moscow several times weekly from US$650, Beijing almost daily from US$300, Tokyo and Seoul several times weekly). Outbound air tickets are generally easy to buy a few days ahead (but see the following note about the Nadaam Festival).

Trans-Siberian specialist agencies such as those listed on pp24-40 can arrange rail tickets for specific segments, although buying these on arrival is quite feasible and gives you more flexibility to alter your plans. You needn't book more than a few days ahead for small segments but you may need more time for longer ones such as Irkutsk–Moscow. Sleeping berths may be scarce on services not originating in your proposed departure town. From October to April it's easy to book almost any train at short notice.

Possibilities include the No 5/6 Ulan Bator–Moscow, No 9/10 Irkutsk–Moscow, No 23/24 Beijing–Ulan Bator, No 25/26 Novosibirsk–Moscow and No 263/264 Ulan Bator–Irkutsk. Certain services and times get heavily booked – eg, those to and from Ulan Bator around the time of Mongolia's Nadaam Festival in mid-July.

cities, including Khabarovsk and Vladivostok, have good four-star places. Hotel prices in Moscow and St Petersburg are higher than anywhere else in the country.

Most visitors still stay in former Intourist hotels, paying US$40-100/£25-60 for a single or US$50-130/£30-80 for a double with attached bathroom. Independent travellers who search out basic rooms in cheaper hotels can expect to pay US$10-40/£6-25 for a single or US$15-50/£10-30 for a double with attached bathroom. Breakfast is sometimes included in the price.

Hostels and guest-houses have sprung up in Moscow, St Petersburg and Irkutsk and are opening in other places, charging about US$15-30/£10-20 for bed and breakfast. Homestays are an option available in most larger Trans-Siberian towns, at about US$25-40/£20-30 per person per night including some or all meals.

For more information on accommodation see p65.

Train classes and prices

Most Trans-Siberian train carriages intended for foreigners are classed as either *kupé* (coupé; also called 2nd, hard or tourist class), with four-berth closed compartments; or *SV* (also called 1st or soft class), with comfortable two-berth compartments, sometimes with washbasins.

On Trans-Mongolian trains No 3/4, however, SV compartments are four-berth and identical in layout to all other services' kupé compartments except a bit wider, so they are poor value. But these trains also have an additional '*de luxe 1st*' class, whose carpeted two-berth compartments have armchairs and attached bathrooms, and are the only ones with showers.

Compartments are not single sex. Foreigners may find themselves sharing with other foreigners if they've booked through an agency that deals mainly with non-Russians. For further details on train classes see p70.

Approximate sample prices (including any booking fees) are shown below for a non-stop, no-frills, single (one-way) journey on each of the main routes across Siberia. They range from the cheapest ticket bought over the counter in Moscow or Beijing to those offered by Western travel agents.

● **Trans-Siberian route** (Moscow–Vladivostok): kupé (2nd) US$75-350/£60-275; SV (1st) US$265-900/£210-700.
● **Trans-Manchurian route** (Moscow–Beijing): kupé (2nd) US$160-300/£125-250; SV (1st) US$255-450/£200-350.
● **Trans-Mongolian route** (Moscow–Beijing): kupé (2nd) US$135-300/£105-250; SV (1st) US$230-400/£180-320; deluxe 1st class US$450-650/£350-500

BREAKING YOUR JOURNEY

Most people will want to break their journey and stop off along the way. This is a good idea not only for the chance to stretch your legs and have a shower but also because some of the places you pass through are well worth exploring. You

❏ INTERNET RESOURCES

Many travel agents have their own Web sites, some with useful links; see pp24-40. For some sites with timetable and related information, see Appendix B (Timetables).

Railway Ring – 🖥 parovoz.com/cgi-bin/rrr.cgi
A venerable site for Russian rail fanatics, with an English version and exhaustive links to other sites on railways in Russia, the Baltic States and elsewhere in the CIS.

Library of Congress Russian Info – 🖥 lcweb2.loc.gov/frd/cs/rutoc.html
In-depth Russian history, culture, religion, politics etc: the on-line version of a book published by the LOC under its Country Studies/Area Handbook Program (1996).

Russian Cities On The Web – 🖥 www.city.ru/
A huge series of links to Web sites about individual cities in Russia.

Yahoo! Russia News – 🖥 fullcoverage.yahoo.com/full_coverage/world/russia/
Round-up of current news stories about Russia, culled from the main news-service websites, both Western and Russian.

Russia Today – 🖥 www.russiatoday.com/
An excellent round-up of Russian news and analysis.

Dazhdbog's Grandchildren – 🖥 www.ibiblio.org/sergei/
Russian folklore, traditions, culture, myths; many useful links too.

Oyubilig's Great Mongol Homepage – 🖥 www.mongols.com
Mongolian traditions, folklore, history and culture.

The Buryatia Page – 🖥 www.geocities.com/Athens/Oracle/8226/index.html
A wide-ranging site on Buryat shamanism, folklore, history, and poetry, with very good links.

The Red Book – 🖥 www.eki.ee/books/redbook/foreword.shtml
Scholarly, sobering research (1991) on the ethnic minority communities of the ex-USSR, with lots about 'endangered' Siberian native peoples.

Trans-Siberian Web Encyclopedia – 🖥 www.transsib.ru/eng/
Lots of Trans-Sib memorabilia, pictures, city notes, chat and links.

Clickable Trans-Sib picture collection – 🖥 www.etrema.com/east2000/
You can even check out what the train loos look like on this site.

Jaap Hoogenboom's Trans-Sib Site
🖥 www.ibmail.nl/~hoogboom/english/index.html
A personal trans-Mongolian travelogue with lots of great pictures.

Famous Russian Paintings – 🖥 www.museum.ru/museum/paintings
Browse this on-line gallery or go to the (Russian-only) homepage for a general look at what's on offer from the Russian Museum.

Russian Cuisine – 🖥 www.ruscuisine.com/

Cyrillic-English Language Support
🖥 www.russialink.org.uk/keyboard/russify.htm
Teach your computer to display Russian (Cyrillic) fonts.

won't learn much about life in Siberia by looking through a train window, especially if you're sharing a compartment with other foreigners. With the exception of a few military centres, all cities on the Trans-Siberian can be visited. If you're booking through an agency, plan carefully: once you have started on your trip, it's too late to change your itinerary. But if you travel independently you can just buy tickets as you go along, and stop off whenever and wherever you like.

If your trip starts in **Moscow** (see p152) it's usually necessary to spend a night there, although you'd need several days to see the main sights. A side-trip to **St Petersburg** (p130) is highly recommended. At the other end, it's certainly worth spending several days in **Beijing** (p315).

In between there's the 'Golden Ring' city of **Nizhny Novgorod** (p206) and historically rich **Yekaterinburg** (p214). **Novosibirsk** (p230) is the sprawling capital of Western Siberia, and **Krasnoyarsk** (p239) is among the region's most pleasantly-situated cities. **Irkutsk** (p245), capital of Eastern Siberia, is 64km from beautiful Lake Baikal, the world's deepest freshwater lake; a stay beside the lake at **Listvyanka** (p258) is highly recommended. **Ulan Ude** (p266) is worth a stop for the Buddhist monastery nearby, and **Khabarovsk** (p278) is surprisingly pleasant. **Vladivostok** (p287), the brawny home port of Russia's Pacific Fleet, is the eastern railway terminus. Also recommended for those headed to Beijing is a visit to **Ulan Bator** (p297), the capital of Mongolia. Irkutsk and Ulan Bator are the most popular stopovers for Trans-Siberian travellers.

When to go

The mode of life which the long dark nights of winter induce, the contrivances of man in his struggle with the climate, the dormant aspect of nature with its thick coverage of dazzling snow and its ice-bound lakes now bearing horses and the heaviest burdens where ships floated and waves rolled, perhaps only a fortnight ago: – all these scenes and peculiar phases of life render a journey to Russia very interesting in winter.
Murray's Handbook for Travellers in Russia, Poland and Finland (1865)

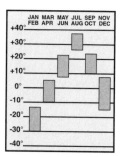

Irkutsk – temperature (average max/min °C)

For most people 'Siberia' evokes a picture of snowy scenes from the film *Dr Zhivago* and if they are not to be disappointed, then winter is probably the best time to go. It is, after all, the most Russian of seasons, a time of fur coats, sleigh-rides and chilled vodka. In sub-zero temperatures, with the bare birch and fir trees encased in ice, Siberia looks as one imagines it ought to – a barren, desolate wasteland (the train, however, is well heated). Russian cities, too, look best and feel most 'Russian' under

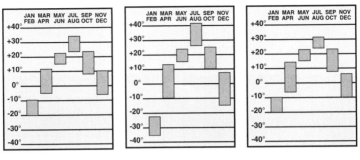

Moscow – temperature (average max/min °C)   **Ulan Bator – temperature (average max/min °C)**   **Beijing – temperature (average max/min °C)**

a layer of snow. St Petersburg with its brightly painted Classical architecture is far more attractive in the winter months when the weather is crisp and skies clear. But if you want to spend time in any Siberian city you'll find it more enjoyable to go in late spring, summer or autumn, when there is more to do.

In Siberia the heaviest snowfalls and coldest temperatures – as low as minus 40°C (minus 40°F) in Krasnoyarsk and some other towns the train passes through – occur in December and January. From late January to early April the weather is generally cold and clear. Spring comes late. In July and August it is warm enough for an invigorating dip in Lake Baikal. The birch and aspen provide a beautiful autumnal display in September and October.

In Moscow the average temperature is 17°C (63°F) in summer and minus 9°C (+16°F) during the winter; there are occasional heavy summer showers.

Tourist season

The tourist season runs from May through September, peaking from mid-July to early September. In the low season, between October and April, some companies offer discounts on tours; you'll also find it much easier to get a booking for the train at short notice at this time. During the summer it can be difficult to get a place on the popular Moscow–Beijing route without planning several weeks ahead.

❏ **Winter travel**
'I've just got back from a round-the-world journey that began with a trip on the Trans-Siberian Railway. We knew what to look out for, were informed about what we were seeing and, to a certain extent, had an idea of what to expect. Nothing, though, could really prepare one for the pleasure of seeing acres of snow, the tracks going seemingly nowhere, the groups of trees, the delicate reeds and huge frozen rivers and lakes'.   **Elizabeth Watson** (UK)

Bookings and visas

ORGANIZED TOURS OR INDIVIDUAL ITINERARIES?

Note that regulations governing the issuing of Russian visas are particularly susceptible to change. Check the latest situation with your embassy or through the organizations listed on pp19-20.

Group tours

Many visitors come to Russia in organized groups. This is still how the Russian authorities would prefer you to travel: groups are easier to control and tend to spend more money than itinerant backpackers. Going with a tour group certainly takes much of the hassle out of the experience, but it also means there isn't much room for doing your own thing. Most tours are accompanied by an English-speaking guide from the moment you set foot in the country until the moment you leave. See pp24-40 for information on tour companies.

Semi-independent travel

This is the easiest and most popular way for foreigners to travel on the Trans-Siberian. A specialist agency makes all accommodation and train bookings (with or without stops along the way), providing you in the process with the documentation needed for obtaining a Russian tourist visa. You choose departure dates and number and length of stops, in effect designing your own trip. Once in Russia you're usually on your own, although some agencies offer guides to meet you at the station and help you organize your time in stopover cities. You'll often get good quality accommodation in Moscow as part of the deal. Numerous travel agents in the West can make these arrangements (see pp24-40), or you can deal directly with locally-based Trans-Siberian specialists such as the St Petersburg International Hostel (see p19) or The Russia Experience (see p19) in Moscow, or Monkey Business in Beijing (see p38).

Fully independent travel

Getting a tourist visa which allows you to wander around freely in Russia is no longer difficult. Along with your visa application you must present confirmation of hotel bookings, furnished by a registered Russian tourist organization. Various hotels and agencies can do this for you (see p19). Some will furnish documentation of accommodation for the duration of your visa, in exchange for your booking only your first night's stay with them. Once you have your visa, you are free to travel wherever you want, irrespective of what the documentation says (although this situation is under official scrutiny and may change).

Although few Russians outside the largest cities speak English and tourist infrastructure is limited, this shouldn't put you off. Most Russians are friendly and generous, and learning a bit of basic Russian before you go will help communication. Travelling independently is not difficult and is the best way to gain an insight into the 'real' Russia. Nevertheless many Russians seem baffled by the notion of making up your itinerary as you go along!

ROUTE PLANNING

Main services

The table below is a summary of some major Siberian train services. For detailed timetables (updated with each reprint of this book) and other details see pp418-26 but note that timetables are subject to change, nowhere more so than in this part of the world. There may be occasional one-hour variations on account of differences between countries in implementing Daylight Savings Time. Local times are given below, but note that official Russian timetables use Moscow Time only.

The trains which run across Siberia are not tourist specials but working services used by local people, and they're very popular. On most routes they run to capacity, especially in summer (when additional services may be laid on). Buying tickets as you go along shouldn't be too difficult as Russians usually seem to leave it to the last minute. If you book a couple of days before you want to travel, you'll probably get what you want on the smaller sections, but you'll need more time if you want a ticket for the whole route or for a longer section such as Irkutsk–Moscow.

Train	Leaves	on	at	Arrives	on	at
1, *Rossiya*	Vladivostok	Even-no days	17.50	Moscow	Day 7	16.42
2, *Rossiya*	Moscow	Odd-no days	17.16	Vladivostok	Day 8	05.35
3 (Mongolia)	Beijing	Wed	07:40	Moscow	Mon	14:20
4 (Mongolia)	Moscow	Tue	22.05	Beijing	Mon	14.30
5	Ulan Bator	Tue, Fri	13:50	Moscow	Sat, Tue	14:20
6	Moscow	Wed, Thu	22.05	Ulan Bator	Mon, Tue	07.35
9, *Baikal*	Irkutsk	Even-no days	16.35	Moscow	Day 4	16.52
10, *Baikal*	Moscow	Odd-no days	23.30	Irkutsk	Day 5	09.06
19, *Vostok* (Manchuria)	Beijing	Sat	22.50	Moscow	Fri	17.55
20, *Vostok* (Manchuria)	Moscow	Fri	23:58	Beijing	Fri	05:20
23*	Beijing	Tue	07:40	Ulan Bator	Wed	13:20
24*	Ulan Bator	Thu	08.05	Beijing	Fri	14.30
263	Ulan Bator	Daily	20.45	Irkutsk	Day 3	08:30
264	Irkutsk	Daily	20.30	Ulan Bator	Day 3	06.20

additional service in summer only, dep Beijing (No 23) Mon, Ulan Bator (No 24) Sat

Moscow to Vladivostok

There are many trains on the line between Moscow and Vladivostok, but the famous No 1/2 *Rossiya* train is the top choice for service. Other very good trains which cover shorter segments include the No 9/10 *Baikal* between Moscow and Irkutsk; these increase your options if you are making stopovers along the way.

There are weekly ferries from Vladivostok to Japan in the summer months (see p296) but increasing numbers of travellers are opting for the cheaper alternative of ferry crossings to Japan from various ports in China (see p36).

Moscow to Beijing: Trans-Manchurian or Trans-Mongolian?

You have two route choices between Moscow and Beijing: the Trans-Mongolian route via Ulan Bator in Mongolia, and the Trans-Manchurian route via Harbin in China. There are advantages and disadvantages with each.

The Trans-Manchurian Moscow–Beijing train is the No 19/20 *Vostok*. This currently departs from Beijing at a more civilized time (in the evening) than the Trans-Mongolian (crack of dawn) but costs a bit more. Moscow departure is in the evening for both routes.

The Trans-Mongolian Moscow–Beijing service is the No 3/4, although there are additional, shorter-distance options including the No 23/24 (Beijing–Ulan Bator) and No 263/264 (Irkutsk–Ulan Bator). Only the No 3/4 offers de luxe 1st class carriages (see p118), although travellers who opt for kupé will find these carriages identical on both routes. You need a Mongolian transit visa on this route, even if you do not stop along the way. The Trans-Mongolian journey takes about 12 hours less than the Trans-Manchurian.

Despite long-standing Trans-Siberian lore, there's no difference between the restaurant cars on the two routes as these are supplied by the country through which you're travelling.

Both trains have weekly departures in each direction. Summer is the most difficult time to book a place on long-distance trains on either route, so make arrangements several months in advance.

Stopping off in Mongolia

If you're taking the Trans-Mongolian route, breaking your journey in Ulan Bator (see p297) is highly recommended. It's easy to organize either through a specialist agency or independently.

A related option, though not in Mongolia, is a stop at Hohhot (Huhehot) in China's Inner Mongolia province, where you'll find a similar rural Mongolian Buddhist culture and similar grassland tours.

Side trips

There are numerous possibilities for side trips by rail, including on the **Siberian BAM Railway** (from Tayshet) and the **Turksib Railway** (from Novosibirsk), with links via the Turksib to the **Kazakhstan–China Railway**. See pp127-9 for more on all these lines.

From **Blagoveshchensk** (see p376), on a spur off the Moscow–Vladivostok line at Belogorsk, you can cross the Amur River by boat to Heihe in China. With onward connections via Harbin, this little-known alternative to the Trans-Manchurian line is actually the cheapest land route from Moscow to Beijing at present.

A branch line runs from Sibirtsevo, near Vladivostok, via Ussurisk to Pyongyang in **North Korea**, although at the moment such a journey is hard to organize. Russia is keen to foster the extension of this line into South Korea and its deep-water port at Pusan, tying the Trans-Siberian into a potentially very profitable Asia–Europe network.

From Beijing it's easy to continue by rail into **Vietnam**, a three-night journey.

VISAS

Visas are required by most foreigners visiting Russia, Mongolia and China. Getting a Russian visa is not always straightforward (largely because of the need to obtain an invitation and confirm your accommodation). It's simple to get a Chinese visa from most embassies, and relatively easy to get a Mongolian visa. Visa regulations change regularly, and even border guards and local police officials don't always know the latest. Check with travel agents or embassies.

You'll always need to show your visa when staying at a hotel and whenever you buy a rail ticket.

Russia visa invitations

To get a visa to Russia, you must first obtain an invitation or equivalent document (*podtverzhdenie* подтверждение) confirming your accommodation details while in Russia, plus one or more vouchers (*order* ордер) confirming payment for this accommodation. These documents may only be issued by travel agencies, hotels or other organizations registered to do so with the Russian Ministry of the Interior (a responsibility recently transferred from the Ministry of Foreign Affairs). The documents must all state your passport details, itinerary and duration of stay, along with the inviting organization's address and registration number. If you are going on a package tour your travel agent will organize everything and you will see little of this paperwork.

Although an itinerary must be specified, the visa itself no longer lists all your proposed destinations (as it did in Soviet days), making it far easier for independent travellers to visit places on the spur of the moment. Most travel companies will issue an invitation/confirmation only for the days for which you have paid to stay with them, but some will confirm accommodation for the duration of your visa in exchange for your booking just your first night's stay with them, leaving you free to go where you like after that (this situation, however, was under review at the time of writing and is subject to change).

Costs for documentation in support of a one-month tourist visa (**not** for the visa itself, although the price may include registration of the visa upon arrival: see p22) are approximately US$25-50/£20-40 (single entry) or US$40-65/£30-50 (double entry). Support for a three-month visa costs about US$10-15/£8-12 more. Costs in support of multiple-entry and/or business visas will be higher still.

Following are some trustworthy companies which are either Russia-based or have offices in Russia, and which can issue you with an invitation (although terms and conditions may vary). Most will accept credit cards for online payment.

● **St Petersburg International Hostel** (☎ +7-812-329 8018, 🖹 +7-812-329 8019, 🖳 www.ryh.ru), ul 3rd Sovietskaya 28, St Petersburg 193036, Russia, are recommended.

● **The Russia Experience** (UK ☎ 020-8566 8846, 🖹 020-8566 8843, 🖳 www.trans-siberian.co.uk), Research House, Fraser Rd, Perivale, Middlesex UB6 7AQ, UK.

- **ATH** (Andrew's Travel House; UK ☎ 020-7727 2838, 🖹 020-7727 2848, 🖳 www.andrews-consulting.com), 23 Pembridge Square, London W2 4DR, UK. Their main office (☎ +7-095-916 9898, 🖹 +7-095-916 9828, 🖳 moscow @ath.ru) is at ul Volkhonka 18/2, Moscow.
- **Host Families Association** (HOFA; ☎t/🖹 +7-812-275 1992, mobile ☎ +7-911-914 2762, 🖳 www.hofa.us), ul Tavricheskaya 5/25, St Petersburg 193015, Russia. This is a network of academic and professional families offering home-stays, flat rental and budget hotels in some 60 Russian cities and elsewhere in the CIS. See p66 for further details.
- **Russia-Rail.com** (Passport Travel; ☎ +61-3-9867 3888, 🖹 +61-3-9867 1055, 🖳 passport@travelcentre.com.au, www.russia-rail.com), Suite 11, 401 St Kilda Rd, Melbourne, Victoria 3004, Australia.
- **G&R International** (☎ +7-095-374 5731, 🖹 +7-095-374 7506, 🖳 grtour @online.ru, www.hostels.ru), Block 6, Office 40, Institute of Youth, ul Yunosti 5/1, Moscow, Russia 111395. Parent company of G&R Hostel Asia in Moscow (see p169 and p170).
- **Infinity Travel** (visa department ☎ +7-095-234 6999, 🖹 +7-095-234 6556, 🖳 www.infinity.ru), Komsomolsky prospekt 13, Moscow 119146. Associated with Travellers Guest House in Moscow (see p170).
- **Hostel Sherstone** (☎/🖹 +7-095-797 8075, 🖳 sherstone@mail.ru, www.sher-stone.ru), Gostinichny proezd 8, korpus 1, room 324, Moscow, Russia 127106.
- **Hostel Tramp** (☎ +7-095-187 5433, ☎/🖹 +7-095-551 2876, 🖳 www.hostel ling.ru), Room 524, building 7, Hotel Turist, Selskokhozyaystvennaya ul 17/2, Moscow 129226.
- **Russian Visa Express** (☎ +7-095-955 4254, ☎/🖹 +7-095-955 4279, 🖳 www.visaru.com), Room 609, Leninsky pr 29, Moscow 117912.

Russian visa

In Cold-War days many Western countries frowned on those who visited the Soviet Union, so Soviet visas took the form of a separate, passport-sized document. A Russian visa is now a one-page form stuck directly into your passport, containing your passport information, entry and exit dates, and the name and registration of the organization that has invited you.

Application is normally made at the nearest Russian embassy or consulate. In addition to a completed visa application form you will be asked for your passport (preferably a 10-year passport, in good condition and with two facing blank pages), invitation/confirmation document, accommodation voucher(s), one to three passport-sized photos and the visa fee. Some embassies will accept faxed copies of visa-support documents, but not all, so check before you apply and don't take your 'host's' word on this.

Any foreigner visiting Russia for more than three months requires a doctor's certification that they are not HIV-positive, a requirement introduced to placate anti-West forces in Russia.

The visa fee depends on where you apply (and sometimes on your nationality), the type and duration of the visa, and how quickly you want it. For most nationalities a one-month, single-entry tourist visa delivered in one to two weeks costs US$40-60/£30-50, although you can usually get faster service by paying more.

● **Tourist visa** There are one-month and three-month tourist visas, and single-entry and double-entry versions. A tourist visa requires an invitation and a hotel booking, but to secure the invitation this may be for as little as just one night.

● **Business visa** A business visa allows you to stay for up to a year, but requires an invitation from a registered Russian business. In the past many tourists have managed to get business visas but there is growing official pressure for a better-documented connection between visitor and inviting organization, and the use of business visas for tourism looks increasingly problematic.

● **Private visa** This visa is for foreigners who are invited by Russian friends or relatives, but it can take three months or more to get. The process involves your Russian friend getting an authorization (*izveshchenia* извещение) from their home-town OViR/PVU (Passport & Visa Unit) office and mailing it to you. You must then take it to your Russian embassy, which confirms it with OViR/PVU back in Russia. You can get a private visa for a stay of up to three months, though extensions are common. Non-Russian friends in Russia cannot invite you.

● **Transit visa** Transit visas are normally given only to those who are in transit through Russia and not staying overnight in any city. Most Russian embassies issue transit visas for only 72 hours; Russian embassies and consulates in China, however, will issue them for up to 10 days which allows you to travel on the Trans-Siberian, stay in Moscow for a night and then leave. You will probably have to show your Russian rail ticket, and sometimes your onward ticket, when applying for the visa. If you intend to stay anywhere other than Moscow you must get a tourist visa.

Russian visa extension In any country it's always best to arrive with a visa that is certain to cover the length of your stay, rather than having to go to the trouble of extending it.

The situation with visa extensions changes all the time. Provided you have registered your visa (see below), it's possible to get a visa extension but currently not easy. The organization which issued your visa invitation must submit an official request for an extension.

❏ **Health insurance**
Citizens of countries signatory to the Schengen Convention (Austria, Belgium, Denmark, Finland, France, Germany, Greece, Iceland, Italy, Luxembourg, Netherlands, Norway, Portugal, Spain and Sweden) who apply for a Russian visa are expected to produce proof of medical insurance valid in Russia, although this is unevenly enforced. Some embassies will accept just about any insurance document while others insist on coverage by a company having an agreement with Ingosstrakh/Rosno, the Russian state insurance agency.

Sometimes an international train ticket is all the proof you need. It's wise to take your original visa invitation and at least three passport photos with you in case you have to extend or replace your visa.

Russian visa registration All visitors staying in Russia for more than 72 hours must register their visas with the local police or OViR/PVU within 72 hours of arrival. If police check your papers and find that your visa is not registered, they may fine you. Border officials at your exit point can also fine you for having an unregistered visa.

That, at least, is the official line, although it doesn't always work like that. At least in Siberia you may be forgiven for an unregistered visa if you have a sound excuse (you just got off the train from Beijing, or arrived on a weekend or during a holiday, for example). After arriving in Chita from Beijing, I dutifully went to register with OViR/PVU and was told to wait until I got to Khabarovsk, even though this would be well past the 72-hour limit. You may not find officials so forgiving in Moscow or St Petersburg.

In any case you should make every effort to register within 72 hours, and certainly as soon as possible after arriving at your first town in Russia. The organization that issued your invitation is expected to handle this, but if you are travelling independently it can be taken care of by staff at your first hotel stop. You may be charged a fee for the service, typically US$5-10. If the hotel can't or won't do it, take yourself to the nearest OViR/PVU office as soon as you can. There you may have to pay a late-registration fee of a few US dollars, but if you're stopped by an unscrupulous police officer before you do it, you could end up forking over much more, even if the statutory 72 hours has not yet elapsed.

Even though you only need to register once, most hotels will hold your passport for a few hours after you arrive in order to register you, whether you ask them to or not. Registration usually takes the form of a hotel stamp on the reverse of your immigration departure card, with dates written in, and there is no charge. In the Soviet era you had to have registration stamps covering every day, and old habits die hard. A page full of registration stamps won't do you any harm. Don't forget to pick up your passport from reception.

Mongolian visa

Mongolian tourist visas are issued for up to 90 days and there are single, double and triple-entry versions. A single-entry visa costs around US$40-45/£30-35 and takes three or four working days; quicker service is available for higher fees. Only US dollar cash is accepted at Mongolian embassies in China and Russia. Confusingly, you can also get separate visas for entry and for exit; be certain that your visa is valid for exit too, as the process of getting an endorsement for this once you're in the country is time-consuming.

Transit visas are available for stays of 48 hours or less and cost US$30-35/£25-30. Embassy officials may ask to see an onward (eg, Russian or Chinese) visa.

Mongolia has consular offices along the route of the Trans-Siberian, in Moscow (p167), Irkutsk (p255) and Beijing (p39), and visas may also be available at the Mongolian border or at the airport, but it's wise to try and get your visa before you leave home.

In the past visas have been full-page stamps in your passport, although embassies are moving towards full-page stickers. The application process is usually straightforward. You will need a valid passport, one or two photos and the visa fee. An official letter of invitation from a Mongolian organization or individual is no longer necessary for a transit or 30-day tourist visa, although you'll need one for any visit of more than 30 days.

American citizens need no visa for a stay of up to three months.

Mongolian visa extension Extending your visa once you are in Mongolia can be a trying experience. The Ministry of Foreign Affairs will invariably tell you that it is impossible but be persistent: anything is possible, although it might cost you a few dollars. To do this in Ulan Bator, see p305. A seven-day extension costs around US$15, plus US$2 for each additional day. You can be fined for overstaying your visa.

Mongolian visa registration There is no registration requirement for transit or 30-day tourist visas. If you are staying for more than 30 days you must register with the police as soon as possible after arriving in Mongolia and definitely within 10 days of arrival.

Chinese visa
Tourist visas are generally given for up to a month, although if you apply for a shorter period you may only be granted a visa for the period you request. There are single and double-entry versions, as well as multiple-entry visas for long stays. One-month extensions are easy to arrange in most cities within China, though they're easier in smaller towns where there aren't so many tourists.

The process of getting a visa is straightforward at most Chinese embassies. In addition to your passport and the application form you'll need one photo and the visa fee (eg, single/double-entry for £20/30 if obtained from the UK or US$30/45 from the US). Processing usually takes about three working days. Where you are asked on your application to list the places you wish to visit, just write something like Beijing, Shanghai and Guangzhou. It's not checked and doesn't limit you to those places, but is a safer bet than revealing your true intentions (Tibet for example).

If you're planning on entering the country via Russia or Mongolia, try to get your Chinese visa **before** you reach Moscow as the Chinese embassy in Moscow is not easy to deal with.

Other visas
If you are starting from Beijing and planning to continue westward through Europe after you leave Moscow or St Petersburg, depending on your own nationality you may need transit visas for some countries bordering Russia, including Estonia, Latvia, Lithuania, Poland, Belarus or Ukraine. You may find it much easier to get these visas in Beijing than in Moscow; in particular the Ukrainian Embassy in Moscow is notoriously unpredictable and difficult.

At the time of writing, nationals of most English-speaking countries needed a visa to visit or transit Belarus and Ukraine. Citizens of EU countries and the US can visit Poland visa-free for up to 90 days (180 days for UK citizens). Nationals of Australia, New Zealand, the USA, Canada and EU countries can visit Estonia, Latvia and Lithuania visa-free, except for Canadians who need a visa for Lithuania.

MAKING A BOOKING IN BRITAIN

The following companies offer Trans-Siberian or more general Russia packages, and some produce their own very informative brochures.

● **The Russia Experience** (☎ 020-8566 8846, 🗎 020-8566 8843, 💻 www.trans-siberian.co.uk), Research House, Fraser Rd, Perivale, Middlesex UB6 7AQ. Recommended specialists in budget and medium-priced travel for individuals. Their innovative system of guides ('buddies') is popular: if there are places you want to visit they'll take you there, if you want to sit in a bar all day they'll happily sit with you. Homestays can be arranged in most cities, as well as in Siberian villages or Mongolian yurts. They offer a variety of packages, eg Moscow to Beijing with two nights' accommodation in Moscow, or Moscow to Vladivostok, both from £439. They also offer trekking and rafting in the Altai, trips to Tuva, and Beetroot Backpackers trips (see p169) by bus or train on interesting routes such as Moscow-Blagoveshchensk-Harbin.

● **Regent Holidays UK** (☎ 0117-921 1711, 🗎 0117-925 4866, 💻 www.regent-holidays.co.uk), 15 John St, Bristol BS1 2HR. Recommended by many readers, Regent specialize in independent travel to Russia and the CIS, China, Mongolia, Vietnam and North and South Korea, but also offer group tours. Moscow–Beijing tickets via the Trans-Mongolian or Trans-Manchurian route cost from £420 (£400 going the other way); stopover packages at Lake Baikal and in Irkutsk or Ulan Bator are available. Bookings are accepted from outside the UK. They can arrange visas (allow at least six weeks), flights, tours and accommodation.

● **China Travel Service and Information Centre** (CTSIC; ☎ 020-7388 8838, 🗎 020-7388 8828, 💻 www.chinatravel.co.uk), 124 Euston Rd, London NW1 2AL. Friendly staff here can help with tickets from Beijing to Moscow (this direction only) as well as tours throughout China. Prices for Beijing–Moscow start at £200/245/300 (hard/soft/soft de luxe class) on the Trans-Manchurian or Trans-Mongolian route; Beijing–Ulan Bator costs £89/135 (hard/soft de luxe). You're given a voucher which you exchange in Beijing for a confirmed ticket.

● **Intourist Ltd** has offices in London (☎ 020-7727 4100, 🗎 020-7727 8090, 💻 www.intourist.co.uk), 7 Wellington Terrace, Notting Hill, London W2 4LW; Manchester (☎ 0161-872 4222, 🗎 0161-872 4888), Duckworth House, 32 Talbot Rd, Manchester M32 0FP; and Glasgow (☎ 0141-204 5809, 🗎 0141-204 5807), 29 St Vincent Place, Glasgow G1 2DT. Intourist Ltd now concentrates on independent travel, and for some reason most of its Trans-Siberian clients book through the Glasgow branch. They tend to be hard to reach except by telephone or visit. They'll take care of flights, accommodation, train tickets, transfers, visas and excursions.

● **Adventure Bound/The Imaginative Traveller** (☎ 01473-667337, 🖹 01473-614565, 🖳 info@abounduk.net, www.adventurebound.co.uk), 19 Gloster Rd, Martlesham Heath, Suffolk IP5 3RB, is the UK agent for Sundowners (see p34). This efficient company offers tickets for all Trans-Siberian routes, for individual travellers as well as package tourists. Moscow–Vladivostok with two nights in Moscow and one in Vladivostok costs £460. The cheapest Trans-Manchurian trip costs £435 and includes two nights in Moscow. They can also arrange flights, visas, and accommodation en route.

● **CTS Horizons** (☎ 020-7836 9911, 🖹 020-7836 3121, 🖳 cts@ctsuk.com, www.ctshorizons.com), 7 Upper St Martin's Lane, London WC2H 9DL. The new-look China Travel Service office can book individual itineraries across China. A summer-season, 2nd (kupé) class Trans-Manchurian journey for one person, with budget B&B accommodation (two nights each in Beijing and Moscow) and no stopovers costs about £850; visas are extra.

● **Steppes East** (☎ 01285-651010, 🖹 01285-885888, 🖳 www.steppes east.co.uk), The Travel House, 51 Castle St, Cirencester, Glos GL7 1QD, offers tailor-made individual Trans-Siberian itineraries and tours, plus options for Moscow, St Petersburg and the Russian Far East (eg, 19 days for about £1600, with flights). Even if you stay home, their catalogue is an excellent dream-book.

● **The Trans-Siberian Express Company / GW Travel** (☎ 01565-754540, 🖹 01565-634172, 🖳 www.gwtravel.co.uk), 2 Tabley Court, Moss Lane, Over Tabley, Knutsford, Cheshire WA16 0PL, runs distinctly upmarket tours by air-conditioned private train, including en-suite facilities for each sleeping compartment. A two-week escorted tour from Moscow via St Petersburg to Vladivostok (or vice-versa), with approximately one day off the train touring for every day on board, costs from about £3300, including flights from/to London. There are regular summer departures and occasional winter ones, plus an annual July trip to Ulan Bator for the Naadam festival. Many other agencies also feature The Trans-Siberian Express Company's tours.

Budget travellers booking from Britain should note that they can also arrange Trans-Siberian rail tickets through specialist agencies in Hong Kong (see p40) and Russia (pp19-20).

 If it's just a flight-only deal you're looking for, get in touch with a bargain-ticket agency such as **STA Travel** (☎ 0870-160 0599, 🖳 www.statravel.co.uk), **Travel Cuts** (☎ 020-7255 2082, 🖳 www.travelcuts.co.uk), **Trailfinders** (☎ 020-7937 1234, 🖳 www.trailfinders.co.uk) or **Flight Centre** (☎ 0870-890 8099, 🖳 www.flightcentre.co.uk).

Further information Russia has no state tourism office in Britain, although from time to time some travel agent with Moscow links sets itself up as the 'Official Russian Tourist Office' in an effort to sell more of its own tours.

For information on the Chinese section of the journey, visit the **China National Tourist Office** (☎ 020-7373 0888, brochure line ☎ 0900-160 0188, 📠 020-7370 9989), 71 Warwick Rd, London SW5 9HB.

Embassies in Britain The **Russian Embassy** (☎ 020-7229 3628, visa information service ☎ 0891-171 271, 🖳 www.rusemblon.org) is at 5 Kensington Palace Gardens, London W8 4QS; it's open for applications 09:00-12:30 (last application 11:45) Monday to Friday. Queues here can be long, and you may wish to pay for the visa service offered by most Russia-specialist travel agencies (prices vary). Your visa invitation must specify accommodation for all nights you will be in Russia. In order for you to get a visa most of the companies listed on pp19-20 will state on their support documents that you're staying with them for the duration of your trip, even though they know you may not do so. A single-entry tourist visa available in six working days costs £30, with higher fees for faster service, from £60 for three to five days up to £120 for one-hour service. A double-entry visa costs £10 extra. For postal applications allow at least three weeks. There's also a **Russian consulate** (☎ 0131-225 7121, 🖳 visa @edconsul.demon.co.uk) at 58 Melville St, Edinburgh, EH3 7HL.

The **Mongolian Embassy** (☎ 020-7937 0150, 📠 020-7937 1117, 🖳 www .embassyofmongolia.co.uk) is at 7 Kensington Court, London W8 5DL; the visa section is open 10:00-12:30 Monday to Friday. A transit visa costs £30 (rail confirmation is not required) and a single-entry/exit tourist visa costs £35; visas take two to five working days to process. You'll need one photo.

The **Chinese Embassy** (visa information ☎ 09001-880808 or, between 14:00-16:00, ☎ 020-7631 1430, 📠 020-7636 9756, 🖳 www.chinese-embassy.org.uk) is at 31 Portland Place, London W1B 1QD; the visa section is open 09:00-12:00 Monday to Friday. A one-month tourist visa is quite easy to obtain yourself, and takes three working days. You'll need one passport photo and the fee of £20/30 (single/double-entry). Check the dates on the visa before leaving the embassy. There are **Chinese consulates** in Manchester (☎ 0161-2248672; Denison House, 49 Denison Road, Manchester M14 5RX) and Edinburgh (☎ 0131-3164789; 43 Station Rd, Edinburgh EH12 7AF).

The **Belarus Embassy** (consular section ☎ 020-7938 3677, 📠 020-7361 0005, 🖳 www.belemb.freeserve.co.uk) is at 6 Kensington Court, London W8 5DL; visa section open 9:00-12:30 Monday to Friday. For the mandatory 48-hour Belarussian transit visa you'll need one photo plus a fee of £10; you may also be asked to show your onward visa. Processing takes five working days.

The **Ukrainian Embassy** (☎ 020-7243 8923, 📠 020-7727 3567, 🖳 www .ukremb.org.uk) is at 78 Kensington Park Rd, London W11 2PL; visa section open 9:30-12:00 Monday to Friday. For a five-day Ukrainian transit visa you need two photos and the £15 fee, and the visa is ready in three working days. You must also present a photocopy of your onward visa.

Getting to Moscow or Beijing from Britain
● **By air**: Flights to Moscow start at around £145 one-way, £220 return. Aeroflot (☎ 020-7355 2233) offers the cheapest seats most often, all to Sheremetyevo-2 airport. Transaero (☎ 0870-850 7767) is another Russian carrier, with connections from Gatwick to Moscow's Domodedovo airport. Beijing is more expensive: at least £380 one way, £450 return. Air China is a good bet for cheap seats and can be booked through CTSIC or other UK agencies; see p24.
● **By rail**: Deutsche Bahn Travelservice (☎ 0870-243 5363, ▤ 020-8339 4700, ▣ www.reiseauskunft.bahn.de) can book a one-way ticket from London to Moscow for as little as £207 (advance purchase); they also sell return tickets but say the return sleeper bookings are not always honoured in Moscow. The daily train service takes about 44 hours, with train changes in Brussels and Cologne. Tickets to a range of European cities (but not currently in Russia) can be booked through Rail Europe (☎ 08705-848848) or Eurostar (☎ 08705-186186).

MAKING A BOOKING IN CONTINENTAL EUROPE

From Denmark
● **Albatros Tours** (☎ 36 98 00 00, ▤ 36 98 00 20, ▣ www.albatros-travel.dk), Kultorvet 11, 1175 Copenhagen K.
● **Kilroy Travels** (☎ 70 80 80 15, ▣ www.kilroytravels.com) is a youth/student agency with half a dozen branches around the country, which sells Trans-Mongolian and Trans-Manchurian tickets and can arrange visas and flights as well as accommodation in some Russian cities.
● **MyPlanet** (☎ 97 42 50 11, ▤ 96 10 02 53, ▣ hol@myplanet.com), Nørregade 51, 7500 Holstebro; and (☎ 33 55 75 55, ▤ 96 10 02 55, ▣ cph@my planet.com), Frederiksberg Álle 18-20, 1820 Frederiksberg.

From Finland
● **Kilroy Travels** (☎ 0203-545769, ▣ www.kilroytravels.com) is a youth-student agency with branches around Finland; see under Denmark for services.
● **OY Finnsov Tours** (☎ 09-694 2011, ▤ 09-694 5534, ▣ www.finnsov.fi), Eerikinkatu 3, 00100 Helsinki, is an Intourist affiliate agency.

From France
● **Inexco Voyages** (☎ 01 47 42 25 95, ▤ 01 47 42 26 95, ▣ www.inexco-voy ages.com), 29 rue Tronchet, 75008 Paris. Inexco is a Switzerland-based agency with expertise in tourism from France to states of the former CIS.
● **Elytoor** (☎ 01 42 25 33 09, ▤ 01 42 25 09 70), 34 Ave des Champs Elysees, 75008 Paris, has been recommended by readers.
● **CGTT** (☎ 01 40 22 88 88), 82 rue d'Hauteville, 75010 Paris: group tours.
● **China Travel Service** (☎ 01 44 51 55 66, ▤ 01 44 51 55 60, ▣ www.cts france.com), 32 rue Vignon, 75009 Paris, offers bargain Paris–Beijing airfares and help with China visas. Recommended by readers.
● **Office du Tourisme de Chine** (☎ 01 56 59 10 10, ▤ 53 75 32 88, ▣ paris @cnta.gov.cn), 15 rue de Berri, 75008 Paris. This official tourist information

office can also help with China visas and air tickets, though not railway bookings.
● **Transtours** (☎ 01 53 24 34 00), 42 av de l'Opéra, 75002 Paris: group tours.

From Germany

● **Travel Service Asia** (☎ 07351-373210, ▤ 07351-373211, ▣ www.tsa-reisen
.de), Schmelzweg 10, 88400 Biberach/Riß. TSA offers a range of independent
journeys and budget tours on the Trans-Siberian, Trans-Manchurian and Trans-
Mongolian routes, including in Mongolia. Through Baikal Complex in Irkutsk
(see p253) they offer Lake Baikal hiking tours. They can also arrange visas and
visa support, and are worth contacting even if you don't live in Germany.
● **Eurasia Erlebnisreisen** (☎ **07821-955970**, ▤ **07821-955972**, ▣ **mochel@t-
online.de**), **Schwarzwaldstr 101**, **D-77933 Lah**: **China and Trans-**Siberian.
● **Lernidee-Erlebnisreisen** (☎ 030-786 0000, ▤ 030-786 5596, ▣ www
.transsiberian-railroad-travel.com, www.lernidee.de), Eisenacherstrasse 11,
10777 Berlin. Siberian itineraries range from a 2nd-class ticket on the

---

❑ **Trains from Germany**
'It comes as no surprise to those who know some geography that Deutsche Bahn,
German Rail, has the best (and oldest) rail connections with Russia. There are sever-
al options:
● The old 'Est–West-Express', formerly going Paris–Moscow, still operates
Cologne–Moscow. The train starts every evening, and leaving Friday night means
arriving 9am on Sunday.
● There is a daily (winter: Tu/Th/Su) train from Berlin (departure from Lichtenberg
Station) to Moscow; this train contains a carriage to St Petersburg. The train doesn't
operate on Saturdays.
● Every Saturday a train departs from Berlin-Lichtenberg to Samara (south of
Moscow), which itself somehow sounds to me like a place at the end of the world.
Things get even better: this train contains through cars to the Kazakhstan capital,
Astana, and to the capital of Siberia, Novosibirsk. So after visiting the Siberian tigers
in the Lichtenberg zoo, just walk to your train, lie down for 100 hours and wake up
in Siberia!

Reservations Ask at any German railway station or at their telesales office for tickets inside Russia and their reaction sounds like you are already in Russia: 'That's
impossible!' Well, it's somehow tricky because reservations must not be sold for
every train, but with insistence I got myself a ticket for the Moscow–Irkutsk train at
Dusseldorf railway station. Also ask for special return offers, e.g. Cologne–Irkutsk
–Cologne for about $350!
    Reservation can also be done by phone (☎ +49-1805-996633, speaking some
German may be helpful but someone will speak English). You will then get a reservation number: quote this number at any German ticket counter and your reservation
will be printed.

Information Linked via the website of Deutsche Bundesbahn (▣ www.bahn.de), go
to – **http://reiseauskunft.bahn.de/bin/query.exe/en?L=adr& newrequest=yes&
protocol=http:&** – and simply enter time and date you want to go from and to. The
server knows all European and CIS long-distance-trains'.

Benedikt Jaeger (Germany)

Moscow–Beijing train to stopovers in Mongolia (three nights including full board, with English-speaking guide). Other routes include Moscow to Vladivostok. Homestay and hotel accommodation are offered in several cities.

● **White Nights** (☎ 06221-166505, 🖳 www.wnights.com), Pleikartsfoersterhof 9, 69124 Heidelberg, is the German agent for this St Petersburg-based budget travel operator; see also p31.

● **Die Bahn** (☎ 1805-996633, 🖳 www.reiseauskunft.bahn.de). With Deutsche Bahn's switched-on, multilingual travel service, you can make Trans-Siberian rail bookings by telephone or online.

● **Mongol Juulchin Foreign Tourism Corporation** (☎ 030-440-57-646, 🖹 030-440-57-645, 🖳 jlncorp.repofficeuro@berlin.snafu.de), Chausseestrasse 84, D-10115 Berlin. This branch of the Mongolian state tourism office also accepts bookings from outside Germany.

● **China Tourist Office** (☎ 069-520135, 🖹 069-528490, 🖳 frankfurt@cnta.gov.cn), Ilkenhanstrasse 6, D-60433 Frankfurt am Main. This is the official government tourism information office for Germany, Austria and the Netherlands.

From the Netherlands
● **Circ Rusland Reizen** (☎ 020-625 3528, 🖹 020-620 55 54, 🖳 circ@euronet.nl), Honthorststraat 42, 1071 DH Amsterdam, recommended by readers, can organize train tickets, visas and accommodation.

● **Tozai Travel** (☎ 020-6262272, 🖹 020-6279736, 🖳 info@tozai.nl, www.transsiberie.nl), Nieuwezijds Voorburgwal 175,1012 RK Amsterdam. This agency, also recommended by readers, concentrates on itineraries for individual travellers.

● **White Nights** (☎ 070-360 7785, 🖳 www.wnights.com), Jan van Nassaustraat 47M, 2562 BN The Hague, is the Dutch agent for this St Petersburg-based budget travel operator; see also p31.

● **VNC Travel** (☎ 030-231 1500, 🖹 030-231 0232, 🖳 www.vnc.nl), Catharijnesingel 70, 3500 AB Utrecht, can organize trips for independent travellers as well as group tours.

● **Tiara Tours** (☎ 076-565 28 79, 🖹 076-560 26 30, 🖳 tiara@tref.nl, www.tiaratours.nl), Charles Petitweg 35/10, 4827 HJ Breda. This Trans-Sib specialist has a user-friendly Web site.

● **Eurocult** (☎ 030-243 9634, 🖹 030-244 2475, 🖳 www.eurocult.nl), Wittevrouwenstraat 36, 3512 CV Utrecht, can book Trans-Siberian tickets.

From Norway
● **Kinareiser** (☎ 22-98 22 00, 🖹 22-98 22 01, 🖳 www.kinareiser.no), Hegdehaugsveien 10, 0167 Oslo. This company arranges Trans-Siberian trips, and also represents Nomadic Journeys, a licensed tour operator and train-ticket consolidator based in Ulan Bator (see p303).

● **Intourist Norway** (☎ 22-42 28 99, 🖹 22-42 62 01), Fr Nansens Plass 8, 0160 Oslo, can arrange tickets for all routes (in either direction) as well as visas, accommodation and flights.

❏ **Cheap tickets via Poland**
'I live in Poland and this information concerning getting to Russia from Poland may
be useful for travellers planning to travel to Moscow because all the main routes from
Western Europe to Russia cross Poland. If you want to go from Berlin, for example,
to Moscow, the cheapest way is not to take international direct trains. Do the journey
in stages and take the EuroCity train Berlin–Warsaw (€33, six hours), then the rapid
train Warsaw–Terespol (around €5). This city is located right next to the border with
Belarus, and on the other side of the River Bug that separates Poland from Belarus is
the city of Brest. You can either cross the border by foot or take a train. In Brest you
can buy a plastcartny ticket to Moscow ($20) or even buy a ticket for the whole
Trans-Siberian route'.   **Jakub Pilch** (Poland)

From Poland
● **Intourist Warsawa Ltd** (☎ 22-625 0852, 🖹 22-629 0202, 🖳 www
.intourist.pl), 10 Nowogrodzka str, 00-509 Warsaw.

From Russia
Many organizations within Russia can arrange visa support (see pp19-20). For
others, refer to the travel agents in each city (see Part 4: City Guides and
Plans).

From Sweden
● **Eco Tour Production** (☎ 0498 487 105, 🖹 0498 487 115, 🖳 www
.nomadicjourneys.com), Norra Kustvägen 17, 620 20 Klintehamn, Gotland, is a
Swedish partner with Nomadic Journeys, an Ulan Bator-based tour operator and
one of the few locally-based consolidators for train tickets. On offer are horse
riding, sports fishing, popular *ger* (yurt) camp stays and longer horseback expeditions. Camps are low-impact and quiet, with wind and solar power instead of
generators. Eco Tour can also help with train journeys starting from Ulan Bator.
● **Swedish-Chinese Travel** (Svensk-Kinesiska Reserbyran; ☎ 08-108824, 🖹
08-411 0888, 🖳 www.svenskkinesiska.se), Sveavägen 31, 103 68 Stockholm.
This agency pioneered tourism from Scandinavia to China and is now Sweden's
largest tour operator specializing in China and its neighbours.
● **Iventus International Travel** (☎ 08-651 4523, 🖹 08-651 2558, 🖳 www
.iventus.se), Eriksgatan 19, Box 12313, 102 28 Stockholm, is an outlet for Eco
Tour/Nomadic Journeys and a specialist in travel to (and onward from) China.
On offer are air, train and ferry bookings; hotels and homestays; Baikal, Ulan
Bator and China programmes; and Russia, Mongolia and China visa services.

From Switzerland
● **White Nights** (☎ 079-463 8967, 🖳 www.wnights.com), Freiburgstrasse 18,
2500 Biel, is the Swiss agent for this St Petersburg-based budget travel operator; see also p31.

MAKING A BOOKING IN NORTH AMERICA

From the USA

● **Adventure Center** (☎ 510-654-1879, 🖹 510-654-4200, 🖳 silkroad@adventurecenter.com), Suite 200, 1311 63rd Street, Emeryville, CA 94608. Agents for the popular Sundowners Adventure Travel trips (see p34).

● **White Nights** (☎/🖹 916-979-9381, 🖳 wnights@concourse.net, www.wnights.com), 610 La Sierra Drive, Sacramento, CA 95864, is the US office of a Russia-based budget travel operator (☎/🖹 812-268-2515, 🖳 wn@wnights.com, 5th Sovietskaya ul 6A, St Petersburg 193130). Moscow to Vladivostok costs from US$378.

● **Mir Corporation** (☎ 206-624-7289, toll-free ☎ 1-800-424-7289, 🖹 206-624-7360, 🖳 www.mircorp.com), 85 South Washington St, Suite 210, Seattle, WA 98104. Mir offer a range of individual and small-group escorted tours on the Trans-Siberian, with homestay or hotel accommodation; they're also the USA agent for the Trans-Siberian Express Company (see p25). They have branch offices in Moscow, St Petersburg, Irkutsk and Ulan Ude.

● **Asia Voyages** (☎ 510-559-3388, toll-free ☎ 1-800-914-9133 ext 202, 🖹 510-291-8448, 🖳 www.asiavoyages.com), 1650 Solano Ave, Suite A, Berkeley, CA 94707. The company markets a range of independent and group tours in Russia, Mongolia and China, and offers a 20-day trip from Moscow to Hong Kong.

● **Go to Russia Travel** (☎ 404-497-9190, toll-free ☎ 1-888-263-0023, 🖹 404-827-0435, 🖳 www.gotorussia.net), 309A Peters St, Atlanta, GA 30313. This Russia specialist company offers both individual travel assistance (including flights and visa support) and package tours (eg, an 11-night Trans-Siberian tour from US$3120).

● **Boojum Expeditions** (☎ 406-587-0125, toll-free ☎ 1-800-287-0125, 🖹 406-585 3474, 🖳 www.boojum.com), 14543 Kelly Canyon Rd, Bozeman, MT 59715. Through its office in Ulan Bator (🖳 boojum@mongol.net) Boojum organizes horse-riding trips in Mongolia's Hovsgol region, on the border with Siberia and Tuva, as well as jeep tours.

● **General Tours** (toll-free ☎ 1-800-221-2216, 🖹 603-357-4548, 🖳 www.generaltours.com), 53 Summer St, Keene NH 03431, a venerable agency organizing mainly escorted tours and cruises, including on the Trans-Siberian.

● **The Society of International Railway Travelers** (☎ 502-454-0277, 🖹 502-458-2250, 🖳 www.irtsociety.com), 1810 Sils Ave, Louisville, KY 40205, is a membership organization which organizes de luxe train trips all over the world, including Siberian journeys with the Trans-Siberian Express Company (see p25).

● **Mongolian Travel USA** (☎ 609-419-4416, 🖹 609-275-3827, 🖳 mongol@juno.com, www.mongoltravel.com), 707 Alexander Rd, suite 208, Princeton NJ 08540, is US representative for Juulchin, the Mongolian state tourism corporation.

Two major airfare specialists are **Council Travel** (toll-free ☎ 1-800-226-8624, 🖳 www.counciltravel.com) and **STA Travel** (toll-free ☎ 1-800-781-4040, 🖳 www.statravel.com). Both have offices all over the country.

You can get information from the **Russian National Tourist Office** (☎ 212-575 3431, toll-free ☎ 1-877-221-7120, 💻 www.russia-travel.com), 130 West 42nd St, Suite 412, New York, NY 10036. The **China National Tourist Office** has branches in New York (☎ 212-760-8218, 💻 ny@cnto.org, 350 5th Avenue, Suite 6413, New York, NY 10118) and Los Angeles (☎ 818-545-7507, 💻 la@cnto.org), 600 W Broadway, Suite 320, Glendale, Los Angeles, CA 91204).

Embassies in the USA The consular office of the **Russian Embassy** (☎ 202-939-9907, 📠 202-483-7579, 💻 www.russianembassy.org) is at 2641 Tunlaw Rd NW, Washington, DC 20007. There are also **consulates** in San Francisco (☎ 415-928-6878, 2790 Green St, CA 94123), New York (☎ 212-348-0926, 11 E 91st St, NY 10128) and Seattle (☎ 206-728-1910, 2323 Westin Building, 2001 6th Ave, Seattle, WA 98121).

The **Chinese Embassy** (☎ 202-328-2500, 📠 202-328-2582, 💻 www.china-embassy.org) is at 2300 Connecticut Ave NW, Washington, DC 20008. There are **consulates** in New York (☎ 212-244-9392, 520 12th Ave, New York, NY 10036), Chicago (☎ 312-803-0095, 100 W Erie St, Chicago, IL 60610), Houston (☎ 713-524-0780, 3417 Montrose Blvd, Houston, TX 77006), Los Angeles (☎ 213-807-8088, 443 Shatto Pl, Los Angeles, CA 90020) and San Francisco (visa office ☎ 415-674-2925/6, 1450 Laguna St, San Francisco, CA 94115).

The **Mongolian Embassy** (☎ 202-333-7117, 📠 202-298-9227, 💻 www.mongolianembassy.us) is at 2833 M Street NW, Washington DC 20007.

The **Belarus Embassy** (☎ 202-986 1606, 📠 202-986-1805, 💻 www.belarusembassy.org) is at 1619 New Hampshire Ave NW, Washington DC 20009. There's a consulate in New York (☎ 212-682 5392, 708 3rd Ave, New York, NY 10017).

Getting to Russia or China from the USA Numerous airlines fly from the US to Russia. Aeroflot is among the cheapest, with departures from many US cities. From New York, one-way flights to Moscow cost US$450-700 depending on the season. Aeroflot also flies direct from Seattle to Moscow every day. Korean Air has flights from several west-coast cities via Seoul to Vladivostok. Magadan Airlines (☎ 206-433-8905) operates daily direct flights from Anchorage to Magadan (on Russia's Pacific coast), from where you can fly to major Siberian cities.

One-way flights to Beijing start at about US$650 from New York or US$550 from Los Angeles.

From Canada
● **Adventure Centre/Westcan Treks** offers a range of individual and group Trans-Siberian itineraries. The Adventure Centre (☎ 416-922-7584, toll-free ☎ 1-800-267-3347, 📠 416-922-8136, 💻 www.theadventurecentre.com) is at 25 Bellair St, Toronto M5R 3L3. Westcan Treks has branches in Vancouver (toll-free ☎ 1-800-663-5132, 2911 West 4th Avenue, Vancouver V6K 1R3), Edmonton (toll-free ☎ 1-800-387-3574, 8412 109th St, Edmonton T6G 1E2)

and Calgary (toll-free ☎ 1-800-690-4859, 336 14th St NW, Calgary T2N 1Z7).
● **Intours Corp** (☎ 416-766-4720, toll-free ☎ 1-800-268-1785, 🖹 416-766-
8507, 🖳 intours@on.aibn.com), 2150 Bloor St West, Suite 308, Toronto,
Ontario M6S 1M8. This Intourist affiliate can organize individual or group trips
on all Trans-Siberian routes, including arrangements in neighbouring countries.
● **Exotik Tours** (☎ 514-284-3324, 🖹 514-843-5493, 🖳 exotictours@exotic-
tours.com), Suite 806, 828 Ste Catherine St East, Montreal, Quebec H2L 2E3.
Exotik sells packages for the Trans-Mongolian and Trans-Manchurian routes,
with options to stop in Novosibirsk and Irkutsk. Sightseeing tours in Mongolia
are available. In addition the staff can arrange scheduled flights and visas for
Russia, Mongolia and China.
● **Travel CUTS/Voyages Campus** (toll-free ☎ 1-866-246-9762, 🖳 www.trav
elcuts.com) is Canada's best bargain-ticket agency, with offices countrywide.

The **China National Tourist Office** (☎ 416-599-6636, 🖹 416-599-6382, 🖳 cn
to@tourismchina-ca.com) is at 480 University Ave, Suite 806, Toronto, Ontario
M5G 1V2.

Embassies in Canada The consular department of the **Russian Embassy**
(☎ 613-336-7220, 🖹 613-238-6158, 🖳 otconsul@intranet.ca) is at 52 Range
Rd, Ottawa, Ontario K1N 8J5. There is a **consulate** (☎ 514-842-5343, 🖳 con-
sulat@dsuper.net) at 3655 Ave du Musée, Montreal, Quebec H3G 2E1.
   The **Chinese Embassy** (☎ 613-789-3434, 🖹 613-789-1911, 🖳 www.china
embassycanada.org) is at 515 St Patrick St, Ottawa, Ontario K1N 5H3. There
are **consulates** in Vancouver (☎ 604-734-7492, 3380 Granville St, Vancouver,
BC V6H 3K3), Toronto (☎ 416-964-7260, 240 St George St, Toronto, Ontario
M5R 2P4) and Calgary (☎ 403-217-3816, 1011 6th Ave, Suite 100, Calgary,
Alberta T2P 0W1).
   The **Mongolian Embassy** (☎ 613-569-3830, 🖹 613-569-3916, 🖳 www
.mongolembassy.org) is at 151 Slater St, Suite 503, Ottawa K1P 5H3.
   The **Belarus Embassy** (☎ 613-233-9994, 🖹 613-233-8500, 🖳 canada
@belembassy.org) is at 130 Albert St, Suite 600, Ottawa K1P 5G4.
   The **Polish Embassy** (☎ 613-789-0468, 🖹 613-789-1218, 🖳 polamb@
hookup.net) is at 443 Daly Ave, Ottawa K1N 6H3. There is a consulate (☎ 514-
937-9481) at 1500 Pine Ave West, Montreal, Quebec H3G 1B4.

MAKING A BOOKING IN AUSTRALASIA

From Australia
● **Travel Directors** (☎ 08-9322 5155, toll-free ☎ 1-800-641236, 🖹 08-9322
1310, 🖳 www.traveldirectors.com.au), 177 Oxford St, Leederville, Perth, WA
6007. This recommended Trans-Siberian specialist agency offers high-quality
tour packages strong on person-to-person contact, along with basic visa support.
● **Passport Travel** (☎ 03-9867 3888, 🖹 03-9867 1055, 🖳 passport@travelcen
tre.com.au, www.russia-rail.com), Suite 11, 401 St Kilda Rd, Melbourne,
Victoria, 3004. See p20.

- **Sundowners Adventure Travel** (☎ 03-9672 5300, 🖷 03-9672 5311, 💻 www
.sundownerstravel.com), Suite 15, 600 Lonsdale St, Melbourne, Vic 3000, is
recommended by several readers. They offer both independent and group Trans-
Siberian, Trans-Mongolian and Trans-Manchurian trips. Sample group trips
include a 19-day St Petersburg to Vladivostok journey including 11 nights in
hotels and guesthouses, and a 28-day rail odyssey from Hong Kong via Xi'an
to Beijing, Ulan Bator, Irkutsk, Moscow and St Petersburg. Under the name
Vodkatrain (💻 www.vodkatrain.com) they also offer loosely-structured,
unescorted group journeys for people aged 18-35, with young local guides at
stopover towns.
- **Russian Travel Centre/Eastern Europe Travel** (☎ 02-9262 1144, 🖷 02-
9262 4479, 💻 www.eetbtravel.com), Level 5, 75 King St, Sydney, can arrange
Trans-Mongolian and Trans-Manchurian trips, with options for homestay
accommodation. They also have a branch in Brisbane (☎ 07-3395 4008, 🖷 07-
3395 4770, 18 Bodian Street, Carindale).
- **Russia and Beyond** (☎ 02-9299 5799, 🖷 02-9262 3438, 💻 info@russiabe
yond.com.au), 191 Clarence St, Sydney 2000, can arrange Trans-Siberian travel packages starting in Moscow, St. Petersburg, Vladivsotok, Shanghai or
Beijing, and including stopovers, transfers, accommodation, sightseeing, flights
and visa support.
- **Eastern European & Russian Travel Centre** (☎ 618 9322 6812, 9322 4522,
🖷 618 9321 4351, 💻 living@jazzline.net.au), 9th floor, 5 Mill Street, Perth,
WA.
- **Gateway Travel** (☎ 02-9745 3333, 🖷 02-9745 3237, 💻 www.russian-gate
way.com.au), 48 The Boulevarde, Strathfield, NSW 2135.

The **China National Tourist Office** (☎ 02-9252 9838, 🖷 02-9252 2728, 💻 www
.cnto.org.au) is at 234 George Street, 11th floor, Sydney, NSW 2000.

Embassies in Australia The **Russian Embassy** (☎ 06-6295 9033, 🖷 6295
1847, 💻 rusemb@dynamite.com.au) is at 78 Canberra Ave, Griffith, ACT 2603.
There's also a **consulate** (☎ 02-9326 1866, 💻 russcon@ozemail.com.au) at 7-
9 Fullerton St, Woollahra, NSW 2025.

The **Chinese Embassy** (☎ 02-273 4780, 🖷 02-273 4878, 💻 www.china
embassy.org.au) is at 15 Coronation Dr, Yarralumla (Canberra), ACT 2600.
There are **consulates** in Sydney (☎ 02-9319 0678, 💻 www.chinacon
sulatesyd.org, 539 Elizabeth St, Surry Hills, NSW 2010), Perth (consular office
☎ 02-9481 3278, 3rd Floor, Australia Place, 15-17 William St, Perth, WA 6000)
and Melbourne (☎ 03-9822 0604, 💻 www.chinaconsulatemel.org, 75-77 Irving
Road, Toorak, Victoria 3142).

Australia has no consular offices for Mongolia, Belarus or Poland.

From New Zealand
- **Sundowners Adventure Travel** (toll-free ☎ 0800-447 506, 🖷 03-9672 5311,
💻 www.sundownerstravel.com); these contact details connect to the
Sundowners office in Australia (see above).

● **Adventure World** (☎ 09-529 4782, 🖹 09-520 6629, 🖳 www.adventure-world.co.nz), 101 Great South Rd, Remuera, PO Box 74007, Auckland. New Zealand's biggest adventure-travel wholesaler offers individual and group Trans-Siberian, Trans-Mongolian and Trans-Manchurian journeys, and is an agent for The Russia Experience (see p24) and Sundowners (see opposite).
● **Innovative Travel** (☎ 03-365 3910, toll-free ☎ 0508-700700, 🖹 03-365 5755, 🖳 www.innovative-travel.com), Innovative House, 269 Cashel St, PO Box 21247, Christchurch, is an agent for the Russian Travel Centre (see p34).

Embassies in New Zealand The **Russian Embassy** (consular office ☎ 04-476 6742, 🖹 04-476-3843, 🖳 embassyofrussia@xtra.co.nz) is at 57 Messines Rd, Karori, Wellington.

The **Chinese Embassy** (☎ 04-472 1382, 🖹 04-499 -419, 🖳 www.chinaembassy.org.nz) is at 2-6 Glenmore St, Wellington. There is a **consulate** (☎ 09-525 1587, 🖳 www.chinaconsulate.org.nz) at 588 Great South Rd, Greenlane, Auckland.

Belarus, Mongolia and Poland do not have embassies in New Zealand.

MAKING A BOOKING IN SOUTH AFRICA

● **Concorde Travel** (☎ 011-532 8000, 🖹 011-486 1876), Nedcor Investment Bank Building, 1 Newtown Avenue, Killarney (Johannesburg) 2193, can do Trans-Siberian railway bookings as well as hotels and transport.
● **STA Travel** (☎ 011-706 0052, 🖹 011-706 0227, 🖳 www.statravel.co.za), 1st floor, Coachmans Crossing, Lyme Park, Sandton. STA South Africa, with 14 branches including in Pretoria, Bloemfontein, Durban and Cape Town, can make Trans-Siberian bookings.

Embassies in South Africa The consular office of the **Russian Embassy** (☎ 012-334 4812, 🖹 012-343 8636, 🖳 ruspospr@mweb.co.za) is at 135 Bourke Street, Sunnyside 0132, PO Box 5715, Pretoria 0001. There is also a **consulate** (☎ 021-418 3656, 🖹 021-419 2651, 🖳 rusco@icon.co.za) at 2nd Floor, Southern Life Centre, 8 Riebeek St, Cape Town.

The **Chinese Embassy** (☎ 012-3424194, 🖹 012-3424154, 🖳 www.chinese-embassy.org.za) is at 972 Pretorius St, Arcadia, Pretoria. There are **consulates** at Durban (☎ 031-208 0540, 26 Springfield Rd, Berea), Cape Town (☎ 021-674 0579, 25 Rhodes Ave, Newlands) and Johannesburg (☎ 082-660 3680, 25 Cleveland Rd, Sandhurst, Sandton).

MAKING A BOOKING IN JAPAN

Ferries from Japan
In addition to flights you have several options for travel by ferry from Japan. You may sail to the Russian port of Vladivostok, or to various Chinese ports, all within easy reach of Beijing: Shanghai, Tianjin or Qingdao.

Fushiki to Vladivostok From mid-June to late December a weekly ferry service operates between Fushiki and Vladivostok, a 40- to 45-hour journey. One-way tickets cost ¥22,800-88,800 (US$190-740),including meals and the port tax at Vladivostok, with 10% off for students. Agencies where you can purchase tickets include the following:

● **FKK Air Service** (☎ 0766-222 212, 🖳 fkk-air@toyama-net.com), Duo Bldg, Shimonoseki-machi 4-56, Takaoka-shi, Toyama 933-0021. FKK also sells tickets for flights to Vladivostok.

● **United Orient Shipping & Agency Co** (Tokyo Kyodo Kaiun; ☎ 03-5541 7511, 🖹 03-3552 7322, 🖳 h.tazaki@uniorient.co.jp), 4th Floor, Shuwa-Sakurabashi Bldg, 4-5-4, Hatchobori, Chuo-ku, Tokyo 104-0032.

For information on the journey **from** Vladivostok, see p296.

Osaka/Kobe to Shanghai The Chinese-run Japan-China International Ferry Co (JIFCO) runs weekly ferries to Shanghai, with departures from Osaka or Kobe on alternate weeks; and the Shanghai Ferry Co operates a weekly service from Osaka. One-way fares range from ¥20,000 to ¥50,000 including breakfast, with 10% discounts for students. The journey takes approximately 48 hours. From Shanghai it's a 15-hour train journey on to Beijing.

● **Japan-China International Ferry Co** has offices in Tokyo (☎ 03-5489 4800, 🖹 03-5489 4788, 🖳 jifcot@dream.com, Daikanyama Pacific Bldg, 10-14 Sarugaku-cho, Shibuya-ku, Tokyo 150-0033) and Osaka (☎ 06-6536 6541, 🖹 06-6536 6542, 🖳 jifcot@oregano.ocn.ne.jp, Room 201, Sanai Bldg, 1-8-6 Shinmachi, Nishi-ku, Osaka 550-0013).

● **Shanghai Ferry Company** has offices in Osaka (☎ 06-6243 6345, 🖹 06-6243 6308, 🖳 pax@shanghai-ferry.co.jp, 5F Dai Building, Midosuji, 4-1-2 Minami Kyuhoji-cho, Chuo-ku, Osaka 541-0058) and Shanghai (☎ 021-6537 5111, 🖹 021-6537 9111, 🖳 sfco@shanghai.cngb.com, 4th floor The Panorama Shanghai, 53 Huangpu Rd, Shanghai 20080).

Tickets can also be bought from branch offices of Japan Travel Bureau and Kintsuri (Kinki Nihon Tourist).

Kobe to Tianjin China Express Line sails weekly between Kobe and the Chinese port of Tanggu, near Tianjin, a 48-hour trip. One-way fares start at ¥20,000 with a 10% student discount. From Tianjin it's a 1¹/₂ to two-hour train journey to Beijing.

● **China Express Line** (☎ 078-321 5791, 🖹 078-321 5793, 🖳 pax@ celkobe.co.jp) is at 4-5 Shinkocho, Chuo-ku, Kobe 650-0041. Their Chinese counterpart is the **Tianjin Jinshen Ferry Co** (☎ 022-2420 5777, 🖹 022-2420 5970), 22nd floor, Ocean Shipping Plaza, Hebei District, Tianjin.

Shimonoseki to Qingdao Japanese-owned Orient Ferry Ltd operates a twice-weekly, year-round service between Shimonoseki, on the western tip of Honshu island, and Qingdao, a 40-hour voyage. One-way tickets cost ¥19,000-70,000 with a 20% student discount; those departing from Shimonoseki pay an additional ¥600 charge.

● **Orient Ferry Ltd** has offices in Shimonoseki (☎ 0832-326615, 🖹 0832-326616, 🖳 orient.f@crocus.ocn.ne.jp, 10-64-1 Higashi-Yamato-cho,

Shimonoseki 750-0066) and Qingdao (☎ 0532-389 7636, ▤ 0532-389 7637, ⌨ ao lin@public.qd.sd.cn, Haitian Hotel, 48 Xiang Gang Xi Rd, Qingdao 266071).

Other services
● **Euras Tours Inc** (☎ 03-5562 3381, ▤ 03-5562 3380, ⌨ euras-tyo@ma.neweb.ne.jp), 1-26-8 Higashi-Azabu, Minato-ku, Tokyo 106-1044. This friendly, efficient agency handles bookings for rail journeys to Europe. They also have a branch in **Osaka** (☎ 06-6531-7416, ▤ 06-6531-7437, ⌨ euras-osa@me.neweb.ne.jp, 1-11-7 Nishi-Honcho, Osaka City). Euras offers a choice of itineraries combining flights, ferries and trains, directly into Russia or via China.
● **Intourist Japan** (☎ 03-3238-9118, ▤ 03-3238 9128, ⌨ info@intourist-jpn.co.jp), 3rd floor, Saiwai Bldg, 4-19 Gobancho, Chiyoda-ku, Tokyo 102-0076.
● **Mongol Juulchin Tours Co** (☎ 03-3486 7351, ▤ 03-3486 7440, ⌨ www .mongol.co.jp), 3rd floor, Dai-2 Kawana Bldg, 14-6 Shibuya 2-chome, Shibuya-ku, Tokyo 150-0002. This is the Tokyo office of Mongolia's Juulchin Foreign Tourism Corporation.

The **China National Tourist Office** has branches in Tokyo (☎ 03-3591 8686, ▤ 03-3591 6886, 8th floor, Air China Bldg, 252 Toranomon, Minato-ku, Tokyo) and in Osaka (☎ 06-635 3280, ▤ 06-635 3281, 4th floor, Ocat Bldg, 141 Minato-machi, Naniwaku, Osaka).

Embassies in Japan
The consular division of the **Russian Embassy** (☎ 03-3583 4445, ▤ 03-3586 0407, ⌨ rosconsl@ma.kcom.ne.jp) is at 1-1 Azabudai, 2-chome, Minato-ku, Tokyo 106-0041. There are **consulates** in Osaka (☎ 06-848 3452, Toyonaka-shi, Nishi Midorigaoka 1-2-2), Niigata (☎ 025-244 6015, Fai-Biru, 1-20-5 Sasaguchi) and Sapporo (☎ 011-561 3171, 826 Nishi 12-chome, Minami 14-jo, Chuoku).

The **Chinese Embassy** (☎ 03-3403 3388, ▤ 03-3403 3345) is at 3-4-33 Moto-Azabu, Minato-ku, Tokyo 106-0046.

The **Mongolian Embassy** (☎ 03-3469 2088, ▤ 3469 2216, ⌨ www .embassy-avenue.jp/mongolia/index.htm) is at 21-4 Kamiyama-cho, Shibuya-ku, Tokyo 150-0047.

There is a **Belarus Embassy** (☎ 03-3584 8054, ▤ 03-3584 8064) at 3-3-25 Roppongi, Minako-ku, Tokyo 106.

MAKING A BOOKING IN CHINA
From Beijing
In the summer trains fill up quickly so if you plan to spend some time travelling around China make Beijing your first stop and get your onward travel nailed down. Once you've made your train reservations and paid your deposit, do the rounds of the embassies and collect your visas. You'll need RMB (yuan) as well as crisp US dollar cash, and a stock of passport photos.

Alternatively you may be able to reserve a place on the train while you're in Shanghai (ask at the travel bureau in the Peace Hotel). Shanghai has a Russian consulate (see below) but no Mongolian consulate.

● **Monkey Business Infocenter** (☎ 010-6591 6519, 🖹 010-6591 6517, 🖳 mon keychina@compuserve.com, www.monkeyshrine.com), 12 Dongdaqiao Xie Jie, Nan Sanlitun, Chao Yang District, 100027 Beijing. The Infocenter, open 10:00-19:00 Monday-Saturday, is above the Hidden Tree Belgian Beer Bar, a great place to meet fellow Trans-Sib travellers or unwind at the end of the journey with first-rate pizza washed down with Belgian beer.

The 'monkeys' are André and Patrick, Belgian brothers who by now have put literally thousands of budget travellers on trains across Siberia. They'll organize everything for you, provide vital visa support for Russia stopovers, even put you on the train. They sell a range of individual packages from Beijing to Moscow (from US$355) and various stopver packages (eg, from US$620 with stops in Mongolia, Lake Baikal and Yekaterinburg). They can even book a journey from Moscow **to** Beijing.

● **CITS Beijing** (☎ 010-6512 0507, 🖹 010-6512 0503, 🖳 tianwei @cits.com.cn), West Lobby, Beijing International Hotel. The cheapest, quickest Trans-Siberian tickets you're likely to find are sold here, although staff aren't keen to spend a lot of time answering questions, and availability can be a problem in summer owing to high demand. They're open 08:30-12:00 and 13:30-17:00 Monday to Friday.

● **Beijing Tourism Group** (BTG; ☎ 010-6515 8562, 🖹 010-6515 8603), Beijing Tourism Bldg, 28 Jianguomenwai Dajie, between the New Otani and Gloria Plaza Hotels. This CITS offshoot caters for independent travellers (including on the Trans-Siberian) and is easier to deal with than CITS. Try them even if CITS says there are no tickets. They're open 08:30-11:30 and 13:30-17:00 Monday to Friday.

Further information The Beijing office of **Juulchin**, the Mongolian state tourism corporation (☎ 010-6512 6688, 🖹 010-6525 4339, 🖳 julpek@public .bta.net.cn) is at the Beijing International Hotel, 9 Jianguomennei Dajie, Beijing.

Embassies in Beijing Of course you'll need to visit the Russian embassy and, for the Trans-Mongolian route, the Mongolian embassy. If you're continuing through Europe after Moscow you will probably need a transit visa for Belarus or Ukraine, and possibly for Poland (see pp19-24 for further information on visa requirements for these countries). If you don't have all your visas already, it may be easier to get them here than in Moscow.

● **Russia** (consular department ☎ 010-6532 1267, 🖹 010-6532 4853, 🖳 rusemb @public3.bta.net.cn), 4 Dongzhimen Beizhong Jie, Beijing 100600; open for applications 09:30-12:00 Monday to Friday, but you are strongly advised to get there before 10:30.

There are **Russian consulates** in Shanghai (☎ 021-6324 8383, ☐ consul @online.sh.cn, 20 Huangpu Lu, Shanghai 200080), Shenyang (☎ 024-611 4963, ☐ ruscons@pub.sy.ln.cn, Fenghuang Hotel, 109 Huange Nan Lu, Shenyang 110031) and Hong Kong (☎ 2877 7188, ▤ 2877 7166, ☐ cg rushk@hknet.com, 29th floor, Sun Hung Kai Centre, 30 Harbour Rd, Wanchai).

A single-entry tourist or transit visa costs US$50 plus a consular fee which varies with your nationality (typically US$25, although Brits and Canadians paid no extra fee at the time of writing); double-entry costs US$50 extra. Processing normally takes five working days; add US$30 for three working days or US$70 for 24 hours. Prices are displayed in US$ and that is what for-eigners are expected to use, although Chinese can pay in RMB. Officially you must present the originals of visa-support documents (plus a photocopy of each) although faxed copies are normally accepted. You'll also need one photo, and photocopies of the information pages of your passport.

Transit visas from this embassy are normally valid for 10 days from your departure from Beijing, giving you just enough time to get to Moscow and stay a night or two. Check this before you leave the embassy. For a transit visa you will probably have to show onward visa and tickets. If you're stopping off any-where or spending more than two days in Moscow, you'll need a tourist visa.

Note that German nationals cannot currently get a Russian tourist visa in Beijing unless they are resident in China, although transit visas are available. At the time of writing this rule was not enforced at the Russian consulate in Hong Kong. Some European nationalities also need health insurance to qualify for a Russian visa (see p21).

● **Mongolia** (☎ 010-6532 1203, ▤ 010-6532 5045, ☐ monembbj@public 3.bta.net.cn), 2 Xiushui Beijie, Jianguomenwai Dajie, Beijing; the consular sec-tion is open for applications 9:00-11:00 Monday to Friday. There is also a Mongolian consular office in Hong Kong but only Hong Kong residents may apply there. Visas must be paid for in US$ cash – for example US$40 for a 30-day tourist visa, US$30 for a two-day transit visa, or US$60 for either one if you want it the next day – plus an additional Y25 charge in all cases. You'll need one photo, but you're not required to show onward visas or tickets. Procedures are formal but staff are helpful.

● **Belarus** (☎ 010-6532 1691, ▤ 010-6532 6417, ☐ china@belembassy.org), 1 Dong Yijie, Ritan Lu, Jianguomenwai, Beijing 100600; open for applications 10:00-12:00 Monday, Wednesday and Friday. For the mandatory 48-hour tran-sit visa you'll need one photoand US$30 in US dollar cash. Processing takes five working days. To get your visa in three working days costs US$57. You may be asked to show your Russian visa.

● **Poland** (☎ 6532 1235), 1 Ritan Lu, Jianguomenwai, Beijing 100600; open for applications 9:00-10:30 Monday, Wednesday and Thursday. Australians, New Zealanders, Canadians and others (but not USA or EU nationals) need a visa to cross Poland. You'll need one photo and a copy of the information pages of your passport, plus Y700 (US$85) for a tourist visa or Y430 (US$52) for a transit visa. Processing takes two working days.

For information on other embassies in Beijing see p320.

From Hong Kong

Hong Kong can be a good place to arrange a ticket or stopover package on the Trans-Siberian. Most visitors do not require a visa to enter Hong Kong, and this is an easy place to get a visa for onward travel into the rest of China.

Agencies here offer a range of services and booking with them from abroad is usually no problem. Several travel agencies in the Nathan Road area can arrange tickets with a few weeks' notice. Some will sell you a voucher to exchange in Beijing for a reserved ticket. Others sell you an open ticket with a reservation voucher, leaving you to get the ticket endorsed by CITS in Beijing; don't accept an open ticket without a reservation voucher. But to visit any Russian cities apart from Moscow you'll need a tourist visa and therefore visa support.

● **Monkey Business/Moonsky Star** (☎ 2723 1376, 🖹 2723 6653, 🖳 mon keyhk@compuserve.com, www.monkeyshrine.com), E-Block, 4th Floor, Flat 6, Chungking Mansions, 36-44 Nathan Rd, Kowloon; open 10:00-18:00, Monday to Saturday. This office concentrates on journeys commencing in Hong Kong. If you want to make advance plans, get in touch with their Beijing office (see p38).

● **Phoenix Services Agency** (☎ 2722 7378, 🖹 2369 8884, 🖳 phoenix1@netvi gator.com, info@phoenixtrvl.com), Room A, 7th Floor, Milton Mansion, 96 Nathan Rd, Kowloon.

● **Time Travel Services** (☎ 2366 6222, 🖹 2739 5413, 🖳 timetrvl@hkstar.com), Block A, 16th Floor, Chungking Mansions, 36-44 Nathan Rd, Kowloon.

● **Shoestring Travel** (☎ 2723 2306, 🖹 2721 2085, 🖳 shoetvl@hkstar.com), Flat A, 4th Floor, Alpha House, 27-33 Nathan Rd, Kowloon.

What to take

Woollen underwear is the best safeguard against sudden changes in temperature. High goloshes or 'rubber boots' are desirable, as the unpaved streets of the towns are almost impassable in spring and autumn; in winter felt overshoes or 'arctics' are also necessary. A mosquito-veil is desirable in E. Siberia and Manchuria during the summer. It is desirable to carry a revolver in Manchuria and in trips away from the railway.
Karl Baedeker *Russia with Teheran, Port Arthur and Pekin, 1914,*

The best advice today is to travel as light as possible. Some people recommend that you put out everything you think you'll need and then pack only half of it. Remember that unless you're going on an upmarket tour, you'll be carrying your luggage yourself.

Clothes

For summer in Moscow and Siberia pack as for an English summer: thin clothes, a sweater and a raincoat. In every hotel you will be able to get laundry done, often returned the same day, for a few roubles. Take shirts and tops of a quick-drying cotton/polyester mixture if you are going to wash them yourself.

Winter in Russia and northern China is extremely cold, although trains and most buildings are kept well-heated: inside the train you can be quite warm enough in a thin shirt as you watch Arctic scenes pass by your window. When you're outside, however, a thick winter overcoat is an absolute necessity, as well as gloves and a warm hat. It's easy to buy good quality overcoats/jackets in Beijing for about £30/US$45. If you're travelling in winter and plan to stop off in Siberian cities along the way you might consider taking thermal underwear. Shoes should be strong, light and comfortable; most travellers take sturdy trainers. On the train, Russians discard their shoes and wear flip flops – the type you can wear with socks. This is a good idea and you can buy them at any station or on virtually any street. Russians also wear track-suits throughout the journey whilst the Chinese might resort to pyjamas.

If you forget anything, clothes are expensive in Japan, cheap but shoddy in Russia, cheap and fashionable in Hong Kong, and very cheap in China.

Luggage

If you're going on one of the more expensive tours which include baggage handling, take a suitcase. Those on individual itineraries have the choice of rucksack (comfortable to carry for long distances but bulky) or shoulder-bag (not so good for longer walks but more compact than a rucksack). Unless you are going trekking in Russia or China, a zip-up holdall with a shoulder strap or a frameless backpack is probably the best bet. It's also useful to take along a small daypack for camera, books etc. Since bedding on the train and in hotels is supplied you don't need to take a sleeping-bag even when travelling in winter, although

---

❏ **Luggage limits**
On my first Trans-Siberian trip from Beijing we had so much luggage that several taxidrivers refused to take us to the station. Unfortunately all thirteen bags were necessary as we were moving back from Japan. On the train we'd managed to get some of them stowed away in the compartments above the door and under the seats when we were joined by a German woman travelling home after three years in China. Her equally voluminous baggage included two full-size theatrical lanterns which were very fragile. Then the man from Yaroslavl arrived with three trunks. We solved the storage situation by covering the floor between the bottom bunks with luggage and spreading the bedding over it, making a sort of triple bed on which we all lounged comfortably – eating, drinking, reading, playing cards and sleeping for the next six days. Dragging our bags around Moscow, Berlin and Paris was no fun, however. On subsequent journeys I didn't even take a rucksack, only a light 'sausage' bag with a shoulder strap and a small day-pack. Never travel with an ounce more than you absolutely need. Nowadays a 35kg luggage limit in compartments is strictly applied in Beijing and to a lesser extent in Moscow.

some travellers prefer to carry their own sleeping sheet (a sheet used inside a sleeping bag).

Medical supplies

Essential items are: aspirin or paracetamol; lip salve; sunscreen lotion; insect repellent (vital if you're travelling in summer); antiseptic cream and some plasters/bandaids; an anti-AIDS kit containing sterile syringes and swabs for emergency medical treatment. Note that Western brands of tampons and condoms are not always easily available in Russia or China. Bring an extra pair of glasses or contact lenses if you wear them.

You may want to take along something for an upset stomach (Arrêt, for example) but use it only in an emergency, as changes in diet often cause slight diarrhoea which stops of its own accord. Avoid rich food, alcohol and strong coffee to give your stomach time to adjust. Paradoxically, a number of travellers have suggested that it's a good idea to take along laxatives. For vaccination requirements, see p49.

General items

A money-belt is essential to safeguard your documents and cash. Wear it underneath your clothing and don't take it off on the train, as compartments are very occasionally broken into. A good pair of sun-glasses is necessary in summer as well as in winter when the sun on the snow is particularly bright. A water bottle (two-litre) which can take boiling water is essential as is a mug (insulated is best), spoon and knife.

The following items are also useful: a few clothes pegs, adhesive tape, ballpoint pens, business cards, camera and adequate supplies of film (see p44), flashlight, folding umbrella, games (cards, chess – the Russians are very keen chess players – Scrabble etc), lavatory paper, calculator (for exchange rates), notebook or diary, penknife with corkscrew and can-opener (although there's a bottle opener fixed underneath the table in each compartment on the train), photocopies of passport, visa, air tickets, etc (keep them in two separate places), sewing-kit, spare passport photographs for visas, string (to use as a washing-line), the addresses of friends and relatives (don't take your address book in case you lose it), tissues (including the wet variety), universal bathplug (Russian basins usually don't have a plug), walkman (batteries are easily found locally), washing powder (liquid Travel Soap is good) and hand soap. Some people take along an electric heating coil for boiling a mug of water when staying in a hotel. A compass is useful when looking at maps and out of the window of the train. Earplugs are useful on the train and in noisy Chinese hotels. Don't forget to take a good book (see p46).

It's also a very good idea to bring things to show people: glossy magazines (the more celebrity pictures the better), photos of your family and friends, your home or somewhere interesting you have been. Everyone will want to look at them, and will often get out photos of their own to show you; the Chinese in particular adore looking at photographs of people. This is a great way to break the ice when you don't speak much of the local language.

❏ **Platform food – see also p123**
'I rather regretted having taken on so many supplies at Moscow before the journey, when I saw how much was on offer at the informal markets en route. Gastronomic offerings available from the hawkers at the various stations on the route included: fresh fruit and vegetables, bread, savoury pastries, pancakes, ice-cream, potatoes and various other hot dishes. Big city stations, however, often have no hawkers at all.'

Anthony Kay (UK)

Gifts

Once the sale of a pair of Levis in Moscow could cover your spending money for the entire trip but this is just not the case any more. It is now very hard for foreigners to trade anything on the black market.

What you should bring in abundance is gifts. The Russians are great present givers (see p84) and there's nothing more embarrassing than being entertained in a Russian home and then being presented with a truckload of souvenirs when you have nothing to offer in return. In the major cities, most Western goods can be purchased; however in Siberia it can be harder. Rather than give something that can be bought locally, bring things that are harder for Russians to get. These include postcards of your country, key rings and baseball caps. Bring a few foreign coins and badges as Russia is full of collectors.

It is essential to ensure that you have things to share while you're on the train, such as chocolate biscuits, sweets or other snacks. Forget Twixes, Mars Bars or Snickers, as they're all widely available. If you're trying to impress a Russian with chocolate it has to be good since Russian chocolate, the Red October brand in particular, can be excellent. Red October's Gold Label bar has been on the market since 1867.

Provisions

The range of food and drink available on the train is improving and you can now buy numerous things in the dining car that weren't previously available, such as beer, chocolate and biscuits. There's also a good selection of things to eat available from hawkers on station platforms along the way.

But it's still wise to buy some provisions before you get on the train, especially if you are going the whole way without a break. Take along fruit, cheese and sausage; you can almost always buy bread, tomatoes, boiled eggs or boiled potatoes on the platforms. Vodka is not sold on station platforms, but Russians always know where to find it! If you are sharing a compartment with Russians, they will probably insist that you share their food. To refuse would be rude but you should obviously offer some of your food as well, though often it will not be accepted as they will see you as their guest.

Some travellers bring rucksacks filled with food, though it's more realistic to bring just some biscuits and tea-bags or instant coffee (with whitener and sugar if required); hot water is always available from the samovar in each carriage. Other popular items include drinking chocolate, dried soups, tinned or fresh fruit, fruit-juice powder, peanut butter, Marmite or Vegemite, chocolate, crackers, cheese and pot noodles. If you forget to buy provisions at home there are Western-style supermarkets in both Moscow and Beijing where you can stock up with essentials.

Money – see also p74
With certain exceptions, you will have to pay for everything in local currency (roubles in Russia, RMB/yuan in China). Russian hotels must accept roubles even though some may ask you for dollars.

There are now abundant, well-signposted, 24-hour international ATMs in Moscow and St Petersburg, in all major cities along the Trans-Siberian, and in Beijing. Most accept Visa, MasterCard and other major cards and give cash advances from your own account, in local currency. All you need is your PIN number from home. Exchange rates are based on daily international rates, and the only commission you pay is to your own bank, about 1.5% per transaction. This is generally the most convenient way to maintain a supply of local currency without carrying a huge stash of US$ cash around with you. Cards are also accepted by many hotels and a growing number of guesthouses, restaurants and shops.

In Russia you're only likely to succeed in cashing travellers' cheques at banks, and therefore only during weekday banking hours; and few banks are interested in anything but US$ cheques. In China travellers' cheques are accepted at better hotels, though most are very fussy about signatures and will ask for your passport, which can be a problem if you're busy applying for visas. The exchange rate is usually slightly better than for cash, but the difference is too small to matter. You will probably also be asked to show your original purchase receipts. If your cheques are lost or stolen, you're unlikely to get a swift refund or replacement, so they are hardly any safer than cash.

But there are many times when cash is essential, for example when the banks are closed or there are no ATMs, for visa fees at many embassies, and in Mongolian restaurant cars on the Trans-Siberian. It's essential to have a stash of cash, and by far the most useful currency in Russia, Mongolia and China is US dollars. Carry only a small amount in your pocket and the rest safely under your clothing in a moneybelt (worn in bed at night as well as during the day). Keep a second stash somewhere else for emergencies. Although cash may seem more risky than travellers' cheques many Russians carry far larger stashes around with them than you will probably have.

See p75 for tips on what kind of banknotes to bring, and on places in Russia where other currencies are commonly accepted. See p63 for important information about declaring your foreign currency at customs.

Because of the circulation of outdated and worthless Russian bank notes, and the small difference in the legal and black markets, exchanging money on the street is not recommended.

Photographic equipment
Bring more film than you think you'll need, as you'll find there's a lot to photograph. Don't forget to bring some faster film for shots from the train (400

❏ **Window cleaning**
A squeegie, an instrument used by window-cleaners to remove water, can be easily
obtained in a small size for car windows. This tool is an invaluable aid for cleaning
the train's windows for photography or, for that matter, just for passengers' viewing.
Robert Bray (UK)

ASA). It's wise to carry all your film in a lead-lined pouch (available from camera shops) if you are going to let them go through Russian X-ray machines at
airports.

Most major brands of film are available in Russia cities, but slide or
high/low ASA film may be difficult to find outside Moscow and St Petersburg.
In the large cities in Siberia and China, you can have your film processed in one
hour and the quality is acceptable. In Ulan Bator there seem to be plenty of
newly-opened developers with imported machines. Film development is natu-
rally of a high standard in Japan but, unless you request otherwise, prints will
be small.

What not to photograph
Taking pictures from the train used to be forbidden but now it's OK, although
it would be wise not to get trigger-happy at aerodromes, military installations or
other politically sensitive areas. In addition, many Russians still believe it is
illegal to take any photos from a train and they may tell you in no uncertain
terms to stop.

Remember that in Russia, as in most other countries, it's considered rude to
take pictures of strangers, their children or possessions without asking permission. Often people are keen to have their picture taken but you must always ask.
This is particularly the case during political demonstrations or rallies: the
updater of an earlier edition of this guide got stoned by a group of pensioners
outside the White House in September 1993 for trying to get the next cover for
Time magazine. Beware!

Refrain from photographing touchy subjects such as drunks, queues and
beggars. Photography in churches is normally discouraged, and taking a photo
of someone in front of an icon is considered disrespectful. A useful phrase is
'Mozhno vas snimat?' (Можно вас снимать?) meaning simply, 'Can I take a
photo of you?' When asking for permission, offer to send them a copy: and keep
your word. If travelling in winter always carry your camera inside your pocket
or elsewhere near your body as film gets brittle and batteries get sluggish in the
intense cold.

Photography from the train
The problem on the train is to find a window that isn't opaque or one that opens.
They're usually locked in winter so that no warmth escapes. Opening doors and
hanging out will upset the carriage attendants if they catch you; if one carriage's
doors are locked try the next, and remember that the kitchen car's doors are

always open. Probably the best place for undisturbed photography is right at the end of the train: 'No one seemed to mind if we opened the door in the very last carriage. We got some great shots of the tracks extending for miles behind the train'. (Elizabeth Hehir, The Netherlands).

Background reading
A number of excellent books have been written about the Trans-Siberian railway. Several are unfortunately out of print, though they're often available through inter-library loan. The following are well worth reading before you go:
● *Journey Into the Mind's Eye: Fragments of an Autobiography* by Lesley Blanch (1988, out of print) is a fascinating book: a witty, semi-autobiographical story of the author's romantic obsession with Russia and the Trans-Siberian Railway.
● *To the Great Ocean* by Harmon Tupper (1965, out of print) gives an entertaining account of Siberia and the building of the railway.
● *Guide to the Great Siberian Railway 1900* by AI Dmitriev-Mamanov, a reprint (David and Charles 1971 and also out of print) of the guide originally published by the Tsar's government to publicize their new railway. Highly detailed but interesting to look at.
● *Peking to Paris: A Journey across two Continents* by Luigi Barzini (1973, out of print) tells the story of the Peking to Paris Rally in 1907. The author accompanied the Italian Prince Borghese and his chauffeur in the winning car, a 40 hp Itala. Their route took them across Mongolia and Siberia and for some of the journey they actually drove along the railway tracks.
● *The Big Red Train Ride* by Eric Newby. This is a perceptive and entertaining account of the journey he made in the Soviet era, written in Newby's characteristically humorous style.
● *In Siberia* by Colin Thubron is the best modern book for background on Siberia and certainly one you should either read before you go or take with you on the trip. Thubron's excellent earlier travelogue, *Among the Russians*, was written after his travels in Soviet times.
● *The Trans-Siberian Railway: A Traveller's Anthology*, edited by Deborah Manley, is well worth taking on the trip for a greater insight into the railway and the journey, through the eyes of travellers from Annette Meakin to Bob Geldof. Now out of print but available in libraries.
● Paddy Linehan's *Trans-Siberia* (2001) is a warm and easily-readable account of a trip made recently – the contemporary flavour shines-out a-plenty. You quickly warm to the author's unpretentious style.
● *The Princess of Siberia* (1984) is Christine Sutherland's very readable biography of Princess Maria Volkonskaya, who followed her husband Sergei Volkonsky to Siberia after he'd been exiled for his part in the Decembrists' Uprising. Her house in Irkutsk is now a museum.
● *As Far As My Feet Will Carry Me* (1955, reprinted 2003) is the true story of the escape of German prisoner of war, Clemens Forell, from the Siberian gulag where he was serving a 25-year hard-labour sentence. It's a gripping adventure tale.

● *Stalin's Nose: Travels Around the Bloc* by Rory Maclean (1992). Maclean explores the former Eastern Bloc in a battered Trabant with his elderly aunt Zita and a pig named Winston. He recounts the histories of some of his more notorious relatives, providing in the process a surreal, darkly humorous commentary on communism and its demise.

● *Lenin's Tomb* by David Remnick (1993) is an eyewitness account of the heady Gorbachev era by this articulate former *Washington Post* correspondent.

● *Between the Hammer and the Sickle: Across Russia by Cycle* by Simon Vickers (1994) is a highly entertaining account of an epic bicycle journey from St Petersburg to Vladivostok in 1990. Out of print but available from libraries.

● *East of the Sun: The Conquest and Settlement of Siberia* by Benson Bobrick (1993, reprinted 1997). A readable narrative of Russia's conquest of Siberia, a saga which in colour and drama rivals the taming of the American West.

● *Around The Sacred Sea: Mongolia and Lake Baikal on Horseback* by Bartle Bull (1999). In 1993 Bull and two photographers rode north from Mongolia into Siberia and around Lake Baikal, partly a Boys-Own adventure and partly to report on the growing environmental threat to the lake after the collapse of the USSR. The result is an engaging true-life adventure story.

● *A People's Tragedy: The Russian Revolution 1891-1924* by British historian Orlando Figes (1997) is a scholarly work of social and political history that brings this turning point in Russia's history to life. Winner of the 1997 NCR Book Award.

● *A History of Twentieth-Century Russia* by Robert W Service (1997). The eminent British scholar of Russian history looks back at the entire Soviet experiment, from the rise of communism to the collapse of the USSR.

● *Holy Russia* by Fitzroy Maclean (1979, out of print), probably the most articulate and readable of many summaries of European Russian history, includes several topical walking tours.

However well written and accurate they may be, these books are only the impressions of foreign scholars and visitors. You will get a better idea of the Russian mind and soul from Russians' own literature, even from the pre-Revolution classics. If you haven't already read them you might try some of the following:

● Dostoyevsky's thought-provoking, atmospheric *Crime and Punishment* (set in the Haymarket in St Petersburg).

● Tolstoy's *War and Peace*.

● Mikhail Bulgakov's surreal masterpiece, *The Master and Margarita*.

● *Dr Zhivago* by Boris Pasternak (whose grave you can visit in Moscow).

● *Memories from the House of the Dead*, a semi-autobiographical account of Dostoyevsky's life as a convict in Omsk.

● *A Day in the Life of Ivan Denisovich* by Alexander Solzhenitsyn, detailing 24 hours in the life of a Siberian convict.

● *The Gulag Archipelago* by Alexander Solzhenitsyn.

Other guidebooks

● *Siberian BAM Guide: Rail, Rivers and Road* by Athol Yates and Nicholas Zvegintzov (also from Trailblazer) is a comprehensive guide for travellers in north-east Siberia, including the 3400km BAM (Baikal-Amur Mainline) railway in Eastern Siberia and good coverage of the northern end of Lake Baikal and Lena River routes.

● *Trekking in Russia & Central Asia* by Frith Maier (1994) covers parts of Siberia and includes a look at the history of mountaineering in Russia, although it's now a bit out of date.

● *Russia & Belarus* (Lonely Planet) is comprehensive. LP has guides to most of the countries on or around the Trans-Siberian route.

For further rail travels in Russia there's *Russia by Rail with Belarus and Ukraine* by Athol Yates (Bradt, 1996), covering 50 cities and 300 towns along major rail lines. Trailblazer publishes guides to rail travel in China, Japan, Vietnam and several other countries – see p446-7 for more information.

For information on locomotives, *Soviet Locomotive Types: The Union Legacy* by AJ Heywood and IDC Button is invaluable. It's co-published by Luddenden Press (UK) and Frank Stenvalls (Sweden).

Health precautions and inoculations

No vaccinations are listed as official requirements for Western tourists visiting Russia, China, Mongolia or Japan. Some may be advisable, however, for certain areas (see below). If you plan to spend more than three months in Russia evidence of a recent negative AIDS test is required. Russia now has one of the highest incidences of AIDS infection in the world, 90% of it drug related. Since the 1990s there has been a worrying decline in public health in Russia: an outbreak of diphtheria in 1993, a rise in tuberculosis particularly amongst prison inmates and the reappearance of diseases such as anthrax and bubonic plague.

Vaccination services are available in London through **Trailfinders** (☎ 020-7938 3999, 🖳 www.trailfinders.co.uk, 194 Kensington High St) and **British Airways Travel Clinic** (☎ 0845-600 2236, 🖳 www.britishairways.com/travel/healthclinintro, 213 Piccadilly and 101 Cheapside). **Nomad Travellers Store & Medical Centre** (☎ 020-8889 7014, 🖳 www.nomadtravel.co.uk, 3-4 Wellington Terrace, Turnpike Lane, London) offers travel medical advice, inoculations and supplies.

In the USA the **Centers for Disease Control and Prevention** (toll-free ☎ 1-800-311-3435, 🖳 www.cdc.gov) in Atlanta is the best place to contact for worldwide health information.

Wherever you're travelling you should have health insurance, available through any travel agent. The UK has reciprocal health-care agreements with some 40 other countries, including Russia but neither China nor Mongolia.

> ❑ **Drinking water**
> Although tap water is safe to drink in some Russian cities, it's wise to stick to bottled mineral water or boiled water. At all costs, avoid tap water in St Petersburg since it is infected with *giardia*, which can cause a nasty and persistent form of diarrhoea. In Irkutsk and Listvyanka you can safely drink the tap water, which comes directly from Lake Baikal.
>
> In Mongolia and China, drink only boiled or bottled water; thermos flasks of boiled water are routinely provided on trains and in hotels. Tap water is safe in Japan and Hong Kong.
>
> On the train, boiled water is always available from samovars in each carriage.

Treatment in Russian hospitals is free as long as you collect Form E-111 from a UK post office before you go; but given the state of most Russian hospitals, you're advised to arrange proper health insurance and go to a private clinic if you get ill. Some other nationalities will need **health insurance** before they can get a Russian visa (see p21).

INOCULATIONS

● **Diphtheria** Ensure that you were given the initial vaccine as a child and a booster within the last 10 years. The World Health Organization recommends a combined diphtheria-tetanus toxoid (DTT) booster.

● **Tetanus** A booster is advisable if you haven't had one in the last 10 years: if you then cut yourself badly in Russia you won't need another.

● **Hepatitis A** Those travelling on tight budgets and eating in cheaper restaurants run a risk of catching infectious hepatitis, a disease of the liver that drains you of energy and can last from three to eight weeks. It's spread by infected water or food, or by utensils handled by infected persons. Gamma globulin antibody injections give immediate but short-term protection (two to six months). A vaccine (trade names Havrix or Avaxim) lasts for twice that time (and up to 10 years if a booster is given within six to 12 months).

● **Malaria** If you plan to visit rural areas of south-western China you may be at risk of malaria, a dangerous disease which is on the increase in parts of Asia. The malaria parasite (carried by the Anopheles mosquito) is now resistant to chloroquine, so you may need a complex regimen of **anti-malarial tablets** starting before you go and continuing for weeks after you leave the malarial zone.

● **Other** Ensure you've had recent **typhoid**, **polio** and **BCG** (tuberculosis) boosters. Most people are vaccinated against these diseases in childhood. If you're planning to go off the beaten track it's advisable to have a vaccination against **meningococcal meningitis**. Those going on a long trek in Siberia may want to consider a vaccination against **tick-borne encephalitis**. It's also worth considering a pre-exposure rabies vaccination course.

If you're arriving from Africa or South America you may be required to show a **yellow fever** vaccination certificate.

MEDICAL SERVICES

Those travelling with tour groups will be with guides who can contact doctors to sort out medical problems. Serious problems can be expensive, but you'll get the best treatment possible from doctors used to dealing with foreigners. If you're travelling independently and require medical assistance, contact an upmarket hotel for help. In Moscow or St Petersburg the best place to go in an emergency is the American Medical Center. In St Petersburg, Moscow, Yekaterinburg, Novosibirsk, Irkutsk and Khabarovsk, medical assistance is available at clinics beside MNTK-Iris hotels.

Large hotels in China usually have a doctor in residence. In Beijing, Shanghai and Guangzhou (Canton) there are special hospitals for foreigners. Take supplies of any prescription medicine you may need. Medical facilities in Mongolia are very limited and some medications are unavailable.

❏ **SARS**

A mysterious viral infection characterized by high fever, coughing and breathing difficulties appeared for the first time in China's Guangdong province in November 2002. Only three months later did its seriousness become apparent, when the Chinese Ministry of Health made the sheepish admission that there were some 300 cases in the province and that five people had already died from it.

Within weeks it appeared in hospital workers in Hong Kong, and the World Health Organization (WHO) declared the disease, called Severe Acute Respiratory Syndrome (SARS), a worldwide health threat. Further cases were quickly identified in Canada, Indonesia, the Philippines, Singapore, Thailand and Vietnam, and within weeks SARS had reached Europe, Africa and South Asia.

The virus is believed to spread mainly via infectious droplets such as from coughing or sneezing. Most cases have involved people in close contact with (eg, caring for or living with) SARS-infected persons. Treatment is with antibiotic or antiviral drugs; there is no specific vaccine.

But strict screening measures appear to have paid off. By the time of writing the WHO had declared the virus under control, with infection rates dropping, although concerns remained that it could reappear during subsequent winters.

All advisories against travel to China have now been lifted. For current information on SARS consult your local health authority or visit official websites such as those maintained by WHO (🖳 www.who.int/en/), the USA's Centers for Disease Control (CDC; 🖳 www.cdc.gov/) or the UK Department of Health (🖳 www.doh .gov.uk/).

RUSSIA

Facts about the country

GEOGRAPHICAL BACKGROUND

The Russian Federation includes over 75% of the former USSR, but even without the other old Soviet republics it remains the largest country in the world, incorporating 17,175,000 sq km (over 6.5 million square miles) and stretching from well into the Arctic Circle right down to the northern Caucasus in the south, and from the Black Sea in the west to the Bering Strait in the east, only a few kilometres from Alaska. Russia is twice as big as the USA; the UK could fit into this vast country some 69 times.

Climate

Much of the country is situated in far northern latitudes. Moscow is on the same latitude as Edinburgh, St Petersburg almost as far north as Anchorage, Alaska. Winters are bitter: the coldest inhabited place on earth, with temperatures as low as -68°C (-90°F), is Oymyakon, in Yakutia in north-eastern Siberia.

Geography is as much to blame as latitude. Most of Russia is an open plain, stretching across Siberia to the Arctic, and while there is high ground in the south, there are no northern mountains to block the cold Arctic air which blows across this plain. To the west are the Urals, the low range which divides Europe and Asia. The Himalaya and Pamir ranges beyond the southern borders stop warm tropical air from reaching the Siberian and Russian plains. Thus isolated, the plains warm rapidly in summer and become very cold in winter. Olekminsk, also in Yakutia, holds the record for the widest temperature range in the world, from -60°C (-87°F) to a breathtaking summer high of 45°C (113°F). Along the route of the Trans-Siberian, however, summers are rather milder.

Transport and communications

Railways remain the principal means of transport for both passengers and goods, and there are some 87,500km of track in Russia. The heaviest rail traffic in the world is on certain stretches of the Trans-Siberian, with trains passing every few minutes. Although the **road network** is comparatively well-developed (624,000km) few people own cars. As a result some 31% of all passengers, and 47% of all freight, go by rail.

Russia's **rivers** have historically been of vital importance as a communication network. Some of these rivers are huge, and even navigable by ocean-going ships for considerable distances. But ice precludes year-round navigation, and **air travel** is gradually taking over.

Landscape zones: flora and fauna

The main landscape zones of interest to the Trans-Siberian traveller are as follows:

● **European Russia** Flora and fauna west of the Urals are similar to those elsewhere in northern Europe. Trees include oak, elm, hazel, ash, apple, aspen, spruce, lime and maple.

● **Northern Siberia and the Arctic** The *tundra* zone (short grass, mosses and lichens) covers the tree-less area in the far north. Soil is poor and much of it permanently frozen. In fact *permafrost* affects over 40% of Russia and extends down into southern Siberia, where it causes building problems for architects and engineers. Wildlife in this desolate northern zone includes reindeer, arctic fox, wolf, lemming and vole. Bird life is richer, with ptarmigan, snow-bunting, Iceland falcon and snow-owl as well as many kinds of migratory water and marsh fowl.

● **The Siberian plain** Much of this area is covered in *taiga*, a Russian word meaning thick forest. To the north the trees are stunted and windblown; in the south they form dark impenetrable forests. More than 30% of all the world's trees grow in this zone. These include larch, pine and silver fir, intermingled with birch, aspen and maple. Willow and poplar line rivers and streams. Much of the taiga forest along the route of the Trans-Siberian has been cleared and replaced with fields of wheat or sunflowers. Parts of this region are affected by permafrost, so that in places rails and roads sink, and houses, trees and telegraph poles often keel over drunkenly. Fauna includes species once common in Europe: bear, badger, wolverine, polecat, ermine, sable, squirrel, weasel, otter, wolf, fox, lynx, beaver, several types of rodent, musk deer, roebuck, reindeer and elk.

● **Eastern Siberia and Trans-Baikal** Much of the flora and fauna of this region is unique including, in Lake Baikal, such rarities as the fresh-water seal. Amongst the ubiquitous larch and pine there grows a type of birch with dark bark, *Betula daurica*. Towards the south and into China and Mongolia, the forests give way to open grassy areas known as *steppes*. The black earth (*chernozem*) of the northern steppes is quite fertile and some areas are under cultivation.

● **The Far Eastern territories: the Amur region** Along the Amur River flora and fauna are similar to those of northern China, and it is here that the rare Amur tiger (see p381) is found. European flora, including trees such as cork, walnut and acacia, make a reappearance in the Far East.

HISTORICAL OUTLINE

The first Russians

Artefacts uncovered in Siberia (see p89) suggest that human history in Russia may stretch back much further than previously believed: 500,000 or more years. In the 13th millennium BC there were Stone Age nomads living beside Lake Baikal.

By the 2nd millennium BC when fairly advanced civilizations had emerged here, European Russia was inhabited by Ural-Altaic and Indo-European peoples. In the 6th century BC the Scythians (whose magnificent goldwork may be seen in the Hermitage) settled in southern Russia near the Black Sea.

Through the early centuries of the 1st millennium AD trade routes developed between Scandinavia, Russia and Byzantium, following the Dnieper River. Trading centres (including Novgorod, Kiev, Smolensk and Chernigov) grew up along the route and by the 6th century AD were populated by Slavic tribes known as *Rus* (hence 'Russian').

The year 830 saw the first of the Varangian (Viking) invasions and in 862 Novgorod fell to the Varangian chief Rurik, Russia's first sovereign.

Vladimir and Christian Russia

The great Tsar Vladimir (978-1015) ruled Russia from Kiev and was responsible for the conversion of the country to Christianity. Until then Slavs worshipped a range of pagan gods, and it is said that in his search for a state religion Vladimir invited bids from Islam, Judaism and Christianity. Islam wasn't compatible with the Slavs' love of alcohol and Judaism didn't make for a unified nation. Vladimir chose Christianity, had himself baptized at Constantinople in 988 AD, and ordered the mass conversion of the Russian people, with whole towns being baptized simultaneously.

The 11th century was marked by continual feuding between his heirs. It was at this time that the northern principalities of Vladimir and Suzdal were founded.

The Mongol invasion and the rise of Muscovy

Between 1220 and 1230 the Golden Horde brought a sudden halt to economic progress in Russia, burning towns and putting the local population to the sword. By 1249 Kiev was under their control and the Russians moved north, establishing a new political centre at Muscovy (Moscow).

All Russian principalities were obliged to pay tribute to the Mongol khans but Muscovy was the first to challenge their authority. Over the next three centuries Moscow gained control of the other Russian principalities and shook off the Mongol yoke.

Ivan the Terrible (1530-84)

When Ivan the Terrible came to the throne he declared himself Tsar of All the Russias and by his successful military campaigns extended the borders of the young country. He was as wild and bloodthirsty as his name suggests: in a fit of anger in 1582 he struck his favourite son with a metal staff, fatally injuring him (a scene conjured by Ilya Repin in one of his greatest paintings). Ivan was succeeded by his mentally-retarded son Fyodor, but real power rested with the regent, Boris Godunov. Godunov himself later became Tsar, ruling from 1598 to 1605.

The early 17th century was marked by dynastic feuding which ended with the election of Michael Romanov (1613-45), first of a line that was to rule until the Revolution in 1917.

An English Tsarina for Ivan Bazilovitch?

In Elizabethan times there were diplomatic and trading links between England and Muscovy whose emissaries and merchants came to London 'dripping pearls and vermin' while Englishmen went to Moscow. Indeed the Tsar had occasion to complain of the behaviour of some of them thereby eliciting a tactful letter from the Queen.

Elizabeth's diplomatic skills brought about a peace between Ivan Bazilovitch and John, King of Sweden, and the former was so grateful to her that 'imagining she might stand his friend in a matter more interesting to his personal happiness, he made humble suit to her majesty to send him a wife out of England'. The Queen chose Anne, sister of the Earl of Huntingdon and of royal Plantagenet blood, but the lady was not willing to risk 'the barbarous laws of Muscovy which allowed the sovereign to put away his czarina as soon as he was tired of her and wanted something new in the conjugal department. The czar was dissatisfied and did not long survive his disappointment', dying in 1584. He is better known to history as Ivan the Terrible and his reputation may well have affected the Queen's thinking when she sorely tried Tsar Boris Godunov's patience with her diplomatic procrastination over his attempts to get an English bride for one of his sons.

(Sources: *The Letters of Queen Elizabeth*, ed. Harrison; *Lives of the Queens of England*, Agnes Strickland; *History of England from the Accession of James II*, Lord Macaulay; Camden's *Annals*).   **Patricia Major**

Peter the Great and the Westernization of Russia

Peter (1672-1725) well deserves his sobriquet, 'the Great', for it was his policy of Westernization that helped Russia emerge from centuries of isolation and backwardness into the 18th century. He founded St Petersburg in 1703 as a 'window open on the West' and made it his capital in 1712. During his reign there were wars with Sweden and Turkey. Territorial gains included the Baltic provinces and the southern and western shores of the Caspian Sea.

Peter's extravagant building programme in St Petersburg continued under Catherine the Great (1762-96). While her generals were taking the Black Sea steppes, the Ukraine and parts of Poland for Russia, Catherine conducted extensive campaigns of a more romantic nature with a series of favourites in her elegant capital.

Alexander I and the Napoleonic Wars

In 19th century Russia the political pendulum swung back and forth between conservatism and enlightenment. The mad Tsar Paul I came to the throne in 1796, only to be murdered five years later. He was succeeded by his son Alexander I (1801-25) who was said to have had a hand in the sudden demise of his father. Alexander abolished the secret police, lifted the laws of censorship and would have freed the serfs had the aristocracy not objected so strongly to the idea. In 1812 Napoleon invaded Russia, and Moscow was burnt to the ground (by its inhabitants, not by the French) before he was pushed back over the border.

Growing unrest among the peasants

Nicholas I's reign began with the first Russian Revolution, the Decembrists' uprising (see p97), and ended, after he had reversed most of Alexander's enlightened policies, with the Crimean War against the English and French in 1853-6. Nicholas was succeeded by Alexander II (1855-81) who was known as the Tsar Liberator, for it was he who finally freed the serfs. His reward was his assassination by a student in St Petersburg in 1881. He was succeeded by the strong Alexander III, during whose reign work began on the Trans-Siberian Railway.

Nicholas II: last of the Tsars

The dice were heavily loaded against the unfortunate Nicholas. He inherited a vast empire and a restless population that was beginning to discover its own power. In 1905 his army and navy suffered a humiliating defeat at the hands of the Japanese. Just when his country needed him most, as strikes and riots swept through the cities in the first few years of the 20th century, Nicholas's attention was drawn into his own family crisis. It was discovered that Alexis, heir to the throne, was suffering from haemophilia. The Siberian monk, Rasputin, ingratiated his way into the court circle through his ability to exert a calming influence on the Tsarevich. His influence over other members of the royal family, including the Tsar, was not so beneficial.

October 1917: the Russian Revolution

After riots in 1905, Nicholas agreed to allow the formation of a national parliament (Duma), though its elected members had no real power. Reforms came too slowly for the people and morale fell further when, during the First World War, Russia suffered heavy losses.

By March 1917 the Tsar had lost control and was forced to abdicate in favour of a provisional government led by Alexander Kerensky. But the Revolution that abruptly changed the course of Russian history took place in October of that year, when the reins of government were seized by Lenin and his Bolshevik Party. The Tsar and his family were taken to Siberia where they were murdered (see p214). Civil war raged across the country and it was not until 1920 that the Bolsheviks brought the lands of Russia under their control, forming the Union of Soviet Socialist Republics.

The Stalin era

After Lenin's death in 1924 control passed to Stalin and it was under his leadership that the USSR was transformed from a backward agricultural country into an industrial world power. The cost to the people was tremendous and most of those unwilling to swim with the current were jailed for their 'political' crimes. During the Great Terror in the 1930s, millions were sentenced to work camps, which provided much of the labour for ambitious building projects.

During the Second World War the USSR played a vital part in the defeat of the Nazis and extended its influence to the East European countries that took on Communist governments after the war.

Khrushchev, Brezhnev, Andropov and Chernenko

After Stalin died in 1953 Nikita Khrushchev became Party Secretary and attempted to ease the strict regulations which governed Soviet society. In 1962 his installation of missiles in Cuba almost led to war with the USA.

Khrushchev was forced to resign in 1964, blamed for the failure of the country's economy and for his clumsy foreign policy. He was replaced by Brezhnev who continued the USSR's policy of adopting friendly 'buffer' states along the Iron Curtain. He ordered the invasion of Afghanistan in 1979 'at the invitation of the leaders of the country'.

When Leonid Brezhnev died in 1982, he was replaced by the former head of the KGB, Yuri Andropov. He died in 1984 and was succeeded by the elderly Konstantin Chernenko, who managed a mere 13 months in office before becoming the chief participant in yet another state funeral.

Gorbachev and the end of the Cold War

Mikhail Gorbachev, the youngest Soviet premier since Stalin, was elected in 1985 and quickly initiated a process of change known by the terms *glasnost* (openness) and *perestroika* (restructuring). He is credited in the West with bringing about the end of the Cold War (he received the Nobel Prize in 1990) but it would be misguided to think of him as sole architect of the changes that took place in the USSR: it was widely acknowledged before he came to power that things had gone seriously wrong.

Gorbachev launched a series of bold reforms: Soviet troops were pulled out of Afghanistan, Eastern Europe and Mongolia, political dissidents were freed, laws on religion relaxed and press censorship lifted. These changes displeased many of the Soviet 'old guard,' and on 19 August 1991, a group of senior military and political figures staged a coup. Gorbachev was isolated at his Crimean villa and Vice-President Gennadi Yanayev took over, declaring a state of emergency. Other politicians, including the President of the Russian Republic, Boris Yeltsin, denounced the coup and rallied popular support. There were general strikes and, after a very limited skirmish in Moscow (three casualties), the coup committee was put to flight.

The collapse of the USSR

Because most levels of the Communist Party had been compromised in the failed coup attempt, it was soon seen as corrupt and ineffectual. Gorbachev resigned his position as Chairman in late August and the Party was abolished five days later. The Party's collapse heralded the demise of the republic it had created, and Gorbachev began a desperate struggle to stop this happening. His reforms, however, had already sparked nationalist uprisings in the Baltic republics, Armenia and Azerbaijan. Despite his suggestions for loose 'federations' of Russian states, by the end of 1991 the USSR had split into 15 independent republics. Having lost almost all his support, Gorbachev resigned and was relieved by Yeltsin.

Yeltsin vs the Congress of Deputies

Yeltsin's plans for economic reform were thwarted at every turn by the Congress of People's Deputies (parliament). Members of Congress, elected before the collapse of communism, were well aware that by voting for reforms they were, in effect, removing themselves from office. In the Western press this struggle was described as the fight between reformists (Yeltsin and his followers) and hardliners (Vice President Alexander Rutskoi, Congress Speaker Ruslan Khasbulatov and the rest of Congress). Yeltsin's hard-won referendum in April 1993 gave him a majority of 58% but not a mandate to overrule parliament.

On 22 September 1993 Yeltsin suddenly dissolved parliament and declared presidential rule (some have suggested that this swift action was to avert another coup attempt). The Congress denounced his action, stripped him of power and swore in Rutskoi as President. The Constitutional Court ruled that, having acted illegally, Yeltsin could now be impeached. Khasbulatov accused him of effecting a 'state coup' and appealed for a national strike.

The deciding factor in the confrontation between parliament and president was the loyalty of the military. Rutskoi, an Afghan war veteran with a keen military following, ordered troops to march on Moscow. They never did, but some 5000 supporters responded by surrounding the White House. Inside, the Congress voted to impeach Yeltsin, who retaliated by severing their telephone lines. The White House vigil turned into a siege; electricity lines were cut and the building surrounded by troops faithful to Yeltsin.

On 3 October a crowd of 10,000 communist supporters converged on the White House where Rutskoi exhorted the people to seize the Kremlin and other strategic locations around the city. All through the night there were confrontations as rioters attacked the mayor's office, the Tass news service building and the main TV station. At dawn on 4 October Yeltsin's troops stormed the White House. Fighting went on for most of the day but by evening the building, charred and battered, was taken. By the end of the week, when order had been restored, 171 people had been killed.

Zhirinovsky and Chechnya

State elections in December 1993 supported Yeltsin's draft constitution, which outlined Russia's new democratic architecture. Although the immediate threat was seen to be rejection of the constitution (Yeltsin warned that this might lead to civil war), the election revealed a new problem in the form of the Liberal Democrat Party. Its leader, Vladimir Zhirinovsky, espoused some extremely sinister policies. Particularly worrying were his comments about reuniting the former USSR, his racist jibes and his aim of re-establishing a Russian empire reaching 'from Murmansk to Madras'.

Yeltsin, in a move to demonstrate his leadership, warn other republics against separatism and regain control over the region's oil industry, ordered Russian troops into the breakaway Russian republic of Chechnya in December 1994. This attempt at a military solution to a political problem was to saddle

Russia with its deadliest domestic issue for decades. By the time a truce was signed in May 1996 over 80,000 Russian and Chechen soldiers and civilians had died. The refusal to countenance Chechen demands for independence has made the issue all but intractable. The truce, and a subsequent ceasefire and peace accord have all failed to quench the violence.

1996 presidential elections

Zhirinovsky's star had fallen by the start of the 1996 election campaign: it appeared that the winner would be communist leader Gennadi Zyuganov, but Yeltsin showed his formidable political skills, winning the first round with a fist-ful of electoral bribes, a promise of strict media control and the backing of the nation's richest entrpreneurs. Interestingly, Gorbachev polled less than 3%. The popular General Alexander Lebed posed a last-minute threat but finally support-ed Yeltsin in return for appointment as chairman of the powerful National Security Council, tipping the scales in Yeltsin's favour.

Immediately after his victory Yeltsin disappeared from public view and it soon became obvious that the campaign had taken a serious toll on the hard-drinking president. For nearly four months Russia was virtually leaderless, and power plays were the only decisions being made in the Kremlin. In early 1997 Yeltsin was back and by the end of the year some progress had been made. Inflation was under control and the rouble had been stabilized. Unfortunately the Asian economic crisis of 1998 spoiled Russia's success, and a huge drop in oil exports was followed by the withdrawal of many foreign investors.

Putin's rise to the presidency

In August 1999 Yeltsin fired his fourth prime minister in 18 months and installed Vladimir Putin, an ex-KGB officer, in the post. On New Year's Eve, to everyone's surprise, Yeltsin resigned and handed presidential power to Putin. Three months later Putin won the presidential election with just 52.5% of the vote, pledging to clean up Russia and transform it into a 'rich, strong and civi-lized country'.

Continuing violence in Chechnya began spilling beyond its borders. After a series of deadly apartment-block bombings in Moscow and other Russian cities were blamed on Chechen terrorists, Putin sent Russian troops back into the province in September 1999. An estimated 200,000 civilians fled into neigh-bouring republics, and by early 2000 much of Grozny, the Chechen capital, had been razed to the ground. In October 2002 Chechen rebels seized a Moscow the-atre, holding 800 people hostage until Russian troops stormed the building, killing most of the rebels and some 180 hostages. Two suicide bombers blew themselves up at a Moscow rock concert in July 2003, officials blamed the Chechens. These and the September 11 attacks in the USA have given free rein to the president's hard-line approach in Chechnya, though no solution is in sight.

Putin's past career as a KGB spy has clearly left him with authoritarian ten-dencies, and he has shown himself to be no friend of free speech. Email and Internet usage is monitored, and reporters and press barons have been hounded. Most worryingly, the Duma has approved a law giving the president the right to declare a state of emergency and close down political parties whenever he sees fit to do so.

On the positive side, Putin has overhauled the tax system, making it simpler to operate and harder to evade, and seems committed to protecting property rights and a liberalized economy. Most Russians seem to believe that if an authoritarian approach is needed to bring order and prosperity to their country then so be it. But many in Russia and the West worry that he may take things too far and send Russia spiralling back into a police state.

ECONOMY

Russia has vast natural resources and in this sense is an extremely rich country. It has the world's largest reserves of natural gas as well as deposits of oil, coal, iron ore, manganese, asbestos, lead, gold, silver and copper that will continue to be extracted long after most other countries have exhausted their supplies. Russia's forested regions cover an area almost four times the size of the Amazon basin. Yet, owing to gross economic mismanagement under communism and continuing corruption since the privatization of state industries, the country is experiencing severe financial hardship and has been receiving Western aid since 1990.

Privatization

Mass privatization started in the early 1990s. In an attempt to win public approval for the process, in October 1992 every citizen received vouchers worth 10,000 roubles (about US$60 at that time), which could be sold for cash or exchanged for shares in the growing number of private companies. Although the idea of buying and selling stocks caught on, confusion remained over how exactly the market works. Western economic advisers were often asked such questions as 'If I own part of the company, why can't I take the computer home?'

Over 150,000 organizations were privatized but it is now obvious that privatization did nothing to benefit the average Russian. The country's raw materials and viable industries were mostly sold at closed auctions to officially-preferred banks and tycoons, with workers left to purchase economically unviable factories and collective farms. Consequently a relatively small number of well-connected business people pocketed most of Russia's new wealth while millions of workers were lumbered with worthless investments.

Hyperinflation

When once-regulated commodities markets were freed in January 1992, prices immediately soared by 300-400%. Inflation had already been stoked by a 1990 law allowing possession of hard currency, which led to a rush for dollars. Another factor fuelling inflation was an old agreement allowing former Communist Bloc countries to pay off some debts to Russia in roubles. These countries simply printed up rouble notes, further aggravating Russia's problems. In late 1993 inflation was running at around 25% per month. By the end of 1996 it had dropped to 2% but in 1997 the rouble started to dive again, and Russians sought desperately to change rouble savings into dollars before they became worthless. Foreign investment started to dry up.

In August 1998 Yeltsin took the major decision to devalue the currency: three zeros were knocked off to make the exchange rate six roubles to the dollar; new banknotes were printed and strict new rules governed access to foreign currency. After dropping further to about 50 roubles to the dollar, the rate has more or less stabilized, wavering around 30 roubles to the dollar in mid-2003, with inflation running at around 15-20%.

Economic future

Russia is heavily dependent on its energy resources, mainly oil and gas, which account for about 40% of exports, and the economy is very sensitive to global energy prices. High world oil prices in 1999-2000 gave the country a revenue windfall, a jump of 8% in Gross Domestic Product (GDP) and a big boost in its recovery from the 1998 crisis, although growth has been slower since then and the outlook for the future is cloudy. In June 2002 the G8 group of industrialized countries agreed to explore the cancellation of some of Russia's Soviet-era debts.

Putin has brought in a much-needed reform of the tax system. In 1996 only 16% of Russian enterprises paid their taxes in full and on time and only 14 regions out of Russia's 75 paid their tax bills in full. For most people there's now a flat tax rate of 13% with 1% set aside for welfare; corporate taxes have been simplified, too, the idea being that if taxes are low and fair people will pay. It is estimated that over the last decade taxes amounting to US$150 billion have not been collected.

The country's enormous backlog of wages is gradually being addressed and government coffers are slowly filling. In 2002 Russia had its first surplus budget since the fall of the Soviet Union. On paper things seem to be looking up, but ask anyone in the street and you'll find that real life for the vast majority of Russians is as tough as ever.

THE PEOPLE

Russia is the sixth most populous nation in the world with an estimated 141.4 million people (about half the population of the former USSR), but it is also one of only a few countries in the world with a declining population: Russia's is dropping by some two-thirds of a million per year, with drug use, alcoholism, sexually transmitted diseases and deteriorating medical care among suggested causes. Average life expectancy is 72 years for Russian women and just 59 years for men.

A high proportion of Russia's people (82%) are ethnic Russians. The rest belong to nearly 100 ethnic minorities, the most numerous being Tatars (4%) and Ukrainians (3%). In the former USSR it was never wise to refer to people as 'Russian' because of the many other republics they might have come from. With the establishment of independence for many of these states you must be even more careful: Kazakhs or Ukrainians, for example, will not appreciate being called Russians.

Russia is divided into *oblasts* (the basic administrative unit), *krays* (smaller territories) and *autonomous republics* (special territories containing ethnic minority groups such as the Buryats in Siberia). Siberia is part of the Russian Federation and exists only as a geographical, not a political, unit.

Government
Russia moved briskly down the political path from autocracy to 'socialist state', with a period of a few months in 1917 when it was a republic. From November 1917 until August 1991 the country was in the hands of the Communist Party, and until September 1993 it was run by the Congress of People's Deputies. This 1068-seat forum was elected from throughout the USSR. At its head sat the Supreme Soviet, the legislative body, elected from Congress. Since only Party members could stand for election in Congress, only Party members could ever run the country.

The approval of a new Russian Constitution in December 1993 means that the country is now governed by a European-style two-tier parliament very similar to that of France. The head of state is the Russian president, currently Vladimir Putin.

Despite the theory, Russia is far from democratic. The power of the country is vested in a few hundred chief executives of huge corporations who picked up enormous wealth through the corrupt privatization of state enterprises. These so-called 'oligarchs' now monopolize the media, gas and oil, military production and banking sectors, in effect controlling the entire Russian state. Seven of these tycoons bankrolled the 1996 Yeltsin re-election and were rewarded with powerful government positions. With these monopolistic and in many cases criminal power merchants securely lodged in the Kremlin, true democracy is a long way off. Under Putin's autocratic control the situation has not changed.

Education and social welfare
Education and health care are provided free for the entire population but standards for both are falling. School is compulsory between the ages of seven and 17, with the result that Russia has a literacy rate of 98%. Although funding for research is currently at an all-time low, until a few years ago the country ploughed some 5% of national income directly into scientific research in its 900 universities and institutes. Russia's present inability to maintain its scientists has led to a severe brain drain; certain states in the Middle East are very keen for Russian scientists to help them with their nuclear programmes.

The national health care programme is likewise suffering through lack of funds. Russia has produced some of the world's leading surgeons, yet recent outbreaks of diseases extinct in the developed world have demonstrated that health services here were never comprehensive. The most publicized epidemic in the last few years has been diphtheria, with the death of hundreds of Russians who should have been inoculated at birth.

On his re-election in 1996 Yeltsin promised a high priority for social reform and for raising the living standards of ordinary Russians. Market reforms had seen real incomes fall by 40% between 1991 and 1996, boosted unemployment to 6.6 million and driven a quarter of Russians below the poverty line (US$70 a month). Salaries have risen, but unemployment is sharply up and the fraction of Russians living below the poverty line has continued to rise. The country's external debt, US$38 million in 1987 under the communists, is now US$157 **billion**.

Recent government programmes aim to stabilize living standards, gradually reduce poverty and mass unemployment, and create conditions for real growth in income. To even the most optimistic Russian, these programmes have virtually no chance of success.

Religion

Russia was a pagan nation until 988 when Tsar Vladimir ordered a mass conversion to Christianity. The state religion adopted was that of the Greek Orthodox Eastern Church (Russian Orthodox) rather than Roman Catholicism. After the Revolution religion was suppressed until the late 1930s when Stalin, recognizing the importance of the Church's patriotism in time of war, restored Orthodoxy to respectability. This policy was reversed after the war and many of the country's churches, synagogues and mosques were closed down. Labour camps were filled with religious dissidents, particularly under Khrushchev.

Gorbachev's attitude towards religion was more relaxed and the 1990 Freedom of Conscience law took religion off the blacklist. In 1991 Yeltsin even legalized Christmas: Russian Christmas Day, celebrated on 7 January, is now an official public holiday again. Numerous churches have been restored to cater for the country's estimated 50 million Orthodox believers. In 1997 the Cathedral of Christ the Saviour, demolished by Stalin to make way for a public swimming-pool, was rebuilt in Moscow (see p164). The new cathedral was the setting for a magnificent service on 20 August 2000 in which Tsar Nicholas II and his family, the arch-victims of communism and the Revolution, were made saints in an elaborate canonization ceremony.

As well as Russian Orthodox Christians there are also about 1.4 million Roman Catholics. Numbers of Christian sects are growing. Sects as diverse as the so-called 'Old Believers' (who split from the Orthodox church in the 17th century), Scientology and Jehovah's Witnesses are looking for converts here. This has worried some Russians, and on 14 June 1993 the Supreme Soviet passed an amendment to the Freedom of Conscience law banning foreign organizations from recruiting by 'independent' religious activities without permission.

Although the number of Muslims has fallen with the independence of the Central Asian Republics, there are still about 11 million in Russia.

Russian Jews, historically subject to the most cruel discrimination, have been less trusting of the greater religious freedoms. Their position has been made even less comfortable by the recent growth of Russian neo-Nazi groups and by the canonization of the last tsar, a confirmed anti-Semite. In 1990 more than 200,000 Jews moved to Israel, pouring in at a rate of up to 3000 per day. By 1998 over half a million had left, though there are still large Jewish communities in Moscow and St Petersburg.

In Buryatia, the centre of Russian Buddhism, many monasteries have reopened. Since all are a long way off the tourist track, they have not been kept in good repair as museums, unlike churches in European Russia.

Religious freedoms have also brought a growth in animism and Shamanism, particularly in Siberia.

Practical information for the visitor

ESSENTIAL DOCUMENTS

(Also see Part 1: Planning Your Trip.) One 19th-century English traveller who left his passport and tickets behind in London still managed to travel across Siberia carrying no other document than a pass to the Reading Room at the British Library. Entry requirements for foreigners are somewhat stricter nowadays.

The essential documents are your passport, a Russian visa (a page-sized sticker in your passport) and, if appropriate, a visa for the first country you'll be entering after Russia. If you are travelling with an organization (eg Intourist) which has issued you with vouchers to exchange for accommodation or train tickets, don't forget these. **Always carry your passport on you in Russia**: if the police stop you and you don't have it on you, you'll be fined.

It's worth bringing some additional identification (eg driver's licence) as your passport will be taken by the hotel when you check in so that they can register you with the authorities. Don't forget, as many travellers do, to get your passport back before you leave the hotel. Note that **all visas must be registered within three days of your arrival in the country**. Failure to do this will make leaving the country difficult without payment of a fine (as high as US$500!) and will make extending a visa almost impossible.

If you want to rent a self-drive car in Russia you'll need an international driving licence (available from your country's automobile club). International student cards are useful for discounts.

If you're arriving from Africa or South America you may be required to show a yellow fever vaccination certificate.

CROSSING THE BORDER

Customs declaration form

At the Russian border you will be given a Customs Declaration Form (*tamozhennaya deklaratsiya*, таможенная декларация) on which you must declare the total amount of money (cash and travellers' cheques) you are carrying if it exceeds US$1500, and list the number of pieces of luggage you have. **Be sure to get both the entry and exit pages of this form stamped on arrival** (see the boxed text on p64). You must keep this form to be checked when you leave the country, at which time you fill out the exit portion of the form, or another identical form.

Customs-form scam

Travellers continuing via the Trans-Siberian into Mongolia or China – and indeed probably anyone planning to leave Russia from anywhere other than Moscow or St Petersburg – **must** get both the entry and exit pages of their Customs Declaration Form (CDF) stamped on arrival.

Nobody will stamp your CDF in the 'green' customs channel on arrival. You must take the 'red' channel if there is one, demand that someone confirm your hard currency (no matter how little you have, and even if it means having all your belongings pawed over) and insist on a stamp. Ignore anyone who says not to bother, or claims that it doesn't matter provided you have less than US$1500. Of course you'll need to be honest about what you're carrying.

If you fail to get the form stamped you run the risk of being fleeced by bent customs officials at your exit point. There you may be given the choice of either handing over your remaining hard currency or leaving the train and hunting for a way to exchange it back into roubles, at extortionate rates. Arguing will get you nowhere. This has now happened to so many people that it has become the stuff of Trans-Siberian legend. Some travellers have lost hundreds of dollars. The officials are actually doing nothing illegal, merely keeping to a strict interpretation of customs regulations.

At the time of writing there was no need to do this if you intend to fly back out from Moscow or St Petersburg – but better safe than sorry.

In the past, customs officials required documentation of all currency-exchange transactions. They would deduct these from your entry declaration and compare the result with your exit declaration, to ensure that you had not done any black-market exchanges. Although this is no longer the case it is still wise to keep records of your exchange transactions.

China no longer requires visitors to fill in a separate customs form.

Customs allowances: entering or leaving the country

You should not have any problem bringing into Russia any items for personal use or consumption, including modest amounts of spirits or wine. Note that you need a special permit to export 'cultural treasures', a term used to include almost anything that looks old or valuable. Paintings, gold and silver items made before 1968, military medals and coins attract the attention of customs officials and may be confiscated or charged at 100% or more duty if you do not have a permit from the Ministry of Culture.

Border-crossing procedure

Border-crossing procedures in the train may take anywhere from three to seven hours. The first step is for immigration and customs officers of the country you are leaving to check passports and visas and collect customs forms. They may disappear with your passport for half an hour or so, and the train might even move during this time; don't worry, but of course don't forget to get it back! The compartments are then searched by border guards looking for stowaways. On the other side of the border the entire procedure is repeated.

As rails in Russia and Mongolia are of a wider gauge (ie wider apart) than those in China and most of Europe, bogies have to be changed at the borders. The carriages are lifted individually and the bogies rolled out and replaced. If you do not want to stay on the train during this time, you can wait at the border station. If you do get off, carriage attendants won't normally let you get back on before the official boarding time, which is when the train returns to the station to pick up the passengers. Don't leave valuables behind.

Bear in mind that during the entire border crossing procedure the train's lavatories remain locked. This is not purely for security reasons since changing the bogies requires workers operating beneath the train.

❏ **Yes sir, whatever you say, sir**
It's never a good idea to act smart in front of border guards, but this is perhaps nowhere more true than in Russia. A disturbing study reported by the Russian ITAR-TASS news service states that about 60% of Russia's border guards are so unstable they shouldn't be allowed to carry guns. The study, released two days after a guard in eastern Siberia killed five of his colleagues on a shooting rampage, was based on tests conducted by doctors, psychologists and lawyers following a series of similar shootouts by border guards over the previous two years.

WHERE TO STAY

There's now a wide range of places to stay in Russia: everything from B&Bs (homestays) to luxurious hotels of an international standard. Generally, though, Russian hotels are of gargantuan proportions and about as architecturally interesting as a multi-storey car park. This having been said, some old hotels in Moscow and St Petersburg have been restored to a very high standard. It will be interesting to see what becomes of the Hotel Moskva in Moscow, once the biggest hotel in the world and now closed for renovation or demolition.

Note that some hotels may still operate a two-tier pricing system, with higher prices for foreign 'guests'. Except in upmarket hotels, it's actually very difficult to pin down hotel prices: quoted prices seem to vary widely from month to month. Note that hotel prices are normally per person, not per room.

Types of accommodation
Top hotels Many are owned by large Western chains such as Marriott, Radisson and Novotel. While they look glitzy like international hotels everywhere, the service still has a touch of Soviet reticence about it. Their restaurants are normally excellent, they have banking facilities, room service and shops, and their staff are motivated. These hotels are mostly found in Moscow and St Petersburg and prices are what you would expect in the West – US$200-500/£120-300 per night.

Standard hotels These are mostly solid old Intourist hotels. They have all the tourist facilities of restaurants, banks and shops. Their rooms were once good but lack of maintenance and interest has resulted in some decay. In Moscow and St Petersburg standard hotel rooms cost US$50-200/£30-120 and in other cities US$25-60/£15-35.

Basic hotels Once impossible for foreigners to stay in, these places are usually clean if basically equipped. They normally have a restaurant but no shops, foreign exchange or room service. Rooms are simple with a TV and fridge; you will probably be offered one with a bathroom. As long as you don't look too closely the rooms are generally adequate. The best rooms are referred to as *lyuks* ('luxury') and most hotels have at least one such room. This is a relative term and just means that it's the best of all the rooms in that hotel. Basic hotel rooms range from US$15-50/£9-30.

Very basic hotels/hostels These come in many forms; some are quite good and others lousy. They're often attached to an industrial enterprise or a market to accommodate visiting workers or farmers. Sometimes foreigners are turned away at these hotels because staff feel that this isn't quite the sort of place a foreigner should stay in, and they'll direct you to the local Intourist hotel. If you are refused, be persistent or return later when reception staff have changed. These hotels will often not even have a restaurant or café. Very few rooms will have an attached bathroom and many will have up to four beds.

Most train stations have a Rest Room (Komnata otdykha Комната отдыха) where you can stay overnight if you have a ticket for a train departing the next morning. Rooms at very basic hotels cost US$5-15/£3-9.

Youth hostels A few cities in Russia, including Moscow, St Petersburg and Irkutsk, have youth hostels. Standards are surprisingly high and about what you would expect in the West. Dormitory beds cost about £11-14/US$14-18 a night including basic breakfast. Information on youth hostels can be obtained from the Russian Youth Hostel Association (🖳 www.hostelling-russia.ru) or Hostels.com (🖳 www.hostels.com/ru.html).

Holiday homes (Dom otdykha Дом отдыха) In the Soviet era these were holiday destinations for city dwellers. They were like country hotels and offered meals and some organized activities. Today the ones that still operate are mostly run-down and often do not even have a restaurant. A few are excellent and remain the holiday choice of the country's élite.

Sanatoria (Sanatory Санаторий) These are similar to holiday homes with the addition of a sauna, therapeutic services and mud or spring pools. You do not have to be sick to stay at one and many locals visit them once a year in the belief that this will keep them healthy for another year.

Homestays These can be organized in most cities along the Trans-Siberian for £20-30/US$25-40 per person per night including some or all meals, with additional charges for any tours, ticketing, transport or other services. A reliable agency is Host Families Association (HOFA; ☎/📠 +7-812-275 1992, 📧info@hofa.us, www.hofa.us); also see p20 and p146.

To minimize any misunderstandings, agree in advance on meal times, and on how much you can afford for food if this is not included. When you visit markets it's customary and polite to supplement your host's supplies with ingredients they might not otherwise have or be able to afford.

At some railway stations you may be approached by locals offering to put you up in their houses for around £8/US$10 per night. Look the place over before agreeing, and don't allow yourself to be persuaded if you feel in any way uncomfortable about the arrangement.

Checking in at a hotel

Checking in is never the swift procedure it should be. After the receptionist has kept you waiting for a while, serving other customers and occasionally glancing at you, you'll be relieved of your passport and payment and handed a small pass-card. You must present this to the *dezhurnaya* (floor attendant) on your floor in exchange for your room key; in some upmarket hotels you may be given your key by the receptionist.

The dezhurnaya, often an elderly female busybody, seems to spend most of her time drinking tea in a little den, gossiping with friends and keeping an eagle eye on all that happens on her floor. She usually turns very friendly when she figures out that you are a foreigner. As with provodniks on the trains, it's wise to keep on good terms with her (see Tipping on p76). She can provide boiling water or mineral water at all hours, and arrange to get laundry done.

Most hotels have a midday check-out time but you can usually pay for a couple of extra hours or a half day if your train leaves in the evening.

Bedrooms

Rooms are vast and comfortable in some older hotels but rather smaller in more modern places. Mid-range hotels are generally furnished in the worst possible taste, often verging on the schizophrenic: pink roses on the wallpaper matched with purple nylon curtains. Beds are often too short, usually of orthopaedic hardness or so old that every spring digs into you. Bedding, usually consisting of blankets in a duvet cover, is always clean though sometimes a bit threadbare.

There's usually an internal phone, and wake-up calls may be arranged at the reception desk; these seem to be reliable and often the dezhurnaya will knock on your door as well to make sure. You may get phone calls to your room in the evening from women offering 'personal services'; a firm 'no' usually ends the calls.

Bathrooms

Most places now provide toilet paper, soap and a clean towel or two. Bathrooms are usually clean but, except in smarter hotels, tend to be in poor repair. Sink and bath plugs are rare, so it's wise to carry your own universal plug.

It may take five or ten minutes before the tap water comes out hot. Hot water is centrally supplied and because pipes need an annual cleaning, your hotel and every other building in the city may be without hot water for up to four weeks (more in some Siberian cities) during the summer. Only some top-end hotels with independent hot-water systems may escape this. Don't expect a discount on your bill just because you don't have hot water.

TOURS

While guided tours allow you to cover a lot of ground quickly, you can easily get around by yourself in all the cities in this book. You'll learn far more on the buses and metro than you will inside a tour bus. There are some tours that are worth going on, though, and these are mentioned in the relevant city section of this book.

If you fancy a tour of Moscow, St Petersburg and Golden Ring cities there's a backpacker tour bus to take you around: the Beetroot Bus (UK ☎ 020-8566 8846, 🖥 beetroot@beetroot.org, www.beetroot.org).

LOCAL TRANSPORT

If you are booking an independent trip through an agency you may be encouraged to purchase 'transfers' so that you will be met at the airport or station on arrival and taken to your hotel. Prices tend to be high (typically £30-60/US$40-80, depending on distance) but it can be money well spent. If you intend to take a taxi from the airport in particular, it may be worth booking a transfer instead, if only to keep yourself out of the hands of the taxi mafia.

Taxis

Virtually every car in Russia is a taxi: stand in the street with your arm outstretched and someone will pull over and ask where you want to go. Negotiate a price and get in. It's illegal, but if drivers are going your way it makes sense for them to take paying passengers. But while this may be very convenient it can also be dangerous, as you have no idea of the driver's intentions. Women travelling alone would be unwise to hitch rides, and no one should get into a car that has more than one occupant. Don't put your luggage in the boot (trunk) or your driver could simply pull away when you get out to retrieve it. Russians seem to delight in worrying about crime and if you ask them they'll tell you numerous stories about unwary passengers being driven into the countryside and robbed.

Official taxis are safer but harder to find. You'll recognize them by the chequerboard pattern on the door and the green 'for hire' light. Although they have meters, few use them. You should agree on a price before you even get in since once the driver realizes you're a foreigner, he'll bump it up accordingly. Ask a local beforehand what the taxi trip should cost and don't be afraid to haggle; even if you haven't a clue, at least get the price down a bit. You'll find that taxi drivers stick together and one won't offer you a lower price than the others. You're more likely to be charged local rates if you don't pick up taxis outside big hotels or major tourist spots.

Metro
The metro is a very cheap way to get around, with a flat fare of R7 (about £0.14/US$0.18) and trains every few minutes. In Moscow it's worth using the metro just to see the stations, which are more like subterranean stately homes, with ornate ceilings, gilded statues and enormous chandeliers.

Be careful boarding metro-station escalators as they move about twice as fast as Western ones. Russian metro stations are deeper underground than their Western counterparts, perhaps in order to double as bomb shelters, so their escalators are long and swift. The one at St Petersburg's Ploshchad Lenina station rises 59m (194 ft).

At street level, metro stations are indicated by a large blue or red 'M'. Lines are named after their terminal stations, as on the Paris metro. Where two lines intersect the transfer station may have two names, one for each line. As trains move off from the station, the next station is announced. The counter above the end of each tunnel indicates how long it's been since the last train left. In Siberia there are metros in Novosibirsk and Yekaterinburg.

Buses
Every major city has a bus service (fixed-fare and often very crowded) and usually also trolley-buses and trams. Some buses have conductors, some have ticket machines and in others tickets are purchased from the driver in strips or booklets. If there's no conductor you must validate your own ticket, using one of the punches by the windows. If the bus is crowded and you can't reach, pass your ticket to someone near a punch and they'll do it for you. Occasionally, inspectors impose on-the-spot fines for those without punched tickets.

Domestic flights
Domestic flights usually involve long delays and far too much sitting around in airports. Safety standards are not high: if you must fly use one of the larger carriers such as Aeroflot or Transaero. Getting airline tickets is considerably easier than getting tickets for some trains because most Russians can't afford to fly. Nearly all upmarket hotels have airline ticket booking offices.

Boat
Most of the cities you will visit are built on rivers and short trips on the water are usually possible. In St Petersburg the most interesting way to reach Petrodvorets is by hydrofoil. From Irkutsk you can get to Lake Baikal by boat up the Angara River. There are also some long-distance options: for example, a four-day trip up the Yenisey from Krasnoyarsk to Dudinka.

Car rental
In St Petersburg, Moscow and some other cities it is possible to rent self-drive cars. Charges start at about £25/US$35 a day and you will need an international driving licence. You're unlikely to be allowed to drive east of the Urals, however.

BUYING RAIL TICKETS

Classes of service

There are four main classes of service on Russian trains. *Obshchy* (meaning general) signifies carriages with unreserved seating only. *Platskartny* (3rd class) is the most basic of sleeping carriages, an open-plan arrangement of doorless compartments, each with four bunks in tiers of two plus another bunk beside the corridor.

Kupé (coupé; also called 2nd, hard or tourist class) refers to carriages with four-berth closed compartments. *SV* (*spalny vagon*, literally 'sleeping car'; also called 1st or soft class) has comfortable, two-berth compartments which sometimes have washbasins. Some Trans-Siberian trains have an additional *deluxe 1st class* (see p118).

The term *firmenny* refers not to carriages but to certain train services, including all international trains and many domestic ones. On firmenny trains you can expect extra attention to detail and comfort in all classes.

Russian Railways Ticket

BUYING A TRAIN TICKET

Within Russia you will probably want a ticket for travel either the same day or within a couple of days. In either case it's usually possible to go to the station or ticket office, find the correct window, buy your ticket and be out again fairly quickly. If you don't speak Russian you can use the form on p73. Payment is in rouble cash only.

Which train?

The timetable displayed in the booking hall states the train's number, the time of departure and the days on which it travels.

● The train number indicates its direction, with even numbers indicating generally eastbound or northbound travel, and odd numbers westbound or southbound.

● Timetables invariably use Moscow Time. Across a network covering eight time zones this is the only way the system could work. The clock in the booking hall is normally set to Moscow Time. Some station clocks have two hour-hands, black for local time and red for Moscow Time.

● Most trains depart daily, but some run only on odd-numbered days of each month (1st, 3rd, 5th etc) and some only on even-numbered days.

Which ticket window?

There are usually several ticket windows (kassa касса) depending on your destination and possibly on whether you want a same-day or advance-purchase ticket. Staff may not always be very helpful. If the choice is not obvious, go to the administrator's window (Администратор) where you'll either be sold a ticket or told where to get one. If there's a queue and you want to return later, take note of the window's closing times.

Larger stations may have an Intourist window, though it may only be marked Иностранцы (inostrantsy, meaning foreigner). The main stations in Moscow and St Petersburg have 'service centres' with English-speaking staff, though at these you must pay a small extra service fee, typically a few dollars.

Which ticket?

At the window you'll need to tell them your destination, train number; date of departure and compartment class: Л (L = two-berth SV), М (M = four-berth SV), К (K = kupé), П (P = platskartny), О (O = obshchi), either verbally or in writing (see p72). There are several types of long-distance tickets but the most common is a long computer-printed one (see opposite). It contains not only information about the train but also your name and passport number (so don't buy someone else's ticket from them). If you are buying for yourself and others you may have to present passports for everyone; a requirement designed to stop speculators from buying tickets and reselling them for a profit when the train is otherwise sold out. The only way for a ticket to be legally renamed once it is bought is for the ticket seller to cover the original name with an official sticker and write your name on it. In the Soviet era a rail ticket would be sold to a foreigner only if the destination was written on their visa, but this is no longer the case.

On the train the conductor tears off a portion of the ticket, which prevents it being used again. If your ticket is for a train originating somewhere other than your own boarding station, you get a berth number only after you board the train.

TICKET BUYING FOR NON-RUSSIAN SPEAKERS

If you can't speak enough Russian to buy a ticket write what you need on a piece of paper as shown below. The clerk will usually write down a suggested train number and departure time and hand it back to you. Say *Da* (Yes) and you'll get the ticket. Check that the time the clerk writes down is Moscow Time by pointing to it and saying *Moskovskoye vremya*?

For more complex enquiries use the form opposite. If there's a long queue, however, it would be better to transcribe the question you need answered from the page opposite onto a piece of paper rather than trying to get the clerk to look through the whole page.

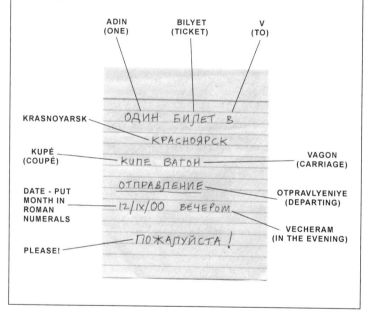

ADIN (ONE)
BILYET (TICKET)
V (TO)
KRASNOYARSK
KUPÉ (COUPÉ)
VAGON (CARRIAGE)
DATE - PUT MONTH IN ROMAN NUMERALS
OTPRAVLYENIYE (DEPARTING)
VECHERAM (IN THE EVENING)
PLEASE!

ОДИН БИЛЕТ В КРАСНОЯРСК
КУПЕ ВАГОН
ОТПРАВЛЕНИЕ
12/IX/00 ВЕЧЕРОМ
ПОЖАЛУЙСТА !

Prices

Overnight rail tickets in Russia are considerably cheaper than in the West; a kupé ticket for a 24-hour journey costs as little as £12/US$15. Supply varies, and the official response appears to be to raise prices when demand seems to be exceeding supply.

The ticket price comprises a booking fee (about US$4 to US$7 depending on where you buy the ticket) plus a charge depending upon the class of service and the distance travelled. Most popular for overnight journeys is the four-berth *kupé* ticket. A two-berth *SV* ticket is 1.5 to 2 times the cost of kupé, and tickets for firmenny trains cost about 1.2 to 1.5 times non-firmenny tickets.

TRAIN INFORMATION AND TICKET BUYING FORM

Please help me.
I don't speak Russian.
Please read the question I point to and
    write the answer
Or * = circle your choice.
Q = question / A = answer
MT = Moscow Time

Будте любезны, помогите мне.
Я не говрю по-русски.
Прочтите вопросы на которые я
    укажу, и напишите ответ
Или * = кружите свой выбор.
Воп. = вопрос / Отв. = ответ
МВ = Московское Время

Information   Информация

Q. When is the next train with available
    SV* kupé* platskartny* spaces
    to ....?
A. The train No. is ....
    It departs at .... : .... (MT).

Воп. Когда следующий поезд со
    свободными местами (СВ*
    купе* плацкарт*) до ....?
Отв. Номер у поезда ....
    Отправляется в .... : ....(МВ).

Q. Are there SV* kupé* platskartny*
    tickets to ....
    on train No. ....?
A. Yes / No

Воп. Есть свободные места
    (СВ* купе* плацкарт*) до ....
    в поезде No ....?
Отв. Да / Нет

Q. When does the train depart and
    arrive?
A. It departs at .... : .... and
    ...arrives at .... : .... (MT).

Воп. Когда поезд отправляется и
    прибывает?
Отв. Отправляется в .... : ....
    и прибывает в .... : .... (МВ).

Q. How much does a SV* kupé*
    platskartny* ticket cost?
A. It costs .... roubles.

Воп. Сколько стоит билет в СВ*
    купе* плацкарт*?
Отв. Билет стоит .... рублей.

Q. Which ticket window should I go to?
A. Ticket window No. ....

Воп. К какой кассе мне подойти?
Отв. Касса номер ....

Q. What platform does train
    No. .... leave from?
A. Platform No. ....

Воп. С какой платформы
    отправляется поезд номер ....?
Отв. Платформа номер ....

Buying tickets   Покупка билетов

Q. May I buy .... SV* kupé*
    platskartny* tickets to ....
    on train No. ..... leaving on ....?
    (DD/MM/YY format, eg 31/12/00.)
A. Yes, it costs .... roubles.
A. No.

Воп. Можно купить ... (СВ* купе*
    плацкарт*) билет до ....
    на поезд номер .... который
    отправляется до ....?
Отв. Да. Билет стоит .... рублей.
Отв. Нет.

Q. Why can't I buy a ticket?
A. There is no train.
A. The train is fully booked.
A. You must buy your ticket at
    window No. ....
A. You can only buy a ticket .... hours
    before the train arrives.

Воп. Почему я не могу купить билет?
Отв. Нет поезда.
Отв. Нет мест.
Отв. Вы должны купить билет в
    кассе номер.............
Отв.Вы можете купить билет за
    ...... часов до прибытия поезда.

Thank you for your help.   **Большое спасибо за помощь.**

Stations in Moscow or St Petersburg will issue domestic tickets up to 45 days in advance and international tickets up to 40 days ahead. Larger stations elsewhere may only allow 30 days' advance purchase. Locals can hold reservations without paying until 10 days before departure, at which point unsold tickets are released and resold.

Getting off in the middle of a journey

It is possible to break your journey once on any through ticket, but it's hardly worth the effort. You must get the stationmaster to validate your ticket within 30 minutes of arrival, then re-book a berth for the onward journey (which can often be done only by the chief ticket officer). If you don't speak Russian, don't even attempt this.

Buying a ticket with 'built-in' stopovers is almost as difficult. Most ticket sellers will advise you to wait and buy tickets for onward segments at your stopover towns. But if you do this you may find that sleeping berths are available only on those few services that **originate** at the stopover town, with none available on through services originating elsewhere, so think first before stopping off at obscure villages or towns.

ELECTRICITY

In almost all Russian cities electricity is 220V, 50 cycle AC. Sockets require a continental-type plug or adaptor. In some places the voltage is 127V so you should enquire at the reception desk before using your own appliances. Sockets for electric razors are provided on trains.

TIME

Russia spans 10 time zones, and on the Trans-Siberian you will be adjusting your watch by an hour almost every day. Russian railways run entirely on Moscow time, and timetables do not list local time. It can be disconcerting to cross the border from China at breakfast-time, only to be informed by station clocks that it's just 02:00.

Moscow Time (MT) is four hours ahead of Greenwich Mean Time when the country is on 'summer time': from the last Sunday in March to the last Saturday in October. Outside that period MT = GMT+3. Siberian local time zones are listed throughout the route guide; those for the main cities are: Novosibirsk (MT+3), Irkutsk (MT+5), Khabarovsk (MT+7) and Vladivostok (MT+7).

MONEY

(See also p44). The basic unit of Russian currency is the rouble, which is divided into 100 kopecks. There are 1, 5, 10 and 50-kopeck and 1, 2, 5 and 10-rouble coins; banknotes come in denominations of 10, 50, 100, 500 and 1000 roubles. When the currency was devalued in 1998 by a factor of 1000, all old notes ceased to be legal tender.

The use of US dollars is illegal in Russia with a few exceptions including airline ticket sales and visa fees. Upmarket hotels and restaurants may quote prices in US$ but will expect payment in roubles. Some Russians still change their roubles to dollars for security, although as the rouble stablizes they are gaining confidence in their own currency. Note that this guide mainly quotes US dollar prices, as these appear fairly steady from year to year: convert at the current exchange rate for rouble prices.

What to bring

US dollars are the easiest currency to exchange throughout Russia. Euros are close behind although many Russians are still unfamiliar with them. UK pounds and a few other non-EU currencies can be changed in Moscow and St Petersburg, and Swedish kroner and Finnish marks in St Petersburg. Japanese yen are easily exchanged in Khabarovsk and Vladivostok.

Foreign banknotes should be as new, crisp and clean as possible. US dollar notes should ideally be dated 1996 or later, as these provide good protection against counterfeiting. Every foreign banknote you exchange will be examined closely and older ones, especially if they're torn, soiled or have writing or ink stamps on them, are likely to be rejected, especially in smaller towns. Your bank at home may hate you for insisting on clean, new notes but it will save you many headaches on the road.

Encashing travellers' cheques is nearly impossible outside weekday banking hours, and difficult at any time outside larger cities. If you do decide to bring travellers' cheques, you will have the fewest problems with American Express or Thomas Cook cheques denominated in US dollars.

Exchanging dollars for roubles

You'll have no problem finding somewhere to change money as there are hundreds of official currency-exchange offices (*obmen valyuty*) in hotels, banks, stores and kiosks in most cities. It's a wise precaution to keep all your currency-exchange receipts until you leave the country. The difference in banks' buying and selling rates is about 2-4%. Rates at currency-exchange offices may vary according to supply and demand and whether banks are open. Out of hours you will get a worse deal than during bank hours.

One traveller remarked that Russia is a country with no change. Steer clear of R1000 notes from banks or currency exchanges, as you will have difficulty getting change back from them in shops. For the same reason you should always keep a stash of coins and small-denomination rouble notes.

❏ **Exchange rates**
To get the latest rates of exchange visit www.oanda.com/convert/classic.

US$1	R29.90
UK£1	R50.74
Euro €1	R35.29
Aus $1	R20.94
Can $1	R22.87
China Y10	R36.19
Japan ¥100	R27.36
Mong T1000	R26.70
NZ$	R18.23
Sing$	R17.20

Credit/debit cards and ATMs

Credit cards – especially Visa, MasterCard and Cirrus, less readily American Express and

Diners Club – are now accepted in many of Russia's upmarket shops, hotels and restaurants. In most cities, including those along the Trans-Siberian, banks, upper-end hotels and even metro stations have automated teller machines (ATMs) where a range of debit cards can be used for rouble cash advances at international exchange rates, with commissions to your home bank of up to 5%. Indeed ATMs are plentiful enough that a Trans-Siberian traveller could confidently carry less than half their money requirements in cash, relying for the rest on a debit card.

The black market
With little difference between bank rates and black market rates the risks involved in changing money this way far outweigh the benefits. There's also nothing to be gained from bringing in articles from the West to sell in Russia, as most Western goods can now be bought locally.

Tipping
Soviet policy outlawed tipping, see as nothing less than bribery: the thin end of the corruption wedge. Glasnost changed all that and you'll find that waiters and others have come to accept the practice. It's really up to you, though. Russians generally don't tip.

If you've agreed a price with a taxi driver there's no need to add a tip. In restaurants you should tip whatever you feel is deserved, up to a maximum of 10% in better restaurants. Porters expect about US$1 and guides US$5-10 per day.

If you want to thank your carriage attendant on the train or your hotel floor attendant, a good way of doing so is with a small gift, preferably something obviously imported. Scented soap, perfume or any particularly exotic Western food product will go down well. Note that with most foreign items now available in Russia, people are much more brand-conscious than they were in Soviet days.

POST AND TELECOMMUNICATIONS
Post
Outbound airmail to the UK and USA takes about two weeks and is reliable. Inbound mail is less reliable and can take more than three weeks. Letters may be opened in transit by thieves looking for money, so don't send anything valuable or important in either direction. To send a parcel from Russia you must have it wrapped and sealed with a wax stamp at the post office.

On international mail to and from Russia, addresses may be written in English and in standard Western format. For domestic mail the usual format is the following, and should be all in Russian:

> Six-digit postal code
> Name of city or town
> Street name, with house number set off by a comma
> Name of addressee
> followed below by the return address.

On international mail it is helpful to write the country name in Cyrillic:

UK: **Великобритания**, USA: **США**
Canada: **Канада**, Germany: **Германия**
Australia: **Австралия**, New Zealand: **Новая Зеландия**

If you wish to send something urgent or valuable out of Russia you should use one of the courier companies such as DHL that have branches around Russia.

Email
Internet access is becoming more widespread in Russia. There are Internet cafés in most cities covered in this book (see the City Guides chapter for addresses). New ones are opening all the time; check the locations of new ones at 🖳 www.cybercafes.com. Access costs US$1-2 per hour. If email contact is important to you it's worth setting up a Web-based email account, eg with Hotmail or Yahoo, before you go.

Telephone
The Russian telephone system has greatly improved and it's now relatively easy to dial into or out of the country. To make an international call dial 8, then wait for a secondary tone and dial 10 followed by the country code and number.

To call from a street telephone (*taksofon*) you need a prepaid telephone card (*kartochka dlya taksofona*) or, for some older telephones, a metal token (*zheton*). Both are available from kiosks and metro station ticket windows, although tokens appear to be on the way out. When placing a call from a taksofon it's important to remember that, as soon as the other party answers, you must press a button to 'start' the call; otherwise you cannot be heard! This button can be a separate button on the telephone, or a number (usually the number 3).

However, taksofon cards are only useful for local calls. For intercity and international calls you should purchase one of a variety of international cards printed with a toll-free or local-rates telephone number and a PIN number. These cards are widely available in shops and kiosks, and all have similar rates. To navigate voice prompts with these cards your telephone must have '*' and '#' keys. Most Russian telephones are pulse-dial so you must switch to tone-dial after being connected, usually by pressing '*'. Some cards (eg, Elvis) have a further option for English-language voice prompts.

You can also make calls from telephone offices, usually part of the post office. Leave a deposit with the cashier who will assign you a booth from which you make your call. Pay the balance after the call.

Upper-end hotels in most Russian cities may also have telephones which take credit/debit cards or the hotel's own brand of card, but calls from such telephones tend to be very expensive.

Fax
The main city post offices often have public fax machines, with typical international rates of around US$5/£3 per minute (one to two pages).

MAGAZINES AND NEWSPAPERS

Two free, visitor-friendly, English-language newspapers worth looking out for in their respective cities are the daily *Moscow Times* and the twice-weekly *St Petersburg Times*. They're easy to find in hotels, hostels, cafés and supermarkets frequented by foreigners.

Western news magazines such as *Time* and *Newsweek* are sold at kiosks and better hotels.

PUBLIC HOLIDAYS

National holidays

If a holiday falls on Thursday, then Friday and Saturday may also be holidays. If a holiday falls on Saturday or Sunday, then Monday will be a holiday.

- 1 January: New Year's Day
- 7 January: Russian Orthodox Christmas Day
- 13 January: New Year's Day according to the old Julian calendar
- 15 February: Defenders of the Motherland Day
- 8 March: International Women's Day
- Late April/early May: Russian Orthodox Easter
- 1 May: Day of Spring and Labour (formerly May Day or International Working People's Solidarity Day). The following work day is also a holiday.
- 9 May: Victory Day, commemorating the end of World War II (known in Russia as the 1941-45 Great Patriotic War)
- 12 June: Independence Day for Russia
- 7-8 November: Grief Day or Reconciliation Day (formerly the Anniversary of the October Revolution)
- 12 December: Constitution Day

School and university holidays

Schools start 1 September and finish 31 May with a week's vacation in November, two weeks in January at the New Year and one week in March. Universities usually start on 1 September and finish on 25 June with the winter break from 25 January to 8 February.

FESTIVALS

Annual arts festivals in Moscow include Moscow Stars (5-15 May) and Russian Winter (25 December to 5 January).

The most interesting festival is St Petersburg's White Nights, held around the summer solstice, when the sun does not set. The days are separated by only a few hours of silvery light: a combined dusk and dawn. Theatres and concert halls save their best performances for this time and a festival is also held at Petrodvorets.

FOOD AND DRINK

There's more to Russian cuisine than borscht and chicken Kiev, but if you eat
most of your meals on the train you'll have little chance to discover this. You'll
probably leave with the idea that Russian cooking is of the school-dinner variety, with large hunks of meat, piles of potatoes and one vegetable (the inter-
minable cabbage), followed by tinned fruit or ice cream. On the whole Russian
cuisine is bland, but you will occasionally be surprised by the delicious food
which seems to appear in the most unlikely restaurants.

Food is no problem if you have money. You can now buy a Mars bar in the
middle of Siberia, although it may be desperately expensive. There are food
shortages in some parts of the country, but Westerners are well catered for. A substantial breakfast will provide you with enough energy to tackle even the heaviest sight-seeing schedule.

The first meal of the day consists of fruit juice (good if it's apple), cheese,
eggs, sausage, bread, jam and *kefir* (thin, sour yoghurt). Lunch and dinner will
be of similarly large size, each consisting of at least three courses. Meat dishes
can be good but there is still a shortage of fresh fruit and vegetables except at the
best hotels.

Zakuski
Russian hors d'oeuvres (*zakuski)* consist of some or all of the following: cold
meat, sausages, salmon, pickled herring, paté, tomato salad, sturgeon and
caviare. Large quantities of vodka are drunk with zakuski.

Soups
Soups are on the watery side but tasty, and make meals in themselves with a
stack of brown bread. Best known is *borscht* (beetroot soup) which often
includes other vegetables (potatoes, cabbage and onion), chopped ham and a
swirl of *smetane* (sour cream).

Caviare
The roe of the sturgeon is becoming more expensive as the fish itself
becomes rarer. Four species are acknowledged to produce the best caviare: beluga,
sterlet, osetra and sevruga, all of them from the Caspian and Black Seas. To produce
caviare's characteristic flavour (preferably not too 'fishy') a complicated process is
involved. The female sturgeon is stunned with a mallet, her belly slit open and the roe
sacs removed. The eggs are washed and strained into batches of uniform size. The
master-taster then samples the roe and decides how much salt to add for preservation.

Processed caviare varies in colour (black, red or golden) and also in the size of
the roe. It is either eaten with brown bread or served with sour cream in *blinis* (thin
pancakes). If you want it you can get it in most tourist hotels and on the train.

A recent report from the World Wide Fund for Nature warns that the sturgeon is
on the brink of extinction because of aggressive fishing by Russia. The report says
that up to 90% of caviare is now obtained illegally and that Russian authorities are
doing nothing because of corruption.

You don't eat meat?!

Vegetarian cooking isn't widely understood in Russia, and with the exception of one or two Hare Krishna-style Asian restaurants there are no genuinely vegetarian restaurants. Vegetarians can manage in Russian restaurants if they choose carefully, but they shouldn't rely on the waiter's imagination or assistance!

Amongst **appetizers**, *shchi* (cabbage soup) is often meatless; suluguni cheese is very similar to Greek halloumi and usually served grilled; and carrot, tomato and cucumber salads are also available.

Main courses are harder; one option is to order a double portion of a starter found on almost every Russian menu: *Julienne*, also known as *griby v smetane* – wild mushrooms baked in cream sauce. Omelettes are another option, if a horribly predictable one. Perversely, you can often do better in cheap cafés than in fine restaurants because meatless food is regarded as rather down-market. Items to look for in cafés are *piroshkie* (dough-pastries with fillings like onion, cabbage or carrot), *vatrushkie* (cream-cheese pastries) and *vareniki* (cheese-filled dumplings). You can almost always find *blini* or *oladi* (different kinds of Russian pancakes) served with either sour cream or jam. In Georgian restaurants *lobio* (spicy bean stew) is a vegetarian mainstay, and a few Georgian places also serve *achma* (a kind of cream-sauce lasagne) – combined with *khachapuri* cheesebreads and some salads, this is about as good as it gets.

Neil McGowan

Shchi (cabbage soup) is the traditional soup of the proletariat and was a favourite of Nicholas II, who is said to have enjoyed only plain peasant cooking, to the great disappointment of his French chef. *Akroshka* is a chilled soup of meat, vegetables and *kvas* (a beer-like brew made from fermented bread). *Rassolnik* is a soup of pickled vegetables.

Fish

Fish common in Russia include herring, halibut, salmon and sturgeon. These last two may be served with a creamy vegetable sauce. In Irkutsk you should try *omul*, the famous Lake Baikal fish, which has a delicious, delicate flavour.

Meat

The most famous Russian main course is chicken Kiev (fried breast of chicken filled with garlic and butter). Almost as famous is *boeuf* Stroganov (named after the wealthy merchant family who financed the first Siberian explorations in the 1580s), a beef stew made with sour cream and mushrooms. Other regional specialities you're likely to encounter include *shashlyk* (mutton kebabs) and *plov* (rice with mutton and spices) from Central Asia, chicken *tabaka* (with garlic sauce) from Georgia, and a Ukrainian dish worth avoiding at all costs, *salo* or pig's fat preserved with salt, said to be good for hangovers. From Siberia comes

---

Opposite Top: Train No 3 (Beijing–Moscow on the Trans-Mongolian route) crossing the rolling hills south of Ulan Bator. (Photo © Nick Hill). **Bottom:** The *Rossiya* is the name the Russians give to the train which crosses Siberia from Moscow 9289km to Vladivostok. (Photo © Tatyana Pozar-Burgar).

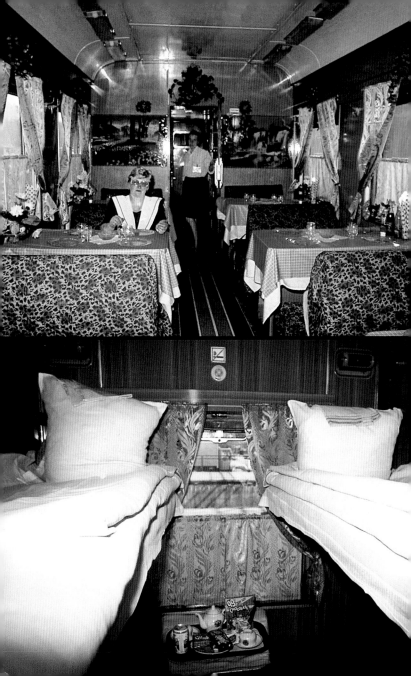

pelmeni, small meat-filled dumplings served in a soup or as a main course. If you're expecting a rump steak when you order *bifstek* you'll be disappointed: it's just a compressed lump of minced meat, usually swimming in grease and grey in colour.

Puddings

Very often the choice is limited to ice cream (*morozhenoye* – always good, safe, and available everywhere) and fruit compôte (a disappointing fruit salad of a few pieces of tinned fruit floating in a large dish of syrup). You may, however, be offered delicious *blinis* (thin pancakes, like crepes) with sour cream and fruit jam; *vareniki* (sweet dumplings filled with cheese or fruit) or rice pudding. Unless you are staying in one of the more expensive hotels there won't be much fresh fruit on offer, although it is now easily available from street vendors.

Bread

Russian bread, served with every meal, is wholesome and filling. Tourist brochures boast that over 100 different types are baked in Moscow. Soviet-era 'bread technology' was allegedly in such great demand in the West that Russian experts were recruited to build a brown-bread factory in Finland.

Drinks

Non-alcoholic Most popular is tea, traditionally served black with a spoonful of jam or sugar. Milk is not always available so you may want to take along some powdered creamer. Russians have been brewing coffee since Peter the Great introduced it in the 17th century, but standards have dropped since then and even a jar of instant coffee from home may taste better.

Bottled mineral water is available everywhere, often carbonated and frequently tasting rather strongly of all those natural minerals that are supposed to be so good for you. There are several varieties of bottled fruit juice (*sok*), of which apple seems to be the most consistently good. The Pepsi and Coca Cola companies fought bitterly over distribution in the USSR and in the 1980s Pepsi was awarded sole rights. Now both are widely obtainable, as are other Western soft drinks.

Alcoholic Vodka predominates, of course, and Russians will be disgusted if you do anything other than drink it straight. The spirit originated in Poland (although some say that it was brought back from Holland by Peter the Great) and means 'little water', something of an understatement. If you tire of the original product, there's a range of flavoured vodkas to sample, including lemon, cherry, blackberry and pepper.

Be warned that the standard vodka measure in Russia is *sto gram* (100g), compared to 25g in the UK. Vodka is traditionally served ice cold and drained in one go from a shot glass. Men are expected to keep this up but a woman might be permitted to drop out after a couple of shots. It can be easy enough to

Opposite Top: Dining car. **Bottom:** Russian Railways compartment (see p118). (Photos: © Tatyana Pozar-Burgar).

drink but it will quickly catch up with you. You may be asked to give a toast and you should take this seriously – a short speech about your subject is enough.

Note that a shot of vodka ought to be followed immediately by zakuski (see p79): a popular Russian saying is that 'only drunkards drink without food'. Another goes: 'Drinking vodka without beer is like throwing money to the wind'. If someone flicks their throat with their forefinger, it usually means 'How about a drink?'. It's considered impolite to refuse.

If you're buying your own vodka, stick with popular brands like Gzhelka. Cheap vodka from street kiosks is often bootleg, and drinking it could give you much worse than a bad hangover. There's also wine: most varieties tend to be rather sweet for the Western palate but Georgian wines are worth trying. Russian champagne is surprisingly good and very cheap. Beer is widely available, popular and cheap; a good brand is Baltika, which comes in nine different types – No 3 is the most popular, while No 7 is a tasty dark brew.

You should also try *kvas* (a beer-like, fermented mixture of stale brown bread, yeast, malt sugar and water). A popular summer cooler sold on the streets from yellow tankers, its alcohol content is so low as to be unnoticeable.

BUYING YOUR OWN FOOD

The once sparse self-serve Soviet supermarkets *(universam)* have rapidly modernized and improved their quality and selection. Canned and packaged goods, juices, pots, tableware, soap, paper products and dry goods, as well as meat, bread, fruits and vegetables, can be found here. *Produkty* stores sell a limited range of fresh vegetables, fruit, bread, meat, eggs and manufactured products. Western-style supermarkets in larger cities have a wide range of products, both imported and local. A *gastronome* is a delicatessen; a *dieta* sells products for diabetics and others on special diets.

Markets *(rynok)* range from clusters of old people selling garden produce at metro exits to large covered markets with dozens of stalls offering everything from home-made honey to dried mushrooms, from meat to imported pineapples.

WHERE TO EAT

It used to be very difficult to get a good meal in Russia. Because all restaurants were state-run, waiters had no incentive to serve you, chefs couldn't be bothered and you were lucky if you managed to bribe your way to a table. All that has changed now and there are restaurants as good as in any Western city. Not surprisingly, prices in top places are also a match for those in the West.

The cheapest places to eat are **self-service cafés** (*stolovaya*) found in most shopping streets, where a filling but stodgy meal of salad, bread, potatoes, meat and tea costs about US$1. In many cities there are also Western **fast-food chains** such as McDonald's (recommended at least for their clean loos) and Patio Pizza, plus Russian derivatives such as Russkoye Bistro. In Moscow, St Petersburg and a few other large cities, **cafés** are good places for an interesting and still reasonably cheap meal.

Food and drink prices
Only a few products such as bread, milk and eggs are still subsidized and regulated. Some examples of current prices:

Hot dog (cheapest)	US$0.30
Hot dog (better quality: eg 'Stop Top')	US$0.80
Georgian cheese bread (*khajapuri*)	US$0.70
McDonald's Big Mac (US$2 in Moscow)	US$1.30
Large loaf of tasty white bread	US$0.30
Sweet cake	US$0.50
Russian 'Edam' style cheese (1kg)	US$3.30
Large jar of Nutella spread	US$2.00
Cheap Russian beer (500ml bottle)	US$0.50
Heineken beer (330ml can)	US$1.05
Cheap vodka (1 litre)	US$1.60
Moskovskaya vodka (1 litre)	US$1.80
Gzhelka vodka (1 litre)	US$4.35
Georgian red wine (1 litre)	US$6.50
Sekt Russian champagne (1 litre)	US$4.60

When you buy **vodka** check the seal on the bottle to make sure it hasn't been diluted. It's wise to go for the bigger brands: some smaller distilleries reportedly cut costs by producing low-grade alcohol, which has resulted in blindness and death amongst some drinkers.

In **restaurants**, service varies wildly: sometimes it's a struggle to get anyone to notice you, while at other times there's a friendly English-speaking waiter or waitress who can't do enough to help you. Russians rarely dine out and when they do it's always a big occasion. They go in large groups and like to make a meal last the evening. Staff give guests ample time to interpret the menu and do their best to ensure that no dish arrives too quickly. While you await your food a dance-band may entertain you with folk-songs and 1960s Western hits at a volume that prohibits conversation; there may even be a cabaret show (of sorts). If you get invited to join a Russian party, a visit to a restaurant can be a very entertaining, often drunken affair. Note that tsarist traditions die hard: if a man wishes to invite a woman from another table to dance he must first ask permission of the men at her table.

In some upmarket restaurants you may find cover and/or entertainment charges of up to 10% added to your bill. Sometimes they'll just round up the total by about this amount to save the bother of doing an accurate calculation.

WHAT TO DO IN THE EVENING

Nightlife in Moscow and St Petersburg is now as good as you'll get in any big city in the West. These cities have lots of nightclubs, discos and bars, and it really helps to have Russian friends to show you the best places. In smaller towns your major options are the hotel bars and discos which often stay open late,

❏ RUSSIAN CUSTOMS AND ETIQUETTE

Customs

● Wine, cake, candy or flowers are traditional gifts if you're invited to dinner in someone's home. A small gift for any children is also appropriate. If you bring flowers be sure the number of flowers is uneven: even numbers are for funerals.

● Shaking hands or kissing across the threshold of a doorstep is considered to bring bad luck.

● Take off your gloves when shaking hands.

● Be prepared to remove your shoes upon entering a home. You will be given a pair of slippers (*tapki*) to help keep the apartment clean.

● Do not cross your legs with the ankle on the knee, as it's impolite to show people the soles of your shoes. When in the metro or sitting on a bus, don't let your feet even come close to a seat or to another passenger.

● Smoking is common and accepted in Russia.

● Be prepared to accept all alcohol and food offered when visiting friends, and this can be quite a lot. Refusing a drink or a toast is a serious breach of etiquette. An open bottle must be finished.

● Be prepared to give toasts at dinners, etc. Be careful, the vodka can catch up with you.

● Dress up for the theatre. Check your coat and any large bags at the garderobe.

● Be careful how you admire something in a home. Your host may offer it to you to take away.

● Russian men still expect women to act in a traditional manner. It's bad form for a woman to be assertive in public, to carry heavy bags if you're walking with a man, to open doors, uncork bottles or pay your own way in social situations. A woman alone in a restaurant or hotel risks being taken for a prostitute.

● Dress casually for dinner in someone's home. Wear a hat in cold weather, or babushkas will lecture you on your foolishness!

● In a Russian Orthodox church women should cover their heads with a scarf or hat and wear a skirt. Men should remove their hats.

● Putting your thumb between your first two fingers is a very rude gesture.

Superstitions

Russians remain remarkably superstitious; many of the following were once also common elsewhere in Europe:

● Never light a cigarette from a candle. It will bring you bad luck.

● Do not whistle indoors or you will whistle away your money.

● Never pour wine back-handed, it means you will also pour away your money.

● A black cat crossing your path is bad luck.

● A woman who finds herself sitting at the corner of a table will be single for the next seven years.

● If you spill salt at the table you will be plagued by bad luck unless you immediately throw three pinches over your left shoulder.

● If someone offers you good wishes, or if you are discussing your good fortune, you must spit three times over your left shoulder and touch (knock on) wood to keep your good fortune.

casinos which you may find difficult to get into and want to leave as soon as you do, and cultural activities such as opera, theatre, ballet or circus. Performances usually start early: between 18:00 and 19:00; don't be late or ushers may not let you in until the interval.

Ballet
Many of the world's greatest dancers have been from Russia's Bolshoi and Kirov companies. Some defected to the West including the Kirov's Rudolf Nureyev, Russia's most famous ballet star, who liked to say he was 'shaken out' of his mother's womb on the Trans-Siberian as it rattled towards Lake Baikal.

Don't miss the chance of a night at the magnificent Bolshoi Theatre; the season runs from September to May. Note that many touring groups dance at the Bolshoi so it may not be the famous company you see.

Opera and theatre
In the past, opera was encouraged more than theatre as it was seen as politically neutral. Glasnost, however, encouraged playwrights to dramatize Russian life as it is, rather than as the government wanted people to see it. This has led to a number of successful new theatre groups opening in Moscow and St Petersburg. There are also several puppet theatres which are highly recommended.

Cinema
In the 1980s the Soviet film industry benefited from the greater freedoms that came with glasnost. In early 1987 one of the most successful and controversial films was *Is It Easy To Be Young?*, which was deeply critical of the Soviet war in Afghanistan. In the 1990s the pessimism of the people towards life is reflected in films made in the country. *Little Vera* (1990) is the story of a provincial girl who sinks into small-time prostitution and finally drowns herself (Gorbachev walked out of it saying he disapproved of the sex scenes). In *Executioner* (1991) a female journalist takes on the mafia in St Petersburg and loses. But by the late 1990s Russian film output began to drop as state sponsorship of the arts shrank.

Nowadays Western, and especially American, films are everywhere. Every sizeable town has a cinema, with shows starting early in the evening. There is a thriving black market in bootleg American movies; don't be surprised to find *Harry Potter* showing in your restaurant car.

Television
Russian television has evolved fast in recent years, with news and current affairs programmes of quite high quality. Hotel TVs often have satellite channels, a welcome break from the usual round of garish game-shows. Moscow time rules the airwaves, so children's programmes broadcast at 16:00 in Moscow come on at 23:00 in Vladivostok!

Rock concerts and sports matches
Rock concerts and sports fixtures are invariably held in stadiums. These are usually well worth attending, and very safe as the arenas swarm with police and soldiers to keep order. Football is very popular, as is ice hockey in winter.

Tennis has grown in popularity following the success of Wimbledon semifinal-ist Yevgeny Kafelnikov.

SHOPPING

Shopping was a complicated, frustrating affair in the USSR. Shops were crowd-ed and if they weren't this was a sign that there was nothing worth buying in them. The common view on market reform is that while 20 years ago there was not much in the stores, at least everyone could afford what there was. Now shelves overflow with goods but no one has the money to buy them, and many Russians are starting to get nostalgic for the old days.

Although Russian shoppers tend to flock to stores with the lowest prices, you are unlikely to see food queues. Nevertheless Russians still carry around their *avoska* (a 'just in case' bag) and are quick to spot a queue and join it even before they know what it is for, in the hope of a bargain.

For foreigners shopping is no problem at all: you only have to wander into a main street to see the wide variety of goods on sale. In the electronics section of any department store you'll find quality merchandise on a par with anything available in the West. Whereas previously this was all sold for hard currency, now it's for roubles, although that doesn't mean ordinary Russians can afford it.

Making a purchase

Although many shops now have a Western-style system for choosing and pay-ing, the procedure in some, such as bakeries and bookshops, is more complicat-ed. First you must decide what you want and find out the price (the assistant may write this down on a ticket for you); then you must go to the cash desk (where an abacus may be used to calculate your total bill) and pay, getting a receipt; then you take the receipt back to the first counter and exchange it for your purchases.

Department stores

Department stores (*univermag*) sell a variety of manufactured goods such as clothing, linens, toys, homewares and shoes. No visit to Moscow would be complete without a visit to GUM, Russia's largest department store. It com-prises an enormous collection of arcades (now largely occupied by upmarket Western chains and boutiques), housed in an impressive glass-roofed building resembling a giant greenhouse. There is another department store chain: TsUM, which has branches in Moscow and most larger cities.

Kiosks

Outdoor kiosks are shops in small booths on the sidewalks, squares, markets and around the metros and stations. They often remain open late and a few are open 24 hours. Most sell telephone cards, alcohol, drinks and cigarettes, while others specialize in newspapers, ticket sales, lotto, milk, souvenirs, fruit and vegetables, bootleg cassettes and CDs or clothing.

Opening hours

Large department stores are open from 09:00 to 20:00 Monday to Saturday. Smaller stores have a wide range of opening times, anywhere from 08:00 to

11:00, closing between 20:00 and 23:00, with an hour's lunch-break either from 13:00 to 14:00 or 14:00 to 15:00. Most shops are closed on Sundays. Many modern shops and large department stores now work without a lunch-break.

WHAT TO BUY

Handicrafts

These include attractively decorated black lacquer *palekh* boxes (icon-painters started making them when religious art lost popularity after the Revolution); enamelled bowls and ornaments; embroidered blouses and tablecloths from the Ukraine; large black printed scarves; guitars and *balalaikas*; lace tablecloths and handkerchiefs; jewellery and gemstones from Siberia and the Urals, and painted wooden ornaments including the ubiquitous *matrioshka* dolls which fit one inside the other. Modern variations on the matrioshka include leaders of the former USSR, the Beatles and even South Park cartoon characters.

Old communist memorabilia have long disappeared from shops but are still sold to tourists and make interesting souvenirs. There is much military memorabilia on sale: anything from hats and hip flasks to diving suits and medals. Check what you're buying carefully as it might not be genuine, and don't declare any of it when you leave Russia. This is equally true with the old bank notes you can buy.

Beware of buying paintings, especially if they are expensive, as duty of 100% or more may be imposed on them when you leave the country. If you are going to buy one, make it a small one so that it will fit into your bag easily. If the painting looks old and potentially valuable, it may well be confiscated by customs officials unless you have a permit from the Ministry of Culture. Customs officials always make a point of looking at paintings when you leave the country.

Books

You'll find few English-language books in the shops but upmarket hotel gift shops usually have a small selection of novels. If you haven't already got one, it's well worth buying an English–Russian/Russian–English dictionary (US$2 or less in most bookshops) to supplement your phrasebook.

Russian-language art books are worth buying for their cheap but usually high-quality reproductions. There are branches of Dom Knigi (House of Books) in Moscow, St Petersburg and most other large cities.

Cassettes, CDs and CD-ROMs

Pirated Russian and Western hit music is available everywhere, at around US$1 for tapes, US$2-3 for CDs and US$10 for DVDs; the quality is generally good.

Russian music runs the gamut from pop to metal. Pop groups with staying power over recent years include Ruki Vverkh (Hands Up), Gosti iz Budushchevo (Guests from the Future), Premier Ministr and Ivanushky International. Chai-F is a long-running rock band preferred by older fans. A popular young female vocalist is Alsu. Alla Pugacheva is an older female singer with a loyal following, particularly among women over 40.

CD-ROMs with pirated computer software are widely available, many with English-language versions included. Virtually any application is available, though you need to know what you are looking for. They can be very cheap (as little as US$3) but it's impossible to know what viruses they may contain.

Clothes

There is a huge market for fake sports clothes and there are now also dozens of trendy foreign fashion shops in the biggest cities. Russian or old Soviet military clothing is a popular buy for foreigners but this should be concealed as you leave the country or it may be confiscated.

CRIME

Russia is as safe a place for tourists as London or New York, with much the same amount of petty crime. It can, however, be a dangerous place if you're involved in business.

In December 2000 gunmen opened fire on the car of Moscow's deputy mayor, Josif Ordzhonikidze, just after he had brokered a deal to open the city's first Formula One racetrack. Seriously injured, he became another statistic confirming that doing business in Russia is dangerous, despite Putin's pledge to establish a 'dictatorship of the law'. There are believed to be over 8000 gangs operating in the country, many of whom, using 'heavies' recruited from the army, extort protection money from businesses. Taxi-drivers have been threatened with having their cars damaged or families attacked. There are even occasional shoot-outs between rival gangs. St Petersburg is considered the most dangerous city in which to operate a business, followed by Moscow and Krasnoyarsk. It seems that it's not the local councils but the mafia who now run Russia's cities.

Crimes against tourists were almost unimaginable in the communist era, when Moscow's streets were safer than those of New York, but now a branch of the police force has been set up especially to protect foreigners. The situation is not as bad as in some other European or American cities, but you shouldn't wander around late at night, especially in Moscow or St Petersburg. The mafia aren't really interested in tourists; they deal in far more money than they could get from you.

Be sensible about your safety: as a Russian woman warned me, 'Where there is big crime, there will also be small crime'. Don't dress ostentatiously or wear expensive watches or jewellery. Watch out for pickpockets. Travellers report that petty pilfering from hotel rooms has increased considerably in recent years. You're better off leaving your valuables at home. A money-belt for your passport, credit cards, travellers' cheques and foreign currency is essential. Also see the warnings on p125 for Trans-Siberian travellers.

The foreign media have exaggerated the dangers of the mafia as far as tourists are concerned – only bad news sells. After visiting Russia you will remember, more than anything else, just how friendly and genuine the people were to you.

SIBERIA AND THE RAILWAY

Historical outline

EARLY HISTORY

Prehistory: the first Siberians

Discoveries at Dering Yuryakh, by the Lena River 100km south of Yakutsk, have indicated that man has lived in Siberia for far longer than had previously been thought. Archaeologist Yuri Mochanov, who led excavations there in the 1980s and 1990s, believes that the thousands of stone tools he found embedded in geological stratum dating back over two million years suggests human habitation stretching back this far, which would place the site on a par with Professor Leakey's discoveries in East Africa. It's a highly controversial theory as it would mean that initial human evolution also occurred outside Africa. Western archaeologists who have studied the material believe, however, that it cannot be more than 500,000 years old; that would still give the Siberians an impressively long history.

There is evidence of rather more recent human life in the Lake Baikal area. In the 13th millennium BC, Stone Age nomads roamed round the shores of the lake, hunting mammoths and carving their tusks into the tubby fertility goddesses that can been seen in the museums of Irkutsk today. Several sites dating back to this early period have been excavated in the Baikal area; the railway passes near one at the village of Malta (see p357), 85km west of Irkutsk.

There is far more archaeological evidence from the Neolithic Age (12th to 5th millennia BC) and it shows that nomadic tribes had reached the Arctic Circle, with some even moving into North America via the Bering Strait (then a land bridge) and Alaska. These northern nomads trained dogs to pull their sledges, but remained technologically in the Stone Age until Russian colonists arrived in the mid-17th century.

In the south, several Bronze Age cultures emerged around the central parts of the Yenisey River. Afanassevskaya, south of Krasnoyarsk, has given its name to the culture of a people who lived in this area in the 2nd millennium BC and decorated their pottery with a characteristic herringbone pattern.

The first evidence of permanent buildings has been found near Achinsk, where the Andronovo people built huge log cabins in the 1st millennium BC. Excavations of sites of the Karassuk culture, also dated to the 1st millennium BC, have yielded Chinese artifacts, indicating trade between these two peoples.

Early civilizations

The Iron Age sites show evidence of more complex and organized societies. The clear air of the Altai Mountains has preserved the contents of numerous graves of the 2nd century BC Tagar Culture. Their leaders were embalmed and buried like Egyptian pharaohs with all that they might need in the afterlife. In their burial mounds archaeologists have found perfectly preserved woollen blankets, decorated leather saddles and the complete skeletons of horses, probably buried alive when their masters died.

In the 3rd century BC the Huns moved into the region south of Lake Baikal where their descendants, the Buryats, now live. The Huns' westward progress continued for five centuries until the infamous Attila, 'The Scourge of God', having pillaged his way across Europe, reached Paris where he was defeated in 452 AD.

The ancestors of the Kyrgyz people were the Tashtyks of Western Siberia, who built large houses of clay (one found near Abakan even has an under-floor central heating system), moulded the features of their dead in clay death masks and decorated their bodies with elaborate tattoos. The tiny Central Asian republic of Kyrgyzstan, south of Kazakhstan, is all that remains of a once mighty empire that stretched from Samarkand to Manchuria in the 12th century.

In the following century the Kyrgyz were defeated by the rapidly advancing Mongols. Genghis Khan's Mongol empire grew to become history's largest land empire, including the Tartars of South Russia, and the peoples of North Asia, Mongolia and China.

The first Russian expeditions to Siberia

In mediaeval times Siberia was known to Russians only as a distant land of valuable fur-bearing animals. Occasional expeditions from Novgorod in the 15th century became more frequent in the 16th century, after South Russia was released from the Mongol grip by Tsar Ivan the Terrible. Ivan's seizure of Kazan and Astrakhan opened the way to Siberia. Yediger, leader of a small Siberian kingdom just over the Urals, realized his vulnerability and sent Ivan a large tribute of furs, declaring himself a vassal of the Tsar.

Yediger's son Kuchum was of a more independent mind and, having murdered his father, he put an end to the annual tribute, proclaiming himself Tsar of Siberia. Ivan's armies were occupied on his western frontiers, so he allowed the powerful Stroganov family to raise a private army to annex the rebel lands. In 1574 Ivan granted the Stroganovs a 27-year lease on the land over the Urals as far east as the Tobol River, the centre of Kuchum's kingdom.

Yermak: the founder of Siberia

The Stroganovs' army was a wild bunch of mercenaries led by an ex-pirate named Yermak, the man now recognized as the founder of Siberia. They crossed the Urals and challenged Kuchum, gaining control of his lands after a struggle that was surprisingly long considering that Russian muskets faced only swords and arrows.

On 5 November 1581 Yermak raised the Russian flag at Isker, near modern Tobolsk, and sent the Tsar a tribute of over 2500 furs. In return Ivan pardoned him for his past crimes, sent him a fur-lined cape that had once graced the royal shoulders, and a magnificent suit of armour. Over the next few years Yermak and his men were constantly harassed by Kuchum, and on 16 August 1584 were ambushed as they slept on an island in the Irtysh. The story goes that Yermak drowned in the river, dragged under by the weight of the Tsar's armour. Yermak's name lives on as the top brand of Russian rucksack.

The quest for furs

Over the next 50 years Cossack forces moved rapidly across Siberia, establishing *ostrogs* (military outposts) as they went and gathering tributes of fur for the Tsar. Tyumen was founded in 1586, Tomsk in 1604, Krasnoyarsk in 1628 and Yakutsk in 1633. By 1639 the Cossacks had reached the east coast.

Like the Spanish Conquistadors in South America they dealt roughly with the native tribes they met, who were no match for their muskets and cannon. The prize they lusted after was not gold, as it was for the Spaniards in Peru and for later Russian adventurers in Siberia, but furs. In the days before fur farms, certain pelts were worth far more than they are today; from the proceeds of a season's trapping in Siberia a man could buy and stock a large farm with cattle and sheep. The chances of a Russian trapper finding his way into and out of the dark, swampy forests of the taiga were not very high, but quite a few did it.

Khabarov and the Amur

In 1650 a Russian fur merchant named Khabarov set out from Yakutsk to explore the Amur region in what is now the Far Eastern Territories, fertile and rich in fur-bearing animals. Khabarov found the local tribes extremely hostile, as the Russians' reputation for rape and pillage had spread before him. He and his men committed such atrocities that the news reached the ears of the Tsar, who ordered him back to the capital to explain himself. Bearing gifts of fur, he convinced the Tsar that he had won valuable new lands which would enrich his empire.

The local tribes, however, appealed to the Manchus, their southern neighbours, who sent an army to help them fight off the Russians. The Tsar's men were gradually beaten back. Periodic fighting went on until 1689, when the Russians were forced out of Manchuria and the Amur by the Treaty of Nerchinsk.

18th-century explorers

Peter the Great became Tsar in 1696 and initiated a new era of exploration in the Far East. By the following year the explorer Vladimir Atlasov had claimed Kamchatka for Russia. In 1719 the first scientific expedition set out for Siberia. Peter commissioned the Danish seaman Vitus Bering to search for a northern sea-passage to Kamchatka and the Sea of Okhotsk (unaware that such a route had been discovered by Semyon Deshnev 80 years earlier). However, the Tsar did not live to see Bering set out in 1725.

Between 1733 and 1743 another scientific expedition, comprising naval officers, topographers, geodesic surveyors, naturalists and astronomers, made detailed charts of Russians lands in the Far East. Fur traders reached the Aleutian Islands and in 1784 the first Alaskan colony was founded on Kodiak Island by Gregory Shelekhov (whose grave is in the cemetery of Znamensky Convent in Irkutsk.) Russian Alaska was sold to the United States in 1868 for the bargain price of two cents an acre.

THE 19TH CENTURY

There were two developments in Siberia in the 19th century which had a tremendous effect upon its history. First, the practice of sentencing criminals to a life of exile or hard labour in Siberia was increased to provide labour for the mines and to establish communities around the military outposts. The exile system, which caused a great deal of human misery, (see below) greatly increased the population in this vast and empty region. Secondly, and of far greater importance, was the building of the Trans-Siberian Railway in the 1890s (see p106).

Colonization

By the end of the 18th century the population of Siberia was estimated to be about 1½ million people, most of whom belonged to nomadic native tribes. The policy of populating the region through the exile system swelled the numbers of settlers, but criminals did not make the best colonists. The government therefore tried to encourage voluntary emigration from overcrowded European Russia. Peasant settlers could escape the bonds of serfdom by crossing the Urals, although Siberia's reputation as a place of exile was not much of an incentive to move.

As the railway penetrated Siberia, the transport of colonists was facilitated. Tsar Alexander's emigration representatives were sent to many thickly-populated regions in European Russia in the 1880s, offering prospective colonists incentives including a reduced rail fare (six roubles for the 1900km/1200-mile journey) and a free allotment of 27 acres of land. Prices in Siberia were high, and colonists could expect get up to 100% more than in European Russia for produce grown on this land. Many peasants left Europe for Siberia after the great famine of 1890-91.

Further exploration and expansion

Throughout the century scientists and explorers continued to make expeditions to Siberia. In 1829 an expedition led by the German scientist, Baron von Humboldt, already famous for his explorations in South America, investigated the geological structure of the Altai plateau in southern Siberia.

In 1840 the estuary of the Amur was discovered, and colonization was encouraged after Count Muravyev-Amursky, Governor General of Eastern Siberia, annexed the entire Amur territory for Russia, in flagrant violation of the 1689 Russo-Chinese Treaty of Nerchinsk. But the Chinese were in no position to argue, being threatened by the French and English as well as by internal troubles in Peking. By the Treaty of Peking (1860) they ceded the territory north of the Amur to Russia, and also the land east of the Ussuri, including the valuable Pacific port of Vladivostok.

THE EXILE SYSTEM

The word 'Siberia' meant only one thing in Victorian England and 19th century Russia: an inhospitable land of exiled murderers and other evil criminals who paid for their sins by working in its infamous salt mines. While some of the first exiles sent over the Urals did indeed work in salt mines, most of them mined gold, silver or coal.

By 1900 over a million people had been exiled and made the long march to the squalid and overcrowded prisons of Siberia.

George Kennan

In 1891 a book entitled *Siberia and the Exile System*, written by George Kennan, was published in America. It exposed the truly horrific conditions under which prisoners were kept in Siberia and aroused public opinion in both America and Britain. Kennan was a journalist working for the *New York Century Magazine*. He knew Siberia well, having previously spent two years there. At that time he had been unaware of how badly convicts were treated and in a series of lectures before the American Geographical Society had defended the Tsarist government and its exile system.

When his editor commissioned him to investigate the system more thoroughly, bureaucrats in St Petersburg were happy to give him the letters of introduction which allowed him to venture into the very worst of the prisons and to meet the governors and convicts.

The government doubtless hoped that Kennan would champion their cause. Such had been the case with the Rev Dr Henry Landsell who had travelled in Siberia in 1879. In an account of his journey, *Through Siberia*, Landsell wrote that 'on the whole, if a Russian exile behaves himself decently well, he may in Siberia be more comfortable than in many, and as comfortable as in most of the prisons of the world.' After the year he spent visiting Siberian prisons, Kennan could not agree with Landsell, and revealed the inhumanity of the exile system, the convict mines and the terrible conditions in the overcrowded prisons.

The first exiles

The earliest mention of exile in Russian legal documents was in 1648. In the 17th century exile was used as a way of banishing criminals who had already been punished. In Kennan's words: 'The Russian criminal code of that age was almost incredibly cruel and barbarous. Men were impaled on sharp stakes, hanged and beheaded by the hundred for crimes that would not now be regarded as criminal in any civilized country in the world, while lesser offenders were flogged with the knut (a whip of leather and metal thongs, which could break a man's back with a single blow) and bastinado (cane), branded with hot irons, mutilated by amputation of one or more of their limbs, deprived of their tongues, and suspended in the air by hooks passed under two of their ribs until they died a lingering and miserable death.' Those who survived these ordeals were too mutilated to be of any use so they were then driven out of their villages to the lands beyond the Urals.

The Siberian Boundary Post (circa 1880) In this melancholy scene, friends and relatives bid exiled prisoners farewell by the brick pillar that marked the western border of Siberia, on the Great Post Road.

Exile as a punishment: the convict mines

With the discovery of valuable minerals in Siberia and in light of the shortage of labourers, the government began to use criminals to work the mines. Exile was thus developed into a form of punishment and extended to cover a range of crimes including desertion, assault with intent to kill and vagrancy (when the vagrant was of no use to the army or the community). According to Kennan, exile was also a punishment for offences that now seem nothing short of ridiculous: fortune-telling, prize-fighting, snuff-taking (the snuff-taker was not only banished to Siberia but also had the septum between his nostrils torn out) and driving with reins (traditionally Russian drivers rode their horses or ran beside them: reins were regarded as too Western, too European)

Abolition of the death penalty

In the 18th century the demand for mine labour grew, and the list of crimes punishable by exile was extended to include drunkenness and wife-beating, the cutting down of trees by serfs, begging with a pretence to being in distress, and setting fire to property accidentally. In 1753 the death penalty was abolished (for all crimes except an attempt on the life of the Tsar) and replaced by exile with hard labour. No attention was given to the treatment of exiles en route, who were simply herded like animals over the Urals, many dying on the way. The system was chaotically corrupt and disorganized, with hardened murderers being set free in Siberia while people convicted of relatively insignificant offences perished down the mines.

Reorganization in the 19th century

In the 19th century the system became more organized but no less corrupt. In 1817 a series of *étapes* (exile stations) was built along the way to provide overnight shelter for the marching parties. They were nothing more than crude log cabins with wooden sleeping platforms. Forwarding prisons were established at Tyumen and Tomsk from where prisoners were sent to their final place of exile. From Tyumen convicts travelled by barge in specially designed cages to Tomsk. From there some would be directed on to Krasnoyarsk or to Irkutsk, a 1670km (1040-mile), three-month march away. Prisoners were sent on to smaller prisons, penal colonies and mines. The most infamous mines were on the island of Sakhalin, off the east coast, where convicts dug for coal; the gold mines of Kara; and the silver mines of Nerchinsk.

Records were started in 1823 and between this date and 1887, when Kennan consulted the books in Tomsk, 772,979 prisoners had passed through on their way to Siberia. They comprised *katorzhniki* (hard labour convicts), distinguishable by their half-shaved heads; *poselentsi* (penal colonists); *silni* (persons simply banished and allowed to return to European Russia after serving their sentence); and *dobrovolni* (women and children voluntarily accompanying their husbands or fathers). Until the 1850s convicts and penal colonists were branded on the cheek with a letter to indicate the nature of their crime. More than half of those who crossed the Urals had had no proper trial but were exiled by 'administrative process'. As Kennan states: 'Every village commune has the right to banish any of its members who, through bad conduct or general worthlessness, have proved themselves obnoxious to their fellow citizens.'

Life in the cells
The first prison Kennan was shown on his trip in 1887 was the Tyumen forwarding prison. He records the experience thus: 'As we entered the cell, the convicts, with a sudden jingling of chains, sprang to their feet, removed their caps and stood in a dense throng around the *nari* (wooden sleeping platforms).... "The prison" said the warden, "is terribly overcrowded. This cell for example is only 35 feet long by 25 wide, and has air space for 35, or at most 40 men. How many men slept here last night?" he inquired, turning to the prisoners. "A hundred and sixty, your high nobility", shouted half a dozen hoarse voices.....I looked around the cell. There was practically no ventilation and the air was so poisoned and foul that I could hardly force myself to breathe it in.'

The hospital cells
None of these dreadful experiences could prepare Kennan for the hospital cells, filled with prisoners suffering from typhus, scurvy, pneumonia, smallpox, diphtheria, dysentery and syphilis. He wrote afterwards: 'Never before in my life had I seen faces so white, haggard, and ghastly as those that lay on the gray pillows in the hospital cells....As I breathed that heavy, stifling atmosphere, poisoned with the breaths of syphilitic and fever-stricken patients, loaded and saturated with the odor of excrement, disease germs, exhalations from unclean human bodies, and foulness inconceivable, it seemed to me that over the hospital doors should be written "All hope abandon, ye who enter here".'

From the records he discovered that almost 30% of patients in the prison hospital died each year. This he compared with 3.8% for French prisons of the time, 2% for American prisons and 1.4% for English prisons.

Corruption
As well as the inhuman conditions he saw in the prisons, Kennan found that the whole exile system was riddled with corruption. Bribes were regularly accepted by warders and other officials. One provincial administrator boasted that the Governor of Tobolsk was so careless that he could get him to sign any document he was given. As a wager he wrote out The Lord's Prayer on an official form and placed it before the Governor, who duly signed it. The St Petersburg government was too far away to know what was going on in the lands beyond the Urals.

Many high-ranking officials in Siberia were so tightly bound by bureaucratic ties that change was impossible, even if they desired it. An officer in the Tomsk prison confided in Kennan: 'I would gladly resign tomorrow if I could see the (exile) system abolished. It is disastrous to Siberia, it is ruinous to the criminal, and it causes an immense amount of misery; but what can be done? If we say anything to our superiors in St Petersburg, they strike us in the face; and they strike hard – it hurts!'

Opposite Top: Plinthed loco by the line at km3333, Novosibirsk. **Bottom**: Changing the bogies at the Chinese border (see p392).

(**Above**): Political exiles (circa 1880), many of whom came from aristocratic families, were free to adopt whatever lifestyle they could afford within the confines of Siberia, once they had completed their prison sentences.

Political exiles

Life for the so-called 'politicals' and 'nihilists', banished to prevent them infecting European Russians with their criticisms of the autocratic political system that was choking the country to death, was generally better than that for other prisoners. Many came from aristocratic families and, once out of prison, life for them continued in much the same way as it had west of the Urals.

The most famous political exiles were the 'Decembrists', men who took part in an unsuccessful coup in 1825. Many were accompanied into exile by their wives. Some of the houses in which they lived are now preserved as *dom* (house) museums in Irkutsk (see p249). Kennan secretly visited many of the politicals in Siberia and was convinced that they did not deserve being exiled. He wrote later: 'If such men are in exile in a lonely Siberian village on the frontier of Mongolia, instead of being at home in the service of the state – so much the worse for the state.'

A few politicals were sentenced to exile with the native Yakuts within the Arctic Circle. Escape was impossible and life with a Stone Age tribe must have seemed unbearable for cultured aristocrats who had until recently been part of the St Petersburg court circle.

Opposite Top: The house of Decembrist, Maria Volkonskaya, the 'Princess of Siberia' (see p249) in Irkutsk is now a museum. **Bottom**: There are still some traditional wooden buildings to be seen in Siberian cities such as this house in the back streets of Ulan Ude.

Temporary abolition of the exile system

The exile system was abolished in 1900. But however corrupt the system and inhuman the conditions in these early Siberian prisons, worse was to come only 30 years later. Under Stalin, vast concentration camps were set up, in European Russia as well as Siberia, to provide a huge slave-labour force to build roads, railways and factories in the 1930s and 1940s. Prisoners were grossly overworked and undernourished. The mortality rate in some of these camps is said to have been as high as 30%. Reports of the number of people sentenced to these slave labour camps range from three million to 20 million. Some researchers place the death toll up to the late 1950s as high as 18 million.

Early travellers

VICTORIAN ADVENTURERS

The Victorian era was the great age of the gentleman (and gentlewoman) adventurer. Many upper-class travellers spent the greater part of their lives exploring lesser-known regions of the world, writing long and often highly readable accounts of their adventures and their encounters with the 'natives'. Siberia attracted almost as many of this brave breed as did Africa and India. Once travel across the great Siberian plain by normal forms of transport of the time (carriage and sledge) had been tried, some resorted to such new-fangled inventions as the bicycle (RL Jefferson in 1896), the train (from 1900) and the car (the Italian Prince Borghese in an Itala in 1907). Some even crossed the country entirely on foot.

THE GREAT SIBERIAN POST ROAD

Before the railway was built there was but one route across the region for convicts, colonists or adventurers: a rough track known as the Great Siberian Post Road or *Trakt*. Posting stations, where travellers could rent horses and drivers, were set up at approximately 40km (25-mile) intervals. Murray's 1865 *Handbook for Russia, Poland and Finland* tells travellers: 'Three kinds of conveyances are available: the *telega*, or cart without springs, which has to be changed at every station, and for which a charge of about 8d is made at every stage; the *kibitka* or cart (in winter a sledge) with a hood; and the *tarantass*, a

---

❏ **Travel by tarantass**
Kate Marsden, a nurse travelling in 1894, recalled the agony of days spent in a tarantass in the following way: 'Your limbs ache, your muscles ache, your head aches, and, worst of all, your inside aches terribly. "Tarantass rheumatism" internal and external, chronic, or rather perpetual, is the complaint.'

(**Above**): Until the building of the Trans-Siberian, the Great Post Road formed the life-line for hundreds of tiny communities such as this. (**Below**): There were few bridges on the Road – crossing frozen rivers and lakes was treacherous in early winter and spring.

❏ KATE MARSDEN VISITS SIBERIAN LEPERS

Miss Marsden was a nurse with a definite mission in Siberia. In the 1880s she learnt, through travellers' accounts, of the numerous leper colonies north of Yakutsk. There were rumours of a special herb found there which could alleviate the symptoms of the disease. After an audience with Queen Victoria, during which she was given useful letters of introduction, she travelled to Moscow. She arrived in mid-winter, wearing her thin cotton nurse's uniform and a white bonnet, which she immediately exchanged for thick Russian clothes.

Crossing Siberia

After meeting the Empress Maria, who gave her 1000 roubles for her relief fund, she started on her long sledge ride. It was not a dignified send-off – 'three muscular policemen attempted to lift me into the sledge; but their combined strength was futile under the load'. She got aboard eventually and was soon experiencing the extreme discomfort of Siberian travel. She said it made her feel more like 'a battered old log of mahogany than a gently nurtured Englishwoman'.

Distributing tea, sugar and copies of the Gospels to convicts in the marching parties she encountered along the Post Road, she reached Irkutsk in the summer. She boarded a leaky barge on the Lena River north of Lake Baikal, and drifted down to Yakutsk, sitting on the sacks of potatoes with which the boat was filled. Of this part of the journey she wrote: 'Fortunately we had only about 3,000 miles of this but 3,000 miles were enough'.

Her goal was still a 3200km (2000 mile) ride away when she reached Yakutsk. Although she had never been on a horse before, this brave woman arranged an escort of 15 men and rode with them through insect-infested swamps and across a fiery plain, below which the earth was in a constant state of combustion, until she reached the settlement of Viluisk.

The Lepers of Viluisk

On her arrival the local priest informed her that 'On the whole of the earth you will not find men in so miserable a condition as the Smedni Viluisk lepers'. She found them dressed in rags, living in hovels and barely existing on a diet of rotten fish. This was in an area where, in winter, some of the lowest temperatures in the world have been recorded. Unfortunately she did not find the herb that was rumoured to exist there but left all the more convinced that finances must be raised for a hospital.

Although she managed to raise 25,000 roubles towards the enterprise, her task was not made any easier by several individuals who took exception to her breezy style of writing, accusing her of having undertaken the journey for her own fame and fortune. Some even suggested that the journey was a fiction invented so that Miss Marsden could collect charitable sums for her own use. In the end she was forced to sue one of her attackers who wrote a letter to *The Times* describing her journey as 'only a little pleasure trip'.

Nevertheless she achieved her aim: a hospital opened in Viluisk in 1897. It still stands and her name is still remembered in this remote corner of Russia.

kind of carriage on wooden springs which admits of the traveller lying down full length and which can be made very comfortable at night. The two latter vehicles have to be purchased at Perm, if the *telega*, or postal conveyance be not accepted. A *tarantass* may be bought from £12 to £15.'

George Kennan called the Imperial Russian Post System 'the most perfectly organized horse express service in the world'.

The discomforts of Siberian travel

Since a visit to Siberia could rarely be completed in a single season, most travellers had the opportunity to try the various modes of transport used in summer and winter. While most found the sledge more comfortable than the tarantass, no 19th century travelogue would be complete without a detailed description of the tarantass.

This unique vehicle had a large boat-shaped body, and travellers stored their belongings on the floor, covering them with straw and mattresses on which they lay. This may sound comfortable, but when experienced at speed over atrocious roads and for great distances, by contemporary accounts it was not. SS Hill wrote in 1854: 'The worst of the inconveniences arose from the deep ruts which were everywhere...and from the necessity of galloping down the declivities to force the carriage upon the bridges. And often our carriage fell with such force against the bridges that it was unsafe to retain our accustomed reclining position...'

The yamshchiki

The driver (*yamshchik*) of the tarantass or sledge was invariably drunk, and had to be bribed with vodka to make good time between post stations. Murray's 1865 guidebook thoughtfully includes in its Useful Russian Phrases section 'Dam na vodki' ('I will give you drink money'). Accidents were commonplace; RL Jefferson (on a trip without his bicycle in 1895) wrote that his yamshchik became so inebriated that he fell off the sledge and died. The same fate befell one of Kate Marsden's sledge-drivers who had gone to sleep with the reins tied around his wrists. She wrote: 'And there was the poor fellow being tossed to and fro amongst the legs of the horses, which, now terrified, tore down the hill like mad creatures.... In a few minutes there was a fearful crash. We had come into collision with another tarantass and the six horses and the two tarantasses were mixed up in a chaotic mass'.

The horses

Sledges and tarantasses were pulled by a *troika*, a group of three horses. These were small furry specimens, 'not much larger than the average English donkey', noted RL Jefferson. They were hired between post stations and usually belonged to the yamshchik.

SS Hill was shocked at the way these animals were treated. He remarked: 'The Arab is the friend of his horse. The Russian or Siberian peasant is his severe master who exacts every grain of his strength by blows accompanied with curses....lodges him badly or not at all, cares little how he feeds him, and never cleans him or clips a hair of his body from the hour of his birth to that of his death.' Horses were worked literally until they died. RL Jefferson recalls that two of his animals dropped dead in harness and had to be cut free.

> ❏ **Dangers**
> Travel in Siberia was not only uncomfortable, it was also dangerous. Wolves and
> bears roamed the forests and when food was scarce would attack a horse or man
> (although you were safe in a tarantass). In the Amur region lived the world's largest
> cat, the Amur tiger. Just as wild as these animals, and probably more dangerous, were
> the *brodyagi*, escaped convicts in search of money and a passport to readmit them to
> Europe.

Dirt and disease
As well as the discomfort of the 'conveyance' and the dangers along the Trakt,
travellers were warned about the dirt and disease they could encounter. RL
Jefferson wrote: 'No wonder that Siberia is looked upon by the traveller with
abhorrence. Apart from its inhabitants, no one can say that Siberia is not a land
of beauty, plenty and promise; but it is the nature of its inhabitants which make
it the terrible place it is. The independence, the filth and general want of comfort which characterize every effort of the community, serve to make a visit to
any Siberian centre a thing to be remembered for many years and an experience
not desirable to repeat.'

Hotel rooms were universally squalid. Kate Marsden gives the following
advice to anyone entering a hotel bedroom in Siberia: 'Have your pocket hand-
kerchief ready...and place it close to your nostrils the moment the door is
opened. The hinges creak and your first greeting is a gust of hot, foetid air.'

Insects
Especially in the summer months, travellers were plagued by flies and mosquitoes. Kate Marsden wrote: 'After a few days the body swells from their bites
into a form that can neither be imagined nor described. They attack your eyes
and your face, so that you would hardly be recognized by your dearest friend.'

At night, travellers who had stopped in the dirty hotels or posting stations
were kept awake by lice, bedbugs and a variety of other insects with which the
bedding was infested. RL Jefferson met a man who never travelled without four
saucers and a can of kerosene. In the hotel room at night he would put a saucer
filled with kerosene under each bed-leg, to stop the bugs reaching him in bed.
However, Jefferson noted that: 'With a sagacity which one would hardly credit
so small an insect, it would make a detour by getting up the wall on to the ceil-
ing, and then, having accurately poised, drop down upon the victim – no doubt
to his extreme discomfort.'

Bovril and Jaeger underwear: essential provisions
RL Jefferson (see 'Jefferson's Bicycle Jaunts', opposite) never travelled without a large supply of Bovril and a change of Jaeger 'cellular' underwear – 'capital stuff for lightness and durability' he wrote after one long ride on his
Imperial Rover bicycle. Kate Marsden shared his enthusiasm for Dr Jaeger's
undergarments: 'without which it would have been quite impossible to go

through all the changes of climate; and to remain for weeks together without changing my clothes', she wrote. On the subject of provisions for the trip, Murray recommended taking along basic foodstuffs. Miss Marsden packed into her tarantass 'a few boxes of sardines, biscuits, some bread, tea and one or two other trifles which included 18kg (40 lb) of plum pudding'.

SS HILL'S *TRAVELS IN SIBERIA*

This account of Hill's Siberian adventures was the result of a journey made in the early 1850s to Irkutsk and Yakutsk. Armed with a pistol loaded with goose-shot (the law forbade a foreigner to shoot at a Russian, even in self-defence), he travelled by tarantass and lived on *shchi* (soup) and tea most of the time. He makes some interesting observations upon the culinary habits of the Siberians he met along the way.

He records that on one occasion, when settling down to a bowl of shchi after a long winter's journey, 'we found the taste of our accustomed dish, however, today peculiar'. He was made aware of the main ingredient of their soup later, 'by the yamshchik pointing out to us the marks of the axe upon the frozen carcass of a horse lying within a quarter of a verst of the site of our feast'. In some places even tea and shchi were unavailable and they could find only cedar nuts ('a favourite food article with the peasants of Eastern Siberia'). He ate better in Irkutsk, where, at a dinner party, he was treated to *comba* fish, 2m (6 ft) in length and served whole. 'I confess I never before saw so enormous an animal served or cooked whole save once, an ox roasted at a 'mop' in Worcestershire', he wrote later. He was shocked by the behaviour of the ladies at the table, who, when bored, displayed 'a very droll habit of rolling the damp crumb of rye bread... into pills'. He remarks with surprise that in Siberian society 'a glass of milk terminates the dinner'.

JEFFERSON'S BICYCLE JAUNTS

RL Jefferson was also an enthusiastic cyclist and made several bicycle journeys to Siberia in the 1890s. A year after cycling from London to Constantinople and back, he set out again from Kennington Oval for Moscow on his Imperial Rover bicycle. Twelve hours out of Moscow, a speeding tarantass knocked him down, squashing the back wheel of his 'machine'. Repairs took a few days but he still managed to set a cycling speed record of just under 50 days for the 6890km (4281-mile) journey from London to Moscow and back.

His next ride was to the decaying capital of the Khanate of Khiva, now in Uzbekistan. The 9700km (6000-mile) journey took him across the Kyrgyz Steppes in south-west Siberia, along the coast of the Aral Sea and over the Karakum Desert. When the bicycle's wheels sank up to their axles in the sand he had the Rover lashed to the back of a camel for the rest of the journey. While in Central Asia he lived on a diet of boiled mutton and *koumis* (fermented mares' milk). He travelled in a camel-hair suit (Jaeger, of course) and top boots, with a white cork helmet to complete the outfit.

Across Siberia

Jefferson made two more trips to Siberia. In *Across Siberia by Bicycle* (1896), he wrote that he left Moscow and 'sleeping the night in some woodman's hut, subsisting on occasional lumps of black bread, bitten to desperation by fearful insects, and tormented out of my life during the day by swarms of mosquitoes, I arrived in Perm jaded and disgusted'. He then cycled over the Urals and through the mud of the Great Post Road to Yekaterinburg. Here he was entertained by the Yekaterinburg Cyclists' Club whom he described as 'friends of the wheel – jolly good fellows all'.

Declaring that 'from a cyclist's point of view, Russian roads cannot be recommended', he abandoned his Rover in 1897 for the adventure described in *Roughing it in Siberia*. With three chums he travelled by sledge from Krasnoyarsk up the frozen Yenisey ('jerking about like peas in a frying pan') to the gold mines in Minusinsk district, spending several weeks prospecting in the Syansk Mountains.

Building the railway

The first railway to be built in Russia was Tsar Nicholas I's private line (opened in 1836) which ran from his summer palace at Tsarkoye Selo (Pushkin) to Pavlovsk and later to St Petersburg, a distance of 23km (14 miles). The Tsar was said to have been most impressed with this new form of transport and over the next 30 years several lines were laid in European Russia, linking the main cities and towns. Siberia, however, was too far away to deserve serious consideration since most people went there only if they were forced to as exiles. As far as the Tsar was concerned traditional methods of transport kept him supplied with all the gold and furs he needed.

PLANS FOR A TRANS-SIBERIAN RAILWAY

Horse-powered Trans-Siberian Express?

The earliest plans for a long-distance railway in Siberia came from foreigners. Most books which include a history of the Trans-Siberian give passing mention to a certain English engineer, if only because of his wildly eccentric ideas and his unfortunate name. Thus it is a Mr Dull who has gone down in history as the man who first seriously suggested the building of a line from Perm across Siberia to the Pacific, with carriages being pulled by wild horses (of which there were a great many in the region at the time). He is said to have formally proposed his plan to the Ministry of Ways of Communication who, perhaps not surprisingly, turned it down.

In fact the Englishman's name was not Dull but Duff, and it's not only his name that has been distorted through time. His descendants (John Howell and William Lawrie) have requested that the story be set straight. Thomas Duff was an enterprising adventurer who went to China to seek his fortune in the 1850s. He returned to England via Siberia, spending some time in St Petersburg with wealthy aristocratic friends. Here he was introduced to the Minister of Ways of Communication and it was probably during their conversation that he remarked on the vast numbers of wild horses he had encountered on his journey. Could they not be put to some use? Perhaps they might be trained to pull the trains that people were saying would soon run across Siberia. It is unlikely that this remark was meant to be serious but it has gone down in history as a formal proposal for a horse-powered Trans-Siberian Express.

More serious proposals

At around this time the American Perry McDonough Collins was exploring the Amur river, having persuaded the US government to appoint him as commercial agent in the region. After an enthusiastic welcome by Count Muravyev-Amursky, Governor-General of Siberia, Collins set off to descend the Amur in a small boat. Collins envisaged a trade link between America and Siberia with vessels sailing up the Amur and Shilka rivers to Chita, where a railway link would shuttle goods to and from Irkutsk. He sent his plans for the building and financing of such a line to the government but they were rejected. His next venture, a telegraph link between America and Russia, also failed but not before he had made himself a considerable fortune.

It took a further 20 years for the government to become interested enough in the idea of a Siberian railway to send surveyors to investigate its feasibility. Plans were considered for lines to link the great Siberian rivers, so that future travellers could cross Siberia in relative comfort by a combination of rail and ship. European lines were extended from Perm over the Urals, reaching Yekaterinburg in 1878.

Tsar Alexander III: the railway's founder

In 1881 Alexander III became Tsar and in 1886 gave the Trans-Siberian project his official sanction with the words: 'I have read many reports of the Governors-General of Siberia and must own with grief and shame that until now the government has done scarcely anything towards satisfying the needs of this rich, but neglected country! It is time, high time!'

He was thus able to add 'Most August Founder of The Great Siberian Railway' to his many other titles. He rightly saw the railway as both the key to developing the land beyond the Urals and also as the means to transport his troops to the Amur region which was being threatened by the Chinese. When the commission looking into the building of the new line declared that the country did not have the money to pay for it, the Tsar's reply was to dismiss the committee and form a new one.

THE DECISION TO BUILD

The new commission took note of petitions from Count Ignatyev and Baron Korf, the Governors-General of Irkutsk and the Amur territories, respectively. They had proposed rail links between Tomsk and Irkutsk, Lake Baikal and

Sretensk (where passengers could board ships for the journey down the Shilka and Amur Rivers to the coast) and for the Ussuri line to Vladivostok. Baron Korf considered it imperative for the Ussuri line to be built as soon as possible if the valuable port of Vladivostok was not to be cut off by the advancing Chinese. The Tsar took note and declared: 'I hope the Ministry will practically prove the possibility of the quick and cheap construction of the line'.

Surveys were commissioned and detailed plans prepared. In 1891 it was announced that the Trans-Siberian Railway would indeed be built and work would start immediately. It was, however, to be constructed as cheaply as possible using thinner rails, shorter sleepers and timber (rather than stone) for the smaller bridges.

The route
The railway committee decided that the great project should be divided into several sections, on which work would commence simultaneously. The West Siberian Railway would run from Chelyabinsk (the railway over the Urals reached this town in 1892) to the Ob River where the settlement of Novo Nikolayevsk (now Novosibirsk) was being built. The Mid-Siberian Railway would link the Ob to Irkutsk, capital of Eastern Siberia. Passengers would cross Lake Baikal on ferries to Mysovaya, the start of the Transbaikal Railway to Sretensk. From there they would continue to use the Shilka and Amur River for the journey to Khabarovsk, until the Amur Railway could be built between these towns. The Ussuri Railway would link Khabarovsk with Vladivostok.

There were also plans for a shortcut from the Transbaikal area to Vladivostok, across Manchuria. This would be known as the East Chinese Railway.

Nicholas lays the foundation stone
After the decision to start work, the Tsar wrote the following letter to his son, the Tsarevich, who had just reached Vladivostok at the end of a tour around the world: 'Having given the order to build a continuous line of railway across Siberia, which is to unite the rich Siberian provinces with the railway system of the interior, I entrust you to declare My will, upon your entering the Russian dominions after your inspection of the foreign countries of the East. At the same time I desire you to lay the first stone at Vladivostok for the construction of the Ussuri line forming part of the Siberian Railway...'.

On 31 May 1891 Nicholas carried out his father's wishes, filling a wheelbarrow with earth and emptying it onto what was to become part of the embankment for the Ussuri Railway. He then laid the foundation stone for the station.

RAILWAY CONSTRUCTION: PHASE 1 (1891-1901)

● **The Ussuri, West Siberian & Mid-Siberian Railways (1891-98)** Work started on the Ussuri line (Vladivostok to Khabarovsk) some time after the inauguration ceremony and proceeded slowly. In July 1892 construction of the West Siberian line (Chelyabinsk to the Ob River) was begun. In July 1893 work started on the Mid-Siberian line (Ob River to Irkutsk).

The West Siberian reached Omsk in 1894 and was completed when the rails reached the Ob in October 1895. The Ussuri Railway was completed in 1897. In the following year the final rails of the Mid-Siberian were laid, finally linking Irkutsk to Moscow and St Petersburg.

● **The Transbaikal Railway (1895-1900)** The rail link between the Lake Baikal port of Mysovaya and Sretensk on the Shilka River was begun in 1895. In spite of a flood which swept away part of the track in 1897, the line was completed by the beginning of 1900.

Passengers could now travel to Irkutsk by train, take the ferry across Lake Baikal and the train again from Mysovaya to Srtensk, where steamers would take them to Khabarovsk.

● **The East Chinese Railway (1897-1901)** Surveys showed that the proposed Amur Railway between Sretensk and Khabarovsk would be expensive to build because of the mountainous terrain and the large supplies of explosives required to deal with the permafrost. In 1894 the Russian government granted China a generous loan to help pay off the latter's debts to Japan. In exchange a secret treaty was signed which allowed Russia to build and control a rail link between the Transbaikal region and Vladivostok, across the Chinese territory of Manchuria.

Every difficulty encountered in building railways in Siberia (severe winters, mountains, rivers, floods, disease and bandits) was a feature of the construction of the East Chinese Railway, begun in 1897 and opened to light traffic in 1901.

The labour force
The greater part of the Trans-Siberian Railway was built without heavy machinery, by men with nothing more than wooden shovels. They nevertheless managed to lay up to 4km ($2^1/_2$ miles) of rail on a good day. Most of the labour force had to be imported as local peasants were already fully employed on the land. They came not only from European Russia but from as far away as Italy and Turkey. Chinese coolies were employed on the Ussuri Railway but overseers found them unreliable and terrified of the Amur tigers with which the area was infested.

The government soon turned to the prisons to relieve the shortage of labour, and gangs of convicts were put to work on the lines. They were paid 25 kopecks (a quarter of a rouble) a day and had their sentences reduced – eight months on the railways counted for a year in prison. The 1500 convicts employed on the Mid-Siberian worked hard but those brought in from Sakhalin Island to work on the Ussuri line ran riot and terrorized the inhabitants of Vladivostok.

Shortage of materials
On many parts of the Siberian Plain engineers discovered that although there were vast forests, the trees were unsuitable for use as sleepers (ties). Timber had to be imported over great distances. Rails came from European Russia and some even from Britain. They were shipped either via the Kara Sea (a southern extension of the Arctic Ocean) and up the Yenisey River to Krasnoyarsk,

or right around the continent by boat to Vladivostok (which took two months). From here, when work started on the Transbaikal line in 1895, materials were shipped up the Ussuri, Amur and Shilka Rivers to Sretensk (over 1600km/1000 miles). Horses and carts were scarce in Siberia and these, too, had to be brought in from Europe.

Difficult terrain

When the railway between St Petersburg and Moscow was being planned, the Tsar took ruler and pencil and drew a straight line between the two cities, declaring that this was the route to be followed, with almost every town by-passed. For the Trans-Siberian, Alexander ordered that it be built as cheaply as possible which is why in some places the route twists and turns so that expensive tunnelling might be avoided. There were few problems in laying foundations for the rails across the open steppeland of the Siberian plain, but cutting through the almost impenetrable forests of the taiga proved extremely difficult. Much of this area was not only thickly forested, but swampy in summer and frozen until July. Consequently the building season lasted no more than four months in most places.

Parts of the route in eastern Siberia were locked in permafrost and, even in mid-summer, had to be dynamited or warmed with fires before rails could be laid. The most difficult terrain was the short line around the southern end of Lake Baikal, the Circumbaikal Loop, which required over 200 trestles and bridges, and 33 tunnels.

Conditions

For the workers who laboured in Siberia, conditions were hardly the most enjoyable. All were far from home, living in isolated log cabins that were not much cleaner or more comfortable than Tyumen's squalid prison, graphically described by George Kennan in *Siberia and the Exile System*. Winters were very long and extremely cold. The brief summer brought relief from the cold but the added discomfort of plagues of black flies and mosquitoes in the swamps of the taiga. There were numerous outbreaks of disease. Workers on the East Chinese Railway were struck by bubonic plague in 1899 and cholera in 1902. In many places the horses were wiped out by Siberian anthrax.

There were other dangers in addition to disease. In Manchuria and the Amur and Ussuri regions, the forests were filled with Amur tigers for whom the occasional railway labourer no doubt made a pleasant snack. In Manchuria construction camps were frequently raided by *hunghutzes* (bandits) who roamed the country in gangs of up to 700. As a result the Russian government was obliged to allocate considerable money and manpower to the policing of the region.

There were several setbacks that no one could have foreseen. In July 1897 severe flooding swept away or damaged over 300km (200 miles) of track near Lake Baikal on the Transbaikal line, also destroying settlements and livestock. Damage was estimated at six million roubles. In other areas landslides were caused by torrential rainfall.

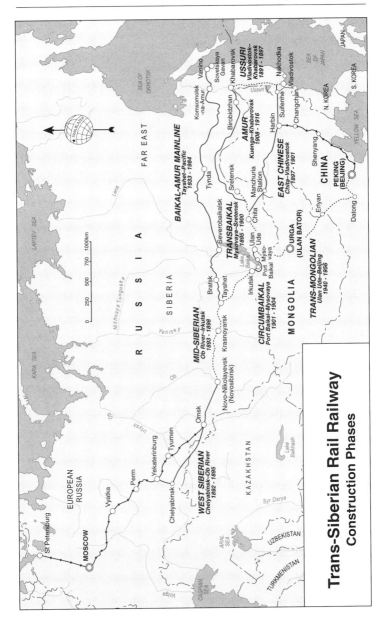

Trans-Siberian Rail Railway
Construction Phases

RAILWAY CONSTRUCTION: PHASE 2 (1898-1916)

Reconstruction

As the first trains began to travel over the newly-laid tracks, the shortsighted-ness of building the railway as cheaply as possible soon became clear. Many of the materials used in its construction were either substandard or unsuitable to the conditions they were expected to withstand. The rails, less than half the weight of those used in North America and fashioned of inferior quality iron, soon bent and buckled and needed replacing. The ballast under the sleepers was far thinner than that put down on the major railways of Europe. As a result the ride in the carriages was bumpy and uncomfortable and speed had to be kept down to 13mph for passenger trains, 8mph for freight. Foreign engineers pro-claimed the whole system unsafe and were proved correct by the frequent derailments which took place.

In 1895 Prince Khilkov became Minister of Ways of Communication. On a tour of inspection along the West and Mid-Siberian lines he quickly realized the need for a massive rebuilding programme. Extra trains were also needed to transport the hundreds of thousands of emigrants who were now flooding over the Urals. In 1899, 100 million roubles were allocated for repairs, work which would have been unnecessary had sufficient funds been made available from the start.

● **The Circumbaikal Loop Line (1901-1904)** In 1901 work began on the 260km Circumbaikal Loop line around Lake Baikal's southern shore. The ini-tial project had been shelved in 1893, the terrain considered too difficult. Passengers used the ferry service across the lake but it was soon found that the ships couldn't cope with the increased traffic. The situation became critical at the start of the Russo-Japanese war in 1904 when troops and machinery being sent to the East by rail were delayed at the lake. Construction of the new line continued as fast as possible and by the end of the year the final section of the Trans-Siberian was opened. Passengers were at last able to travel from Calais to Vladivostok entirely by train.

● **The Amur Railway (1907-1916)** The original plans for a railway from Sretensk to Khabarovsk along the Shilka and Amur Rivers were abandoned because the route would entail expensive engineering work. After the Russo-Japanese war in 1904-5, the government realized there was a danger of Japan taking control of Manchuria and the East Chinese Railway. As this was the only rail link to Russia's naval base at Vladivostok, it was decided that the Amur Railway must indeed be built.

Work began at Kuenga in 1908. There were the usual problems of insects, disease and permafrost but with the rest of the railway operational, it was easier to transport labour and materials to the area. When the bridge over the Amur at Khabarovsk was finished in 1916, the Trans-Siberian Railway was at last com-plete. Since 1891 over 1000 million roubles had been spent on building all the sections (including the East Chinese line).

THE FIRST RAIL TRAVELLERS

Rail service begins

As each of the sectors of the Trans-Siberian was completed, a rail service was begun. To say that there were teething troubles would be a gross understatement: there was a shortage of engines and carriages, most of the system operated without a timetable and there were frequent delays and derailments along the shoddily-constructed line. Nevertheless, to attract foreign travellers, luxury trains and 'Expresses' were introduced. Those run by the government were known as Russian State Expresses while another service was operated by the Belgian Compagnie Internationale des Wagons-Lits. In 1900 the Ministry of Ways of Communication published its English-language *Guide to The Great Siberian Railway*.

Early rail travellers

When RL Jefferson set out to investigate the Minusinsk gold-mining region in 1897, he was able to take the train (travelling this time without his bicycle but no doubt taking along a good supply of Bovril and Jaeger underwear) as far as Krasnoyarsk.

The first Englishwoman to travel the entire length of this route was Annette Meakin, who in 1900 took her aged mother along for company. They travelled via Paris to see the Siberian display at the Paris Exhibition. Having crossed Siberia, they went by ship to Japan and then on to North America, crossing that continent by train, too. Having circumnavigated the globe by rail, Miss Meakin recorded her experiences in the book she called *A Ribbon of Iron*.

The Paris Exhibition

The Russian government was keen to show off to the world the country's great engineering feat and at the Paris 'Exposition Universelle' of 1900, a comprehensive Trans-Siberian exhibit was staged. Amongst photographs and maps of Siberia, with Kyrgyz, Buryat and Goldi robes and artefacts, there were several carriages to be operated by the Wagons-Lits Company on the Great Siberian Railway. They were furnished in the most sumptuous style, with just four spacious compartments in the sleeping carriages, each with a connecting lavatory. The other carriages contained a smoking-room done up in Chinese style, a library and music-room complete with piano.

In the two restaurant cars, decorated with mahogany panelling and heavy curtains, visitors to the exhibition could dine on the luxurious fare that was promised on the journey itself. To give diners the feeling of crossing Siberia, a length of canvas on which was painted a Siberian panorama of wide steppes, dense taiga and little villages of log cabins, could be seen through the windows. To complete the illusion, the painted panorama was made to move past the windows by mechanical means.

Visitors were intrigued and impressed and more than a few soon set off on the epic trip. The reality, they were to discover, was a little different from what they experienced at the exhibition.

Two years later Michael Myres Shoemaker took *The Great Siberian Railway from St Petersburg to Pekin* (the name of his account of the journey). He wrote enthusiastically: 'This Railway will take its place amongst the most important works of the world .... Russia is awakening at last and moving forward.'

It is interesting to compare the descriptions these travellers give of the trains they took, with the carriages displayed at the Paris Exhibition as well as with the service operated today by Russian Railways.

The carriages

In gushing prose, advertising brochures informed prospective Trans-Siberian travellers that the carriages in which they were to be conveyed would be of a standard equal to those used by European royalty. In addition to the luxurious sleeping compartments and dining cars shown at the Paris Exhibition, there would be a bathroom with marble bathtub, a gymnasium equipped with a stationary bicycle and other exercising machines, a fire-proof safe, a hair-dressing salon and a darkroom equipped with all the chemicals a photographer would need. The carriages would be lit by electric lighting, individually heated in winter and cooled by under-floor ice-boxes in summer.

Although more than a few of those luxurious appointments, which they had seen in the carriages of the Siberian exhibit in Paris, were missing on their train, Annette Meakin and her mother found their accommodation entirely satisfactory. The ride was not so comfortable from Mysovaya on the Transbaikal Railway. Only fourth-class carriages were available, and the two ladies were forced to take their travelling rugs and picnic hamper to the luggage van, where they spent the next four days.

Travelling in 1902, Michael Myres Shoemaker was very impressed with the bathing arrangements on the train and wrote: 'I have just discovered that there is a fine bathroom in the restaurant car, large and tiled, with all sorts of sprays, plunges and douches. This bath has its separate attendant and all the bath towels you may demand.' He was less enthusiastic about his travelling companions, a French Consul and family whose fox terrier 'promptly domesticated itself in my compartment'.

> ❏ The Siberian express is a kind of "Liberty Hall", where you can shut your door and sleep all day if you prefer it, or eat and drink, smoke and play cards if you like that better. An electric bell summons a serving-man to make your bed or sweep your floor, as the case may be, while a bell on the other side summons a waiter from the buffet....Time passes very pleasantly on such a train.'
> **Annette Meakin** *A Ribbon of Iron*

The restaurant car

At the Paris Exhibition visitors were led to believe that a good part of the enjoyment of travelling on the Trans-Siberian would be the cordon bleu cuisine served in the restaurant car. It was claimed that the kitchens were even equipped with water tanks filled with live fish. The waiters would be multilingual and a truly international service was promised.

Travellers found this to be something of an exaggeration. Annette Meakin reported the existence of a Bechstein piano and a library of Russian novels in the restaurant car. Shoemaker wrote: 'The restaurant car is just like all those on the trains of Europe. There is a piano, generally used to hold dirty dishes. There are three very stupid waiters who speak nothing save Russian. The food is very poor.'

Travellers were warned by guide-books that there were occasional food shortages on the trains and were advised to take a picnic hamper. The Meakins found theirs invaluable on their four-day jaunt in the luggage van. In fact during the service's first four years there were no restaurant cars. RL Jefferson wrote that at meal-times the train would stop at a convenient station and all passengers (and the engine-driver) would get off for a meal at the station.

❏ Travelling in 1901, John Foster Fraser reports, in *The Real Siberia*, that locals did good business on the platforms selling 'dumplings with hashed meat and seasoning inside... huge loaves of new made bread, bottles of beer, pails of milk, apples, grapes, and fifty other things'. This is still true today.

The church car
Behind the baggage car was a peculiar carriage known as the church car. It was a Russian Orthodox Church on wheels, complete with icons and candelabra inside, church bells and a cross on the roof, and a peripatetic priest who dispensed blessings along the way. This carriage was detached at stations and settlements where churches had not yet been built and services were conducted for railway workers and their families.

Transport of emigrants
While foreign visitors discussed whether or not their accommodation was all that the Paris exhibition had led them to expect, emigrants travelled in the unenviable conditions described by RL Jefferson: 'The emigrants' train is simply one of the cattle trucks, each car being marked on the side "Forty men or eight horses". There are no seats or lights provided, and into each of these pens forty men, women and children have to herd over a dreary journey of fourteen or fifteen days...They have to provide their own food but at every station a large samovar is kept boiling in order to provide them with hot water for their tea.' By the end of the century they were crossing the Urals to Siberia at the rate of about a quarter of a million peasants each year.

Stations
Little wooden station buildings mushroomed along the railway. Russian stations were traditionally given a class number from one to five. Of the stations listed in the official *Guide to the Great Siberian Railway*, none was of the first class and the majority were no more than fifth class. Beside most stations there towered a water-tank to supply the steam engines; many of these towers, their eaves decorated with ornate fretwork, can still be seen today. Most of the larger stations had their own churches and resident priests. If the train did not have a

church car, stops would be made for lengthy services at these railside churches, especially on the eve of important saints' days.

RL Jefferson found that in the early years of the railways, the arrival and departure of every train at a Siberian station was quite an event, being 'attended with an amount of excitement that it is hard to associate with the usually stolid Russian. Particularly is this so in Eastern Russia where railways are new and interesting.' A man 'performs a terrific tintinabulation on a large suspended bell. All the conductors blow whistles.' Jefferson goes on to explain that none of the passengers was allowed out of the train until the engine driver had got down and shaken hands with the station-master and his staff.

Delays

Because the original line was so badly laid, the ride in the carriages was rough and uncomfortable and speed had to be kept down. There were frequent derailments and long delays. Annette Meakin complained: 'We stopped at a great many stations; indeed on some parts of the route we seemed to get into a chronic state of stopping'.

'All day long at a dog trot,' wrote Shoemaker, 'Certainly no more than ten miles an hour.' Over some sections the train went so slowly passengers could get out and pick flowers as they walked along beside it. Still, the delays did give one time to catch up on current affairs, as Miss Meakin observes when her train was delayed for four hours ('a mere nothing in Siberia') at Tayga. She writes: 'As we sat waiting in the station the good news was brought that Mafeking had been relieved.'

Bridges

Although the rails were badly laid and of poor quality, the bridges that were made of stone were built to such a high standard that many are still in use today. They were largely the work of Italian masons, who laboured throughout the winter months: the bridge-building season, since no work could be done on the snow-covered line. Many labourers succumbed to hypothermia in temperatures as low as -40°C, dropping to their death on the ice below.

In winter, where bridges had not been finished when the railway lines reached them, engineers had the brilliant idea of laying rails across the ice. The sleepers were literally frozen onto the surface of the river by large amounts of water being poured over them. When RL Jefferson's train reached the track laid across the Chulim River, passengers were made to get out and walk, in case the train proved too great a weight for the ice to bear. He wrote: 'As it passed us we felt the ice quiver, and heard innumerable cracks, like the reports of pistols in the distance, but the train got across the centre safely.'

Breakdowns

These were all too frequent. A wait of 24 hours for a new engine was not regarded as a long delay. Annette Meakin recorded the following incident: 'Outside Kainsk the train stopped. "The engine has smashed up," said a jolly Russian sailor in broken English. "She is sixty years old and was made in

Glasgow. She is no use any more"....The poor old engine was now towed to her last berth....I had whipped out my "Kodak" and taken her photograph, thinking of Turner's "Fighting Temeraire".'

Cost of the journey
The *Guide to the Great Siberian Railway* informed its readers that, for the journey from London to Shanghai: 'The conveyance by the Siberian Railway will be over twice as quick and two and a half times cheaper than that now existing' (the sea passage via the Suez Canal). The cost of a first class ticket for the sixteen-day journey was to be 319 roubles. From Moscow to Vladivostok the price was 114 roubles.

THE RAILWAY IN THE 20TH CENTURY

After the Revolution
'When the trains stop, that will be the end,' announced Lenin, and the trains, the Trans-Siberian included, continued to run throughout those troubled times.

When the new Bolshevik government pulled out of the First World War in early 1918, a Czech force of 50,000 well-armed men found themselves marooned in Russia, German forces preventing them from returning western Europe. Receiving permission to leave Russia via Vladivostok, they set off on the Trans-Siberian. Their passage was not a smooth one, for the Bolsheviks suspected that the Czechs would join the White Russian resistance while the Czechs suspected that the Bolsheviks were not going to allow them to leave. Violence erupted, several Czechs were arrested and the rest of the legion decided to shoot their way out of Russia. They took over the Trans-Siberian line from the Urals to Lake Baikal and travelled the railway in armour-plated carriages.

The Civil War in Siberia (1918-20)
At this time Siberia was divided amongst a number of forces, all fighting against the Bolsheviks but not as a combined unit. Many of the leaders were nothing more than gangsters. East Siberia and Manchuria were controlled by the evil Ataman Semenov, half-Russian, half-Buryat and supported by the Japanese. He charged around Transbaikalia murdering whole villages and, to alleviate the boredom of these mass executions, a different method of death was adopted each day. Then there was Baron General von Ungern Sternberg, a White Russian commander whose cruelty rivalled that of Semenov.

The Americans, French, English and Japanese all brought troops into Siberia to evacuate the Czech legions and to help Admiral Kolchak, the Supreme Ruler of the White Government based at Omsk. Kolchak, however, failed to win the support of the people in Siberia's towns, his troops were undisciplined and in November 1919 he lost Omsk to the Bolsheviks. He was executed in Irkutsk in early 1920 and the Allies abandoned the White Russian cause. The Japanese gave up Vladivostok in 1922, leaving all Siberia in Communist hands.

Reconstruction

After the Civil War the Soviet Union set about rebuilding its battered economy. High on the priority list was the repair of the Trans-Siberian line, so that raw materials like iron ore could be transported to European Russia. The First Five Year Plan (1928) set ambitious goals for the expansion of industry and agriculture. It also included new railway projects, the double-tracking of the Trans-Siberian and the building of the Turk-Sib, the line between Turkestan and Novosibirsk. Work began on two giant industrial complexes known as the Ural-Kuznetsk Combine. Iron ore from the Urals was taken by rail to the Kuznetsk Basin in Siberia, where it was exchanged for coal for Ural blast furnaces. For all these giant projects an enormous, controllable labour force was needed and this was to a large extent provided by prisoners from the corrective labour camps.

The Second World War

Siberia played an important backstage role in the 'Great Patriotic War', as Russians call the Second World War. Many factories were moved from European Russia to Siberia and the populations of cities such as Novosibirsk rose dramatically. The Trans-Siberian's part was a vital one and shipments of coal and food were continuously despatched over the Urals to Europe throughout the war years.

The Trans-Siberian today

THE TRAIN

Engines

If you're counting on being hauled across Siberia by a puffing steam locomotive you will be sadly disappointed. Soviet Railways (SZD), now Russian Railways (RZD), began converting the system to electricity in 1927. Today the Trans-Siberian line is entirely electrified (25kV 50Hz ac or in some cases 3kV dc).

Passenger engines are usually Czech Skoda ChS4T's (line voltage 25kV 50 Hz; max output 5200kW; max speed 180kph; weight 126 tonnes) or ChS2's (3kV dc; 4620kW; 160kph; 126 tonnes), or Russian-built VL10's, VL60's or VL65's. On the Moscow–St Petersburg route the latest Czech-built engines are used: the CS200 (3kV dc; 8400kW; 200kph; 157 tonnes) and the CS7 developed from it. The most common freight engines are the large VL80S and the newer VL85.

Elsewhere on the Russian system where electrification is incomplete, and for shunting duties, diesel rather than steam engines are likely to be used, typically Russian-built 2TE10L/M/V (with overhanging windscreens) or sometimes 2M62U or 3M62U twin or triple units. If you're continuing on the Trans-Mongolian or Trans-Manchurian, it is quite likely that a steam loco will be hitched to your carriages at the China border, at least for shunting duties.

Although steam engines have been officially phased out in Russia, there are still some on the books, many of them decaying on remote sidings along the Trans-Siberian route. Their numbers are shrinking fast as they are sold off to Western Europe and China for scrap and parts. See p127 for identification information and class numbers.

Carriages and carriage attendants

Most carriages now in use are of East German origin, solidly-built and warm in winter. Each carriage is staffed by an **attendant** (female *provodnitsa* or male *provodnik* in Russian, *fuwuyuen* in Chinese), whose 'den' is a compartment at the end of the carriage. Their duties include collecting your tickets, letting down the steps at stations, coming round with the vacuum-cleaner, and selling you tea (good but without milk) or coffee (utterly disgusting) at around US$0.10 a glass. The attendant also maintains the

❏ **Samovar**

The coal-fired stove-samovar (batchok) provides hot water in each carriage. 'A margarine pot and lid is the perfect preparation pot for noodles! Crush noodles into the pot, add seasoning and fill with water from the samovar. Cover and wait five minutes'. **Will Harrison-Cripps** (UK)

samovar which is opposite his or her compartment, and which provides a continuous supply of boiling water for drinks.

There are doors at both ends of the carriages, and the only place where passengers may **smoke** is in the (unheated) area between the carriages. Travellers on some trains, Nos 3/4 in particular, report that if there are many smokers on board this rule appears to be waived. The no-smoking rule doesn't seem to be applied strictly in the dining car, either.

Carriages are heated in winter and air-conditioned in summer. The air-conditioning system works on the pressure difference between the inside and outside of the carriage and takes about an hour to get going, so all carriage windows must be kept shut. One's initial instinct (certainly that of the Russian passengers) is to throw them open, and carriage attendants wage a constant battle to keep them closed.

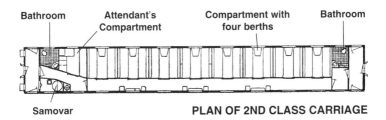

Bathroom   Attendant's Compartment   Compartment with four berths   Bathroom

Samovar   **PLAN OF 2ND CLASS CARRIAGE**

❏ **Hot or cold?**
Many travellers say the carriages are very warm – I far from agree and often found them chilly. However, as a Scandinavian I, like the Americans, also found it cold in Poland, while the Continental Europeans found the temperature on board just fine and the Britons complained about it being too warm! **Matz Lonnedal Risberg** (Norway)

Radio or taped music is piped into the compartments from the attendant's den. A knob above the window controls the volume, although in some compartments you cannot turn it completely off. This can be annoying if you don't happen to share your attendant's taste for early-morning doo-wop or dub reggae.

Compartments

For an introduction to classes of service on trains, and to buying tickets, see p70.

Most Trans-Siberian train carriages are either *kupé* (coupé; also called 2nd, hard or tourist class), whose four-berth closed compartments are favoured option as they're reasonably comfortable and cheap; or *SV* (also called 1st or soft class), with comfortable two-berth compartments, sometimes with washbasins.

Note that in the Chinese-made carriages of Trans-Mongolian trains No 3/4, SV compartments are *four*-berth and identical to all other services' kupé compartments except 16cm wider, so they are conspicuously poor value. But these particular Trans-Mongolian trains also have an additional *deluxe 1st* class, whose two-berth, carpeted, wood-panelled compartments have wider bunks, armchair, wind-down window and attached bathroom with rudimentary hand-held shower. This is the closest you'll get to true luxury on a scheduled train service across Siberia.

Platskartny (3rd), cheap but rough, is adequate for a day or two but do not even contemplate it for a Trans-Siberian journey. *Obshchy* is a dismal step below this, with unreserved seats.

The term *firmenny* refers not to carriages but to certain services, including all international trains and many domestic ones (among them the Nos 1/2 Moscow–Vladivostok and Nos 9/10 Moscow–Irkutsk). Firmenny trains are characterized by extra attention to detail and comfort, in both kupé and SV classes.

Bedding is provided and sheets are supposed to be changed every three days. You may have to pay anything up to US$1 for the sealed bag containing your clean sheets and pillow case. You may also receive a small towel and toiletries for free on firmenny trains. In newer carriages it is possible to move the lower bed up to 10cm away from the wall, giving a wider sleeping area.

Luggage

Each passenger can take up to 35kg of luggage with them for free on the Trans-Siberian. In Beijing this limit is rigidly enforced as baggage is weighed before you are allowed onto the platform.

You can take additional luggage totalling up to 75kg provided you pay an excess-baggage charge (around US$17 per 10kg for Moscow–Beijing). If you're leaving from Moscow, get to the station early to pay the fee; you'll be asked to show a receipt before boarding, and in general you can take the extra baggage to your compartment. If you're departing from Beijing you must box up any excess baggage, with a limit of one box per ticket, and it travels in a separate carriage. Bring only the excess to the Luggage Shipment Office at least 24 hours before departure, along with passport, ticket and customs entry declaration. The office is to the right of the main station and is open 8:00-noon for Trans-Siberian passengers. You may manage to escape the weigh-in, but it can be a major hassle if you're caught out. Mongolian traders seem somehow able to get around most luggage limits.

> ❏ **Varied baggage**
> If you're travelling on local trains between smaller stations in Siberia be prepared to share your compartment with almost any form of luggage, animate or inanimate. Since few people can afford a car, the train is their primary means of transport.
> I have had to politely move over in order to accommodate bicycles, televisions, car windscreens and even several sacks of leeches.
> **Nick Hill** (UK)

In your compartment, luggage can be stored either in the box under the bottom seat (57x134x24cm), in the free space beside the box (57x28x24cm) or in the space above the door (33x190x67cm).

Bathroom

Sadly the marble bathtub (ingeniously designed not to overflow as the train rounded a corner) and the copious hot water and towels that Michael Myres Shoemaker enthused over in 1902 are no more. The lack of proper bathing facilities is usually the biggest grumble from people who have done the trip. Apart from the Trans-Mongolian's deluxe 1st class compartments, there are no showers on the train – a ridiculous oversight (though rumour has it that a single carriage on each No 9/10 'Baikal' service between Moscow and Irkutsk has one for use at about US$2). With the system now electrified there is an obvious cheap power source for heated shower units but no doubt it will be years before they are installed.

> ❏ **Bathing in a Chinese spittoon**
> A week was a short time to go without a bath in Siberia, we were told, but this didn't make the prospect any more appealing. I read somewhere that in pre-Revolution days most Russian peasants spent the whole winter without having a bath.
> Shopping for supplies on a freezing December afternoon in Beijing before we left, we resolved to find some kind of bucket or basin to facilitate washing on the train. In one shop we found weighty china buckets with bamboo handles and in another a plastic bath designed for a large baby and complete with a little holder for the soap. In the end we settled for something smaller, an enamel spittoon (diameter 9ins/23mm) which turned out to exactly fit the basin in the train. It could be filled from the samovar in the corridor (to the astonishment of the Chinese passengers who knew the true purpose of the utensil) and it greatly simplified the difficult process of washing on the train.

❏ **Carriage keys**
On our train (No 6) there were a large number of Mongolian traders who proved to be very entertaining. They had managed to obtain a carriage key so that they could unlock the loo door after it had been locked. They would always oblige us with a quick unlock when we asked. We did notice that this carriage key looked familiar and it may be worth advising British travellers to try taking their British Gas meter cupboard key with them since it looks as if it is identical. **Andrew Wingham** (UK)

Instead, every carriage has a 'bathroom' at each end: a small cubicle with a stainless steel basin and lavatory, with or without a seat. To flush the lavatory, fully depress and hold the foot pedal, and lean back out of the way, as the contents have a nasty habit of going the wrong way if the train is moving fast. Sometimes the carriage attendants will keep the bathroom beside their own compartment locked for their personal use. Complaining is unlikely to achieve anything, but a strategic friendly gift might gain you access.

The taps on the basin are operated by pushing up the little lever located under the tap outlet. You should get hot water by turning the left-hand wheel above the sink (the right-hand wheel controls cold water), but the supply of hot water depends on the whim of the attendant who may not want to switch the system on. Don't forget to bring along a **universal plug** (or a squash ball) for the basin, **soap**, a **sponge** or **flannel**, and **lavatory paper**.

There's a socket for an electric razor but you may need to ask the attendant to turn the power on. Charging video-camera or other batteries from these sockets may blow the fuses. There are two ways to have a shower in these bathrooms: either fill the basin and use a mug to scoop out water and pour it over yourself, or fit a flexible shower hose over the tap nozzle. Some attendants carry these hoses and you may be able to rent one from them. Don't worry about splashing water around as there is a drain in the floor.

The bathrooms are generally kept clean. Note that they are often locked for up to 20 minutes before and after major station stops.

❏ *Baikal* – **the top train**
'I took train No 10, the 'Baikal', from Moscow to Irkutsk. The service is definitely the best of all the trains I've taken in Russia, with each compartment vacuum cleaned twice a day and train staff pushing their carts of food and drinks down the carriage aisles a few times a day'. **Terry Nakazono** (USA)

'On the No 10 train, the 'Baikal', I discovered, thanks to the Russian couple I shared the compartment with, that there is a real shower cubicle, with real hot water, in at least one of the carriages. The water is only a trickle, but it is still very welcome. It costs 50 roubles, its use depends apparently on the good will of the provodnitsa. People don't seem to use it: not the Russians because it's too expensive, and not the foreigners because they don't know about it'. **Claudia Gamperle** (Switzerland)

Restaurant cars

One of the myths that has sprung up amongst prospective travellers is that you get better food on the Chinese (Trans-Mongolian) train. As with most international rail travel, restaurant cars belonging to the country through which the train is travelling are attached at the border. Regardless of which train you're on, when you're passing through China you eat in a restaurant car supplied by Chinese Railways; at the border with Mongolia this is replaced by a Mongolian restaurant car; and while the train is in Russia meals are provided by a restaurant car from Russian Railways.

Note that the Trans-Mongolian usually has no restaurant car between the Russian border and Ulan Bator. Regional trains such as the Irkutsk–Ulan Bator service may have no restaurant car at all.

> ❏ **Getting better service**
> 'The only relevant information about Russian restaurant cars is that the food seems to vary much between one... car and the next, as every Russian restaurant car is its own private enterprise, and I've experienced everything from excellent to disaster. I've found out that a very good way to obtain a good relationship with the staff is simply to be a regular customer and learn a few Russian words'. **Matz Lonnedal Risberg** (Norway)

● **Russian restaurant car** The food was never much to write home about, and financial hardship in Russia has not made things any better. Russian restaurant cars are now run as private franchises, so service, food quality, prices and opening hours are highly unpredictable. Staff shop en route for whatever provisions they can find, so menus are unpredictable too.

On entering the car (having averted your eyes from the kitchen to safeguard your appetite) you may be presented with a menu, almost invariably in Russian and often running to 10 pages or more. The only available dishes will be indicated by a pencilled-in price or added in an indecipherable scrawl. The choice may include egg or tomato salad with sour cream, *shchi* (cabbage soup with meat), *solyanka* (a thick meat soup), meatballs and mash or macaroni, *skumbriya* (mackerel), Beef Stroganov, the ever-present *bifstek*, or rice and boiled chicken. A main course will cost about US$2-3. Payment is in roubles only.

Staff can now sell all sorts of goodies on the side. Banned for several years, alcohol is now sold on trains. In fact you may find your restaurant car offering little more than crisps, instant noodles, chocolate bars and biscuits, plus fruit juice, vodka, beer (pricier than on station platforms) or chilled Russian champagne (around US$6), with no cooked food in sight. Some screen bootleg videos.

> ❏ **Vodka on the train**
> Whilst beer is easily available from kiosks and vendors, they are not allowed to sell spirits on stations. So the only supply of vodka, once you have drunk any that you bought in advance, is the restaurant car, which by the end of the trip was down to some horrible-tasting and dubious brand with unsealed caps.
> **Dmitri Gorokhov** (Russia)

❏ **Platform food**
'What you can buy at stations very much depends upon the season and the stop. 'We stocked up really well in Moscow and I'm glad that we did as we only had two station stops where people were selling things. Maybe our train (No 6) went through stations such as these in the middle of the night but we had fellow travellers who had not brought much food who would have been very hungry were it not for the Mongolian traders selling pot noodles.'
Angela Hollingsworth (UK)

'I was aware that I would be offered food by the Russians we were sharing a cabin with. What I was not expecting was a whole cooked chicken to be sat, unwrapped, on the storage shelf above the carriage walkway. Different food was purchased at each stop. Clearly they knew what to buy and when to buy it'.
Will Harrison-Cripps (UK).

'It is worth stressing the abundance and variety of food on sale at many stations, especially rural ones, during stops. If you see something you want, buy it: the next stop might be a city, where sellers will not appear on the platforms, or rows of babushkas with prams full of raspberries might be replaced by a monotonous offering of, say, fish. Regulars knew what to expect at each stop.'
Howard Dymock (UK)

Russians think of the restaurant car as little more than a bar, and wouldn't think of eating a meal in one. You may find everything overpriced at first, but service tends to get cheaper and friendlier the more often you return. On popular tourist services the restaurant car is a good place to meet other foreigners.

● **Mongolian restaurant car** With luck you'll get a smart new Mongolian restaurant car. Generally the main differences from Russian restaurant cars are that here you're likely to get a menu in English, nearly everything comes with mutton, and you pay (officially) in US$. Take small-denomination notes as staff never seem to have change. Chinese currency is sometimes accepted.

Delicacies include: main course with roast potatoes, main course with rice, main course with noodles, and main course with cabbage, all priced from US$3-5. For breakfast they can do you a one-egg omelette for US$2. Tea is about US$0.50, coffee US$1, Pepsi US$1. Some Mongolian cars have extensive stocks of duty-free goods and even souvenirs, postcards and stamps. Mongolian beer is recommended.

Train Nos 5/6 and 263/264 rarely have a restaurant carriage inside Mongolia. 'Train No 264 did not have any buffet car on it (certainly from Irkutsk to Ulan Bator). Travelling from Ulan Bator to Beijing in Train No 24 we had a buffet car until the Chinese border. The waitress was hiding the menu, and therefore the prices, and telling people that there was only 'beef' stroganoff available. And the cost – $6! We later discovered that if staff were pushed a menu could be found and the prices were far more reasonable' (Will Harrison-Cripps, UK).

● **Chinese restaurant car** Travellers tend to agree that Chinese restaurant cars have the best food, the widest choice and the best service. The cars are full every evening, which is a good sign. For US$3 you can get a breakfast of eggs, bread, jam and tea. For lunch or supper (main courses about US$2-3) you can typically choose from tomato salad, cold chicken or sauté chicken with peanuts, fish, sweet and sour pork, sauté beef or egg plant with dried shrimp. Drinks include beer (US$0.50), cola (US$1) and mineral water (US$1). Payment is in yuan (renminbi).

● **Food at the stations** At many of the stops along the Trans-Siberian locals turn out on the station platform to sell all manner of foodstuffs: fruit, vegetables and even entire cooked meals (cabbage rolls, freshly-boiled potatoes with dill, pancakes filled with goat's cheese, boiled eggs and fresh bread).

Note that some travellers have reported upset stomachs after eating platform food so you should take care with salads, cold meats and fish and anything that looks as if it has been sitting around for too long. Generally, if the food is hot you should be fine; and all fruit should be washed.

LIFE ON THE TRAIN

Most people imagine they'll get bored on so long a journey but you may be surprised at how quickly the time flies.

Don't overdo the number of books you bring: *War and Peace,* all 1444 pages of it, is a frequent choice, although I know of only one person who actually managed to finish it on the trip. There are so many other things to do besides reading. You can have monosyllabic conversations with inquisitive Russians, meet other Westerners, play cards or chess, visit the restaurant car or hop off at the stations for a little exercise.

'Time passes very pleasantly on such a train', as Annette Meakin wrote in 1900. It is surprising how the time drifts by and even though you do very little,

---

❏ **Local travellers**
Unlike the Orient Express, most trains that cross Siberia are working trains, not tourist specials. Russian passengers are extremely friendly and genuinely interested in foreign travellers. Sharing her compartment with three Russians, a winter traveller writes: 'Inside the carriage there's interest on both sides. Great concern all round about my travelling unaccompanied and questions as to the whereabouts of my parents. Much shaking of heads and 'tutting'.

There's plenty for me to find out. The thin man (with cold eyes that have gradually thawed over the last two days) has five children and is going to Moscow to get stomach medicine for one of them (or for himself?). The large motherly babushka in the corner who has been so kind to me is an artist, going to visit her son (or is the son an artist?). The fourth member of the compartment played chess with me last night, totally baffled by my tactics (there weren't any) so that we ended with a stalemate. He hasn't offered again. So much can be achieved with not a word of language in common.' **Heather Oxley** (UK)

you won't be bored. Having said that, the Russian man who bought the Tetris electronic game at the Manzhouli Friendship Store quickly became everyone's best friend.

The Trans-Siberian time warp

During his trip on the Great Siberian Railway in 1902, Michael Myres Shoemaker wrote: 'There is an odd state of affairs as regards time over here. Though Irkutsk is 2,400 miles from St Petersburg, the trains all run on the time of the latter city, therefore arriving in Irkutsk at 5pm when the sun would make it 9pm. The confusion en route is amusing; one never knows when to go to bed or when to eat. Today I should make it now about 8.30 – these clocks say 10.30 and some of these people are eating their luncheon.'

You will be pleased to know that this at least has not changed. The entire system operates on Moscow time (same as St Petersburg time), and all timetables list Moscow time. Crossing the border from China after breakfast, the first Russian station clock you see tells you that it's one o'clock in the morning! The restaurant car, however, runs on local time. Passing through as many as seven time-zones, things can get rather confusing. The answer is to ignore Moscow time and reset your watch as you cross into new time zones (details in the Route Guide). A watch that shows the time in two zones would be handy; otherwise just add or subtract the appropriate number of hours every time you consult the timetable in the corridor.

Stops

Getting enough exercise on so long a journey can be a problem and most people make full use of the brief stops: 'We even managed to persuade our carriage attendant (never seen out of her pink woolen hat) to take part in our efforts to keep fit on the platforms. However, if your attendant indicates that you shouldn't get off at a stop, take her advice. At some stops another train pulls in between the platform and yours, making it almost impossible for you to get back on board.' Jane Bull (UK). Always carry your passport and valuables with you in case you miss your train.

❏ **Stopping off**
'At station stops, before you alight, check with the provodnitsas the time allotted at the particular station. If the train is late stops will be curtailed. If the attendant says 15 minutes (normally signalled in sign language) make it 10. Also check that your compartment door will be locked by the attendant. And take your passport with you in case you get left behind on the platform!'
John Gothard (UK)

Traders' trains

With the growth of free trade in Russia in the 1990s, some Trans-Siberian routes became virtually monopolized by Chinese, Mongolian and Russian shuttle traders. While excess-baggage charges and lower duty-free allowances have stemmed the flow, you may still share a Trans-Mongolian compartment with traders accompanied by anything from a bundle of fake Adidas trainers to several thousand yellow plastic ducks. The Mongolian-run No 5/6 (Moscow–Ulan

❏ Safety tips for Trans-Siberian travellers

There are many stories of crime on the railways. Most are exaggerations, distortions or complete fabrications. The most outrageous story in recent years was the so-called 'Sleeping Gas Incident', in which an entire carriage of a Moscow–St Petersburg train was supposedly put to sleep by gas and everyone robbed. After a week of international media coverage the Russian journalist who wrote the story admitted that it was fictitious, though she maintained that she did lose her purse when she was asleep!

While there is crime on the trains, a few simple precautions will substantially reduce your chances of anything untoward happening to you.

● **Lock your compartment door** from inside when you go to sleep, using both the door-handle lock and the flick-down lock; your Russian companions will do this anyway. The railways are currently installing a plastic device known as a *blokirator* to further thwart break-ins, mainly on firmenny trains, both kupé and SV. It immobilizes the locking handle in the locked position, and is allegedly so effective that even some attendants cannot outwit it from outside. 'Best piece of information I managed to get from Russians on the train was on safety in the carriage – an explanation about the secondary door lock; the main door lock can be undone with a standard triangular UK gas meter box key (worth taking with you). I was recommended to put a cork in the second door catch to stop it being opened with a knife. Therefore worth taking a cork with you'. (Will Harrison-Cripps, UK)

● At night, **put your bags under the sleeping bench** or in the space above the door. It is not necessary to lock them, but don't leave them lying around either. Some people padlock their bags to the compartment wall but this is unnecessary.

● Always **leave someone in the compartment** to look after the luggage. If everyone must leave, ask the attendant to lock the compartment. Valuables can be left in a safe in the chief attendant's compartment but this is not recommended.

● **Dress down**, and always carry your valuables on your person. Stash only non-essentials in shoulder bags, and only a few roubles and US$ in your wallet. Money and important documents should be in a **money belt** under your clothing; even sleep with it on.

● Russians tend to carry things around in tattered old carry-alls; if you do the same you'll attract much less attention than with a flashy sports rucksack.

Few further tips for when you leave the train, especially in larger towns and cities.

● **Change money only at kiosks and banks**.

● Keep a **pocket torch** (flashlight) handy as many entrance halls and stairways are unlighted. This is especially important in winter when it gets dark very early.

● **Never enter a taxi which is carrying anyone other than the driver**. Take a good look at the driver and the car; if you're in any doubt, wave it on. Taxis ordered by telephone or through organized services at hotels are often a better bet.

● A very **common scam** is for someone to drop a roll of cash and then to act as if they are searching for it. If you pick it up and return it, you may then be treated with mock suspicion and asked to show your own cash. A nimble-fingered thief can then slip notes out of your own wad of cash.

● **Street urchins and gipsy children** are the most visible and aggressive thieves. If you don't ignore them they'll swarm around you like bees, begging and even grabbing your legs or arms to distract you, and before you realize it they'll have opened your bag or pulled out your wallet. Their 'controller' is often a dishevelled-looking woman with an infant in her arms. If you're approached, don't look at them but walk away quickly. It you fear you're becoming a victim, go into a shop or towards a group of Russians, who will usually send them packing.

> ❏ **Scams at the borders**
> In recent years official-looking Mongolians have been boarding trains at the Mongolian border at the same time as Immigration officials, and demanding US$10 from foreigners for what they say is mandatory insurance cover for a visit to the country. Travellers with a copy of a legitimate insurance policy are usually ignored; others who pay up are presented with an official-looking document from the Mongol Daatgal National Insurance & Reinsurance Co. Don't fall for this one!
> Also see p64 for details of an ongoing, nasty scheme by some Russian border officials to defraud travellers carrying improperly-validated Customs declaration forms.

Bator) service is heavily subsidized for Mongolian citizens and is therefore a popular traders' train, the scene of frequent tension with non-traders, and not always a peaceful journey.

Traders with goods in excess of customs limits sometimes get help from carriage attendants, who may stash the traders' wares in their own compartments until the police have gone. Some traders get around the regulations by swapping half of their purchases with half of a friend's items, so that neither is over the limit for either type of goods. One traveller recalled how everyone in the carriage was asked by a Mongolian trader to wear one of his leather jackets through customs, though it's hard to imagine officials failing to notice that everyone had identical jackets. Traders are often the target of robbers.

STEAM LOCOMOTIVES IN SIBERIA

In 1956 the USSR stopped producing steam engines, and official policy was to phase them out by 1970. As with most official plans in the country, this one overran a little and a second official end of steam was announced for 1987, when the number of locos stood at over 6000. Some of these were sold as scrap to Germany and Korea but many were stored as a 'strategic reserve' in remote sidings and used very occasionally for shunting work; there are some to be seen along the Trans-Siberian line (see the Route Guide for locations). In 2000, however, it was decided not to retain steam engines within these strategic military reserves so numbers are now falling fast. Each of the country's 32 railway administrations will be allowed to keep just 10 steam engines so in the next few years there will be no more than 320 working steam locos in the whole of Russia. In Northern China there are numerous steam engines still at work.

In 1836 Russia's first locomotive, a Hackworth 2-2-2, was delivered in St Petersburg to pull the Tsar's private carriages over the 23km (14 miles) of six-foot gauge track to his palace at Tsarskoye Selo. The Russians have always been (and still are) conservative by nature when it comes to buying or building engines. Usually large numbers of a few standard locomotives have been ordered so there's not much of a range to be seen today. They seem to be uniformly large, standing up to 5m (17 ft) high, and larger than British locos, partly because the Russian gauge is almost 9cm ($3^{1}/_{2}$ inches) wider than that used in Britain.

They are numbered separately by classes, not in a single series and not by railway regions. If variations of the class have been built, they are given an additional letter after the main class letter. Thus, for example, the first type of 0-10-0 freight locomotive was Class E and those of this class built in Germany were Class Eg. Classes you may see in Siberia include the following (Roman alphabet class letters given in brackets; * = very rare):

● **Class О (O)** The first freight trains on the Trans-Siberian route were pulled by these long-boilered 0-8-0 locos (55 tons) which date back to 1889. The 'O' in the class name stands for *Osnovnoi Tip* meaning 'basic type'. Although production ceased in 1923, as late as 1958 there were 1500 of these locomotives still at work.
● **Class С (S)*** 2-6-2 (75 tons) A highly successful passenger engine. 'S' stands for *Sormovo*, where these locos were built from 1911. **Class Су (Su)** ('u' for usileny, meaning 'strengthened') was developed from the former class and in production from 1926 to 1951.
● **Class Е (Ye)** 2-10-0 (imported from the USA in 1914). There were 1500 Ye 2-10-0s imported.
● **Class Эу/Эм/Эр (Eu/Em/Er)*** (subclasses of the old type (E) 0-10-0, 80 tons, built in Russia from 1926 to 1952. The old type E was also produced in Germany and Sweden, as Esh and Eg subclasses.
● **Class Еа (YeA)*** 2-10-0 (90 tons) Over 2000 were built in the USA between 1944 and 1947 and shipped across the Pacific.
● **Class Л (L)** 2-10-0 (103 tons) About 4130 were built between 1945 and 1956.
● **Class П36 (P36)** 4-8-4 (133 tons) 251 were built between 1950 and 1956 – the last express passenger type built for Soviet Railways. 'Skyliner'-style, fitted with large smoke-deflectors, and painted green with a cream stripe. Preserved examples at Sharya, Tayga, Sibirtsevo, Skovorodino, Belogorsk, Mogzon and Chernyshevsk

Classes **O**, **C/Cy**, **E** (**O**, **S/Su**, **Ye**) have all disappeared from the steam dumps but you will see the occasional one on a plinth.

For more information refer to the comprehensive *Soviet Locomotive Types – The Union Legacy* by AJ Heywood and IDC Button (1995, Frank Stenvalls/Luddenden Press). There's also a good deal of information about Russian trains on the Internet; a good place to start is **www.transsib.ru/Eng/** – the Trans-Siberian Railway Web Encyclopedia.

OTHER RAILWAY LINES LINKED TO THE TRANS-SIBERIAN

BAM – a second Trans-Siberian
In the 1930s another Herculean undertaking was begun on the railways of Russia. The project was named the Baikal-Amur-Magistral (BAM): a second Trans-Siberian railway, 3140km long, running parallel but to the north of the existing line. It was to run through the rich mining districts of northern Siberia, providing an east–west communications back-up to the main line. Work began

in Tayshet and the track reached Ust Kut on the Lena River before the project was officially abandoned at the end of the First World War. Much of the 700km of track that had been laid was torn up to replace war-damaged lines in the west. Construction continued in secret, using slave labour until the gulags were closed in 1954.

In 1976 it was announced that work on the BAM was recommencing. Incentives were offered to collect the 100,000 strong work-force needed for so large a project. For eight years they laboured heroically, dynamiting their way through the permafrost which covers almost half the route, across a region where temperatures fall as low as -60°C in winter. In October 1984 it was announced that the way was open from Tayshet to Komsomolsk-na-Amur. Although track-laying had been completed, only the eastern half was operational (from Komsomolsk to BAM Station, where traffic joined the old Trans-Siberian route).

By 1991 the whole system was still not fully operational, the main obstacle being the Severomuysk Tunnel, bypassed by an unsatisfactory detour with an impressive 1:25 gradient. It took from 1981 to 1991 to drill 13km of the 16km of this unfinished tunnel in the most difficult of conditions. Many were already questioning the point of a railway that was beginning to look like a white elephant. Work has more or less stopped now; the main sections of the line are complete

but traffic is infrequent. The BAM was built to compete with shipping routes for the transfer of freight but the cost has been tremendous: there has been considerable ecological damage and there is little money left for the extraction of the minerals that was the other reason for the building of the railway. It is possible to travel along the BAM route starting near the north of Lake Baikal and ending up at Khabarovsk. You can find full details about the BAM and travel in the BAM region in the *Siberian BAM Guide – rail, rivers and road*, by Athol Yates and Nicholas Zvegintzov (also from Trailblazer).

AYaM and Little BAM

The **AYaM** (Amuro-Yakutskaya Magistral) is the Amur-Yakutsk Mainline, which will eventually run from Tynda on the BAM north to Yakutsk. The project was scheduled for completion at the same time as the BAM but the line has now only reached Tommot, and passenger services operate only as far as Aldan. The final 456km from Tommot to Yakutsk is unlikely to be completed for several years.

The **Little BAM** is the 180km rail link between the Trans-Siberian at Bamovskaya and Tynda, start of the AYaM.

Sakhalin railway

The island of Sakhalin (north of Japan) is currently linked to the Russian mainland by rail ferries operating between Vanino and Kholmsk. Steam specials are occasionally run on the island's 3ft 6in-gauge rail system.

Turkestan–Siberia (Turksib) railway

The Turksib links Novosibirsk on the Trans-Siberian with Almaty in Kazakhstan, a journey of 1678km. It was constructed in the 1930s to make it easier to transport grain from Siberia and cotton from Turkestan between these two regions. For more information visit the website – 🖳 www.turksib.com.

Kazakhstan–China railway

In September 1990 a rail line was opened between Urumqi in north-west China and the border with Kazakhstan, opening a new rail route between east Asia and Europe via the Central Asian Republics. China built this link to create the shortest Eurasian rail route (2000km shorter than the Trans-Siberian) between the Pacific and the Atlantic, enabling freight to be transported faster and more cheaply than by ship.

With the breakup of the Soviet Union, this has not really taken off in the way that the Chinese had hoped. But it does mean that it's now possible to travel along the ancient Silk Route by rail, through the old Central Asian capitals of Khiva, Bukhara and Samarkand and the Chinese cities of Dunhuang, Luoyang and Xi'an. For the adventurous, the trip represents a unique travel opportunity.

Kazakhstan–Iran railway

In May 1996 a 295km cross-border railway line was officially opened between Mashhad in Iran and Saraghs and Tejen in Turkmenistan. This line, it was said, was the forerunner of a network that would join land-locked Central Asia to the Persian Gulf and, via Turkey, to the Mediterranean. The potential was there for a new Silk Route between southern Europe and the Far East, cutting travel times by up to 10 days.

Six years later the line had reached northwards via Turkmenabat (Turkmenistan) and Tashkent (Uzbekistan) all the way to Almaty (Kazakhstan), and southwards to Tehran (Iran). In March 2002, with great fanfare, a weekly service was inaugurated for the 3300km, 70-hour Almaty–Tehran journey. But a month later it was suspended, apparently over disagreements about right of way through Uzbekistan, and by early 2003 it had not resumed.

For the moment, if you want to come this way you must take the train from Tehran to Mashhad, cross the border into Turkmenistan by bus to Ashgabat or via Sarachs to Mary, and continue into Uzbekistan by bus to Bukhara. Alternatively you could take Asseman Airlines' more-or-less weekly flight between Tehran and Ashgabat.

CITY GUIDES AND PLANS

St Petersburg
Санкт-Петербург

'It is in Russia – but it is not Russian!' exclaimed Emperor Nicholas I in the hope of making his country's (then) capital city more appealing to his visitor, the Marquis de Custine. The remark speaks volumes: Russians desperately want their country to be admired by foreigners, and to that end are not above having it rebuilt at gargantuan expense by foreigners.

St Petersburg is named after the patron saint of its founder, Tsar Peter I 'the Great', a man who had toured Europe, who wrote fluently in eight languages and who felt his illiterate, unwashed forebears were a shaming heritage. The city was created as a face Russia could proudly show the world, and remained the capital until the Soviet era, during which Russians officially didn't care what others thought. It can hardly be coincidence that Vladimir Putin, architect of post-Soviet Russia's rediscovered pride in its image abroad, is a St Petersburg lad. Nicholas I's words are the wisest of introductions: allow your senses to be dazzled by its splendours but reserve judgement on Russia until you have seen more typically Russian cities.

A trip to St Petersburg is well worth it if only for a visit to the Hermitage, one of the world's most spectacular collections of European art, partly housed in the fabulously ornate Winter Palace. You can take a side-trip from Moscow by taking the overnight train and staying a night or two, although you'd need at least four days to do the city justice. Other options are to route your Trans-Siberian journey through St Petersburg by starting or finishing in Helsinki (200km from St Petersburg) or to travel directly between St Petersburg and Warsaw, bypassing Moscow.

'The Northern Capital'

Petersburgers persistently refer to their city as the 'Northern Capital' (or more conversationally as 'Peter'). The criteria for its location were strategic rather than climatic. At the same latitude as the Orkney Islands or North Dakota, winter photos taken before about 10:00 or after 14:00 will show the city in half-darkness, while summertime darkens for only a few hours of twilight – down to about 45 minutes during June's 'White Nights' celebrations. Biting winter gales off the Gulf of Finland give way in summer to armies of hungry (but non-malarial) mosquitoes. 'I love this city, but it's bloody cold in winter!' ran the chorus of a Soviet-era hit by local underground rockers Kino.

St Petersburg was Russia's first paved city. These paving-stones were a legacy of Catherine the Great; it is said that they were swept clean each day by prostitutes arrested the previous night. Their modern-day successors escape such duties, and with Soviet potholes to add topographic interest, sturdy footwear is recommended. Winter ice isn't removed but crushed, turning the city into an unofficial skating-rink from October until April – bring ridge-sole boots.

HISTORY

Imperial Glories

At the turn of the 18th century Peter the Great finally defeated Sweden in the Great Northern Wars campaign inherited from his father. Sweden's navy had once sailed unopposed down Russia's rivers and Peter, determined never to be thus humiliated again, in 1703 ordered construction of a defensive garrison, the St Peter and Paul Fortress, on the banks of the River Neva. Russia had no navy, so shipyards were needed too. Then Peter had the audacious idea of simply abandoning Russia's backward, shambling capital in Moscow and moving it here. Swedish POW labour and bottomless reserves of cash saw a complete new city rise in just nine years. By 1712 this was the new Russian capital, and Peter was styling himself not merely 'Tsar' but 'Imperator'.

Falconet's riverside Bronze Horseman statue, the city's virtual trademark, bears the legend *Petrus Primus – Katerina Secunda*, a Latin double-entendre which not only translates their titles but reminds us that 'Peter was first – and Catherine followed through'. The glory-days of the Russian Empire were under a woman born in Germany as Princess Sophie of Anhalt-Zerbst, now known to the world as Catherine the Great. St Petersburg flourished during her reign, benefiting from her skills at empire-building and statesmanship, and her private passions for architecture, the arts, fine conversation, the Russian language, cavalry officers and horsemanship.

Once clear of the threat of Napoleonic France, Catherine's successors ruled over Europe's wealthiest empire, from a capital barely a century old. The fortunes to be made here attracted Europe's highest achievers. The city showcased the neoclassical architecture of Rossi, Rastrelli and Karl Ton. Home-grown writers like Pushkin, Gogol, and Dostoyevsky vied with visitors like Balzac, and Anton Chekhov wrote *Uncle Vanya* and *The Seagull*. The Imperial Opera commissioned Verdi to write 'Don Carlos'. Mikhail Lomonosov, the poet and scientist considered the father of modern Russian literature, was made rector of a new University, and Dmitri Mendeleev conceived his Periodic Table of Elements. Yet in most of Russia, serfs worked the land in conditions bordering on slavery to pay for all this. Change was inevitable, but was resisted until it took control of events by itself.

St Petersburg to Leningrad and back again

It was not only the working classes who envied the wealth and privilege of St Petersburg. Any Russian not of noble birth or military inclination found himself excluded from the capital, and even a century before the Revolution of 1917 Gogol was satirizing the capital's wealth and social iniquities in his surreal tales

The Nose and *The Overcoat*. Most of Dostoyevsky's writing depicts St Petersburg as a force wrecking the lives of its inhabitants. In 1881 Emperor Alexander II was blown to pieces by anarchists in the very centre of the city.

A bungled attempt to quash a protest over the price of bread in January 1905 led to the 'Bloody Sunday' massacre on Palace Square. In February 1917 Emperor Nicholas II retired to private life, with effective power transferred to Parliament. Armed attempts by aristocratic cavalry officers to return Nicholas to the throne created an atmosphere of panic and havoc. This played into the hands of Trotsky's Bolshevists, who in October 1917 arrested the Provisional Government and declared Soviet Power, under a leader freshly returned from discussing Socialism in the tea-salons of Europe, Vladimir Lenin.

With the nearest elements of the German army (suspected of having encouraged Lenin to foment a coup and even of providing the train in which he returned home) only a day's march from St Petersburg, Lenin returned all governmental functions to Moscow – and left them there, making the change of capital official in 1918. The Imperial Capital was left to fall into genteel decay. Gentility descended into barbarity during WWII: for 900 days the city – by now renamed Leningrad – was besieged, and nearly a quarter of the population died of hunger, disease or bombardment.

Yet the communists, resentful of their own Imperial past, starved the city of resources after the war, preferring to develop new industrial centres in Russia's interior. Perversely, this policy – and boggy terrain unconducive to high-rise building – saved it from the excesses of Soviet planning, but left it in a state of disrepair which post-Soviet Russia still cannot afford to put right. Little time was wasted, however, in renaming the city St Petersburg within a year of the fall of communism.

St Petersburg today

Much of the promise the city offered when communism fell in 1990 has gone undelivered. This is the country's second-wealthiest city on paper, although crooked privatizations and robber-barons appear to have spirited away its wealth. Russian TV's most popular police drama is *Criminalny St-Petersburg*.

As this book went to print St Petersburg – now with a population of some 4.6 million – was celebrating its 300th anniversary, having given itself a frantic but largely cosmetic make-over. Its glory still seems sadly faded, but with local hero Vladimir Putin as the nation's president, there is hope that serious-minded improvements will at last grace Russia's second city.

WHAT TO SEE

The State Hermitage Museum

No visit to St Petersburg should omit the Hermitage, combining the city's two must-see attractions. Most famously, this is one of the world's biggest and most splendid collections of fine art. As a bonus, it is housed in the grandest rooms of the former Winter Palace of the Tsars, Europe's wealthiest royal family.

❏ **Rules for social conduct in the Hermitage**
When Catherine the Great held a dinner party the lucky few honoured with an invitation were bound by a list of social rules displayed by the doors to the dining room. Guests were ordered to 'put off their title and rank as well as their hats and swords'. Pretensions were to be left outside; guests were to 'enjoy themselves but break nothing and spoil nothing'; be sparing with their words; eat and drink with moderation and avoid yawning. Those who violated these rules were obliged to undergo the following punishment: the drinking of one glass of fresh water (ladies not excepted) and the recital of a page of poetry.

The collection began with 225 paintings presented to Catherine the Great by a Berlin-based Russian banker named Gotskovsky, the first of many to gain Imperial promotion by sending artworks home to Her Majesty. Catherine displayed them in her Hermitage, a purpose-built annexe of the Winter Palace added by the Italian architect Rastrelli in his 1762 remodelling of the complex.

The collection swelled with gifts from foreign rulers seeking favour or trade agreements, and officers and civil servants looking for a quick promotion. Some pieces were eventually shifted to the Russian Museum (see p139). But the greatest, and most controversial, of the Hermitage's acquisitions came after 1917 with 'nationalization' of the private collections of Russia's aristocracy and bourgeoisie.

The massive collection now numbers more than three million catalogued works. All the state rooms, private chambers and servants' quarters of the Winter Palace, plus the Old and New Hermitage buildings, cannot display more than half the items at one time. This is also a research centre, with priceless works from ancient Rome, Greece, and Egypt amongst many others, and experts on archaeology and ancient cultures in residence.

Indeed there is so much to see here that a single visit can only scratch the surface. Many visitors make several visits, following themed routes. The museum comprises the following main departments:

● **Prehistoric Art**, including the exquisite Scythian gold collection
● **Antiquity**, including Ancient Greece and Rome
● **Western European Art**, which draws the biggest crowds
● **Oriental Art**, including the Middle East, China, Japan and Central Asia
● **Russian Culture**.

There are also special sections including armaments, numismatics and jewellery, and of course the extraordinary 'collection' represented by the setting itself, including grand marble halls with gilded columns, mosaic floors and immense crystal chandeliers.

Most casual visitors follow a well-trodden path combining Western European Art and the most impressive of the Palace State Rooms. The goal of many is the superb French Impressionist collection, which is on the top floor on the Dvortsovaya pl (Palace Square) side. *(continued on p139)*

❏ A walk down Nevsky Prospekt

Nevsky Prospekt has been the main shopping street and most fashionable place to be seen in St Petersburg since the city's founding. A walk along this grand street, past palaces and churches, over canals and beside faded buildings is a walk through the history of the city itself. Nevsky Prospekt starts near the Admiralty Building and, as you walk south-east from here, you can identify the buildings by the numbers beside the doors.

Where to eat There are numerous cafés, bars and restaurants so you can stop for a rest when you want. To name but a few there's *Nevski 40* (Russian-German) at No 40, *Baskin Robbins* at No 79, *Pizza Hut* at No 96, *Balsen* at No 142 and *Zolotaya Rybka* (good fish dishes) at No 166.

No 7 Gogol wrote *The Government Inspector* here in the 1830s.

No 9 This building was modelled on the Doges' Palace in Venice, for the Swedish banker Wawelberg. Now it's the **Airline Ticket Office**.

No 14 A blue and white sign here, dating from the WWII Siege of Leningrad, advises pedestrians to walk on the other side of the street during shelling.

No 17 This impressive building, designed by Rastrelli and completed in 1754, was once the palace of the wealthy Stroganov family. Although they are more famous for the beef stew named after them, it was the Stroganovs who initiated the conquest and colonization of Siberia by sending their private army to the Urals in the 1570s.

No 18 The *Literaturnoye Kafe* (see Where to eat, p148) was Pushkin's favourite café. It's worth seeing but tends to be packed with tourists. The entry fee covers high-class entertainment such as violin concerts.

No 20 The former **Dutch Church**, built in 1837.

No 24 Once the showrooms of the court jewellers Fabergé (creators of the golden Easter eggs now on display in the Kremlin).

No 28 The former showrooms of the Singer Sewing Machine Company with their trademark (a glass globe) still on the roof. Now it's home to the **Dom Knigi Bookstore**, the city's largest bookshop.

Kazan Cathedral was designed by Voronikhin and completed in 1811. Prince Peter Kropotkin, writing in 1911, called it 'an ugly imitation on a smaller scale of St Peter's in Rome'. The large, domed cathedral is approached via a semi-circular colonnade with statues at either end. The one on the left is Mikhail Kutuzov, who prayed here before leading an army to fight Napoleon. After the 1812 victory over the French the cathedral became a monument to Russia's military glory. In an act of supreme taste-lessness the Soviets turned it into a Museum of Atheism. Part of the cathedral still houses exhibits on the history of religion, while the rest has been returned to the Orthodox Church. *(Continued opposite)*

KAZAN CATHEDRAL

❏ A walk down Nevsky Prospekt (cont'd)

Looking north along the Griboyedov Canal you'll see the pseudo-Old-Russian style **Church of the Resurrection**, whose multicoloured onion domes are reminiscent of St Basil's in Moscow. It's also called the Church of the Resurrection Built on Spilt Blood as it's erected on the spot where Alexander II was assassinated in 1881.

No 31 This building housed the City Duma (Municipal Council) in Tsarist times. The tower was used as a fire lookout. Opposite the Duma is Mikhailovskaya ul, running north into pl Iskusstv (Arts Square). In the former Mikhailovsky Palace in the square is the **Russian Museum,** home to over 300,000 paintings, drawings and sculptures. Well worth seeing, it is open 10:00-18:00, closed Tuesday; admission US$5. The **Mussorgsky Opera and Ballet Theatre** (the former Maly Theatre) and the **St Petersburg State Philharmonia** are near the museum. The **Grand Hotel Europe** is a short distance away at Mikhailovskaya ul 32.

No 32 In the **Church of St Catherine** is the grave of Stanislaw Poniatowski, the last king of Poland and one of Catherine the Great's lovers. Local artists sell their sketches and watercolours outside.

No 41 The **St Petersburg Tourist Information Centre** (☎ 311 2943) opened here in 2000.

Gostinny Dvor, the city's largest department store, fills the whole of the next block. This is a good place to buy souvenirs. **Passazh**, across the street, was the city's first privately-owned department store and has a range of goods similar to any large Western department store. There is a large **supermarket** in the basement.

From the street you can see a **statue of Catherine the Great**, surrounded by her lovers (or 'associates' as some guides coyly put it) and other famous people of the time. In the park behind this is the **Pushkin Theatre**.

No 56 **Eliseyevsky Gastronom** was a delicatessen rivalling the Food Hall at Harrods in Tsarist times. After the Revolution it became Gastronom No 1 and the ornate showcases of its sumptuous interior were heaped with jars of boiled vegetables. It is a wonderful example of classic St Petersburg interior design. Exotic Western fare is now on offer.

The building on the south side of the street beside the Fontanka 'Canal' (properly River Fontanka) is known as **Anichkov Palace**, after the nearby **Anichkov Bridge** with its famous equestrian statues.

No 82 **Art Gallery of the Master's Guild** (Gildiya Masterov) offers a good range of graphics, tapestries, ceramics, batik, jewellery and glassware by well-known artists. It's open 11:00-16:00 weekdays.

It's 1km from here to pl Vosstaniya where **Moskovsky station** (for trains to Moscow) is situated.

From pl Vosstaniya it's 700m to the end of the avenue at pl Aleksandra Nevskogo. Here are the **Alexander Nevsky Monastery**, with seven churches in the grounds, and the **Hotel Moskva**.

MOSKOVSOKY
RAILWAY STATION

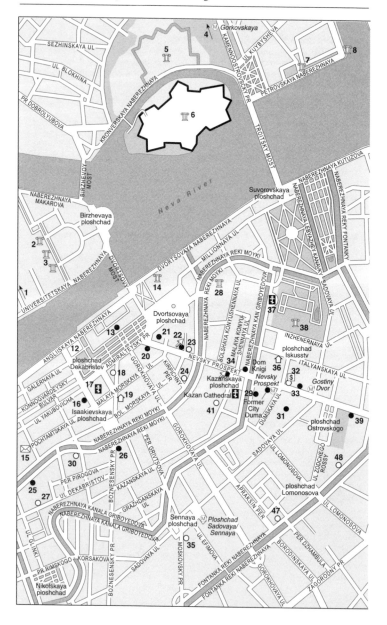

SEZHINSKAYA UL

4 ↑ Ⓜ Gorkovskaya

UL KUYBYSHEVA

Ⓣ 8

5 ♈

7

KAMENNOOSTROVSKY PR

UL BLOKHINA

PETROVSKAYA NABEREZHNAYA

PR DOBROLYUBOVA

KRONVERKSKAYA NABEREZHNAYA

6 ♈

TROITSKY MOST

NABEREZHNAYA MAKAROVA

BIRZHEVOY MOST

Neva River

Suvorovskaya
ploshchad

NABEREZHNAYA KUTUZOVA

NABEREZHNAYA REKI FONTANKY

Birzhevaya
ploshchad

NABEREZHNAYA LEYTENANTA SHMIDTA

2 ♈

DVORTSOVY MOST

DVORTSOVAYA NABEREZHNAYA

MILLIONNAYA UL

3 ♈

1 ↑

UNIVERSITETSKAYA NABEREZHNAYA

ANGLISKAYA NABEREZHNAYA

NABEREZHNAYA REKI MOYKI

SADOVAYA UL

14 ♈

28 ♈

Dvortsovaya
ploshchad

13 ●

21 ●   22 ●

23 ●

NABEREZHNAYA REKI MOYKI

ADMIRALTEYSKY PR

GOROKHOVAYA UL

NEVSKY PROSPEKT

BOLSHAYA KONYUSHENNAYA UL

MALAYA KONYUSHENNAYA UL

37 ♰

INZHENERNAYA UL

38 ♈

ploshchad
Iskusstv

ITALYANSKAYA UL

12 ●

ploshchad
Dekabristov

20 ●

18 ●

24 ●

KIRPICHNY PER

Dom
Knigi

36 ⇑

Nevsky
Prospekt

32 $

33 ●

Gostiny
Dvor Ⓜ

GALERNAYA UL

KONNOGVARDEYSKY BULVAR

UL YAKUBOVICHA

17 ♰

16 ●

19 ⇑

MALAYA MORSKAYA UL

BOL MORSKAYA UL

Kazanskaya
ploshchad

Kazan Cathedral ♰

29 ●

Former
City
Duma

31 ●

ploshchad
Ostrovskogo

39 ●

Isaakievskaya
ploshchad

41 ●

POCHTAMTSKAYA UL

NABEREZHNAYA REKI MOYKI

GOROKHOVAYA UL

SADOVAYA UL

UL ZODCHEGO ROSSY

15 ✉

30 ○

PER GRIVTSOVA

26 ●

BOZNESENSKY PR

KAZANSKAYA UL

48 ○

PER PIROGOVA

ploshchad
Lomonosova

UL LOMONOSOVA

25 ●

27 ○

UL DEKABRISTOV

GRAZHDANSKAYA UL

AFRAKSIN PER

UL GLINKI

PR RIMSKOGO

NABEREZHNAYA KANALA GRIBOYEDOVA

NABEREZHNAYA KANALA GRIBOYEDOVA

47 ●

KORSAKOVSKY PR

SADOVAYA UL

MOSKOVSKY PR

Sennaya
ploshchad

Ⓜ Ploshchad
Sadovaya/
Sennaya

UL EFIMOVA

35 ○

FONTANKA REKI NABEREZHNAYA

GOROKHOVAYA UL

PER DZHAMBULA

BORODINSKAYA UL

ZAGORODNY PR

Nikolskaya
ploshchad

FONTANKA REKI NABEREZHNAYA

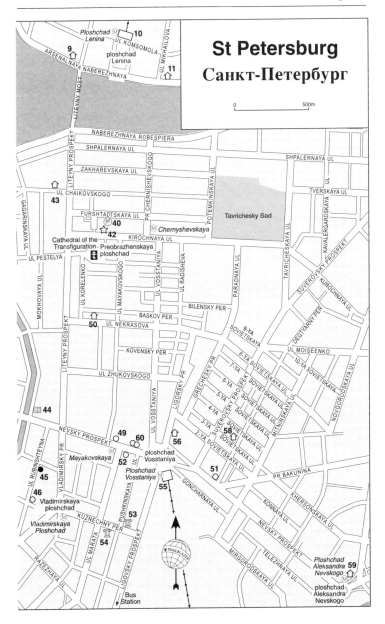

St Petersburg
Санкт-Петербург

0   500m

Ploshchad Lenina
UL KOMSOMOLA
10
9
ploshchad Lenina
11
UL MIKHAILOVA
ARSENALNAYA NABEREZHNAYA
LITEYNY MOST

NABEREZHNAYA ROBESPIERA
SHPALERNAYA UL
SHPALERNAYA UL
ZAKHAREVSKAYA UL
LITEYNY PROSPEKT
PR CHERNISHEVSKOGO
TVERSKAYA UL
KAVALERGARDSKAYA
UL CHAIKOVSKOGO
43
Tavrichesky Sad
GAGARINSKAYA UL
FURSHTADTSKAYA UL
40
POTEMKINSKAYA UL
42
Chernyshevskaya
KIROCHNAYA UL
Cathedral of the Transfiguration
Preobrazhenskaya ploshchad
TAVRICHESKAYA UL
SUVOROVSKY PROSPEKT
KUROCHNAYA UL
UL PESTELYA
PARADNAYA UL
UL VOSSTANIYA
UL RADISHEVA
MOKHOVAYA UL
UL KORELENKO
UL MAYAKOVSKOGO
DEGTYARNY PER
BILENSKY PER
BASKOV PER
UL NEKRASOVA
50
9-YA SOVIETSKAYA
UL MOISEENKO
LITEYNY PROSPEKT
KOVENSKY PER
8-YA SOVIETSKAYA UL
10-YA SOVIETSKAYA
7-YA SOVIETSKAYA UL
UL ZHUKOVSKOGO
GRECHESKY PR
6-YA SOVIETSKAYA UL
NOVGORODSKAYA UL
5-YA SOVIETSKAYA UL
44
LIGORSKY PR
UL VOSSTANIYA
SUVOROVSKY PROSPEKT
4-YA SOVIETSKAYA UL
MITNINSKAYA UL
3-YA SOVIETSKAYA UL
NEVSKY PROSPEKT
49 60
58
2-YA SOVIETSKAYA UL
56
Mayakovskaya
ploshchad Vosstaniya
51
PR BAKUNINA
VLADIMIRSKY PR
52
45
Ploshchad Vosstaniya
55
GONCHARNAYA UL
UL RUBINSHTEYNA
46
KONNAYA UL
Vladimirskaya ploshchad
PUSHKINSKAYA UL
53
NEVSKY PROSPEKT
KHERSONSKAYA UL
Vladimirskaya Ploshchad
KUZNECHNY PER
UL MARATA
54
TELEZHNAYA UL
TRAILBLAZER
Ploshchad Aleksandra Nevskogo
59
RAZEZHAYA UL
LIGOVSKY PROSPEKT
MIRGORODSKAYA UL
ploshchad Aleksandra Nevskogo
Bus Station

WHERE TO STAY AND EAT

1 To Restaurant Kalinka (200m)
Ресторан Калинка
4 To Café Troitsky Most (200m)
Кафе Троицкий Мост
9 Hotel St Petersburg
Гостиница Санкт-Петербург
11 Hostel Holiday Гостиница Holiday
18 Tandoor Indian Restaurant
Индийский Ресторан Тандур
19 Hotel Astoria & Angleterre Wing
Гостиница Астория
23 Literaturnoye Kafe
Кафе Литературное
24 Pizza Hut Пицца Хат
27 Dvoryanskoye Gnezdo
30 Idiot Café Кафе Идиот
32 Grillmaster & ATM
35 McDonald's Restaurant
Макдоналдс
36 Grand-Hotel Europe
Гостиница Гранд
41 Tinkoff
43 Hotel Neva Гостиница Нева
46 Mollie's Irish Bar
Ирландский Бар Моллиз
47 Jazz Club
48 La Cucuracha
49 KFC/Pizza Hut Пицца Хат
50 St Petersburg Puppet Hostel
51 Bahlsen Bakery
52 Baskin-Robbins Ice Cream
56 Hotel Oktyabrskaya
Гостиница Октябрьская
58 St Petersburg International Hostel
Sindbad Travel
59 Hotel Moskva Гостиница Москва
60 Café Marko & Idealnaya Chaska

OTHER

2 Literature Museum/Geological
Museum Музей Русской
Литературы/Карпинский
Геологический Музей
3 Naval Museum
Военно-Морской Музей
& Anthropology Museum
Музей Антропологии
5 Artillery Museum
Артиллерийский Музей
6 Peter and Paul Fortress
Петропавловская Крепость

7 Peter the Great's Log Cabin
Домик Петра
8 Cruiser *Aurora* Аврора
10 Finlandsky Station
Финляндский Вокзал
12 Decembrists' Square
Площадь Декабристов
13 Admiralty Адмиралтейство
14 Hermitage/Winter Palace
Эрмитаж/Зимний Дворец
15 Central Post Office Главпочтамт
16 St P Travel Co Ст.Петербургская
Компания Путешествий
17 St Isaac's Cathedral
Иссакиевский Собор
20 Central Air Ticket Offices
Аэровокзал
21 Former General Staff Building
Здание Главного Штаба
22 Telephone Office Центральний
Переговорный Пункт
25 Yusupov Palace
Юсупов Дворец
26 Mariinsky Palace
Мариинский Дворец
28 Pushkin House Дом Пушкина
29 Railway Ticket Office
Центральные
Железнодорожные Кассы
31 Gostiny Dvor
Универмаг Гостиный Двор
32 ATM Банк
33 Theatre Tickets Kiosk
Театральная Касса
34 Quo Vadis
37 Church of the Resurrection
Церковь Воскресения Христова
38 State Russian Museum
Русский Государственый Музей
39 Anichkov Palace Аничков Дворец
40 US Consulate Консульство США
42 Central OViR/PVU ОВИР
44 Anglia Book Shop
Книга магазин Англия
45 Mussorgsky (Maly) Theatre
Театр Мусоргского (Малый)
53 Arctic Museum Музей Арктика
54 Dostoyevsky House-Museum
Музей Ф.М. Достоевского
55 Moskovsky Station
Московский Вокзал

(Cont'd from p133) You enter via the splendid Jordan Staircase. Of the **State Rooms**, don't miss the Malachite Hall, designed by Brullov, and the adjacent Small Dining Room, where the 1917 revolutionaries arrested the Provisional Government (who had made the Palace their headquarters). Perhaps most impressive are three adjacent rooms: the Royal Throne Room, the Great Banquet Hall and the Gallery of Heroes of 1812, the last decorated with over 1000 portraits of officers who served in the Napoleonic campaign. Various stories are told about the missing canvases – that their subjects died before the portraits were finished or, more credibly, that they were subsequently disgraced by their involvement in the 1825 Decembrist plot to depose Nicholas I.

The museum is so vast that it's easiest to navigate by looking out of the windows and using the river and Palace Square as landmarks. For a virtual preview, visit the museum's excellent website (🖳 www.hermitagemuseum.org).

Entry is on the river-facing side, at Dvortsovaya naberezhnaya 34. The Hermitage is open 10:30-18:00 (to 17:00 on holidays and days preceding holidays) daily except Monday, with the last admission one hour before closing. Admission costs R300 (free for students and those aged under 17). A permit to take photos/videos costs R100/250 extra, and you might be thrown out if you shoot without one.

The State Russian Museum

Given the size of the Hermitage collection, it seems almost impossible that there could be another art museum of similar scope anywhere in the world – but there is, just halfway down Nevsky Prospekt. The Russian Museum, the country's first public art gallery, is housed in the former Mikhailovsky Palace on pl Iskusstv (Arts Square). While the Hermitage contains almost uniquely non-Russian works, the Russian Museum is home to the finest of the country's own 'Old Masters'.

The original collection, which opened in 1895, is displayed in chronological order around the palace, while later acquisitions are in the adjacent Benois Wing. You begin with icons and applied art from as early as the 12th century, including those by legendary 14th-century master Andrei Rublyov. The heart of the collection, however, is the work of Russian painters of the 18th to mid-19th centuries, rarely exhibited abroad. Don't miss the chance to see Brullov's *The Last Days of Pompeii*, Vasnetsov's over-the-top medieval heroes or Aivazovsky's boiling seascapes. Perhaps the finest of all are the portraits of Ilya Repin, whose monumental *The State Parliament* fills a whole room and depicts the last tsar, Nicholas II, with his ministers.

The museum is open 10:00-18:00 daily except Tuesday (to 17:00 Monday). Admission costs US$5. For a virtual tour check out the museum's website, 🖳 www.rusmuseum.ru.

Canals and embankments

Peter the Great imagined his city as a 'Northern Venice', and many of its finest buildings are meant to be approached by water. A canal-boat ride saves much hoofing round the central city where metro stations are scarce, although operators can be rude and commentary may be only in Russian. Trips starting from the junction of Nevsky Prospekt with the Moyka Canal (properly Reka Moyka, 'River Moyka') are the most enjoyable and imaginative. You shouldn't have to pay more than R200. Take sun-hat, sun-cream, cold drinks and a map.

Sights on most routes include **St Isaac's Cathedral** (see below); the **Church of the Resurrection** (see p135); **Mariinsky Theatre**, the blue-and-white home of top-rated opera and ballet (see p149); **Mariinsky Palace**, built without stairs for the invalid Princess Marie, and now the City Hall; **Kazan Cathedral** (see p134); and **Yusupov Palace** (see below). Some trips also go out onto the Neva.

St Isaac's Cathedral

The colossal bronze dome of St Isaac's dominates the city skyline. Its 40-year construction, completed in 1859, was the life's work of French architect Nicholas Montferrand (whose petition to the Empress to be buried there was refused on the grounds that he was Roman Catholic). The central Cathedral of the Russian Empire is open 11:00-18:00 daily except Wednesday, for R200 (plus R80 to ascend the dome, where the Soviet ban on photography no longer applies).

Adjacent to the cathedral is **Decembrists' Square**, scene of the ill-fated 'patriotic rebellion' of 14 December 1825. It's now dominated by Etienne-Maurice Falconet's **Bronze Horseman**, an equestrian monument to Peter the Great erected in 1782 by order of Catherine the Great.

Yusupov Palace

This stately building is famous as the place where in 1916 the ersatz monk Rasputin was poisoned by his dinner host, young Viscount Felix Yusupov, stabbed and shot by Yusupov's cronies and thrown through the ice of the Moyka Canal. It is also a splendid building inside, especially its private theatre. The palace (☎ 314 9883) is at naberezhnaya Reki Moyki 94, a 20-minute walk from metro Nevsky Prospekt. It's open 11:00-16:00 daily except Wednesday. A 90-minute guided tour, including to the murder site, costs around US$25 (book ahead).

Peter and Paul Fortress

The city's first stone structure, begun in 1703 built to keep Swedish invaders out, was subsequently used to keep prisoners in. Its Trubetskoy Bastion served as a Tsarist political prison, with a roster of inmates including Dostoyevsky and Gorky (who survived) and Lenin's elder brother Alexander (who did not). After the revolution the fortress was turned into a museum.

Time your visit to see the noon-day cannon fired from the ramparts. The highlight of the fortress is the **SS Peter and Paul Cathedral**, where most of Russia's rulers from Peter the Great to Nicholas II (see the boxed text opposite) are buried. Also on offer are reconstructions of the **Trubetskoy dungeons** and a **Cosmonaut Museum**.

The fortress and all its attractions are open 10:00-18:00 daily (except Wednesday and the last Tuesday of the month), for R200.

The Romanov Reburial

Despite considerable controversy, July 1998 saw the remains of the Romanov Royal Family transferred for reburial in SS Peter and Paul Cathedral from the abandoned mineshaft near Yekaterinburg where they had been hidden after the murder in 1918.

The list of those who had much to lose from this event was numerous. Hardline Communists feared the backlash that the story would cause. The City of Yekaterinburg fought long and hard to hold on to the relics (and the tourist trade they brought in). The City of Moscow argued they should be buried in the Kremlin with the earliest Tsars. President Boris Yeltsin felt a lump in his throat – 30 years previously the Communists had razed the holding-place in Yekaterinburg where the murders took place, and as Yekaterinburg's mayor he'd signed the orders himself. Even the Russian Orthodox Church winced: in their haste to damn the Communists for the murders, they'd rushed in in the 1920s to authenticate a set of remains in Paris (purchased for a tidy sum) which had been worshipped as Holy Relics for nearly 50 years, and were now shown up as fakes.

Then there were the embarrassed relatives of the late 'Anna Anderson', the woman who'd hoodwinked even close intimates of the Royal Family that she was the escaped Princess Anastasia, rightful Tsarina (her body was subsequently DNA-tested at the behest of greedy relations and shown to be Franziska Schanzkova, a Polish refugee). Last but not least, Fox Motion Pictures had just released a full-length animation, *Anastasia*, showing her not only escaping but marrying the sensitive young soldier who'd pulled her not-quite-dead body from the corpses, and finding happiness in America...

As you enter the Cathedral take a sharp right before the inner doors, to an anteroom where an official plaque declares that you are surrounded by the complete, authenticated and indubitable remains of those killed in Yekaterinburg on 16 July 1918. Even with such a definitive statement (which sidesteps a short tally of bones, and the whereabouts of the Royal valet, chambermaid and physician who also fell in the hail of bullets), this was to be a burial that refused to go easily to the grave. Opening the catacombs to inter Nicholas with his forebears, workmen found a 'last laugh' from the Communists, who had piped concrete into the foundations to prevent any further burials. Ceremonies were delayed whilst digging equipment blasted enough space for the funereal urns.

With a date set and foreign dignitaries invited (including the British Royal Family, cousins of the Romanovs), Yeltsin's Vice-President Boris Nemtsov went to the Finance Ministry with his budget for the rites, commemorative stones, VIP reception – in all, around US$10m. 'What?', he was told, 'Don't you know the economy's going down the tubes? We can let you have US$1m, but don't hang around, the country will be bust in a month!' Thus, at least most of the Romanovs were finally united with their ancestors – in a hurry, and on the cheap.

Neil McGowan (Russia)

Multiple museums

Many more of St Petersburg's old buildings and palaces conceal other museums of mind-boggling esotericism. Enthusiasts for topics as diverse as railways, the Russian postal service, the Arctic, hygiene, and the history of bread will find something to their taste.

Of wider appeal is the **Russian Vodka Museum**, turning dry academicism into a healthy and interactive practical study, with Slavic snacks to help soak up the hard stuff. The museum (☎ 312 3416), at 5 Konnogvardeysky bulvar, is open 11:00-22:00 daily, with full-scale vodka suppers served in the evenings (book ahead).

EXCURSIONS FROM ST PETERSBURG

Scorching heat and reeking rivers (the waterways doubled as open sewers) drove Imperial St Petersburg's aristocrats into the countryside in the summer, to residences no less grand than their *pied-a-terres* in town. Day-trips to these magnificent mansions make a rewarding change from yet another walk down Nevsky prospekt.

Thirty kilometres west of the city lies **Petrodvorets** (Peterhof), built by Peter the Great as his Versailles-by-the-sea. Its great attractions are the Ornamental Gardens and the Cascades (fountains) whose gilded figures appear in every tourist brochure. Grounds and palace are open 09:00-21:00 daily except Friday (the palace is closed in winter). In summer the nicest way to arrive is by hydrofoil, departing from Palace Pier outside the Hermitage's main entrance, but at over US$15 it's an extravagant ride. Crowded but cheap suburban trains run from Baltiisky station (metro: Baltiiskaya) to Novy Peterhof for a fraction of the price, but from there you must get a local bus or taxi, or take a 50-minute hike. Double-decker excursion buses go directly to the Palace from Baltiisky station but schedules are irregular.

Set in beautiful parklands at **Pushkin** (formerly Tsarskoye Selo, the 'royal hamlet'), 25km south of St Petersburg, is the vast Catherine Palace, completed in 1756. The palace was looted by German soldiers in WWII. Its famous Amber Room (whose original amber panels disappeared during the German retreat and have never been found) has been called the largest piece of jewellery in the world; the room has recently reopened after a multi-million-dollar renovation. The palace is open daily except Tuesday. The adjoining estate, 4km further south at **Pavlovsk** (open daily except Friday), was built by Catherine the Great for her son, 'mad' Tsar Paul I. This and Pushkin are joined by a country path and make a practical full-day's outing. Trains for Pushkin and Pavlovsk leave from Vitebsky station (metro: Pushkinskaya). Alternatively, frequent minibuses run past Pushkin from Moskovskaya metro station.

Lomonosov (Oranienbaum), 12km beyond Petrodvorets, attracts far fewer tourists but its park, extensive and wild, is a quiet spot for a picnic or tryst (bring your own snacks as refreshments are scarce here). The Grand Palace built by Peter's lieutenant, Alexander Menshikov, is largely under renovation. More interesting is Catherine the Great's extravagant rococo Chinese Palace. The estate is closed Tuesday and in winter. Trains leave from Baltiisky station.

If you simply yearn for some greenery and fresh air the metro will get you to **Kamenny ostrov** (metro: Krestovsky Ostrov or Staraya Derevnya), a pleasure-park of natural islands in the city's north-west, where the active can rent a rowing-boat and the contemplative can visit the **Gunzechoiney Buddhist Temple** at Primorsky pr 91.

PRACTICAL INFORMATION
Arriving in St Petersburg
See p64 for important information on potential customs-form rip-offs on the Trans-Siberian.

By air There are two airports, sharing one runway, about 20km south of the city. **Pulkovo 2**, recently renovated and well-designed, is for international flights. Minibus No 13 runs frequently between here and Moskovskaya metro station from 05:30 until the last flight, for R10 (the bus with the same number and routing isn't worth the R5 savings). Taxis into town cost US$30-50 (in roubles) depending on your bargaining power; going to the airport costs US$20-30 due to higher competition.

Most domestic flight use **Pulkovo 1**, a charmless Soviet heap 15 minutes further south. Hang on to your baggage-reclaim tag on domestic flights, as you may have trouble retrieving your bag without it. Minibus No 39 goes to Moskovskaya metro station for R10.

By train The *Sibelius* and *Repin* expresses from Helsinki arrive at **Finlandsky station** (metro: Ploshchad Lenina). **Varshavsky station** (metro: Frunzenskaya) is the arrival point from almost anywhere in north-western Europe; and while **Baltiisky station** is being rebuilt it's also the terminus for trains from Estonia, Latvia and Lithuania. Moscow and Novgorod trains come into **Moskovsky station**, the grandest and most central, on Nevsky pr (metro: Ploshchad Vosstaniya or Mayakovskaya).

By bus There are comfortable coach services from Helsinki, Tallinn and Tartu, and uncomfortable ones from as far away as Tbilisi in Georgia. All arrive at the city's only bus station (called Avtovokzal No 2 for obscure reasons) at naberezhnaya Obvodnogo Kanala 36; Ligovsky Prospekt metro station is a 15-minute hike away. Eurolines tickets are sold from an office at ul Shkapina 10.

By boat Ocean-going cruises anchor in the Neva. River cruises use the river termi-nal (*rechnoy vokzal*) at Obukhovskoy Oborony pr 195 (take tram No 24 or 29 from Proletarskaya metro station).

Local transport
St Petersburg's **metro** is quick, cheap and efficient, and is open from 05:30 to midnight.

A ticket to anywhere on the system costs R7; old-style tokens (*jeton*) are being phased out in favour of multiple-ride magnetic cards. Unlike the 'Stalin-wedding-cake' style of Moscow's stations, many of those in St Petersburg, notably Mayakovskaya, feature bold Soviet-Constructivist designs. Some stations have automatic safety doors, which can make it hard to spot your destination station: just stay alert and count the stops.

But the metro network has great gaps where waterways prevent tunnelling (including vast swathes of the city centre), and for these areas you must square-up to the **buses, trams, trolley-buses** or **minibuses**. The fare on all except minibuses is R5 for any distance, paid to a conductor on board. Minibuses with the same numbers, on the same routes, provide faster, more frequent service and guaranteed seating for a few roubles more.

Orientation and services
St Petersburg stands at the mouth of the Neva, in a web of channels and islands (33 main ones and countless small ones) where the river meets the Baltic Sea's Gulf of Finland. The main axis is 4km-long Nevsky prospekt, with Dvortsovaya pl (Palace Square) and the Hermitage at its north-western end. This square is the ceremonial centre, although the city's heart beats from the block of Nevsky pr between the Nevsky Prospekt and Gostinny Dvor metro stations.

Across the Neva are the city's other main 'quarters', Vasilevsky ostrov (St Basil's Island), Petrograd side (beyond the Peter and Paul Fortress) and Vyborg side to the north-east.

Diplomatic missions China (☎ 114 7670, 🖷 114 4958, 🖳 frchn@mail.w plus.net) naberezhnaya Kanala Griboyed-

ova 134; **Belarus** (☎ 273 0078, ▤ 273 4164, ▣ st_petersburg@belemb assy.org) ul Robespiera 8/46; **Estonia** (☎ 102 0920, ▤ 102 0927) Bolshaya Monyetnaya ul 14; **Finland** (visa dept ☎ 273 7321, ▤ 272 1421) ul Chaykovskogo 71; **Germany** (☎ 320 24008, ▤ 327 3117) ul Furshtadtskaya 39; **Latvia** (☎ 327 6054, ▤ 327 6052) 10-ya liniya 11, Vasilevsky ostrov; **Sweden** (visa dept ☎ 329 1440, ▤ 329 1445) Malaya Konyushennaya ul 1/3; **UK** (☎ 320 3200, ▤ 320 3211, ▣ www.britain.spb.ru) pl Proletarskoy Diktatury 5; **USA** (consular dept ☎ 331 2600, ▤ 331 2852, ▣ usembassy.st ate.gov/stpetersburg) Furshtadtskaya ul 15.

Local publications The best listings freesheet is *Pulse* (which has an English-language version). *Where in St Petersburg* is weightier but heavily slanted in favour of its advertisers. The *St Petersburg Times* is a source of somewhat pedestrian news but preferable to the *Neva News*, English mouthpiece of conservative local politicians. Russian speakers should pick up *Aktivist*, which has the best listings of all.

Medical For medical, dental or emergency services, contact the **American Medical Center** (☎ 326 1730) at Serpukhovskaya ul 10 (metro: Tekhnologichesky Institut or Pushkinskaya) or the **British-American Family Practice** (☎ 327 6030, 24-hour ☎ 999 0949), Grafsky pereulok 7 at the corner of Vladimirsky pr.

Russian visas and extensions If St Petersburg is your first stop in Russia, remember that you should register your visa within three working days. Even if you have already registered elsewhere in Russia, it may be wise to do it again here to avoid the possibility of problems with the city's occasionally zealous policemen. Hotel (and usually hostel) guests are automatically registered at check-in. If you are staying privately you must do this yourself, at the central office of **OViR/PVU** (☎ 278 3486), ul Saltykova-Schedrina 4 (metro: Chernyshevskaya); bring passport, visa, proof of hotel reservation, and a translator

if you don't speak Russian. This is also the place to apply for a visa extension.

Telecommunications Most street telephones (*taksofony*) use pre-paid cards available from kiosks and metro station ticket windows, but they are an expensive way to make long-distance and international calls. For these you should purchase one of the many international phone cards available in shops, kiosks, post offices and metro ticket desks. You can make prepaid, slightly discounted long-distance and international calls from the **Central Telephone Office** at Bolshaya Morskaya ul 3.

The best and friendliest Internet café is **Quo Vadis** at Nevsky pr 24, open 24 hours a day every day. **Tetris**, pioneers of public-access Internet in Russia, is at Chernyakhovskogo 33. For those with their own laptops, pre-paid internet cards are sold at many kiosks. The Central Telephone Office also has Internet access.

Tours Independent sightseeing is easy, but if it's a tour you want, the **St Petersburg Travel Company** (formerly Intourist; ☎ 315 5129), Nevsky pr 100, offers themed half-day trips around the city for US$16-25 and excursions to the country palaces (see p142) from US$40. **Peter's Tours** (☎ 329 8018) operate much-recommended walking tours from the St Petersburg International Hostel (see Where to stay).

The adventurous can join much cheaper jaunts for Russian tourists, who visit St Petersburg in huge numbers. There are daily morning and lunchtime departures from the north-western wing of the Gostinny Dvor department store on Nevsky pr (metro: Gostinny Dvor); if you keep silent you might even enjoy 'local' prices for attractions along the way.

Travel Services **Sindbad Travel** (☎ 324 0740, ▤ 324 0880, ▣ incomingtravel.sind bad.ru), at Universitetskaya naberezhnaya 11 and in the St Petersburg International Hostel (see Where to stay), caters to budget travellers of all ages with train and plane tickets, visa support, tours, theatre tickets and

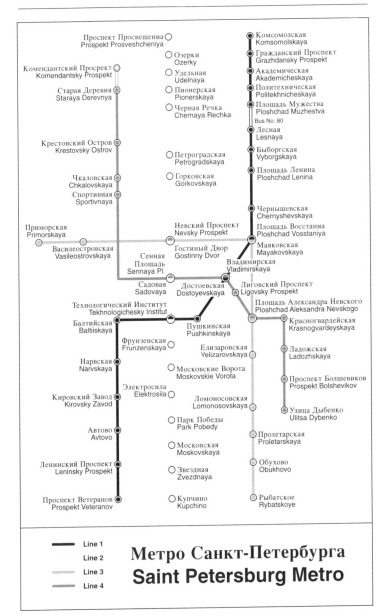

Метро Санкт-Петербурга
Saint Petersburg Metro

Line 1
Line 2
Line 3
Line 4

hostelling information. There is also a student-oriented travel service at the **Quo Vadis** Internet café (see Telecommunications, above). The helpful **Dyum Tourist Agency** (☎ 279 0037) is in the Central House of Actors (Tsentralny Dom Aktyor) at Nevsky pr 86. **American Express** are inside the Grand Hotel Europe.

Where to stay
St Petersburg has a chronic shortage of accommodation at every level, so make arrangements early, especially for May-June.

Budget accommodation Rooms in this bracket normally do not include toilet or bath.

The *St Petersburg International Hostel* (☎ 329 8018, 🖹 329 8019, 🖳 ryh@ryh.ru, www.ryh.ru), ul 3-ya Sovietskaya 28, was Russia's first accredited youth hostel. A bed in a three to five-bed dormitory in summer (March-October)/winter costs US$19/12 for HI cardholders and US$21/15 for others, with breakfast included. In summer it's often full. There is a friendly social atmosphere, helped along by a range of useful services and English-language movies. Sindbad Travel (see Travel services, above) are affiliated to the hostel and located on the premises.

Affiliated to the St Petersburg International Hostel and echoing its services and prices is the small, slick *St Petersburg Puppet Hostel* (☎ 272 5401, 🖳 pup pet@ryh.ru), budget accommodation with no strings attached, on the top floor of the Puppet Theatre at ul Nekrasova 12.

Hostel Holiday (☎/🖹 327 1070, 🖳 www.hostel.spb.ru) is beautifully located on the Vyborg-side waterfront at ul Mikhaylova 1, a five-minute walk from Finland station (metro: Ploshchad Lenina). Dorm beds cost US$15 and doubles with hot breakfast are US$19 per person; winter rates are slightly lower and HI and ISIC card-holders get a further US$1 off. Visa support is also offered.

Catering to German-speaking guests but open to all is the *Hotel Nemetsky Klub* (☎ 371 5104, 🖹 371 5690, 🖳 www.german club.narod.ru), a slightly wacky place in a

Stalin-era building at ul Gastello 20, three blocks from Moskovskaya metro station. Single/double rooms with furnishings in hilariously bad taste start at US$25/30.

The *Sportivnaya Hotel* (☎ 235 0236, 🖹 230 4333), ul Deputatskaya 34, offers truly budget accommodation in a remote but charming part of town, Kamenny ostrov, well-served by Krestovsky Ostrov metro station. Twins start at about US$12 per room, in roubles cash only.

Homestays with an English-speaking host can be organized through Host Families Association (HOFA; ☎ 275 1992, mobile ☎ 914 2762, 🖳 www.hofa.us), Tavricheskaya ul 5/25. Single/double B&B starts at about US$30/50 a night, and support services including visa support are available at additional cost.

Mid-range hotels All rooms in this category have attached bathroom. Many hotels offer weekend discounts (Friday and Saturday nights) of up to 30%, if you ask. Prices include combined 25% Russian Federation and sales taxes.

One of the city's few 'period' hotels, built in 1912, the *Hotel Neva* (☎ 278 0504, 🖹 273 3593), ul Chaykovskogo 12, has spotless three-star rooms and a fantastic central location, though the lobby could use a coat of paint. Singles/doubles are US$35/42 in the old wing and US$80/90 in the new wing.

The standard, well-worn choice is *Hotel Oktyabrskaya* (☎ 277 6330, 🖹 315 7501) with branches on either side of pl Vosstaniya; the main address is Ligovsky pr 10. Singles/doubles cost US$35/42. Recent renovations offer better rooms at higher prices, but a decline in low-price rooms. Noise from the city's two busiest streets and Moskovsky station, plus guests 'in a good mood', are a negative factor.

The non-central location of *Hotel Rossiya* (☎ 294 6322), ul Chernyshevs kogo 11, is offset by its proximity to Park Pobedy metro station. It's no longer the grim Soviet heap it appears from the outside, recently renovated to three-star standards with prices to match at US$58/78 for a single/double.

Matisov Domik (☎ 318 5462, ▤ 318 7419, ▢ www.matisov.spb.ru), naberezhnaya Reki Pryazhky 3/1, is a new three-star hotel much favoured by Russian actors, ballet stars and other luvvies for its charming service (in Russian only). Singles/doubles cost US$60/100. The downside is its location almost 3km south-west of the city centre, far from transport.

A Soviet-era hotel beloved by group tourists, the *Hotel St Petersburg* (☎ 542 9411, ▤ 248 8002, ▢ postmaster@spbho tel.spb.ru) has majestic views from river-facing rooms, although the rooms themselves are less inspiring: green swirly carpets, red curtains and purple bedspreads. Singles/doubles cost US$80/97. It's at Pirogovskaya naberezhnaya 5/2, a 15-minute walk from Ploshchad Lenina metro.

Built in 1980, *Hotel Mercury* (☎ 325 6444, ▤ 276 1977), ul Tavricheskaya 39, was the last of the USSR Top-Party-Boss hotels. Its 16 ample-sized rooms are good value at US$63/75 for a single/twin; book well ahead.

The Austrian *Hotel Neptune* (☎ 324 4610, ▤ 324 4611), newly-built to staid three-star standards, is probably worth the price (single US$80-120, twin US$120-150) for the super facilities including massive swimming pool and sports complex. It's at naberezhnaya Obvodnogo Kanala 93a, a central if unlovely location.

Time has stood still since 1983 at the *Hotel Moskva* (☎ 274 3001, ▤ 274 2130), pl Aleksandra Nevskogo 2, a Soviet monolith with rude staff, overbearing colossal-style lobby, dull rooms and an army of hookers in the bar. Its main business seems to be vodka-fuelled Scandinavian coach tours. Rooms are US$100 for a single or US$130 for a double.

Upmarket hotels   If you can accept a non-central location with a metro near at hand, the *Deson-Ladoga Hotel* (☎ 528 5202, ▤ 528 5220, ▢ www.deson.lek.ru) is astonishing value for money, a four-star hotel with huge luxurious rooms for US$113/153 per single/double. It's at pr Shaumyana 26, a 10-minute walk from metro Novocherkasskaya.

Centrally located in a converted 19th-century mansion block, the *Hotel Corona* (☎ 311 0086, ▤ 314 3865), Malaya Konyushennaya ul 7 (off Nevsky pr), has small but excellently-furnished rooms, and everything is new. Singles cost US$120-156, doubles US$156-180.

Anyone who was anyone in the 19th century stayed either at the Astoria or the Yevropeyskaya (now the Grand-Hotel Europe). The guestbook at *Hotel Astoria* (☎ 313 5757, ▤ 313 5059, ▢ www.asto ria.spb.ru), Bolshaya Morskaya ul 39, features writers, artists and actors in endless streams of great names. Hitler planned to celebrate his victory over the USSR in its ballroom, and even had invitations printed, although he failed to show up for the date. A 1990s refurbishment may have destroyed its charm but it's still a thoroughly excellent five-star hotel, with singles/doubles from US$360/500, or US$276/336 in its lower-priced *Angleterre Wing* (▢ www.angleter rehotel.spb.ru).

The *Grand-Hotel Europe* (☎ 329 6000, ▤ 329 6001, ▢ www.grandhoteleu rope.com) is probably Russia's finest five-star hotel, with a superlative location in the middle of Nevsky pr, a guest-list including heads of state and the crowned heads of Europe, and service so good it's almost worth the breathtaking prices (singles/doubles from US$388/475).

Where to eat

St Petersburg's eating scene has metamorphosed entirely since this guidebook first appeared. In the early editions we listed places which might actually have food, and even sell it. In today's St Petersburg, eating out has become a pleasurable activity where the problem is the range of choice, not the lack of it.

The St Petersburg area code is ☎ 812. From outside Russia dial +7-812.

Russian and other local cuisines

Baronial-style Russian food of the 19th century is the attraction at *Count Suvorov* (☎ 315 4238), ul Lomonosova 6. Restaurant prices are upper-moderate or you can eat the same dishes for less in their bar-lounge.

Centrally-located *Masha i Medved* (Maria & The Bear; ☎ 310 4631), at Malaya Sadovaya ul 1, is a super little Russian-cuisine basement café with different caviars (not just black and red), pies, pastries, soups and complete meals at low prices – authentic and without tourist-style nonsense. Almost next door is *Café Mekong*, with a marvellous Asian buffet spread for just US$4.50.

In an outbuilding of the Yusupov Palace at pl Dekabristov 21, *Dvoryanskoye Gnezdo* (Noble Nest; ☎ 312 3205) offers succulent gourmet food, an exclusive wine list and outstanding service. This is one of those expensive places which are really worth the expense. Dress is formal and booking is recommended.

For luscious and inexplicably cheap Georgian food go to *Kolkhida* (☎ 274 2514), Nevsky pr 176. Supper costs around US$15. Service is cheerful if rather slow.

The *Literaturnoye Kafe* (☎ 312 8543), Nevsky pr 18, may have pleased Pushkin but it's a worn-out old place now, with waiters in nylon '18th century' livery and service so slow you almost need to order a day in advance.

Eccentric

For mid-price Russian and international food in a cloak-and-dagger atmosphere try *Sac-Voyage Beremmenoy Shpionki* (The Pregnant Spy's Travelling-Bag; ☎ 311 7817) at Bolshaya Konyushennaya ul 13 (off Nevsky pr). Eat in the Spy Room, the Stalactite Cave, the Kama Sutra Room or the sort-of-S&M Torture Chamber. The Pregnant Spy and her associates wander around giving out coded messages (in Russian), and there is cabaret some nights.

At barnyard-bizarre *Priut Bodlivoy Kozy* (The Cursed Goat's Manger; ☎ 315 7297), Zagorodny pr 2/4, grills are the thing to choose (and choose them early: they're cooked to order and take a while). Meantime try a Cursed Goat Cocktail if you dare.

The dining rooms at *Federico Fellini* (☎ 311 5078), Malaya Konyushennaya ul 4/2 (off Nevsky pr), are from Fellini film sets: a prison, a palm beach, a luxury hotel suite. The Italian-accented European food or fondue comes at affordable prices (dinner around US$15).

At the Nevsky pr end of the same street is much-liked *Bogart's Bar*, serving brasserie meals and drinks at prices cheaper than all the gin-joints in all the world, eg, US$3.50 for a main course with complimentary wine or beer.

European and International

There's a bit of everything on the menu at *Golden Ostap* (☎ 303 8822) – Russian, European, Asian – plus good service and moderate prices (especially the US$8 set Business Lunch). It's at Italyanskaya ul 4, only steps away from the Griboyedov Canal, and one you come back to again and again.

In the Grand-Café style, *Stroganovsky Dvor* (Stroganov Courtyard; ☎ 315 2315), Nevsky pr 17, nevertheless has some excellent budget options, including an extensive self-serve buffet for under US$5. The location, in a marquee in the courtyard of the Stroganov Palace, is truly regal.

Shalom (☎ 327 5475), ul Koli Tolmachka 8, offers hearty, mid-price Jewish food in the grand style (including kletzmer

---

❏ **Drinking water**

Avoid St Petersburg's tap water at all costs (including as ice in your drinks and for brushing your teeth) as it is infected with giardia, a particularly nasty parasite which can cause stomach cramps, nausea and an unpleasant and persistent form of diarrhoea. Buy bottled water, and stick to fresh fruit that you can peel.

band on big nights), daily except Saturday. Vegetarians might do well here too.

For cheaper kosher eating (dine for US$5) try *Zhemchuzhina*, Skipersky protok 2, although the tacky 80s décor may disturb your digestion.

In the shadow of the Admiralty, *Tandoor* (☎ 312 3886), Voznesensky pr 2, offers classic, spicy Indian dining. If it's budget Asian cuisine you're after, try the plastic tables, neon lighting and super food at *Krasny Terem*, Nevsky pr 78, a bargain-basement Chinese buffet.

La Cucuracha (☎ 110 4006), Fontanka Reki naberezhnaya 39, is a mid-price Mexican spot whose noisy, cheerful atmosphere makes it a favourite for office parties and hen nights.

Vegetarian plus Named after the hero of Dostoyevsky's novel, the *Idiot Café* (☎ 315 1675), naberezhnaya Reki Moyki 82, serves veggie and near-veggie (fish) dishes in a cosy, jokey Bohemian-intellectual basement on the Moyka embankment, a few blocks from St Isaac's.

Kavkaz-Bar (☎ 312 1665), Karavannaya ul 18, is a swish Georgian place which is better value than it looks. Amongst meaty grills and satsivi chicken there are multiple meatless morsels and spicy cheesebreads to munch.

In the 'health food café' tradition – with worthy food and terrible décor – is *Troitsky Most*, at Posadskaya 2.

Fast food and snacks Nevsky pr is lined with *fast-food* eateries – Pizza Hut, KFC, Subway and the rest. For even cheaper eating there are kiosks (along Nevsky pr, around Moskovsky station and near every metro station) selling hot dogs, pizza slices, jacket potatoes and Russian *blini* pancakes, all for around US$1 per meal-sized portion.

Idealnaya Chashka is a chain of Seattle-style coffee shops with several branches, notably at Nevsky pr 112 (metro: Ploshchad Vosstaniya) where rivals *Café Marco* are next door. Both serve top-quality coffee and luscious cakes, and Marco also does salads and light meals.

Bars and nightlife
For Czech beer and set-lunch deals from US$2 try *Gambrinus* at Nevsky pr 126. *Mollie's Irish Bar* serves Guinness until 3am at ul Rubinshteyna 36. **Café Saigon** (Nevsky pr 7-9), original home of 1980s underground rock in the USSR, is still a music venue, much tidied-up although the food is still dreadful. *Tinkoff* brew their own beer on the premises at Kazanskaya ul 7. Leningrad's first foreign bar, in the 1980s, was *Chayka*, and it's still going strong at naberezhnaya Griboyedova Kanala 14.

There are numerous nightclubs offering a Las Vegas style evening, of which *Hollywood Nites* (Nevsky pr 46), *Golden Dolls* (Nevsky pr 60) and *The National Hunt* (Malaya Morskaya ul 11) are strongly promoted. For a less commercialized bop try *Money Honey* in Apraskin Dvor, Sadovaya ul 13, or join a younger crowd at *Metro*, Ligovsky pr 174.

Art-house music/dance venues are dominated by *Fish Fabrique* (Pushkinskaya ul 10 but enter through the arch at Ligovsky pr 53) and nearby *Griboyedov*, in a converted bomb shelter at Voronezhskaya ul 2a (look for the shelter entrance standing alone in the street). *Club 69* (2-ya Krasnoarmeyskaya 6) is a leading gay club, as is **Greshniki** (Sinners; naberezhnaya Gribo-yedova Kanala 28/1). *Cabaret*, ul Dekabristov 34, is presided over by transvestite Lilya, the sharpness of whose tongue may be lost on non-Russian-speakers.

Cultural life
Head and shoulders above the rest in St Petersburg is Valery Gergiev, conductor and Musical Director of the **Mariinsky Opera and Ballet Theatre** (called the Kirov in Soviet days) at Teatralnaya pl 2. Good seats will set you back at least US$100, but this is the finest ballet troupe in the world. Excellent opera and ballet can also be enjoyed, for around one-third of that price, at the **Mussorgsky Theatre** (the former Maly Theatre) at pl Isskustv 1. Unless your Russian is flawless you cannot avoid paying these 'foreigner prices', imposed by the mayor (passports are

checked). Another star is maestro Yuri Temirkanov of the **St Petersburg State Philharmonia,** Mikhailovskaya ul 2, where ticket prices put world-class music within reach of even the destitute.

In July and August all of St Petersburg's theatre companies go on holiday or on tour. But you can pick up tickets for touring companies at the Alexandrinsky Theatre, the massive building dominating pl Ostrovskogo, and see young stars of tomorrow dancing for cruise-line passengers.

Ciniselli's Circus, at Fontanka Reki naberezhnaya 3, has been a city highlight since the 19th century, although animal-lovers may prefer to give it a miss. There are regular **folklore shows** at the Nikolayevsky Palace (☎ 312 5500), pl Truda 4.

Moving on

By air St Petersburg is served by most major European airlines as well as local carrier Pulkovo Aviation, and there are daily flights from London, Berlin, Helsinki, Prague and Warsaw and regular weekly flights from most other European capitals. Most international flights land at Pulkovo 2 while domestic flights use Pulkovo 1. For information on getting to the airport see p143.

Tickets for most airlines can be purchased at Central Air Ticket Offices (☎ 314 6963) at Nevsky pr 7/9 or Kamennoostrovsky pr 27 (open 08:00-19:00 Monday-Friday, 08:00-18:00 weekends). Usually, however, you'll get a better deal through a travel agent (see p144).

By train Check your ticket to see which station you depart from: current rebuilding programmes (especially at Baltiisky station) have relocated some departures.

Trains are usually available for boarding 30 minutes before leaving. They rarely depart late and have been known to roll out of the station a few minutes ahead of schedule. Don't underestimate the time it takes to walk the length of a 16-carriage train! Intercity train timetables are available at all stations and if you can speak Russian, you can call for information on ☎ 162 3344 (domestic) or ☎ 274 2092 (international).

Tickets for same-day departure can only be purchased at the station of departure, at the 'same-day' window (*sutochnaya*) or service centre. Buying last-minute tickets from speculators is risky because of the name-on-ticket/passport rule (see p71).

Advance-purchase long-distance and international tickets can be purchased from the departure station or from the **Railways Ticket Office** at naberezhnaya Kanala Griboyedova 24 (08:00-20:00 Monday-Saturday, 08:00-16:00 Sunday). You'll need your passport, and your name and passport number will printed on the ticket.

If you plan to return from St Petersburg to Europe you must pass through one or more of the Baltic states (Estonia, Latvia and Lithuania), Poland, Belarus and Ukraine. **Belarus** requires visas from almost every visitor, and it can take three days to get one. A Ukrainian visa is so difficult to obtain that most travellers try to bypass the country. Canadians need a Lithuanian visa but may not be able to obtain one here.

Train No 25 goes via the Baltic states and Warsaw to Berlin (32 hours), avoiding Belarus. Train No 57 goes via Belarus to Warsaw (22 hours). You can get to Prague (48 hours) on train No 183 via Belarus and

---

❏ **Bridge raising**

St Petersburg is a working port, and shipping must pass. It does so at night from May to September when the waterways are unfrozen, and **all** the city's bridges are raised from approximately 02:00 until 05:00. There is no alternative way home if you are caught out, and you just have to wait. There are no riverboat services even in daylight hours, and the metro shuts down at midnight.

Ukraine, or save many headaches by changing trains in Warsaw. Some other international journey times from St Petersburg are: Helsinki (8 hours), Tallinn (9 hours), Riga (12 hours), Vilnius (13 hours) and Budapest (44 hours).

By bus In addition to the fairly run-down services leaving from the bus station, there are a few smarter private operators, mainly running to Helsinki (about US$45) and other destinations in Finland. **Sovavto** (☎ 264 5125) sells tickets at pl Pobedy 1 and Kamennoostrovsky pr 39 for daily services to Helsinki, Turku, Lappeenranta, and Yvyaskyulya. **Finnord** (☎ 314 8951), Italyanskaya ul 37, offer student discounts on a twice-daily service to Helsinki.

❏ **Moscow to St Petersburg by train**
The arrow-straight, 650km railway between Moscow and St Petersburg is Russia's busiest and most prestigious line, and high standards are maintained in terms of both facilities and service. When it was opened in 1851 the average travel time was 25 hours. Today most overnight trains take eight hours, with the once-weekly *ER-200* getting there in just five hours (compared to over 10 hours by car).

There are about 10 trains a day in each direction. Most travellers prefer an overnight journey as it saves accommodation costs and leaves more time for sightseeing. Berths are comfortable, and security guards patrol the corridors. The higher-priced *Krasnaya Strela* (Red Arrow), *Nikolayevsky Express* and *Express* have all-night restaurant service. First-class passengers get a packed lunch (daytime trains) or breakfast (overnight trains).

If you buy a ticket yourself, a berth in a two-berth cabin (SV) costs US$60-85; in a four-berth cabin (kupé) it's US$35-58 on the better trains. On a day train (eg No 23/24) you could do it for US$18-24.

Travellers arriving at St Petersburg's Moskovsky station are spurred through the mob of greedy porters and taxi drivers by the loudspeaker strains of Reinhold Gliere's pompous *Anthem to a Great City*.

Origin	Train Name	No	Jny time	Dep	Arr	Destination
St Petersburg	*Krasnaya Strela*	1	8hrs 30mins	23:55	08:25	Moscow
St Petersburg	*Express*	3	8hrs 29mins	23:59	08:30	Moscow
St Petersburg	*Nikolayevsky Exp*	5	7hrs 10mins	23:35	07:47	Moscow
St Petersburg		13	9hrs 23mins	21:55	06:03	Moscow
St Petersburg	*Yunost* (seat only)	23	8hrs 36mins	13:05	21:41	Moscow
St Petersburg	*Smena*	25	8hrs 05mins	23:10	07:15	Moscow
St Petersburg	*ER200**	157	4hrs 59mins	12:15	17:08	Moscow
St Petersburg	*Avrora*	159	6hrs 15mins	15:55	22:10	Moscow
Moscow	*Krasnaya Strela*	2	8hrs 30mins	23:55	08:25	St Petersburg
Moscow	*Express*	4	8hrs 30mins	23:59	08:29	St Petersburg
Moscow	*Nikolayevsky Exp*	6	8hrs 45mins	23:10	07:55	St Petersburg
Moscow		14	8hrs 30mins	20:26	05:00	St Petersburg
Moscow	*Yunost* (seat only)	24	8hrs 34mins	12:16	20:50	St Petersburg
Moscow	*Smena*	26	8hrs 15mins	23:00	07:05	St Petersburg
Moscow	*ER200§*	158	4hrs 59mins	12:11	17:09	St Petersburg
Moscow	*Avrora*	160	6hrs 15mins	17:20	23:55	St Petersburg

* = Thursday only   § = Friday only

Moscow
Москва

All railway lines in Russia lead to the capital so you'll be spending some time here, even if it's just a quick visit to Red Square as you change stations. Moscow is worth much more than that, however. Almost all the resounding changes that have taken place in the country over the past decade have been initiated here and if you're looking for the pulse of the new Russia this is where you'll find it.

Moscow's historic sights alone make it a fascinating place to explore; bank on a minimum of three days to see the main attractions. Finding a place to stay, whatever your budget, is not a problem, and the metro makes getting around easy.

HISTORY

The archaeological record shows that the Moscow area has been inhabited since Neolithic times. However, the first written mention of the city was not until 1147, when Prince Yuri Dolgoruki founded the city by building a wooden fort beside the Moskva River, in the principality of Vladimir. The settlement which grew up around the fort soon developed into a major trading centre.

The Mongols
Disaster struck the Russian principalities in the early 13th century in the form of the Mongol invasion. Moscow was razed to the ground in 1238 and for the next $2^{1}/_{2}$ centuries was obliged to pay an annual tribute to the Mongol Khan. But in 1326 Moscow was made seat of the Russian Orthodox Church, a role carrying with it the title of capital of Russia. Prince Dmitry Donskoi strengthened the city's defences, built a stone wall around the Kremlin and in 1380 defeated a Mongol-Tatar army at Kulikovo. But it was not until 1476 that tributes to the Khan ceased.

The years of growth
The reign of Ivan III 'The Great' (1462-1505) was a period of intensive construction in the city. Italian architects were commissioned to redesign the Kremlin, and many cathedrals and churches date from this period. Prosperity continued into the 16th century under Ivan IV 'The Terrible'; it was at this time that St Basil's Cathedral was built.

The early 17th century was a time of civil disorder, and a peasant uprising culminated in the invasion of Moscow by Polish and Lithuanian forces. When they were driven out in 1612 the city was again burnt to the ground. Rebuilt in stone, Moscow became by the end of the 17th century Russia's most important trading city. It remained a major economic and cultural centre even after Peter the Great transferred the capital to St Petersburg in 1712.

The last sacking of the city occurred in 1812 when Napoleon invaded Russia. Muscovites, seeing the invasion as inevitable, torched their own city rather than let Napoleon have it (Tolstoy describes Count Bekuzhkov being arrested as an arsonist in *War and Peace,* his semi-fictionalized account of the campaign). But recovery was swift and trade increased after the abolition of serfdom in 1861.

Revolution

Towards the end of the 19th century Moscow became a revolutionary centre, its factories hit by a series of strikes and riots. Michael Myres Shoemaker, who was here in 1903, wrote in *The Great Siberian Railway from St Petersburg to Peking*: 'Up to the present day the dissatisfaction has arisen from the middle classes especially the students, but now for the first time in Russia's history it is spreading downward to the peasants... but it will be a century at least before that vast inert mass awakens to life.' But in 1905 there was an armed uprising, and 12 years later 'that vast inert mass' stormed the Kremlin and established Soviet power in the city. The subsequent civil war saw terrible food shortages and great loss of life.

The capital once more

In March 1918 Lenin transferred the government back to Moscow. In the years between the two world wars the city embarked on an ambitious programme of industrial development, and by 1939 the population had doubled to four million. During WWII many factories in the European part of the USSR were relocated across the Urals, a wise move in retrospect. By October 1941 the German army had surrounded the city (getting as close as the present-day site of Sheremetyevo airport) and the two-month Siege of Moscow began.

Moscow was rebuilt following the war, growing in size, grandeur and power. But by the late 1980s services had started to collapse under Gorbachev's reforms and the breakdown of communist power. The years following the 1991 disintegration of the Soviet Union was a time when little worked in the city and roads, buildings and public utilities were continually on the verge of collapse.

Moscow today

The USSR has gone but the Soviet habit of centralized decision-making and financial control remains intact, and has made Moscow vastly wealthier than any other city in Russia, with average wages six to 20 times higher than those in even moderate Siberian cities. But even here remnants of the past coexist incongruously with the elegant shops, restaurants and offices of the 'new Russians'. Lenin's description of 19th-century London as 'two nations living in one city' has become true of Moscow itself.

But the city's pugnacious mayor, Yury Luzhkov, has ensured that those who can afford to pay are made to, and enormous infrastructure projects have gone ahead with little help from the central government. Many, however, blame the city itself for Russia's continuing economic malaise, complaining of a 'robber baron' state in which compliance with impossible regulations can only be achieved by paying off the city officials who uphold them. Yeltsin-era Prime Minister Yevgeny Primakov once noted glumly that 'any new business wishing to open must obtain 57 different authorizations – and we all know that not one of them can be had for the official fee'.

Your Trans-Siberian co-passengers will doubtless include some of Russia's luckless thousands – on a trip to the capital to pay a fortune in bribes for permission to build a Scout hut in Bryansk or lease horses to tourists in the Altai Mountains. Yet many Russians dream of relocating to the capital's bright lights and high incomes. Fewer than half its residents were actually born here.

Visitors, happily, can only benefit from Moscow's luck. No other Russian city offers the enormous range of cultural heritage, entertainment, hotels, dining, nightlife and shopping that Moscow has pilfered from the rest of the country since the 13th century.

WHAT TO SEE

Red Square (Krasnaya ploshchad)
This wide cobbled square extends across the area beside the north-eastern wall of the Kremlin. The name derives from the red cobblestones first laid when the stinking city market was cleared away from the Kremlin's walls in the 16th century, and has no connection with Communism. The main sights in and around the square are St Basil's Cathedral, the History Museum, Lenin's Mausoleum, the GUM shopping arcade and the Kremlin. Note that smoking in Red Square – as in most public places in Russia – could earn you a hefty fine.

Lenin's Mausoleum
Built onto the side of the Kremlin in 1930, the red granite mausoleum and its mummified occupant were the centre of a personality cult that flourished for almost 70 years. (*Continued on p160*).

❏ **Mummification for the masses**
A few years ago the Centre for Biological Researches, responsible for the preservation of Lenin's body, announced the offer of full mummification services to anyone for a mere US$300,000. Previous clients are a testimony to their skill. An independent team of embalmers recently inspected Lenin's corpse and declared it to be in perfect condition.

After Lenin's death on 21 January 1924 an autopsy was carried out and a full report published in *Pravda*, treating the public to the weights and measurements of their dead leader's internal organs. Then the embalmers began their work. One wonders if the Central Executive Committee's 1924 decision to preserve the body had anything to do with the discovery of the Pharaoh Tuthankamun 14 months earlier.

Lenin's brain (1340g, far larger than average, of course) was removed and placed in a specially-founded Institute of Lenin's Brain, where scientists analysed deep-frozen micro-slices in an attempt to discover the secret of his greatness. The Institute was quietly closed in the 1960s and any discoveries it had made went unpublished.

The debate over what to do with Lenin continues, with liberal politicians suggesting that Russia should bury its past and Communists arguing that to move him now would be a denial of the country's history. President Putin left this poisoned chalice to his successor when he announced a moratorium on any decision until 2012.

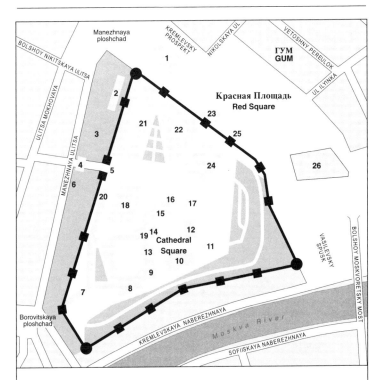

Moscow Kremlin

1 State History Museum
  Государтвенный Исторический Музей
2 Tomb of the Unknown Soldier
  Могила Неизвестнного Солдата
3 Aleksandrovsky Garden
  Александровский Сад
4 Kutafya Tower
  Кутафья Башня
5 Trinity Tower
  Троицкаа Башня
6 Ticket Offices
  Кассы
7 Armoury
  Оружейная Палата
8 Great Kremlin Palace
  Большой Кремлевский Дворец
9 Cathedral of the Annunciation
  Благовещенский Собор
10 Cathedral of the Archangel
  Архангельский Собор
11 Tsar Bell
  Царь Колокол
12 Bell Tower of Ivan III
  Колокольня Ивана Великого
13 Facetted Palace
  Кафель Дворен

Москва Кремль

14 Cathedral of the Assumption
  Успенский Собор
15 Patriach's Palace
  Патриарший Дворец
16 Church of the Twelve Apostles
  Церковь Двенадцать Святой
17 Tsar Cannon
  Царь Пушка
18 Palace of Congresses
  Конгресс Дворец
19 Church of the Deposition of the Robe
  Церковь Ризопогожения
20 Poteshny Palace
  Потешный Дворец
21 Arsenal
  Арсенал
22 Senate
  Сенат
23 Lenin's Mausoleum
  Мавзолей В И Ленина
24 Supreme Soviet
  Верховный Совет
25 Spassky Tower
  Спасский Башня
26 St Basil's Cathedral
  Собор Василия Блаженного

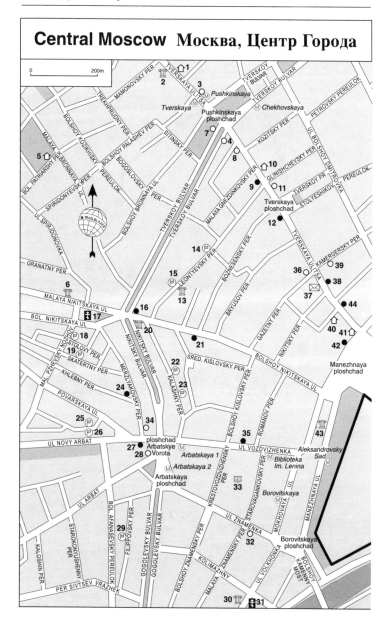

Central Moscow Москва, Центр Города

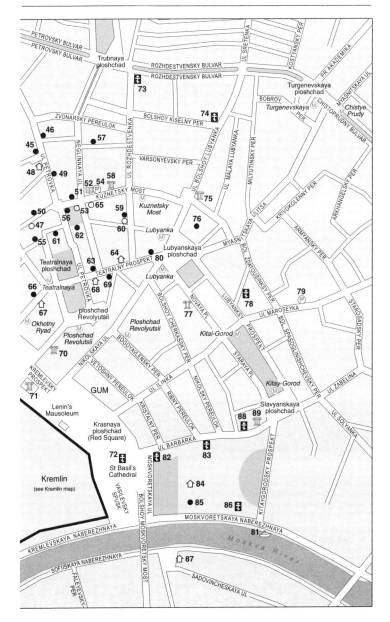

WHERE TO STAY AND EAT

  1 Marriott Grand Hotel Гостиница Марриотт Гранд
  3 Russkoye Bistro/Yolki Palki Restaurants Ресторан Руссое/Елки Палки
  4 Café Pushkin Кафе Пушкин
  5 Marco Polo-Presnya Hotel Гостинца Марко Поло-Пресня
  7 McDonald's Restaurant Макдоналдс
  8 Mesto Vstrechi Restaurant Ресторан Место Встречий
 10 Hotel Tsentralnaya Гостиница Центральная
 11 Pizza Hut Restaurant Пицца Хат
 28 Praga Restaurant Ресторан Прага
 32 Rosie O'Grady's Pub Бар Рози Огрэдис
 34 Dioscuria Ресторан Дюскурия
 36 McDonald's Restaurant Макдоналдс
 39 Tibet Kitchen Ресторан Тибетская Кухня
 40 Hotel Intourist Гостиница Интурист
 41 Hotel National Гостиница Националь
 47 Pelmeshka
 48 Marriott Moscow Aurora Hotel Гостиница Марриотт Аврора
 53 Jugganat Restaurant Ресторан Джэганот
 60 Pizzeria Пиццерия
 64 Hotel Savoy Гостиница Савой
 65 Yolki-Palki Ресторан Елки Палки
 67 Hotel Moskva (currently closed) Гостиница Москва
 68 Hotel Metropole Гостиница Метрополь
 84 Hotel Rossiya Гостиница Россия
 87 Hotel Baltschug-Kempinski Гостиница Балчуг-Кемпинский

OTHER

  2 Museum of Contemporary Russian History (Russian Revolutions)
     Музей Революции
  6 Gorky House Museum Дом-Музей Горького
  9 Moscow Drama Theatre Московсий Драмитический Театр
 12 Moscow City Government Building Мэрия
 13 Museum of Folk Art Музей народного искусства
 14 Azerbaijan Embassy Посольство Азербайджана
 15 Ukraine Embassy Посольство Украины
 16 ITAR-TASS news agency ИТАР-ТАСС
 17 Grand Ascension Church Большая Вознесеная Цекровь
 18 Georgia Embassy Посольство Грузии
 19 Tajikistan Embassy Посольство Таджикистана
 20 Mayakovsky House-Museum Дом-Музей Маяковского
 21 Tchaikovsky Conservatory Консерватория имени Чайковского
 22 Estonia Embassy Посольство Эстонии
 23 Netherlands Embassy Посольство Нидерландов
 24 USA & Canada Institute Институт США и Канады
 25 Norway Embassy Посольство Норвегии
 26 Belgium Embassy Посольство Бельгии
 27 Irish Arbat Department Store Ирландский Дом
 29 Turkmen Embassy Посольство Туркменистана
 30 Pushkin Museum of Fine Arts
     Музей Изобразительных Искусств имени А С Пушкина

31 Cathedral of Christ the Saviour Храм Христа Снасителя
33 Russian State Library Российская Государственная Библиотека
35 Military Department Store Воинторг
37 Central Post Office Центральный Телеграф
38 Finnair & Malev Airline Offices Finnair Malev Авиа Касса
42 Intourist Travel Agency Интурист
43 Central Exhibition Hall Центральный Выставочный Зал
44 Transaero Трансаэро
45 Intourtrans Travel Agency Интуртранс
46 Aeroflot Airlines Office Касса Аэрофлотаа
49 Petrovsky Passazh Department Store Универмаг Петровский Пассаж
50 SAS Airline Office SAS Авиакасса
51 JAL Airline Office JAL Авиакасса
52 Atlas Map Shop Магазин Атлас
54 Moldova Embassy Посольство Молдавии
55 Operetta Theatre Театр Оперетты
56 Air China Airline Office Air China Авиакасса
57 Sandunovskaya Baths Бани Сандуновские
58 Artists' Union Gallery Выставочный Зал
59 City Excursion Bureau Московское Городское Экскурсконное Бюро
61 Bolshoi Theatre Большой Театр
62 TsUM Department Store ЦУМ
63 Maly Theatre Малый Театр
66 State Duma Parliament House Государственная Дума
69 Arkadia Jazz Club Джаз Клуб Аркадия
70 Former Lenin Museum Бывший Центральный Музей Ленина
71 State History Museum Государственный Исторический Музей
72 St Basil's Cathedral Собор Василия Блаженного
73 Nativity of Our Lady Cathedral Рождественский Собор
74 Church of Vladimir Mother of God Церковь Владимирской Богоматери
75 KGB Museum Музей КГБ
76 Former KGB Headquarters Лубянка
77 Moscow City History Museum Музей Истории Города Москвы
78 St Nicholas Church Никольская церковь
79 Belarus Embassy Посольство Белоруссии
80 Detsky Mir Children's Department Store Универмаг Детский Мир
81 Boat Landing Пристань
82 St Barbara's Church Церковь Святово Варвары
83 Monastery of the Sign Belltower Колокольня Знаменского Монастыря
85 Central Concert Hall Центральный Концертный Зал
86 Church of St Anne's Conception Церковь Святой Зачатия Анны
88 St George's Church Церковь Святово Святово Георгия
89 17th Century Art Museum Художественний музей 17 века

❏ **MOSCOW METRO – see colour map at back of book (p449)**

(*Continued from p154*). Nowadays Lenin and his mausoleum are something of an embarrassment, although tourists still queue up to file past the once-revered corpse, laid out in dark suit and tie. The mausoleum was Stalin's idea, and the deceased Stalin lay beside Lenin until his legacy was reassessed by Khrushchev. The tomb's design is the work of one AV Shchusev, who saw the cube, like the pyramid, as a symbol of eternity and envisaged every Soviet home having its own little cube to the memory of the dead leader.

Lenin currently receives visitors from 10:00 to 13:00, except on Monday and Friday; Red Square is closed to other visitors during these hours. The wait is usually no more than 15 to 20 minutes (in Soviet times it was several hours). There's no entry charge. The one-way route, which also features the Tombs Of Soviet Heroes (including Yury Gagarin) in the Kremlin walls, emerges at St Basil's Cathedral. Visitors may not take cameras, large bags, electronic items or sharp objects with them, nor wear 'disrespectful' clothing such as shorts, halter-tops or t-shirts saying things like 'Eat at McLenin's'. The nearest cloakroom where you can leave these items is back in the Kremlin gatehouse.

St Basil's Cathedral

Also known as the Church of the Saviour (and nicknamed the 'Pineapple Church' by Victorian travellers), this whimsical creation is as much a symbol of Moscow as Tower Bridge is of London. It was commissioned by Ivan the Terrible to celebrate his victory over the Tatars, and completed in 1561. So pleased was Ivan with the result, according to legend, that he had the architect's eyes put out so that he could never produce anything to equal or surpass it.

The cathedral is named after a holy hermit known as Basil the Simpleton, who dressed year-round in a loincloth, begging and sleeping in the street out-side. Basil proved less of a simpleton when he denounced Tsar Boris Godunov as the murderer of the rightful ruler, Ivan the Terrible's weakling son Dmitry.

St Basil's is a quite incredible building, with its nine brightly-painted, dis-similar domes, and stonework decorated with intricate patterns more usually found on the wooden buildings of the time. Its painted interiors were burnt off when Napoleon used it as a stable. The domes' paintwork dates from the 18th century. Outside the cathedral is a statue of Kuzma Minin and Prince Dmitry Pozharsky, who saved Russia from the Polish-Lithuanian invasion in the early 17th century.

For many years a museum, the cathedral has now been returned to the Church, although you must still pay US$3.20 to get in (half price with a student card). It's open 11:00-19:00 (11:00-17:00 November-April) daily except Tuesday and the first Monday of each month.

GUM

The remarkable glass-roofed GUM shopping arcade (pronounced 'goom', an acronym for *Generalny Universalny Magazin*) was constructed in 1894 on the site

Opposite: St Basil's Cathedral on Red Square is Moscow's most famous landmark.

of a covered market which was torn down as a health hazard. It was nationalized after the Revolution and turned into a huge department store, a monument to Soviet shortages. Now the Western chains have moved in and you can buy anything from a Benetton sweater to the latest CD, at prices which represent probably the worst value-for-money in Russia.

The chic *Bosco Café* offers a pavement view onto Red Square at monopoly prices (admission only from within GUM). For cheaper coffee go to the ground-floor stand at the intersection of aisles 1 and 2.

State History Museum

This museum, reopened in 1997, is at the north end of Red Square. Extensive collections cover the history of the country up to 1917, and the palatial building is worth seeing in itself. It's open 11:00-19:00 daily except Tuesday and first Monday of the month; entry is US$2.50.

The Tomb of the Unknown Soldier

It is traditional for newly weds to visit this monument in the Aleksandrovsky Gardens (the former Kremlin moat) to be photographed beside its eternal flame. Beneath the marble lies the body of one of the soldiers who helped to stop the German advance on Moscow in 1941. The blood-red marble caskets beside the flame contain soil from Soviet 'Hero-Cities' (those with the greatest number of WWII dead). The honour guard which once stood watch at Lenin's Mausoleum now stands here, with a goose-stepping Changing of the Guard every hour.

The Kremlin

The heart of Moscow and seat of the Russian government, the Kremlin is in fact a large walled citadel. Although the site has been continuously occupied for at least eight centuries, the present walls and many of the cathedrals inside date from the 15th century. There are 20 towers, the most famous being the **Saviour (Spassky) Clock-Tower** above Red Square.

The main visitors' entrance and ticket office for the Kremlin is in the **Kutafya Tower**, on the opposite side from Red Square. You may not take large bags or rucksacks inside (there is a pay-per-item cloakroom in the basement of the Kutafya Tower) and you won't get past the guards if you are wearing shorts.

A ticket for the grounds and the main sights inside costs US$8 (US$5 with a student card) from an office beside the Kutafya Tower in Aleksandrovsky Park (use the public toilets here, as there are none inside). You pay separately (here or inside) for the Armoury Chamber and some other sights; tours for these start at particular times, so check your ticket. To prevent disappointment, you can always buy tickets a few days ahead.

The Kremlin grounds are open 10:00-17:00 daily except Thursday. If the Palace of Congress is in use for a daytime concert or other function you may be

Opposite Top: The Hermitage Museum in St Petersburg (see p132) is the world's largest gallery with over three million works of art in its collection. To walk through each of the 300 galleries you'd cover a total distance of almost 25km!. **Bottom:** Gilded statues gracing the Grand Cascade at Petrodvorets (see p142).

redirected to the Borovitsky Tower entrance at the far end of Alexandrovsky Gardens. The Kremlin may be partly or completely closed without warning if there are VIP visitors.

Cathedral Square [See **map on p155**] Around the Kremlin's central square stand four main cathedrals and the **Bell Tower** of Ivan the Great (81m/263ft high) which Napoleon attempted to blow up in 1812. Beneath the tower stands the **Tsar Bell**, at 200 tons the heaviest in the world; the piece that stands beside it broke off during the fire of 1737. Nearby is **Tsar Cannon**, the largest-calibre cannon in the world. The cannon-balls don't fit the cannon, which never fired a shot.

The **Cathedral of the Assumption**, the work of Italian architect Aristotle Fiorovanti and his sons, was completed in 1479 and was the traditional place of coronation for Russia's tsars. The last coronation, on 26 May 1896, saw what many considered a bad omen: as Nicholas II climbed the steps to the altar the chain of the Order of St Anthony fell from his shoulders. The interior is one of the most richly-decorated in Russia. There are three thrones; the wooden one to the right as you enter belonged to Ivan the Terrible.

The **Cathedral of the Archangel Michael** (1505-09) looks classically Russian from the outside but the hand of its Italian architect, Alevisio Novi, can be seen in the light interior. Forty-six tsars (including Ivan the Great and Ivan the Terrible) are buried here. The smaller **Cathedral of the Annunciation** (1484-89), the tsars' private chapel, was the work of Russian architects and contains icons by the great master, Andrei Rublyov. The **Church of the Deposition of the Robe** (1484-5) was designed as a private chapel for the clergy. The Patriarch worshipped in the **Church of the Twelve Apostles** next door to his residence.

Other buildings in the Kremlin The **Great Kremlin Palace**, now a government building, is only open to Guests of State and other VIPs. A total renovation, to restore the palace to its pre-communist finery, was completed in 1999. 'Put it back as it was before', said Yeltsin, and they did, for a mere US$800 million. Also VIP-only is the only secular building on Cathedral Square, the Italian-designed **Facetted Chamber**, so-called because of its façade of pointed stone blocks. The **Golden Tsarina Palace** or Terem Palace has a striking red and white-tiled roof.

The modern building facing the Kremlin's main entrance is the **Palace of Congress**, formerly the seat of the Parliament of the USSR. It was designed to also do duty as a theatre in the evenings, and now that Parliament meets elsewhere (at the former State Planning Ministry on ul Okhotny Ryad) this building is the full-time home of the Moscow Kremlin Ballet. Ticket-holders get special entrance to the Kremlin in the evenings, but you can't sightsee before the show.

The **Armoury Chamber** contains a dazzling display of tsars' jewellery and regalia, weapons and armour. Of special interest to Trans-Siberian passengers is the ornate Great Siberian Easter Egg (probably the finest of the 56 famous Imperial Easter Eggs made by Carl Fabergé), containing a tiny clockwork model of the train, complete with gold and platinum engine, five gold coaches and a church-car. Entry is US$11 (US$6 for students).

The State Tretyakov Gallery

The best collection of paintings, icons and sculpture in Russia is housed here. Highlights include icons by Andrei Rublyov; two halls devoted to the great Russian masters Ilya Repin and Vasily Surikov, including Repin's boozy, vodka-stricken portrait of the composer Mussorgsky; *Christ's First Appearance to the People* which took Alexander Ivanov 20 years to complete; and Ge's *Peter the Great Interrogates His Own Son* and *Ivan the Terrible, Having Murdered His Own Son*. The gallery (☎ 951 1362), at Lavrushinsky pereulok 10 (metro: Tretyakovskaya), is open 10:00-19:30 daily except Monday. Entry costs US\$8 (US\$4 for students). Go early to avoid long queues; *Aldebaran Café*, at Bolshoy Tolmachevsky pereulok 4, on the square as you turn right from the metro, offers a delicious if pricey breakfast for early starters.

Pushkin Museum of Fine Arts

This excellent museum of non-Russian art is well worth a visit for its large collection of Impressionist canvases (Manet's *Déjeuner sur l'Herbe*, for example,

---

The Moscow metro and the secret metro

Construction of the metro began in the early 1930s, and it was planned that the first line would open on May Day 1935. In late April Stalin was invited to inspect the system but his tour came to an unexpected 30-minute halt following a signal failure. Expecting imprisonment or worse, engineers nearly collapsed with relief when Stalin suggested that it might be better to fix all the problems and delay the opening until 15 May. The honour of driving the first train, which consisted of local copies of 1932 New York carriages, went to the alliteratively-named Ivan Ivanovich Ivanov.

As well as transporting passengers, the metro served as a bomb shelter in 1941-1942. Male Muscovites slept on wooden platforms assembled every evening in the tunnels while women and children slept on camp stretchers on the platforms. During the Cold War the metro was modified to contain fallout shelters, and evidence of both the WWII and Cold War preparations can still be seen today. These include large recessed blast doors at ground-level entrances, collapsible platform edges which become steps, and large storerooms on the platforms for medical supplies.

A second, 'secret' metro was finished in 1967 which would enable government leaders to flee Moscow in the face of a nuclear attack. This 30km line runs from the former Central Communist Headquarters building on Staraya pl (near metro Kitay-Gorod) via the government's underground bunker complex in the Ramenky region (near metro Universitet) to Vnukovo-2 airport. Closed to the public, the line is said to be still operational.

New N5 metro carriages from Moscow's Mytishchi railway factory are being phased in. They are significantly quieter, smoother and safer, with automatic fire quenchers and extensive use of fireproof material.

While women drive many of Moscow's buses and trams, until recently only men were train drivers. The reason for this is the belief that men better handle the stress of suicidal passengers jumping in front of oncoming trains.

The **Moscow Metro Museum** (☎ 222 7309, Khamovnichesky Val ul 35), part of Sportivnaya metro station, contains maps, models and documents about the history of Moscow's public transport system from the early 19th century. It's open 11:00-18:00 Monday, 09:00-16:00 Tuesday-Friday, for about US\$1. Booking is advisable.

and Monet's *Boulevard des Capucines*). There are also galleries of Egyptian antiquities and Old Masters. The gallery (☎ 203 9578), at ul Volkhonka 12 (metro: Kropotkinskaya) is open 10:00-19:00 daily except Monday, for US$5 (US$2.50 for students). Just down the street at No 14 is the **Museum of Private Collections**, displaying the best of many works 'liberated' from wealthy Muscovites during the Revolution.

Cathedral of Christ the Saviour
Moscow's central cathedral church was bulldozed by Stalin to make way for an ambitious Palace Of The Soviets, planned as the world's largest building. But expert opinion concluded that the riverside location, directly opposite the Pushkin Museum, wouldn't support the weight and after an embarrassing hiatus a rather good swimming pool was built there instead. In 1997 a replica of the original cathedral, financed with public and corporate contributions, was opened by Mayor Luzhkov. The view from the dome is worth the climb.

'The Arbat'
Pedestrianized ul Arbat, shopping street and popular tourist-trap, swarms with buskers, street artists and hawkers of everything from matrioshkas to pirated CDs. Bargain hard and watch for pickpockets.

The 'Viktor we still love you' grafitti along Krivoarbatsky pereulok refer to Viktor Tsoy, a cult-status underground rock star killed in a 1990 car crash. Before underground rock came the singer-songwriter 'bards', the most famous of whom, Bulat Okudjava, lived here and wrote *Arbat*, his best-loved song. Banned from recording in Soviet times, his funeral drew 60,000 people.

Muscovites now rarely bother with the Arbat, preferring to hang out along Kuznetsky Most.

Sandunovskaya Baths
If you've just stepped off a Trans-Sib train, a traditional Russian bath in the oldest public banya in the city is an invigorating and interesting experience. On Sandunovsky pereulok (off ul Petrovka), it's beautifully decorated in Classical style. It's open 08:00-22:00 daily except Tuesday; entry is about US$20 for the mens' baths, US$16 for the (separate) ladies'.

Novodevichy Convent
This beautiful 16th-century walled convent has also served as a fortress (holding out against a Polish siege in 1610) and a prison (Peter the Great banished his first wife Sofia here, allegedly bricking her up in a cell with no door, for trying to assassinate him). Many of the nuns here were daughters of noble families who had brought shame upon family honour in the days before contraception. Napoleon tried unsuccessfully to blow it up in 1812: one brave nun rushed in and extinguished the fuses to the powder kegs at the last minute.

The convent church is famous for its frescoes and highly ornate, multi-tiered iconostasis (the backdrop to the altar). It also contains a small museum. The convent's private cemetery was a safe location for graves which might otherwise become unwanted shrines, including those of many Decembrist officers.

Adjacent to the convent is a more public cemetery with some outlandish grave-stones (one soldier lies under a model tank) plus the graves of many an influential Russian, including Chekhov, Prokofiev, Khrushchev and Brezhnev.

The convent (metro: Sportivnaya) is open 08:00-18:00 daily except Tuesday and the first Monday of the month. Behind it is a wooded lake, originally the convent's own fishpond, now a perfect picnic spot and by evening something of a Lover's Lane.

Other museums, galleries and churches
There is not room in a guidebook of this type to give details of more than a few of Moscow's 150-plus museums and exhibitions. However, a few of the best are the **Andrei Rublyov Ancient Russian Culture and Art Museum** (☎ 278 1467, pl Andronyevskaya 10, open 11:00-18:00 daily except Wednesday and last Friday of each month, US$3); the **Museum of Cosmonauts** (☎ 286 3714, ul 1-ya Ostankinskaya 41/9); the **Borodino Battle Field Panorama** (☎ 148 1965, Kutuzovsky pr 38, open 10:30-20:00 Saturday to Thursday); the **Federal Counterintelligence Service (KGB) Museum** (☎ 224 1982, ul Lubyanka 12); and the **Former Political Prisoners Museum** (☎ 925 0144, ul Chaplyghina 15). There are other museums devoted to Gorky, Tolstoy, Dostoyevsky, Pushkin, Chekhov, Gogol, Glinka, Bulgakov and Lermontov.

EXCURSIONS FROM MOSCOW

A visit to the cathedrals and churches of **Sergiev Posad** (formerly Zagorsk; see p179), 75km from Moscow, is the most interesting day trip.

About 80km from Moscow is the estate of **Abramtsevo**, an important centre of Russian culture in the second half of the 19th century. Today it's a museum, and well worth a day trip. The estate was originally called Obromkovo Pustosh when the current wooden house was built in the 1770s. Bought in 1843 by Slavophile writer Sergei Aksakov, it became the regular haunt of eminent Russian writers and actors including Gogol and Turgenev. In 1870 the estate was purchased by railway tycoon and art connoisseur Savva Mamontov and turned into a colony for artists concerned that Russian native art and architecture faced extinction by rapid industrialization – ironic considering the estate's patron. From Moscow's Yaroslavsky station take any suburban (*prigorodny*) train for Sergiev Posad (Сергиев Посад) or Aleksandrov (Александров), and get off at Abramtsevo, a 70-minute trip. The estate is a 30-minute walk from the station. There's a pleasant restaurant opposite the estate entrance.

PRACTICAL INFORMATION
Arriving in Moscow
See p64 for important information on potential customs-form rip-offs on the Trans-Siberian.

By air Moscow has five airports. **Sheremetyevo 2** (SVO), 35km from the city centre, is used only for international flights. Most foreign airlines currently use this inadequate, worn-out airport, built for the 1980 Olympics. The arrivals hall has an information desk whose multilingual staff will at least direct you to the buses. A kiosk in the hall sells city maps. **Sheremetyevo 1** has mainly domestic flights plus some international ones to Mongolia and former-USSR destinations.

Both airports are served by bus No 851 (R7, about US$0.25), shuttling to and from Rechnoy Vokzal metro station every half-hour from 06:00 to 23:00, taking about an hour. Minibuses (*marshrutnoye*, R15) with the same number offer guaranteed seating and a journey time of 30-45 minutes (longer in rush hour). Both leave Sheremetyevo 2 from the third lane outside the arrivals hall. Change a bit of foreign currency into low-denomination rouble notes before boarding as drivers won't accept anything else. You may be charged a nominal extra fare if you have a lot of baggage. There are less frequent minibuses (No 817, same fares) to Planernaya metro station. Going *to* the airport, remember to get off at Sheremetyevo 2, not 1.

City-run **Domodedovo** (DME) airport has metamorphosed into an efficient, modern facility, handling domestic connections to Siberian destinations plus international charter flights. Some international carriers (including Transaero, British Airways and Swiss) are now opting for its modern facilities, and more may follow if the city completes a planned high-speed (about 40 minutes) rail link. Hang onto your baggage-claim receipt as you may be unable to retrieve your bags without it. Minibus No 405 (R25, about US$0.80) runs between here and Domodedovskaya metro station. You're advised to avoid taxis into the city centre, which take at least two hours and could cost you US$75 or more.

Unlovely **Vnukovo** mostly serves lower-budget domestic flights, with bus No 611 connecting to Yugo-Zapadnaya metro station. Tiny **Bykovo** aerodrome is used by a mixture of domestic and cargo flights.

Tenacious taxi drivers swarm around all arrival halls, with official taxis charging US$40-50 between Sheremetyevo 2 and the city centre. At the Web site 🖳 www.taxi.ru you can even book a taxi to meet you on arrival. For your own safety, avoid 'gypsy cabs' (unlicensed private cars) no matter how cheap the fare they offer.

By train Moscow has nine railway stations. The ones you are most likely to use are: **Belorussy** (sometimes incorrectly called Smolensky; metro: Belorusskaya) for trains to and from Western Europe; **Leningradsky** (metro: Komsomolskaya) for Helsinki and St Petersburg; **Yaroslavsky** (beside Leningradsky) for most Trans-Siberian trains; and **Kazansky** (opposite Leningradsky) for Central Asia plus a few Siberian trains (including Nos 15/16 Yekaterinburg and the following, all via Yekaterinburg: Nos 31/32 Novo kuznetsk, Nos 35/36 Barnaul, Nos 37/38 Tomsk, Nos 59/60 Tyumen, Nos 75/ 76 Tynda, Nos 117/118 Novokuznetsk, Nos 121/122 Ulan Ude and Nos 907/908 Novosibirsk and Irkutsk). Some trains to Vladimir and Nizhny Novgorod leave from **Kursky** station. **Kievsky** station (metro: Kievskaya) is for trains to Budapest. See p177 for information on leaving Moscow.

Local transport
Metro The palatial metro system (**see map at back of book: p449**), a tourist attraction in itself, is the best way to travel around Moscow. The metro uses magnetic cards available in denominations of 1, 2, 5, 10 and 20 rides, with a small discount for 10 and 20 rides. A ride to anywhere on the system currently costs R7 (about US$0.25). Buy tickets inside the metro station building at windows marked касса. During peak hours, from about 07:00 to 10:00 and 15:00 to 19:00, trains arrive every 1-2 minutes, and you're unlikely to wait more than five minutes even at midnight. Peak-hour trains are very crowded.

Just before the train leaves a station a recorded message warns you that the doors are about to close and announces the name of the next station. Non-Russian speakers can catch the name of the next station: it's the last word of the message. Each carriage has at least one system map posted inside but, annoyingly, there are none at platform level. Stations at points where two or more lines intersect often have a different name on each line (eg, Pushkinskaya, Chekhovskaya and Tverskaya).

Useful Cyrillic signs to recognize are вход (entrance), выход (exit), переход (crossover between stations) and выход в город (way out or exit to street level).

Other Bus and tram services are comprehensive but overcrowded. Tickets currently cost R5 (about US$0.17). Virtually any Russian car can be a **taxi** but don't get in if there are already passengers.

Self-drive **hire cars** (from bigger hotel service bureaux, or Hertz opposite Belarussky station) might be worth considering for some sights outside the city but are not recommended for city sightseeing; you need an International Driving Licence and a medical certificate, and prices are high.

There's a pleasant **river trip** (US$1.10) which leaves from the Kiev River Terminal (near Kievskaya metro station) and passes the Lenin Hills and Gorky Park on its way towards the Kremlin. The 1¹/₂-hour trip ends at the Novospassky Bridge terminal, about 2km past the Kremlin.

Orientation and services

At the very centre of the city are the Kremlin, Red Square and St Basil's Cathedral. The most conveniently placed (and generally expensive) hotels are in this area. The metro system is efficient, however, so it's not vital or financially sensible to stay at a hotel right on Red Square.

There are no tourist information offices. Larger hotels have service bureaux offering a range of standard tours.

Diplomatic representation

Australia (☎ 956 6070) Kropotkinsky pereulok 13; **Austria** (☎ 201 7317) Starokonyushenny pereulok 1; **Belarus** (visas ☎ 924 7095) ul Maroseka 17/6, open for applications 10:00-12:00 weekdays; **Belgium** (☎ 937 8040) Malaya Molchanovka ul 7; **Canada** (☎ 956 6666) Starokonyushenny pereulok 23; **China** (visas ☎ 143 1543) ul Druzhby 6, metro Universitet, open for applications 09:00-11:30 weekdays (slow service, try to arrive by 07:00; if there are more than 20 people ahead of you it's unlikely you'll get in; consider paying on-the-spot US$20 express surcharge so you don't have to queue again); **Czech Republic** (☎ 251 0145) ul Yuliusa Fuchika 12/14, metro Mayakovskaya/Belarusskaya; **Denmark** (visas ☎ 201 5782) Prechistensky pereulok 9; **Estonia** (visas ☎ 261 5530) Kalashny pereulok 8; **Finland** (☎ 246 4027) Kropotkinsky pereulok 15/17; **France** (visas ☎ 937 1587) Kazansky pereulok 10; **Georgia** (☎ 291 1359) Maly Rzhevsky pereulok 6, metro Pushkinskaya/Alexandrovsky Sad; **Germany** (consulate ☎ 933 4312), Leninsky pr 95A; **Hungary** (☎ 796 9377) Mosfilmovskaya ul 62, metro Kievskaya; **Ireland** (visas ☎ 937 5900) Grokholsky pereulok 5; **Israel** (visas ☎ 230 6700) Bolshaya Ordynka ul 56; **Italy** (visas ☎ 795 9692) Bolshaya Polyanka ul 2/10; **Japan** (visas ☎ 202 3248) Maly Kislovsky pereulok 5A; **Kazakhstan** (visas ☎ 927 1836) Chistoprudny bulvar 3A; **Kyrgyzstan** (☎ 237 3364) ul Bolshaya Ordynka ul 64, metro Dobryninskaya; **Latvia** (visas ☎ 925 2707) Bolshoy Kharitonyevsky pereulok 12; **Lithuania** (visas ☎ 291 6109) Borisoglebsky pereulok 10, metro Arbatskaya; **Moldova** (visas ☎ 928 1050) Kuznetsky Most 18; **Mongolia** (consulate ☎ 241 1458) Spasopeskovsky pereulok 7, metro Smolenskaya, open for applications 09:00-13:00 weekdays; **Netherlands** (visas ☎ 797 2979) Kalashny pereulok 6; **New Zealand** (visas ☎ 956 2642) Povarskaya ul 44; **Norway** (visas ☎ 203 2270) Povarskaya ul 7; **Poland** (visas ☎ 231 1556) ul Klimashkina 4, metro Barrikadnaya; **Slovakia** (visas ☎ 956 4923) ul Yuliusa Fuchika 12/14; **South Africa** (visas ☎ 230 6870) Bolshoy Strochenovsky pereulok 22/25; **UK** (visas ☎ 956 7250) Smolenskaya naberezhnaya 10; **Ukraine** (visas ☎ 229 3442) Leontevsky pereulok 18, metro Pushkinskaya; **USA** (consular section ☎ 728 5599, visas ☎ 728 5588) Novinsky bulvar 19/23.

Local publications

English-language freesheets, available in the lobbies of larger hotels, theatres, supermarkets etc, include the worthy *Moscow Times* (🖳 www.the moscowtimes.com), whose weekend edition has good listings and travel sections, and the rarely-spotted *Moscow Tribune* (🖳 w ww.tribune.ru). The St Petersburg listings magazine *Pulse* has an excellent Moscow edition too. Fun and foul-mouthed, *The eXile* discards political correctness but is worth it for the ruthlessly honest listings. *The Russia Journal*, mainly business and financial news, has some good writing and provocative analysis. Although not free, *Moscow News* appears in English with its special brand of pro-government propaganda (they never run out of it on Aeroflot, even if you're in the back row). Russian-speakers will love *Afisha*, a clone of London's *Time Out*. For cheap Russian-language basic listings pick up *Dosug*, whilst *Bolshoy Gorod* is the art-house freesheet.

It is practically impossible to find foreign publications at normal news stands, but Stockmann's supermarket, in the basement of the Smolensky Passage shopping mall (metro: Smolenskaya), has them at inflated prices.

Medical The **European Medical Centre** (☎ 933 6655, 🖳 www.emcmos.ru), Spiridonyevsky pereulok 5/1, offers medical and surgical services, and have a dental clinic (☎ 933 0002) at Konushkovskaya ul 34 (metro: Barrikadnaya).

The **American Medical Center** (☎ 933 7700, 🖳 www.amcenters.com) at Grokholsky pereulok 1 (metro: Prospekt Mira) also offer medical and dental services.

Reliable pharmacies include **Farmakon** (☎ 292 0301), 4th Tverskaya-Yamskaya ul 2/11; **Eczacibasi** (☎ 928 9189) at Telegrafny pereulok 5/4 and ul Maroseyka 2/15; a 24-hour **Apteka** at Tishinskaya pl 6; and the **American Medical Center** (above).

If you know what you want, especially by generic name, better pharmacies can dispense it cheaply and often without a prescription.

Money Most of Moscow's bigger banks have **ATMs** so you can use your bank card to access your account or get cash advances (in roubles). Many metro stations have stand-alone ATMs in the lobby, but with a R3000 (about US$100) limit. If you need more, don't use one of these as most Russian ATM networks limit you to one daily withdrawal.

Hard currency used to be the number one requirement for travellers in Moscow but there's less demand for it now. US dollars and euros can be exchanged at almost any bank or currency exchange; with other currencies you must go to larger bank branches. The **Exchange Bureau**, with branches at the Kievskaya and Kurskaya metro stations, will exchange just about any world currency.

Travellers' cheques are accepted at major banks but hardly anywhere else, and are tedious to cash (you must show your passport, and often your purchase receipts). **American Express**, Sadovo-Kudrinskaya ul 21A (metro Maykovskaya), will accept only their own cheques, and also have an ATM for American Express cards. It's open weekdays 9:00-17:00, Saturday 9:00-13:00.

Russian visas and extensions The situation with visa extensions is ever-changing. Five-day extensions are currently available if you have a day to spend getting the right documents, including for onward travel. Requests for longer extensions or a second one are often refused.

UViR/PVU (Moscow's name for OViR/PVU, the state visa office) is at ul Pokrovka 42, near metro Kurskaya or Krasnye Vorota. It's open 10:00-13:00 and 15:00-18:00 Monday, Tuesday, Thursday and Friday (to 17:00 Friday); it's also open 10:00-13:00 Saturday but only for emergencies. To apply for an extension take your passport, visa and onward ticket to Room No 1 on the ground floor. When you turn in the application you are given a chit which you must take to Sberegatelny Bank at ul Pokrovka 31, opposite and just west of UViR, and open 8:30-14:00 and 15:00-19:30 weekdays. There you fill in another form, pay the visa fee (in roubles) and get a receipt. Take this back to UViR where your visa will be stamped with an extension.

As the extension starts from the date of application, go to UViR only a few days before your visa expires. It is advisable to take a Russian speaker or a letter from the organization which provided your visa invitation saying that they will provide for you.

If you have difficulty, contact one of the travel agencies listed below or one of the specialist visa agencies listed in the classified section of the *Moscow Times* or *Moscow Tribune*.

Telecommunications The Central Post and Telegraph Office (ul Tverskaya) is the best place for phone calls and faxes, and you may also send email from here. Rates are listed in English and there are some English-speaking staff. They also sell discount phonecards – their own Tsentel as well as rival brands – which offer much cheaper international calls from domestic or hotel telephones. **Street telephones** (*taksofon*) for local calls use cards sold at most kiosks and metro ticket windows. For more on telephone cards and on making local and long-distance calls see p77.

There are numerous places to access the **Internet** in Moscow. **Time On-Line**, on the bottom level of the Manege shopping complex (enter from Okhotny Ryad metro station) is open 24 hours with English-speaking staff, English-language browsers on request, and access for US$1 per hour. The **Internet Café** at Kuznetsky Most 12 offers similar services at similar prices. Friendly **NetBuffet**, Rozhdestvenka 11/1 (in the right-hand wing of the Markhi Institute), charges US$1 per hour and is also a genuine café, serving light meals. **Nice** (☎ 253 3234), ul 1905 Goda 2 is open 24 hours and charges US$1-2 per hour.

Tours Tours of the main sights can be arranged in any of the upmarket hotels or at **Intourist** (☎ 292 1278), ul Mokhovaya 13. Intourist tours include daily or almost-daily tours of the Armoury and Kremlin (four hours, US$25), Kremlin grounds tour (two hours, US$10), Pushkin Museum (three hours, US$15), Tretyakov Gallery (four hours, US$20), plus tours of the city (three hours, US$20), the metro and many other museums.

Patriarshy Dom Tours (☎ 795 0927, 🖳 alanskaya@co.ru) run highly rated, English-language excursions which even have official US Embassy endorsement. Cheaper tours are offered by guides who lurk around the Tomb of the Unknown Soldier; if they are registered they will have ID cards to prove it.

It's worth enquiring about the KGB tour occasionally offered by Intourist and Patriarshy Dom, which includes demonstrations of miniature cameras, micro-dots, bugging techniques and more at the Federal Counterintelligence Service (KGB) Museum, plus a great deal of whitewash about the darker side of the KGB's history. You cannot visit this museum except on a tour.

If you're looking for a backpacker tour bus, Russia has the **Beetroot Backpackers Bus** (☎ 453 4368, 🖳 www.beetroot.org) which takes in the sights of Moscow, Kostroma, Rybinsk, Vologda, St Petersburg, Novgorod and Valdai – one/two weeks for US$370/720, including transport, accommodation, breakfast and guide.

Travel agencies General travel agencies are convenient sources for rail tickets, and most offer good advice and a flexible outlook into the bargain. Most do air ticketing as well, and accept at least some major credit cards.

For those who know exactly what they want, specialist ticket resellers like Galileo-Rus and the service bureaux at the train stations are cheaper and just as competent, and if your itinerary is simple you can go right to the source and avoid any mark-up. For details see Moving on, p177.

● **G&R International** (☎ 374 5731, 🖹 374 7366, 🖳 grtour@online.ru, www.hostels.ru), Block 6, Institut Molodyozh (Institute of Youth), ul Yunosti 5/1 (from Vykhino metro station catch bus No 196 or 197 to Institut Molodyozh stop). G&R can handle Trans-Siberian accommodation, transfers, ticketing, guides and visa support. Affiliate G&R Hostel Asia (see Where to stay) looks after Moscow accommodation and travel services.

● **Star Travel** (☎ 797 9555, 🖹 797 9554, 🖳 help@startravel.ru), Baltiiskaya ul 9, 3rd floor (metro: Sokol). This student-friendly agency affiliated with Travellers Guest House does hotel bookings and air ticketing and sells international youth and student cards. Its sibling agency, **Infinity Travel** (☎ 234 6555, 🖹 234 6556, 🖳 w ww.infinity.ru), Komsomolsky pr 13 (metro: Park Kultury), concentrates on outbound air and rail tickets and visa support.

● **ATH** (Andrew's Consulting; ☎ 916 9898, 🖹 916 9828, 🖳 moscow@ath.ru, www.a th.ru), ul Volkhonka 18/2 (metro Kropot kinskaya), enter via courtyard on Bolshoy Znamensky pereulok. Aimed at corporate clients but prepared to help individuals with visa registration, extensions, ticketing (but no international trains) and excursions. Open 09:00-17:00 weekdays, 10:00-18:00 Saturday-Sunday.

● **Intourist** (☎ 234 9508, 🖹 232 1950, 🖳 via@intourist.ru), pereulok Stoleshnikov 11. This is the Intourist office for buying train and air tickets: not Trans-Sib specialists by any means but competent for standard journeys. Open 09:00-20:00 weekdays, 10:00-19:00 Saturday-Sunday.

Where to stay

All prices given below include Moscow's hefty 24% hotel-tax surcharge. In upper-end hotels you may be quoted a price without tax, so it's worth checking.

Budget accommodation Moscow now has four good hostels, each subletting part of an existing hotel for its own use. While the 'host' hotels may or may not be licensed to register foreigners, the hostels themselves are. All four have English-speaking staff and facilities to satisfy most budget travellers, and offer further services such as transfers to/from the airport (US$25-30) or train station (US$15). All also offer visa support.

Travellers Guest House Moscow (☎ 971 4059, 🖹 280 7686, 🖳 tgh@startra vel.ru, www.infinity.ru/tgh) is on the 10th floor of the rather ropey-looking Hotel Gasis, Bolshaya Pereyaslavskaya ul 50. This is the closest hostel to the city centre, a magnet for budget travellers and a great place to pick up travel tips. Five-bed dorms cost US$18 per bed and spartan singles/ doubles US$36/48, all in pairs sharing toilet and shower. HI cards earn a 10% discount, ISIC cards 5%, and breakfast is included. Rooms are all on one floor and guests have access to a common room, laundry facilities, kitchen, notice-board, travel services (including Trans-Siberian ticketing, weekdays only), café and bar. From Prospekt Mira metro station walk north on pr Mira, turn right at the third street (Bannii pereulok), continue until it ends at Bolshaya Pereyaslavskaya ul, turn left and the building is the first tall one on your right. Alternatively, trolleybus No 14 from Leningradsky station takes you right past the building.

In the south-east of the city is *G&R Hostel Asia* (☎ 378 0001, ☎/🖹 378 2866, 🖳 hostel-asia@mtu-net.ru, www.hostels.ru), based on the 15th floor of the Hotel Asia, ul Zelenodolskaya 3/2, beside metro station Ryazansky Prospekt. The hostel's rooms, all in individually-locked pairs sharing bath and toilet, are scattered round the hotel: two- or three-bedded dorms at US$16 and functional single/double rooms with TV and telephone for US$22/36. HI card-holders get a US$1-per-night discount. A basic breakfast is included.

Quite literally G&R's 'sister' hostel (it's owned by the sister of G&R's owner), *Hostel Sherstone* (☎/🖹 797 8075, 🖳 sher stone@mail.ru) is based in room 324 of the well-run Hotel Sherston at 8 Gostinichny proezd, north of the city centre. Rooms, scattered throughout the hotel, include four-bed dorms at US$14 per bed and sin-gles/doubles/triples for US$25/40/45; HI card-holders save US$1 per night. Each room has attached bath and toilet; non-dorms have TV and telephone. A simple hot breakfast is included. The hostel is a 10-minute walk from Vladykino metro station:

from the exit closest to downtown, follow Botanicheskaya ul to the right for 200m, but where it bends left, leave the road and cross the courtyard of a housing block to the four-lane road beyond, also signposted Botanicheskaya ul; cross, turn right and immediately left before the Hotel Altay into an unnamed street; continue for two long blocks to the end of this street and turn right into Gostinichny proezd. Alternatively, trolleybus No 36 from behind the metro station passes by the hotel.

Tops for setting is **Hostel Tramp** (☎ 187 5433, ☎/🖷 551 2876, 🖳 info@hostelling.ru, www.hostelling.ru) in the quiet, low-rise complex of the Hotel Turist, Selskokhozyaystvennaya ul 17/2. The hostel is based in room 524, building 7. There are no dorms, only singles/doubles with TV, attached toilet and bath for US$27/40. HI and ISIC card-holders get 10% off. Breakfast is included. There are snack bars in each of the hotel's buildings and a restaurant in nearby Hotel Baykal. Guests can use the hotel's laundry and parking lot. From metro station Botanichesky Sad (exit closest to city centre) walk south through parkland beside Vilgelma Pika ul for 10 minutes, to traffic lights at the intersection with Selskokhozyaystvennaya ul; the hotel is just beyond this on the right.

In the region of VDNKh metro station is a cluster of hotels originally built or upgraded for the 1980 Olympics. Several are budget-range and good value, including **Hotel Zolotoy Kolos** (☎ 217 6666, ☎/🖷 286 2932, 🖳 zolotoikolos@mail.ru), in korpus 3 of a low-rise complex at Yaroslavskaya ul 15. It's behind street-facing korpus 2, 15 minutes' walk from the metro station, east along ul Kosmonavtov and right on Yaroslavskaya. Singles/doubles with TV, telephone and bath start at US$25/30. Breakfast is about US$2.50 extra.

Hotel Zvyozdnaya (☎ 215 4292, 🖷 215 4301), ul Argunovskaya 2, is the white high-rise at the end of a 20-minute walk (or a ride on bus No 61) south-west down Zvyozdny bulvar from metro VDNKh. The atmosphere is Soviet but serviceable single/double rooms start at US$15/25, with breakfast.

Quiet, Indian-run **Prakash Guest House** (☎ 334 8201, ☎/🖷 334 2598, 🖳 prakash akhil@yahoo.com) is at ul Profsoyuznaya 83, korpus 1, entrance 2. Homespun, spartan singles/doubles with TV, attached bath and toilet are overpriced at US$30/50 but come with more hospitality than most Russians can manage. Breakfast is US$3 extra and basic Indian meals are available for guests. But they're not licenced to register visas and must do so through a nearby hotel for an extra fee of about US$25. The guest house is near Belyaevo metro station, 20-25 minutes south of the city centre: turn left (north) out of the train, right out of the station to the farthest stairway, left up the stairs and about four minutes along ul Profsoyuznaya to the first cluster of tall buildings. Korpus 1 is the furthest of these from the metro. At the entrance to the right of the Simplex store, ring the bell and say 'Prakash'. Calling ahead is highly recommended.

Small (11-room), quiet, professionally-run **Hotel Gostinny Dvor** (☎ 497 8209, 🖷 492 5315, 🖳 www.q-dom.ru) could be one of Moscow's best bargains but unfortunately they cannot register foreigners, so you'd have to stay somewhere else first. It's at Skhodnenskaya ul 10, unsignposted and set back from the street in an agreeable neighbourhood 20-25 minutes north of the centre by metro. From Skhodnenskaya metro station it's a 15-minute walk south on Skhodnenskaya ul (or three stops on any tram, to the Zapadny Most stop). Single/double rooms with TV but shared bathroom cost about US$25/30, and breakfast is US$1.60.

Several old, rather grim Soviet-era hotels offer reasonably cheap accommodation, although none is worth writing home about. If you just want a comfy room and no service whatsoever, you can't get much more central than the **Hotel Minsk** (☎ 299 1213, 🖷 299 0362, 🖳 hotelminsk.virtu alave.net), Tverskaya ul 22 near Pushkinskaya ploshchad. This Soviet fossil has been stuck in a timewarp since 1978 but so are the prices, at US$30-50 for a single or US$38-60 for a double. The **Hotel Tsentralnaya** (☎ 229 8957, 🖷 220 0848),

Tverskaya ul 10 (metro: Pushkinskaya or Tverskaya), is famously rude but well-run in a Soviet sort of way. Singles/doubles with shared bath start at US$22/$29, including either breakfast or dinner. Equally unenthusiastic about individual tourists is unrenovated, overpriced *Hotel Kievskaya* (☎ 240 1444, 🖳 240 5388), ul Kievskaya 2 (beside Kievskaya metro and train stations), with grim doubles for as little as US$15 with shared bathroom or US$30 with bath.

Homestays are possible from about US$30 per day. Check out the ads in the *Moscow Times* or contact HOFA (see p20).

Mid-range accommodation Prices in this category also seem to vary widely from month to month. Phone ahead to check.

The huge *Hotel Moskva* (☎ 960 2020, 🖳 928 5938), ul Okhotny Ryad 2 (metro: Okhotny Ryad), is well located but currently closed for rebuilding. How much of this hotel will be knocked down remains to be seen as plans to have it razed are being opposed on preservation grounds, presumably by lovers of ugly buildings. The even bigger *Hotel Rossiya* (☎ 232 5000, 🖳 298 5544), a step from Red Square at ul Varvarka 6 (metro: Kitay-Gorod), is the world's second biggest hotel. It's now pretty shoddy and way overpriced at US$95/120 for singles/doubles. There have been numerous reports of petty theft from rooms. Upgrading of this hotel is a permanent promise, but there are no signs of it.

The Soviet-era *Hotel Pekin* (☎ 209 2215, 🖳 200 1420) has a super central location at Bolshaya Sadovaya ul 5/1 (metro: Mayakovskaya), opposite Tchaikovsky Concert Hall and a five-minute walk from Patriarch's Ponds. It was built as offices for the KGB (note the busy/enter lights above each door) but never used. Singles/doubles start at US$60/85.

The four-block, Soviet-era *Hotel Izmaylovo* (☎ 166 4127, 🖳 166 7486), Izmaylovsky shosse 71 (metro: Izmaylovsky Park), is not a bad place once you get inside. Single/double rooms cost US$60/ US$75. Intourist has an office in block D.

AST Gof Hotel (☎ 142 2117, 🖳 142 2384) is a comfortable three-star hotel on ul Bolshaya Filyovskaya, opposite Fili park (metro: Bagrationovskaya). A single/double room with attached shower is US$72/104, with breakfast included. There's a bank adjacent, plus Internet service and a large market opposite the metro station.

The refurbished *Hotel Aeropolis* (☎ 151 0442), Leningradsky pr 37, charges US$75 for a double and boasts a 24-hour restaurant, casino, bar, sauna and laundry. It's between metro stations Dynamo and Aeroport, convenient if you're in transit between airports.

Hotel East-West (☎ 290 0404), Tverskoy bulvar 14/4, is a three-star boutique hotel in a charming 19th-century mansion (part of the former Governor's residence) on a historic central street. Singles/doubles are US$100/160; each room has its own shape, size and design.

The grand, partly-renovated *Hotel Ukraina* (☎ 243 2596, 🖳 243 3092), Kutuzovsky pr 2/1 (metro: Kievskaya plus a 15-minute walk) is in one of Moscow's Stalin-era high-rise buildings. It's a good three-star option, charging US$120/160 for a single/double including breakfast, though you may get a better price for an unrenovated room.

Upmarket hotels It's worth checking whether quoted prices include 24% city tax, and whether they include breakfast, which otherwise may cost you US$30 or more. The best deals are at weekends when business-friendly hotels drop their prices by up to 40%: always ask.

Marriott (🖳 www.marriotthotels.com) has several hotels in Moscow. Charges are per room, not per person, and increase the closer the hotel is to the centre: from US$240 at the *Marriott Tverskaya* (☎ 258 3000, 🖳 258 3099), 1-ya Tverskaya-Yamskaya ul 34; US$310 at the *Marriott Grand* (☎ 935 8500, 🖳 935 8501), Tverskaya ul 26; and US$346 at the well-run, very central *Marriott Moscow Aurora* (☎ 937 1000, 🖳 937 1001), ul Petrovka 11/20.

Close to Red Square is *Hotel Savoy* (☎ 929 8500, 🖂 230 2186, 💻 www.savoy.ru), ul Rozhdestvenka 3 (metro: Lubyanka), charging from US$186/236 for a single/double. You can often get good deals here.

A small, high-standard hotel without the 'grand-hotel' atmosphere is the Austrian-run *Marco Polo Presnya* (☎ 244 3631, 🖂 926 5402) at Spiridonyevsky pereulok 9 (metro: Pushkinskaya). This former Communist Party hotel, in the superchic area of Patriarch's Ponds, is quiet, exclusive and central. Rooms cost US$220-480.

Hotel Radisson Slavyanskaya (☎ 941 8020, 🖂 224 1225, 💻 reserv@mosbusiness.ru), Berezhkovskaya naberezhnaya 1 (metro: Kievskaya), charges from US$221 a room (single or double), including breakfast. There's a swimming-pool, shopping mall and cinema too.

The Canadian joint-venture *Aerostar Hotel Moscow* (☎ 213 9000, 🖂 213 9001, 💻 www.aerostar.ru), Leningradsky pr 37, korpus 9 (7km from the city centre; metro: Dinamo), has single rooms from US$199 and doubles from US$240. A buffet breakfast is included. Also quite distant from the centre is the *Sofitel Iris Hotel* (also called Iris Congress Hotel; ☎ 203 0131), Korovinskoye shosse 10, with swimming-pool and single rooms from US$260. It's convenient for Sheremetyevo airport.

As much a historic monument as a place to stay, it was at the *Hotel Metropole* (☎ 927 6000, 🖂 927 6010, 💻 metropol@metmos.ru), close to Red Square at Teatralny proezd 1, that Rasputin is said to have dined and Lenin to have made several speeches. Its beautiful Art Nouveau interior also featured in the film *Dr Zhivago*. It offers an exotic level of comfort, although service can be patchy. Rooms cost from US$260/297 for a single/double.

It's a short walk to the Kremlin and Red Square from the well-run *Hotel National* (☎ 258 7000, 🖂 258 7100, 💻 www.national.ru), a beautiful period hotel at Mokhovaya ul 15/1 that's now part of the international Le Meridien/Forte group. Prices start at US$334 for a single or

US$446 for a double. Lenin liked the hotel so much he made his office here.

Moscow's best hotel is probably the German-run *Hotel Baltschug Kempinski* (☎ 230 6500, 🖂 230 6502, 💻 www.kempinski-moscow.com), ul Balchug 1. The service is impeccable and the riverside location affords superb views of the Kremlin. Facilities are all you would expect in a hotel of this class, with marble bathtubs and satellite telephones. Rooms cost US$496-2350. High-profile guests have included Helmut Kohl, Tina Turner and Sting.

Where to eat

You can now eat very well in Moscow. The restaurant scene is changing fast, with new places opening daily. Your budget will stretch furthest if you eat your main meal at lunchtime: most restaurants offer cheap weekday 'business-lunch' deals which can save up to 50% compared with the same dishes ordered à la carte.

If you aren't sure what you want to eat and want to browse a bit, the **Arbat** (see p164) is a good place to start. The most interesting prospects are at the Smolenskaya metro station end, the so-called *vostochny kvartal* (oriental quarter), with a mixture of Turkish, Greek, Georgian and Armenian cafés of frequently shifting ownership, and *Rioni* (budget Georgian food) at the mid-point of the street. In Arbatskaya ploshchad, at the far end (of both the street and the price scale) is the *Praga Restaurant*, recognized as one of Moscow's élite dining establishments for the ultra-rich.

Other streets with a fair number of reasonable eateries are **Myasnitskaya**, starting from Lyubyanka metro station, and **Maroseyka**, which runs from Kitay-Gorod metro station.

Budget and fast food You can get hot dogs, burgers, shwarma-kebab, pancakes and snacks of all kinds at stands gathered around most metro stations, for very low prices. One such place is *Rostiks*, at Mayakovskaya metro station and elsewhere, with reliable chicken and sandwiches. 'Summer cafés', serving beer, pizza and snacks at rock-bottom prices, spring up on any spare patch of ground.

For cheap, ultra-convenient fast food close to Red Square, the multi-concession *Food Court* on the bottom level of the Manezhnaya Shopping Centre (entrance opposite Hotel Moskva or directly from Okhotny Ryad metro station) has everything from Russian to Italian to Korean at a few dollars per helping, plus clean loos.

For super-cheap Russian café food – pies, pastries, soups etc – *Russkoye Bistro* has branches all over Moscow, notably on ul Petrovka behind the TsUM department store and Bolshoi Theatre, where you can sit outside in summer. Their biggest drawback: no toilets.

McDonald's is everywhere, most centrally at the junction of Gazetny pereulok and Tverskaya ul; other branches are at ul Arbat 50 near metro Smolenskaya, pr Mira close to metro Prospekt Mira and pl Pushkina 29 near metro Pushkinskaya.

Russian and Slavic There are dozens of branches of *Yolki-Palki* around Moscow; the largest one adjacent to Tverskaya metro station. These rustic-style theme restaurants feature an all-you-can-eat buffet of tasty salads for around US$8, and a wide selection of main courses and drinks. The food is always reliable if a bit mass-produced. Count on US$10-15 per person. The name, a favourite cuss of Russian villagers, roughly translates as 'bleedin' 'ell!'

Balalaika, at 2-ya Brestskaya 52 on the big square by Belorussky Station, is another 'Olde Russia' style place with dinner for about US$15, and more charm than Yolki-Palki. *Shury-Mury* (☎ 929 8755) ul Petrovka 15 (metro: Kuznetsky Most) is another favourite in the same rustic format, great value for around US$10-20.

The attraction at slightly more elegant *Matrioshka,* Triumfalnaya pl 1 (across the square from Mayakovskaya metro station), is the magnificent, all-you-can-eat *shvedsky stol* (buffet), including salads, fish, hot meat dishes and desserts, for US$8 at lunchtime or US$11 in the evening.

Through the arch and 150m through a courtyard at ul Petrovka 26, *Ulitsa OGI* (☎

200 6873) has delicious Russo-European food in a modern soft-industrial setting. Owned by an artists' collective, it's a favourite with the theatre/media crowd. Don't be alarmed by the apparently derelict exterior or the abandoned London phone-box outside. Supper at around US$30 (including drinks) is worth twice that.

Pub-style *Mesto Vstrechi* ('Meeting-Place'; ☎ 229 2373), at Maly Gnezdnikovsky pereulok 9/8 on the corner with Tverskaya ul (metro: Pushkinskaya), is a basement restaurant popular with young professionals.

For hearty Ukrainian dishes at wallet-friendly prices, try *Taras Bulva Korchma* (☎ 200 6082), ul Petrovka 30/7 (metro: Chekhovskaya). The interior is a bit cutesy-folksy but the service is good. Expect to spend US$8-12 for a meal. Another *branch* at Leninsky pr 37 is bigger and even more fun.

Self-service *Pelmeshka*, on Kuznetsky Most near Kammergeysky pereulok (look for the sign of the dancing dumpling), may be the cheapest smart lunch in Moscow, with a chic minimalist dining-room, silent movies playing on the walls, and a portion of *pelmeni* (Siberian dumplings) for just US$1. It's open until 21:00.

If you feel like pushing the boat out for Moscow's top Russian food, *Café Pushkin* (☎ 229 5590), Tverskoy bulvar 26A (metro: Pushkinskaya), is the place to see and be seen, a favourite of government ministers and film stars alike. The interior is in the style of a 19th-century gentleman's study, complete with globes, telescope and leather-bound books. Immaculate cuisine runs at around US$50-60 for dinner.

For a true gourmet experience *Oblomov* (☎ 255 9290), in a palatial 19th-century setting at ul 1905 Goda 2 (metro: Ulitsa 1905 Goda), is highly recommended. There's a different menu each day of the month, and the US$56 per person price includes everything on your bill.

Georgian Russia's favourite 'ethnic food' is Mediterranean-style Georgian food. The winning formula at *Mama Zoya* (☎ 242

8550), on a houseboat at Frunzenskaya naberezhnaya 16D (metro: Frunzenskaya), is fabulous food at cheap prices, around US$10-15 a head, and no rude surprises with wine prices as at many Georgian places. Service is efficient if not exactly charming. Book ahead in summer if you want a waterside table on their floating pontoon verandah.

Another good choice is *Guriya* (☎ 246 0378) Komsomolsky pr 7/3 (metro: Park Kultury). Low prices (about US$12 per person) attract the crowds, so go early. Khachapuri (cheesebreads) are a favourite.

Slightly upscale at about US$15 per person is *Dioscuria* (☎ 290 6908), featuring some Abkhaz dishes too (cheesebreads here are egg-topped). There's a good range of Georgian wines: try Saperavi or Kindzmarauli (red) or Tsinandali (white). It's at Merzlyakovsky pereulok 2; enter through the arch of the post office on ul Novy Arbat, opposite Praga Restaurant.

International In Moscow, Tex-Mex does not get cheaper than at *Moosehead* (☎ 230 7333), a popular Canadian bar and restaurant. Figure US$9-12 per person.

For US-diner favourites at moderate prices the *American Bar & Grill* (☎ 251 7999) on 1-ya Tverskaya-Yamskaya ul (metro: Mayakovskaya) attracts lots of young Americans in Moscow and costs around US$12-15 for a meal (avoid American beer by ordering Russian instead).

For a genuine diner in the heart of Moscow, dishing up shakes, fries, pepper steak and more, visit the *Starlight Diner* (☎ 290 9638), Bolshaya Sadovaya ul 16A, in the Aquarium Garden adjacent to the Satire Theatre: from Mayakovskaya metro station head down the boulevard one block then left into the iron-gated garden.

Authentic Cajun cooking comes to Moscow at *BB King* (☎ 299 8206), Sadovaya-Samotyochnaya ul 4/2 (metro: Tsvetnoy Bulvar). Jambalaya and gumbo jockey for positions on a packed menu, with great business-lunch deals too. Expect to pay US$20 per person.

Tibet-Gimalay (Tibet-Himalaya; ☎ 917 3985), ul Pokrovka 19 (metro: Chistye Prudy), is a rather New-Age but successful restaurant with Tibetan staff, calorie-counted menus and Tibetan-style food for around US$30 per person.

For Serbian food in hearty-sized portions visit *Drago* (☎ 923 0492), Myasnitskaya ul 13 (metro: Chistye Prudy). The US$6 business lunch will have you letting your belt out and includes a drink.

Jagganat (☎ 928 3580), Kuznetsky Most 11, is a vegetarian Indian restaurant in the hyper-trendy Kuznetsky Most area. The cafeteria offers bargain-basement veggie food (and a health-food shop), while the restaurant is pricier (around US$25 per person) and somewhat pretentious. No smoking or alcohol allowed.

Parisian-style brasserie *Soleil Express* (☎ 725 6474), Sadovaya-Samotyochnaya ul 24/27 (metro: Tsvetnoy Bulvar) offers light meals, sandwiches, baguettes and excellent coffee.

Trattoria Mei Amici (☎ 251 1116), 1-ya Tverskaya-Yamskaya ul 22 (metro: Mayakovskaya), has reasonably-priced classic Italian cuisine at around US$12 per head, and great-value, genuine Italian-style pizza.

Coffee and cakes *Coffeebean* (ul Pokrovka 18; Tverskaya ul 10), *Caffe-Inne* (Bolshaya Dmitrovka ul 16), *Kofe-Tun* (Tverskaya ul 18) and *Zen Coffee* (corner of Kammergeysky pereulok and Bolshaya Dmitrovka ul, with a 24-hour branch opposite Belorussky station) all offer the full Seattle experience, most with cakes, sandwiches and salads too.

Great Canadian Bagel (Tverskaya ul 27) has sandwiches, tea and cakes along with the bagels.

Nightlife
Moscow, more than St Petersburg, is where it's at for nightlife. It's all a very far cry from those evenings back in the communist era when the choice was either the ballet or the circus – and so to bed. Now you can have as wild a time as in any Western city.

Anything goes – Lenin must be spinning in his mausoleum.

Among **bars**, the most popular expat place is *Doug'n'Marty's Boarhouse*, Zemlyanoy Val ul 26 opposite Kursky station (metro: Kurskaya), where the beer is free until 21:00 on Wednesday evenings. Popular *Moosehead* (see Where to eat) has a good range of beers. Both places also do good meals. There's no better place for a pint of Guinness than at Irish theme-pub *Rosie O'Grady's* at ul Znamenka 9 (metro: Borovitskaya). *BB King* (see Where to eat) often has live jazz and blues. Good all-Russian beer bars include *Pivnaya 01*, at Vernadskogo 6 adjacent to Universitet metro station, with a fire-station theme (look for the two-storey fire-extinguisher). *Kruzhka* (Beer-Mug), Butyrsky Val ul 4 (metro: Belorusskaya), has a top-floor beer garden for those hot Moscow summer evenings.

The **club** scene seems to change every few weeks, but reliable Moscow favourites include *Propoganda* at Bolshoy Zlatustinsky pereulok 7, a top club with notoriously vicious face-control; *Karma-Bar*, Pushechnaya ul 3, a friendly club with a large dance floor and popular with expats; *Art Garbage*, Starosadsky pereulok 5/6, a club/bar/art-centre popular with students.

If dancing isn't your thing you could always go **bowling**: Moscow has a swathe of 'fun clubs' that feature bowling, bar, snooker, karaoke, games and more, of which the biggest is *Champion* at Leningradskoye shosse 16 (metro: Voykovskaya, and about 100m past M-Video), which has free admission too.

The season at the fabulous **Bolshoi Theatre** (☎ 292 0050), Teatralnaya pl 1 (metro: Teatralnaya) runs from October to June with alternating programmes of ballet and opera. Many of the world's greatest dancers were trained here and despite defections to other companies the Bolshoi

is still brilliant. But be sure it's really the Bolshoi Ballet that you will be seeing and not a visiting company. To watch classical ballet here is an experience made more magical by the ambience of the 1½-century-old theatre.

The adjacent, newly-opened **Bolshoi New Stage** usually offers a choice of nightly performances (the same company performs at both venues). Tickets are easy to come by for around US$50 (more for star performances).

The theatre has a ticket office but most tickets are bought up in advance by touts; stand around outside the theatre before a performance and they'll find you, assess your gullibility and quote prices of US$25-100. Bargain hard, and remember that the later you leave it before the performance starts the more anxious they'll be to get rid of their tickets. Check the date and time on the ticket before you buy.

For ballet or opera on a budget, there are equally good (some would say better) performances at the **Kremlin Palace of Congresses** (although the music is on tape) and the **Stanislavsky Musical Theatre** (up the street from the Bolshoi at Bolshaya Dmitrovka ul 17). Tickets for either venue are available for US$2-10 at any theatre-kiosk, such as the one at Teatralnaya metro station, but like the Bolshoi both close in summer. The *Moscow Times* has what's-on listings, as does 🖳 www.expat.ru.

Moscow is also home to the **Helikon Opera**, with extreme avant-garde productions at Bolshaya Nikitskaya 19. Splendid classical-music concerts can be heard at the **Tchaikovsky Concert Hall** (metro: Mayakovskaya) and the **Conservatoire**, Bolshaya Nikitskaya ul, for US$2-8.

Moscow has two permanent **circuses**. The **New Circus** (metro: Universitet) is more spectacular while the **Old Circus** (metro: Tsvetnoye Bulvar) has a more traditional show. In both the human performers are generally excellent, although

Opposite: Cathedral of the Ascension, Novosibirsk (see p234). (Photo © Nick Hill).

Western visitors tend to be dismayed by the animal acts. Tickets are readily available for US$2-5.

Undubbed English-language **films** are sometimes shown at **Kodak Kinomir** on Nastasin pereulok (metro: Pushkinskaya), behind TGI Fridays.

What to buy

Most foreigners end up buying their matrioshkas, ceramic boxes and furry hats from street sellers, although you should check quality first and bargain hard.

The best **market** is at Ismaylovsky Park at the weekend, where you'll find everything from stolen icons to Stalin photos. Some of it is just clothing and shoes but if you head towards the old-style wooden buildings you'll find the part aimed at tourists. Prices get lower the further in you go. Visitors are charged R10 to go in. From Ismaylovsky Park metro station just follow the crowds to the market, a five-minute walk away.

Moscow's main general shopping streets are ul Novy Arbat and Tverskaya ul.

Moving on

By air For tickets go to one of the travel agents on p169 or directly to the airlines. **Aeroflot** has numerous branches around the city, including at ul Petrovka 20 (☎ 150 3883) and Korovy Val ul 7 (☎ 156 8019). **Transaero** (☎ 241 4800, 241 7676, 292 7526) is at the Hotel Moskva, ul Okhotny Ryad 2.

Other major carriers with Moscow services include: **Air China** (☎ 292 5440), Kuznetsky Most 1/8; **Air France** (☎ 937 3839), Korovy Val ul 7; **Alitalia** (☎ 258 3601), Olimpeysky pr 18/1; **ANA/All Nippon Airways** (☎ 253 1546), Krasnopresnenskaya naberezhnaya 12, room 1405; **British Airways** (☎ 363 2525), 1-ya Tverskaya-Yamskaya ul 23; **Delta** (☎ 937 9090), Gogolevsky bulvar 11; **Finnair** (☎ 933 0056), Kropotkinsky pereulok 7;

JAL (☎ 921 6448), Kuznetsky Most 3; **KLM** (☎ 258 3600, 956 1666), ul Usacheva 33; **LOT** (☎ 229 5771) Tverskoy bulvar 26; **Lufthansa** (☎ 737 6400), Olimpeysky pr 18/1; **MIAT-Mongolian Airlines** (☎ 241 3757), Spasopeskovsky pereulok 7/1; **SAS** (☎ 925 4747), Kuznetsky Most 3; and **Swissair** (☎ 937 7767), Gogolevsky bulvar 3.

There are frequent daily flights to St Petersburg from Sheremetyevo 2, plus daily flights from Domodedovo airport to many Siberian cities including Yekaterinburg, Irkutsk, Khabarovsk, Novosibirsk, Ulan Ude and Vladivostok. Sample prices: St Petersburg (US$60-80), Irkutsk (US$180-220) and Vladivostok (US$280-340).

By train Trains to Siberia use either Yaroslavsky or Kazansky stations (both at Komsomolskaya pl). There are also some trains to Vladimir and Nizhny Novgorod from Kursky station. For details of these and other connections see p166.

If you're unsure of your plans the easiest source of tickets is one of the **travel agencies** listed on p169. Those with a straightforward itinerary can save a bit at one of the **service centres** in the stations: Yaroslavsky, Kazansky, Leningradsky, Belorussky (in the building across the tracks behind the station, at the end nearest the station), Paveletsky or Kievsky. Service is quick, some English is spoken and the price includes a mark-up of about US$4.25 **for each ticketed segment**.

If you know exactly what you want you'll do even better with a rail ticket consolidator such as **Galileo-Rus** (☎ 256 9771, ▤ 256 8910, ▭ train@galileo.ru), ul 1905 Goda 5; from Ulitsa 1905 Goda metro station, cross Zvenigorodskoye shosse/ Krasnaya Presnya ul, walk 1½ blocks south on ul 1905 Goda and it's on the right just beyond ul Kostikova. The office is open 9:00-20:00 Monday-Friday, and they also do air ticketing.

Opposite Top: Lake Baikal, the world's deepest lake (over 1500m deep) does not freeze over until late December, in spite of the extreme cold. **Bottom:** Many Muscovites own small cottages (*dacha*, see p328) outside the capital where they spend weekends and holidays.

To avoid the mark-up altogether you can go to one of the city's four offices of the **Central Railway Agency** (Tsentralnoye or Moskovskoye Zheleznodorozhnoye Agentstvo), all open 08:00-13:00 and 14:00-19:00 (to 18:00 on Saturday and 17:00 on Sunday). Each office can issue tickets to all destinations served by all Moscow train stations, although the one on the east side of Yaroslavsky station (metro: Komsomolskaya) is the best choice for Trans-Siberian tickets. Others are at Maly Kharitonevsky pereulok 6/11, korpus 2 (metro: Chistye Prudy or Krasnaya Vorota); Leningradsky pr 1, in the building across the tracks behind Belorussky station, at the end farthest from the station (metro: Belorusskaya); and Mozhaysky Val ul 4/6 (metro: Kievskaya). Relevant window numbers change all the time, but look for

key words to help you find the right one, for example *vnutrenny* (internal or domestic) or *mezhdunarodny* (international).

You could even brave the relevant **train station** (see pp433-4 for useful phrases), although these can be quite baffling and chaotic, with long, scrum-like queues. Note that at a station you can only buy tickets for trains departing from that station. Russian speakers can try calling ☎ 266 9333 for train information.

Payment at Central Railway Agency offices and stations is with rouble cash only. Domestic tickets are sold for departures up to 45 days ahead, and international tickets up to 40 days ahead. Timetables (*raspisanie*) for all Moscow arrivals and departures are on sale at ticket offices for about US$0.75.

🚂 Luggage lockers

Using one of the *avtomaticheskie kamery khranenia* (combination-lock luggage lockers) at stations is not as straightforward as it looks. To store your bags, buy a token (typically about US$0.85-1.30, in roubles) from the supervisor and choose a locker within view of him or her. On the inside of the locker door is a set of four dials, on which you select your own combination of three numbers and a Cyrillic character. **Before you shut the locker, write down the locker number and your chosen combination**. Then insert the token, close the door and twirl the knobs on the outside.

To get your bags out, set the combination on the knobs and wait two seconds until you hear the electric lock click back (some lockers require you to put in a second token before this happens).

If you have a problem or forget the combination, call the supervisor, who can open any locker, although you must first describe your luggage. If you forget the locker number they'll open up to three of them for you. If none of these is yours and more must be opened the supervisor must summon a police officer. After your things have been found you pay a small fine, fill in a form and show your passport. This process of tracking down a locker can take up to an hour and could cause you to miss your train, so don't forget to write down the combination; never rely on your memory.

Although lockers function 24 hours a day, they're closed several times a day for breaks of up to 30 minutes, so you should find out when these breaks are. If you leave luggage later than 23:59 on the following day the locker will be cleared.

Sergiev Posad
Сергиев Посад

Sergiev Posad, known as **Zagorsk** in the communist period, is the most popular tourist attraction in the Golden Ring (see p330) and a must even for those who are 'all churched out'. The town (pop: 110,000) contains Russia's religious capital, the Exalted Trinity Monastery of St Sergius (Troitse-Sergiyeva Lavra). Entering the white-walled, six-century-old monastery is like taking a step back into mediaeval Russia, with long-bearded monks in traditional black robes and tall *klobuki* hats, and continuous chanting emanating from lamp-lit, incense-filled churches.

HISTORY

The monastery was founded in 1340 by Sergius of Radonezh (1321-1391), who was later to become Russia's patron saint. The power of his monastery grew quickly because he was closely allied to Moscow's princes, and actively worked for the unification of Russian lands by building a ring of 23 similar monastery-fortresses around Moscow. His friendship with Moscow's ruler, Grand Prince Dmitry Donskoi, was so strong that when Dmitry asked for the church's blessing in 1380 before leaving to fight the Tatar-Mongols at Kulikovo, Sergius himself delivered the service. While the resultant victory had already indicated to Sergius's followers that he had God's ear, 17 years after his death it became obvious that he also had divine protection: in 1408, after the Tatar-Mongols levelled the monastery, the only thing to survive unscathed was Sergius's corpse.

Between 1540 and 1550 the monastery was surrounded with a massive stone wall and 12 defensive towers. Never again was it to fall, even after an 18-month siege by 20,000 Poles against 1500 defenders in 1608. Both Ivan the Terrible and Peter the Great hid here after fleeing plotting princes in Moscow.

Besides its military function, the monastery was a great centre of learning. It became famous for its *Sergievsky* style of manuscript illumination, with hand-copied pages adorned with gold and vermilion letters. Several of these manuscripts are on display at the museum inside the monastery. It is thought that Ivan Fedorov, Russia's first printer, studied here.

During the 18th century the monastery's spiritual power grew considerably. In 1744 it was elevated to a *lavra* or 'most exalted monastery'. At the time there were only four such monasteries in Russia, the other three being Kievo-Pechorskaya in Kiev, Aleksandro-Nevskaya in St Petersburg and Pochayevsko-Uspenskaya in Volyn. In 1749 a theological college was opened here, and in 1814 an ecclesiastical academy.

Two years after the communists came to power the monastery was closed down. It was reopened only in 1946 as part of a pact Stalin made with the Orthodox Church in return for the Church's support during WWII.

WHERE TO STAY & EAT

1 Hotel Zagorsk/Druzhba Гостиница Дружба/Загорск
4 McDonald's Макдональдс
27 Restaurant Trapeza na Makovtse Ресторан Трапеза на Маковце
31 Restaurant Russky Dvorik Ресторан Русский Дворик
32 Café Minutka Кафе Минутка
39 Restaurant Zolotoe Koltso Ресторан Золотое Кольцо
44 Hotel Russky Dvorik Гостиница Русский Дворик

OTHER

2 Church Церковь
3 Architecture & History Museum, in former stables
    Музей Истории и Конный Двор
5 Duck Tower Уточья Башня
6 Pilgrim Gate Tower Каличья Воротная Башня
7 Bathhouse Баня
8 Tsar's Palace Царский Дворец
9 Smolensk Church Смоленская Церковь
10 Bell-tower Колокольня

TRINITY CATHEDRAL

11 History Museum in Church of Saints Zosima & Savvaty
    Исторический Музей и Церковь Зосимы и Савватия
12 Former Treasurer's Wing Казначейский Корпус
13 Assumption/Dormition Cathedral Успенский Собор
14 Red Gate, Holy Gates & John the Baptist Gate Church
    Красные Ворота, Святые Ворота и Надвратная Церковь Иоанна
    Предтечи
15 Chapel above the Well Надкладезная Часовня
16 Museum Ticket Kiosk Музейная Касса
17 Museum of Ancient Russian Art, in vestry
    Музей Древнерусского Прикладного Искусства (Ризница)
18 Trinity Cathedral Троицкий Собор
19 Descent of the Holy Spirit Church Духовная Церковь
20 St Micah's Church Михеевская Церковь
21 Metropolitan's Chambers Митрополичьи Палаты
22 Refectory & St Sergius's Church
    Трапезная Палата и Церковь Святого Сергия
23 Former Hospital of the Trinity Monastery of St Sergei
    Больница-Богодельня Троице-Сергиевой Лавры
24 Elijah the Prophet's Church Ильинская Церковь
25 Water Gate/Tower Водяные Ворота/Башня
26 Lenin Bust Бюст Ленина
28 Krasnogorskaya Chapel Красногорская Часовня
29 Sberbank Сбербанк
30 Currency Exchange Обмен валюты
33 St Paraskeva Pyatnitsa Church Пятницкая Церковь
34 Telephone & Telegraph Office Телефон и Телеграф
35 Presentation of the Mother of God Church Введенская Церковь
36 War Memorial Военный памятник
37 Chapel over St Paraskeva Pyatnitsa's Well Часовня Пятницкого Колодца
38 Toy Museum Музей Игрушки
40 Ascension Church Вознесенская Церковь
41 Dormition Church Успенская Церковь
42 Bus Station Автовокзал
43 Railway Station Железнодорожний Вокзал

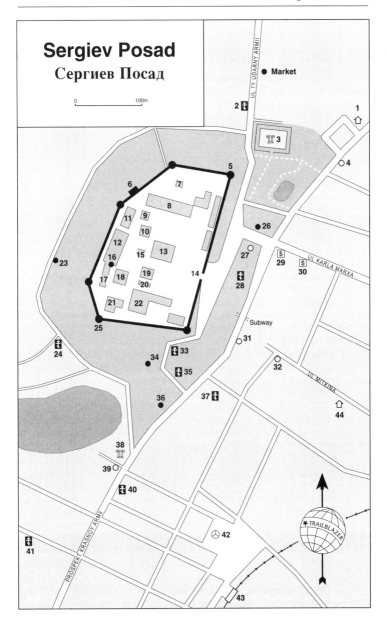

Sergiev Posad
Сергиев Посад

0   100m

Market

UL 1Y UDARNY ARMII

1

2

3

4

5

6

7

8

9

10

11

12

13

14

15

16

17

18

19

20

21

22

23

24

25

26

27

28

29

30

UL KARLA MARXA

31

32

UL MITKINA

33

34

35

36

37

38

39

40

41

42

43

44

Subway

TRAILBLAZER

PROSPEKT KRASNOY ARMII

The monastery was the seat of the Patriarch of Russia until the latter was moved to Moscow's Danilovsky Monastery in 1988. Five years later Unesco declared the monastery a World Heritage Site.

WHAT TO SEE

Exalted Trinity Monastery of St Sergius

The monastery is spread over six hectares and ringed by a whitewashed, 1km long wall which is up to 15m thick. Of its 13 defensive towers, note the Duck Tower: the metal duck on its spire was put there for the young Peter the Great to use for archery practice.

Many of the churches are open for services, although you may be turned away if you are wearing shorts or have bare shoulders. You may only take pictures within the monastery if you queue up and pay a fee (photos US$3, video US$5) at a kiosk near the entrance. You should not take flash photos, as this damages the icons, nor have your picture taken in front of an icon as this is considered disrespectful.

The monastery grounds are open daily 09:00-18:00; entry is free. You enter via the **Red Gate** and the inner **Holy Gates**. Above the latter is the **Church of St John the Baptist**, paid for by the wealthy Stroganov family in 1693.

The sky-blue and gold-starred, five-cupola **Assumption Cathedral** is the heart of the complex. It was consecrated in 1585 in honour of Ivan the Terrible's victory over the Mongols near Astrakhan and Kazan, and is the church in which many of the Tsars were baptized. Outside the western door is the tomb of Tsar Boris Godunov, his wife and two of their children.

The **Chapel over the Well** was built over a spring said to have appeared during the Polish siege of 1608. Here you'll find the longest queues, of pilgrims waiting to fill their bottles with holy water. The **Bell Tower** is the monastery's tallest building, 93m high. Construction began in 1740 and took 30 years.

The **Refectory and Church of St Sergius**, completed in 1693, served as a dining hall for pilgrims. You can't miss this red, blue, green and yellow chequered building with its carved columns. Outside it is the squat **Church of St Sergius**, crowned with a single golden dome. The **Church of the Descent of the Holy Spirit** contains the grave of the first Bishop of Russian Alaska.

Trinity Cathedral is the monastery's most sacred place, being the site of St Sergius' original wooden church. It contains Sergius's corpse in a dull silver sarcophagus donated by Ivan the Terrible. Built in 1422 in honour of Sergius' canonization, the cathedral contains 42 icons by Andrei Rublyov, Russia's most revered icon painter.

The **Church of Our Lady of Smolensk** was built to house the icon of the same name in 1745. Decorated in baroque style, it resembles a rotunda.

The **Tsar's Palace** was built at the end of the 17th century to house Tsar Alexei and his entourage of over 500 people when they came calling. It now houses the theological college and ecclesiastical academy.

The large, peach-and-white **Dormition Church** is finally open after years of restoration. Inside are photos of the church before and during that restoration.

About 200m south of the monastery are several other churches. Both the **Church of St Pareskeva Pyatnitsa** and the **Church of the Presentation of the Mother of God** were built in 1547, the year Ivan the Terrible was crowned Tsar. Across the road is the attractive **Pyatnitsa Well Chapel**. One of the most photogenic views of Sergiev Posad is with these three churches in the foreground.

Museums
The **Museum of Ancient Russian Art**, in the monastery's vestry (*riznitsa*, ризница), contains one of Russia's richest collections of ancient religious art (14th-17th centuries), plus gifts presented to the monastery over the centuries. The gifts are displayed in the order they were given, and it is interesting to see how tastes changed over the centuries. The museum is open 10:00-17:00 (closed Monday and Tuesday). The ticket window is opposite the vestry entrance; foreigners pay US$5. Tickets can be used only at the time printed on them; at peak times you may have to wait several hours so it's best to buy your ticket on arrival.

There is a less spectacular museum on the monastery's architecture and history, plus more recent art and handicrafts, in the renovated **stables** (*konniy dvor*, конный двор) about 200m north of the monastery entrance. This is open 10:00-17:00 (closed Monday and Thursday); foreigners pay US$2.

English-language tours can be arranged at the respective ticket offices.

PRACTICAL INFORMATION
Sergiev Posad has always been associated with carved wooden toys, as St Sergius used to give them to children. Before you buy any toys visit the **Toy Museum** for a look at the variety that's available. Locally-produced matrioshkas are distinctive, painted with gouache and varnished.

You can change money during normal business hours at Sber Bank on ul Karla Marxa, or at other times at a no-commission exchange bureau two doors eastward.

Where to stay
Hotel Zagorsk/Druzhba is on pl Sovetskaya. It's a typical huge concrete structure with single rooms costing from US$30 and doubles from US$45 with attached bathroom and breakfast included. The rooms are large but spartan and getting shabby. A better option is *Russky Dvorik*, a small hotel on ul Mitkina, run by the restaurant of the same name (see below). There are rooms from $48/68 for a single/double.

Where to eat
Restaurants near the monastery tend to be full of tourists, and charge tourist prices. *Restaurant Russky Dvorik*, just across pr

Krasnoy Armii from the monastery entrance, is an agreeable place with kitschy rustic decor and live music, offering soups or pelmeny from about US$6 and hot courses for US$6-10.

Just north of the monastery entrance is the somewhat more pretentious and pricey *Restaurant Trapeza na Makovtse*, although the food is well-prepared. *Restaurant Zolotoye Koltso* (Golden Ring), closer to the train station, is popular with tour groups and has a downstairs café.

There is a branch of *McDonald's* on pr Krasnoy Armii north of the monastery. You can find basic local eateries in the town centre beyond McDonald's, or try *Café Minutka* behind the Russky Dvorik.

Getting there
Around two trains per hour run to Sergiev Posad from suburban (*prigorodnie*, пригородние) platforms behind Moscow's Yaroslavsky station; take any train bound for Sergiev Posad or Aleksandrov. It's about US$2 return for the 95-minute trip. The slightly pricier 08:30 *Yaroslavl Express* also stops at Sergiev Posad, taking one hour. The monastery is a 20-minute walk from the station.

Rostov-Yaroslavski (Rostov-Veliki)
Ростов-Ярославский (Ростов-Великий)

Also known as **Rostov-Veliki**, this is one of the most attractive Golden Ring cities to visit. Although it's no longer on the main Trans-Siberian route, if you're travelling via Yaroslavl it's well worth stopping off here. It's 225km from Moscow and 60km from Yaroslavl.

Packed with interesting places, Rostov-Yaroslavski is a small city in a beautiful location beside scenic Lake Nero. It has a wonderfully sleepy atmosphere; and the added attraction of being able to stay right in the kremlin itself makes it worth a visit.

Founded in 862, Rostov-Yaroslavski played a major role in the formation of Russia and at one time was as big as the mighty capitals of Kiev and Novgorod. Yuri Dolgoruky, who founded Moscow in 1147, gave Rostov the honourable and rare title of *veliki,* meaning great. Rostov-Veliki soon became an independent principality.

Rebuilt after the Tatar-Mongol sacking, Rostov-Veliki continued to have political importance for two more centuries until the local prince sold the remainder of his hereditary domain to Moscow's Grand Prince Ivan III in 1474. The city remained an important ecclesiastical centre as it was the religious capital of northern Russia and home to the senior religious leader called the Metropolitan. In the 17th century, however, the Metropolitan was moved to the larger city of Yaroslavl. No longer called Rostov the Great, the city became known as Rostov-Yaroslavski, rapidly became a backwater and has remained one ever since.

CATHEDRAL OF THE ASSUMPTION

Much of Russia's lousy coffee originates here as Rostov-Yaroslavski boasts a factory for roasting chicory roots which are often substituted for or added to coffee beans.

WHAT TO SEE

Cathedral of the Assumption

The cathedral, just north of the kremlin, is a 16th-century, 60m-high, five-domed building with white stone friezes decorating the outside. The cathedral contains the tomb of the canonized Bishop Leontius who was martyred by Rostov's pagans in 1071 during his Christianity drive. The Metropolitan Ion is also buried here. The **bell-tower** contains superb examples of 17th-century Russian bells, the largest weighing 32 tons. There are 13 bells in all and they can be heard up to twenty kilometres away. They're rung at 13:00 on Saturday and Sunday. There are also occasional bell-ringing concerts.

The Rostov Kremlin

The white-walled Rostov Kremlin is one of the most photogenic in the country. It is spread over two hectares, has six churches and is ringed by 11 towers. The kremlin was founded in 1162 by Prince Andrei Bogolybusky, son of Yuri Dolgoruky; all traces of the original buildings disappeared in the 17th century when the kremlin was rebuilt.

Despite its mighty 12m high and 2m thick walls and towers, this reconstructed kremlin is actually an imitation fortress. All the elements of real fortifications are missing. The ambitious 17th-century Metropolitan, Ion Sisoyevich, wanted a residence to reflect his importance. After the 17th century when the Metropolitan was moved to nearby Yaroslavl, the kremlin became derelict. Today most of the buildings have been restored to their 16th- and 17th-century condition, though work still continues.

The central part of the kremlin contains five churches. The religious part of each church occupies only the 2nd floor as the ground floor was left for animal husbandry, storage and accommodation.

The kremlin grounds are always open as the gate on the eastern wall is never locked. The kremlin's **main entrance** is on its western side through the **St John the Divine Gateway Church** built in 1683, which has a richly decorated façade. The ticket office is in this building and charges US$3 for entrance to everywhere in the kremlin. The museums are normally open 10:00-17:00 and are staffed by the usual plethora of babushkas, each insisting on adding another tear to your disintegrating ticket.

The entrance to the kremlin's northern part from the central part is through the **Resurrection of Christ Gate Church** built in 1670. This church has a stone iconostasis instead of the traditional wooden one.

The **Transfiguration of the Saviour above the Cellars Church** is one of the gems of the kremlin as it was the private church of the Metropolitan. It is quite austere from the outside but its interior is lavish. This church is the tallest in the kremlin and has a single dome. The **White Chamber** next door was designed as a sumptuous dining hall; it now houses a museum for local Rostov crafts.

The **Church of the Virgin Hodegetria** was erected 20 years after the death of Metropolitan Ion and has a Moscow baroque interior. It now contains an exhibition of church vestments.

The building housing the **Prince's Chambers** is the oldest here, dating from the 16th century. It's claustrophobic with small dark passages, narrow doors and slit windows filled with slivers of mica. This is a good place to get an impression of the daily life of 16th-century Russian nobility.

The **Metropolitan's House** is now a museum and has a large collection of stone carvings, wooden sculptures, and 14th and 15th-century doors from local churches. The **Red Chamber**, built as a residence for visiting tsars and their large retinue, is now the hostel of the International Youth Tourism Centre.

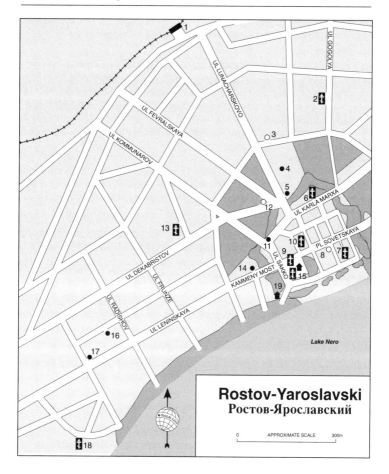

Rostov-Yaroslavski
Ростов-Ярославский

0   APPROXIMATE SCALE   300m

Other places of interest

In front of the eastern entrance of the kremlin is the **Saviour on the Market Place Church**. It was built in the late 1600s and is now a library. The name comes from the rows of shops and stalls around the church that have stood there for centuries.

Beside the church is the Arcade built in the 1830s and on the opposite side of the street is the Traders' Row.

The neoclassical **St Nicholas in the Field Church** on ul Gogola was built in 1813 and has recently been well restored. It has a golden iconostasis with finift enamel decorations and icons from the 15th to 19th centuries. This was

ROSTOV-YAROSLAVSKI – MAP KEY
 1 Railway and Bus Stop Железнодорожний Вокзал
 2 Church of St Nicholas (Nikola) in the Field Церковь Святого Николая
 3 Café Кафе
 4 Lenin statue Ленин
 5 Market Рынок
 6 Church of St Isidore the Blessed Церковь Вознесения
 7 Church of the Virgin Birth Церковь Рождества Богородицы
 8 Restaurant Slavyanskii Ресторан Славянский
 9 Cathedral of the Assumption Успенский Собор
10 Saviour on the Market Place Church Церковь Спаса на Торгу
11 Main Bus Station Автовокзал
12 Restaurant Teremok Ресторан Теремок
13 Church of the Tolg Virgin Церковь Толгской Богоматери
14 Metropolitan's Horse Stables Конный двор и Музей
15 Rostov Kremlin, Churches and Hotel Ростовский Кремль и Гостиница
16 Market Рынок
17 Kiosks Киоск
18 St Jacob Monastery Яковлевский Монастырь
19 Khors House of Art Хорс

one of two main churches in Rostov that conducted services during the communist era (the other was the **Church of the Tolg Virgin**).

The single-domed **Church of St Isidore the Blessed**, ul Karla Marxa, dates from the 16th century and was originally called Ascension Church. It is hidden partly by the old Kremlin walls and seems out of use.

In front of the kremlin's main gate on the western side, ul Kamenny Most, are the **Metropolitan's Horse Stables**. It was planned to demolish this nondescript two-storey building recently. After the plaster was knocked off the walls, however, it was discovered that the building was part of a 300-year-old complex which included stables, rooms for tack, sledges and carriages, and quarters for grooms, coachmen and watchmen.

It's worth walking the 1500m to the **St Jacob Monastery**. Although it seems almost deserted, it is still functioning and you might glimpse a monk walking silently between the buildings. There is a shop that stocks a wide range of icons in the main church and a courtyard of beautifully-scented flowers.

If you walk through an archway between houses on pl Sovetskaya into a courtyard you will come upon the **Church of the Virgin Birth**. It's a big church but out of use at the moment. The babushkas in the courtyard will tell you it's 'ne rabota', then rattle on for ages; you may not understand a word but it's well meant.

PRACTICAL INFORMATION
Services
There are two small **markets** in town. One just outside the old Kremlin walls on ul Belinskovo and the other on ul October where you can buy all sorts of things from fruit to a three-piece suite.

You can hire rowing boats at the **river station** near Khors House of Art.

Where to stay
One of the most appealing places to stay is in the **Rostov Kremlin (Dom)**. The former servants' quarters have been turned into a

basic hotel run by the International Tourist Centre (☎ 318 54). The rooms cost from US$9 with common bath. There are also some rooms with attached bath. The other interesting place to stay here is *Khors* (around US$10 per room) but it's usually reserved for visiting artists – see the box item on Finift, below – and there are only a couple of rooms.

Where to eat

The *café* near the Red Chamber and the Metropolitan's House inside the kremlin is good, both for meals and for snacks and cakes.

You can get a filling three-course meal at *Restaurant Teremok*. It looks pretty awful from the outside and not so much better inside but it's always busy, the food is good and it's absurdly cheap. Three

courses will cost less than US$2. Open 12:00-24:00.

The *Restaurant Slavansky* on pl Sovetskaya is much smarter, and recommended. There's a large restaurant and a dark bar. The salads are particularly good and three courses will cost around US$4; drinks are extra.

Getting there

Rostov is about 60km from Yaroslavl and there are trains and buses almost every hour. From Moscow, Rostov is five hours by train (US$3).

To get from the railway station to the kremlin and the main bus station, take bus No 6. To get from the main bus station to St Jacob Monastery, take bus Nos 1 or 2; for St Avraamy Monastery, take bus No 1.

🚂 Finift

Rostov-Yaroslavski's most famous handicraft is *finift* multi-coloured enamel work. This craft originated in Byzantium: the name derives from the Greek *fingitis* meaning colourful and shiny. Finift was used to decorate icons, sacred utensils and bible covers, as well as in portraits of people. The enamel's greatest advantages are that it cannot be damaged by water and does not fade with time.

The process of making the enamel is extremely complex and involves oxidizing various metals to produce different colours. Iron produces yellow, orange-red and brown, copper produces green and blue, tin produces a non-transparent white, and gold with tin produces a cold ruby red.

Finift has been produced here since the 12th century and the **Rostov Finift Factory** has been operating since the 18th century. While there are no regular tours, it's sometimes possible to organize one by contacting the factory's director (☎ 352 29). Far more accessible is the **Khors House of Art** (☎ 324 83, 🖳 enamel.by.ru), a small gallery between the kremlin and the lake, in the home of artist Mikhail Selishchev. He uses different materials such as wood, metal and stone in combination with enamel and it's an interesting place to visit. He also has a couple of rooms to rent but these are usually reserved for visiting artists.

Yaroslavl
Ярославль

Yaroslav's old central section and the tree-lined streets and squares make this one of the most attractive cities in Russia. In many ways, the buildings in this old section surpass those of Moscow as they have not suffered as much from the ravages of war and rapid industrialization. With most Trans-Siberian trains now going via Vladimir, however, Yaroslavl sees fewer Siberian-bound travellers than it used to. It's 260km from Moscow.

Yaroslavl is the Volga River's oldest city, founded in 1010 by Grand Prince Yaroslav the Wise. With the expansion of river trade from the 16th century, Yaroslavl became the second most populous city after Moscow. Until the opening of the Moscow-Volga River Canal in 1937, which gave Moscow direct access to the Volga, Yaroslavl was Moscow's main port.

WHAT TO SEE

Transfiguration of Our Saviour Monastery

This attractive white monastery was founded in the 12th century but the oldest building to be seen today dates from 1516 when the wooden walls were replaced with stone and brick. As it was considered impregnable, part of the tsar's treasury was stored here, protected by a garrison.

The **Transfiguration of Our Saviour Cathedral** occupies central place in the monastery. This three-domed cathedral was built in 1516 after the original building was destroyed in a fire in 1501 and is currently being renovated. Sixteenth-century frescoes include depictions of John the Baptist on the eastern wall, Christ Pantokrator on the cupola in the central dome, and the Last Judgement on the western wall.

The **Refectory** was built in the 16th century. On the second floor a single mighty pillar supports the vaults, creating a large open dining area. It's now a history museum. The Refectory Church became a natural history museum in the communist era but may now be restored.

Climb the **bell tower** for a panoramic view of the city. There are four flights of stairs, each getting narrower and you'll end up standing on the wooden roof. Directly above you is the main bell which was cast in 1738. The bell-tower's clock was installed in 1624 after being brought from the Saviour (Spassky) Tower in the Moscow Kremlin.

The **Monks' Cell Block** consists of four buildings and was built at the end of the 17th century. It now contains a large museum of Old Russia which includes icons, handicrafts, weapons, armour and books.

Entry into the grounds (open daily) is free; entry to each museum and exhibition (open 10:00-17:00 daily except Monday) costs US$0.70.

Around the monastery
This area is rich in churches and other historic buildings. Directly opposite the monastery on the Moscow Highway is the **Epiphany Church**. The five-domed church was completed in 1693 and has nine large windows which make the interior extraordinarily light. It is an excellent example of the Yaroslavl school of architecture with its glazed tiles and festive decorations. Most of the church has been restored save for the dangerously-leaning tower near the entrance. It's open 10:00-17:00, closed Tuesday.

THE EPIPHANY TOWER

The **House of Ivanov**, ul Chaikovskovo 4, is a typical two-storey residence of a well-to-do town dweller built at the end of the 17th century. The ground floor was used for storage and the sleeping and living rooms are upstairs.

The **Church of St Nicholas on the Waters**, ul Chaikovskovo 1, was built from 1665 to 1672 in red brick and has marvellous glazed bands around the altar windows. The five green onion-domes complement the red brick and make for an impressive sight. The white **Church of the Tikhvin Virgin** next door is a small church dwarfed by its neighbour but specially designed for winter worship as it can be heated. It has extensive glazed-tile work on its exterior.

Volga River Embankment
A stroll down the landscaped high right bank of the Volga River from the river station to the Metropolitan's Chambers is an enjoyable way of exploring this area. At the end of ul Pervomaiskaya is the **river station**: one section is for long-distance hydrofoils and, slightly downstream, there's another for local passenger ferries.

The tent-roofed **Nativity Church**, ul Kedrova 1, built over nine years starting in 1635 consists of two buildings and is famous as being the first church to use glazed tiles for external decoration. This practice was soon adopted everywhere and led to the development of the Yaroslavl Architecture style (see p194). The names of those involved in the building of the church have been inscribed on the tiles and if you look closely, you can still see them. Unfortunately, this church is in desperate need of restoration and much of the tilework is disappearing. Nearby is an interesting private gallery – **Mostoslavski's Music and Time** – a collection of timepieces and musical instruments. It's open daily except Monday and entry is $0.70.

St Nicholas-Nadeyina Church, per Narodny 2a, was funded by the wealthy merchant, Nadey Sveshnikov, hence its name. The Annunciation Chapel here was built for Nadey's private use so that he could pray in the company of only his closest friends. It has an interesting iconostasis framed in ornamental lead. The church is now a museum (entry US$0.40), open 1 May to 30 September, 10:00-17:00, closed Sunday and Monday.

The **Art Museum** is housed in the former governor's residence and it contains European works of art and furniture from the 15th to 19th century watched over by a friendly retired English teacher. Rooms of Russian art cover the 18th-20th centuries. You'll have to dodge around the art students practising there but a visit makes an interesting break from all the churches. Located at nab Volzhskaya 23, entry is US$1 and it's open 10:00-18:00, closed Friday.

The **Volga Tower**, also known as the Arsenal Tower, sits on the river bank at nab Volzhskaya 7. It is one of two towers which remain from the former Yaroslavl Kremlin. This citadel consisted of earth ramparts with wooden fortress walls and stone towers. This tower was finished in 1668 and is now a naval club.

The **Metropolitan's Chamber**, nab Volzhskaya 1, was built in the 1680s for the Metropolitan of the nearby city of Rostov-Yaroslavski. The two-storey building is now one of the country's richest museums of **old Russian Art**. While Yaroslavl's most revered icon, *The Sign of the Virgin*, painted in about 1218, now sits in Moscow's Tretyakov Gallery, the museum contains a number of other notable icons. Particularly interesting are the 13th and 14th centuries Mongolian icons. Entry is US$1, the museum is open 10:00-17:30, closed Monday.

Yaroslavl centre

The centre of the city is Soviet Square (pl Sovetskaya). On the east side of the square is the Church of St Elijah the Prophet and on the north side is a government office building of circa 1780.

The imposing **Church of St Elijah the Prophet** is well worth seeing for its superb 17th-century frescoes, still in excellent condition. The church was commissioned by one of the richest and most influential Russian merchant dynasties, the Shripins. It's open daily from 1 May to 30 September, from 10:00 to 18:00.

The **Vlasyevskaya Tower**, ul Pervomaiskaya 21, is the second of the two towers that remain from Yaroslavl's original kremlin. It's also known as the Sign (Znamenskaya) Tower and flower sellers gather underneath it everyday.

The **Volkov Drama Theatre**, pl Volkova, was built in 1911 and is named after Fedor Volkov (1729-1763) who is considered the founder of Russian national theatre. He inherited his stepfather's factories in Yaroslavl which enabled him to organize his own private theatre company before moving on to bigger and better things. Amongst his claims to fame was that he organized the first staging of *Hamlet* in Russia. The theatre is currently being restored and the finished parts look beautiful.

Although the Rostov Finift Enamel factory is based in the nearby city of Rostov-Yaroslavski, the **factory shop** is here at ul Kirova 13, next to the Hotel Volga. It has a great range of *finift* enamel gifts.

The **planetarium** is on ul Trefoleva and open 10:00-18:00. It is frequently used for teaching local school groups.

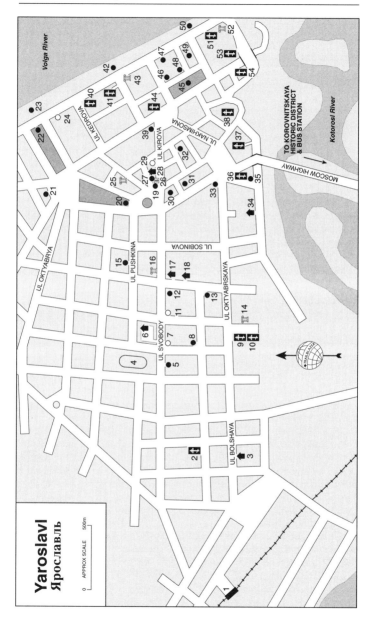

WHERE TO STAY AND EAT
3 Hotel Kotorosl Гостиница Которосль
6 Hotel Stariy Gorod Гостиница Старый Город
7 McDonald's Макдоналдс
11 Restaurant Vlasyevsky Ресторан Власьевский
17 Hotel Vest Гостиница Вест
18 Hotel Yuta Гостиница Юта
24 Café Lira Кафе Лира
28 Hotel Volga Гостиница Волга
29 Restaurant Rus Ресторан Русь
34 Hotel Yubileynaya Гостиница Юбилейная

OTHER
1 Yaroslavl Main Station Ярославль-Главный Вокзал
2 Church of Vladimir Mother of God
 Церковь Владимирской Богоматери
4 Stadium Стадион
5 Circus Цирк
9 Bell-tower of St Nicholas Колокольня Николы
9 Church of St Nicholas on the Waters
 Церковь Святого Николы
10 Church of Tikhvin Virgin Церковь Тихвинской Богоматери
12 Youth and Puppet Theatres Театры Юного Зрителя и Театр Кукол
13 Seminary Духовная Семинария
14 House of Ivanov Дом Иванова
15 Airlines Office Авиаагентство
16 House of Nikin Дом Никина
19 Book Store Дом Книги
20 Volkov's Theatre Драматический Театр имени Волкова
21 University Университет
22 Nekrasov Monument Памятник Некрасову
23 River Station Речной Вокзал

OTHER (cont)
25 Planetarium Планетарий
26 Sberbank Сбербанк
27 Philharmonic Hall Филармония
30 Vlasyevskaya Tower Власьевская Башня
31 Arcade Гостиный Двор
32 Market Рынок
33 Post Office Почтамт
35 Descent of Holy Spirit Consistorium Духовная Консистория
36 Epiphany Church Церковь Богоявления
37 Transfiguration of our Saviour Monastery
 Спасо-Преображенский Монастырь
38 Church of St Michael the Archangel Церковь Михаила-Архангелского
39 Government Offices Присутственные Места
40 Church of the Nativity Церковь Рождества Христова
41 Church of St Nicholas-Naden Церковь Цвятого Николы Надена
42 Provincial Governor's Rotunda-Pavilion Павильон
43 Art Museum Художественный Музей
44 Church of Elijah the Prophet Церковь Ильи Пророка
45 Chelyuskintsev Park Парк Челюскинцев
46 House of Matreev Дом Матреева
47 Physicians Society House Дом Врачей
48 House of the Vakhrameevs Дом Вахрамеевых
49 Medical Institute Медицинский Институт
50 Volga Tower Волжская Башня
51 Church of Patriarch Tikhon Церковь Патриарха Тихона
52 Metropolitan's Chamber Метрополита Палаты
53 Church of St Nicholas in Log Town Церковь Святого Николы
54 Church of Saviour in the Town Церковь Спаса

❏ **Yaroslavl style**
The Yaroslavl school of architecture dates from the second half of the 16th century and is epitomized by tall, pointed tent roofs, free standing bell-towers, large airy churches with side chapels, external glazed tiles, and large interior frescoes and mosaics. Yaroslavl has many buildings in this style as its evolution coincided with a massive reconstruction drive after the great fire in 1658. The city had developed a rich merchant class which commissioned churches to its own taste. As this style also appealed to hereditary nobles and peasants, it became widespread throughout Russia, much to the chagrin of the conservative clergy.

Korovnitskaya Sloboda Historic District
Korovnitskaya Sloboda, which means 'cattle breeding settlement on the outskirts of town', sits on the right bank of the Kotorosl River as it flows into the Volga River.

The district's focal point is the **Church of St John Chrysostom**, nab Portovaya 2, which was built from 1649 to 1654. It has four domes and two tent-shaped side chapels which makes it appealingly symmetrical. As it was built at the height of the decorative arts in Yaroslavl, its ornamentation is very elaborate. The **Church of Vladimir Mother of God**, surrounded by apartment blocks is very similar in style but significantly smaller. It's in a very poor state now and seems closed.

The most obvious building in this historic area is the pointed 37m-high **bell-tower** which carries the nickname of the Candle of Yaroslavl. There isn't much left of it except the brickwork now.

Church of St John the Baptist
In the Tolchkovski district, once famous for its leather work, this impressive 15-domed church (1671-87) is considered the architectural pinnacle of Yaroslavl. From a distance it looks as if it is trimmed in lace and carved of wood but this deception is created by carved and patterned bricks. It consists of two side chapels, unusual in that they are practically as tall as the church and each is crowned with five domes. Inside is a mass of frescoes – reputedly more than in any other church in Russia. The church is open daily 10:00-18:00 except Tuesday.

You can see this church from the train as you cross over the Kotorosl River.

PRACTICAL INFORMATION
Orientation and services

There are two railway stations. **Yaroslavl-Glavny** (*Yaroslavl-Main*) is on the north side of the Kotorosl River and **Yaroslavl-Moskovski** is on the south side. All trains to Yaroslavl go through Yaroslavl-Glavny while only those trains travelling along the east and west line (such as from Ivanovo and St Petersburg) go through Yaroslavl-Moskovski.

To get from the station to pl Volkova (for Hotel Yaroslavl), catch trolley-bus No 1. From the station to Hotel Kotorosl, take tram No 3.

Aeroflot is at ul Svobody 20. The airport is to the north and its closest railway station is Molot (Мотол) on the line to St Petersburg. Bus No 140 from pl Sovetskaya runs to the airport.

You can change money and travellers' cheques at **Sberbank** which is on the pedestrianized section of ul Kirova.

In the summer there are various **river trips** leaving from the river station. Tolga, 30 minutes along the Konstantinovo route, is worth visiting.

Where to stay

Hotel Yuta (☎ 218 793), ul Respublikanskaya 79, looks newish but the rooms are fast becoming tatty. A single with attached bathroom costs US$18; there are doubles for US$25. The *Hotel Volga* (☎ 229 131), ul Kirova 10, formerly known as the Bristol Hotel, is in a fine location. It's US$18 for a double with shared bath. Rooms with attached bath cost US$22/32 for a single/double.

Hotel Kotorosl (☎ 212 415), ul Bolshaya Oktyabrskaya 87, is a good choice although it is 2km from the centre. They charge from US$17 for a single and from US$25 for a double.

Hotel Stariy Gorod (☎ 320 488/321 327), ul Svobody 46, is a curious place tucked away at the back of a courtyard –

see map (p192). It's very quiet and is run by a friendly and helpful woman. It costs US$24 for a single, US$30 for a double. Rooms have bathroom attached.

Currently the best option is the *Hotel Yubileynaya* (☎ 726 565, 730 704, 🖃/☎ 726 565, 🖳 www.yubil.yar.ru), nab Kotoroslennaya 11A. It's US$46/68 for a single/double room with attached bath if you book in advance but you should be able to get a better deal if you simply turn up. There's a health club, business centre and views over the river.

Where to eat

McDonald's is very popular. You can't miss the giant M emblem erected with the company's usual sensitivity not far from the war memorial. There are several other cheap places to eat nearby along ul Svobody.

The upmarket *Restaurant Rus* is at the end of the pedestrianized section of ul Kirova and serves traditional Russian food. It's probably the best that Yaroslavl currently has to offer. There's a much cheaper version, *Café Rus*, on the ground floor, that's recommended.

Restaurant Vlasevski is a good place on the corner of ul Svobody and ul Tchaikovskogo. Downstairs is a café and upstairs is the restaurant serving a variety of dishes for around US$4. The food is tasty and the portions are generous. Other places to eat are *Restaurant Staroe Mesto*, and *Restaurant Volga* at the River Station.

Moving on

There are about 10 trains a day to Moscow (US$3, five hours).

The bus station is about 2km south of the city. There are buses to many destinations including about six buses a day to Rostov-Yaroslavski (US$1, 90 minutes).

In the summer from the river station it's possible to get a boat along the Volga to Moscow. The trip takes 40 hours.

The Yaroslavl area code is ☎ 0852. From outside Russia dial +7-852.

Vladimir
Владимир

Vladimir is a rewarding place to visit as part of a day trip or an extensive Golden Ring tour from Moscow, or even as a Trans-Siberian stopover. To enjoy Vladimir plus nearby Suzdal, Bogolyubovo and the lovely Church of the Intercession on the Nerl you'd need to spend two nights here.

HISTORY

Vladimir was officially founded in 1108, although there was a village here as early as 500BC. During the great migration of Slavs from the disintegrating Kievian Rus empire in the late 10th and early 11th centuries the Vladimir region was settled and its ancient inhabitants evicted.

In 1108 Grand Prince Vladimir Monomakh of Kiev, after whom the town is named, built a fortress here to protect his eastern lands. Vladimir's grandson, Andrei Bogolyubsky, stormed and pillaged Kiev in 1157 and took its master craftsmen away to build a new Russian capital at Vladimir. By the time of

CATHEDRAL OF ST DEMETRIUS OF SALONICA

Andrei's murder at Bogolyubovo in 1174, Vladimir surpassed Kiev in grandeur and had become the centre of a powerful principality. Unfortunately Andrei's brother and successor, Vsevolod III, was unable to hold the principality together and it was soon divided amongst family members.

Despite its defeat by Tatar-Mongols in 1238 the town remained the political centre of north-eastern Russia. It became the religious centre of the entire country in 1300 when the seat of the Metropolitan of All Rus was moved here from Kiev, but this power too disappeared when the seat was shifted to Moscow 20 years later. Vladimir's glory came to an end in 1392 with its absorption into the Moscow Principality. It rapidly became a backwater and by 1668 its population numbered just 990.

Vladimir slowly recovered from this low point (its current population is about 350,000) but it played no role in the revolutionary turmoil at the turn of the 20th century. During the early years of communism, central planners decided that Vladimir should become an industrial centre, and some 50 factories were built, including the big Vladimir tractor factory and the Avtopribor automotive engineering plant.

WHAT TO SEE

Almost everything of interest in Vladimir lies along the main road, known variously from west to east as pr Lenina, ul Pushkina, Moskovskaya ul, ul 3-ya Internatsionala and ul Frunze.

The Golden Gates

Vladimir was once ringed by several kilometres of earth ramparts topped with oaken walls. Traditionally a city *kremlin* consisted of a small, heavily fortified citadel with an unprotected settlement beyond its walls. With a defensive wall around the entire city, the town's population swelled as settlers arrived seeking security.

The only surviving remnants of these defences are the so-called Golden Gates. Built by Andrei Bogolyubsky in 1158, they were modelled on those of Kiev, which in turn were based on the Golden Gates of Constantinople. To further emphasize Vladimir's inherited majesty, the heavy oaken outer doors were covered in gilded copper. Adorning the gates is a copy of the Byzantine icon of Our Lady of Vladimir (the original went to Moscow when the Metropolitan's seat was moved there in 1320). In 1785 two ornamental towers were added as buttresses, and most earth ramparts removed to make way for increased traffic.

Above the gates is the golden-domed Gate-Church of the Deposition of the Robe. This now serves as a **Military Exposition**, centred on a diorama of the storming of Vladimir by the Tatar-Mongols. It's open 10:00-17:00, closed Monday and Tuesday; entry is US$1. Remnants of the earthen walls can be seen beside the gates.

In front of the gates is the **Museum of Crystal**, **Lacquer Miniatures and Embroidery**, Moskovskaya ul 2. The red-brick building was formerly the Old Believers' Trinity Church, built in 1913. Entry is US$1.

Just to the south of the gates is the **Exhibition of Old Vladimir**, housed in a 19th-century water tower on val Kozlov; it's open 10:00-17:00 daily except Monday. On the top floor is an observation deck offering panoramic views of Vladimir.

Assumption Cathedral

The city is justifiably proud of its cathedral, built by Andrei Bogolyubsky in 1160 to rival Kiev's St Sophia Cathedral. At the time this was the tallest building in all of Russia. Following a fire in 1185 it was enlarged to hold 4000 worshippers. All of Russia's rulers from Andrei Bogolyubsky to Ivan III (the Great) were crowned here. This served in turn as the 15th-century model for its namesake in Moscow's kremlin.

The cathedral's 25m-high iconostasis contains 100 icons. These once included works by Andrei Rublyov, now held in Moscow's Tretyakov Gallery and St Petersburg's Russian Museum. But Rublyov's work can still be seen in the form of frescoes done in 1408.

The cathedral is normally open to (appropriately dressed) tourists from 13:30-16:30 only and there's a charge of US$1. Adjacent to the cathedral are the

Chapel of St George, a 'winter church' (meaning it could be heated) built in 1862, and a three-storey **bell tower** built in 1810 after the original tent-roofed tower was destroyed by lightning.

Cathedral of St Demetrius of Salonica

The unusual, single-domed, square Cathedral of St Demetrius of Salonica was completed in 1197 as Vsevolod III's court church. It is built from white lime-stone blocks and its exterior walls have over 1300 bas-relief carvings showing a range of people, events, animals and plants. The cathedral is managed by the nearby History Museum, whose staff may open it up if asked – but it's the exterior that's of real interest.

Other attractions

The **House of Officers**, ul Bolshaya Moskovskaya 33, formerly the Noblemen's Assembly Club, was built in 1826. The building, opposite the Assumption Cathedral, played an interesting role in the anti-religion campaign of the 1970s and 1980s. Every time a major service was held in the cathedral, loudspeakers in the House of Officers blared out (rarely-heard) Western rock music. The decision to use decadent music to destroy insidious religion must have been full of anguish for the local Soviet leadership.

The **Monument to the 850th Anniversary of Vladimir**, unveiled in 1958, symbolizes, with its bronze figures of an architect, a soldier and a worker, the communist theory that ordinary people are the makers of history.

The **Traders' Row Arcade**, completed in 1792, is being renovated into a retailing district and many of the shops are now open again.

The **Vladimir Museum of History**, ul Bolshaya Moskovskaya 43, contains archaeological finds, coins, weapons and rare books. Its most interesting exhibits are the so-called Vladimir Mother of God icon, attributed to Andrei Rublyov, and the white stone sarcophagus of the great Russian hero Alexander Nevsky. The museum is open 10:00-16:00, closed Monday. Entry is US$1.

The **Nativity Monastery**, ul Bolshaya Moskovskaya 33, was completed in 1196 and was the city's most important monastery until the end of the 16th century. Alexander Nevsky was buried here in 1262, until Peter the Great had him reinterred in St Petersburg in 1724.

The **Frunze Monument** honours communist hero Mikhail Frunze, who carried out revolutionary work in this region. Just 300m away is the maximum-security prison where Frunze was imprisoned in 1907. The walls around this part of the city followed the Lybed River which now flows through large pipes under the road. The **Princess' Convent** is Vladimir's third-oldest building and the first one erected after the town was sacked by the Tatar-Mongols. The monastery was founded in 1220 by Maria Shvarnovna, wife of Vsevolod III. The monastery cathedral was made into a museum of atheism in Soviet times but has now been reconsecrated.

The Vladimir area code is ☎ 09222. From outside Russia dial +7-09222.

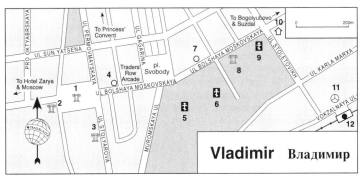

WHERE TO STAY AND EAT
4 Restaurant Zolotye Vorota
  Ресторан Золотое Ворота
7 Cafés Кафе/Столовая
10 Hotel Vladimir Гостиница Владимир

OTHER
1 Golden Gates Золотое Ворота
2 Museum of Crystal Хрусталя Музей
3 Exhibition of Old Vladimir
  Выставка Старого Владимира

5 Assumption Cathedral
  Успенский Собор
6 Cathedral of St Demetrius of Salonica
  Дмитриевский Собор
8 Vladimir Museum of History
  Исторический Музей
9 Nativity Monastery Рождества
  Монастырь
11 Bus Station Автовокзал
12 Railway Station Вокзал

EXCURSIONS FROM VLADIMIR

Bogolyubovo (Боголюбово)
Ten kilometres from Vladimir, this ancient town was the site of the royal palace of Prince Andrei Bogolyubsky, who developed Vladimir into the capital of Rus. He chose this site rather than Vladimir because of its strategic position at the junction of the Klyazma River, which runs through Vladimir, and the Nerl River, which runs through the rival city of Suzdal.

This quickly became Vladimir's real power centre, but following Andrei's murder here in 1174, the whole lot was turned over to the Bogolyubovo Monastery. Andrei's assassins, powerful *boyars* from Suzdal, wounded him in his bed chamber before stabbing him to death on a staircase.

Today only one tower and a covered archway date from Andrei's time, the rest from 19th-century renovations. Major buildings still standing include the Holy Gates, a bell tower from 1841 and the huge five-domed Bogolyubovo Cathedral of the Icon of the Mother of God, built in 1866. The cathedral, slowly being renovated, is open for services.

Getting there To get to Bogolyubovo, take a suburban train from Vladimir. There are 13 suburban trains a day to Bogolyubovo and the trip takes 14 minutes. The station is about 400m from the walled Bogolyubovo Monastery. You can also catch one of the numerous buses from Vladimir's central bus station, opposite the railway station, to Bogolyubovo.

The Church of the Intercession on the Nerl

About 1.5km east of Bogolyubovo, alone in a field at the junction of the Nerl and Klyazma rivers, is one of Russia's loveliest churches, the simple, white stone Church of the Intercession on the Nerl.

It was built in a single summer in 1165 on the orders of Andrei Bogolyubsky, for a number of symbolic reasons. Rising like an apparition beside a tributary of Russia's major trading waterway, the Volga, it would be visible to all official visitors. As if to emphasize Vladimir's power and independence, it was consecrated to the Intercession of the Virgin on a holiday declared by Andrei without the permission of the patriarchs of Byzantium or Kiev. Legend also says that Andrei dedicated it to the memory of his son, killed in battle against the Volga Bulgars.

The church is open 10:00-16:00 during the summer, closed Monday. But go even if it's closed, for it's the outside of the church which is most appealing.

Getting there There are no roads to the church so you must walk the 1.5km from Bogolyubovo, most quickly from Bogolyubovo railway station. Cross the tracks and follow any of the paths through the adjacent woods into the open field beyond. The church is off to your left, a 20-minute walk from the station. During the spring thaw, floodwaters cut it off from the path.

PRACTICAL INFORMATION
Orientation and services
The long-distance **bus station** and the **railway station** are opposite one another. Trolleybus No 5 starts at the railway station and travels east then north until trolleybus runs westward along the main street. Bus No 14 also travels along the main road but does not go to the station.

There's an **internet café** opposite the Vladimir Museum of History, ul Bolshaya Moskovskaya.

Where to stay and eat
The closest hotel to the station is the *Hotel Vladimir* (☎ 323041), ul Bolshaya Moskovskaya 74. Rooms cost US$7/12 for a single/double with common bathroom. There are also some rooms from US$20 with bath attached. From the station, you can reach the hotel more quickly on foot than you can by catching trolleybus No 5 which does a big loop from the station

before passing the hotel. If you can't get into the Vladimir you could try *Hotel Zarya* (☎ 325219), ul Pushkina 36 (trolleybus No 5 stops directly in front of it), or *Hotel Klyazma*, (☎ 324237), shosse Sudogorodskoye 15, both more expensive and less appealing than Hotel Vladimir.

There are numerous places to eat along ul Bolshaya Moskovskaya including two *cafés* 200m east of pl Svobodny. The long-running *Zolotye Vorota* (Golden Gate), ul Bolshaya Moskovskaya 13-15, is a smart place.

Moving on
Vladimir is 180km from Moscow. There are rail services from Yaroslavl and Kursk stations in Moscow: the quickest services being the early morning and early evening departures from Kursk station (US$3.50; 2 hours, 35 minutes).

There are numerous buses to Suzdal (US$0.40; 1 hour).

Suzdal
Суздаль

Suzdal is well worth seeing. It must hold the record for the largest number of churches per capita in Russia: incredibly, at one time there was a church for every 12 of its citizens, along with 15 monasteries (more than any other Russian city except Moscow) and over 100 major architectural monuments, all in the space of just eight square kilometres.

Even today over 40 old religious buildings survive in Suzdal. The explanation for this is that in medieval times just about every street in every town had its own small, invariably wooden, church. This tradition was effectively sustained as a result of Suzdal's shrinking population, even as it was forgotten elsewhere, and taken a step further with the gradual replacement of wooden churches with durable stone ones.

Two other historical events contributed to this unprecedented degree of historical preservation. In 1788 a new town plan limiting building heights to two storeys forced urban growth outwards instead of upwards, leaving many older, central buildings still standing instead of bring replaced. And in 1862 the railway from Moscow to Nizhny Novgorod bypassed Suzdal by 30km, reducing the town to an underdeveloped backwater until its renaissance, in the last years of the communist era – as a tourist attraction.

HISTORY

The first recorded mention of Suzdal was in 1024 when many townsfolk were put to the sword by the local prince after a peasant rebellion. By the end of that century the town's first major fortification had been built and in 1152 Yuri Dolgoruky, son of Prince Vladimir Monomakh, transferred the seat of princely power here. Within a few years Suzdal had more people than London at that time.

Despite the shift of power by Dolgoruky's son, Andrei Bogolyubsky, to Vladimir, Suzdal continued to grow until 1238, when it was devastated by the Tatar-Mongols. The town tried to rebuild itself as a trading and political centre but its dreams were shattered after another rebellion was put down by Moscow in the mid-15th century. Although most of its people eventually moved elsewhere, Suzdal remained a strong religious centre. At one point there were seven churches and cathedrals in the kremlin, 14 within the city ramparts and 27 more scattered around various local monasteries.

In 1573 the town had just 400 households, and disasters over the next few centuries ensured that the number didn't rise much. Between 1608 and 1610 the town was raided several times by Polish and Lithuanian forces; in 1634 it was devastated by Crimean Tatars; in 1644 most of its wooden buildings were burnt down; in 1654 the plague wiped out almost half the population; and in a huge fire in 1719 every remaining wooden building in the centre was destroyed.

WHAT TO SEE

Kremlin
The Suzdal kremlin of the 11th century was ringed by 1400m of earth embankments topped with log walls and towers. These fortifications survived until the 18th century but the only sections left today are the small earth walls dotted around the city.

The enormous **Cathedral of the Birth of the Mother of God**, its five blue onion domes dotted with golden stars, is the most striking building within the kremlin. It was begun in 1222 and completed in just two years; the upper tier was rebuilt in 1530. It's currently undergoing restoration and may be closed. The octagonal **bell tower**, added in 1635, was once fitted with bells that chimed not only hourly but on the minute.

Attached to the bell tower by a gallery is the 15th-18th century **Archbishop's Chambers**, which now houses the **Suzdal History and Art Museum**. This and the Cross Chamber, a vast ceremonial reception hall on the 1st floor, are open 10.00-17.00, closed Tuesday. Entry is US$1.

Also within the old walls are two **churches** dedicated to St Nicholas: a stone one to the south-east, completed in 1739 and considered one of Suzdal's finest 18th-century buildings, and a wooden one to the south-west, brought here from the nearby village of Glotovo.

Trading Square (Torgovaya ploshchad)
On one side of the Trading Square (Torgovaya ploshchad) is a traders' arcade built at the turn of the 19th century, now containing tourist shops, bars and restaurants. Originally there was a second arcade facing the Kamenka River. Nearby are several more 18th-century churches, including the **Church of the Resurrection**, now with an exhibition of 17th- to 19th-century peasant wood carving.

Museum of Wooden Architecture
This museum near the kremlin was opened in 1960 to preserve examples of vanishing regional wooden architecture, including churches, peasant houses, windmills, barns and granaries. Among the most striking buildings are the **Church of the Transfiguration**, erected in 1756 at the ancient Monastery of St Demetrius in the village of Kozlyatevo, and the **Church of the Resurrection**, built in 1776 in Potakino village. A two-family **peasant house**, carved with the date 1862, came from the village of Kamenevo. This and other buildings are fitted out with a display of period clothes, hand looms, kitchen utensils and agricultural equipment. You can visit the site 09:30-16:30 (closed Tuesday) year-round, although most interiors are only open from May to September. Entry is US$1.

Nearby is the 18th-century **Church of SS Boris and Gleb**, the only church in Suzdal with any baroque features.

Convent of the Intercession

This convent offers an insight into the patriarchal nature of traditional Russian society. Euphemistically referred to as a retreat for high-spirited women, it was in fact a place of banishment for infertile wives, victims of dynastic squabbles and women who broke any of the harsh customs of medieval society.

First to use it in this way, in 1525, was Moscow's Grand Prince Vasily, whose wife Solomonia Saburova bore him no heirs. Solomonia, whose revenge was to outlive Vasily and his second wife, is buried in the **Intercession Cathedral**, completed in 1518. Other famous women discarded here were Praskovya Solovaya, second wife of Ivan the Great; Anna Vasilchikova, Ivan the Terrible's fourth wife; and Evdokya Lopukhina, Peter the Great's first wife.

The three-domed **Gateway Church of the Annunciation** sits above the Holy Gates. The two-storey **Refectory Church of the Conception of St Anna** was built in 1551 on the orders of Ivan the Great. By the convent's south-western wall, in the 17th-century Administrative Office, is a **Museum of the Convent's History** including an exhibition of 19th- and early 20th-century linen embroidery and a re-creation of the furnished cells of a nun and the novice who attended her. The museum is open 10:00-17:00, closed Tuesday.

Near the convent is the five-domed **Church of SS Peter and Paul**, built in 1694. Evdokia Lopukhina, banished to the convent by Peter the Great, founded a small side-chapel here in honour of her son Aleksei, murdered on Peter's orders. Beside the church is the single-domed winter **Church of St Nicholas**.

Monastery of the Saviour and St Euthimius

This fortified monastery was founded in the mid-14th century to protect Suzdal's northern approaches, although the present fortifications – a 12km-long stone wall reinforced with 12 towers – date from three centuries later. The monastery is home to five museums, all open 10:00-17:00, closed Monday. Entry is US$3.

You enter the monastery via a 22m-high tower gate and beneath the **Gate-Church of the Annunciation**. In the church is an exhibition on a local prince, Dmitry Pozharsky, who with Kuzma Minin, a village elder in Nizhny Novgorod, raised the volunteer army which liberated Moscow from Polish-Lithuanian forces in 1612 (Pozharsky and Minin are immortalized in a statue in front of St Basil's Cathedral in Moscow).

Pozharsky's grave is by the eastern wall of the **Cathedral of the Transfiguration of the Saviour**. The 17th-century frescoes here are particularly impressive. At 10.15 most mornings a choir gives a short recital in the cathedral and this is followed by the ringing of the bells. In a side chapel is the grave of St Euthimius, who founded the monastery in 1352.

Adjoining the 16th-century **Church of the Assumption** is the Father Superior chambers, with a **Museum of Six Centuries of Books**. Beside the 17th-century Church of St Nicholas is the **Infirmary**, where a museum called the **Golden Treasury** features Russian decorative art of the 13th-20th centuries.

The long, single-storey building nearby was the monastery **prison**, used until 1905 for those who had committed crimes against the faith. Now it's become the **Convicts of the Monastery Prison Museum**. The **Monks' Cells** now contain the weird and wonderful **Folk Art Museum of Russian Amateurs**, with everything from boxes made of carved bone to pictures made with coloured rice.

Monastery of the Deposition of the Robe

Founded in 1207, this is Suzdal's oldest monastery, although only a few of its original buildings remain: the asymmetrical, double-arched **Holy Gates** (1688), topped with tiny onion domes; the plain **Cathedral of the Deposition of the Robe**, dating from the first half of the 16th century; and a 72m-high **bell tower** visible from all over town and thought to have been erected in honour of Napoleon's defeat in 1812. There is an observation deck on its upper floor.

Convent of St Alexander Nevsky

The original convent is thought to have been founded in 1240 by Alexander Nevsky for the wives of noblemen killed in the Tatar-Mongol invasion. It was closed in 1764 and little remains of its original buildings except the white **Church of the Ascension**, built in 1694 and funded by Peter the Great's mother, Natalia Naryshkina. Today the convent serves as a research and education centre for restoration techniques.

Kideksha

About 4km east of Suzdal in the village of Kideksha (Кидекша) is the 12th-century former royal estate of Yuri Dolgoruky, who founded Moscow and made Suzdal the capital of his principality. The original estate included a wooden fortress and watch tower, and a white stone church. Only the church remains, renovated beyond recognition.

Today the estate's main draw is the charming **Church of SS Boris and Gleb**, built in 1152 and restored in the 17th century, and one of the two oldest buildings in north-east Russia (the other is the cathedral in the Golden Ring city of Pereslavl-Zalesski). Inside are traces of 12th-century frescoes. The church is now a museum, open 10:00-17:00, closed Tuesday. Other attractions include the winter **Church of St Stephen** (1780) and the **Holy Gates**.

To get to Kideksha you can either walk or catch a bus for Kameshkovo (Камешково) from Suzdal's long-distance bus station.

The Suzdal area code is ☎ 09231. From outside Russia dial +7-9231.

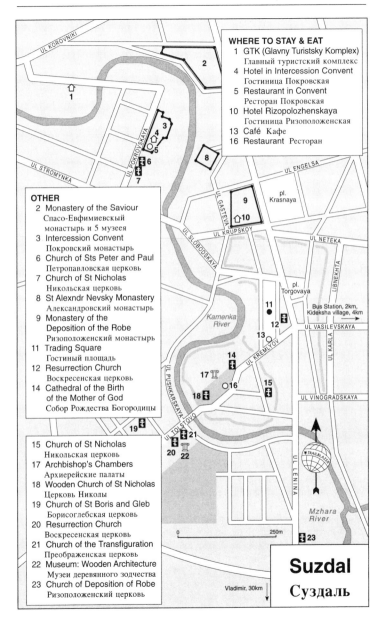

WHERE TO STAY & EAT

1 GTK (Glavny Turistsky Komplex)
  Главный туристский комплекс
4 Hotel in Intercession Convent
  Гостиница Покровская
5 Restaurant in Convent
  Ресторан Покровская
10 Hotel Rizopolozhenskaya
  Гостиница Ризоположенская
13 Café Кафе
16 Restaurant Ресторан

OTHER

2 Monastery of the Saviour
  Спасо-Евфимиевский
  монастырь и 5 музеев
3 Intercession Convent
  Покровский монастырь
6 Church of Sts Peter and Paul
  Петропавловская церковь
7 Church of St Nicholas
  Никольская церковь
8 St Alexndr Nevsky Monastery
  Александровский монастырь
9 Monastery of the
  Deposition of the Robe
  Ризоположенский монастырь
11 Trading Square
  Гостиный площадь
12 Resurrection Church
  Воскресенская церковь
14 Cathedral of the Birth
  of the Mother of God
  Собор Рождества Богородицы

15 Church of St Nicholas
  Никольская церковь
17 Archbishop's Chambers
  Архиерейские палаты
18 Wooden Church of St Nicholas
  Церковь Николы
19 Church of St Boris and Gleb
  Борисоглебская церковь
20 Resurrection Church
  Воскресенская церковь
21 Church of the Transfiguration
  Преображенская церковь
22 Museum: Wooden Architecture
  Музеи деревянного зодчества
23 Church of Deposition of Robe
  Ризоположенский церковь

Bus Station, 2km,
Kideksha village, 4km

Kamenka River

Mzhara River

Vladimir, 30km

Suzdal
Суздаль

0   250m

PRACTICAL INFORMATION
Orientation and services
Virtually everything to see is within walk-ing distance of the centre of town with the exception of Yuri Dolgoruky's estate at Kideksha.

Where to stay and eat
Most visitors stay at the large sprawling *GTK – Glavny Turistsky Komplex* (Main Tourist Complex, ☎ 20889 or 20908, 🖹 20666) on the north-western outskirts of the town.

This complex was built in 1976 with beds for 430 people. Spread out along a bend in the River Kamenka, it is just 350m from the nearest monastery. By road it's about 1.5km from Suzdal's main street but, by a footbridge over the river, it's only 500m away. The complex includes a motel, concert hall, cinema, sauna and swimming pool. Rooms cost US$16/20 for a single/double. There is a *restaurant* and canteen here.

There are 30 rooms in wooden *cabins* at the Intercession Convent. A double room costs US$50. The cabins are currently run by GTK (above) but there's a chance that they may close as the convent has been handed back to the church.

There is an excellent *restaurant* in the refectory church. There are also several *cafés* in the Traders' Arcade.

The best place to stay is *Likhoninsky Dom* (☎ 21901), ul Slobodskaya 34, which provides bed and breakfast for US$15/22 per person. The building is a renovated 17th-century house. It has only a few rooms so booking is advisable.

If everywhere else is full try *Hotel Rizopolozhenskaya* (☎ 214 08) in the Monastery of the Deposition. Double rooms cost US$9.

Moving on
Suzdal is not on any railway but it is easy to get to by bus from Vladimir which is 35km away. Buses leave every hour from Vladimir's central bus station opposite the railway station.

Suzdal's long-distance bus station is just under 2km east of the centre of the town and local bus No 3 runs from the bus station through the town to the Main Tourist Complex.

Nizhny Novgorod
Нижний Новгород

Nizhny Novgorod was founded in 1221 by Prince Vladimir Monomakh at the junction of the Oka and Volga Rivers. This strategic location on two central shipping routes virtually guaranteed its growth and prosperity, and its impor-tance as a major trading centre was consolidated with the opening in 1817 of the Nizhny Novgorod Fair. By the 1870s this fair had a turnover of some 300 mil-lion gold roubles. To put this into perspective, the entire Trans-Siberian railway cost about 1000 million roubles to build.

In the 1930s Nizhny Novgorod was turned into a major Soviet military-industrial centre, closed to foreigners and renamed Gorky, after the Russian novelist and playwright Maxim Gorky (1868-1936), who was born here. In the 1980s it was best known outside the USSR as a place of internal exile for dis-sidents, most famously the nuclear physicist and Nobel Peace Prize winner Andrei Sakharov.

Following the collapse of communism the city was in 1991 reopened and given back its old name, and its fair was reborn in the fabulously renovated 1800s Empire-style Fair Building. Nizhny Novgorod's history and its attractive old centre have turned it into a major tourist destination. The city (population about 1.9 million, fourth largest in Russia after Moscow, St Petersburg and Novosibirsk) is still listed as Gorky in many railway timetables.

WHAT TO SEE

Kremlin
The well-preserved kremlin, with its 12 impressive towers, sits on a hill dominating the area. There are good views from here. Inside are the City Hall, the **Cathedral of the Archangel Michael**, and the **Fine Arts Museum** (open 10:00-17:00, closed Tuesday; entry US$1.50) in the former Governor's House, featuring icons and paintings by Russian masters.

Old Nizhny Novgorod
The old town has two interesting pedestrian-only streets. One-km-long **ul Bolshaya Pokrovskaya** runs from pl Gorkogo to pl Minina i Pozharskogo (in front of the kremlin), past one of the city's biggest food markets, the Drama Theatre, the impressive art nouveau State Bank building and the Duma parliamentary building. Typical of Russian cobbled streets of the late 18th century is **Rozhdestvenskaya ul**, whose most appealing section is from the river station to the northern gate of the kremlin.

The **Ostrog** is where prisoners exiled to Siberia were kept overnight on their forced march to the east. Its most famous prisoner was the USSR's first prime minister, Mikhail Sverdlov. The building, later a science library, is expected to reopen as a museum.

Museums
Maxim Gorky, born here in 1868, wrote of the cruelty and injustice of rural Tsarist Russia, making his books compulsory reading for Soviet children. Gorky historical sites include his **birthplace** on Kovalikhinskaya ul (open 10:00-17:00, closed Wednesday); **Domik Kashirin**, his grandfather's house on Pochtovy sezd, where he and his mother moved in 1870; and the **Gorky Apartment-Museum** (open 09:00-17:00, closed Monday and Thursday), in the house at ul Semashko 19 where he lived from 1902-04. Every Sunday at 15:00 there is a reading of Gorky's works at the Apartment-Museum.

The dissident nuclear physicist Andrei Sakharov was exiled to Gorky from January 1981 to December 1986. His old flat at pr Gagarina 214 has been turned into the **Andrei Sakharov Apartment-Museum** (open 10:00-17:30, closed

STS PETER & PAUL CHURCH

The Nizhny Novgorod area code is ☎ 8312. From outside Russia dial +7-8312

Friday; entry US$0.50). The hour-long tour (US$1) is highly recommended.

Another famous regional son is air pioneer Valery Chkalov, famous for circumnavigating the USSR in June 1936 and flying non-stop from Moscow via the North Pole to Vancouver in June 1937. In a hangar at the **Chkalov Museum**, ul Chkalova 5 (open 10:00-17:00, closed Monday), are several well-preserved planes, including the ANT-25 Chkalov flew to North America. Chkalov's **statue** stands by the Alexandrovsky Gardens.

The best place to appreciate regional arts and crafts is the **Arts Museum**, with exhibits on *khokhloma* lacquered-wood articles, hand-painted Gorodets toys, filigree jewellery and feather-light Balakhna lace. The museum, at naberezhnaya Verkhne-Volzhskaya 3, is open 10:00-17:00, closed Friday.

The **Museum of Architecture** (open 10:00-16:00, closed Friday) is set in the park area known as Shcholokovsky Khutor, south-east of the centre and on bus route No 28. There's an interesting collection of old wooden buildings including an Old Believers' Church.

Other specialist museums, all open 10:00-16:00 weekdays, include the **City History Museum**, naberezhnaya Verkhne-Volzhskaya 7; the **Tank Guards Army Museum**, ul Shkolnaya 9; the **River Fleet Museum**, ul Minina 7; and the **Radio Technology Museum**, naberezhnaya Verkhne-Volzhskaya 10.

Gorodets
The village of Gorodets (Городец) is famous for its hand-painted toys. You can see them being made at the Gorodetskaya Rospis handicraft factory (closed weekends). On the way you pass the Gorkovsky hydro-electric station with its 15km-long dam. To get to Gorodets, take a northbound suburban train to Zavolzhe (Заволже) and then a river boat across the Volga. Ferries also travel regularly between Nizhny Novgorod and Gorodets.

PRACTICAL INFORMATION
Orientation and services
The central part of Nizhny Novgorod and the kremlin lie at the junction of the Volga and Oka rivers. The railway station is across the river from the centre. Pedestrianized Bolshaya Pokrovskaya, running from pl Gorkogo to the kremlin, is the main shopping street.

Nizhny Novgorod's **metro** was opened in 1985 with 14 stations but it's still not extensive enough to be much use to the visitor. There's a good network of **trams** and **buses**. Tram No 1 runs from the railway station across the river and up to the kremlin.

Komanda Gorkiy (Team Gorky Adventure Travel, ☎ 651-999, ☎ 317-004, 🖹 651-999, 🖳 www.teamgorky.ru), 1a, ul 40 Let Oktiabria, organizes weekend rafting in the Nizhny Novgorod region on the Kerzenets River, trekking, fishing and white-water rafting in Siberia and bicycling around the Golden Ring. Their website has an English-language section.

Where to stay and eat
Hotel Volzhsky Otkos (☎ 391641, 🖹 363894), formerly Hotel Rossiya, is at nab Verkhne-Volzhskaya 8. It's a reasonable place with basic rooms from US$12/15 and

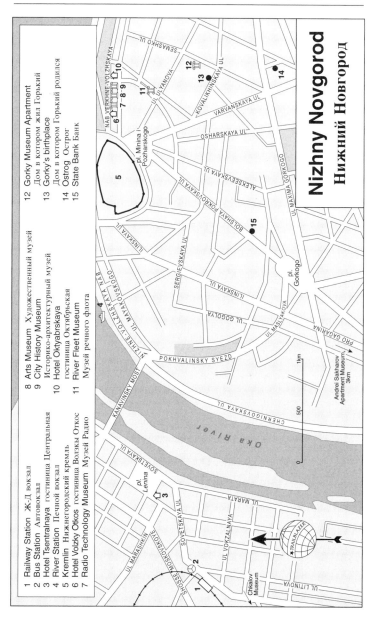

Nizhny Novgorod
Нижний Новгород

1 Railway Station Ж-Д вокзал
2 Bus Station Автовокзал
3 Hotel Tsentralnaya гостиница Центральная
4 River Station Речной вокзал
5 Kremlin Нижегородский кремль
6 Hotel Volzky Otkos гостиница Волжкы Откос
7 Radio Technology Museum Музей Радио

8 Arts Museum Художественный музей
9 City History Museum
   Историко-архитектурный музей
10 Hotel Oktyabrskaya
   гостиница Октябрьская
11 River Fleet Museum
   Музей речного флота

12 Gorky Museum Apartment
   Дом в котором жил Горький
13 Gorky's birthplace
   Дом в котором Горький родился
14 Ostrog Острог
15 State Bank Банк

modernized doubles from US$50. *Hotel Tsentralnaya* (☎ 775934, 🖳 775500), at Sovetskaya 12, is close to the station. Standard singles/doubles cost US$25/30; renovated rooms are US$48/56. You can check your email here.

Hotel Oktyabrskaya (☎ 320670, 🖳 320550), nab Verkhne-Volzhskaya 9a, is centrally-located and a good choice. Standard rooms cost US$58/90; the renovated rooms are US$92/138.

The top hotel is the four-star *Hotel Volna* (☎ 961900, 🖳 961414), quite a long way out from the centre at ul Lenina 98. Single rooms cost US$85-130; doubles

US$125-215. This is essentially a business hotel so rooms are cheaper at the weekend.

There's a good range of **places to eat and drink** on Bolshaya Pokrovskaya. *Gardinia*, on Verkhne-Volzhskaya, is a fast-food restaurant opened in 1992 by a Palestinian-American couple.

Moving on
By air There are daily flights to and from Moscow, St Petersburg, Vyatka and most major Russian cities.
By rail There are suburban trains between Nizhny Novgorod and Vladimir ($4^{1}/_{2}$ hours).

Vyatka (Kirov)
Вятка (Киров)

Vyatka was founded on the banks of the Vyatka River in 1181, as Klynov. It developed into a fur-trading centre entirely dependent on the river for transport and communication with the rest of the country. In the 18th century it fell under the rule of Moscow and was renamed Vyatka, soon gaining a reputation as a place of exile.

In 1934 the name was changed once more, this time to Kirov, in honour of the communist leader assassinated earlier in the same year. Sergei Kirov was at one time so close to Stalin that most people assumed he would succeed him as Party General Secretary. But he subsequently broke away, and it is more than likely that Stalin had a hand in his death, and moreover used it as an

---

🚂 Vyatka to Velikoretskaya Pilgrimage
Every year on 3 June, 1000-odd worshippers join the Russian Orthodox Church's longest procession: a 170km trek from Vyatka to the village of Velikoretskaya. At the head of the procession is carried the icon of St Nikolai, the miracle curer.

According to religious lore, in 1383 a peasant found this icon, surrounded by candles, up a tree on the outskirts of Velikoretskaya. The villagers agreed to house the icon in Klynov (as Vyatka was then known) providing it was brought back to the village annually. This condition has been met every year since then, even during the communist era when the icon was kept hidden, the tree in Velikoryetskaya had been chopped down and the devout had to pretend that they were out strolling.

Today the procession is regaining popularity as more people seek the miracles that they believe result from taking part in it. Everyone is welcome but you must bring your own blanket, food and drink for three days of walking.

excuse for his own Great Purge in the mid-1930s, during which several million people died in labour camps.

Modern Vyatka, still sometimes referred to as Kirov (on railway timetables, for example), is a large industrial and administrative centre with a population of 463,000. It's not of great interest but there's enough to keep you occupied for a day, and the river front is attractive.

WHAT TO SEE

Russia's answer to Joseph Conrad was AC Grin (1880-1932), born 35km away at Slobodskoy. Grin's adventure novels, set in mysterious places, are still popular today. His works are on display in Vyatka's **AC Grin Museum**, ul Volodarskogo 44. This and most of the town's other museums are open 10:00-18:00 daily except Monday.

Other attractions include the **Museum of Aviation and Space**, ul Engelsa; the **Museum of Vyatka Local Handicrafts**, ul Drelevskogo 4B, with a large collection of Dymkovo clay toys; and the **United Historical Archive and Literary Museum**, ul Lenina 82. The **Exhibition Hall of the Kirov Region**, ul Gertsena, exhibits works of local artists, with a different exhibition each month.

The **Assumption Cathedral** at the Trifon Monastery dates from the late 17th century.

PRACTICAL INFORMATION
Orientation and services
Vyatka is spread out and has no real main street which means that you need to do a lot of walking to get around.

To get from the train station (which some railway timetables still call Kirov) to the Hotel Administratsii Oblast and the Drama Theatre, take bus No 23 from in front of Detsky Mir department store. To get from the train station to the Hotel Vyatka, take trolley bus No 2, 3 or 6 from Detsky Mir.

Aeroflot (☎ 44 472, 25 287) is at ul Gorkogo 56.

For Internet access go to **InetCafé** (☎ 624 984, 🖳 www.inetcafe.vyatka.ru) at ul Svobody 67. For US$2 you get one hour's access and a cup of tea.

Where to stay
The *Kirov Regional Administration Hotel* (Gostinitsa Administratsii Oblast; ☎ 381

018, 🖾 381 016), ul Gertsena 49, has single rooms for US$25. The *Hotel Vyatka* (☎ 644 503, 🖾 646 410), Oktyabrsky pr 145, charges US$30/70 for a basic single/double. *Motel Kolos* (☎ 671 689), ul Bolshevikov, has dorm beds for US$6 and singles for US$30.

Where to eat
The best restaurant is the *Rossiya* at ul Lenina 80, near the Saltykov-Shchedrin House-Museum. There is a restaurant in the *Hotel Vyatka* and three canteens near the puppet theatre.

Moving on
At the station you can buy tickets only for trains departing the same day; for advance bookings you must go to the Advance Railway Ticket Booking Office. Note that queues can be very long.

On the fastest trains it's 15 hours to Moscow and eight hours to Perm.

The Vyatka area code is ☎ 8332. From outside Russia dial +7-8332.

Perm
Пермь

The city of Perm, Pasternak's Yuryatin in *Dr Zhivago*, is the gateway to Siberia. Lying in the foothills of the Ural Mountains it's an industrial city of just under a million people, and the focus of the region. The surrounding area is good for hiking and skiing, and some operators offer white-water rafting trips.

Perm dates back to 1723 and the construction of the Yegoshikhinsky copper foundry, established by VN Tatichev, a close associate of Peter the Great. Its location on two major trading rivers ensured that Perm grew as both an industrial and a trading city. Salt caravans arrived along the Kama River while wheat, honey and metal products from the Urals travelled along the Chusovoy River. The arrival of the railway in 1878, the discovery of oil in the region and the transfer of factories from European Russia during WWII all boosted the local economy further.

The city's most familiar product is the Kama bicycle which, while rarely seen on the streets of Russian cities, is still widely used in the country. Nearly all of Russia's domestic telephones are made here too, but Perm's most specialized products are the first-stage engines for Proton Heavy-Lift rockets.

Despite its industrial history Perm has a tradition of culture and scholarship, thanks largely to the revolutionaries, intellectuals and political prisoners exiled here in the 19th century. Perm had the Urals' first university, whose most famous student was Alexander Popov (1859-1905), a local boy (born in nearby Krasnoturinsk) and, according to Russian historians, the inventor of the wireless. Popov is said to have demonstrated his invention in 1895, the same year that Marconi proved his concept.

From 1940 to 1957 Perm was called Molotov, after the subsequently-disgraced Soviet Foreign Minister who signed the 1939 Ribbentrop-Molotov Pact, dividing up Poland with the Nazis.

WHAT TO SEE

The most interesting part of town is the old quarter around Perm 1 train station. Old churches here include the baroque **Cathedral of Peter and Paul** (1757-1765, with a 19th-century belfry) and the Empire-style **Cathedral of the Saviour**, part of the **Transfiguration Monastery** (1798-1832). There are also numerous examples of eclectic and art nouveau architectural styles, of which the old building of Perm 2 station is one. The river station is near Perm 1.

Perm Art Gallery, Komsomolsky pr 2, is one of the largest galleries in Russia, with a collection of wooden sculptures that includes a figure of Jesus with Mongolian features. It's open 11:00-18:00, daily except Monday. The city also boasts a **terrarium** in Gorky Park, a **planetarium** and a **Museum of Local Studies**.

About 45km out of town near the village of **Khokhlovka** is a year-round, open-air ethnographic museum with a collection of 16th-20th century buildings.

About 100km from Perm are the fabulous **Kungur Ice Caves**, among the biggest in the Urals, 5.6km long including 58 grottos, 60 lakes and hundreds of stalactites and stalagmites. Some 1.3km of the caves are open to the public and fitted with electric lights. Take warm clothes. There are several direct trains a day from Perm to Kungur (two hours); the caves are 6km from the town.

PRACTICAL INFORMATION
Orientation and services
The town is spread along the Kama River with its centre around Perm 1 station, on the left (eastern) bank. At the southern end of Perm, also on the left bank, is Perm 2 station where Trans-Siberian trains stop. Suburban trains run the 5km between Perm 2 and Perm 1.

The city has two airports: Bolshoye Savino, 20km to the west, which handles most traffic, and the older Bakharevka airport, 10km south in the suburb of Balatovo.

Recommended travel agencies include **JSC Permtourist** (☎ 348 703, 🗎 342 609, 💻 www.permtourist.ru) at the Hotel Ural, and **Galakon** (☎ 338 087, 🗎 341 568), ul Kuybysheva 14. Both can arrange boat trips along the Kama and Chusovoy rivers and day trips to the Kungur Ice Caves.

Aeroflot (☎ 334 668) is at ul Krisanova 19. You can also buy air tickets from the Ural and Prikamiye hotels.

You can access the Internet at the **post office**, near the corner of ul Lenina (Glavny) and ul Popova.

Where to stay
The best choice is the big *Ural Hotel* (☎ 906 220, 🗎 906 208, 💻 www.perm tourist.ru), ul Lenina 58. Basic singles/dou-

bles cost US$13/25 but first they'll offer you a smarter room for US$40/60. They also have a business centre and travel agency (Permtourist).

Hotel Prikamiye (☎ 349 428, 🗎 348 662), Komsomolsky pr 27, is not bad and has singles/doubles for US$14/18.

Tops in Perm is the four-star *Hotel Mikos* (☎ 241 999, 🗎 221 198, 💻 micos@nevod.ru), Stakhanovskaya ul 10A.

At the Kungur Ice Caves (see above) the *Hotel Stalagmit* (contact through Ural Hotel) has double rooms from US$10.

Where to eat
All the hotels have restaurants. The one at the *Ural Hotel* is on the 7th floor; in the basement is the *Grot Bar* (better than it sounds). Probably the best place to eat is the *European* (☎ 338 716), ul Lenina 72B, but it's expensive.

Moving on
Aeroflot flies daily to Moscow, and Lufthansa has two weekly flights between Perm and Frankfurt. By rail it's 7hrs to Yekaterinburg and 28hrs to Novosibirsk.

The Perm area code is ☎ 3422. From outside Russia dial +7-3422.

Yekaterinburg
Екатеринбург

Yekaterinburg's role in shaping Russian history has been both immense and par-
adoxical: ushering in the Socialist era in 1918 with the murder of the Romanov
family, providing the setting for the 1960s 'U2 Affair' (effectively a caricature
of the Cold War itself) and giving the country Boris Yeltsin, who played a key
role in dismantling the Soviet myth. The city seems to act as Russia's litmus
paper: as a harbinger of what is to come.

Its historical significance alone justifies a visit and while there is not much
to see here in real terms, the wealth of pre-Stalinist architecture makes a change
from other Siberian cities, harking back to the days before the Revolution when
Yekaterinburg was already the centre of a rich mining region. From 1924 to
1992 the city was known as Sverdlovsk, the name that Russian Railways still
uses on its timetables.

HISTORY

The earliest settlers in the area were 'Old Believers', religious dissidents fleeing the reforms of the Russian Orthodox Church in 1672. They created the
Shartash township here and were the first to discover that the area was rich in
iron ore. This discovery was the key to later development: Peter the Great,
embroiled in the Great Northern War against Sweden, gave instructions for new
sources of iron to be sought, and the first ironworks were established here just
as the war ended in 1721. A fortress was built a year later and in 1723 the town
of Yekaterinburg was founded, in honour of Peter's new wife, Catherine. The
railway arrived in 1888 bringing foreign travellers on their way to Siberia.

The murder of the Romanovs

The Romanov family was moved from Tobolsk to Yekaterinburg in May 1918
and imprisoned in a house belonging to a rich merchant named Ipatyev. Here
they spent the last two months of their lives being tormented by the guards, who
openly referred to Nicholas as the 'Blood Drinker' and scrawled lewd pictures
on the walls depicting the Tsarina with Rasputin.

Several attempts were made to save the royal family, and eventually the
Bolshevik government, deciding that the Tsar was too great a threat to its security, ordered his elimination. Shortly before midnight on 16 July, Nicholas,
Alexandra, their four daughters and their haemophiliac son Alexis, were taken
to the cellar where they were shot and bayonetted to death. The bodies were
then taken to the Four Brothers Mine, 40km outside the city, where guards spent
three days destroying the evidence. The corpses were dismembered, doused
with petrol and burned.

The road to Romanov sainthood

The story behind the discovery of the Romanov remains is almost as bizarre as that of their 'disappearance'. In July 1991 it was announced that parts of nine bodies had been found and that these were almost certainly those of the Imperial Family. Perhaps the most intriguing aspect of the discovery was that three of the skulls, including that of the Tsar himself, had been placed in a wooden box. In fact the bodies had been discovered some 20 years before by a local detective-novel writer named Geli Ryabov. He deduced from the skulls' immaculate dental work that these were indeed the bodies of the Royal Family, but reburied them for fear of persecution by the secret police. In December 1992, DNA testing at the Forensic Science Service laboratory in Aldermaston (UK) matched samples from the bodies with those from a blood sample provided by Prince Philip, Duke of Edinburgh (Tsarina Alexandra's sister was Philip's maternal grandmother).

The state burial of the royal remains was delayed for several years following a disagreement between the government, which favoured burial of the bones in St Petersburg, and surviving members of the Romanov family who wanted them returned to Yekaterinburg as a memorial to the millions killed by the Communists. On 19 August 1998 the remains were finally interred in the Romanov vault in St Petersburg's Peter and Paul Cathedral (see p140). At the service, then President Boris Yeltsin made the first official apology: 'The massacre of the Tsar was one of the most shameful pages of our history....We are all guilty. It is impossible to lie to ourselves by justifying the senseless cruelty on political grounds'.

On 20 August 2000, at a special ceremony in Moscow's Cathedral of Christ the Saviour, Patriarch Alexi II canonized the Tsar, the royal family and hundreds of priests who died as 'zealots of faith and piety' during the Communist era.

A week later the White Army took Yekaterinburg, and their suspicions were immediately aroused by the sight of the cellar's blood-spattered walls. In the garden they found the Tsarevich's spaniel, Joy, neglected and half starved. However, it was not until the following January that investigators were led to the mineshaft, where they found fragments of bone and pieces of jewellery that had once belonged to members of the Imperial Family. They also found the body of Jimmy, Anastasia's dog, which the murderers had callously flung down the mineshaft without bothering to kill it first. All the evidence was identified by the Tsarevich's tutor, Pierre Gilliard. At first the Bolsheviks would not admit to more than the 'execution' of Nicholas, accusing a group of counter-revolutionaries of the murders of his family. Five of them were tried, 'found guilty' and executed. However, in 1919 after the death of Party official Yacob Sverdlov, it was acknowledged that it was in fact he who had arranged the massacre. In his honour the town was renamed Sverdlovsk.

The U2 Affair

The next time the town became the focus of world attention was in May 1960 when the American U2 pilot, Gary Powers, was shot down in this area (see p339). He survived the crash, parachuting into the arms of the Soviets and confirming that he had been spying. The ensuing confrontation led to the collapse of the Summit conference in Paris.

The city today

With a population of 1.26 million Yekaterinburg is Russia's fifth-largest city (after Moscow, St Petersburg, Novosibirsk and Nizhny Novgorod) and one of the country's most important industrial centres. The city's most famous son is, of course, Boris Yeltsin: coup-buster, economic reformer, referendum winner, dissolver of parliament and former Russian President.

Industries include heavy engineering and chemical production, with some 200 complexes. The city is also a transport hub, with seven radiating railway lines. It is educationally rich with over 200 schools, 50 technical schools and 14 higher education institutions. It also has over 600 libraries including the 15-million-volume Belinsky Library, founded in 1899. The city once specialized in armaments research and production but munitions factories, including the vast 'Pentagon' building in the eastern part of town, are being closed down. The area's biggest employer, Uralmash, which makes machine tools, has slashed its original 40,000 workforce. There has been some foreign investment, including by Coca Cola, Pepsi and the mobile phone company, USWest.

If Yekaterinburg is an indicator of the state of affairs in Russia, things don't look too good: I asked if anything important had happened here recently and was told only that there had been 'a number of mafia funerals'. Local mafia gangs hold a lot of power here: Yekaterinburg is a transit point on the 'heroin route' between Asia and Europe. But unless you're also involved in this trade you'll be all right.

WHAT TO SEE

The Romanov Memorial

The site of the murder of the Imperial family is 500m north of pr Lenina and marked by a **white metal cross**, a **marble cross** and a **plaque** inscribed with the names of Romanov family members. Yeltsin had the original building (Ipatyev House) demolished in 1976; at the time of writing the large memorial **Church of the Blood** was nearing completion on the site.

Also here is a small wooden **chapel**, built in the late 1980s and repeatedly burnt down by anti-monarchists. It's dedicated to St Elizabeth (Elizabeth Fyodorov), Alexander II's sister-in-law who, following the Romanov murders, was thrown down a mineshaft and left to die. Local villagers claimed to have heard her miserable wailings for two days as she prayed for the souls of her attackers who, when they realized that she was still alive, piped poisonous gas into the well and filled the hole with earth.

The grand building opposite the Romanov site now houses the headquarters of the Children's Movement. The building was commissioned by a merchant named Rastorguiev who, legend says, was so rich that he minted his own gold coins in the basement. He is said to have bailed an architect out of jail and offered to buy the man's freedom if he designed him a beautiful-enough house. The architect laboured hard to complete his side of the bargain but, when Rastorguiev did not keep his promise, hanged himself.

Next door to this building is the **Ascension Cathedral**, impressive from the outside but containing nothing of particular note. It was closed following the Revolution, its treasures removed and its murals painted over.

Military Museum
There is a small exhibit on the U2 incident in the Military Museum at the House of Officers (Dom Ofitserov) near the city centre, though staff are sometimes unwilling to let foreigners in. On display upstairs are a few pieces of the aircraft, photos of the wreckage and of Gary Powers in court, plus items from his survival kit. There is no sign of the U2 camera which so impressed Nikita Khrushchev: 'It must be said that the camera is not a bad one,' he said, 'the photographs are very accurate. But I must say that our cameras take better pictures and are more accurate'. The House of Officers is easily recognizable by the massive armoury outside; around the back is a collection of Soviet military hardware including fighter planes, a helicopter, tanks and a Soyuz cosmonauts' re-entry capsule. The Military Museum (☎ 552 106) is open 09:00-13:00 and 14:00-17:00 Tuesday to Saturday (to 15:00 Saturday); entry US$0.50.

Museum of Decorative Arts
Here you'll find a fine collection of 19th-century iron sculpture, a gallery of Russian paintings including works by Ivanov and Tarakanova, a portrait of PA Stroganov (of Beef Stroganov fame) and a famous painting of Christ by Polenov. Pride of place goes to the iron pavilion, which won first prize in the Paris Exposition in 1900; it's very impressive but you can't but wonder what it's for. Open 11:00-19:00 daily except Sunday; entry US$1.

Museum of Local History
The Museum of Local History (☎ 511 819) is at ul Malysheva 46, relocated from Alexander Nevsky Cathedral. There are interesting displays on 19th-century Yekaterinburg, the Revolution, the murder of the Romanovs and the discovery of their remains. It's well worth a visit and is open daily 11:00-18:00; entry US$0.30.

Street name changes
Like many Russian cities, Yekaterinburg changed the names of many of its streets after the fall of communism in hopes of erasing old memories. Some government offices and businesses made the changes on letterhead and business cards but in general the revised names have been met with a yawn, and the old street signs are still in place. We use old names, but here are a few major streets in the town centre where you may find revised names used occasionally (revised names in parentheses):
● prospekt Lenina (Glavny prospekt)
● ulitsa Malysheva (Pokrovsky prospekt)
● ulitsa Kuybysheva (Sibirsky prospekt)
● ulitsa Sverdlova (Arsenevsky prospekt)
● ulitsa Lunacharskogo (Vasentsovskaya ulitsa)

WHERE TO STAY
 2 Hotel Sverdlovsk Гостиница Свердловск
26 Atrium Palace Hotel Гостиница Атриум Дворец
32 Hotel Tsentralnaya Гостиница Центральная
35 Hotel Eurasia Гостиница Уразия
38 Hotel Bolshoi Ural Гостиница Большой Урал
42 Hotel Iset Гостиница Исет

WHERE TO EAT
11 Stolovaya Столовая
16 Subway
19 Akvarium Аквариум
20 Astoria Астория
22 Mak Pik Мак Пик
27 Café Pekin Кафе Пекин
34 Fridays Фрайдис
43 Central Asian Food Среднеазиатское Кушанье

OTHER
 1 Railway Station Вокзал
 3 Former Rastorguiev-Kharitonov Estate
    Быв. Усадьба Расторгуева-Харитонова
 4 Church of the Blood
 5 Romanov Memorial (former Ipatyev House)
    Белый Крест (Быв. Дом Ипатьева)
 6 Monument to Urals Young Communists
    Памятник Комсомолу Урала
 7 Ascension Cathedral Церковь Вознесения
 8 Afghan War Memorial Памятник Военный Афганистанскйи
 9 Military Museum, in the House of Officers
    Музей «Боевая Слава Урала», в Доме Офицеров
10 Photography Museum Музей Фотографий
12 Literary Quarter Museum Литературный Музей
13 Master & Margarita Club Клуб Мастер и Маргарита
14 Central Post Office & Internet Почтамт и Интернет
15 ATMs Банк
17 Sputnik Travel, Transaero & Lufthansa Спутник, Трансаэро, Луфтганса
18 Museum of Decorative Arts Музей Изобразительных Искусств
21 Clone Internet Клоне Интернет
23 Museum of Local History Краеведческий Музей
24 Urals Geology Museum Уралский Геологический Музей
25 Circus Цирк
28 Bookshop Дом Книги
29 British Consulate Консулъство Британское
30 US Consulate Консулъство США
31 Popov Radio Museum Музей Радио имени Попова
33 Bookshop Дом Книги
36 Sverdlov Statue Памятник Свердлову
37 Opera & Ballet Theatre Театр Оперы и Балета
39 Mineralogy Museum Минеральный Музей
40 OBK Bank & ATM ОБК-Банк
41 Puppet Theatre Кукольный Театр

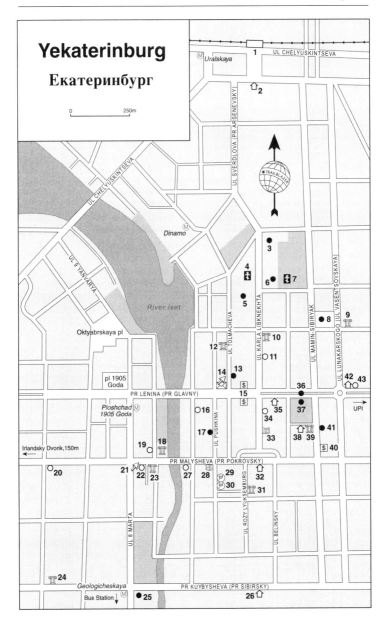

Yekaterinburg

Екатеринбург

0 _____ 250m

1

Ⓜ Uralskaya

🏛 2

UL CHELYUSKINTSEVA

UL SVERDLOVA (PR ARSENEVSKY)

UL CHELYUSKINTSEVA

⭑TRAILBLAZER

UL 9 YANVARYA

Ⓜ Dinamo

● 3

4 🚻

● 6   ✝ 7

River Iset

● 5

Oktyabrskaya pl

UL TOLMACHEVA

UL KARLA LIBKNEKHTA

UL MAMIN-SIBIRYAK

UL LUNAKARSKOGO (UL VASENTSOVSKAYA)

● 8

🏛 9

12 🏛   🏛 10

○ 11

pl 1905
Goda

14 ✉   13 🏛

$

PR LENINA (PR GLAVNY)

15
$

36 ●

42 🏛 43

UPI

Ⓜ Ploshchad
1905 Goda

○ 16

○ 35   37

34

Irlandsky Dvorik,150m ←

17 ●

UL PUSHKINA

33   38 🏛 39   🏛 41

19 ○   18 🏛

$ 40

20 ○

21 🔧○   🏛   ○ 27   28   29 🅿   🏛 32

22   23

30 🅿   🏛 31

PR MALYSHEVA (PR POKROVSKY)

UL ROZY LYUKSEMBURG

UL BELINSKY

UL 8 MARTA

🏛 24

Geologicheskaya

Bus Station ↓ Ⓜ

● 25

PR KUYBYSHEVA (PR SIBIRSKY)

26 🏛

Other things to see in Yekaterinburg

The **Urals Geology Museum** (☎ 223 109) at ul Kuybysheva 30 is good; try to track down the curator, who speaks perfect English and enjoys showing visitors around. It is open 11:00-18:00, closed at weekends. The **Mineralogy Museum** next to the Hotel Bolshoi Ural has a large collection of regional minerals and an extensive gift shop. It's open 10:00-19:00 Monday-Friday and 10:00-17:00 at weekends; entry US$1.

Other museums include the **Literary Quarter Museum**, ul Tolmacheva 41, and the **Popov Radio Museum**, ul Rozy Lyuksemburg 9; the latter includes a **planetarium**. The **Photography Museum**, above a photo shop at ul Karla Libknekhta 36, has some great early 20th-century photos of Yekaterinburg and its inhabitants. It's open 11:00-18:00; entry US$0.50.

There are several interesting buildings in the city including the classical-style **Mining Office** and the former **Rastorguiev-Kharitonov Estate** (1794-1824), both at ul Karla Libknehkta 44 opposite the Romanov memorial. At the eastern end of pr Lenina is **UPI**, the Urals Polytechnical Institute, an impressive building which often features on postcards (it is in fact a university but the old name has stuck). The building beside it with the cannons outside is the city's military college.

The **Opera and Ballet Theatre** (☎ 558 057) at pr Lenina 46a is Russia's third most important such theatre after those in Moscow and St Petersburg. There is a **Puppet Theatre** on ul Mamin-Sibiryak. In the square opposite the House of Officers is a powerful **Afghan War Memorial**. The pose of the soldier, very different from most such memorials around Russia, offers an interesting insight into how people feel about the war. At ul Mamin-Sibiryak 189 there is a depressing **zoo** which looks more like a prison.

Excursions from Yekaterinburg

● **Europe/Asia marker** About 40km to the west along the main road to Moscow (Novy Moscovsky Trakt) is the point which the German scientists Humboldt and Roze designated as the border between Europe and Asia while doing barometric surveys in 1829. The original marker was destroyed in the 1920s and replaced with a concrete obelisk faced with granite. Intourist runs trips to this obelisk for US$45. There's a another marker beside the railway line, 36km west of Yekaterinburg at Vershina (Вершина).

● **Museum of Wooden Architecture** It's a long way away (120km to the north) and not as good as the one outside Irkutsk but bus No 31 from the railway station will get you here. The most interesting building is the old church, closed since the Revolution. During recent restoration work many of its carved floor tiles were found to be missing. As work proceeded the 'lost' tiles began to show up, returned by pensioners who had long ago removed them as mementos. Incredibly, every single tile has now been returned.

The Yekaterinburg area code is ☎ 3432. From outside Russia dial +7-3432.

PRACTICAL INFORMATION
Orientation and services
The main street, pr Lenina, runs east-west through the city. The point where it is bisected by the River Iset is more or less the city centre, and most of the hotels, restaurants and sights are within walking distance of here.

For local information and maps look for the *City Guide* (US$2) in hotels and other places frequented by foreigners.

Travel agents include Intourist (☎ 518 434, 🖹 518 230), room 339, Hotel Eurasia, pr Lenina 40; Sputnik (☎ 513 743, 519 157, 🖹 513 483), ul Pushkina 5; Miklukho-Maklay (☎ 237 596, 🖹 518 087), ul Shaumyana 100; and Globe Tour (☎ 589 819, 🖹 516 455), ul Dzerzhinsky 2.

Aeroflot (☎ 299 298) is at ul Bolshakova 99A. **Lufthansa** (☎ 598 300) and **Transaero** at ul Pushkina 5.

For **rail tickets**, you have to go to the second floor of the **Central Railway Ticket Booking Office**, on the west side of the main railway station.

There are numerous **ATMs** around town. **OBK-Bank**, ul Mamin-Sibiryak 145, can cash travellers' cheques. You can change money at various places including the post office and Hotel Eurasia.

The **Central Post Office**, pr Lenina 51, has all the usual services plus **Internet access** for US$1.60 per hour. It's open 08:00-20:00 Monday-Friday and 08:00-18:00 at weekends. There is also Internet access at **Clone Internet** at the corner of ul 8 Marta and ul Malysheva.

There's a **British Consulate** (☎ 564 931, 🖹 592 901, 🖳 brit@sky.ru), ul Gogolya 15A, and a **US Consulate** (☎ 564 619, 🖹 564 515, 🖳 usc gyekat@gin.ru) also at ul Gogolya 15A.

Local transport
Yekaterinburg has a good bus and trolley-bus system, and a rather limited metro. To get to the centre from the station, take bus Nos 1, 13, 21, 23, 31, or trolley-bus Nos 1, 3, 5, 9, 12.

From the station to the Hotel Tsentralnaya, take trolley-bus Nos 1, 5, 9 down ul Karla Libknekhta. For Hotel Iset and Hotel Bolshoi Ural, take tram No 27 or 29; both go down ul Lunacharskogo, then pr Lenina.

To get to the airport, catch a bus from the Air Station (Aerovokzal) beside the Aeroflot office, ul Bolshakova 99A.

Where to stay
All hotels in this section have attached bathrooms, except as noted.

Hotel Eurasia (☎ 578 028) at pr Lenina 40 is a busy place with a wide variety of rooms from US$12/20 for a single/double. There is an Intourist office on the 3rd floor.

Directly opposite the railway station is the vast *Hotel Sverdlovsk* (☎ 536 261), ul Chelyuskintseva 106, which is a conventional, Intourist-style place, partly renovated. Rooms cost from US$14/20 for a single/double, though the cheaper rooms are falling apart.

Hotel Bolshoi Ural (☎ 556 896), ul Krasnoarmeyskaya 1, offers an interesting insight into how hotels were run years ago. It's often full but it's worth asking because it's fairly cheap at US$21 for a double (single rate US$10.50); singles with shared bath cost US$8.

Hotel Iset (☎ 506 943, 🖳 hotel_resr@etel.ru), pr Lenina 69/1, has singles/doubles from US$60/74. You can pay US$37 for one bed in a double room and chances are you won't have to share the room. It's a quiet place with friendly, English-speaking staff, and better than it looks from the outside. It was built to resemble a hammer and sickle from above. The sickle, which one imagines would be

THE MODERNIST CENTRAL POST OFFICE

the tricky bit, turned out well but the hammer never really quite happened.

Hotel Tsentralnaya (☎ 551 109), ul Malysheva 74, is worth trying. It has singles/doubles for US$30/50 plus a few cheaper rooms. It's friendly enough and is popular with business people.

The top place to stay is the *Atrium Palace Hotel* (☎ 556 076, 📠 555 136) at the World Trade Centre, Sibirsky pr 44. There are rooms from US$200 to US$700.

Homestays These can be organized by *HOFA* and by Moscow-based *G&R International* (see p20 and p169 for contact information).

Where to eat

There are plenty of fast-food places in Yekaterinburg including the very popular *Mak Pik* on pr Lenina, which serves burgers, pizzas and pelmeni. *Fridays* on ul Karla Libknekhta serves similar food. *Subway* on ul Gorkogo makes filling sandwiches for US$2.

There is a basic *stolovaya* on ul Karla Libknekhta where you can get a meal and drink for US$1. Next to Hotel Iset is a place selling tasty **Central Asian food** such as plov and shashlyk for US$1.50. The pelmeni at *Hotel Iset* are good, although the place is a bit dingy and service can be casual.

Café Pekin on ul Malysheva serves delicious Chinese food in atmospheric surroundings and is deservedly popular. It's open from noon to midnight.

The *Astoria* (☎ 510 161), ul Malysheva 28, is a small smart restaurant that is among the city's best. Main dishes cost US$10-15, service is quite good and it's popular amongst business people. Nearby is *Irlandsky Dvorik*, an Irish pub and restaurant. It often gets busy in the evenings here.

The *Akvarium* restaurant, opposite the Museum of Decorative Arts is a small place which serves a range of fish dishes for around US$5.

There is a bearable restaurant at the *Master & Margarita Club*, just around the corner from the post office. Restaurant patrons get in to the nightclub for free; it's usually US$2 after 23:00. It's a stylish place which attracts mainly 25-35 year olds.

Moving on

By rail Yekaterinburg is 22 hours from Novosibirsk (US$29) and 30 hours from Moscow (US$33). There are also numerous services to Tyumen (five hours, US$10) and Omsk (12 hours, US$24).

Note that certain trains to/from Moscow use Moscow's Kazansky station rather than Yaroslavsky; these include the No 15/16 (terminating here), No 31/32 Novokuznetsk, No 35/36 Barnaul, No 37/38 Tomsk, No 59/60 Tyumen, No 75/76 Tynda, No 117/118 Novokuznetsk, No 121/122 Ulan Ude and No 907/908 Novosibirsk and Irkutsk.

The railway station is often very busy and ticket queues can be daunting. Window No 17 is for international tickets but will probably sell you domestic tickets if they know you are a foreigner.

If you are waiting for a train, or arrive late at night, there is a comfortable waiting room with soft seats, toilets and a bar. The entrance is to the left of the main station entrance and it costs US$1.60 for a minimum of three hours.

By air The main airport is 16km south of the city. There are three flights a week to **Frankfurt** with Lufthansa, weekly connections to **Prague** or **Cologne** with Ural Airlines (🖳 www.uralairlines.com) and daily flights to **Moscow** and **Irkutsk** with Transaero and Aeroflot. You can also fly to St Petersburg, Novosibirsk, Vladivostok, Krasnoyarsk, Almaty or Tashkent from here.

Tyumen
Тюмень

The only city in Asia to have hosted a European cup, Tyumen is the booming oil capital of Western Siberia, its wealth confirmed by the expensive goods in the shops.

Founded in 1586, Tyumen's location on a major trading river, the Tura, made it an important transit point for goods between Siberia and China. It was also a major transit point for settlers and convicts destined for Siberia and the Russian Far East. By 1900 over a million convicts had tramped through the town.

During WWII, many of European Russia's people, treasures and factories were relocated to Siberia. The greatest treasure to be transferred from Moscow to Tyumen during this time was Lenin's corpse. For years he rested secretly in a building of the Agricultural Institute, tended by a team of specialists.

Prior to the drilling of the region's first oil well in 1960, Tyumen was just a dusty backwater of 150,000 inhabitants. Since then its population has grown to an estimated 509,000. The importance of oil to the city can be seen in the two giant crude-oil pipelines running through it. Tyumen is a pleasant-enough place and certainly feels more affluent than many other Siberian cities.

WHAT TO SEE

All museums in Tyumen are closed on Monday and Tuesday. The most interesting buildings are in the so-called **History Museum Complex** at ul Kommunisticheskaya 10.

The complex, open 09:30-17:00, includes the Church of Saints Peter and Paul, Trinity Cathedral (built in 1616) and surviving walls of the adjacent monastery (unusual in Siberia in having been built of stone), plus displays on local history and Siberian religious history.

The **Household Goods and Architecture Museum** (formerly the Blyukher Museum) on ul Respubliki is a wooden house built in 1804 and owned at one time by the town's 1830s mayor, Ikonikov. The **Masharov House-Museum**, ul Lenina 24, provides an insight into the life and times of a wealthy 19th-century factory owner.

Specialist museums include the **Fire Technology Museum** on ul Gorkogo, and the **Geology Museum** (☎ 227 426) at ul Respubliki 42. The **city park** is the local Hari Krishna hangout. **Bookstores** sell old Tsarist coins. Don't declare them at customs when you leave Russia as it's illegal to export them.

PRACTICAL INFORMATION
Orientation and services
From the train station all buses and trolley-buses take you along ul Pervomayskaya, then either down ul Respubliky or ul Lenina.

Travel agencies include **Intourist** (☎ 322 782), ul Melinkite 93, and **Sputnik** (☎ 240 721), ul Respubliki 19. **Aeroflot** (☎ 223 252, 262 946) is at ul Respubliki 156, or you can get flight information at the airport (☎ 232 124).

Credit card **cash advances** can be obtained from the exchange office at the Hotel Prometey and from Credo Bank at ul Pervomayskaya 8.

Where to stay
The cheapest accommodation is in one of the railway station's spartan *rest rooms (komnata otdikha;* ☎ 292 073), where a single/double/triple room costs US$6/10/12; bathrooms are in the corridor. The entrance is on the street at the front of the station.

Hotel Vostok (☎ 225 205), ul Respubliki 159, is a huge characterless place with singles/doubles from US$12/25; all rooms have bathroom attached. It's a half-hour walk from the Central Square, or you can take trolley-bus No 14 along ul Respubliki.

Hotel Prometey (☎ 251 423), ul Sovietskaya 20, charges US$30/60 for a single/double. Although it looks shabby from the outside, rooms have been renovated, with all the charm of a portakabin.

Hotel Zapsibgazprom, on ul Respubliki near the Geology Museum, is a quiet place with rooms from US$25-70. All rooms have bathroom attached.

Opened in 1995, the 230-room *Hotel Quality Tyumen* (☎ 394 040, 🖷 394 050), ul Ordzhonikidze 46, is the town's top hotel. It's well run and often full of business people. If you could pay Russian prices it would be a bargain, but foreigners must ante up US$95/105 for a single/double. There's a sauna, gym and excellent restaurants.

Where to eat
A popular fast-food place is *Fridays*, on the corner of ul Ordzhonikidze and ul Respubliki. The food is nothing special but it's only US$2 for a meal and a drink. Another good place for snacks is *Pizza Tyumen* (☎ 261 868), ul Lenina 61 (opposite the city park), which has a good range of fast food such as pizza (US$1), pelmeni (US$1) and salad (US$1). In summer the patio upstairs is open and becomes *Café Letnee*.

Restaurant Slavutich (☎ 465 013), ul Respubliki 62, is Tyumen's best Russian restaurant, with friendly service and large portions. It has a wide range of meals including assorted salads (US$2), *vareniki* (potato-filled dumplings; US$3), stuffed tomatoes (US$2) and soups (US$2). In the evenings it's popular with wealthy locals who all seem to want a turn at the piano, singing old folk songs.

Restaurant Tyumen (☎ 394 040) at the Hotel Quality Tyumen is one of the top places in town. Main dishes cost US$8-12. Many guests at the Hotel Prometey next door walk across in the evening to eat here.

Moving on
Tyumen is about halfway between Moscow (US$40) and Irkutsk (US$40), each about 41 hours away by rail. It's just under 7 hours to Omsk (US$12), 5 hours to Yekaterinburg (US$10) and 17 hours to Novosibirsk (US$26).

Note that certain trains to/from Moscow use Moscow's Kazansky station; these include No 59/60 (terminating here), No 75/76 Tynda and No 121/122 Ulan Ude.

The Tyumen area code is ☎ 3452. From outside Russia dial +7-3452.

WHERE TO STAY
24 Hotel Prometey Гостиница Прометей
25 Hotel Quality Tyumen Гостиница Тюмень
33 Hotel Zapsibgazprom
    Гостиница Запсибгазпром
36 Hotel Vostok Гостиница Восток

WHERE TO EAT
17 Pizza Tyumen Пицца Тюмень
27 Market Рынок
28 Restaurant Slavutich Ресторан Славутич
29 Fridays Фрайдис

OTHER
 1 History Museum Complex (Saints Peter &
    Paul Church & Cathedral of Trinity Monastery
    Музей Истории Города (Петропавловская
    Церковь и Троицкий Собор Троицкого
    Мужского Монастыря)
 2 Elevation of the Cross Church
    Крестовоздвиженская Церковь
 3 Remains of the Kremlin Walls
    Остатки Земляных Валов быв. Кремля
 4 Local Studies Museum
    Краеведческий Музей
 5 Church of Mikhaila Maleina
    Церковь Михаила Малеина
 6 Masharov House-Museum
    Дом-музей Машарова
 7 Household Goods & Architecture Museum
 8 University Университет
 9 Puppet Theatre Кукольный Театр
10 Cathedral of the Holy Cross
    Знаменский Собор
11 Church of the Saviour Спасская Церковь
12 Philharmonic Hall Филармония
13 Sputnik Travel Agency Спутник
14 Credo Bank Кредо Банк
15 Drama Theatre Театр Драмы
16 Circus Цирк
18 Police Station Милиция
19 City Park Парк
20 Central Stadium Центральный Стадион
21 Parliament House Дом Советов
22 Central Square Центральная Площадь
23 Central Post Office Почтамт
26 Department Store Универмаг
30 Fire Technology Museum
    Музей Противолознарной Техники
31 Old Cemetery Старое Кладбище
32 Geology Museum Музей Геологиуеский
34 Aeroflot Касса Аэрофлота
35 Book Shop Дом Книги

Omsk
Омск

Omsk, now Siberia's second largest city, was founded in 1719 as a small fortress on the west bank of the River Om, to be used as the military headquarters of the Cossack regiments in Siberia. It had been considerably enlarged and included a large *ostrog* (prison) by the time Fyodor Dostoyevsky arrived in 1849 to begin four years of hard labour for political crimes. His unenviable experiences were recorded in *Buried Alive in Siberia*. He was twice flogged, once for complaining about a lump of dirt in his soup; the second time he saved the life of a drowning prisoner, ignoring a guard who ordered that the man be left to drown. Dostoyevsky received so severe a flogging for this charitable act that he almost died and had to spend six weeks in the hospital.

During the Civil War Omsk was the capital of the White Russian government of Admiral Kolchak, until November 1919 when the Red Army entered and took the city. The population grew fast after the war and now an estimated 1.1 million people live here. Textiles, food, agricultural machinery and timber products are the main industries. There is also an important petrochemical complex here, supplied by a pipeline from the Ural-Volga oil region.

Omsk has a sister-city relationship with Milwaukee, Wisconsin.

WHAT TO SEE

Omsk prides itself on its numerous parks and is a pleasant place to spend a day,

**REBUILT CHAPEL
OMSK RIVERFRONT**

but there isn't really a lot to see here unless you're into museums of the 'Former Home of Unknown Artist and Obscure Soviet Poet' variety. But the **Literature Museum** (☎ 242 965) on ul Dostoyevskogo is fairly interesting, and has a section on Dostoyevsky. It's open 10:00-18:00 daily except Wednesday; entry US$0.70.

The **Omsk State History Museum**, ul Lenina 23, is a standard Russian museum and if you've been to a few before, this one might not be too inspiring. Visitors are heavily outnumbered by staff. It's open 10:00-19:00; entry US$0.50.

The **Military Museum**, ul Taube 7, has displays on WWI, WWII, and the Afghan and Chechnya conflicts.

Near the junction of the Om and Irtysh rivers are the ramparts and **Tobolsk Gate** of the old Omsk fortress.

Tobolsk

Probably the most interesting thing to do in the area is to take a trip 235km north to the historic town of Tobolsk. This was the capital of Siberia until 1824 and some of its old buildings still survive. The Tobolsk Kremlin sits high above the river; the Bishop's Chambers, Gostiny Dvor and bell-tower are also worth seeing, and there are daily hydrofoil trips along the Irtysh River. Stay either at the railway station: US$4 per bed at the *resting rooms*, or at the *Sibir Hotel* near the Kremlin (US$ 12/20 for a single/double).

From Omsk you can get to Tobolsk by train via Tyumen. The No 273N leaves at 15:57, arriving in Tobolsk at 09:58 the following morning. For the journey back, train No 273E leaves Tobolsk at 11:50, arriving in Omsk at 04:46; alternatively the 375E leaves at 20:55 and arrives in Omsk at 12:38. Remember that these times are all Moscow Time. If you're not in a hurry, the boat from Tyumen can be a pleasant way to reach Tobolsk.

River trips

There are two river stations in Omsk. Long-distance vessels, such as those for Tobolsk, leave from the **River Station**. Timetables and the ticket office are in the large station building.

Tourist trips along the Irtysh depart from a separate **Excursion River Station**, with tickets and timetables available from a kiosk under the Lenin Bridge. A one-hour trip costs about US$3. The river is navigable from late May through September.

PRACTICAL INFORMATION
Orientation and services

Most hotels and museums are located in the city centre which is about 4km from the station around the junction of the Om and Irtysh rivers. There are many minibuses from the railway station to pl Lenina for R7 (about US$0.20).

If you need a travel agency, **Intourist** (☎ 311 490) is at pr Karla Marxa 4 and **Turist** (☎ 250 624) at ul Gagarina 2.

There are **ATMs** at the Hotel Turist and next to Patio Pizza. You can change money at the **exchange office** (obmen valyuty) on the corner of ul Lenina and Pochtovaya ul.

The **Central Post Office** at ul Gertsena 1 is open 08:00-19:00 daily (except 08:00-17:00 Sunday).There is Internet access at **Navigator Internet Café**, open 09:00-23:00 daily, for US$1 per hour.

Where to stay

Only the very basic *Hotel Avtomobilist* (☎ 411 700), pr Karla Marxa 43, and the stan-

dard *Hotel Omsk* (☎ 310 721), Irtyshskaya naberezhnaya 30, are within walking distance (but only just) of the railway station. Bus Nos 11, 24 and 60 and trolley-bus Nos 3, 4 and 7 run this way.

The best of the hotels in downtown Omsk is the *Hotel Mayak* (☎ 315 431), ul Lermontova 2. There are single/double rooms for US$50/75 (with student discounts available) and executive suites from US$100. The rooms are clean and the Russian décor rather kitsch.

Other good choices include *Hotel Turist* (☎ 316 414), ul Tito 2, which has singles/doubles with bathroom on the renovated 7th floor for US$30/45. The staff are friendly and a bland breakfast is included. *Hotel Sibir* (formerly Hotel Europa) (☎ 312 571), ul Lenina 22, has singles for US$40 and de luxe double rooms at US$80.

Where to eat

For a basic but filling meal for about US$1 you could try the *stolovaya* opposite Navigator Internet Café. For something

WHERE TO STAY AND EAT
5 Sibirya Korona Сибирья Корона
7 Stolovaya Столовая
10 Shashlik stands Шашлык
14 Hotel Mayak Гостиница Маяк
15 Hotel Turist Гостиница Турист
16 Hotel Sibir Гостиница Сибирь
19 Old Omsk Restaurant Ресторан Старый Омск
21 U Shvenka; Rostik's; Patio Pizza; ATM; Intourist
   У Швенка; Ростикс; Патио Пицца; Банк; Интурист

OTHER
1 Central Post Office Почтамт
2 Drama Theatre Театр Драмы
3 Military Museum Музей Истории Войск
4 Literature Museum Литературный Музей
6 Navigator Internet Café Кафе Навигатор Интернет
8 Bookshop Дом Книги
9 Turist Турист
11 Excursion River Station
12 Tobolsk Gate Тобольский Ворота
13 River Station & Airline tickets Речной Вокзал и Касса Аэрофлота
17 Currency Exchange Обмен валюты
18 Omsk State History Museum
   Омский Государственный Историко-Краевадуеский Музей
20 Musical Theatre Музыкальный Театр
22 St Nicholas Cathedral Никольский Собор
23 Atlantida Клуб Атлантида

tastier, *Sibirya Korona* by the river serves good Russian/European food in a cosy atmosphere, with mains at around US$3. The *Old Omsk* restaurant is more expensive but always popular and serves similar food.

In a cluster at pr Karla Marxa 5 are three modest choices: *U Shvenka*, *Rostik's* and *Patio Pizza*. For beer with your meal, go to U Shvenka; Rostik's does roast chicken and Patio Pizza serves what you'd expect plus pasta and salads. Expect to pay about US$5 for a large pizza.

There are a number of clubs along ul Lenina north of the bridge, but the best choice is *Atlantida*, south of the centre at pr Karla Marxa 18. With a restaurant, night-club and bowling alley, it's packed at the weekends. Entry is US$7 or half that during the week.

Moving on
By rail it's 9$^{1}/_{2}$ hours to/from Novosibirsk on the overnight No 88/87 train (US$21). This train has fake marble walls in each compartment, everything is of a higher than usual standard and you can often buy tickets just a few hours before departure.

Trains to Yekaterinburg (US$24) take 12 hours. For suggested rail services between Omsk, Tyumen and Tobolsk see p227.

Note that certain trains to/from Moscow use Moscow's Kazansky station, including the No 75/76 Tynda and No 117/118 Novokuznetsk.

The Omsk area code is ☎ 3812. From outside Russia dial +7-3812.

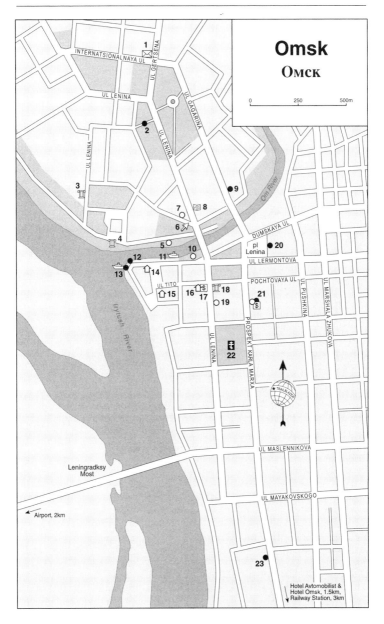

Novosibirsk
Новосибирск

With a population of just under 1.4 million, this is Siberia's largest city and its industrial centre, and Russia's third most populous city after Moscow and St Petersburg. But among the Trans-Siberian cities that foreigners usually visit, Novosibirsk has the least to offer the tourist; it's a relatively young city and has few buildings of historic interest. But it's a pleasant-enough place for a day or two and the vast scale of parts of the centre is amazing. 'Space', writes Colin Thubron in *In Siberia*, 'in the end, may be all you remember of Novosibirsk'.

You can visit the enormous opera house, the museums and the nearby town of Akademgorodok, the 'City of Scientists' where hundreds of researchers live in a purpose-built, lakeside town. Winters here are particularly harsh, with temperatures falling as low as minus 35°C.

Novosibirsk is also the terminus of the Turksib railway (see p129). Travellers can catch a train from here to Almaty in Kazakhstan and then continue east into China.

HISTORY

Novosibirsk didn't exist before the Trans-Siberian was built. Its spectacular growth in the 20th century is largely due to the railway. In 1891 it was decided that a railway bridge over the Ob should be built here, and two years later a small settlement sprang up on the river bank to house the bridge builders. The town was named Novo-Nikolayevsk in honour of the accession of the new Tsar.

By 1900 over 15,000 people lived here and the numbers grew as railway and water-borne trade developed. As far as tourists were concerned there was only one reason to get off the Trans-Siberian here, as Baedeker's 1914 *Guide to Russia* points out: 'It is a favourite starting point for sportsmen in pursuit of the wapiti, mountain sheep, ibex and other big game on the north slopes of the Altai'. The town suffered badly during the Civil War when 30,000 people lost their lives. During the first four months of 1920 a further 60,000 died of typhus. In 1925 Novo-Nikolayevsk was re-christened Novosibirsk ('New Siberia').

Between 1926 and 1939 the population mushroomed as smelting furnaces were built and fed with coal from the nearby Kuznetsk Basin and iron ore from the Urals. The early 1930s saw the laying of the final sections of the Turksib Railway (a project begun in the years just before World War I), completing a 2600km line from Novosibirsk across Kazakhstan via Semey (Semipalatinsk) and Almaty to Arys in the fertile valley of the Syr-Darya river in Central Asia. Grain from the lands around Novosibirsk could now be exchanged for cotton, which grew best in Central Asia. A film of the final stages of construction of this line, the jewel in the new government's first Five Year Plan, provides a fascinating early example of documentary cinema.

During World War II many civilians and complete factories were shifted to Novosibirsk from

NOVOSIBIRSK RAILWAY STATION – SIBERIA'S LARGEST

European Russia, and the city has been growing ever since. It's now the area's busiest river port and Siberia's major industrial centre, with many people employed in engineering and metallurgy factories.

WHAT TO SEE

Lenin Square and the Opera House

Ploshchad Lenina (Lenin Square) is the heart of the city. It's dominated by the vast **Opera and Ballet Theatre**, one of the largest in the world, with its silver dome and gigantic portico. The theatre was completed in 1945 after most able-bodied young men had been sent off to war. The effort was seen as all the more heroic in that many of the city's women and children helped the few builders who remained behind. You can get tickets from the kiosk on the left side of the theatre, or book them by phoning ☎ 223 866. Cheap seats cost just over US$1 and if the theatre isn't full you can move to more expensive seats for free.

In the middle of the square is a **statue of Lenin**, his coat blowing behind him in the cold Siberian wind, a rather more artistic representation than most. He is flanked by three soldiers on his right and by two 'Peace' figures on his left, who look as if they are directing the traffic that flows around the great square.

In the winter there are troika rides here, and people build ice-sculptures. The low building above the metro station is the oldest stone structure in the city.

Museum of Local Studies

The Museum of Local Studies (☎ 218 630) has two branches, at Vokzalnaya Magistral 11 and at Krasny pr 21. The bulk of the collection is housed at the former address, on the ground floor of the block right behind TsUM. It's a good museum, although you will need a guide to explain some of the historical exhibits.

A display on life before the Revolution includes a Singer sewing machine, a rusty British Norton motorbike (built in 1909) and an early piece of rail (stamped 'Birmingham 1899'). There's also a special section recording the agonizing times during the Civil War, when the city was occupied by White Russians and then Bolsheviks, before being devastated by typhus in 1920.

The extensive display of Siberian flora and fauna includes some of the 50 species of mammals, 30 species of fish and 30 species of birds that are found only in Novosibirsk Oblast. There's also a collection of Siberian trees and grasses, a geological display and the skeleton of a mammoth. The labels on the natural history exhibits are in Latin as well as Russian: for translations see p427. The museum is open 10:00-18:00 daily except Monday and Tuesday; entry US$0.50.

WHERE TO STAY
2 Hotel Novosibirsk Гостиница Новосибирск
17 Hotel Sibir, Intourist & Business Centre Гостиница Сибирь
34 Hotel Tsentralnaya Гостиница Центральная

WHERE TO EAT
9 Restaurant Sobek Ресторан Собек
11 Stolovaya Столовая
22 Stolovaya Столовая
23 New York Pizza & New York Times Нью Йорк Пицца и Нью Йорк Таймс
25 Stolovaya Столовая
28 Zolotoy Kolos Булочная Золотой Колос
33 Grill Master Гриль Мастер
35 Stolovaya Столовая

OTHER
1 Central Railway Station Железнодорожный Вокзал
3 Sports Shop Магазин Спорта
4 Circus Цирк
5 Cathedral of the Ascension Вознесенский Собор
6 Aeroflot & Lufthansa Аэрофлот и Люфтанза
7 Inkom Bank Инком Банк
8 Sputnik Travel Agency Спутник
10 Market Рынок
12 Banya Баня
13 Museum of Local Studies Краеведческий Музей
14 TsUM Department Store ЦУМ
15 Santafe Bar Сантафе Бар
16 Kirov House-Museum Дом-Музей Кирова
18 Internet Centre (in pedestrian subway) Интернет Центр
19 Steam Engine Паровоз
20 Puppet Theatre Кукольный Театр
21 Pub 501
24 Irish Pub
26 Telephone Office & Internet Междугородний Переговорный Пункт и Интернет
27 Central Post Office Почтамт
29 Sibirsky Bank Сибирский Банк
30 Tsentralny Dom Knigi Bookstore Центральный Дом Книги
31 Medical Institute Медицинский Институт
32 Opera & Ballet Theatre Театр Оперы и Балета
36 Museum of Local Studies Extension Краеведческий Музей (Присртойка)
37 Chapel of St Nicholas Часовня Святителя Николая
38 Sobi-Bank Соби-Банк
39 German Consulate Консольство Германии
40 Airlines Office Авиа Касса
41 Synagogue Синагога
42 Art Gallery Картинная Галерея
43 Symphony & Orchestra Halls Симфония Зал
44 Alexander Nevsky Cathedral Собор Александра Невского
45 Long-distance Bus Station Автовокзал
46 Oktyabrsky Commercial Port Октябрьский Порт

METRO STATIONS Станция Метро
A Ploshchad Garina-Mikailovskovo Площадь Гарина-Михайловского
B Ploshchad Lenina Площадь Ленина **C** Ploshchad Gagarinskaya Площадь Гагаринская
D Krasny Prospekt Красный Проспект
E Ploshchad Oktyabrskaya Площадь Октябрьская **F** Rechnoy Vokzal Речной Вокзал

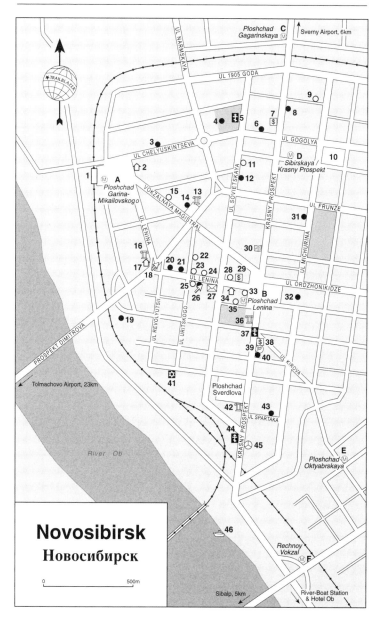

Ploshchad C
Gagarinskaya Ⓜ

Sverny Airport, 6km

UL 1905 GODA

UL NARIMSKAYA

9 ○

7 ○ 8 ●
4 ● ✚ 5 $
6 ●

UL GOGOLYA

3 ●

UL CHELYUSKINTSEVA

Ⓜ D
Sibirskaya /
Krasny Prospekt

10

🏠 2

11 ○

12 ○

1 ▯
Ⓜ A
Ploshchad
Garina-
Mikailovskogo

UL SOVETSKAYA

KRASNY PROSPEKT

15 ○ 13
14 🏛

UL FRUNZE

31 ●

UL MICHURINA

VOKZALNAYA MAGISTRAL

UL LENINA

16 🏛

30 📖

17 🏠

18

20 ● 21 ●
22 ○
23 ○
24 ○

28 ○ 29
$

UL LENINA

25

26

27 ⊠

34 ○
33 ○
Ⓜ B
Ploshchad
Lenina

32 ●

UL ORDZHONIKIDZE

35

36 🏛

UL REVOLYUTSII

UL URITSKOGO

37 ✚
$ 38
39 ●
Ⓟ
40 ●

UL KIROVA

19 ●

PROSPEKT DIMITROVA

Tolmachovo Airport, 23km

41 ✡

Ploshchad
Sverdlova

42 🏛 43 ●

KRASNY PROSPEKT

UL SPARTAKA

44 ✚
❀ 45

River Ob

E
Ploshchad Ⓜ
Oktyabrskaya

46 ⛵

Rechnoy
Vokzal
Ⓜ F

Novosibirsk
Новосибирск

0   500m

Sibalp, 5km

River-Boat Station
& Hotel Ob

Other things to see

Alexander Nevsky Cathedral, at the south end of Krasny pr near the river, has been fully restored and is well worth a visit. Just south of pl Lenina is the tiny **Chapel of St Nicholas**, in the middle of the road and reached from beneath via the pedestrian subway. It was built on the spot said to mark the geographic centre of Russia, and opened during the city's centenary celebrations in 1993. The original church here was destroyed after the Revolution. On ul Sovetskaya, the **Cathedral of the Ascension** with its blue dome was built just 100 years ago.

The **Kirov House-Museum**, on ul Lenina and now overshadowed by the adjacent Hotel Sibir, is devoted to Sergey Kirov, a rising Communist Party leader who was assassinated in 1934 on Stalin's orders. It's an attractive log cabin, one of the few to have survived here. It's open 10:00-13:00 and 14:00-18:00. In the neighbouring apartment block there is a small exhibition of local handicrafts, mainly wood-carvings.

There is a good **Art Gallery** at Krasny pr 5, near the regional administration building on Sverdlovsk Square. It is open 11:00-18:30, closed Tuesday.

PRACTICAL INFORMATION
Orientation and services
The fifth largest city in Russia, Novosibirsk was designed on a grand scale. Krasny prospekt, its main street, extends for over 10km. The mighty River Ob bisects the city, leaving the main hotels, sights and railway station on the east bank. Although there were plans to rid the city of its Communist-era street names, the signs are still in place.

Recommended local travel agents include the adventure travel company **Sibalp** (☎ 495 922, 🖹 541 374, 🖳 sibalp @online.nsk.su), ul Nemirovicha-Danchenko 155/1, apt 47, who offer tours of the Altai region and can arrange climbing and rafting expeditions; Altai specialists **Magic Tours** (☎ 204 252), Krasny pr 62; and sports specialists **Tourist Guide Union** (☎ 297 561, 🖹 239 529), ul Lenina 30/2. **Intourist** (☎ 237 870) is in the Hotel Sibir at ul Lenina 21. **Sputnik** (☎172 382), on Krasny pr, is open 09:00-18:00 on weekdays.

You can access the Internet at the **Internet Centre**, open round the clock in the pedestrian subway near the Hotel Sibir, for US$0.50 an hour, or at the **long-distance telephone office** on ul Lenina for US$0.80 an hour.

There are numerous **ATMs** around Novosibirsk. Currency can be exchanged at most banks, at the Central Post Office on ul Lenina and in the service centre of the railway station. Sibirsky Bank on ul Lenina offers Visa card cash advances and Sobi-Bank on Krasny pr cashes Visa and Amex travellers' cheques.

There is a **banya** on ul Sovietskaya which costs about US$1 and is open 12:00-21:00. Buy your birch leaves, as everyone else does, from vendors outside.

For a good 'virtual guide' to Novosibirsk go to the Web site 🖳 www .olympia-reisen.ru/nskgue_e.phtml.

Local transport
On foot, pl Lenina is about 20 minutes from the railway station, straight down Vokzalnaya Magistral. Novosibirsk has a good but limited **metro** system (including some stations panelled in Siberian marble). To reach pl Lenina from the railway station (metro: Ploshchad Garina-Mikhailovskogo), go one stop to Sibirskaya/Krasny Prospekt station, change to the Studentskaya line and go one stop to Ploshchad Lenina station.

Novosibirsk has two airports: the international **Tolmachovo airport**, 23km from the city centre on the western bank, and the domestic **Sverny airport**, 6km to the north of the centre. Buses No 122 and 111 run between the two via the railway station and bus station, although minibuses covering the same routes are quicker.

Near metro station Rechnoy Vokzal (meaning 'river station') are the **river-boat station** and the **long-distance bus station**.

To get to Akademgorodok, see p238.

Tours

Travel desks at most hotels offer a morning **city tour** as well as tours to the sights and museums described below, for about US$25. Tours to **Akademgorodok** usually include a visit to the Geological Museum and in summer a boat trip on the Ob Dam reservoir. They can also arrange tickets for the **circus** (closed in summer) and for opera and ballet at the Opera House.

From the landing near Rechnoy Vokzal metro station you can organize your own boat trip to Korablik Island, popular with Novosibirskians for swimming and sunbathing from May to September.

Where to stay

The railway station's *rest rooms* (komnata otdikha), upstairs at the station, cost from US$6.50/13 for 12/24 hours for a bed in a double room, and there are private doubles for about US$36. Most rooms share bathrooms which are clean and have good hot showers. However, it's often full. You must show a ticket for onward travel.

Hotel Novosibirsk (☎ 201 120) is right opposite the railway station at Vokzalnaya Magistral 1. It's a typical Soviet place even down to the offhand receptionists; they might tell you they are full, in which case hang around for a few minutes, then ask again and they'll probably find a room, unless they really are full! Single rooms with attached bath cost US$31 and double rooms from US$40. Breakfast is included; whether you'll want it or not is another matter.

Hotel Tsentralnaya (☎ 227 294) is right in the city centre on ul Lenina 3; and was renovated in 2001. The staff are friendly and singles go for US$20 with shared

bath. Doubles are US$66 with bath and you can pay for one bed in a double room for half the price.

Hotel Ob (☎ 667 401), ul Obnaya 49, is on the banks of the Ob about 3km south of the city centre; it's next to the River Station, 10 minutes' walk from Rechnoy Vokzal metro station. Singles start from US$21 and doubles from US$34.

The most upmarket place in the centre is the *Hotel Sibir* (☎ 231 215), ul Lenina 21, a Polish/Russian joint venture and Intourist's standard pad. Rooms start at US$55/86 single/double including breakfast. The rooms are clean and well maintained. There's a classy souvenir shop in the foyer, several bars, a business centre and an Intourist counter which can book rail and air tickets.

For *homestays* contact HOFA (p20).

Where to eat

There are numerous fast-food places in the centre including the American-owned *New York Pizza & Traveler's Coffee* on the corner of ul Lenina and ul Uritskogo. A slice of good pizza and a drink costs around US$1. There are several other branches around town. There's also a busy branch of *Grill Master* on ul Lenina.

There are several *stolovaya* around town. Most are pretty basic but one (No 34 on the map key) around the corner from Ploshchad Lenina metro station is excellent. It serves a wide range of Russian dishes and is very popular. All the food is on display so it's easy to order if you can't speak much Russian. Three very filling courses will cost about US$2 and it's open 09:00-21:00.

There is a surprisingly good snack bar in *TsUM* where the pastries are excellent and the coffee thoroughly drinkable.

Zolotoy Kolos, opposite Hotel Tsentralnaya, is a recommended bakery and a good place to stock up for the Trans-Siberian trip as it sells a range of bottled and tinned foods.

The Novosibirsk area code is ☎ 3832. From outside Russia dial +7-3832.

A night at the Korean *Restaurant Sobek* (☎ 205 867), ul Dostoevsky 19, can be exciting. It's an intimate little place normally packed with racketeers and mafiosi. The food's not bad, about US$5 per person, drinks and live ammunition extra.

A reasonable choice is the downstairs restaurant at *Hotel Sibir*. The service is good, as is the food, but it tends to fill up with leather-jacketed, shell-suited 'businessmen' in the evenings. The upstairs restaurant is better and often has live music. Expect to pay US$20 without drinks; if you want wine it's best to buy it at the kiosk outside the restaurant.

Entertainment
Good places for a drink and live music in the evening are the *New York Times* (☎ 227 809, ul Lenina 12), below New York Pizza, where there's a band most nights, kicking off at 21:00; and *Pub 501*, ul Lenina 20.

Santafe Bar on Vokzalnaya Magistral, a large place serving a wide range of beers, is popular with people after work. It's open 11:00-23:00. There is a cloned *Irish Pub* on ul Lenina which serves Guinness for a most un-Irish price, nearly US$10.

Novosibirsk boasts numerous cultural options besides its famous Opera and Ballet Theatre. Traditional venues include the **Circus** (☎ 237 584), ul Sovietskaya 11; a **Puppet Theatre** (☎ 221 202), ul Revolyutsii 6; and **Symphony and Chamber Orchestra Halls** (☎ 224 880), ul Spartaka 11. Possibly more interesting might be the **Chaldony Song and Dance Company** (☎ 418 889), ul Zabaluyeva 47; the **Siberian Dixieland Jazz Band** (☎ 235 642), ul Kirova 3; and the **Siberian Russian Folk Chorus** (☎ 202 269), ul Krasnoyarskaya 117.

Where to shop
There are the usual souvenir shops in the hotels. The main street for shopping is Vokzalnaya Magistral. The **market** is one block east of Krasny pr.

Tsentralny Dom Knigi Bookstore on Krasny pr has a good selection of maps and dictionaries. The **TsUM Department Store** on Vokzalnaya Magistral is surprisingly well stocked.

Moving on
By rail On the ground floor of the station at the northern end there is a service centre, open 08:00-19:30, which charges a US$1.60 service charge for tickets. Some staff speak English and it's usually quiet so you're more likely to get help here.

On the Trans-Siberian line Novosibirsk is 50 hours from Moscow (US$50), 9^1/$_2$ hours from Omsk (US$21), 12 hours from Krasnoyarsk (US$24), 32 hours from Irkutsk (US$33) and 4^1/$_2$ days from Vladivostok (US$70). Note that certain trains to/from Moscow use Moscow's Kazansky station; these include No 31/32 Novokuznetsk and No 907/908 Irkutsk.

On the Turksib railway, Novosibirsk is 33 hours from Almaty and 68 hours from Tashkent.

By air Most international and long-distance domestic flights use **Tolmachovo airport**; other domestic air traffic uses **Sverny airport**.

An airlines office at Krasny pr 28 includes ticket and information desks for several carriers serving Novosibirsk, including **Siberian Airlines** (Aviacompaniya Sibir; ☎ 276 353, 🖃 227 572, 🖳 www.s7.ru), **Transaero** (☎ 231 917, 🖃 230 321) and **Olympia-Reisen-Sibir** (☎/🖃 233 735). **Aeroflot** and **Lufthansa** have ticket offices at ul Gogolya 3.

There are daily flights to Moscow (four hours) from about US$130 with Transaero and Siberian Airlines. Siberian Airlines also has connections several times each week to St Petersburg, Vladivostok, Frankfurt and Hanover, and a weekly flight to Seoul.

EXCURSIONS FROM NOVOSIBIRSK

River cruises

The River Ob which flows through Novosibirsk is the busiest river in Siberia. The most popular cruise is a 65-minute round trip from the river station to Korablik Island. Most passengers get off there as it is a favourite swimming spot. The ferry travels this route three times a day from May to September. To get to the river station, take the metro to Rechnoy Vokzal station; you can see the landing from the exit.

Akademgorodok (Академгородок)

Akademgorodok, 30km from Novosibirsk, was established in the 1950s as a university and research centre for scientists. It soon grew into an élite township of over 30,000 of the Soviet Union's top intellectuals and their families. In this pleasant sylvan-setting researchers and students grappled with scientific problems with a two-fold aim: to push ahead of the West in the arms race and to harness the wealth of Siberia for the good of the USSR. As with its Olympic athletes, the Soviet Union believed in training its academics from a very early age, spiriting them away from home to attend special boarding schools for the gifted in Akademgorodok. Compared to the ordinary citizen they were well looked after here, the shops stocked with little luxuries hard to find elsewhere. As government funding slowed to a trickle in the early 1990s the utopian dream ended

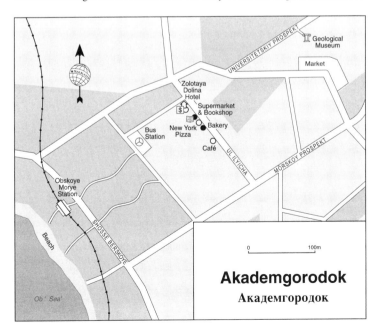

Akademgorodok

Академгородок

and many scientists were lured abroad. But the university still has a good reputation and since 1998 funding has been on the rise.

This is well worth a visit. The forested, lakeside setting offers a relaxing opportunity to get away from polluted Novosibirsk. There's little to see and the town, with its badly maintained buildings, now has a rather melancholic atmosphere, but it still offers a glimmer of the old Soviet utopian dream.

The **Geological Museum** in the Institute of Geology and Geophysics is open to tour groups only. You could follow one in or just say 'moozay' to the doorman, and you may be let into the museum which is straight ahead, up the stairs. The overpowering mineral wealth of Siberia is displayed here, including the purple mineral chaorite, found only in this part of the world.

After looking round Akademgorodok you can walk through the birch forest and over the railway track to the **beaches** of the **Obskoye Morye** ('Ob Sea'), the vast reservoir created by construction of the Novosibirskaya power station, Siberia's first large hydroelectric project. This is a good place to swim in summer, when the water is surprisingly warm: 18°C for two to three months and up to 22°C around July. In winter **cross-country skiers** converge on Akademgorodok, site of some good tracks maintained by the Alik Tulskii ski centre.

Where to stay and eat The *Hotel Zolotaya Dolina* (☎ 3832-356 609), ul Ilyicha 10, charges US$13/28 for a single/double room, and has a good *restaurant*. They may be reluctant to let you stay if they discover you're not a visiting scientist, but hang around for a few minutes and they'll probably find you a room.

For cheap food try the *café* beside the nearby commercial centre (*torgovy tsentr*). There is also a branch of *New York Pizza* in Akademgorodok. In the same street is a **bookshop** which has a small selection of maps, posters and books in English.

Getting there The easiest option for getting to Akademgorodok is the No 15 minibus from outside Novosibirsk's central railway station. These leave every 10 minutes and cost about US$0.50. A **taxi** from Novosibirsk costs about US$20 one way but you may be able to beat them down.

Alternatively you can take a **train** to Obskoye Morye (Обское Море), a slow 50-minute trip from Novosibirsk's suburban station (*prigorodny vokzal*), located south of the central station. There is a timetable at the entrance to the station; trains run from about 06:00 to 23:00. From Obskoye Morye station head away from the reservoir, crossing shosse Berdskoye and continuing on any of the paths through the park for about 10 minutes.

Tomsk (Томск)

Founded in 1604 on the River Tom, Tomsk developed into a large administrative, trading and gold-smelting centre on the Great Siberian Post Road. For a time it was the most important place in Siberia, visited by almost every 19th-century traveller. The city was an important exile centre and had a large forwarding prison. Having almost succumbed to the stench from the overcrowded cells in 1887, Kennan wrote: 'If you visit the prison my advice to you is to breakfast heartily before starting, and to keep out of the hospital wards.'

Tomsk was bypassed by the original Trans-Siberian railway, and began to lose out to stations along the main line. But it remains a robust city of 485,000 people, administrative capital of Tomksaya Oblast and a centre for industrial engineering. The city achieved international notoriety when a radioactive waste reprocessing plant blew up at nearby Tomsk-7 on April 6 1993, contaminating some 120 sq km.

Some finely-preserved wooden architecture and leafy streets make this a pleasant place to spend a few days. At the time of writing it was difficult for foreigners to stay the night without personally going through the tedium of registering with Tomsk OViR/PVU.

Practical information Tomsk's railway and bus stations are next to each other in the south-east of the city, about 2km from the centre. Buy a map from the station and walk up ul Krasnoarmeyskaya where there are many old wooden buildings. The **post office** is in the centre of town at pr Lenina 95. Around the post office are various places to eat and the best shops.

Hotel Tomsk (☎ 524 115) is directly opposite the railway and bus stations. It's a nice enough place for the location, with singles/doubles for US$18/30 with shared bathroom or US$26/41 with attached bathroom. Often there is no hot water here, and if you arrive at lunchtime you may find the sole receptionist on her break.

Also opposite the station is *Trattoria*, a restaurant which serves decent pizza and salads.

Getting there There are trains between Novosibirsk and Tomsk (US$15) but as they depart about 02:00 in either direction, you're better off on a bus. There are also two trains daily to/from Tayga (US$2, 3 hours).

Buses leave several times per hour from 07:00 to 19:30 from Novosibirsk's long-distance bus station (*avtovokzal*), taking 4¹/₂ hours and costing US$5. There are also minibuses running the same route, departing when full, taking four hours and costing US$10.

Krasnoyarsk
Красноярск

Krasnoyarsk is a major industrial centre, producing a quarter of Russia's aluminium, almost a quarter of its refrigerators and millions of truck and car tyres a year. As a result air pollution can be bad at times but Krasnoyarsk is nevertheless worth a visit. The city centre is quite attractive and with hills on the outskirts it's certainly more pleasantly located than some other Siberian cities.

Russian settlement dates back to the construction of Krasny Yar fort on a hill overlooking the River Yenisey in 1628. By 1900 the population was 27,000 and the town boasted 20 churches and two cathedrals, a synagogue, 26 schools, a railway technical college and a botanical garden reputed to be the finest in Siberia.

RL Jefferson visited Krasnoyarsk in 1897 and was impressed: 'Its situation cannot fail to elicit admiration – the tall mountains rear up around it.' Most of the townsfolk he met here were ex-convicts. So used were they to their own kind that they were particularly suspicious of anyone who lacked a criminal record. He was told of a certain merchant in the city who found it difficult to do

>
> **Yudin's library**
> Travelling intellectuals in the 19th and early 20th century were advised to
> visit the library of a Krasnoyarsk merchant named Gennadi Yudin. This bibliophile
> had assembled a collection of 100,000 volumes, including almost every publication
> ever issued in Siberia. At the end of the 19th century, while sentenced to exile in
> Krasnoyarsk, Lenin spent several months working in this library.
>   In 1906 Yudin sold his valuable collection to the US Library of Congress for just
> US$40,000, though it was valued at US$114,000. He did this 'with the sole idea of
> establishing closer relations between the two nations,' he wrote to the Congressional
> Librarian.

business, never having been behind bars. To remedy the situation this merchant
is said to have travelled back to St Petersburg and deliberately committed a
crime punishable by exile to Siberia. After a short sentence in Irkutsk he
returned to his business in Krasnoyarsk and 'got on famously' thereafter.

During the Second World War many factories were relocated here from
European Russia. The city grew as a trading centre and in the course of the
Soviet Union's early five-year plans underwent massive industrialization to
become Siberia's third largest city, now with a population of about 867,000.

A recent local governor was the late army hardliner, General Alexander
Lebed. In the 1996 presidential elections Lebed challenged Boris Yeltsin but
finally stood down and supported him, earning Yeltsin's backing for his own
election campaign in Krasnoyarsk.

WHAT TO SEE

The terraced hill around the old part of town is an interesting place for a walk.
The restored **Annunciation Cathedral** is worth visiting; it's on ul Lenina. The
old **Catholic Church**, which contains an organ, is
near the Central Park.

The tiny **Chapel of St Parasceva Pyatnitsa**
stands above the city and there are good views
from here. It takes about 40 minutes to reach the
chapel from the Hotel Krasnoyarsk.

There are several museums including the
Surikov Art Museum (☎ 272 558), ul Parizhskoy
Kommuny 20, open 10:00-18:00 (closed Monday),
and the renovated **Museum of Local Studies**, ul
Dubrovinskogo 84. The former House-Museum of
V I Lenin (he stayed here for all of two months in
1897) on ul Lenina is now a **Literature Museum**,
and the *SS Nikolay*, the steamship on which Lenin
sailed to exile in Shushenkoye, is now a bar. What
would he think?!

STALINIST-GOTHIC
RIVER STATION
KRASNOYARSK

The Krasnoyarsk area code is ☎ 3912. From outside Russia dial +7-3912.

PRACTICAL INFORMATION
Orientation and services
Krasnoyarsk has two parts, separated by the Yenisey River. The north bank is a mass of terraces and is bounded on the north by a steep hill known as Karaulnaya Mountain and on the west by the forested Gremyachinskaya Ridge. The railway station, museums and hotels are on this side. Just south of the station is the academic area (another Akademgorodok). The south bank is relatively flat and is mostly factories and multi-storey apartment blocks.

Alf Tour (☎ 217 626, 🖹 274 630, 🖳 alftur@hotelkrs.ru), in the Hotel Krasnoyarsk, offers a range of tours, including US$20 for a city tour, US$40 for a tour to Stolby and US$25 to Divnogorsk (see the Excursions section p244). At **Paradise Travel Agency** (☎ 652 650, 🖹 652 649, 🖳 paradise@paradise-travel.ru), ul Lenina 24, staff speak good English and can help with tours, boat tickets and other requests.

There's an **ATM** in the Hotel Krasnoyarsk. Visa and MasterCard cash advances are possible from Avtovazbank at pr Mira 39 and Sinto Bank at pr Mira 87.

For more information on Krasnoyarsk, the online **Krasnoyarsk City Guide** is at 🖳 http://tlcom.krs.ru, which has an English version.

Local transport
For the airport catch bus No 135 from the **bus station** (US$0.50) or take a taxi (US$20). To go between the bus station and Hotel Krasnoyarsk, take trolley bus No 2.

Where to stay
HOFA offer homestays in Krasnoyarsk, see p20.

There's accommodation on the water in the *Mayak*, a boat moored by the river station. They charge only US$5/8 for a single/double although cabins are small and bathrooms are shared. There are also some upmarket double cabins with attached bathrooms.

The *Hotel Enisey* (☎ 278 262), ul Dubrovinskogo 80, is pretty basic and charges from US$5 for a two-bed room. *Hotel Sever* (☎ 224 114), on the corner of ul Lenina and ul Dzerzhinskogo, is also basic but it's adequate and charges US$10-20 for a single and US$15-30 for a double. Both of these places might, or might not, let you stay.

The best-value hotel is the large, standard *Hotel Krasnoyarsk* (☎ 273 769), ul Uritskovo 94, charging from US$20/25 for a single/double without breakfast. All rooms are large and have a bathroom attached.

Intourist groups usually stay at the 103-room *Hotel Oktyabrskaya* (☎ 271 916, 🖳 october@krsk.ru, http://tlcom.krs.ru/october), pr Mira 15, with rooms from US$40/60 for a single/double unless you're Russian in which case you'll pay around a third of that.

Where to eat
While all the hotels have restaurants, the best choice is the *Hotel Krasnoyarsk*, with three cafés, a restaurant and a bar-grill. A good meal in the restaurant will cost about US$10. The square in front of the hotel has many cafés and is a lively place on summer evenings. Another good choice is *Café Shakhmatnoye*, pr Mira 85.

Quite possibly the best pizza in Siberia is served at the *Rosso Italian Restaurant*, next door to the Hotel Sever on ul Lenina. You can buy pizza by the slice.

The attractive *Kofeynya* (literally 'coffee house') on ul Dubrovinskogo between the Hotel Yenisey and the Museum of Local Studies is a good place. Their roast chicken is recommended.

The *SS Nikolay*, the steamship on which Lenin sailed into exile in Shushenkoye, has now been turned into a bar, open daily 14:00-02:00.

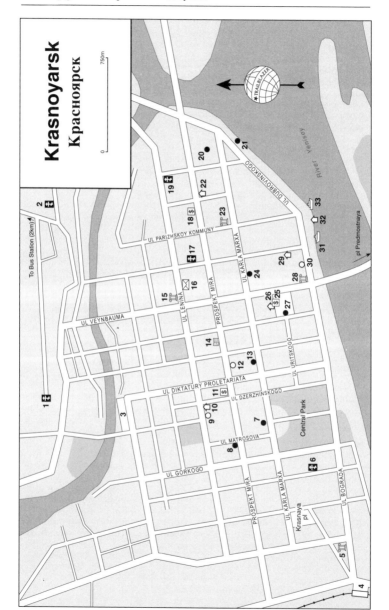

Krasnoyarsk
Красноярск

750m

0

To Bus Station (2km)

2

19

22

20

21

18 $

23

UL PARIZHSKOY KOMMUNY

17

16

15

UL LENINA

UL VEYNBAUMA

PROSPEKT MIRA

UL KARLA MARKA

UL DUBROVINSKOGO

River Yenisey

pl Predmosthaya

33

32

31

30

29

28

24

26

$ 25

27

1

3

14

13

12

11 $

10

9

8

7

UL DIKTATURY PROLETARIATA

UL DZERZHINSKOGO

UL URITSKOGO

UL MATROSOVA

Central Park

UL GORKOGO

6

PROSPEKT MIRA

UL KARLA MARKA

Krasnaya
pl

UL BOGRADA

5

4

★TRAILBLAZER

WHERE TO STAY AND EAT

9 Rosso Italian Restaurant Ресторан Россо
10 Hotel Sever Гостиница Север
12 Café Shakhmatnoye Кафе Шахматное
22 Hotel Oktyabrskaya Гостиница Октябрьская
26 Hotel Krasnoyarsk Гостиница Красноярск
29 Hotel Enisey Гостиница Енисей
30 Kofeynya Кофейня
32 Hotel-Boat Mayak Гостиница Маяк

OTHER

1 Chapel of St Parasceva Pyatnitsa
   Часовня Святой Великомученицы Параскевы Пятницы
2 Trinity Church Троицкая Церковь.
3 Market Рынок
4 Railway Station Железнодорожный Вокзал
5 Palace of Culture of the Combine Harvester Builders (!)
   Дворец Культуры Комбайностроителей
6 Catholic Church Католическая Церковь
7 Lenin Statue Памятник Ленину
8 Aeroflot Office Агентство Аэрофлота
11 Sinto Bank Синто Банк
13 TsUM Department Store ЦУМ
14 Book Shop Книжный Мир
15 Literature Museum Литературный Музей
16 Central Post Office Почтамт
17 Intercession Church Покровская Церковь
18 Avtovaz Bank Автовазбанк
19 Annunciation Cathedral Благовещенский Собор
20 Main Concert Hall Большой Концертный Зал
21 SS Nikolay Пароход «Св. Николай»
23 Surikov Art Museum
   Художественный Музей В И Сурикова
24 City Administration Building
   Здание Городской Администрации
25 ATM (in Hotel Krasnoyarsk)
27 Opera & Ballet Theatre Театр Оперы и Балета
28 Museum of Local Studies Краеведческий Музей
31 Boats to Divnogorsk
33 River Station Речной Вокзал

Moving on

By rail Krasnoyarsk is 65 hours from Moscow (US$55), 12 hours from Novosibirsk (US$24) and 20 hours from Irkutsk (US$27). The 'Yenisey' train (No 55/56) runs between Krasnoyarsk and Moscow. As its SV compartments are often empty, you can watch videos in them for US$0.60 per person. The provodnitsa has a range of videos to choose from.

By river The Yenisey River is a major communications link and passenger ferries sail nearly 2000km along it from Krasnoyarsk. For three months in the summer, twice-weekly boats go north to Dudinka or on to Dickson on the Arctic Ocean, a 4-5 day trip northbound and about a week coming back, but at the time of writing Dudinka and neighbouring Norilsk were closed to foreigners so you could only go as far as Igarka. Tickets are available from **Yenisey Steamship Line** (☎ 274 845, 🖩 236 567) on the 2nd floor of the river station. It's usually unnecessary to book more than a few days in advance if you don't mind which class you travel in; 1st class costs about US$100 each way.

By air Krasnoyarsk's Yemelyanovo-1 airport is 40km north of the railway station. There are daily flights to Moscow (5 hours) and several flights a week to Novosibirsk, Yekaterinburg, Khabarovsk and Yakutsk. There are also occasional charter flights to Hannover in Germany There is an office of **Aeroflot** (☎ 222 156) at ul Matrosova 4), and you can buy tickets for **Krasnoyarsk Airlines** (☎ 236 366, 🖩 234 896) at the Hotel Krasnoyarsk.

EXCURSIONS AROUND KRASNOYARSK

Stolby Nature Sanctuary (Заповедные Столбы)

An excursion to this 17,000-hectare recreational area is probably the most pleasant thing to do from Krasnoyarsk. It's just upstream on the Yenisey and there are over 100 rock pillars (*stolby*), some up to 100m high, that look like people and have been given fanciful names like The Grandfather and The Woman.

Getting there Take the **suburban train** to Ovsyanka (Овсянка), 5km from the city, or to Turbaza (Турбаза). Or you could take **bus** No 7 from pl Predmostnaya (площадь Предмостная) to the Turbaza stop, though from here it is a 5km uphill walk to the first of the pillars. If you stay on the bus to the village of Bazaykha (Базайха), a few stops further on, you can take a **chairlift** (if it is working) to the top and walk to the pillars from there. Another option is to take a tour (see p241).

Divnogorsk (Дивногорск)

About 30km away on the railway past Stolby Nature Sanctuary is the town of Divnogorsk and the Yenisey Hydroelectric Dam. The 100m-high dam has a huge 'escalator', a kind of mobile basin mounted on a cog railway, to lift ships right over the dam. You can see this unusual system operating until late October when the river freezes over.

Where to stay *Hotel Biryusa*, on ul Naberezhnaya, charges US$30 for a double.

Getting there **Hydrofoils** travel between Krasnoyarsk's river station and Divnogorsk from May through August, departing every two hours. The trip takes about 45 minutes and costs US$5 return. There are also **buses** from the bus station behind Hotel Krasnoyarsk which take about 90 minutes, or you can catch a suburban **train** (three times a day). Travel agents in Krasnoyarsk (see p241) can arrange tours to Divnogorsk.

Irkutsk
Иркутск

Irkutsk is the most popular stop for Trans-Siberian travellers. In this city, which was once known as the 'Paris of Siberia', you'll find people rather more friendly and relaxed than those in European Russia. Along many of the streets you can still see the cosy-looking log cabins (eaves and windows decorated with intricate fretwork) which are typical of the Siberian style of domestic architecture.

Some 64km from Irkutsk is Lake Baikal, set within some of the world's most beautiful countryside. Trekking, camping, boat excursions, diving and riding are just a few of the pursuits available in this outdoor paradise.

HISTORY

Military outpost

Irkutsk was founded as a military outpost in 1652 by Ivan Pakhobov, a tax collector who had come to encourage the local Buryat tribesmen to pay their fur tribute. By 1686 a church had been built and a small town established on the banks of the Angara. Tea caravans from China passed through Irkutsk, fur-traders sold their pelts here and the town quickly developed into a centre for trade in Siberia.

By the beginning of the 19th-century Irkutsk was recognized as Siberia's administrative capital. The Governor, who lived in the elegant white building that still stands by the river (opposite the obelisk), presided over an area 20 times the size of France. Being the capital it was the destination of many exiled nobles from Western Russia. The most celebrated exiles were the Decembrists, who had attempted a coup in St Petersburg in 1825. The houses in which some of them lived are now museums.

Boom town

With the discovery of gold in the area in the early 19th century, 'Gold Fever' hit Irkutsk. Fortunes were made in a day and lost overnight in its gambling dens. In spite of a great fire in 1879 which destroyed 75% of its houses, the city had by the end of the century become the financial and cultural centre of Siberia. Its cosmopolitan population included fur traders, tea merchants, gold prospectors, exiles and ex-convicts. A few lucky prospectors became exceedingly rich, amassing personal fortunes equivalent to £70-80 million today. Often no more than illiterate adventurers, they spent their money on lavish houses, French tutors for their children and Parisian clothes for their wives.

By far the most exciting occasion in the Irkutskian social calendar for 1891 was the visit of the Tsarevich (later Nicholas II), who stayed only a day but had

🚂 **How to get on in society**

Travelling along the Trans-Siberian at the end of the 19th century, John Foster Fraser spent several days in Irkutsk. Recording his observations on the city's social order he wrote, 'To do things in the proper way and be correct and Western is, of course, the ambition of Irkutsk. So there is quite a social code. The old millionaires, who for forty years found Irkutsk society – such as it was before the coming of the railway – quite satisfied with a red shirt and a pair of greased top boots, are now "out of it". A millionaire only becomes a gentleman when he tucks in his shirt and wears his trousers outside and not inside his boots. It is etiquette to put on a black coat between the hours of ten in the morning and noon. No matter how sultry the evening is, if you go for the usual promenade and not wear a black overcoat you proclaim you are unacquainted with the ways of good society. As to wealth, there is but one standard in Irkutsk. A man is known by his furs, and his wife by her furs and pearls'.

In Irkutsk Fraser was unimpressed by the standards of hygiene exhibited by all classes of society and declared that 'certainly the Russian is as sparing with water as though it were holy oil from Jerusalem'.

John Foster Fraser, *The Real Siberia* (1902)

time to visit the museum, a gold-smelting laboratory and the monastery, to consecrate and open a pontoon bridge over the Angara (replaced only in 1936), to review the troops and to attend a ball.

The first rail travellers arrive

On 16 August 1898 Irkutsk was linked by rail to Europe with the arrival of the first Trans-Siberian Express. The train brought more European tourists than had dared venture into Siberia in the days when travelling meant weeks of discomfort bumping along the Trakt (the Post Road) in a wooden tarantass (carriage).

Their guidebooks warned them of the dangers awaiting them in Irkutsk. Bradshaw's *Through Routes to the Capitals of the World* (1903) had this to say: 'The streets are not paved or lighted; the sidewalks are merely boards on crosspieces over the open sewers. In summer it is almost impassable owing to the mud, or unbearable owing to the dust. The police are few, escaped criminals and ticket-of-leave criminals many. In Irkutsk and all towns east of it, the stranger should not walk after dark; if a carriage cannot be got as is often the case, the only way is to walk noisily along the planked walk; be careful in making crossings, and do not stop, or the immense mongrel mastiffs turned loose into the streets as guards will attack. To walk in the middle of the road is to court attack from the garrotters with which Siberian towns abound.' The dangers that Bradshaw warned his travellers against were no exaggeration for at the time the average number of reported murders per year in Irkutsk was over 400, out of a population of barely 50,000.

Irkutsk today

Today's Irkutskians are rather better behaved, although as everywhere in Russia, mafia-related crime is on the increase. A city of about 594,000, Irkutsk is still one of the largest suppliers of furs to world markets, although engineering is now the main industry.

In the 2000 elections Putin polled just over 50% of votes in Irkutsk oblast. On a campaign visit to Irkutsk in February 2000 he highlighted the problems of the region: 'The economic successes of the oblast are modest...More than four million people live in extreme poverty'. He added that he wanted to encourage the creation of large companies able not only to extract the region's mineral resources but also to develop and sell them on Russian and world markets. It's now well over a decade since the dawn of the market economy in Russia but the Siberian dream has yet to come true.

WHAT TO SEE

Cathedrals and War Memorial

Irkutsk in 1900 had two cathedrals. The splendid Cathedral of Our Lady of Kazan, bigger than Kazan Cathedral in St Petersburg, was damaged during the Civil War. It was demolished and now the ugly bulk of the **Central Government Headquarters** stands in its place, opposite the **WWII Memorial**.

The **Cathedral of the Epiphany** (1724) is across the road. In the great fire of 1879 it was badly damaged and the heat was so intense that it melted one of the 12-ton bells. It served for a time as a museum of icons but is now a practising church again; the icons have been relocated to the Art Museum.

Church of Our Saviour

This boat-shaped church contains the **Museum of Local Studies**. There are some interesting exterior frescoes which depict, from left to right, Buryats being baptized, Christ being baptized and the local bishop, Innocenti, being canonized. The museum inside contains a small display of stuffed local animals. Upstairs there's an interesting religious history display including the robes, human-bone rattle and feathered head-dress of a shaman (see p248); masks and robes used in Tibetan Buddhist mystery plays; and prayer wheels and Buddhist texts from monasteries south of Irkutsk. Up a very narrow staircase is a small exhibition of bells. The museum is open 10:00-18:00, daily except Tuesday; entry US$2 (photos US$2 extra).

CHURCH OF OUR SAVIOUR (1706)

Polish Catholic Church

Opposite the Church of Our Saviour is a Catholic church with a tall steeple. It is Siberia's only neo-Gothic church, built in 1883 by exiled Poles, and services are held on Sundays for their descendants. During summer there are usually organ concerts on Sundays and Wednesdays, starting around 19:30.

Shamanism
Shamanism is a primitive religion centred around the shaman, a medium and healer. Although the concept of the shaman is fairly common throughout the world, the word itself comes from the language of the Tungus tribes of Siberia.

Wearing spectacular robes, the shaman beats a drum and goes into a trance in order to communicate with the spirits. From them the shaman discovers the cause of an illness, the reason for the failure of the crops, a warning of some approaching disaster. Commonly, spirits are thought to select their shamans before they are born and brand them with distinguishing features: an extra finger or toe or a large birthmark. During their adolescence they may be 'tortured' by the spirits with an illness of some kind until they agree to act as shaman. Some shamans may be physically weak, epileptic, mentally disordered, but through their spiritual power they gain authority and perform rituals.

'Shamanism played an extremely negative role in the history of the Siberian peoples... In status, activity and interests, the shamans were hand in glove with the ruling cliques of the indigenous populations', wrote the Marxist anthropologists MG Levin and LP Potapov in *The Peoples of Siberia*. Other anthropologists have been less severe, noting that shamanism gave those with mental and physical disorders a place in society at a time when most other societies shunned the handicapped.

In the spirit of freedom of religious expression in Russia today shamanism is undergoing something of a revival. The Republic of Tuva, west of Irkutsk, is the modern centre of Shamanism.

Regional Museum
This museum of local history, beside the river just south of the Hotel Intourist, has some interesting exhibits. Upstairs is a 'local achievements' gallery including a model of part of the BAM railway. Above the stairs is a panorama showing the Great Irkutsk Fire of 1879. Ethnographic galleries downstairs include flints and bones from an archaeological site at nearby Malta, where evidence of human habitation has been found dating back 24,000 years; the inside of an early 20th century settler's house with a carved wooden sideboard, HMV gramophone and 78rpm records; a shaman's robes, antlers and drum; old photographs; and a most peculiar article of clothing: a suit made completely of fish skins, standard summer attire of the Goldi tribe who lived in the Far Eastern Territories. The museum (☎ 333 449), ul Karla Marxa, is open 10:00-18:00, except Monday; entry US$2.50, with discounts for student-card holders.

Other places of worship
At the turn of the century Irkutsk boasted 58 places of worship. This fell to only three or four after the Revolution but many are now reopening.

Znamensky Monastery (Apparition of the Virgin), with its turquoise domes, lies north-east of the city and is well worth a visit. Services are held regularly. The frescoes inside are impressive but recent restoration has left the interior looking rather modern. The casket containing the body of **St Innokent**, a Siberian missionary who died here in 1731, was returned to Irkutsk in the 1990s and may be moved to the cathedral when restoration there is complete. It is said that his body is incorruptible and has been the source of many miracles.

Beside the church are the graves of Yekaterina Trubetskaya (see p249) and Gregory Shelekhov who founded the colony of Alaska in 1784 (sold to the USA in 1868). Shelekhov's grave is marked by an obelisk decorated with cartographic instruments. To get here, take trolley-bus No 3 from the south end of pl Kirova.

It's also interesting to visit the old **synagogue**, a large blue building at ul Karla Libknekhta 23, the lower storey of which has been converted into a factory. Enter through the door on the left with the three stars above it. There is a **mosque** at ul Karla Libknekhta 86.

Art Museum
Comprising works by 18th and 19th century Russian, German, Flemish, French, Italian and English painters, this collection was begun by Vladimir Sukachev in the 1870s and 'donated' to the city after the Revolution. There are, however, the inevitable modern Soviet masterpieces, such as AA Plastov's *Supper of Tractor Operators* and AV Moravov's *Calculating of Working Days*. The gallery devoted to 19th century local scenes is particularly interesting; in the gallery of Western Art (15th-19th centuries) you'll find a small canvas labelled 'Landsir 1802-73' which is *The Family of Dogs* by Sir Edwin Landseer, who designed the lions in Trafalgar Square. The Art Museum (☎ 244 336), ul Lenina 5, is open 10:00-18:00, closed Tuesday; entry US$3.50.

Trubetskoy House
The wooden house once occupied by Sergey Trubetskoy and Yekaterina Trubetskaya and other nobles involved in the unsuccessful coup of 1825 is preserved as a museum, kept as it was when the exiles lived here. In the cellar there is a display of old photographs showing life in the Nerchinsk silver mines and a prison cell in Chita. There is also a picture of Maria Volkonskaya (see below) and her child. The house-museum (☎ 275 773), at ul Dzerzhinskogo 64, is open 10:00-18:00, closed Tuesday; entry US$2.50. ('With thermopane windows it would be a great place'. Louis Wozniak (USA): Visitors' book in this museum.)

Maria Volkonskaya's house
The large, attractive blue and white house of this famous Decembrist who followed her husband into Siberian exile is open to the public. If you've read Caroline Sutherland's *The Princess of Siberia* then you must visit the house, a grand old building but sparsely furnished and without the lived-in feel of other house-museums. Displays include Maria's clothes, letters and furniture, and church robes of the 18th and 19th centuries. In the yard there are several wooden buildings and a well. The house (☎ 277 818), at pereulok Volkhonskogo 10, is open 10:00-18:00, closed Monday; entry US$3.50.

Angara steamship
The *Angara*, commissioned in 1899, was partially assembled in England and then sent to Irkutsk in pieces by train. Until the completion of the Circumbaikal

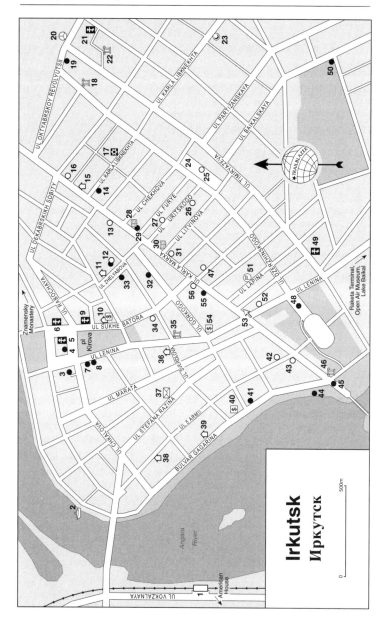

Irkutsk
Иркутск

WHERE TO STAY
10 Hotel Angara & ATM Гостиница Ангара
11 Hotel Arena Гостиница Арена
15 Hotel Kech Гостиница Кэч
36 Hotel Rus Гостиница Русь
38 Hotel Agat Гостиница Агат
39 Hotel Baikal-Intourist Гостиница Байкал-Интурист

WHERE TO EAT
12 Restaurant Aura Ресторан Аура
13 Niva Bakery Пекарня Нива
16 Beer Bar U Shveyka Бар У Швейка
25 Bar Tsentralny Бар Центральный
26 Café Vernysazh Кафе Вернисаж
27 Café Belgrad Кафе Белград
31 Café Snezhinka Кафе Снежинка
34 Café Blinnaya Кафе Блинная
42 Restaurant Drakon Ресторан Дракон
43 Bar Efimich Бар Эфимич
47 Maradona Sports Café
52 Café Karlson Кафе Карлсон
56 Café Havana

OTHER
1 Railway Station Железнодорожный Вокзал
2 River Station Речной Вокзал
3 Sputnik Спутник
4 Central Government Headquarters Дом Правительства
5 Museum of Local Studies, in Church of Our Saviour
   Краеведческий Музей и Спасская Церковь
6 Cathedral of the Epiphany Богоявленский Собор
7 Irkutsk State Teachers' Training Institute of Foreign
   Languages Педагогический институт иностранных языков
8 Ploshchad Kirova Bus Stop Остановка «Пл. Кирова»
9 Polish Church Польский Костёл
12 Circus Цирк
14 Aqua Eco Аква Эко
17 Synagogue Синагога
18 Trubetskoy House Музей-усадьба Трубецкого
19 Titanic Nightclub Клуб-Титаник
20 Long-distance Bus Station Автовокзал
21 Church of the Transfiguration Преображенская Церковь
22 Maria Volkonskaya's House Музей-усадьба Волконского
23 Mosque Мечеть
24 Central Market Центральный Рынок
28 Sitborg Books Ситборга Книги
29 Turbasa Bukhta Peschanaya Office
   Турбаза Бухта Песчаная Контора
30 Rodnik Books Подника Книги
32 Aeroflot & Baikal Airlines
   Касса Аэрофлота и Авиакомпания Байкал
33 Central Telegraph Office Центральный Телеграф
35 Art Museum Художественный Музей
37 Central Post Office Почтамт
40 Alfa-Bank Альфа-Банк
41 Transaero Авиакомпания Трансаэро
44 Gagarin Pier Причал Гагарина
45 Trans-Siberian Builders' Monument
   Обелиск Транссибирской
46 Regional Museum Краеведческий Музей
48 Philharmonic Hall Филармония
49 Church of the Elevation of the Cross Крестовоздвиженская Церковь
50 Aistenok Puppet Theatre Театр Кукол Аистенока
51 Mongolian Consulate Консульство Монголии
53 Internet Centre Интернет Центр
54 Inkom Bank Инком Банк
55 Stratosfera Nightclub Клуб-Стратосфера

line she ferried rail passengers across the lake together with her bigger sister, the *Baikal*. Following the line's completion in 1904 the *Angara* performed a series of menial tasks before being abandoned, partially submerged, in 1958. She was later restored as a Museum of Nautical Navigation. In 1995 the ship was again converted and this time became the office of a local newspaper. Unfortunately you can't wander around the vessel although there are plans to reopen part of it, so it may be worth asking. Trolley-bus No 5 passes this way.

Other sights

In the summer, touring companies perform in the imposing **Drama Theatre**, built at the turn of the 20th century, on ul Karla Marxa.

There are 1- to 2-hour **boat trips** along the river to the dam and power station, leaving daily from Gagarin Pier near the **Trans-Siberian Builders' Monument**. This statue has Yermak and Count Muravyev-Amursky on its sides and the double-headed Imperial eagle on the railings surrounding it. The building beside the obelisk may look like a mini-Sydney Opera House but its main use is for dog shows. You can take a pony ride from here as well.

In the **Fur Distribution Centre**, on the southern outskirts of the city, visitors are shown some of the 18 varieties of mink and also the pelts of the Barguzinsk sable, which sell for over US$750 each. It's open to tours only, and only between October and May.

Also worth a visit is the **House of Artists** (Dom Khudozhnikov) at ul Karla Marxa 38, which has the occasional exhibition.

RIVER CRUISES

Rivers are navigable from mid May to September. There are three river stations in Irkutsk, each for a different destination. Scenic cruises depart from Gagarin Pier, at the intersection of bulvar Gagarina and ul Gorkogo. Boats travel upstream to the Angara Hydroelectric Power Station dam; departures for the 80-minute return trip leave every hour. Tickets can be bought at the pier. For long-distance boats and those to Lake Baikal see p256.

PRACTICAL INFORMATION
Orientation

Irkutsk railway station is on the west bank of the river; the city centre and tourist hotels are on the east. The city centre is along two intersecting arteries, ul Lenina and the shopping and museum street, ul Karla Marxa. Ul Lenina runs north-west from the administrative and public transport centre of pl Kirova.

Any bus heading north from the railway station should take you over the bridge; from here all the main hotels are within walking distance.

Services
Information

On the Internet a good starting place is 🖥 **www.irkutsk.org** which has links to numerous other Irkutsk-related sites.

Locally, you can get good **maps** from Hotel Baikal-Intourist, and from the Sibtorg Bookshop at ul Karla Marxa 24.

Irkutsk State Teachers' Training Institute of Foreign Languages (☎ 333 246, 🖷 333 244), Room 201/203, ul Lenina 8, has **Russian-language courses** lasting anywhere from a week to four years. The cost is US$350 per month for tuition and US$60 a month for accommodation.

Communications

Faxes can be sent from the Central Telegraph Office or the Central Post Office, both open daily 08:00-20:00. For **courier services**, DHL (☎ 290 307) is at Hotel Baikal-Intourist.

There is an **Internet** connection at the Central Telegraph Office which costs US$1 per hour, but there is only one terminal and the queue can be long. The **Internet Centre**, downstairs at the corner of ul Karla Marxa and ul Lenina, charges the same price.

Banks

There are **ATMs** at Hotel Angara and at Alfa-Bank, bulvar Gagarina 38, open 10:00-19:00. You can also cash travellers' cheques at the bank. Other banks with exchange facilities include Inkombank on ul Lenina and Sberbank at ul Furye 2.

You can exchange only US$ cash at Hotel Baikal-Intourist (open 24 hours) and at the office on the 2nd floor at the central market (open daily, 09:00-18:00).

Travel agents

A recommended budget agency is **Baikal Complex** (☎ 390 756, 510 934, 🖷 432 060, 🖳 baikal@online.ru, travel@angara.ru, www.baikalcomplex .irk.ru), Yubileyny 67-35, PO Box 30, Irkutsk-29. It's run by the friendly Yuri Nemirovsky. Call ahead for directions to the office (it's not in the town centre) or for a visit by staff.

Another helpful tour operator is Andrey Berenovsky whose company, **AquaEco** (☎ 201 000), is at ul Karla Libknekhta 12. **Sputnik** (☎ 341 733, 🖷 341 629, 🖳 baikalsp@online.ru) is at ul Chkalova 39A; enter through the courtyard behind the big grey building. They will register your visa for US$11 the same day if you give it to them in the morning. **Maria Travel** (☎ 240 168, 🖷 341 492, 🖳 mariatravel@mail.ru), ul Kievskaya 2, room 211, can arrange trips in the Baikal area. **Intourist** (☎ 290 161) runs overpriced tours from the Hotel Baikal-Intourist, though staff are helpful if you have any questions.

Tours

The travel agents listed above run similar tour programmes which include city tours, day trips and **adventure tours** such as hiking, skiing and trekking. They also offer two-day trips along the **Circumbaikal Railway Line**. See p260 for information on this trip.

Also on offer are **scuba diving** (US$55, PADI or BSAC certificate required) and **horse riding** (US$10 per hour). A four-day trip to **Olkhon Island** (200km north in Lake Baikal), costing about US$60 a day per person, includes accommodation in a wooden hotel (no hot water) in Khuzhir village and visits to several Buryat sacred sites and a Stalin-era gulag camp.

Mirage (☎ 461 921, 464 943 🖳 miraj @irk.ru), run by Igor Sher and recommended by several readers, does trips in their own boat, the *Mirage*. Maximum group size is six, meals are said to be superb and there are hot showers on board. Other programmes include day trips for fishing, and a 10-day Baikal cruise for about US$900 per person.

Local tour guide **Dmitry Meleshko** (🖳 www.irkutsk.ru/baikaladventure, dmel@ irkutsk.ru) has been recommended by readers for homestays and nice inexpensive tours of Irkutsk and Lake Baikal.

Local transport

Since most sights, restaurants and shops are within walking distance of the hotels, this is the most pleasant and interesting way to get around.

Bus No 20 runs between the train station and the airport down ul Lenina. Trams No 1 and 2 go from the station over the bridge and into the centre of town. Tram No 4 goes out to the airport (25 minutes) and back from ul Lenina near the Art Museum.

Shared minibuses (*mikriki*) which run on fixed routes are even more useful: you can see what other passengers pay – R7 (about US$0.20).

The Irkutsk area code is ☎ 3952. From outside Russia dial +7-3952.

Where to stay
Baikal Complex (see p253), HOFA (see p20) and G&R International (see p169) are among companies offering *homestays* in Irkutsk, Listvyanka, Bolshie Koty and Khuzhir for US$35-45 per person per night including some or all meals. You may also be approached at the station by people offering rooms in their houses for US$5-10. Don't agree to anything without seeing the place and the family first.

A cheap hotel in the town is *Hotel Agat* (☎ 297 325), ul 5 Armii 12, which charges US$15/22 for singles/doubles. Bathrooms are shared and clean. It's in an apartment block, partly hidden by trees; a wooden sign on the door says 'Agat' in handwritten Cyrillic. *Hotel Kech* (☎ 335 972), ul Karla Marxa 34, is very basic but clean and friendly. Singles with shared bathroom are US$7, although at the time of writing they weren't taking foreigners.

Near the circus is *Hotel Arena* (☎ 344 642), ul Zhelyabova 8a. It looks better inside than out, although staff seem reluctant to provide any form of service. Rooms with shared bathroom cost from US$23/36 for a single/double, or US$17 for one bed in a double room.

Hotel Angara (☎ 293 616), ul Sukhe Batora 7, is in a good location and always busy with Trans-Sib tourists on pre-booked tours. Singles/doubles with attached shower cost from US$36/53; there are pricier rooms on the renovated 6th floor which they'll offer you first. A remarkably good buffet breakfast is included. A bus service along the endless corridors might be a good idea.

A bit more expensive but worth it is *Hotel Rus* (☎ 343 715), ul Sverdlova 19. Prices for singles are US$36-55 and it's US$63-90 for double rooms, all including breakfast and attached bathrooms. It has a very good restaurant and the whole place is well run.

By far the best choice for budget travellers is the *American House* (☎ 432 689), ul Ostrovsky 19, a very relaxed place with friendly proprietors who speak a little English. It has three singles, two doubles and overflow areas, and bed and breakfast

costs US$15-20. From the railway station you must either take a taxi (ask for 'Americansky Dom') or walk (15 minutes). On foot, leave the station and cross the road. An opening in the row of kiosks takes you to some stairs, and at the top a dirt road leads between apartment blocks to a larger dirt road. This goes up a very steep hill and near the top on the left is a brick church. Opposite, on the right, is ul Ostrovsky. From the city centre you can take bus No 11 from in front of Hotel Angara, across the river, along ul Mayakovskogo and left into ul Chaykovskogo. Get off at the first stop along this street, which is on the corner of the dirt road from the railway station. Walk down the street for about 20m and you will see the church on the right; turn left down ul Ostrovsky.

Hotel Baikal-Intourist (☎ 290 171, ▤ 277 872), bulvar Gagarina 44, is good but seems overpriced compared to Irkutsk's other hotels. Singles/doubles start from US$70/80. The price includes breakfast and the hotel offers a wide range of tourist services.

Where to eat
One local delicacy worth looking out for on menus is *omul*, a delicious fish native to Lake Baikal.

Quiet, friendly *Café Karlson*, on ul Lenina, serves good snacks amidst fairytale décor. Delicious blinis are served at *Café Blinnaya*, near the corner of ul Sukhe Batora and ul Sverdlova.

Other good cheap cafés include the popular *Café Teatralnoye*, ul Lenina 23, open 12:00-04:00; and *Café Belgrad*, ul Uritskogo 7, which offers Yugoslav dishes for around US$5. This is also a good place for a drink.

Café Vernysazh, ul Uritskogo 16, serves tasty Russian food; count on around US$10 for a meal. *Café Snezhinka*, ul Litvinova 2, also serves good Russian dishes and is similarly priced. It's open until 02:00.

An excellent place for traditional Siberian meals is *Restaurant Rus* in the Hotel Rus (☎ 277 315), ul Sverdlova 19. A three-course meal costs US$10-15. The food in the restaurant at the *Hotel Angara* is also good, and even the live singer isn't too bad. A three-course meal is around US$10.

The best oriental food is at the Chinese *Restaurant Drakon*, ul 5 Armii 67, but it's difficult to get in for dinner without a reservation.

Another good choice is *Bar Efimich*, ul Karla Marxa 5, which has a pleasant garden and serves excellent shashlyk for US$5. It's open until 01:00 but the food stops around 22:00.

Restaurant Aura (☎ 336 139), on the 1st floor of the circus building, offers authentic Siberian fare: their pelmeni are recommended. A meal without drinks will cost about US$10. The drawback is the nightly cabaret act (striptease at weekends): an entry fee will indicate that there's a show in progress.

Self-caterers should visit the *central market*. The best bread in town comes from *Niva Bakery*, ul Karla Marxa, and you can also get a good cup of coffee here.

Entertainment
This is Siberia, not New York, but Irkutsk is at least livelier in the evenings than it was in the communist era.

For bars, try the *Belgrad* or *Bar Efimich* (see Where to eat), *Beer Bar U Shveyka* (ul Karla Marxa 34), *Maradona*

Sports Café (ul Kievskaya 1), *Café Havana* (next to the Stratosfera club; see below) and *Bar Tsentralny* (ul Litvinova 17). There are also bars in the larger hotels such as the Baikal-Intourist.

There are several nightclubs: the *Butterfly* is at the Hotel Baikal-Intourist. There's also the *Titanic*, ul Oktyabrskoy Revolyutsii 25. The *Stratosfera*, ul Karla Marxa 15, also has a bowling alley; entry is US$1 and it's open until 05:30.

Irkutsk also has a **circus**. The **Aistenok Puppet Theatre** (☎ 270 666) is at ul Sovietskaya 1. Concerts are given at the **Philharmonic Hall** (☎ 345 873), ul Dzershinskogo 2, and there are organ recitals at the Polish Church.

Where to shop
The heart of the city is the **central market** on ul Dzerzhinskogo. Long before you see it you'll hear the many bootleg cassette dealers demonstrating their 'latest' releases. Good-quality CDs sell for about US$2. Other stalls sell everything from Sindy dolls and Snickers bars to sports shoes and switchblades.

The best local bookshops are **Rodnik Books**, ul Litvinova 1, and **Sibtorg**, ul Karla Marxa 24. Next to Sibtorg is an **art shop** which sells semi-precious gems, some such as chaorite which is found only in the Baikal area.

 Mongolia Travel Services in Irkutsk
Irkutsk has a Mongolian Consulate, Mongolia-specialist travel agents, and daily trains to Mongolia.

The **Mongolian Consulate** (☎ 342 145, 🖹 342 143), ul Lapina 11, is open 09:30-12:00 and 14:30-17:00, Mon, Tues, Thurs, Fri. A transit visa good for 10 days in the country is available in only 45 minutes for US$30 here or in three to four days for US$15; bring two passport photographs and your ticket out of Mongolia. To get a tourist visa, you need US$40 and two photos. Processing takes three to four days or for US$60 a faster service is possible.

Travel agents that can organize train tickets, accommodation and tours to Mongolia include Baikal Complex, Intourist and Sputnik. Baikal Complex offers the cheapest deals.

To buy **train tickets** from Irkutsk to Mongolia, go to the International Ticket Office at Irkutsk railway station. Train No 264 leaves daily for Ulan Bator; a kupé ticket should cost around US$35.

Moving on

By rail There is an International Ticket Office on the 1st floor (north end) of Irkutsk station, open 08:00-13:00 and 14:00-22:00. You can also get domestic tickets there. There is also a rail-ticket booth at the Hotel Baikal-Intourist, charging US$3 commission.

By rail, Irkutsk is 86 hours from Moscow (US$62), 32 hours from Novosibirsk (US$33), 20 hours from Krasnoyarsk (US$27), 8 hours from Ulan Ude (US$13), 36 hours from Ulan Bator (US$35) and 72 hours from Vladivostok (US$58). Note that the daily train No 907/908 serving Irkutsk via Yekaterinburg and Novosibirsk uses Moscow's Kazansky station.

By bus For Listvyanka see p258.

By river Boats for **Lake Baikal** and **Listvyanka** depart from Raketa Terminal (☎ 238 072) above Angara Dam; the dam is 5km upstream (south) of Irkutsk. Bus No 16 runs to the terminal from pl Kirova; the trip takes 45 minutes.

From Raketa Terminal there are also hydrofoils to **Nizhneangarsk** (12 hours) via **Severobaikalsk** on Wednesday (returns Friday), to **Ust Barguzin** (Monday), to **Bukhta Peschanaya** (three per week) and to **Bolshie Koty** (three per day).

Hydrofoils for **Bratsk** (12 hours, three per week) via **Angarsk** depart from the River Station, near the bridge from the railway station. Buy your ticket two days in advance. Avoid the area around the River Station after dark as it's notoriously dangerous.

By air There are direct international flights from Irkutsk to Ulan Bator, Niigata (Japan) and Shenyang (China).

Transaero (☎ 330 891) is at bulvar Gagarina 38. **Aeroflot** (☎ 276 917) is at ul Gorkogo 29, and next door is **Baikal Airlines**, which has services to Moscow and Khabarovsk. Air tickets can also be purchased from the Flight Ticket Office (☎ 293 415) in the Hotel Angara.

Opposite Top left: Permafrost and mammoth tusks in the caverns under the Permafrost Institute in Yakutsk (see p265). **Top right:** Obelisk to the builders of the Trans-Siberian Railway (see p252) in Irkutsk. **Bottom:** Specimens of the unique local wildlife at the Baikal Ecological Museum (see p260) include the *golomyanka*, a fish that lives at depths of up to 1500m and does not lay eggs but gives birth to live young.

Lake Baikal
Озеро Байкал

The world's deepest lake

Lake Baikal, 64km (40 miles) south-east of Irkutsk, is 1637m (5371ft) deep and estimated to contain more than 20,000 cubic kilometres of water, roughly 20% of the world's freshwater supplies. If all the rest of the world's drinking water ran out tomorrow, Lake Baikal could supply the entire population of the planet for the next 40 years.

Known as the 'Blue Eye of Siberia,' it is also the world's oldest lake, formed almost 50 million years ago. It is also among the planet's largest lakes, being about 400 miles long and between 20 and 40 miles wide. The water is incredibly clear and, except around Baikalsk and the Selenga delta, completely safe to drink owing to the filtering action of numerous types of sponge which live in its depths, along with hundreds of other species found nowhere else.

Holy Sea

Russian colonists called Baikal the 'Holy Sea' since there were so many local myths and legends surrounding it. The Buryats believed that the evil spirit Begdozi lived on Olkhon Island in the middle of the lake, though Evenki shamans held that this was the home of the sea god Dianda. It is hardly surprising that these primitive tribes were impressed by the strange power of the lake for at times sudden violent storms spring up, lashing the coast with waves 2m high or more. It freezes to a depth of 3m for four months of the year, from late December. The Angara is the only river that flows **out** of the lake. Since a dam and hydroelectric power station were built on the Angara in 1959 the level of the lake has been slowly rising.

Environmental threats

The lake's remoteness kept it safe from environmental damage until the building of the Trans-Siberian railway at the end of the 19th century. The risk of damage has further increased with the construction of new towns on the northern shores for the construction of the BAM line, and because of industrial waste from Ulan Ude (the Selenga River flows past this city into the lake via one of the world's last large wetlands, the Selenga delta).

The most famous campaigner for the protection of the lake is author Valentin Rasputin. Demonstrations in Irkutsk in 1987 resulted in filtration equipment being installed in the wood pulp mill at Baikalsk on the edge of the lake but cur-

---

Opposite Top: Climb the hill above Listvyanka (see p260) for a good view over Lake Baikal. People tie ribbons to branches of the trees here while sending up a prayer to the local deities. **Bottom:** A picnic in the woods near Listvyanka.

Life-enhancing waters
Guides never fail to recount superstitions concerning the power of Baikal water. Dip your hands in, they say, and you will add a year to your life. Dip your feet in too and this becomes five years. Brave the icy waters for a swim and, if the shock doesn't kill you instantly, you'll be around for 25 extra years.

A world record was set in here in 1991, as a team of relay swimmers managed to cross the width of the lake in 17 hours. But even these intrepid athletes had trouble: because of the extreme cold, the longest period any one of them could spend in the water at one time was 30 minutes.

---

rent reports suggest that it is inefficient and that pollution is continuing. A coastal protection zone was established around the entire lake in 1987 but campaigners bemoan the fact that government anti-pollution laws have no teeth. They believe the lake should be placed under the independent protection of UNESCO.

For more on environmental issues related to Lake Baikal see the Web site ▣ www.greenpeace.ru/english/enbaykal, or contact Greenpeace's Moscow-based Baikal Campaign Coordinator, Roman Pukalov (▤ 095-257 4110, ▣ bru ssia@ru.greenpeace.org).

GETTING TO LAKE BAIKAL

You can get from Irkutsk to Lake Baikal by boat (see p256) or by bus. Buses depart from Irkutsk's long-distance bus station on ul Oktyabrskoy Revolyutsii; the trip takes about 90 minutes and costs US$1.60. In summer, buses depart from Irkutsk at 09:00 and 11:00 and from Listvyanka at 07:30, 11:00, 16:45 and 18:00. The bus will stop on request virtually anywhere, with major stops at the Open Air Museum, Baikal Ecological Museum, Listvyanka village and Listvyanka pier. There are also minibuses running the same route for US$3.30

Open Air Museum
On the road between Irkutsk and Listvyanka is the Museum of Wooden Architecture (☎ 145 249), a collection of reconstructed traditional wooden houses. It is located at the km47 marker from Irkutsk or the km23 marker from Listvyanka; ask the bus driver for 'moozay'. There is a large farmhouse, a bathroom with a vast wooden tub, a water-mill and a post-house, complete with Imperial crest on its roof-top. When the only way to cross Siberia was by road and river, fresh horses and simple accommodation were available from post-houses such as this. The museum is open only in the summer but you can wander round outside in spring and autumn.

LISTVYANKA

Listvyanka is an attractive village of wooden houses beside Lake Baikal. There's also a shop, two small cafés and a jetty. The Baikal Ecological Museum and above it the Hotel Baikal-Intourist are about 2km before the village on the road from Irkutsk. Behind the hotel is a hill with a fine view over the water to

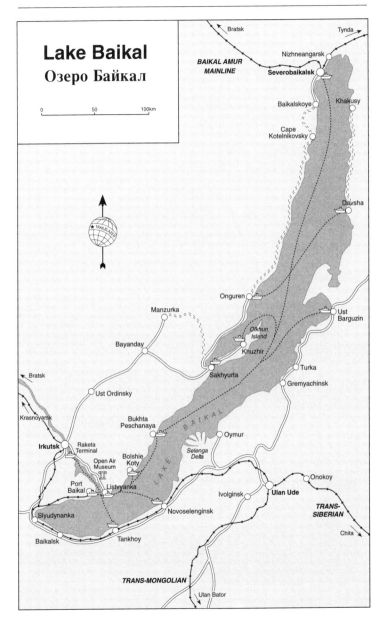

Lake Baikal
Озеро Байкал

0   50   100km

Bratsk
Tynda
BAIKAL AMUR
MAINLINE
Nizhneangarsk
Severobaikalsk
Baikalskoye
Khakusy
Cape
Kotelnikovsky
Davsha
Onguren
Manzurka
Ust
Barguzin
Olkhun
Island
Bayanday
Khuzhir
Sakhyurta
Turka
Bratsk
Gremyachinsk
Ust Ordinsky
LAKE BAIKAL
Krasnoyarsk
Bukhta
Peschanaya
Oymur
Irkutsk
Raketa
Terminal
Selenga
Delta
Open Air
Museum
Bolshie
Koty
Onokoy
Port
Baikal
Listvyanka
Ivolginsk
Ulan Ude
Slyudynanka
TRANS-
SIBERIAN
Novoselenginsk
Baikalsk
Chita
Tankhoy

TRANS-MONGOLIAN

Ulan Bator

the Khamar-Daban Mountains. The half-hour hike up is well worth it. At the top there's a little shelter and a tree decorated with paper ribbons that people have tied to it for good luck, an old Siberian custom.

Baikal Ecological Museum

The Baikal Ecological Museum (formerly Limnological Museum, ☎ 460 324), has a number of fascinating displays of the unique marine life and animals in the Baikal area. Entry is US$2 and it's open 09:00-19:00.

Over 80% of the species in Lake Baikal cannot be found anywhere else in the world. These include 1085 types of algae, 250 mosses, 450 lichens, 1500 vascular plants, 255 small crustaceans, 83 gastropods, 86 worms and 52 fish. Exceptionally high oxygen levels in the lake create an ideal environment for many creatures which have become or are becoming extinct elsewhere. These include freshwater seals, until recently threatened with extinction by the Buryats who turned them into overcoats. They are now a protected species, listed in the *Red Book of Endangered Species* and currently numbering about 60,000. A unique Baikal fish is the tiny *golomyanka*, which lives at depths up to 1¹/₂km and is made up of 35% fat. Surprisingly, it gives birth to its young alive and fully formed.

The museum also contains a model of the *Angara* and a collection of the sponges which keep the water so clean. Colonists' wives discovered that they were also very useful for polishing the samovar.

St Nicholas Church

A pleasant 10 minute walk through the village takes you to a tiny church where an old woman sells cheap-looking icons. Although the village is worth seeing, one feels that this church has been part of the tourist 'milk-run' for a long time. 'No smoking on the territory of the Church', warns a sign in English. Concessions to tourists have their advantages: five-star lavatories are thoughtfully located behind the building.

Shaman Rock

In the stretch of water between the Baikal Ecological Museum and Port Baikal it's possible to make out a rock sticking out of the water. According to local legend, Old Man Baikal had 336 sons (the number of rivers which flow into the

---

Riding the Circumbaikal Railway

A trip on the Circumbaikal Railway (see p361) should not be undertaken lightly. There are two daily trains each way but they're unreliable and very slow. As there is no accommodation in Port Baikal, and it is difficult to get between there and Listvyanka you should be well prepared – you may be up all night. Confirm the times of all services before you set out. Theoretically it is possible to catch a train at the weekend from Irkutsk to Slyudyanka, then take the afternoon Circumbaikal train to Port Baikal. You should reach the station in time for the last ferry from Port Baikal to Listvyanka, which departs at 20:00. Don't expect anything to run to schedule. The easiest way to travel this route is to take one of the tours organized by Irkutsk travel agents (see p253).

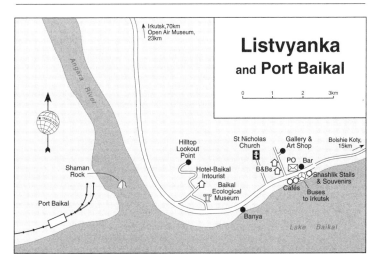

lake) and one daughter, the beautiful but headstrong Angara. She enraged him by refusing to marry the feeble Irkut, preferring the mighty Yenisey (Russia's longest river). The old man chained her up but one stormy night she slipped her bonds and fled north to her lover. As she ran her furious father hurled a huge boulder after her. She got away but the rock remains to this day. The level of the lake has since risen and very little of Shaman Rock is now visible.

Where to stay
There are many **B&Bs** in the village, generally charging about US$20. If you just turn up and ask around, it won't be long before you find one. Near Baikal Ecological Museum is the pleasant *Hotel Baikal-Intourist* (☎ 3952-290391) where most tours stop for lunch. Rooms are US$60/80 for a single/double. Services offered here include bike hire (US$6 per day), skiing, sleigh rides, boat trips and horse riding. There is an expensive sauna, too.

Several travel agencies in Irkutsk (see p253) offer **homestays** in the Listvyanka area; Baikal Complex charges US$30 a night including meals. Baikal Complex also has its own year-round **hostel** at ul Gudina 75, near the public bus line. Its eight twin rooms (US$40 for two) have toilet and shower attached. An alternative is the *Sand Bay Holiday Home* (Turbasa Bukhta Peschanaya), a tourist camp on the lakeshore about 80km north of Listvyanka. To book ahead, visit their Irkutsk office (☎ 243 515) ul Karla Marxa 22, apt. 17.

Where to eat
The restaurant at *Hotel Baikal-Intourist* is excellent; try their omul soup. Other options include two *cafés* (including the *Last Century Café* which was recommended by a reader) in Listvyanka. In summer you can always pick up freshly smoked or barbecued omul fish from local traders on the jetty. There is also a **bar**, popular with locals and tourists, which stays open late.

Banya
There is a banya in Listvyanka which is cheaper than the one at the Hotel Baikal-Intourist. It's beside the lake on the road between the village and the museum, and signposted as a sauna. You can dive into the lake to cool off afterwards.

PORT BAIKAL

Across the water from Listvyanka is the attractive village of Port Baikal. Prior to 1904 Trans-Siberian passengers had stop here and cross the lake by steamer to Mysovaya, from where the trains continued. The largest steamer was a 90m ice-breaker, the *Baikal*, which transported train carriages on her deck. She was built by the English firm of Sir W G Armstrong, Whitworth and Co. in Newcastle, UK, and delivered in sections by train. She was sunk in 1919 during the Civil War. Her smaller sister ship, the *Angara*, supplied by the same firm, survived (see p249).

Four ferries a day run between Port Baikal and Listvyanka from May to December. The first leaves Port Baikal at 06:30 and Listvyanka at 07:00, and the last leaves Port Baikal at 20:00 and Listvyanka at 20:30. In summer a hydrofoil also runs from Port Baikal and Listvyanka all the way along the lake to Severobaikalsk (see p263).

Travel agents in Irkutsk can organize trips to Port Baikal along the old Circumbaikal Railway (see p260).

BOLSHIE KOTY

Bolshie Koty is a small village north of Listvyanka. Its main attraction is Irkutsk University's Limnological Institute where students do their practical work. Gold used to be extracted from the Bolshie Koty River and the rusting dredges can still be seen 1km beyond the village. Baikal Complex organizes trips here, offering **homestays** (US$30).

Three hydrofoils a day link Irkutsk's Raketa terminal with Listvyanka and Bolshie Koty. If you miss the hydrofoil back, you'll have to walk the 15km to Listvyanka on a dirt track along the lake. Note that in some seasons parts of the track may become submerged. Ask locals before setting out.

Other Siberian excursions

The excursions mentioned below are covered in detail in the *Siberian BAM Guide – rail, rivers & road*, also from Trailblazer (see p128).

BRATSK (Братск)

About 470km north of Irkutsk on the BAM line lies one of the world's largest dams. The hydroelectric power station at Bratsk, Russia's second largest after the one at Krasnoyarsk, is the chief attraction of the town. Founded in 1631, Bratsk remained a tiny village until dam construction started in 1955. The station is reputedly capable of generating 4500 MW (the world's biggest hydroelectric project is the 12,600 MW Itaipu Dam on the Brazil-Paraguay border), although lack of customers means it has never run at full capacity. Though it's one of Russia's ten most polluted cities, Bratsk is awe-inspiring considering the achievement of constructing a modern city, a giant dam and massive industrial enterprises in just two decades. But unless you're riding the BAM anyway, or are especially interested in power stations, it's probably not worth the effort.

What to see
The top site is the impressive **Bratsk Hydroelectric Station** and dam. Bus Nos 4, 102, 103, 104, and 107 run along the dam, and you can also visit the power-house. On the outskirts of Angara Village there's an open-air **ethnographic museum** containing a reconstructed Evenki camp, a watchtower and a fort. There's a history museum at ul Komsomolskaya 38.

Orientation and hotels
Bratsk is not one town but a ring of connected settlements around the so-called Bratsk Sea, the reservoir created by the hydroelectric dam. From the south in a counter-clockwise direction, the towns are Port Novobratsk, Bratskoye Morye, Bratsk Tsentralny (the administration centre), Padun, Energetik on the dam's west bank and Gidrostroytel on the east bank.

Padunskie Porogi railway station, which serves the suburbs of Padun and Energetik, is the closest one to the Hotel Turist. Padun is the most attractive part of Bratsk as it has a pleasant promenade with an old log watchtower and the city's only church. Bratsk airport is to the north of Padunskie Porogi and can be reached by a 40-minute bus trip from the station.

Hotel Taiga (☎ 39531-413 979), ul Mira 35, charges US$60/80 for a single/double room and is overpriced. Intourist is on the 2nd floor.

Other choices are the *Hotel Turist* (☎ 39531-378 743), ul Naymushina 28 in Energetik, with rooms from US$15/25, and *Hotel Bratsk* (☎ 39531-438 436), ul Deputatskaya 32, at US$20/30.

Getting to Bratsk
From Irkutsk you can take a hydrofoil (US$10 one way) which leaves at 08.30, arriving in Bratsk at 20.50. On the return journey it leaves at 07.50 arriving at 20.40 in Irkutsk. Hydrofoils travel three times a week from May to September. Trains run daily (18 hours) between Bratsk and Irkutsk.

SEVEROBAIKALSK (Северобайкальск)

Severobaikalsk, on the BAM railway, is the 'capital' of the northern end of Lake Baikal. The town provides excellent access to north Baikal attractions, which include trekking and mountaineering in the Baikal Mountains, downhill skiing, sailing, seal-watching and visits to indigenous villages and a Stalin-era gulag.

What to see
Railway-related attractions are the **BAM Museum**, ul Mira 2, open 10:00-18:00 daily except Monday, and the **BAM Art Museum**, ul Druzhba. Bus No 3 goes past the railway museum.

Akikan Gulag (Акикана ГУЛаг) was a mica mining camp in the late 1930s. The residue of those terrible years consists of several collapsed wooden and stone buildings, towers and barbed wire fences. The camp is a two-hour walk from Kholodnoye (itself 60 minutes by bus or train from Severobaikalsk); BAMTour can provide a guide.

Orientation and services

Everything in Severobaikalsk is within walking distance with the exception of the hydrofoil port. Bus No 1 runs between the port and the central bus station, which is in front of the railway station.

BAMTour (☎/🖷 30139-21560, 🖳 rashit.yahin@usa.net), ul Oktyabrya 16-2, is a recommended company organizing BAM and north Baikal tours. It's run by Rashit Yakhin who worked on the railway in the early 1970s.

The *BAM Railway Cottages* are a 10-minute walk from the train station, and with a view of the coast. Booking is done via BAMTour and costs US$17 a night per person.

Hotel Podelmore, by the railway station, charges US$10 for a double.

Getting to Severobaikalsk

The easiest way to get between Severobaikalsk and Irkutsk is by hydrofoil (see p256). You can also get there by train from Tayshet on the Trans-Siberian. Unfortunately there is no direct Severobaikalsk–Irkutsk train: change at Tayshet or Bratsk.

NIZHNEANGARSK (Нижнеангарск)

Nizhneangarsk is 40km east of Severobaikalsk, wedged on a narrow strip between Lake Baikal and steep mountains. The 20km-long town has a large port for a small fishing fleet. The harbour was built for construction of the BAM but the railway arrived before it was needed. Although the regional airport is located here, Nizhneangarsk is smaller than neighbouring Severobaikalsk.

The town is pleasant to stroll around with its mainly wooden buildings. Despite being built mostly since the mid-1970s it's not dominated by multi-storey concrete flats and prefabricated buildings. Even the two-storey City Council building is wooden. An architectural oddity is the wooden boat-rental and water-rescue station on the lake's edge. The fish-processing factory can be visited and gives an interesting insight into Russian methods and working conditions. The plant makes delicious smoked or salted *omul*.

Nizhneangarsk is linked to Irkutsk by hydrofoil (see p256).

YAKUTSK

This is the capital of Sakha, the vast Yakut Republic (see p372). Lying only 600km south of the Arctic Circle, it is one of the world's coldest cities (average temperature in January is minus 32°C) although summers are pleasantly mild (plus 19°C in July). It is also one of Siberia's oldest settlements, founded in 1632 on the banks of the mighty Lena River as a base for exploration and a trading centre for gold and furs. There is little left of historic interest in this polluted city, but it is worth visiting for the excursions on the Lena and to see the effects of permafrost. All the buildings here have to be built on massive stilts or they would sink into the ground as their heat melted the permafrost.

Only about 30% of the people are ethnic Yakuts, most of the rest being Russians and Ukrainians. Like other minority groups in Russia the Yakuts are now making themselves heard in Moscow. In 1991 an agreement was signed between the presidents of Russia and Sakha, giving the latter a certain degree of autonomy within the Russian Federation and more control over proceeds of gold and diamond mining in this immensely mineral-rich region.

What to see

The most interesting place to visit in Yakutsk is the **Permafrost Institute**. You are taken 12m underground to see part of the old river bed, where the temperature never varies from -5°C. Permafrost is said to affect 25% of the planet and 50% of Russia. Outside is a model of a baby mammoth (the original is in St Petersburg's Natural History Museum) found preserved in permafrost. Entry is US$10. Soon to be relocated, the **State Museum of the History and Culture of the Peoples of the North**, is currently housed in the former Bishop's Palace, and is one of Siberia's oldest museums. It is said to include over 140,000 items illustrating Yakut flora, fauna and anthropology. Outside is part of the old wooden fort. The **Museum of Yakut Music and Folklore**, ul Kirova 8, has an interesting display about Yakut shamanism. There's also a **Yakut Literature Museum** in a large yurt, and a **Geological Museum** crammed full of Yakutia's geological wealth. Tours can be arranged to reindeer-breeding farms.

Getting to Yakutsk

Until the rail link is finished (which will be many years from now as there is still 800km to cover) the only way in is by plane from Irkutsk, Moscow or a few other cities. Local airline agencies are located at ul Ordzhonikidze 8 (☎ 420 204, 425 139). A new airport was built by Canadians in 1995 after the last one burned down.

Where to stay

Hotel Sterkh (☎ 242 701), pr Lenin 8, is centrally-located and has singles/doubles from US$25/40.

The Canadian-built *Hotel Ontario* (☎ 422 066, 🖹 259 438), Viliusky trakt 6, has 12 rooms from US$20 for a single. It is in a quiet location in a park zone about 20 minutes out of the city centre.

At the top end is the *Hotel Tygyn Darkhan* (formerly President Hotel; ☎ 435 109, 🖹 435 004), ul Ammosov 9, in the heart of the city. Recently renovated by a Swiss company, it has 46 rooms from US$70 to US$200. The restaurant is excellent but very pricey.

Excursions on the Lena River

The geological formations known as the **Lena Pillars** have fascinated travellers here since the 17th century. About 140km upriver from Yakutsk, the rock of the cliffs alongside the river has been eroded away into delicate shapes of a reddish brown colour. Two-day cruises leave each Friday evening in summer. Tickets cost from US$200 and are available from LenaRechFlot (☎/🖹 422 762, 425 761), ul Dzerzhinskogo 2. From the landing it's an hour's strenuous climb to the top, for a magnificent view of the river and the cliffs. Tour groups are sometimes brought here on hydrofoil day trips from Yakutsk, leaving early in the morning and getting back after dark.

The Yakutsk area code is ☎ 4112. From outside Russia dial +7-4112.

On the way to the Lena Pillars you pass the archaeological site of **Dering Yuryakh** (see p89).

The luxury cruise ships *M/S Demyan Bedny* and *M/S Mikhail Svetlov* do 7-10 day trips along the Lena River starting from Yakutsk, passing the Lena Pillars and continuing to the river port of **Lensk**. It's also possible to make a trip down the Lena from Yakutsk to Tiksi on the Arctic Ocean. For more information contact LenaRechFlot.

Ulan Ude
Улан Уде

Ulan Ude, the capital of the Buryat Republic, is well worth a stop if only to visit **Ivolginsky Datsan**, the centre of Buddhism in Russia. Rail enthusiasts may also enjoy a visit to the **locomotive repair workshops**. The people of Ulan Ude are very friendly and hospitable and the place has a relaxed atmosphere, with quite a few traditional Siberian wooden buildings still standing.

HISTORY

In 1668 a military outpost was founded here, in a valley between the Khamar-Daban and Tsaga-Daban ranges. Strategically located beside the Selenga and Ude rivers, it was named Verkhneudinsk. A cathedral was built in 1745 and the town became a key centre on the route of tea caravans from China. The railway reached the town in 1900 and in 1949 the branch line to Mongolia was opened.

Ulan Ude is now a pleasant city of some 371,000 (only about a fifth of whom are Buryats, the rest being mainly Russians). Local industries include the large railway repair workshop and locomotive plant, food processing, helicopter assembly and glass-making.

Buildings here require firm foundations since the city is in an earthquake zone. The most recent tremor, measuring 9.5 on the Richter scale, was in 1959 but because its epicentre was directly beneath Lake Baikal there were no fatalities in Ulan Ude. Military bases in the area meant that Ulan Ude was off-limits to foreigners until the thaw in East-West relations. In 1990 Princess Anne led the tourists in with the first royal visit to Russia since the Tsar's execution. A local official declared that her visit was probably the most exciting thing to have happened since Genghis Khan swept through on his way to Moscow in 1239.

WHAT TO SEE

Giant Lenin Head
Ploshchad Sovietov is dominated by the sinister bulk of the world's biggest **Lenin's head**; standing in front of it you feel like Dorothy meeting the Wizard of Oz.

History Museum

This collection has been greatly enriched by the recent transfer from the Virgin Hodegetria Cathedral of a fantastic collection of items relating to Lamaism (Tibetan Buddhism) and the spiritual culture of the Buryats. Assembled from monasteries closed after the Revolution, the collection includes Buddha figures; the robes of a Buryat shaman; musical instruments (conches and horns and a beautiful guitar with a carved horse's head); a large collection of masks used in Buddhist mystery plays; and a valuable collection of Tibetan *thangkas* (paintings). In addition to thangkas used by monks practising traditional medicine, there's a unique *Atlas of Tibetan Medicine*. Local Russian history is also covered: there are icons dating back to the 17th century and day-to-day objects from the houses of the rich traders of Kyakhta. The History Museum, at ul Profsoyuznaya 29, is open 10:00-18:00 daily except Monday; entry US$3.30 for each of the two floors.

Open-Air Ethnographic Museum

One of the best of Russia's numerous open-air museums, this collection of reconstructed buildings is about 6km north of Ulan Ude. Exhibits include a Bronze Age stone circle, an Evenki camp with birchwood wigwam, and a shaman's hut and wooden carvings. The Buryat area contains *gers* (yurts) of felt and wood and a log cabin stocked with day-to-day items. You can also see reconstructed Kazakh, Cossack and Old Believer settlements. There's also a dreadful zoo with camels standing in the mud, bears in tiny cages and disconsolate reindeer (the more people who complain to the guides about this the better). Except in mid-summer it gets very cold here; bring warm clothing.

The museum is open 10:00-17:00 daily in summer. There's no bus to the museum but bus No 8 drops you at a T-junction from where it's a 20-minute walk. This bus also passes a new monastery with a homeopathic shop and a restaurant offering tasty Buryat meat *pozi* (dumplings) and delicious *ponchike* (jam-filled doughnuts).

Locomotive Works

Ulan Ude's railway factory is definitely worth a visit even if you are not interested in trains. The conditions under which people work are surprising, as is the age of most of the equipment. The factory was founded in 1932 to repair steam locomotives and passenger carriages and from 1938 to 1956 it built large SO series locomotives. After a massive refit in 1959 it shifted to electric locomotives and today it repairs VL60 and VL80 locomotives and passenger carriages. Intourist organizes visits to the factory.

There's a preserved SO17 on the right-hand side of the road to the Open-Air Ethnographic Museum.

The Ulan Ude area code is ☎ 3012. From outside Russia dial +7-3012.

WHERE TO STAY AND EAT
4 Hotel Geser Гостиница Гэсэр
7 Stolovaya Столовая
11 Café Buterbrodnya
    Кафе Бутербродная
12 Hotel Baikal Гостиница Байкал
15 Hotel Buryatia Гостиница Бурятия
18 Hotel Barguzin Гостиница Баргузин
19 Letny Café Кафе Летний

OTHER
1 Railway Station
    Железнодорожный Вокзал
2 Internet Centre Интернет Центр
3 Fresh Food Market Рынок
5 Central Post Office Почтамт
6 Geological Museum
    Геологический Музей
8 Giant Head of Lenin Бюст Ленина
9 Sputnik Supermarket
    Спутник Супермаркет

10 History Museum Музей Истории
13 Aeroflot Касса Аэрофлота
14 Opera and Ballet Theatre
    Театр Оперы и Балета
16 Mongolian Consulate
    Кулсульство Монголии
17 Bus Station Автовокзал
20 Shopping Arcade Гостиный Двор
21 T-34 Tank Monument Памятник-
    монумент «Танк Т-34»
22 Trinity Church Церковь Троицы
23 Buryat Drama Theatre
    Бурятский Театр Драмы
24 Market Рынок
25 Buses to Ivolginsk Datsan
    Автобус в Датсан
26 Virgin Hodegetria Cathedral
    Одигитриевский Собор
27 River Station Речной Вокзал

Other sights

It's worth spending some time wandering around the town as there are quite a few interesting buildings. The **Virgin Hodegetria Cathedral**, built from 1745 to 1785, is being very slowly renovated. For many years it was used as a warehouse for the History Museum (which has photographs showing the cathedral in happier days). The streets around the cathedral are lined with picturesque old wooden buildings, some now being restored.

The attractive **Trinity Church**, built in 1798, was closed during the communist era but has now been reopened and renovated; new bells were added in 1993. As at many Russian churches, begging babushkas crowd around the entrance.

The **Opera and Ballet Theatre** has splendid socialist-realist paintings and murals inside but the doorman won't be keen to let you wander round without a ticket for a performance. The theatre was built by some of the 18,000 Japanese prisoners of war interned in Buryatia between 1945 and 1948.

The **Geological Museum**, ul Lenina 57, is open 10:00-16:00 on Tuesday and Friday only.

IVOLGINSK DATSAN

This Tibetan Buddhist monastery, the centre of Russian Buddhism, stands on a wide plain 35km outside the city, and is a fascinating place to visit. Before the Revolution there were hundreds of similar monasteries in the area with the largest and most important at Selenginsk. Almost all were closed and the monks sent to the gulags in the 1930s. When Stalin sanctioned greater religious toler-

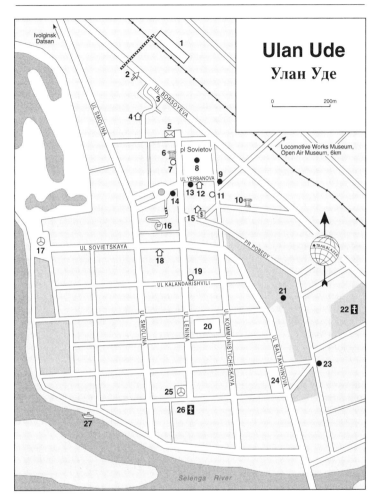

ance in the 1940s astrologers selected this site for a new monastery, which was completed in 1946. There are now 30 lamas, some of them very elderly, but novices join each year; most spend up to five years studying in Ulan Bator. The Dalai Lama has visited the Datsan five times.

Getting there

Bus No 104 from the bus station near the Virgin Hodegetria Cathedral passes the Datsan on its way to Kalenovo village. There are departures at 08:30 and 12:00 and the trip takes 45 minutes. A not very convenient alternative is bus No 130 to Ivolga village, from where it's a two-hour walk through beautiful countryside to the Datsan. Going back, you could try hitching a ride in a tour bus.

Visiting the Datsan

As you stroll around the Datsan don't forget that you should walk clockwise around objects of Buddhist veneration (prayer wheels, temples and stupas), and that hats must be removed inside the buildings. Visitors are shown round by a monk. Be sure to make a donation.

The **largest temple**, a three-storey building constructed in 1971, burnt down four months after completion with the loss of numerous valuable *thangkas* (devotional paintings). It was rebuilt in just seven months. Its joyous technicolour interior seems rather incongruous in grey Russia: golden dragons slide down the 16 wooden columns supporting the upper galleries (where there is a library of Tantric texts), and hundreds of incarnations of the Buddha line one wall. Easy to recognize is Manla, the Buddha of Tibetan medicine, with the dark blue face. The largest thangka hanging above the incarnations is of the founder of the Gelugpa (Yellow Hat) sect of Tibetan Buddhism. Juniper wood is burnt and food and money offered to the incarnations.

Beside this is a smaller stupa, and the **green temple** behind it is the oldest building in the complex, constructed in 1946. The octagonal white building houses a model of **Paradise** (*Devashin*) and a library of several hundred Tibetan and Mongolian texts, each wrapped in silk. In the big **white stupa** nearby are the ashes of the most famous of the Datsan's head lamas, Sherapov, who died in 1961. There is even a **Bo tree** growing very successfully in its own green-house from seeds brought in 1956 from Delhi. Visiting Buddhists stay in the 'hotel' and students now come from all over the region to study Buddhism here.

Snacks are available at the kiosk outside.

PRACTICAL INFORMATION
Orientation and services

To reach the town centre from the railway station, cross the lines via the pedestrian bridge. It takes about 10 minutes to walk to pl Sovietov. The main hotels are all in this area.

The helpful office of **Buryat-Intour** (☎ 216 954, 🖹 219 267, 🖳 bintur@bur net.ru) is in rooms 206-211 of the Hotel Baikal. The **Mongolian Consulate** (☎ 220 499, 🖹 214 188, 🖳 mnc@burnet.ru) is in the Hotel Baikal, and is open 10:00-13:00 and 15:00-17:00 on Monday, Wednesday and Friday; for information on Mongolian visas see p22.

You can send **emails** for US$1 per hour from the Internet Centre on ul Borsoyeva. It's open 09:00-22:00.

You can change money from 09:00-17:30 in the Hotel Buryatia. There is an **ATM** here as well.

Local transport

Most places, except the Datsan and the Open-air museum, are within walking distance. Buses No 7 and 10 from in front of the station run beside pl Sovietov and past the Hotel Baikal; No 7 terminates at the central bus station and No 10 continues to the airport. Bus No 35 travels between the airport and pl Sovietov.

Taxis congregate in the usual places: outside the hotels and by the railway and bus stations, but are not in great supply.

Tours The resurgence of Buddhism here has resulted in the rebuilding or new construction of many temples and monasteries. Buryat-Intour will take you to any of them, the closest being **Ivolginsk Datsan** (see p268) at US$30 for a three-hour tour with a guide. A day trip to **Tamcha Datsan** which is 150 km away costs US$80 for a car or US$20 as part of a group on a bus tour. A visit to **Atsagat Temple**, 50km away, costs US$50 for a car or US$12 on a group tour.

Buryat-Intour also goes to most other local sights, including the **locomotive museum and workshops** for US$30. Other options include **Lake Baikal**, some of the old cities along the tea route to China (including **Kyakhta** and **Novoselenginsk**) and remote villages with interesting ethnic roots, such as **Bolshoi Kunali**.

Where to stay
There are numerous cheap hotels in Ulan Ude but none is particularly good.

Hotel Barguzin (☎ 219 58), ul Sovietskaya 28, charges US$8/15 for a single/double. Staff are friendly but the place is looking very tired; even the stuffed bear in the foyer looks on the verge of collapse. *Hotel Baikal* (☎ 213 718), ul Yerbanova 12, is similarly priced and similarly scruffy. *Hotel Buryatia* (☎ 211 835) on pr Pobedy charges US$12/24 for a single/double with attached bathroom, and has a few cheaper rooms. They have renovated the lobby but seem to have forgotten to refit the rooms. The old Communist Party hotel, the *Hotel Geser* (☎ 218 151), ul Ranzhurova 12, is the best choice. Service is good and the rooms are comfortable. Singles/doubles with attached bathroom cost from US$30/45.

Where to eat
Inside a ger tent at the intersection of ul Lenina and ul Kalandarishvili is the *Letny Café*, a pleasant, friendly place with a range of snacks. *Hotel Buryatia* has some tasty dishes and rather reluctant service. Three courses cost around US$6. The restaurant has a nightly disco which can be entertaining. The food in the main restaurant at the *Hotel Geser* is good and the service efficient but there's usually a live band in the evening. There's also a buffet (open late) down the hall. *Café Buterbrodnya*, ul Kommunist cheskaya, serves excellent pelmeni. There is a basement *stolovaya* opposite Lenin's head, open 10:00-18:00. Everything about the place is basic but a filling meal is only US$1.

Where to shop
There is a **Buryat Crafts Store** in the Shopping Arcade.

Moving on
By rail You can buy domestic and international tickets at the international ticket kassa, on the far left side of the ticket hall.

To Irkutsk (US$13) it's eight hours, Moscow (US$65) is 94 hours, Chita (US$13) is 10 hours and Vladivostok (US$53) is 64 hours away. Note that the No 121/122 train from/to Moscow via Yekaterinburg and Tyumen uses Moscow's Kazansky station.

By air There are regular connections to Moscow and Irkutsk (a 45 minute flight). **Aeroflot**, **Buryat Avia** and **Transaero** have offices in the Hotel Buryatia.

Chita
Чита

Chita is at the junction of the Trans-Siberian and Trans-Manchurian railway lines. The city was closed to foreigners until the late 1980s as it was the military centre for the sometimes-tense Siberian/Chinese border. There's just about enough to keep you occupied for a day here: a Decembrists museum, a museum full of military hardware and an interesting Army Officers' Club where non-members are welcome.

HISTORY

Founded in 1653, Chita became a *sloboda* (tax-exempt settlement) in 1690, populated by Cossacks and trappers. It was famous in the 19th century as a place of exile for many revolutionary Decembrists. George Kennan was here in 1887 and wrote: 'Among the exiles of Chita were some of the brightest, most cultivated, most sympathetic men and women we had met in Eastern Siberia.'

By 1900 more than 11,000 people lived here. There were nine churches, a cathedral, a nunnery, a synagogue, 13 schools and even a telephone system. Soviet power was established in the city on 16 February 1918 but on 26 August the city was captured by the White Army. On 22 October, however, it was firmly back in Soviet hands.

Chita is now a city of about 305,000, Eastern Siberia's major industrial and cultural centre and still of military importance. The numerous army buildings around the city look much like ordinary office buildings but their foyers are hidden from the street and armed guards lurk just inside the doorways.

WHAT TO SEE

The **Army Officers' Club**, ul Lenina 80, is well worth a visit. On the 2nd floor, opposite the bar, is the entertainment room with eight full-size billiard tables. These are surrounded by chess tables with another balcony above, also full of tables. Despite the fact that few people speak, the noise level is unbelievable as each chess player punches his time clock every 30 seconds. The bar is open 12:00-23:00 every day except Monday and there is a popular disco here every weekend. The **Military Museum** is next door, open 10:00-18:00 Wednesday, Thursday and Friday, and 10:00-17:00 at weekends.

Opposite Top: View over Vladivostok (see p288) from Eagle's Nest Hill, reached on the funicular railway. (Photo © Nick Hill). **Bottom left:** The ashes of Sherapov, former head lama of Ivolginsk, are contained in this stupa at the Datsan (see p268) near Ulan Ude. **Bottom right:** The world's biggest sculpted head (see p266) looms over the main square in Ulan Ude. (Photo © Nick Hill).

> The Chita area code is ☎ 30222. From outside Russia dial +7-30222.

The **Decembrists' Museum** (☎ 34803) is housed in the former Archangel Michael Church on ul Dekabristov 3b. It's open 10:00-18:00, closed Monday.

There is an interesting **Art Museum** in a modern-looking building on ul Chkalova, above a furniture shop. Entry is US$0.50 and it's open 10:00-18:00.

The **Museum of Local Studies**, ul Babushkina 113, has the usual array of stuffed animals and some beautiful photographs of winter woodlands on the lower floor, and sections on the Evenki people. Upstairs it seems as if every aspect of life in Chita and the region has been scrutinized and put on display; you can learn about anything from dentistry to dog shows. It's well worth a visit and is open from 10:00-18:00. Entry appears to be free.

There is also a **Geological Museum**, open for no charge. Exhibits aren't that inspiring but you're apt to have several 'guides' following you around, eager to practise their English and ask you questions.

If you're interested in traditional medicine, check out the **Centre for Eastern Medicine** (☎ 66520), housed in a grand old building at ul Lenina 109.

PRACTICAL INFORMATION
Orientation and services
The railway station is a short walk from the centre of the town and most hotels. The airport is 13km east of the city (take bus No 4 or 14 from pl Lenina).

There is internet access for US$1.60 per hour at **Magellan Internet**, just round the corner from the City Administration building. It's open 09:00-20:00, closed Sunday.

There is an **ATM** in Hotel Zabaikalye.

Where to stay
The recently renovated *Hotel Dauriya* (☎ 62365), ul Profsoyuznaya 17 above the Café Harbin, charges US$18/25 for a single/double. The centrally-located *Hotel Zabaikalye* (☎ 64520), ul Leningradskaya 36, seems to be disguised as a shopping centre. They charge US$10/17 for a no-frills single/double.

Hotel Obkomovskaya (☎ 65270), the old Oblast Committee (Obkom) hotel at ul Profsoyuznaya 18, has also been renovated. It's the best place to stay in Chita and is often full. Singles go for US$13 and doubles for US$17, and there's a good café downstairs.

Hotel Turist (☎ 65270), ul Babushkina 42, has a snooker hall below, and charges US$10/14 for single/double rooms. The *Krasny Drakon Motel* (☎ 11973) is out on the road to the airport at ul Magistralnaya; take bus No 14 and tell the driver 'motel' so you're let out at the stop just before it.

Where to eat
The *café* below the Hotel Obkomovskaya is good for lunch. There is a restaurant serving standard Russian dishes in *Hotel Turist*.

Café Harbin, below the Hotel Dauriya, serves a good range of Chinese food and is popular with businessmen.

The most expensive place to eat is *Restaurant Krasny Drakon* (☎ 14288) at the motel of the same name. Bookings are recommended as it is a long trip there.

Opposite: **Ulan Bator** (see pp297-308). **Top:** Gandan Monastery (Photo © Nick Hill). **Bottom**: Bogd Khan Palace (see p299) was the last Mongolian king's winter residence in Ulan Bator.

Moving on

By rail Chita is 4½ days from Moscow (US$68), 18 hours from Irkutsk (US$26), 10 hours from Ulan Ude (US$13), 41 hours from Khabarovsk (US$40) and 54 hours from Vladivostok (US$51).

There is an Intourist window at the station (the middle kassa) but you're better off at the service centre on the left side of the station (enter from outside). The centre is open 08:00-20:00 and the staff are very helpful at getting long-distance tickets at short notice.

Map Key

⇧	Place to stay	☆	OViR	✡	Synagogue
○	Place to eat	🏛	Museum	Ⓟ	Embassy / Consulate
⊠	Post Office	📖	Bookshop	Ⓐ	Bus Station
⁄	Internet	ⓘ	Tourist Info	Ⓜ	Metro Station
$	Bank / Moneychanger	✚	Church / Cathedral	⛴	Ferry / Boat Landing
		◪	Buddhist Temple	●	Other
		☾	Mosque		

CHITA MAP KEY

WHERE TO STAY AND EAT
8 Hotel Zabaikalye Гостиница Забайкалье
15 Hotel Turist & Restaurant Гостиница Турист и Ресторан
19 Hotel Obkomovskaya Обкомовская Гостиница
20 Hotel Dauriya & Café Harbin
   Гостиница Даурия и Кафе Харбин

OTHER
1 Market Рынок
2 Old Church Старая Церковь
3 Teaching Institute Педагогический Институт
4 Magellan Internet Магеллан Интернет
5 City Administration Building Дом Советов
6 Centre for Eastern Medicine Центр Восточной Медицины
7 Central Post Office Почтамт
9 Military Museum & Officers' Club
   Музей Истории Войск и Дом Офицеров
10 Art Museum Художественный Музей
11 Museum of Local Studies Краеведческий Музей
12 Tank Monument Памятник
13 Medical Institute Медицинский Институт
14 Geological Museum Геологический Музей
16 Church Церковь
17 PVU ПВУ
18 Drama Theatre Драматический Театр
21 Bus Station Автовокзал
22 Railway Station Железнодорожный Вокзал
23 Tatar Mosque Татарская Мечеть
24 Decembrists' Museum Музей Декабристов

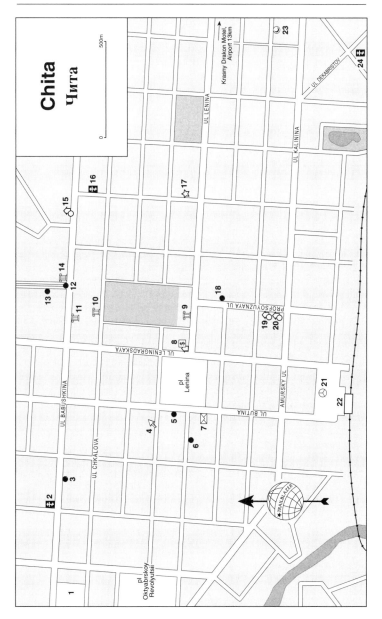

Chita
Чита

500m

pl Lenina

UL LENINGRADSKAYA

UL BABUSHKINA

UL CHKALOVA

pl
Oktyabrskoy
Revolyutsii

UL LENINA

UL KALININA

UL DEKABRISTOV

PROFSOYUZNAYA UL

AMURSKY UL

UL BUTINA

TRAILBLAZER

Krasny Drakon Motel,
Airport 13km

1
2
3
4
5
6
7
8
9
10
11
12
13
14
15
16
17
18
19
20
21
22
23
24

Birobidzhan
Биробиджан

Birobidzhan is the capital of the so-called Jewish Autonomous Region, a remote site selected in 1928 as a 'homeland' for Soviet Jews. An effective propaganda campaign plus starvation in Eastern Europe encouraged 41,000 Soviet Jews to move here in the 1930s. Jewish schools and synagogues were established and a considerable effort was made to give the city a Jewish feel. This included Hebrew street signs, designation of Hebrew as the region's official language and the founding of Russia's only Hebrew-language newspaper, *Birbobidzhaner Stern*.

It soon became obvious, however, that this was no Promised Land. Conditions were extremely harsh with winter lows of minus 40°C and things were made worse in 1937 by a resurgence of religious repression, including closure of the synagogues and the banning of Hebrew and Yiddish. By 1938 60% of the Jewish population had left.

In the 1950s the town developed into an agricultural and industrial centre. Birobidzhan's most famous export was rice combine harvesters from the Dalselmash factory on the western outskirts of town, but this is now on the brink of closure. Many Jewish people have moved to Israel and today less than 6% of the population has Jewish ancestry.

Birobidzhan is not a 'must see' but could make an interesting day trip from Khabarovsk, 180km to the east.

WHAT TO SEE

The **Museum of Local Studies**, ul Lenina 24, is open 10:00-18:00, closed Mondays. There is a new **synagogue** at ul Lenina 19. A **beach** on the River Bira is packed on summer weekends; walk down ul Gorkogo to the river and you'll see it on the left beside the Park Kultury.

PRACTICAL INFORMATION
Orientation and services
Everything is within walking distance of the railway and bus stations.

The town's only travel agent is **Intour-Birobidzhan** (☎ 61573), ul Sholom-Aleykhema 55. There is **Internet access** at the main post office at pr 60 Let SSSR.

Where to stay and eat
The only hotel is the standard *Hotel Vostok* (☎ 65330), ul Sholom-Aleykhema 1, charging US$35/50 for a single/double. There's

also a decent restaurant here. *Restaurant Birobidzhan* on the corner of ul Lenina and ul Gorkogo has a standard Russian menu. Opposite the train station is a *pelmennaya* serving large portions of tasty pelmeni. There is a fresh *produce market* near the Hotel Vostok and a well-stocked *supermarket* a bit further along ul Sholom-Aleykhema.

Moving on
Although major Trans-Siberian trains all pass through Birobidzhan, it's difficult to

buy tickets for them here. There are several local trains daily to Khabarovsk (three hours, US$2), where Trans-Siberian tickets are much easier to buy. A better option to Khabarovsk are local buses, which leave frequently throughout the day from the bus station, take just under three hours and cost US$3.

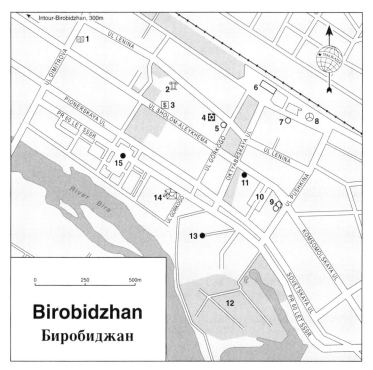

Birobidzhan

Биробиджан

WHERE TO STAY AND EAT
5 Restaurant Birobidzhan
  Ресторан Биробиджан
7 Pelmennaya Пелменная
9 Hotel Vostok & Restaurant
  Гостиница Восток

OTHER
1 Bookshop Дом Книги
2 Museum of Local Studies
  Краеведческий Музей
3 Sber-Bank Сбер-Банк

4 Synagogue Синагога
6 Railway Station
  Железнодорожний Вокзал
8 Bus Station Автовокзал
10 Market Рынок
11 Supermarket Супермаркет
12 Park Парк
13 Philharmonic Hall Филармония
14 Post Office & Internet
  Почтамт и Интернет
15 Lenin Statue Памятник Ленину

The Birobidzhan area code is ☎ 42145. From outside Russia dial +7-42145.

Khabarovsk
Хабаровск

Khabarovsk is a relaxed provincial city of 604,000, picturesquely situated on three hills above the junction of the Amur River and its tributary, the Ussuri.

It's well worth stopping here for a day or two. In summer, holiday crowds flock to the sandy river banks, giving the place the atmosphere of a friendly English seaside resort (except that for some reason Russians often sunbathe standing up). It's bitterly cold in winter and when the river freezes, people drive their cars onto it and fish through holes chopped in the half-metre-thick ice.

Apart from the river, other sights include an interesting Museum of Local History, an Art Museum, a Military Museum, and an arboretum founded over a century ago to supply the city's numerous parks and gardens.

HISTORY

In 1858 a military settlement was founded here by Count Muravyev-Amursky, the Governor-General of East Siberia who did much to advance Russia's interests in the Far East. It was named Khabarovka, in honour of the Cossack explorer who conquered the Amur region in the 17th century, and whose statue now stands in the square in front of the railway station.

By 1883 the town was known as Khabarovsk and the following year, when the Far Eastern Territories were made a region separate from Eastern Siberia, it became the administrative capital and home of the governor-general of the area.

Until the railway arrived the town was just a trading and military post, and a junction for passengers arriving by steamer along the Shilka and Amur rivers from Western Siberia. Here they would transfer to another ship for the voyage down the Amur and Ussuri to Vladivostok.

From 1875 onwards several plans were submitted for the building of the Ussuri Railway, which now runs along the great river between Khabarovsk and Vladivostok. Work began in 1893 and on 3 September 1897 a train completed the first journey between these two towns. A railway technical school was opened in the following year on what is now ul Karla Marxa.

Early visitors

As more sections of the Trans-Siberian Railway were built, greater numbers of foreign travellers arrived in Khabarovsk. The *1900 Guide to the Great Siberian Railway* did not encourage them to stay long, reporting that: 'The conditions of life in Khabarovsk are not attractive, on account of the absence of comfortable dwellings, and the expensiveness of some products and of most necessary articles ... Imported colonial goods are sold at a high price and only fish is very cheap.' Tourists were also advised against trying Mr Khlebnikov's locally produced wine, made from the area's wild vines, because 'it is of inferior quality and without any flavour'. Recommended sights included the wooden triumphal arch (now demolished) erected in commemoration of the visit of Tsarevich Nicholas in 1891, and the bronze statue of Count Muravyev-Amursky on the promontory above the river. After the Revolution the Count was traded in for an image from the Lenin Statue Factory, but he has reappeared in front of the railway station.

The city today

The railway brought more trade than tourists, and though it suffered during the Civil War, the town quickly grew into the modern city it is today. Few of its old wooden cabins remain but there are some attractive stone buildings from Imperial times. It is the capital of Khabarovsk Territory, surrounded by some of the richest mineral deposits in Russia, although the land is little more than a gigantic swampy forest. Khabarovsk is now a major industrial centre involved in engineering, petroleum refining and timber-working.

In the last few years Japanese and South Koreans have moved in, opening factories and businesses. Most of the city's foreign visitors now come from these two countries.

WHAT TO SEE

Museum of Local Studies

The museum, based on the extensive collection of Baron Korff, a former governor-general of the Amur region, was opened in 1894. In 1897 it was moved into its present three-storey building, and was renovated in 1999. With donations from hunters and explorers over the last century, the collection has grown into an impressive display of local history, flora and fauna. In the first few rooms labels are in Cyrillic, English and Latin but after that it's only Cyrillic and Latin (see p427).

Among stuffed animals in the ground-floor galleries are two Amur tigers. Also known as the Siberian or Manchurian tiger (*Felis/Panthera tigris altaica*), this is the largest member of the cat family and can weigh up to 350kg, about twice the average weight of an African lion. In the same gallery are various fur-bearing animals including the large sea-otter or Kamchatka beaver (*Enhydra lutris*) from which come the highest-priced pelts in the world. Before this animal came under official protection in the early 20th century its pelts were selling for over US$2000 each.

The upper galleries are devoted to local history and ethnography. The area was inhabited by several tribes at the time of the Revolution. The Goldi and Orochi lived near the mouth of the Ussuri, and Olchi and Giliak beside the Amur. Each tribe had its *shaman*, and some of their robes and equipment are on display as well as a suit made entirely of fish-skins (the skin of a common fish, the *keta*, was used not only for clothing but also for tents, sails and boots). There's also a display of early settlers' furniture, samovars and other utensils, including some bread baked by the original colonists.

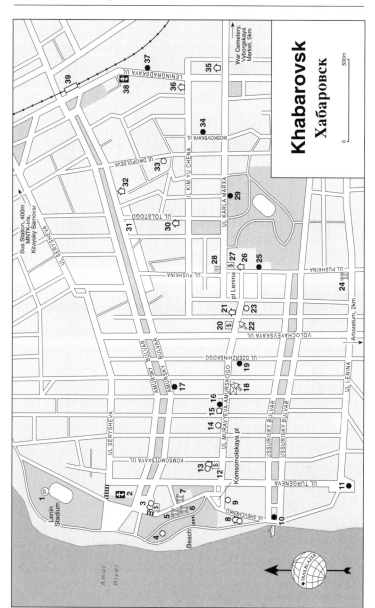

Khabarovsk
Хабаровск

WHERE TO STAY
3 Hotel Intourist & Unikhab Restaurant
Гостиница Интурист и Ресторан Унихаб
8 Hotel Parus & Restaurant Гостиница Парус и ресторан
13 Hotel Sapporo & Restaurant
Гостиница Саппоро и ресторан
21 Hotel Lyudmila Гостиница Людмила
26 Hotel Tsentralnaya Гостиница Центральная
30 Hotel Amethyst Гостиница Аметист
32 Hotel Versailles Гостиница Версаль
35 Hotel Turist Гостиница Турист
36 Hotel Zarya Гостиница Заря

WHERE TO EAT
4 Café Utos Кафе Утос
9 Syangan Restaurant Ресторан Сянган
14 Bistro Yerofe Бистро Ерофе
15 Pelmennaya Пельменная
23 Café Kasam Кафе Касам
33 Stolovaya Столовая

OTHER
1 Chinese Consulate Кунсульство Китайский
2 Church of St Innocent Церковь Святого Иннокентия
5 Museum of Local Studies Краеведческий Музей
6 Art Museum Художественный Музей
7 Military Museum Музей Истории Краснознаменного
Дальневосточного Военного Округа
10 River Station & Ticket Kiosks for Fuyuan Речной Вокзал

11 Victory Monument Монумент Победы
12 ATM
16 Tayny Remesla Art Store
Художественный Магазин Тайны Ремесла
17 Airlines Office Авиа Касса
18 Central Post Office & Internet Почтамт и Интернет
19 Drama Theatre Театр Драмы
20 ATM
22 Internet Интернет
24 Geology Museum Музей Геологии
25 Telephone Office Переговорный Пункт
27 Alfa Bank Альфа Банк
28 Knizhny Mir Bookshop Книжный Мир
29 Theatre of Musical Comedy Театр музыкальной комдеии
31 Market Рынок
34 Sauna Баня
37 Advance-purchase Rail Ticket Office
Предварительная Железнодорожная Касса
38 Church Церковь
39 Railway Station Железнодорожный Вокзал

The museum, at ul Shevchenko 11, is open 10:00-18:00, closed Monday. Entry is US$3 for foreigners or US$0.50 for students.

Art Museum

Next to the Museum of Local History is the Art Museum, renovated in 2002 and featuring a mix of permanent and temporary exhibitions. Permanent exhibits include art and craftwork, mainly carpets and footwear, of the Nanai, Nivkh, Udeghe, Evenki and Negidal peoples. There are also carved walrus tusks by Chukchi and Eskimos. On the 2nd floor there is a selection of exquisite 17th and 18th century religious icons. The galleries have paintings by German and Italian as well as Russian artists, and there is one work by Titian. The gift shop has a good selection of old banknotes, coins, medals and clothing. Entry to the museum is U$3 for foreigners and it's open 10:00-17:00, closed Monday.

Military Museum

This museum opposite the Museum of Local History provides a record of military activity here since the city was founded. There are numerous pictures of

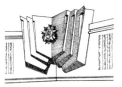

THE MEMORIAL OF GLORY
KHABAROVSK

Russian soldiers, as well as photographs of British, French, Italians and Americans in Vladivostok in 1918. The walls are decorated with medals and old weapons, including a weather-beaten Winchester rifle and a few Smith & Wesson pistols. There's a small display on Mongolia including a photo of Lenin and Sukhe Bator sharing a joke.

Upstairs you'll find WWII memorabilia and an interesting display on the war in Afghanistan.

Behind the building there's a row of armoured vehicles including a tiny MC-1 two-man tank, as well as a MiG fighter plane and a train carriage (usually locked) once used by the commander of the Russian Far East military forces. Entry to the museum is US$2 for foreigners or US$0.50 for students; it's open 10:00-17:00, closed Monday.

Geological Museum

The Geological Museum, on the corner of ul Lenina and ul Pushkina, contains a well laid-out display of local minerals. You've heard how rich Siberia is in natural resources: now come and see what they look like. Paradoxically, pride of place goes to some moon rocks, tiny fragments under a microscope. The museum is open 10:00-18:00 (not Monday); entry US$0.50.

Arboretum

Founded long before the railway arrived, the arboretum is an interesting place to visit. Originally set up to provide trees and shrubs for the new town's parks, it now claims to have a specimen of every plant species found in the Far Eastern Territories. It's on Volochayevskaya ul, and open 09:00-18:00 weekdays. Take bus No 1 to the corner of Volochayevskaya ul and ul Lenina, then bus No 25 to the Ussurisky stop.

Other sights and things to do

The **Amur River** is a focus of interest in winter or summer. In winter when it freezes, locals drill holes through the ice and set up little tents from which they fish. In summer the banks are crowded with swimmers and sun-worshippers. Although the water is not crystal clear it's refreshing on a hot summer's day, but watch out for the strong current. There are also boat trips on the river.

There are regular services at the **church** on Leningradskaya ul, the interior of which is beautifully decorated.

An excellent **sauna** at Moskovskaya ul 7 is very popular with foreigners. It also includes a pool, billiards room and a restaurant. Bookings are not necessary; a visit costs US$10.

PRACTICAL INFORMATION
Orientation and services

Khabarovsk is a large city: the railway station and the Hotel Intourist are almost 3km apart, a half-hour walk. The main street is ul Karla Marxa to the east of the city's central square, pl Lenina, and ul Muravyeva-Amurskogo to the west of it. Many tourist sights are within walking distance of the Hotel Intourist.

Banks Alfa Bank is on ul Karla Marxa near Hotel Tsentralnaya. There are **ATMs** near Hotel Sapporo and Hotel Lyudmila on ul Muravyeva-Amurskogo and in the Hotel Intourist. You can change travellers' cheques at the exchange booth in the Hotel Intourist.

Communications There is **Internet access** at the Internet Centre at Muravyeva-Amurskogo 44 (open 08:30-22:30 daily) for US$1 an hour; and at the central post office at ul Muravyeva-Amurskogo 28 (open 08:00-20:00 weekdays and 09:00-18:00 weekends) for US$1.50 an hour. *Knizhny Mir Bookshop*, ul Pushkina 56, has an excellent range of maps for Khabarovsk and surrounding oblasts and cities; it's open 09:00-20:00.

Consulates The **Chinese Consulate** (☎ 328 390, ▤ 649 094, ▣ gcchina@gcchi

na.khv.ru, www.chinaconsulate.khv.ru) is at Lenin Stadium, and open 10:00-13:00 Monday, Wednesday and Friday for visas. See p23 for details about Chinese visas.

There is a **Japanese Consulate** (☎ 326 907, satellite ☎ 50985-21 002, ▤ 327 212, ▣ consul@japan.khv.ru) at ul Pushkina 38/A. It's open Monday to Friday, 09:00-12:30, 14:00-17:30 for visas.

Travel agents Numerous travel agencies here include the helpful **Intour-Khabarovsk** (☎ 387 919, ▤ 328 774, ▣ info @intour.khv.ru) at Hotel Intourist, open 09:00-21:00. **Dalgeo Tours** (☎ 305 550) at the Hotel Versailles is open 09:00-19:00 (Sundays 11:00-16:00) and offer a wide range of tours and homestays.

Local transport

There are regular **bus**, **trolley-bus** and **tram** services. From the train station bus No 1 travels down ul Karla Marxa and ul Muravyeva-Amurskogo, returning to the station along ul Lenina. Bus No 2 from the station runs down ul Serysheva, returning via ul Karla Marxa and ul Muravyeva-Amurskogo. Many buses and minibuses run between the airport and Komsomolskaya pl.

Boats operate along the Amur River from June to October. Local ferries and long-distance hydrofoils all depart from the

The Khabarovsk area code is ☎ 4212. From outside Russia dial +7-4212.

river station at ul Shevchenko 1. While Intourist can organize tickets for river journeys, it's easy enough to do it yourself.

Tours

Staff at **Intour-Khabarovsk** (☎ 387 919, 📠 328 774, 🖳 info@intour.khv.ru) at the Hotel Intourist are friendly and helpful. They offer the following tours: **city tour** (2½ hours by car; US$35); **museum tours** (US$10); **arboretum** (one hour; US$20); **Nanai village folk show** (four hours; US$75) including a visit to nearby **petroglyphs** (rock carvings). They can also arrange **boat trips**, with a folk group performing on deck.

Where to stay

HOFA (see p20) can organize **homestays** in Khabarovsk.

The **Hotel Lyudmila** is in an excellent location on ul Muravyeva-Amurskogo. The cheapest singles/doubles (with shared bathroom) are US$8/16. It's basic but fairly clean, and often full.

Most centrally-located and possibly the best value is the **Hotel Tsentralnaya** (☎ 327 233), ul Pushkina 52. Comfortable rooms cost from US$25/30 for a single/double with attached bathroom., or you can pay US$15 for one bed in a double room.

The recently renovated **Hotel Zarya** (☎ 327 075), ul Kim Yu Chena 81/16, is a good choice. It's friendly enough, but often full. The cheapest singles/doubles are US$21/40.

The old **Hotel Turist** (☎ 370 417), ul Karla Marxa 67, is extremely popular with Chinese traders but has a run-down feel to it. There's a range of rooms for US$30 for a single (US$20 for one bed in a double) or US$40 for a double. The best have fridges and attached bathrooms.

The old bargain Hotel Mayak has now mutated into the expensive, comfortable **Hotel Versailles** (☎ 305 550) at Amursky bulvar 46a. Good singles/doubles with all mod-cons cost US$40/70. Staff are friendly and speak English; even the free breakfast is better than normal. There is a 24-hour café here as well.

Hotel Amethyst (☎ 334 699, 📠 334 699), ul Tolstogo 5a, has singles/doubles for US$60/100.

The main tourist hotel is **Hotel Intourist** (☎ 399 313, 📠 338 774) at Amursky bulvar 2. At US$70/80 per single/double it's expensive, but it's well organized and pleasant. There are several good shops on the ground floor and an excellent restaurant on the 11th. The service bureau offers a wide range of excursions.

There is a growing number of excellent hotels, popular with business travellers. You're advised to book in advance, but you might be lucky if you just turn up. **Hotel Parus** (☎ 324 414, 327 270, 📠 327 609), ul Shevchenko 5, was undergoing renovation at the time of writing but has single/double rooms for US$90/120. There is a business centre in the hotel and the restaurant serves European food reputed to be the best in town.

Hotel Sapporo (☎ 306 745, 📠 304 418) at Komsomolskaya ul 79 caters for Japanese business people and tour groups, charging US$80/100 for a single/double, though it's nearly always fully booked.

Where to eat

Café Kasam, at the top of ul Muravyeva-Amurskogo, has an extensive menu, most of it illustrated with photos, a boon for non-Russian speakers. It's always busy and has friendly staff. Tasty pelmeni cost US$1.50. Further down the same street is **Bistro Yerofe** which sells coffee, cakes and savoury pastries.

There are various riverside cafés which are pleasant places for a drink and a bite to eat. **Café Utos**, in a tower in the park, overlooking the river, serves good food and is open until midnight.

In the basement on the corner of ul Muravyeva-Amurskogo and ul Kalinina is a **pelmennaya** serving delicious and filling pelmeni from 09:00 to 21:00.

There is a decent **stolovaya** on ul Dikopolseva, normally open 10:00-19:00 but sometimes only until 18:00. The food is basic but filling and of course, very cheap: about US$1 for three 'courses'.

On Komsomolskaya pl you could join the tour groups downstairs in the *Syangan* Chinese restaurant.

The *Kitaysky Samovar* (Chinese Samovar) is a 45-minute tram ride out of town. Despite being only 50m from the main road, it's difficult to locate. Take tram No 5 to the Avtodorozhny Tekhnikum stop.

The Japanese restaurant *Unikhab* (☎ 399 315), on the top storey of Hotel Intourist, is reliable but expensive. For some reason the floor slopes on the southern side of the building, creating a somewhat unsteady feeling even before the vodka appears, but the food more than makes up for this.

Sapporo Restaurant (☎ 236 745) on ul Muravyeva-Amurskogo 3 is the best place to eat. There are three storeys, with Russian cuisine on the first two floors and sushi and other Japanese food on the third. It's expensive and an ATM has been thoughtfully positioned just outside the restaurant to ensure that you will have enough roubles on hand!

Entertainment

Khabarovsk doesn't offer much in terms of nightlife but gamblers may be interested in **Casino Tourist** (☎ 370 473) in the Hotel Tourist, ul Karla Marxa 67. It's an ideal place for encounters with the city's petty criminals.

Most locals seem to dress up in the evenings and walk along busy ul Muravyeva-Amurskogo or sit in its open-air cafés and people-watch. There is quite a Western atmosphere to this part of town and it's difficult to believe that China is less than 30km away.

Intour-Khabarovsk (see p284) can arrange tickets for the **Drama Theatre** or the **Musical Comedy Theatre**, though these are easily done yourself. Note that these venues are all closed on Mondays, and that tickets must be booked before 13:00 on the performance day.

Where to shop

Interesting local products include ginseng and a special blend of vodka and herbs known as *aralyevaya vodka*.

Attractive ul Muravyeva-Amurskogo is the place to shop, although everything closes from 14:00-15:00 for lunch. The best souvenir shop is the **Tayny Remesla** art store, ul Muravyeva-Amurskogo 17. **Hotel Intourist** also has a good selection.

The best clothing and electronics market is the open-air **Vyborgskaya Market**, otherwise known as the Oriental Bazaar. As the name suggests, pretty much everything for sale here has come over the river from China. Trolley-bus No 1 runs to Vyborgskaya ul where you catch a cab for 3km to the market.

Moving on

By rail Khabarovsk is 13 hours from Vladivostok (US$24). The best train for this journey is the No 6 Okean which leaves in the early evening. Khabarovsk is 41 hours from Chita (US$40) and 59 hours from Irkutsk (US$52). There are also daily links to Tynda on the BAM railway and to Port Vanino for ferries to Sakhalin Island.

Buying tickets at the station is no problem. There is also an **advance-purchase ticket office** at ul Leningradskaya 56, where you pay a US$1 commission.

By bus Buses leave frequently from the bus station for Birobidzhan. They take about three hours and cost US$3.

By boat A boat runs from Khabarovsk to **Fuyuan** in China every day from June through October, and sometimes earlier/later in the season depending on the river ice. The boat leaves Khabarovsk at 08:00, and gets back to Khabarovsk at 21:00. Customs precedures are straightforward. Tickets are sold from kiosks prominently signposted 'Fuyuan', near the River Station. You must show a Chinese visa to buy a boat ticket. Expect to pay around US$50 one way. From Fuyuan it's a 15-hour bus ride on to Harbin, or a shorter one

---

Excursions from Khabarovsk
Khabarovsk is an ideal base for trips into the Siberian outback. Intour-Khabarovsk (see Tours, p284) offers special-interest tours and excursions to many distant and not so distant regions. Some are listed below but as the region opens up to tourism other places will become available.

Sakhalin is an island off the East Siberian coast. Its main attraction is the great variety of wildlife which foreigners may photograph, study, ride amongst or hunt. Most popular are fishing trips and bird watching trips. Vanino, from where you catch a ferry to Sakhalin Island, is on the **BAM Railway**.

Other destinations in Eastern Siberia and the Far Eastern Territories that can be visited from Khabarovsk include **Yakutsk** (see p265), **Kamchatka** (for fishing, hunting and adventure tours), **Perelk** in the Arctic Circle (to see the Northern Lights) and **Magadan** (a former gulag centre).

These destinations are covered in detail in the *Siberian BAM Guide – rail, rivers & road*, also from Trailblazer.

---

to Jiamusi from where there are trains to Harbin.

Hydrofoils run between Khabarovsk and Nikolayevsk via Komsomolsk in the summer months.

By air The airport is 8km east of the city centre. Domestic and international air bookings can be made at the **Airlines Office** (Avia Kassa) (☎ 335 346) at Amursky bulvar 18, or through **Intour-**

Khabarovsk (see p284). Both sell tickets for **DAL Avia** (flights to Harbin, Seoul and Singapore) and for **Asiana Airlines** (to South Korea). Other airlines include **Chosonminhang Airlines** of North Korea (at airport, ☎ 373 204), **Japan Airlines** (at airport, ☎ 370 686) and **China Northern Airlines** (☎ 373 440). Flights for Harbin (US$170) leave on Monday, Wednesday and Friday.

Vladivostok
Владивосток

Vladivostok is a robust city of some 592,000 people, the eastern terminus of the Trans-Siberian line and home of Russia's Pacific Fleet, but until 1990 it was off-limits to all visitors. Even Soviet citizens needed special permits, and foreigners, with a few notable exceptions (such as US President Gerald Ford in 1975), required nothing short of divine intervention.

Ferries link Vladivostok with several ports in Japan and Korea. The weather here never seems to be very good; a local saying is that 'It rains only twice in June: once for 13 days and then for 14!'. Nevertheless, whether you're heading east or west, it's well worth stopping off to explore one of the former USSR's biggest Cold War secrets and to enjoy the seaside town atmosphere. Just remember your umbrella.

HISTORY

This region has been occupied for many thousands of years, certainly back at least to the 2nd millennium BC; but inhabitants were largely nomadic so few relics remain. Eastern chronicles reveal that this was considered part of the Chinese empire at a very early stage but also that it was so remote and conditions so harsh that it was left well alone.

The Russians arrive

In the mid-19th century the Russians were concentrating on expanding their territory eastwards at China's expense. At the head of the exploratory missions was Count Muravyev-Amursky, who from his steamer, the *Amerika*, chose this site for a harbour in 1859. A year later a party of 40 soldiers landed to secure the region. The port was named Vladivostok ('Rule the East').

In 1861 more soldiers arrived to protect Russia's new eastern frontier, with settlers not far behind. It soon became apparent just how important a find this city was: Vladivostok's harbour, one of the few deep-water ports on the east coast, remains unfrozen for longer than any other in Siberia, being inaccessible for an average of just 72 days per year, compared with Nakhodka's 98. This and the city's strategic location resulted in the shift to here of Russia's eastern naval base in 1872 from Nikolaevsk-na-Amur (frozen for an awkward 190 days per year).

Conflict in the east

In 1904 the Russo-Japanese war broke out. Vladivostok was heavily bombarded and trade virtually ceased but while large parts of the port were destroyed, the war was ultimately to prove beneficial: peace settlements with Japan left

Vladivostok as Russia's prime east coast port although Japan gained Port Arthur and parts of Sakhalin Island.

During WWI the city served as the chief entry point for supplies and ammunition from the USA, and British, Japanese, American, Canadian and Italian troops streamed in to support the White Russians' struggle against the Bolsheviks. The most notorious foreign 'visitors' were Czech legions who had fought their way east all the way from the Ukraine in a desperate bid for freedom (see p115). The graves of many of them, and of other foreigners, can still be found in the cemetery here.

As it became clear that the Bolsheviks were gaining the upper hand, the foreign forces departed. Most had left by 1920 although some Japanese stayed on until October 1922. Finally, on 25 October, the city was 'liberated' and Soviet power established, prompting Lenin's famous comment about Vladivostok: 'It's a long way away. But it's ours'.

The Soviet period

The Soviet period was good for the city. Money poured in, along with orders to develop the port and build more ships. In the last days of WWII Vladivostok assumed a key role as the centre of operations for the fight against the Japanese in Manchuria. In the space of four years 25 ships were sunk here and some 30,000 sailors perished.

As the Cold War set in, the city was sealed off from the outside world and the Pacific Fleet expanded fast. The West heard little more of this protected port until 1986 when Gorbachev made his 'Vladivostok Initiative' speech, highlighting a grand new plan for Soviet economic and military commitments in the Far East. Echoing Peter the Great, he announced that Vladivostok was to become 'a wide open window on the East'.

Vladivostok today

The city is keen to establish itself as a major player on the Pacific Rim. There are periodic murmurs of a movement to make the entire Primorsky region an independent economic zone. Undoubtedly it is an area of enormous potential and, not surprisingly, it has attracted mafia gangs from all over Russia who deal in every commodity imaginable. (Don't let this put you off; the criminal underworld isn't interested in small fry such as tourists.)

WHAT TO SEE

The Pacific Fleet

Don't miss this unique opportunity to see some of the world's finest naval technology, although owing to a lack of funds it's beginning to look a little weatherbeaten now. Locals will tell you it's all right to take photographs, but telephoto lenses and too many pictures of radar sites might arouse suspicion; caution is advised. A good place to watch the ships is from **Eagle's Nest Hill** (*Orlinoye Gnezdo*). To get to the top take the **funicular railway** from Pushkinskaya ul.

Arsenyev History Museum

This is the biggest and best of Vladivostok's museums, recalling the history of the city and the region, and named after a local writer. The impressive wildlife display has labels in English: local sea life, an Ussuri leopard, a large Amur tiger and a couple of moose locking antlers in the corner. Rarer specimens include a goral (a small goat-like antelope), a Steller's albatross, an Amursky leopard and a Chinese soft-shelled turtle. There's a display of early settlers' belongings, the robes of a Tungus shaman and the safe from the first bank here, stuffed with old rouble notes. Upstairs there's a small exhibition about actor Yul Brynner (whose family lived here before the Revolution), naval memorabilia and local art (the wood carvings are particularly attractive). The museum, at Svetlanskaya ul 20, is open 10:00-19:00 (ticket office closes 18:00), closed Monday. Entry is US$0.60.

Pacific Fleet Military Museum & Border Guard Museum

Displays at the Pacific Fleet Military Museum include model ships and miscellaneous items from various conflicts: muskets, propaganda posters, a flame-thrower, an ejector seat and the twisted propeller and gun from a ditched fighter plane. The Border Guard Museum collection details the history of protecting the nearby frontier with China and has some interesting recent photos showing patrolling activities. Both displays are at Semyononvska ul 18 and open 10:00-18:00, closed Monday. Entry is US$0.60.

Submarine Museum

On the waterfront next to the eternal flame is an old S56 submarine, housing a display on the history of submarines in Vladivostok. There are early uniforms, ships' instruments, pictures of the earliest submarine (1865) and the first flotillas (1906). Much of it consists of old photographs, although you can also see some gifts to submarine commanders from foreign hosts including, strangely enough, a ceremonial key to the City of San Diego and (Tom Cruise fans, take note) a US Navy Fighter Weapons School Top Gun shield. The display is open 10:00-18:00 Wednesday to Saturday, although you might persuade them to open up on other days; entry US$1.60.

Krasny Vympel

Although marginally less interesting than the Submarine Museum, the Soviet Pacific Fleet's first ship, launched on 24 January 1923, is moored just opposite and can also be visited. Displays include photographs of early crew members, medals, uniforms and other salty memorabilia. Some of the machinery is preserved down below. If you're interested in buying bits and pieces of naval uniforms (belt buckles, cap badges etc) the sailors who run the museum may be able to help. The ship, beside Korabelnaya naberezhnaya, is open 09:30-17:45, closed Sunday, Monday and Tuesday.

Vladivostok Fortress Museum

This place, up on the hill behind the Oceanarium, consists of a large array of military hardware and a museum housed in the fortress. All labels are in

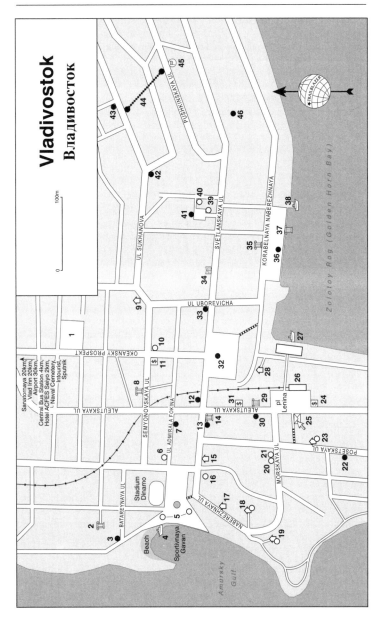

Vladivostok
Владивосток

0 ___ 100m

Zolotoy Rog (Golden Horn Bay)

Amursky Gulf

Russian and English which makes it more interesting than usual. Outside you can see sea mines, torpedoes and supersonic missiles, and join the school children clambering over the tanks and guns. There is also a well-camouflaged toilet amongst the hardware. Inside there is an excellent museum about the region's many fortresses and some history of the Russian-Japanese struggle for control of the Kurile Islands. There are also some great photos of old Vladivostok. The museum is open 10:00-18:00 daily; entry is US$2.30 for foreigners.

Other things to see

The **Primorsky Art Gallery**, Aleutskaya ul 12, is worth a visit. There's a lot to see in here, most of the art having been donated by the Tretyakov Gallery in Moscow. It's open 10:00-18:30 Tuesday to Saturday, 11:00-17:00 Sunday, closed Monday; entry US$0.50. Opposite at No 15 is the **House of the Brynner Family**. You can't enter the former residence of Yul Brynner's family but it's a real pilgrimage for some.

The city's **Oceanarium**, on Batareynaya ul, features stuffed birds and marine life and many species of live fish. It's open 10:00-18:00 during the week and 10:00-20:00 on weekends; closed Monday. Entry is US$0.60.

Vladivostok's **railway station** is one of the city's most impressive buildings, constructed in 1911-12.

VLADIVOSTOK RAILWAY STATION

In the well-tended **Naval Cemetery** are graves of Russians and foreigners who died fighting the Communists in 1919-20. It's a fair way away, on a hill overlooking Zolotoy Rog Bay, so you would be wise to take a car.

PRACTICAL INFORMATION
Orientation and services

Vladivostok is built along the Muravyev Peninsula, which stretches south-west into the Sea of Japan. Scattered around it is a series of islands, of which Russia Island (Russky Ostrov) remains the most important. It's still very much off-limits and protected by ferocious guard dogs so don't try any sightseeing there.

The city's focal point is **Zolotoy Rog** (Golden Horn) **Bay**, so called because of its resemblance to Istanbul's Golden Horn. It's here that most ferries, warships and fishing boats dock.

The **railway station** is conveniently located on the waterfront, ideal if you're transferring directly to the **marine terminal** (*morskoy vokzal*). The railway station faces pl Lenina and Aleutskaya ul (formerly ul 25 Oktyabra). Central hotels are within walk-

ing distance of the station; indeed almost everything is within walking distance but Vladivostok is a hilly place so distances can seem longer.

Note that the **Central Bus Station** is not at all central, being near Vtoraya Rechka suburban railway station (see under Local transport, p293).

Information *Vladivostok News,* on the internet at 🖳 http://vn.vladnews.ru, is a good source of local information.

The **American Business Center** (☎ 226 948, 🖳 abcvlad@sovam .com) is at the US Consulate, Pushkinskaya ul 32. The top hotels also have their own business centres offering everything from email to full secretarial services.

Banks There are **ATMs** at a business centre in the same building as the post office, and at major banks including V-Bank by the railway station, Sber-Bank at Aleutskaya ul 12 and Alfa Bank on Semyonovskaya ul. Sber-Bank, open 08:45-19:00 weekdays and 10:00-17:00 on weekends, can do currency exchange, cash travellers' cheques and give cash advances on Visa cards.

Communications The **central post office** is on Aleutskaya ul opposite the railway station. The adjacent business centre is also a convenient place for **Internet access**, available from 08:00-20:00 daily for US$1.50 per hour.

Travel agents Helpful **Lucky Tour** (☎ 223 333, 🖹 267 800, 🖳 lucky@online.vladivostok.ru, www.lucky tour.com) is at ul Sukhanova 20. Alternatives include **Intourist** (☎ 256 210, 🖹 258 839), Okeansky pr 90; **ACFES Tour Centre** (☎ 319 000) in Hotel Acfes Seiyo, pr 100th Vladivostoka 103; and **Sputnik** (☎ 423 556, 🖹 428 474, 🖳 www.marine.su/sputnik), Partizanskaya ul 2.

For adventure travel try **Dalintourist** (☎ 222 949, 🖹 228 055, 🖳 dalint@mail.primorye.ru, www.dalintourist.ru), ul Admirala Fokina 8.

Tours All sights are within easy walking distance so there's little need for a tour. If, however, you want to see something further away contact one of the travel agencies above.

Boat trips around the harbour are highly recommended: the chance to take pictures of Russian nuclear submarines doesn't arise that often. One-hour ferry cruises around Vladivostok's harbours and straits, with commentary in Russian, leave from **Sportivnaya Gavan Pier** approximately hourly between 11:00 and 16:00 in summer. The boat has a bar and the trip costs US$2.

Local transport
The **airport** is 30km outside Vladivostok. A taxi from the airport to Vladivostok railway station costs about US$50.

Bus No 101 runs from the airport to the 'central' bus station (9km north of the city centre); from Vtoraya Rechka railway station opposite the central bus station there are regular suburban trains and buses to Vladivostok railway station.

The cheapest way from the airport to Vladivostok is also the slowest: take bus No 7 to nearby Artem-Primorsky railway station, get on a local train heading west and at the fourth stop (Amursky Zaliv) change trains for Vladivostok.

There are numerous daily ferries from the **local ferry terminal** opposite the Submarine Museum. Destinations include the popular swimming spots of Russian Island, Popov Island, Reyniky Island and Cape Peshanaya. There are also two hydrofoils a day to Slavyanka Beach (US$6).

Diplomatic representation
● **US Consulate** (☎ 300 070, 🖹 300 091, 🖳 conssect@gin.ru), ul Pushkinskaya 32; American citizen services 14:30-16:00 weekdays.
● **Australian Consulate** (☎ 427 464, 🖹 426 9167), pr Krasnogo Znameny 42.
● **Japanese Consulate** (☎ 267 502, satellite ☎ 509-851 1001, 🖹 267 541), Verkhne-Portovaya ul 46.
● **Indian Consulate** (☎ 413 920, 🖹 413 956, 🖳 cgivlad@online.su), Aleutskaya ul 14.
● **Vietnam Consulate** (☎/🖹 226 948), Pushkinskaya ul 107/1.

Where to stay
Hotel prices in Vladivostok seem to vary wildly from month to month depending on demand. Take the following prices as a rough guide only. Don't expect hot water unless you're in one of the top hotels; even then it may be available only during speci-

The Vladivostok area code is ☎ 4232. From outside Russia dial +7-4232.

fied hours. Note that there are often power and heating shortages in parts of Vladivostok and the surrounding oblast.

HOFA can arrange homestays in Vladivostok, see p20.

Hotel Malaya Venetsiya, wedged beside the railway tracks just behind the station, is better inside than out. It's a motel-style place; rooms cost US$25 for a single, US$60 for a *luks* double and US$75 for a triple. Bring your earplugs as the walls are thin.

The friendly *Hotel Amursky Zaliv* (☎ 267 102), Naberezhnaya ul 9, is a bit of a maze and the cheaper rooms are a bit dingy. Singles/doubles start at US$28/40. Smarter rooms with sea view cost US$76. There are two restaurants, one serving good Georgian food.

Near the station, *Hotel Primorye* (☎ 411 422, 🖳 admin@primorye.ru), Posets kaya ul 20, is a recommended place with rooms from US$33/40 for a single/double. Staff speak English and are friendly. There is a swimming pool here.

At *Hotel Vladivostok* (☎ 412 808), up on the hill at Naberezhnaya ul 10, standards are almost Western. It's where a lot of Westerners on pre-booked Trans-Sib packages stay and costs US$50-66 for a double. There are various bars and a restaurant which are aimed at Chinese tour groups. Within Hotel Vladivostok, on the 4th floor, is the *Hotel Vizit-Vladivostok* (☎ 413 453, 🖳 vizit@hotbox.ru, www.vizit.vl.ru) with singles/doubles for US$60/73, better than the hotel that surrounds it.

Just around the corner from Hotel Vladivostok but in a less desirable state is *Hotel Ekvator* (☎ 410 673) at Naberez hnaya ul 20. Surly staff will charge you US$16/24 for a single/double, but don't expect to be treated like a guest.

One of the top hotels is the Japanese-owned *Hotel Versailles* (☎ 264 201, 🖳 ver sal@mail.primorye.ru), Svetlanskaya ul 10. Luxurious rooms cost US$110-230.

The other top hotel, probably the best, is the fairly new *Hotel Hyundai* (402 233, 🖹 407 007, 🖳 www.hotelhyundai.ru) at the three-way junction of Semenovskaya ul, ul Sukhanova and ul Uborevicha. It offers a quite bewildering range of services, including the Vladivostok Business Centre. Room prices range from US$200 to US$1000.

About 20km north of Vladivostok is the *Vlad Inn* (☎ 331 351, satellite ☎ 504-916 3607, 🖹 330 717, 🖳 www.vlad-inn.ru), Vosmaya (8th) ul 11. This Canadian-Russian joint venture is well-run and recommended. A double costs US$160 including breakfast. Take a suburban train from Vladivostok station for six stops to Sanatornaya (Санаторная).

Where to eat

The best restaurant within easy reach of the railway station is *Café Nostalgia*, Morskaya ul 6/25, which serves genuinely good coffee (most unusual in Russia). The tiny restaurant is clean and offers good Russian dishes: zakuski for about US$2 and main courses for US$4-6.

Next door, behind an ornate Oriental doorway, is the Korean *Restaurant Morambom* (☎ 227 725) which is probably better known for being difficult to get into than for its good food. It's expensive and you will need to book ahead.

There's excellent vegetarian food at *Café Krishna*, Okeansky pr 10/12, open 10:00-19:00 except Sunday. You get three filling courses for US$2 in a serene atmosphere, disturbed only by typical Russian service. They often stop serving food around 16:00.

There are several places serving pizza including *Pizza M*, with a branch at Hotel Primorye and another near the Drama theatre; delicious pizzas cost US$2-10. At *Restaurant Zhemchuzhina* pizzas cost from US$3.

Down by the waterfront there are several *cafés* serving drinks and various snacks all day. You can buy prawns, crabs and other seafood here for US$3-6, with beer to go with them.

Paparatsi, ul Admirala Fokina 5, is a trendy place though not many people order the food. Still, you can have a decent spaghetti bolognese for US$6.

Hotel Amursky Zaliv has an excellent

Georgian restaurant with main courses costing US$2-5. It's well worth a visit and is open 11:00-02:00.

Good upmarket places include the Japanese **Sakura Restaurant** (☎ 260 305) in the Hotel Vladivostok, with mains for US$6-9; and the somewhat cheaper Chinese **Restaurant Harbin** (☎ 268 186) at ul Naberezhnaya 3 (above Okean Cinema).

The **Vlad Inn** serves de luxe hamburgers that actually taste like de luxe hamburgers, for US$6, and some of the biggest steaks you'll ever see for US$20. Their Kamchatka crabs are another speciality.

Main courses cost US$13-25. Book in advance and wear reasonably smart dress when dining here.

Up the block in the Hotel Pensionat is the equally good but cheaper **Captain Cook Restaurant** (☎ 215 341), an Australian-Russian joint venture. The steaks (US$9-12) are recommended.

Restaurant Volna (☎ 219 340), at the top of the marine terminal, offers splendid views but usually caters for pre-booked groups. In the evening this place becomes a popular disco.

Vladivostok-Harbin border crossing

If you decide to take the No 185 train from Vladivostok to Harbin, you should have plenty of time on your hands. The train leaves Vladivostok at 22:44 Vladivostok time. Two hours later it stops at Ussurisk, where your Harbin-bound carriage is detached. After sitting in a siding for eight hours, it is then attached to a new engine and you begin the next stage of the journey; a three-hour jaunt to the border at Grodekovo. So far it has taken you 13 hours to travel just 225km. About now you realize why the carriage is nearly empty: everyone else has taken the four-hour bus journey from Vladivostok to the border.

About 13:00 you disembark with your bags. In the customs and immigration building there is a kassa selling train tickets to Harbin. Customs and immigration officials here won't be working yet, but you can fill out your declaration form and wait upstairs. Three hours on, the officials arrive and it's time to leave Russia. Bags are searched with varying degrees of enthusiasm. Customs forms are requested and they may ask to look in your wallet – but they don't seem too interested. At immigration you might be asked, 'Where are you going after Russia?', though it would seem fairly obvious that the answer is China. My visa wasn't registered with the company that issued it, and four French tourists had all overstayed their visas by a day, but none of this caused a problem.

The train leaves Grodekovo at 17:20, now filled to capacity with all those Russians who took the bus from Vladivostok. During the two-hour journey from Grodekovo to the Chinese border town of Suifenhe, Chinese customs and immigration officials enter your compartment and do their job efficiently and politely. Due to the international time difference it is now 16:20, Chinese time.

On arrival the train is taken off to have the bogies changed, and for three and a half hours you are free to explore the delights of Suifenhe: an OK place, better than most border towns. You can change money in a hotel and get a decent meal.

You set off again at 20.05, and arrive in Harbin at 06:30 the next morning, but this is Harbin North station. Even though everyone else gets off here, you should wait until the train arrives at the main railway station about 15 minutes later. If you get off at Harbin North by mistake, it's about Y20 by taxi to the main station.

Congratulations: you have travelled a grand total of 783km in 35 hours, at an average speed of about 22 km per hour. **Nick Hill**

Ferries from Vladivostok to Japan and Korea
A ferry plies between Vladivostok and Fushiki (Japan) weekly through-out the year. In the past the season has been shorter, typically summer through mid-autumn, and Russia being Russia, there's always a chance that it may revert. The two-night crossing takes about 40 hours. At the time of writing ferries departed Vladivostok at 18:00 Monday, reaching Fushiki at 09:00 Wednesday; and departed Fushiki at 18:00 Friday, arriving in Vladivostok at 09:30 Sunday. The Vladivostok–Fushiki trip costs from US$190 per bed in a lower-deck, four-berth cabin, up to US$740 for higher decks, with discounts for students. Fares includes Vladivostok port tax and all meals. There is a luggage limit of 50kg per person though you can pay US$5 for every extra 5kg. The ships are fairly modern and comfortable.

There are also weekly ferries to Sokcho in Korea for around US$110. For more information and bookings contact:
● **United Orient Shipping and Agency Co**, (☎ 03-5541 7511, 🖷 03-3552 7322, 🖳 h.tazaki@uniorient.co.jp), 4th floor, Shuwa-Sakurabashi Bldg, 4-5-4, Hatchobori, Chuo-ko, Tokyo 104 0032, Japan.
● **Business Intour Service** (Biznes Intur Servis; ☎ 497 391, 🖷 411 829, 🖳 bis@ints.vtc.ru) have an office, open 10:00-18:00 weekdays for tickets, on the 3rd floor of Vladivostok's marine terminal.

Where to shop
The best souvenirs in town are sold at the **Café Nostalgia Art Shop**, Morskaya ul 6/25. Many items are expensive but they seem to be of a high standard. The **Collector's Shop**, next to the Arsenev History Museum, sells a range of old bank notes, coins, medals and other souvenirs.

Entertainment
There's a smart bar at **Hotel Hyundai**. Rather less salubrious places of entertainment include casinos at Hotel Amursky Zaliv and at Hotel Versailles. The popular **Sinyaya Zvezda Café Dancing Club** is open 20:00-06:00.

Inline skates can be hired on the deck at the **Okean cinema** for US$2 an hour between 10:00 and 20:00. **Rowing boats** (US$2 an hour) can be hired near the **barge** which doubles as a disco in summer.

Moving on
By rail Long-distance tickets are sold downstairs at the station, and local tickets upstairs. Doing it yourself is easy, or you can buy your ticket from the station's Service Centre at the south end of the main building. It's open 09:00-12:00 and 13:00-17:45 and charges about US$1.50 commission per ticket.

Khabarovsk (US$24) is 13 hours away on the excellent, nightly No 6/5 Okean train. Irkutsk (US$61) is 83 hours away from Vladivostok.

For Harbin (China), you can go to kassa No 1 and get a ticket on train No 185. This train is actually bound for Blagoveshchensk, but one carriage is redirected at Ussurisk. The train departs on Monday and Thursday evenings, arriving in Harbin in the morning two days later. Only kupé is available, for US$35; as the carriage is rarely full you can buy a ticket at fairly short notice. See the box on p295 for more on this snail's-pace experience.

By bus If you're heading into China, you can take a bus or share a taxi to the border at Grodekovo, four hours from Vladivostok. Because there is no road across the international no-man's land at Grodekovo, you must then rejoin the twice-weekly Vladivostok-Harbin train, but you have knocked about 11 hours off the train journey time.

The signs are that Grodekovo will eventually be developed into a major border crossing, by road as well as rail. Meanwhile many Russians take a bus or share a taxi to the border at Pokrovka where there is a road across the border. On the other side they take a local bus or taxi up to Suifenhe and catch one of the twice-daily trains from there to Harbin (departing at 16:02 and 20:05).

By air Vladivostok's new international air terminal building opened in 1999. Several airlines are represented at the office of the Primorsky Agency of Aviation Companies (☎ 260 880) at ul Posetskaya 17; these include Transaero, Korean Air, British Airways, Aeroflot and numerous 'babyflots', including the regional airline Vladivostok Air (🖥 www.vladavia.ru).

Vladivostok has international air links with Harbin, Niigata, Osaka, Niigata, Toyama, Seoul, Pusan, Bangkok and Seattle. There are also flights to many Siberian cities. Sample fares include Moscow (US$350), Seoul (US$330), Osaka (US$280) and Niigata (US$280).

Ulan Bator
Ulaan Baatar

The world's coldest capital is a fascinating place to visit even if it does, at first sight, look like just another Soviet-style city. Things are changing fast here now though, as the free market takes hold and many more foreigners are visiting the country than ever before.

Ulan Bator (population: 804,000) sits in a basin surrounded by four mountains: Bogd Uul, Songino Khairkhan, Chingeltei and Bayanzurkh, all part of the beautiful Khentii range, the southernmost boundary of the great Siberian taiga. The city experiences great climatic extremes; the temperature ranges from -49°C (-46°F) in winter to 38°C (93°F) in summer. Average annual precipitation is only 236mm and there are on average 283 sunny days in the year. Ulan Bator is 1350m above sea level. Among the industrial suburbs and concrete tower blocks there are vibrant splashes of colour in the temples and old palaces. The Mongolian people are charming and cheerful (Luigi Barzini, driving across the country in 1907, was amazed at their high spirits; the nomads he encountered galloped alongside his car roaring with laughter).

The best time to visit Ulan Bator is during the **Naadam Festival**, usually held between 11 and 13 July (although you'll find many other travellers heading there too, and demand for Trans-Mongolian train tickets can outstrip supply). The festival involves the three traditional Mongolian sports of horse riding, wrestling and archery.

HISTORY

Home of the Living Buddha
For much of its 350-year existence the town was little more than a semi-nomadic settlement. From 1639 to 1778 it moved some 30 times, like a migrat-

ing *ger* (yurt) city. The Da Khure Lamasery, built here in 1639, was the abode of one of the three most important lines of 'Living Buddhas', the others being the Dalai Lama in Tibet and the Panchen Lama in Peking. The one at Da Khure was usually a child who died, or rather was murdered, shortly before reaching puberty, since it was believed that the soul of a deity could dwell only in the body of a child.

From 1639 to 1706 the town was known as Örgöö, from the Mongolian word for 'palace'. From 1706 to 1911 it was Ikh Khuree or Da Khure to Mongolians, or Urga to foreigners.

Independence
When Mongolia declared itself independent of China in 1911 the city was renamed Niislel Khurehe. By this time it had become a large trading centre on the route between China and Russia. There were, in fact, three separate cities here: the Chinese, the Russian and the Mongolian. The Chinese and Russian cities were engaged in the tea and silk trades but the Mongolian city's concern was the salvation (or rather the liberation) of souls. There was a population of some 30,000 Buddhist monks in the lamaseries here.

Ulan Bator today
After the Communist Party came to power in 1921 the capital was renamed Ulan Bator, meaning 'Red Hero'. With considerable help from the USSR, the city was redesigned; the architectural origins of its austere tower blocks and municipal buildings are recognizably Soviet. In the mid 1990s the city experienced a private-sector boom with new buildings springing up everywhere and shops and restaurants opening. As in Russia, most of the money for this came from Communist-era power brokers who quickly took control of privatized state assets.

In 1999-2000 Mongolia was hit by severe weather conditions: a serious drought followed by an extremely cold winter. This led to food shortages although the capital escaped the worst of these. Ulan Bator continues to develop with speed, but it's still easy to see that under this surface layer of development the people and traditions remain largely unchanged.

WHAT TO SEE

Sühbaatariin Talbai (Sukhe Bator Square)
A mounted statue of the Mongolian revolutionary leader Damdinii Sühbaatar in heroic pose stands in the centre of this large square, opposite his mausoleum (modelled on Lenin's Mausoleum in Red Square). His preserved body does not receive visitors but newlyweds queue up to have their photos taken at the foot of his statue, more out of tradition than inclination. In 1990 the square was the scene of the pro-democracy demonstrations that led to the first free elections.

Gandan (Gandantegchinlen) Monastery
Mongolia once had 700 monasteries but virtually all were destroyed in the communist crackdown at the end of the 1930s. More than 14,000 monks were

killed and tens of thousands forced to give up their vows. Following the pro-democracy movement in 1990, restrictions were eased allowing some monasteries to reopen and Gandan to operate as something more than a tourist showpiece.

The original monastery on this site was built in 1785. The first group of new buildings was put up in 1938; along with the main temple there are stupas, a library and accommodation for the monks. Powdered juniper, to be thrown into the big burner outside the temple as an offering, is dispensed in a side building. Many of the buildings have been recently renovated.

It's best to visit the monastery in the morning; watch out for pickpockets when concentrating on the ceremony, and don't wander round this district after dark.

Bogd Khan Palace and Museum

The palace of the last Bogd Khan ('holy king') of Mongolia is a wonderful old place, full of ghosts and rather like Beijing's Forbidden City on a smaller scale. Exploring the palace one gets the impression that the owners walked out just a few years ago, leaving it in the hands of rather relaxed caretakers who have forgotten to mow the lawn.

Entered through a gateway guarded by four fierce-looking incarnations, the palace comprises two courtyards with small pavilions on each side. There are exhibits of *thangkas* (Buddhist devotional paintings), musical instruments and Buddha figures, as well as the day-to-day furnishings of the buildings. Unfortunately there are very few labels telling you what's what.

The Bogd Khan museum is beside the palace complex. Exhibits include Bogd Khan's throne, fur-lined robes and crown, and his luxurious ger (the exterior covered with the skins of 150 snow leopards and containing stove and portable altar). His collection of stuffed animals is also displayed somewhat haphazardly: a moth-eaten lion sharing the same quarters as a grubby polar bear. Outside is an interesting display of palanquins and carriages.

The museum is open 10:00-16:30 (only until 16:00 on Tuesday and Wednesday) and closed Thursday and the last Wednesday of each month. Entry is US$2 plus US$5 for a camera permit. Take any bus heading south from Bayangol Hotel and get off when you see the tank memorial (about five minutes).

Natural History Museum

Mongolia is well known for its dinosaur graveyards and some of the discoveries are on display here, including several fossilized nests of dinosaur eggs. These come in a fascinating range of shapes: cannon balls, ostrich-eggs, even Cornish pasties. Also worth seeing are the stuffed animals arranged in quite imaginative panoramas of the Gobi and the mountains in the west. Here are many of the animals in the *Red Book* for endangered species including the snow leopard, wild Bactrian camel, Gobi bear, khulan (wild ass), red wolf, northern otter, snow griffon and Przewalski's horse. On the top floor are displays of national dress (smelling strongly of moth-balls).

Street names

Finding your way around Ulan Bator is tricky: Russian street names have been abandoned wholesale for Mongolian ones in the last few years, and the script is now Mongolian Cyrillic, which has a few more characters than Russian Cyrillic. There is no single accepted way for names to be transliterated into Latin letters: Ulan Bator, for example, is often written Ulaanbaatar. Following is a table of some old Russian street names plus current Mongolian versions. The Mongolian word for 'street' is *gudamj*, 'avenue' is *örgön chuluu* (meaning 'wide space') and 'square' is *talbai*.

Russian	Mongolian
pl Sukhe Batora	Sühbaatariin Talbai (Sukhe Bator Sq)
pr Karla Marxa	Olimpiin Örgön Chuluu (Olympic Ave)
pr Lenina	Chinggis Khaan Örgön Chuluu (Ghengis Khan Ave)
pr Mira	Enkhtaivanii Örgön Chuluu (Peace Ave)
Ikh Toirog	Ikh Toiruu (Big Ring Rd)
Baga Toirou	Baga Toiruu (Small Ring Rd)
ul Zaluuchuudyn	Zaluuchuudiin Örgön Chuluu (Youth Ave)
ul Khasbatora	Khuvsgalchidiin Örgön Chuluu (Hovsgol Ave)
ul Obedinennykh Natsii	Negdsen Undestnii Gudamj (United Nations St)
ul Stalina	Natsagdorj Gudamj
ul 40-letiya Oktyabrya	Zamchid Gudamj
ul Brezhneva	Khatanbaatar Magsa Iav Gudamj
ul Gagarina	Amarsanaa Gudamj
ul Gorkogo	Ard-Ayush Örgön Chuluu
ul Konstitutsii	Zanabazar Gudamj
Oktyabrskaya ul	Khudaldaanii Gudamj
Universitetskaya ul	Ikh Surguul Gudamj
Irkutskaya ul	Eldiv-Ochir Gudamj

The museum is open 10:00-16:30 daily, but open only Monday and Tuesday in winter. Entry is US$3 plus about US$10 for using cameras and US$20 for video cameras (each section of the museum has different camera charges).

Choijin Lama Monastery

Preserved for many years as a museum of religion, this temple complex has been handed back to the monks in the new spirit of religious freedom. It was the former home of Luvsan Haidav Choijin Lama, the brother of the 8th Bogdo Gegen (Bogd Khan). Both of them were born Tibetans.

The brightly-coloured temple buildings are set amongst overgrown grassy gardens and house a large collection of ornate masks for Buddhist mystery plays. Take a close look at the golden seated Buddha figure, not a statue but the mummified body of a lama, encased in gold. In the northern pavilion you may also want to take a close look at the statues, which graphically depict Tantric rituals involving complex sexual positions.

Ulan Bator
(Ulaanbaatar)

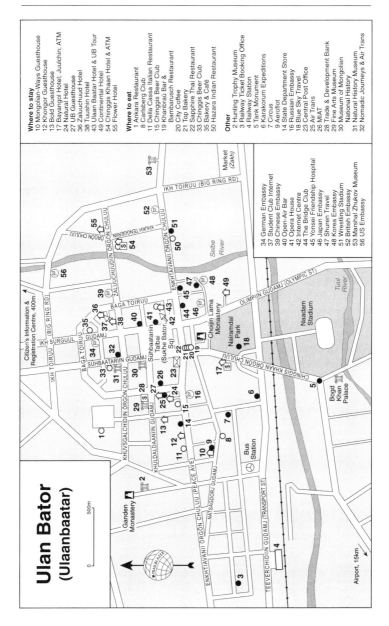

0   500m

Where to stay
10 Mongolian-Ways Guesthouse
12 Khongor Guesthouse
13 Bold Guesthouse
17 Bayangol Hotel; Juulchin; ATM
24 Natural Hotel
27 UB Guesthouse
36 Zaluuchuud Hotel
38 Tuushin Hotel
43 Ulaan Baatar Hotel & UB Tour
49 Continental Hotel
54 Chinggis Khaan Hotel & ATM
55 Flower Hotel

Where to eat
1 Ankara Restaurant
8 Carlsberg Club
11 Della Cassa Italian Restaurant
15 Chinggis Beer Club
19 Khanbrau Bar &
   Bambarusch Restaurant
20 City Coffee
21 Top Bakery
22 Sapphire Thai Restaurant
33 Chinggis Beer Club
35 Bakery & Café
50 Hazara Indian Restaurant

Other
2 Hunting Trophy Museum
3 Railway Ticket Booking Office
4 Railway Station
5 Tank Monument
6 Karakorum Expeditions
7 Circus
9 Aeroflot
14 State Department Store
16 Russian Embassy
18 Blue Sky Travel
23 Central Post Office
25 Air Trans
26 MIAT
28 Trade & Development Bank
29 Fine Arts Museum
30 Museum of Mongolian
   National History
31 Natural History Museum
32 Nomadic Journeys & Air Trans
34 German Embassy
37 Student Club Internet
39 Chinese Embassy
40 Open-Air Bar
41 Opera House
42 Internet Centre
44 The Bridge Club
45 Yonsei Friendship Hospital
46 Japan Embassy
47 Shuren Travel
48 Korea Embassy
51 Wrestling Stadium
52 British Embassy
53 Marshal Zhukov Museum
56 US Embassy

The complex is open 10:00-17:00 daily except Tuesday; entry US$2 plus US$8 for a camera. Immediately to the south of the museum is a statue of the Mongolian writer Natsagorj.

Fine Arts Museum

The museum includes a comprehensive display of thangkas, one more than 15m long. There are copies of prehistoric cave paintings, robes and masks from Buddhist Tsan dances and a gallery of modern paper-cutting art. Open 10:00-17:00; entry US$2.

Other museums and sights

Many of the city's smaller, less significant museums have been closed down, a fact which seems to have disappointed few visitors. A few will reopen after renovation or their displays may eventually be moved to other museums. It is no longer possible to visit the museum in Sühbaatar's bungalow or the Lenin Museum which has recently suffered the humiliation of being turned into a shopping centre. The huge Lenin head is still in place looming down on shoppers.

The **Marshal Zhukov Museum** is still open, probably because there is no Zhukov museum in Russia. The small building is filled with military and Soviet memorabilia including Zhukov's pipe and shoes. The man who runs it sometimes dresses up in the marshal's old uniform.

The former Revolutionary Museum, at the north-west corner of Sühbaatariin Talbai, is now the **Museum of Mongolian National History**, open 10:00-16:30, closed Wednesday, entry US$2.

The **Hunting Trophy Museum** near Gandan Monastery focuses on a highly controversial issue: the lucrative sale of hunting packages to foreign tourists. It's open 09:00-17:00 daily except Monday, but closes at 14:00 at weekends.

Nairamdal Park is where locals go to relax and it has a boating lake, ferris wheel, camel rides and model dinosaurs.

PRACTICAL INFORMATION

Orientation

From Ulan Bator railway station to Sühbaatariin Talbai (Sukhe Bator Sq) is about 1¹/₂km.

Although Ulan Bator is relatively safe compared to some cities in the West, crime is on the increase. Hassle from drunks is probably the most trouble you'll have. Don't wander round the streets alone after dark. Take particular care at the railway station and the market, where **pickpockets** and **bag-slitters** operate. The post office and buses have also been reported as prime locations for petty theft of this kind.

Information

The weekly *Mongol Messenger* (US$1) is a good local newspaper, available from Ulaan Baatar Hotel among other places. There's also a freebie, the *UB Guide*, available at hotels.

There are several useful **websites** with information on Mongolia. The *Mongol Messenger* is online (in English) at 🖳 www.mongolnet.mn/mglmsg.

Try 🖳 www.ulaanbaatar.net for local business listings, information on Mongolian food including recipes, plus weather reports and TV listings.

The US Embassy's website, 🖳 www

❑ **Visiting Mongolia**

Visas Some nationalities, including Americans, no longer need a visa to visit Mongolia. For details see p22.

Individual travel vs package tours While individual travel around Mongolia is perfectly possible, potential problems with language, accommodation, food and organizing travel make joining or assembling a group a popular option, especially if time is limited. If you are visiting only Ulan Bator you can get by on your own but it's not so easy outside the capital. It is easy to organize personal tours once you arrive in Ulan Bator but be sure to check what you are getting for your money. Following is a rough indication of what you should expect to pay for various excursions: Terelj Camp (1 night, 2 days) US$50, extra day US$15; Karakorum (3 days, 2 nights) including van, gas, driver, interpreter, US$210 (four people); car, driver and gas (one day) US$80; car and driver (one day) US$40.

Travel agents in Ulan Bator The former state-run travel bureau, **Juulchin** (Zhuulchin; ☎ 312 095 ▤ 320 246, 🖳 web.mol.mn/~jlncorp), 5B Chinggis Khaan Örgön Chuluu, still has enormous clout and charges as if it were a monopoly. **Shuren Travel** (☎ 310 869, ▤ 450 781, 🖳 shuren@magicnet.mn), 8 Olimpiin Gudamj, arranges trekking, riding and jeep trips all over Mongolia, mainly for groups. **Nomadic Journeys** (☎ 328 737, ▤ 321 489, 🖳 www.nomadicjour neys.com), 1 Sühbaatariin Gudamj, is recommended: as well as offering local tours, it runs the trekking, riding and fishing trips of Eco Tour Production (see p30). **Blue Sky Travel** (☎ /▤ 312 067, 🖳 www.travel2mongolia.mn) has been recommended by several readers. **Karakorum Expeditions** (☎ /▤ 315 655, 🖳 www.gomon golia.com), in the Jiguur Grand Hotel on Teeverchidiin Gudamj, is also recommended. **Mongol Khaan Travel** (☎ 312426, ▤ 312426, 🖳 www.mol.mn/mongolkhaan, mma-prg@magicnet.mn has also been recommended. **UB Tour** (☎ 324 740, ▤ 324 730, 🖳 ubtour@magicnet.mn), on the 4th floor of the Ulaan Baatar Hotel, is a helpful source of international train tickets.

.us-mongolia.com, has business listings and general information about the country.

Local transport
There are **buses** and **trolley-buses** in Ulan Bator (tickets cost the equivalent of US$0.20) but you may prefer to walk as most of the sights are in the city centre. Watch for pickpockets on the buses.

To get a **taxi**, simply put out your hand by the side of the road and a motorist will usually stop. Point to the odometer to show the driver that you expect to pay the prevailing Mongolian rate of T250 (US$0.25) per kilometre. **Official taxis** with meters are also available but they're not in great supply; you'll usually find them outside top hotels.

It's possible to rent **bicycles** in Ulan Bator too. Try Bike Mongolia (☎ 327 423)

or Suren (☎ 453 347). Note that Mongolian dogs like nothing better than to chase foreigners on bicycles.

Services
Post and telecommunications The **Central Post Office** is on Sühbaatariin Talbai but it's better to buy those wonderful Mongolian stamps from the hotels since they often have a greater range.

The most reliable **courier company** is DHL, with representatives at the more expensive hotels including the Ulaan Baatar Hotel. Parcels to the US or Europe take three to five days.

International telephone calls are expensive but can be made from cardphones in many hotels, as well as from the post office and from a 24-hour, AT&T direct-call telephone in the lobby of the

> **❑ Prices in this section**
> Note that prices in this section are quoted in US$ but must usually be paid for in Mongolian togrogs. From year to year, as the togrog exchange rate rises against the dollar, the dollar value seems to stay relatively constant. Convert the US$ price given in this section to togrogs at the going rate and that should be approximately the right price to pay in local currency.

Flower Hotel. Hotels will send **faxes**, but check charges first as some are very high.

There are scores of **Internet cafés** in town and going online seems swift and reliable. Most charge around US$0.60 per hour. The Student Club near the Zaluuchuud Hotel is good; so is the internet centre next to the Ulaan Baatar Hotel.

Currency and banks The *togrog* (or tugrik, or MNT) is the Mongolian unit of currency. Approximate exchange rates at the time of writing were MNT 1120 per US$1, MNT 1904 per UK£1, MNT 1307 per euro, MNT 37 per R1 (Russia) and MNT 136 per Y1 (China).

Many hotels and banks will exchange hard currency or travellers' cheques for togrogs, and buy togrogs. The best place to do this is at the Trade and Development Bank (next to the Fine Arts Museum), where you can also get US$ **cash advances** on Visa or MasterCard. The post office changes cash only. There are **ATMs** (Visa cards only) in the Chinggis Khaan, Bayangol and other better hotels.

Black market and official exchange rates are almost identical so the only reason to use the former is convenience. You can find semi-legal 'grey market' money changers outside the old cinema on Baga Toiruu, who will change US$ and Japanese yen and buy all your unspent roubles or yuan. The usual caveats apply: count your money carefully and be aware that there is always a certain risk in changing money in

this way. Fresh US$ bills printed after 1996 are what everyone wants, preferably US$50s or US$100s.

Diplomatic representation Embassies and consulates in Ulan Bator are listed below.
● **China** (☎ 323 940, ▤ 311 943, 💻 chinaemb_mn@mfa.gov.cn), 5 Zaluuchuudiin Örgön Chuluu, open 9:30-12:00 Monday, Wednesday and Friday; a tourist visa costs US$30 processed in a week, US$50 in three days ot US$60 for a same-day visa.
● **Germany** (☎ 323 325, ▤ 323 905), 7 Negdsen Undestnii Gudamj.
● **Japan** (☎ 320 777, ▤ 313 332), Olimpiin Gudamj.
● **Russia** (☎ 326 037, ▤ 327 018), 6A Enkhtaivanii Örgön Chuluu; open 14:00-15:00 for visas. The visa process is not straightforward here so get your Russian visa elsewhere, even Beijing, if you can. You must go to the consulate in person. Three photographs are required. A visa costs US$30-$95 depending on how quickly you want it. They don't accept fax copies of invitations or vouchers so it's best to get them faxed directly to the consulate. The travel agency at the Aeroflot Office (see p308) might help you get a 90-day business visa in about a week for US$150-180, though you would have to register it in Ulan Ude rather than waiting until you get to Moscow.
● **South Korea** (☎ 321 548, ▤ 311 157), 10 Olimpiin Gudamj.
● **UK** (☎ 458 133, 458 238, ▤ 458 036, 💻 britemb@magicnet.mn), 30 Enkhtaivanii Örgön Chuluu, open 8:30-13:00, 14:00-17:00, Mon-Thurs; 8:30-13:00 Friday.
● **USA** (☎ 329 095, ▤ 320 776), Ikh Toiruu, open 9:00-13:00, 14:00-18:00 weekdays.

Medical Ulan Bator's first non-government hospital, the Yonsei Friendship Hospital (☎ 310 945), opened in 1994. It is sponsored by Yonsei University of Korea and various Christian missionary groups.

For those seeking a traditional cure, the Institute for Mongolian Traditional Medicine is at the Manba Datsan. To get there take bus No 5, 9, 10, 20 or 21 or trolley No 8.

Radio and TV Cable TV (MTV, CNN etc) is available in better hotels. BBC World Service radio broadcasts locally 24 hours a day at FM 103.1 MHz.

Visa extensions and registration It's no longer necessary to register with the police on arrival in Ulan Bator unless you are staying for more than 30 days. To register go to the **Citizens' Information and Registration Centre**, which is hard to find as it doesn't have a street address or look like a police station. It is located about 800m up the road which starts opposite the northern end of Eldiv-Ochir Gudamj. It's on the 3rd floor, on the right, at the end of a hall. It's wise to take a Mongolian speaker with you.

Where to stay
Budget accommodation There are budget guest houses opening up all the time, and many offer trips to the countryside, visa services and onward tickets. Their touts will meet you at the railway station. Some offer ger accommodation or homestays. Prices for a dorm bed are around US$4. Be sure of what is in the price (including breakfast) and don't agree to anything before having a look.

Bold Guesthouse (☎ 9919 6232, ⌨ bold777@hotmail.com) is behind the State Department Store, in building 1, entrance 1, 2nd floor, apartment 8. They charge US$4 per person for dormitory accommodation and arrange visas, tours and train tickets.

UB Guesthouse (⌨ ubguest@hot mail.com) is in an apartment block opposite the MIAT office. There's a sign at the back of the block. Dorm beds are US$4 and double rooms are US$10, with breakfast included, and there is lots of information available.

Khonghor Guesthouse is also located in an apartment block: take the door at the

left end of the block and it's on the 2nd floor, apartment No 6. It's always busy and somewhat cramped, but has cable TV and a kitchen. Dorm beds are US$4. All the usual tours are available from here.

Mongolian-Ways Guesthouse (☎ 320 350, mobile ☎ 91 112 129, ▤ 318 430, ⌨ www.mongolian-ways.com), Civil Defence Board Building, 4th Floor, is more spacious than most other budget guesthouses. A bed in a four-bed room costs US$4. There is also a communal area and a kitchen. The owner can arrange various adventure tours to the countryside.

The *Natural Hotel* is up a small road opposite the Russian Embassy, in an awkwardly located, detached brick building. It's very good value for money, with singles/doubles for US$19/25 with modern fitted bathrooms. Staff are friendly and rooms are well looked after.

Zaluuchuud Hotel (☎ 324 594), 27 Baga Toiruu, is a venerable place that's starting to look a bit tatty. They have a range of rooms and charge from US$16/25 for a single/double with attached bathroom. There is a restaurant here but even the staff will advise you to go to one of the places in town instead.

Mid-range and upmarket hotels All hotel rooms in this section have attached bathroom.

Tuushin Hotel (☎ 323 162, ▤ 325 903, ⌨ tuushot@magicnet.mn) is conveniently located just off Sühbaatariin Talbai. There are singles for US$60 and doubles for US$80-130. There's a sauna, billiard table and travel agency.

Flower Hotel (Mongolian name *Tsetseg*, formerly the Altai; ☎/▤ 358 330, ⌨ flower@magicnet.mn, www.mol.mn/ flowerhotel), 12 Khukh Tenggeriin Örgön Chuluu, is good value at US$44 for a single or US$77-93 for a double. Cheaper rooms have toilet and washbasin but no shower. The hotel caters for Japanese tour groups so standards are high. There is a free sauna.

The Ulan Bator area code is ☎ 1. From outside Mongolia dial +976-1.

The Soviet-style ***Ulaan Baatar Hotel*** (☎ 320 237, 🖻 324 485, 🖳 ubhotel@mag icnet.mn) is the most popular haunt for foreigners and expats, who refer to it as 'the UB'. It's very well located, on Sühbaatariin Talbai. A single is US$70 and doubles range from US$100 to US$190. Rates include breakfast. Credit cards are accepted.

The partly-refurbished, 418-bed ***Bayangol Hotel*** (☎ 326 781, 🖻 326 880) 7 Chinggis Khaan Örgön Chuluu, charges US$70 for a single; doubles cost US$90-180. Breakfast is included. Some rooms are much better than others so you should look at your room before accepting it. The hotel accepts credit cards.

The ***Continental Hotel*** (☎ 323 829, 🖻 329 630, 🖳 continental@magicnet.mn, www.ulaanbaatar.net/continentalhotel~/ho me.html), opposite Nairamdal Park, is an impressive place with a grand pillared entrance. Prices range from US$79 for an economy single to US$168 for a superior double. There's a sauna, and even a heated garage to keep your jeep cosy in winter.

The ***Chinggis Khaan Hotel***, (☎ 313 380, 🖻 312 788, 🖳 www.chinggis-hotel.com), 5 Khukh Tenggeriin Örgön Chuluu, is the city's smartest place to stay. A single room is US$80 and doubles range from US$100 to US$180 including breakfast. There's a casino, a pricey Western restaurant and a business centre.

Where to eat
Mutton still features on nearly every menu but the range of food available is much wider than it was a few years back. If you're a vegetarian you're advised to bring supplies with you as Mongolians have never thought much of veggies: some are even convinced that eating vegetables is not healthy!

Mongolian beer is quite good: Khanbraü is brewed here under a German licence. Another local brand is Chinggis Khan.

In the summer there are many stalls around the city selling a wide range of ***fresh fruit*** and there are plenty of well-stocked ***supermarkets*** for train supplies and

trips into the countryside. A delicious snack, common in the city's many ***cafés***, is steaming hot *khuushuur* (fried, mutton-filled pasties) and Mongolian tea. Three khuushuur cost about US$0.40.

Top Bakery and ***City Coffee***, next door to each other, both serve good cakes and snacks, and City Coffee has a good range of coffees. ***Carlsberg Club*** on Natsagdorj Gudamj serves good ice cream as well as beer.

The best hotel restaurants are in the ***Ulaan Baatar***, ***Bayangol*** and ***Chinggis Khaan*** hotels. Most larger hotels have two restaurants, one cheaper than the other.

The ***Della Cassa*** Italian restaurant on Enkhtaivanii Örgön Chuluu is well worth a visit, with a wide choice of pizzas and pasta. Two main courses and drinks cost around US$10. You can get a great pepper steak at the ***Chinggis Beer Club*** on Sühbaatariin Gudamj.

The ***Khanbraü Bar and Bambarusch Restaurant*** on Chinggis Khaan Örgön Chuluu is popular with expats and wealthy Mongolians. It is always busy and serves great ice creams but prices are relatively high. They brew several of their own beers at the restaurant.

There is a very good Japanese restaurant called ***Hanamasa*** across from the Geser Temple on Ikh Toiruu, with a US$8, all-you-can-eat buffet. If you're big on Asian food you could also try ***Sapphire Thai Restaurant***, on the 2nd floor of the Arts Centre, next to Top Bakery. It's open 11:00-23:00 Monday to Saturday and 11:00-19:00 Sunday. The US$2 set lunch is great value and although it's not exactly authentic Thai, it's very tasty.

Curry has come to UB too: the highly recommended ***Hazara Indian Restaurant*** (☎ 95 157 604) at 16 Enkhtaivanii Örgön Chuluu offers delicious North Indian cuisine for US$10-12, and also does take-aways.

You can find delicious Turkish food at the ***Ankara Restaurant***, in the cinema building on Khuvsgalchidiin Örgön Chuluu. A very filling meal will cost around US$3.

Nightlife
There has been a radical change to evening activities in Mongolia over the last few years and the city seems to be developing something of a taste for decadence.

The **Ministry of Sound** nightclub is very popular on Friday nights. Entry is free, there are several striptease shows and beers cost US$1.50. You should take a taxi as it's outside the city centre.

In the city centre the **Bridge Club** charges US$1.50 at the door and the cheapest drink is nearly US$2. It's open daily until 02:00, later at weekends.

The popular **Chinggis Beer Club** (see Where to eat) is open until 01:00 nightly.

There is a pleasant **open-air bar** set into the corner of the Palace of Culture, and open nightly. Among many other bars, the **Money Train**, **White House** and **Carlsberg Club** have all been recommended. Expats seem to favour the bar at the **Bayangol Hotel**.

More traditional pursuits include ballet or opera at the **State Opera and Ballet Theatre** on Sühbaatariin Talbai; inquire at your hotel for tickets and times or go to the box office on the night. The Song and Dance Show which is on several times a week at the **Drama Theatre** is worth seeing for its excellent traditional dancing. There's also a **circus**, not usually open in the summer.

Where to shop
Things to buy include leather goods, cashmere shawls and sweaters, sheepskin, carpets, jewellery, dinosaur cards and models. Mongolia is also known for its wonderfully bizarre, oversize **postage stamps** with naïve representations of cars and trains. So many are needed for air-mail postage that there is usually little room left on the postcard for a message.

At the fascinating city **market** (*zakh*), at the corner of Ikh Toiruu and Teeverchidiin Gudamj, you can buy anything from a cowbell to a camel and, of course, heaps of imported Russian and Chinese goods fresh off the train. You can benefit from tough economic times by picking up traditional coats, clothes, hats, silks, thangkas, statuettes, daggers and silver buttons. It's open Wednesday, Thursday, Saturday and Sunday. Watch out for unbelievably dextrous bag-slitters and pickpockets.

Less exciting but more convenient is the **State Department Store**. Here you can buy simple Mongolian toys and souvenirs or, if you're lucky, a pair of black riding boots. The boots are normally custom-made, so don't be surprised if they sell you a pair and then tell you to come back in a few weeks. They're worn by men as part of their *del*, the national costume. You will also find fur-lined winter and cotton summer Mongolian hats here. There's a **bookshop** opposite the department store.

You'll see many shops around town selling 'Art' and 'Antiques'. Much of it is very attractive but it's often expensive and most of it nowadays is made solely for tourists.

Moving on
By rail   Tickets for **rail travel within Mongolia** can be booked at an office just east of the station.

International trains can be booked at the Railway Ticket Booking Office just north of the station, open 09:00-13:00 and 14:00-17:00 weekdays and 09:00-14:00 Saturday. It's service with a shrug, but they do speak some English. For a few dollars extra just about any guesthouse or tourist agency will do the legwork for you. Booking office ticket allocations may dry up in peak season, in which case try Nomadic Journeys or Juulchin (see p303), both of them consolidators for outbound rail tickets. Note that with an international student card you can get discounts of around 20% on rail tickets.

The No 263 'Angara' departs every evening, arriving at Ulan Ude late the next evening and Irkutsk early the following morning (at the time of writing there were plans to reduce this service to every other day). Only kupé berths are available, at about US$30 to Irkutsk. For Russia travel beyond Irkutsk take the No 5, departing early afternoon on Tuesdays and Fridays, or get aboard the once-weekly Trans-Mongolian No 3 from Beijing to Moscow, passing through on Thursdays. For Beijing, take the No 24 train on Thursday (plus Saturday in summer) or hop on the Trans-Mongolian No 4 from Moscow on Sunday. For timetables see pp421-5.

By air Ulan Bator's **Buyant Ukhaa International Airport** has been upgraded in recent years. Departure tax at the time of writing was US$12, payable in US$ cash. A taxi between the city centre and the airport costs US$5 and takes about half an hour.

 Mongolian Airlines (MIAT; ☎ 322 273, 🖳 www.miat.com) has direct services to Beijing two to six times weekly for around US$250 one way, and also flies directly to Irkutsk, Moscow (with continuing services to Berlin and Frankfurt), Hohhot, Tokyo, Osaka, Seoul and Hong Kong. **Air China** (☎ 310 061) has flights to Beijing five times a week. **Aeroflot** (☎ 320 720) has once or twice weekly Moscow–Ulan Bator flights. **Korean Airlines** (☎ 326 643) has a weekly Seoul–Ulan Bator flight.

 For good help with airline bookings try the helpful Air Trans, which has offices on Sühbaatariin Gudamj and on Baga Toiruu opposite MIAT.

Excursions from Ulan Bator

ULAN BATOR AREA

To really see Mongolia you must get out into the countryside. There's no better antidote to the polluted city than a night or two camping in a ger and a few days trekking or riding.

 If you're using the services of a **travel agency** (see p303) for an excursion make absolutely sure of what the tour will entail so you know what you'll be getting for your money. Several readers have written to say that they thought the 'excursion' they went on was a rip-off. One paid US$100 to be told by the tour guide that he didn't really know where to go and it all looked the same anyway! Ask travellers who've just been on excursions for the latest recommendations. If you're renting a **jeep** for an out of town expedition for several days it's recommended that you check the odometer reading at stops as well as at the beginning and end of the trip: some operators are not above altering it so as to be able to charge you more.

 Entry to all **national parks** in Mongolia now costs US$1 per foreigner and there is also a charge per vehicle.

 For the practical details of exploring beyond Ulan Bator, get a copy of Lonely Planet's *Mongolia* and their excellent *Mongolian phrasebook*.

Ger encampments

Most groups of travellers are shipped off to **Terelj**, 80km from Ulan Bator, where they sleep out under the stars, drink mare's milk for breakfast and sit around campfires lulled by the sound of gently sizzling mutton kebabs. There are two types of accommodation here: *gers* and *hotels*. Juulchin and a number of other companies offer trips to Terelj. There is one public bus daily (at 15:00) from Ulan Bator's bus station, returning from Terelj at 08:00.

The smaller ger encampments are rather less touristy although the atmosphere often depends as much on your fellow visitors as on the place itself. Each is usually linked to a single travel agency in Ulan Bator, through which you must book. Two such places are **Jalnan Meadows/Khan Khentii Ger Camp** (Nomadic Journeys) and **Elstei Ger Camp** (Shuren Travel). You can rent horses from locals here.

Stars Observatory

A few kilometres west of Ulan Bator is a delightful place called the Stars Observatory. It can be reached on a day trip or with an overnight stay. At the observatory there are two attractive old buildings, one a cheap *hotel* and the other the observatory. The observatory is open weekdays and at night the staff will let you look through the telescope. The view of the city is also worth the trip.

To get there, catch west-bound bus No 14 from the central bus station. Ask to get off at the first left turn on the main highway after the bus gets out of town. Cross the road and walk south-west toward the big railway bridge over the river. Continue south-west across the field for half an hour until you get to a dirt road which goes all the way to the observatory.

Bogd Uul Nature Reserve and Manzshir Monastery

This unique mountain region directly south of Ulan Bator was proclaimed a protected area back in 1778, although conservation of Bogd Uul (which means 'Holy Mountain') actually began in the 12th century when Khan Turil declared the mountains sacred and prohibited logging and hunting in them.

Most of the trees are larch. Rolling, hilly, steppe grasslands stretch to the south. Clouds hang over the mountains in summer, and there are frequent thunderstorms. Snow is abundant in winter. A total of 65,000 hectares of Bogd Uul is a biosphere reserve. The area contains 116 species of birds, including 20 identified as endangered. Other animals in the area include musk deer, ibex, roe-deer, hare and native sable.

Bogd Uul's highest peak is Tsetsee Gun (2268m). It is possible to hike over the ridge to the ruins of the ancient **Manzshir Monastery** and the museum on the southern slope of Bogd Uul. It's well worth visiting the museum to get an idea of the devastation caused in 1937 by the communist crackdown. A German photographer visited in 1926 and took some amazing photos of the monastery which are now on display in the museum. Entry is US$1

Not far from the monastery you can stay at ***Undur Dov Resort***, which has about 40 gers.

FURTHER AFIELD

Hustain Nuruu Reserve

About 110km west of Ulan Bator is this reserve dedicated to the reintroduction and preservation of the last truly wild horse, known in the West as Przewalski's horse and in Mongolia as the *takhi*. Desertification, hunting, cross breeding and competition with domestic livestock resulted in its extinction in the wild by 1969. At that time the world population was down to 161 animals in zoos. A carefully monitored breeding programme has resulted in the wild population increasing to several hundred. It is possible to organize a visit to the reserve but you will have to do it well in advance. Contact the Project Manager, Foundation for the Preservation and Protection of the Przewalski's Horse, PO Box 1160, Central Post Office, Ulan Bator 11. Accommodation consists of basic ***guest gers***.

Karakorum (Harhorin)
This ruined city, now scattered round the modern town of Harhorin, 370km from Ulan Bator, was the capital of the Mongolian Empire in the 13th century. Today its centrepiece is the **Erdene Zuu Monastery** which was built in 1586 and was the first Buddhist centre in Mongolia. At its height the monastery housed about 1000 monks in 100 temples. During the Stalinist purges of the 1930s the monastery was badly damaged but it is once again functioning and open to visitors. Entry costs US$3.

Travel agents offer three-day package trips which are the easiest way to get here. To do the trip yourself by bus you will need to book in advance at the central bus station in Ulan Bator. The trip takes nine hours and the halfway stop is at the little village of Sansar. Remember to take your own food and water. In Harhorin you can stay in the ***Hangayin Hotel***, next to the movie theatre. A room costs US$10 and the hotel has a restaurant. There are also four tourist ***ger camps*** in and around Harhorin.

The Gobi
The Gobi stretches for almost 4000km along the border between Mongolia and China. Only about 3% of the Gobi is true desert. It's said to contain some 33 different ecosystems as well as gazelles, the rare Argali sheep, Asiatic wild ass, wild Bactrian camel, snow leopard and ibex. The site of an ancient inland sea, the Gobi is also a treasure-chest of fossilized dinosaur bones and eggs.

Nestled between the beautiful peaks of the Gurvansaikhan (Three Beauties) Mountains, which tower 3km above the surrounding steppe, is Yol Am Valley. The canyon shelters glaciers which remain frozen in its shadow even through the hottest summers. Camping is not allowed in the **Gurvansaikhan National Park** but there are plenty of tourist ***ger camps*** nearby. Most travel companies organize three-day flying trips to the Gobi from Ulan Bator.

Harbin

Lying on the Songhua river over 1000km north-east of Beijing, Harbin is today a sprawling city of 2.9 million, surrounded by heavy industrial plants and dense forest. This was just another small Manchurian fishing village until the construction of the East Chinese Railway in 1897-1901. The new Russian-built railway passed through Harbin, and this was also the junction for the southern spur to Port Arthur. The former village grew rapidly into a major trading centre, albeit with a wild reputation. The Hon Maurice Baring visited in 1904, expecting to find a modern industrial metropolis, but he was not impressed: 'Harbin is now called the Chicago of the East. This is not a compliment to Chicago'. Harbin continued to grow under Japanese control during the Russo-Japanese War as it served as a supply base for Japanese troops. A great many White Russian refugees settled here following the 1917 Revolution, and the Russian influence remained strong, despite the Japanese presence, until after WWII when Manchuria was officially handed over to the Kuomintang.

Modern Harbin still has a perceptible Russian personality. Most foreign visitors to the city nowadays are Russians on shopping trips, and you might well be mistaken for one of them. There is an affluent air in the main shopping streets and Harbin feels somehow less 'Chinese' than cities further south; pedestrianized Zhongyang Dajie feels almost European. It's an interesting place to spend a day or two on your way into or out of China.

WHAT TO SEE

Church of St Sophia & Harbin Construction Arts Museum

The Russian Orthodox Church of St Sophia, built in 1907, is a five minute walk east of Zhongyang Dajie, facing a square filled with snack stalls, a popular place for locals to sit and relax. The church's exterior has been heavily restored since being damaged during the Cultural Revolution, and looks particularly beautiful when lit up at night. Inside you can see original murals and a huge, ornate chandelier.

This is also the home of the Harbin Construction Arts Museum, which consists mainly of photographs of the city dating back to the turn of the 20th century, and some architectural models. In a passage at the back of the church is a selection of religious icons. The museum is open 08:30-17:30 daily. Entry costs Y20; the ticket office is to the left of the church.

CHURCH OF ST SOPHIA

Where to stay
 4 Gloria Inn
11 Holiday Inn
17 Lungmen Hotel
18 Beiyuan Hotel
19 Kunlun Hotel
22 PSB Hotel

Where to eat
 8 Bakery & Café
 9 Xinjiang-style Restaurants
10 KFC
16 Food Stalls
21 California Beef Noodle King USA

Other
 1 Cable Car to Sun Island Park
 2 Ferry to Sun Island Park
 3 Flood Control Monument
 5 Bank of China
 6 Internet Centre
 7 Zhaolin Park
12 Church of St Sophia; Museum
13 Railway Yards
14 Main Railway Station
15 Post Office
20 Heilongjiang Overseas Travel Corp
23 Construction Bank of China
24 Main Post Office
25 Children's Park and Railway

With your ticket you can also visit what appears to be a nearby annexe of the museum: walk around to a courtyard at the back of the church, where you will see steps leading underground. Down here are more Harbin photographs, including of its annual Ice Festival, but the main attraction is an enormous and impressive scale model of the city. See if you can figure out where your hotel is.

Sun Island Park
This park, on an island in the middle of the Songhua River, is a pleasant and (except at weekends) quiet place to stroll for a few hours. There are boating lakes, water slides and other amusements. Entry costs Y5. To get there you can take a boat (Y1) from near the Flood Control Monument, or a cable car (Y20/30 one way/return) a few hundred metres to the west.

Other sights
Harbin's **markets** are well worth a look. The main market area is in the streets off Zhongyang Dajie where you can choose from a huge variety of food, both Chinese and Russian, and cheap plastic knick-knacks.

A **Children's Park** south-east of the city centre has a small railway which is run by children but big enough to carry adults around the park. There is also table tennis in the middle of the park if you fancy challenging anyone from the world's greatest ping-pong playing nation.

Zhaolin Park, a block east of Zhongyang Dajie, is good for a bit of peace and quiet. If you're here early enough in the morning you can join the people doing Chinese-style aerobics, though anyone under 60 years old may feel a bit conspicuous. Another favourite park, along the river bank, was under renovation at the time of writing.

The **Railway Yards** seem to have run out of steam locomotives, although you can go in and wander around. With some persistence you may find some interesting relics.

The Harbin area code is ☎ 451. From outside China dial +86-451.

PRACTICAL INFORMATION
Information and services

The area around Zhongyang Dajie has more upmarket hotels along with fashionable shops and restaurants. South of the railway line is 'real' Harbin, including cheaper places to stay.

The main **Post Office** is at Dongdazhi Jie, but there is a more convenient branch by the railway station. **Internet access** is available on the 2nd floor of Heilongjiang Information Harbour, 129 Zhongyang Dajie.

Nearly every hotel changes **money** or you can use the Construction Bank of China on Hongjun Lu which also gives Visa and Mastercard cash advances. There are also many banks along Zhongyang Dajie.

Heilongjiang Overseas Travel Corporation (formerly CITS; ☎ 366 1159, ⌨ liguoliucn@yahoo.com), 11th floor, Hushi Building, has helpful, English speaking staff who can assist with Trans-Siberian tickets and flights.

Taxis start at Y7 flagfall, with most trips around town under Y10.

Where to stay

PSB Hotel (the sign says 'Welcome to Hotel') is the only place with dorm beds for foreigners. It's a clean, well, run place with friendly staff. A bed in a six/three-bed room is Y30/38 and they have doubles from Y98.

Opposite the railway station is the big *Beiyuan Hotel*.(☎ 364 3725), with friendly staff and well-appointed but ageing rooms. Doubles/triples are Y160/198, including buffet breakfast.

More or less next door is the ***Lungmen Hotel*** (☎ 363 9701, 🖷 363 9700, 🖳 lmho tel@hotellm.com), similar to its neighbour but of a higher standard. Prices run from Y340 for a double or Y871 for a four-bed room. You can also stay in the 'Honoured Building', the original hotel at the rear of the 'new' block, where you'll have the honour of paying from Y680 for a double.

The ***Kunlun Hotel*** (☎ 360 6688, 🖷 360 0888), 8 Tielu Jie, is favoured by Trans-Siberian package tourists. It's a very comfortable place and costs from Y640 to Y1200 for a double room.

Across the tracks is ***Gloria Inn*** (☎ 463 8855, 🖷 463 8533, 🖳 www.giharbin.com), 257 Zhongyang Dajie. This is one of the top places to stay in Harbin and charges Y588-688/double. Harbin has a ***Holiday Inn*** (☎ 422 6666, 🖷 422 1661, 🖳 holiday@pub lic.hr.hl.cn) at 90 Jingwei Jie, charging Y490 for a standard room including breakfast.

Where to eat

As with every Chinese city, there are scores of places to eat: wander round and see what you find.

Opposite the train station there are many cheap ***food stalls*** selling a variety of food. Just point at what you want and it'll be dished up and shoved at you within seconds.

On Shitou Dajie, just off Zhongyang Dajie, is a row of ***Xinjiang-style restaurants*** serving mutton kebabs and laghman (*la-mian* to the Chinese: long, thick noodles with fried mutton, peppers, tomatoes and onions).

There is a ***California Beef Noodle King*** on Hongjun Lu, open all day and serving large bowls of filling noodles for Y10. There are also several branches of ***McDonald's*** and ***KFC*** around Zhongyang Dajie, and on the street itself is a good ***Bakery & Café***.

Moving on

By rail There are three trains a day to Beijing, taking 12 to 13 hours and costing about Y270 for hard sleeper. You can buy your own ticket at the station if you don't mind the queues, or get it through your hotel for about Y20 commission. You must wait for the train in the assigned waiting room, not on the platform.

There are two daily overnight trains (Y220, 11 hours) to Suifenhe on the China-Russia border, from where you can take a bus to Vladivostok (see the box on p295).

There are also regular, but slow, trains to Jiamusi from where you can take a bus to Fuyuan and cross the river to Khabarovsk. Alternatively, you could endure the 15-hour bus ride straight to Fuyuan from Harbin. See p286 for details.

For Trans-Siberian tickets, contact Heilongjiang Overseas Travel Corporation (see p313). Although they say that they need 20 days' notice for booking Trans-Sib tickets, they are happy to phone the ticketing office to see if there are any spare tickets for an earlier departure.

By air Daily flights to Beijing are about Y800 while flight destinations in Russia include Khabarovsk and Vladivostok; both three times weekly and about US$130. You can book tickets at the Heilongjiang Overseas Tourist Corporation.

Beijing

Both the Trans-Manchurian and Trans-Mongolian routes, by far the most popular with travellers crossing Siberia, start or finish in Beijing, so you'll probably be spending some time here. The city is well worth exploring and is changing fast. Most travellers stay for at least three or four days.

HISTORY

Early history

Remains of China's oldest known inhabitant, Peking Man, were unearthed some 50km south of present-day Beijing in 1921, proving that life in this region dates back at least to 500,000 BC. Chinese records go back only as far as the Zhou dynasty (12th century BC to 771 BC) but indicate that by this period this region was acknowledged as the country's capital.

The city and its environs were to remain at the heart of Chinese culture and politics, although the role of capital was often lost to other cities, including Xi'an (where the 'Terracotta Army' now draws the tourists) and Luoyang. Beijing's strength, however, lay in its proximity to China's northern frontiers: by ruling from here emperors could keep a close eye on military developments to the north, where 'barbarians' were constantly threatening invasion.

Despite the construction of the Great Wall (a continuous process dating from the second century BC) Genghis Khan marched in in 1215, sacked the city and then proceeded to rebuild it as his capital; the Mongols called this Khanbalik (City of the Khan). It was at this stage that the first Westerners visited, including Marco Polo, who liked the place so much that he stayed for 17 years.

The Mongol collapse; further developments

The Mongol empire fell in 1368 and the Chinese shifted their capital to Nanjing. Following a coup led by the son of the first Ming emperor, the government was moved back here and the city renamed Beijing (Northern Capital). The Manchurian invasion in 1644 established the final Chinese dynasty, the Qing, which was to rule from here until the abdication of Pu Yi, the 'Last Emperor', in 1912. Although the early years of Qing dynasty rule were successful, corruption, opium and foreign intervention soon undermined Chinese authority, and there were major rebellions in the city in the late 19th century.

TIAN TAN
THE TEMPLE OF HEAVEN

The Civil War and beyond

Under Chiang Kai-Shek the Kuomintang relocated China's capital to Nanjing in 1928, although following the Communist victory in 1949 it was moved back to Beijing. In October 1949 Chairman Mao declared the foundation of the People's Republic of China in Beijing. The city has hardly been quiet since then: every major movement in the country, notably the mass conventions of the Cultural Revolution and the Democracy rallies (culminating in the Tiananmen Square Incident of 1989, when over 2000 civilians were killed), has had its roots here.

As the capital (now with a population of some 9.4 million) roars through the first decade of the 21st century the economy is booming and Beijing aims to show it off to the world when it hosts the 2008 Olympics. Various grand building projects are underway including the US$430 million National Grand Theatre just west of Tiananmen Square.

WHAT TO SEE

Tiananmen Square and the Forbidden City

Just as Red Square is the best place to begin a tour of Moscow, Tiananmen Square is where you should start your trip around Beijing. At its centre is **Chairman Mao's Mausoleum** (open 08:30-11.30, 14:00-16:00 daily; mornings only in July and August) where, after joining a long but surprisingly fast queue, you can see the body of the great man. Entry is free, but you must leave your bags at one of the nearby kiosks (Y1).

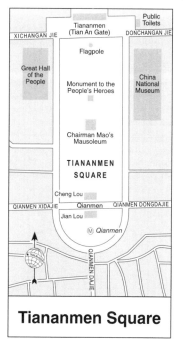

Tiananmen Square

To the east is the **China National Museum**. This huge building, formerly the National Museum of Chinese History and the Museum of the Chinese Revolution, was reopened with a new name in 2003, after a major overhaul. It contains extensive relics from every period of China's history, including much about the post-WWII period, all with English labels. Entry to the museum is Y15; it's open 09.00-16.30.

On the other side of the square is the **Great Hall of the People**, used for meetings of the National People's Congress and featuring an impressive 10,000-seat auditorium. It's open 09:00-14:00, whenever the Congress isn't in session, for Y15.

To the north of the square is the **Imperial Palace**, better known as the Forbidden City, entered through the gate which gives the square its name (Tiananmen means 'Gate of Heaven'). This enclosure, comprising over 70 hectares and 1000 buildings, takes at least a day to explore for even a bare impression; there's so much to see here that really you need much longer.

The palace was erected by the Ming emperor Yong Le in the early 15th century and was thereafter the home of 24 more emperors, up until the abdication of Pu Yi in 1912. The best way to get around is to hire a cassette tour at the main gate and have everything explained to you by Roger Moore. It's a good idea to wander round again afterwards, soaking up the atmosphere. The palace is open 08:30-17:00 daily but ticket offices close at 15:30. Entrance is Y60 and the cassette tour costs a further Y30.

The Great Wall
China's most famous attraction makes an ideal day trip from Beijing. The Wall itself was not built in one massive construction project as many believe; in fact the original scheme under Emperor Shih Huang (1st century BC) was simply to join extant stretches of

> ❏ **Not so Great Wall**
> 'It was one small, throwaway remark for Yang Liwei, but one giant gaffe for millions of his compatriots. When China's first astronaut emerged from his capsule yesterday, touching down near the Mongolian border after orbiting Earth 14 times in 21 hours, there was only one question on the lips of those who gathered around him. "Is it true that you can see the Great Wall of China from space?" asked an eager television interviewer. Yang's answer? "Erm, no".' [Nasa's astronauts have been saying for decades that the Wall cannot be seen from outer space].
> Ian Cobain, *The Times* (17 October 2003)

individual defensive walls together. It was hoped that the resulting fortification would protect China from marauding foreigners but this was not the case. The Wall is currently responsible for drawing more foreigners to China than ever, as those who visit at Badaling or Mutianyu will see.

● **Badaling** This section, 72km from Beijing, has been completely restored and is usually overrun with tourists. Most hotels can arrange tours to the Wall here for around Y50. It's possible to get to Badaling independently by train (the Trans-Siberian route passes by: see p394) from Xizhimen station. Entry is Y40.
● **Mutianyu** Take bus No 6 from outside the north-west entrance of Dong Si Shi Tiao metro station between 06.30 and 10.30. It's 90km from Beijing.
● **Simatai** Less crowded than Badaling but still popular as there's a cable car here. This section is very steep; it's 108km from Beijing. There are tours from Beijing; to get here independently, catch a bus from Dongzhimen bus station to Miyun and then a minibus to Simitai. Entry is Y20.
● **Huanghua** is the new 'untouristy' section but some hotels now operate tours there. Alternatively, take a bus from Dongzhimen bus station in Beijing to Huairou (1 hour) and then a minibus from Huairou to Huanghua. ('We found this trip to be the highlight of our stay in Beijing and a great opportunity to see a more authentic part of the Great Wall'. Felicity Wilcox, UK). Take a copy of Lindesay's book, *Hiking on History: Exploring Beijing's Great Wall on Foot* with you. It's available in Beijing.
● To get to the least touristy section, **Jinshanling**, you'll need to hire a minivan. From here to Simatai is a tough five-hour walk.

Where to stay
1 Bamboo Garden Hotel
11 You Yi Youth Hostel
13 Zhaolong Hotel; International Youth
    Hostel; Indian Restaurant
20 Holiday Inn Crowne Plaza
22 Fangyuan Hotel
23 Donghua Hotel
27 Palace Hotel
31 Beijing Hotel
38 Bei Wei Hotel
43 Beijing International Hotel; CITS;
    Mongol Juulchin; Siberian Airlines

Where to eat
6 Serve The People
9 Mediterraneo
12 1001 Nights
15 The Den
17 Hidden Tree Bar
21 Green Angel Vegetarian Restaurant
24 Donganmen Night Market
26 Deli France, in Sun Dong An Plaza
29 McDonald's
30 Datianshujing Hutong Night Market
32 KFC
35 Qianmen Quanjude Roast Duck
37 Gongdelin Vegetarian Restaurant
40 Bian Yi Fang Roast Duck Restaurant
48 La Vie de France (in Friendship Store)

Other
2 Lama Temple (Yonghegong)
3 PSB
4 Russian Embassy
5 Australian and Canadian Embassies

7 German Embassy
8 Ukraine Embassy
10 French Embassy
14 Minder Café
16 Frank's Place
17 Monkey Business Infocenter
18 Worker's Stadium
19 Airport Bus Stop & CAAC Office
25 Foreign Languages Bookstore
28 ATM
33 Oriental Plaza
34 Old Railway Station
    Shopping Mall & Internet
36 Museum Street
39 Tian Tan Park
41 Beijing Zhan Railway Station
42 P J O'Reilly's Irish Pub
44 Ancient Observatory
45 Beijing Tourism Group (BTG)
46 Scitech Plaza
47 CITIC Bank
48 Friendship Store
49 Sunjoy Mansion
50 International Post Office
51 John Bull Pub
52 Japanese Embassy
53 Polish Embassy
54 Ritan Park
55 Belarus Embassy
56 New Zealand Embassy
57 British Embassy
58 US Embassy
59 Mongolian Embassy
60 Irish Embassy
61 Silk Market
62 World Trade Centre, American Express

Tian Tan (Temple of Heaven)

This is the site from which China's emperors conducted the country's most important religious rituals, upon which depended the well-being of the population. Sights worth noting here include the Hall of Abstinence, the marble circular altar and the Imperial Vault of Heaven (where a whisper towards the surface on one side is perfectly audible around the opposite side). The most famous building is the Hall of Prayer for Good Harvests, to the north, built entirely without the use of glue or nails. The temple, in Tian Tan Park, is open 08:30-18:30; entry to the park is Y2, or Y35 for a tourist ticket.

Summer Palace

This palace, the summer retreat of the Imperial family since 1750, covers an area about four times the size of the Forbidden City. Virtually everything apart from the lake dates back only to the start of the 20th century, thanks to repeated destruction by foreigners. The entire area was razed in 1860 as retribution for

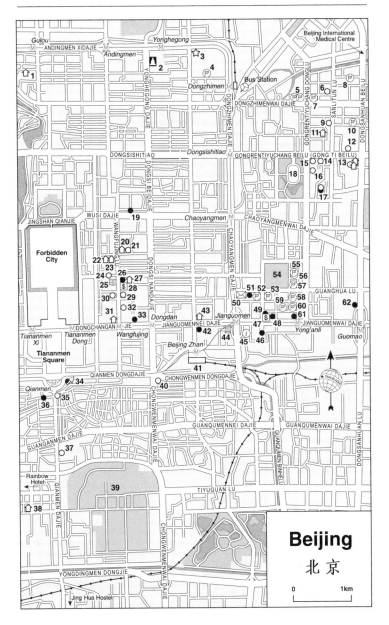

Gulou
ANDINGMEN XIDAJIE
Andingmen
Yonghegong
Beijing International
Medical Centre

3
2
4
Dongzhimen
Bus Station
5
6
8

DONGZHIMENWAI DAJIE
7

9
11
10
12

DONGSISHITIAO
Dongsishitiao
GONGRENTIYUCHANG BEILU (GONG TI BEILU)

15
14
13
18
16
17

JINGSHAN QIANJIE
WUSI DAJIE
19
Chaoyangmen
CHAOYANGMENWAI DAJIE

Forbidden
City
20
21

22
23
24
25
26
27
28
29
30
31
32
33

Dongdan
43
Jianguomen
54
55
56
57
51
52
53
50
59
58
60
61
62
GUANGHUA LU

Tiananmen
Xi
DONGCHANGAN JIE
Wangfujing
JIANGUOMENNEI DAJIE
42
44
47
48
45 46
JIANGUOMENWAI DAJIE
Yong'anli
Guomao

Tiananmen
Dong

Tiananmen
Square
QIANMEN DONGDAJIE
CHONGWENMEN DONGDAJIE
41
Beijing Zhan

Qianmen
34
40
35
36

37

GUANGANMEN DAJIE
GUANQUMENNEI DAJIE
GUANQUMENWAI DAJIE

Rainbow
Hotel
39
TIYUGUAN LU
38

Beijing
北京

0   1km

YONGDINGMEN DONGJIE

Jing Hua Hostel

the Opium Wars, and then again in 1900 after the Boxer Rebellion. It's a great place to explore slowly and if the weather is good it's well worth spending a whole day here wandering around the Royal Residence, the Dragon King Temple, the Long Corridor, the Tower of Buddhist Virtue and the lake. Entry is Y8 (more to enter some sections) and it's open 08:00-17:00. Bus No 808 (aircon) from Tiananmen to the Summer Palace is Y35.

Lama Temple (Yonghegong)

Although firmly on the tour group circuit, this place is well worth a visit. Many of the temples and halls were completed in 1694, though it wasn't a lamasery until 1744. The buildings are colourfully painted both inside and out and all lead you to the centrepiece, a stunning 18m statue of the Buddha carved from sandalwood. It's housed in a small hall which enhances the scale of the statue. The entire temple survived the Cultural Revolution unharmed, some say due to direct orders from Zhou Enlai. Although this is still a working temple there doesn't seem to be much activity apart from the tourists. It's open 09:00-16:00 and costs Y25 to enter. Most tour groups go in the morning, so the afternoon might be a quieter time to visit. It's easily reached from Yonghegong metro station.

Ancient Observatory

If the weather is good you can easily spend an hour or so looking at the bizarre astronomical instruments in the largely open-air Ancient Observatory. It's hard to figure out what most of them were for but they are fantastic pieces of engineering and artistry which wouldn't look out of place in a Harry Potter film. It's often very quiet here which is another attraction. At the south-west corner of the Jianguomen junction, it's open 09:00-18:00 from April to September; entry is Y10.

Chinese Opera

There are numerous performances all over Beijing. The ones at the theatre in the Qianmen Hotel are recommended; there are hour-long performances at 19:30 each evening. The cheapest ticket at Y30 gives a good view.

PRACTICAL INFORMATION
Local transport
The metro system is useful and cheap (Y3 per ride, open 05:00-23:00). There are currently two lines, with another under construction and several more in the planning stages. Buses and trolley-buses are cheap but desperately crowded; **watch out for bag-slitters and pickpockets**. Most travellers end up joining the rest of the city's population on two wheels: there are many places that rent out bikes.

Taxis are easy to flag down anywhere. They're metered (currently Y8-10 flag-fall plus Y1.2/km) and are reasonable value when shared. A taxi from the main train station to Sanlitun is about Y20. If you don't speak Chinese, get your destination written down in Chinese script and show it to the driver.

Orientation and services
Beijing is a large city but finding your way around is not too difficult as most streets are laid out in a neat grid, running either north-south or east-west. Those streets are, however, very crowded.

Trans-Siberian trains use the main railway station, Beijing Zhan. Many other trains arrive and depart from Beijing's smart new West (Xizhan) station, said to be the largest railway station in Asia.

Diplomatic representation See p39 for details on the Beijing embassies of

Mongolia, Russia, Belarus and **Poland**. Note that to cross Belarus or Ukraine you will need a transit visa. There is, however, no Ukrainian consular office in Beijing.

Australia (☎ 6532 2331) 21 Dongzhimenwai Dajie, Sanlitun; **Belarus** (☎ 6532 1691) 1 Dong Yijie, Ritan Lu, Jianguomenwai; **Canada** (☎ 6532 3536) 19 Dongzhimenwai Dajie, Sanlitun; **Czech Republic** (☎ 6532 1531) Ritan Lu, Jianguomenwai; **France** (☎ 6532 1331) 3 Dongsanjie, Sanlitun; **Germany** (☎ 6532 5556) 3 Dongzhimenwai Dajie; **Hungary** (☎ 6532 1431) 10 Dongzhimenwai Dajie, Sanlitun; **Ireland** (☎ 6532 2914) 3 Ritan Donglu, Jianguomenwai; **Japan** (☎ 6532 2361) 7 Jianwai, Ritan Lu, Jianguomenwai; **Mongolia** (☎ 6532 1203) 2 Xiushui Beijie, Jianguomenwai; **Netherlands** (☎ 6532 1131) 1-15-2 Ta Yuan Office Building, Liangmahe Si Nanlu; **New Zealand** (☎ 6532 2732) 1 Dong Erjie, Ritan Lu, Jianguomenwai; **Poland** (☎ 6532 1236) 1 Ritan Lu, Jianguomenwai; **Russian Federation** (☎ 6532 1267) 4 Dongzhimen Beizhong Jie; **Sweden** (☎ 6532 3331) 3 Dongzhimenwai Dajie; **UK** (☎ 6532 1961) 11 Guanghua Lu; **USA** (☎ 6532 3831) 3 Xiushui Beijie, Jianguomenwai.

Travel agencies For more information on many of the following agencies see p37-40.

Trans-Sib specialist **Monkey Business Infocenter** (☎ 6591 6519, 🖷 6591 6517, 🖳 monkeychina@compuserve.com, www .monkey shrine.com) is at 12 Dongdaqiao Xie Jie, Nan Sanlitun, above the Hidden Tree Belgian beer bar. The office is open 10:00-19:00 Monday to Saturday.

CITS (China International Travel Service) has representatives in many of Beijing's larger hotels; its head office (☎ 6512 0507, 🖷 6512 0503, 🖳 tianwei@cits .com.cn), in the West Lobby of the Beijing International Hotel, sells Trans-Siberian tickets. It's open 08:30-12:00 and 13:30-17:00 weekdays. Even if CITS says there are no Tran-Sib tickets available, you could try **Beijing Tourism Group** (BTG; ☎ 6515 8562, 🖷 6515 8603), open 08:30-11:30 and 13:30-17:00 weekdays in the Beijing Tourism Building, 28 Jianguomenwai Dajie.

Mongol Juulchin (☎ 6512 6688, 🖷/🖳 6525 4339, 🖳 julpek@public.bta.net.cn), in the Beijing International Hotel, 9 Jianguomennei Dajie, represents Mongolia's Juulchin Foreign Tourism Corporation.

Medical The best place to go if you need a doctor, dentist or emergency treatment is the International Medical Centre (☎ 6465 1561), next to the Kempinski Hotel.

Money The unit of currency is the *yuan* (Y; also called *renminbi* or RMB) which is divided into 10 *jiao* or 100 *fen*. Exchange rates at the time of writing included Y8.26 per US$1 and Y13.90 per £1

If you need hard currency the CITIC Bank will change travellers' cheques into US$ or arrange credit card withdrawals in US$. There's a branch next to the Friendship Store. American Express has an office in the China World Trade Centre.

China visa extensions The police office, and the place to get your visa extended, is the Public Security Bureau (PSB; ☎ 8401 5292) at 2 Andingmendong Dajie, on the north-east corner of the second ring road in a huge building by the flyover. Take the metro to Yonghegong, turn right out of the station and walk for 15 minutes. It's open 08:30-16:30 daily except Sunday.

Telecommunications The **international post office** is on Chaoyangmennan Dajie, north off of Jianguomen Dajie. There's also a post office opposite Beijing International Hotel.

More and more places are getting **internet access** so you should have no difficulty picking up your email. However, from time to time the government decides to close all the internet cafés, typically for a month or so.

Tours Most larger hotels offer tours to all the major sights, but you can easily visit the Forbidden City, the Temple of Heaven and other attractions independently. It is, however, probably worth joining a tour to see the Great Wall and the Ming Tombs.

Where to stay

Budget accommodation *Zhaolong Hotel & International Youth Hostel* (☎ 6597 2299, 🖹 6597 2288, 🖳 out door@etang.com), 2 Gongrentiyuchang Beilu, is a well-run place and ideally located for Sanlitun nightlife. A bed in a six/four/two-bed dorm costs Y60/70/80, less Y10 for HI members. There is a kitchen, internet access and laundry service. The youth hostel is behind the hotel. The hostel also runs trips out to the non-touristy Huanghua section of the Great Wall. *You Yi Youth Hostel* (☎ 6417 2632, 🖳 poacher43-cn@sina.com, www.poach ers.com.cn), 43 Bei Sanlitun Nanlu, is an independently run hostel that makes a good budget choice. Dorm beds cost Y70 and clean twin rooms are Y180, with breakfast and laundry service included.

Another backpackers' haunt is the *Jinghua Hotel* (☎ 6722 2211) on Nansanhuan Xilu. Dormitories are the best value here: beds in a 20/four/three-bed dorm cost Y30/40/50. There are also doubles with attached bathroom for Y180-500. There's a travel agency and internet access, and you can rent bikes from the restaurant next door. Take bus No 66 south from Qianmen for about 4km to a roundabout called Yangqiao, then walk west for about 500m.

Mid-range hotels The following hotel rooms all have attached bathrooms.

Fangyuan Hotel (☎ 6525 6331, 🖹 6513 8549, 🖳 www.cbw.com/hotel/fang yuan), 36 Dengshikou Xilu, Dongcheng District, is well-located, well-run and friendly. All rooms have air-con, IDD phone, hot shower and TV. Prices for singles/doubles start at Y180/224. Breakfast is included. Just a few doors along from the Fangyuan, and quite similar, is the *Donghua Hotel* (☎ 6525 7532, 🖹 6513 5138), 32 Dengshikou Xilu. Singles/doubles go for Y180/230.

Well located west of Tian Tan Park, the *Bei Wei Hotel* (☎ 6301 2266) at 13 Xinling Lu has singles/doubles for Y240/288. Beside it is the *Rainbow Hotel* with rooms for Y360/590.

Bamboo Garden Hotel (☎ 6403 2229, 🖹 6403 4960, 🖳 www.bbgh.com.cn), 24 Xiaoshiqiao Jiugulou, Xicheng District, is set in quiet gardens a 10 minute walk from Gulou metro station. It's a professionally run 3-star hotel with only 40 rooms so you should book ahead. It costs Y480/580 for a double room without/with a garden view.

Upmarket hotels Note that a 15% tax is applicable. Despite the high prices don't be shy about asking for a discount: if business is slow you may get one.

Palace Hotel (☎ 6512 8899, 🖳 tph@peninsula.com), Chongwenmenwai Dajie, has doubles from US$290 although you may be able to get as much as 50% off just by asking. *Beijing International Hotel* (☎ 6512 6688, 🖳 bih@ht.rol.cn.net), 9 Jianguomennei Dajie, has rooms from US$120 to US$1000.

At the famous *Beijing Hotel* (☎ 6513 7766, 🖳 business@chinabeijinghotel. com.cn) rooms cost from US$180 to US$320. For a night in the best suite here, be prepared to part with US$3900. Being close to Tiananmen Square it's perfectly located.

Where to eat

There's no shortage of places to eat and the best thing to do is to simply give yourself time to wander around the city and see what you come across; you'll never go hungry.

Peking Duck is, of course, the local speciality and there are numerous restaurants where you can sample it: good places include *Qianmen Quanjude Roast Duck Restaurant*, 32 Qianmen Dajie, and *Bian Yi Fang Roast Duck Restaurant* on Chongwen menwei Dajie near the railway station.

Budget food is easy to find in Beijing: try any backstreet for noodles or dumplings. *Donganmen night market,* on Donganmen Dajie off Wangfujing Lu, is big and cheap. The stalls, open from about 18:00 onwards, sell food from all over China, though it's not as varied as it used to be. *Datianshujing Hutong night market*, which has a better selection, is also in a street off Wangfujing Lu. The Datianshujing Hutong has undergone some cosmetic surgery so it looks like an old Chinese lane. It's usually crowded along here but, unlike the Donganmen market, there are places to sit down while you eat.

You'll find numerous choices in the Chaoyang District and around **Sanlitun** ('Bar Street'). Sanlitun is lined with café bars and always busy, and in summer you can sit outside. The *Hidden Tree* bar at 12 Dongdaqiao Xie Jie (locally known as Sanlitun Nan Jie, 'South Bar St') has a pleasant garden and serves a range of food and bar snacks to go with their good Belgian beer (the Monkey Business Infocenter is upstairs; see p38).

Serve the People, at 1 Sanlitun Xiwujie, is recommended for Thai cuisine, with main dishes for Y30-120; it's open 11:00-22:30. Opposite Zhaolong Hotel is *1001 Nights*, a Syrian restaurant with a pleasant terrace; there's even belly dancing some evenings and it's open until 02:00. *Mediterraneo* is another recommended place in this area, with pasta and a range of tapas. Also try *The Den*, next to City Hotel at the corner of Gongrentiyuchang ('Gongti') Beilu and Gongrentiyuchang Donglu, where there's a popular Sunday brunch.

For non-carnivores, the *Gongdelin Vegetarian Restaurant* at 158 Qianmen Dajie is recommended. Another popular vegetarian place is the spacious *Green Angel Vegetarian Restaurant*, just east of the Holiday Inn Crowne Plaza at 57 Denshikou Lu.

The *Indian Restaurant* in the Zhaolong Hotel is recommended for the good food and the dancing shows.

Western fast-food chains have been here in force for years. *McDonald's* is on Chang'an Ave and at around 40 other locations, *Kentucky Fried Chicken* is on Tiananmen Square and *Pizza Hut* has several branches including on Dongzhimenwai Dajie and south of Tiananmen Square on Zhushikou Dajie.

For cakes, pastries and croissants go to *La Vie de France* in the Friendship Store, or *Deli France* in Sun Dong An Plaza.

Nightlife

Beijing nightlife is varied and carries on until late. *That's Beijing* and *City Weekend* are the best of the what's-on magazines; there's also *Metropolis*. **Sanlitun** 'Bar Street' is the place to start: here you'll find *Minder's Café*, with live music, *Frank's Place*, the *Hidden Tree* (see Where to eat) and lots of less salubrious drinking places. The Sanlitun bar area has been marked for demolition for years so don't be surprised if many of these places have relocated by the time you arrive.

The Den (see Where to eat) is popular with students and expats and gets very busy after midnight on Saturday nights. At 44 Guanghua Lu is the *John Bull Pub*. Irish-theme pubs have also reached Beijing: *P J O'Reilly's Irish Pub* is in the Henderson Shopping Centre.

The *Haidian* area near the university is also worth checking out. There's no shortage of bars and it's easy enough to just walk around until you find one that you like the look of.

Where to shop

The **Friendship Store** on Jianguomen Dajie has a huge range of souvenirs spread over three floors. There is also a well-stocked **supermarket** here that's useful for Trans-Sib provisions. The **silk market**, a few hundred metres east of the Friendship Store, is a good place for shopping, though you must bargain hard.

Another good place is the crowded **Qianmen district**, where bartering is in order. **Museum St** (a small side street south-west of Tiananmen Sq) is quite touristy but there's a good range of souvenirs here. A more relaxed area for souvenir shopping is **Liulichang Lu**, about 150m south of Hepingmen metro station

The Beijing area code is ☎ 010. From outside China dial +86-10.

(watch for the 'old' Chinese bridge over the street). Shops here have sold artists' materials, calligraphy and paintings for centuries, although it has now been redeveloped to attract tourists. Art books and decorative items now abound. The **Beijing Ancient Coin Shop**, upstairs at No 22, deals in old Chinese coins and banknotes.

The **Foreign Languages Bookstore** on Wangfujing Lu is a great place for books, maps and postcards about China, and for general reading matter for upcoming long rail journeys.

Be aware that the word 'antique' is used very loosely in Beijing's tourist markets. Genuine antiques are rare except in reputable shops.

Moving on
By rail Domestic tickets can be bought from Beijing Zhan station, at the foreigners' ticket office on the ground floor. Alternatively CITS (at Beijing International Hotel) or your hotel will book a ticket for you for a small fee, saving you the queuing. The train to Hong Kong goes every other day from Beijing West station, taking 28 hours and costing about Y660 for hard sleeper. There are three daily departures for Harbin (13 hours), for Y290.

International tickets must be booked with Monkey Business, CITS, BTG or another registered ticket agency. If you've just arrived on the Trans-Siberian and feel like clocking up a few more kilometres by rail, you could follow the Silk Route back to Europe (see p129).

By air Many major airlines maintain offices in Beijing, so it's usually not difficult finding a seat; the problem is that it can be expensive. Most airlines have offices in the Scitech Plaza, opposite the Friendship Store.

If you'd like to fly the first leg of your Trans-Siberian journey, **Mongolian Airlines** (MIAT; ☎ 6507 9297, 📧 6507 7397), with an office on the 7th floor of Sunjoy Mansion (behind the CITIC Tower), charges Y2100 for a direct Beijing–Ulan Bator flight, departing two to six times a week. **Air China** also flies to Ulan Bator five times weekly. **Siberian Airlines**, with an office in the West Lobby of the Beijing International Hotel, flies to Novosibirsk three times a week (you must have a Russian visa before booking your ticket).

Airport **departure tax** for international flights is Y90, payable before you check in.

The airport is 28km from the city centre. **Buses** (Y16) run about every half-hour between the airport and the city centre (including the Beijing International Hotel and the CAAC office on Wusi Dajie), a 40-minute trip outside rush hour. For a **taxi** between the airport and Tiananmen Square, expect to pay about Y100.

Tickets? Wo mei yo!
Nineteen days to Christmas and the only response I could get from the booking clerk for trains to Europe was: 'Wo mei yo'. He said there were no places. The last train which would get us home for Christmas was leaving in eight days' time. I tried offering a bribe: 'Wo mei yo'. The prospect of spending Christmas in cold, drab Beijing was not a merry one. I asked the clerk to check his reservations list again. We'd been in the office for over an hour by then and he was thoroughly bored with us. Throwing down the comic he'd been trying to read and, thrusting a form at me he said 'Okay'. Not really believing him I asked 'No 19 train okay?'. 'Okay, okay,' he replied. We'd got our reservations. For tickets in the summer, however, you'd need to allow much longer but given enough time, determination and patience, almost anything is possible in China.

ROUTE GUIDE AND MAPS

Using this guide

This route guide has been set out to draw your attention to points of interest and to enable you to locate your position along the Trans-Siberian line. On the maps, stations are indicated in Russian and English and their distance from Moscow is given in the text.

Stations and points of interest are identified in the text by a kilometre number. In some cases these numbers are approximate so start looking out for the point of interest a few kilometres before its stated position.

Where something of interest is on only one side of the track, it is identified after its kilometre number by the approximate compass direction for those going away from Moscow; that is, on the Moscow–Vladivostok Trans-Siberian line (pp327-84) by the letter **N** (north or left-hand side of the train) or **S** (south or right-hand side), and on the Trans-Mongolian branch (pp385-94) and Trans-Manchurian branch (pp395-402) by **E** (east or left-hand side) or **W** (west or right-hand side).

The elevation of major towns and cities is given in metres and feet beside the station name. Time zones are indicated throughout the text (MT = Moscow Time). See inside back cover for **key map and time zones**.

Kilometre posts
These are located on the southern or western side of the track, sometimes so close to the train that they're difficult to see. The technique is either to hang out of the window (dangerous) or press your face close to the glass and look along the train until a post flashes by. On each post, the number on the face furthest from Moscow is larger by 1km than that on the face nearest to Moscow, suggesting that each number really refers to the entire 1km of railway towards which it 'looks'.

Railway timetables show your approximate true distance from Moscow, but unfortunately the distances painted on kilometre posts generally do not: indeed on the Trans-Siberian they may vary by up to 40km, the result of multiple route changes over the years. Distances noted in the following route guide and in the timetables at the back of the book correspond to those on the kilometre posts. Occasionally, however, railway authorities may recalibrate and repaint these posts, thereby confusing us all! If you notice any discrepancies, please write to the author.

Points of interest and stations in this guide are identified by the nearest kilometre post visible from the train.

Station name boards
Station signs are almost as difficult to catch sight of as kilometre posts since they are usually placed only on the station building and not along the platform as in most other countries. Rail traffic on the line is heavy and even if your carriage does pull up opposite the station building you may have your view of it obscured by another train.

Stops
Where the train stops at a station the duration of the stop is indicated by:
  ● (1-5 min) ●● (7-14 min) ●●● (15-25 min) ●●●+ (over 25 min)
These durations are based upon timetables for the No 1/2 Moscow–Vladivostok (*Rossiya*), No 3/4 Moscow–Beijing (Trans-Mongolian) and No 19/20 Moscow–Beijing (*Vostok*, Trans-Manchurian) services. Actual durations may vary widely as timetables are revised, and may be reduced if a train is running late.

Only your carriage attendant knows the precise amount of time for the train you're on. Don't stray far from the train as it will probably move off without a whistle or other signal (except in China) and passengers can be left behind. Three of us, our carriage attendant included, were once almost left in sub-zero temperatures on the platform of a tiny Siberian station when the train left five minutes ahead of schedule.

Time zones
All trains in Russia run on Moscow time (MT). **Siberian time zones** are listed throughout the route guide; major cities include Novosibirsk (MT+3), Irkutsk (MT+5), Khabarovsk (MT+7) and Vladivostok (MT+7). **Moscow time** is four

---

❏ **Speed calculations**
Using kilometre posts and a watch you can calculate how quickly, or more usually how slowly, the train is going. Note the time that elapses between one post and the next and consult the table below. The average speed over the seven-day journey between Moscow and Vladivostok is just 69kph (43mph).

Seconds	kph	mph	Seconds	kph	mph
24	150	93	52	69	43
26	138	86	54	66	41
28	129	80	56	64	40
30	120	75	60	60	37
32	113	70	64	56	35
34	106	66	68	53	33
36	100	62	72	50	31
38	95	59	78	46	28
40	90	56	84	43	27
42	86	53	92	39	24
44	82	51	100	36	22
46	78	49	120	30	18
48	75	47	150	24	15
50	72	45	180	20	12

hours ahead of Greenwich Mean Time (GMT+4) when Russia is on Daylight Savings Time, from the last Sunday in March to the last Saturday in October; for the rest of the year MT = GMT+3 (although time differences with most countries of Europe, which also use DST, remain constant throughout the year). Note that **China** has a single time zone, GMT+8, for the whole country and for the whole year. **Mongolian time** is GMT+8.

TRANS-SIBERIAN ROUTE

Km0: Moscow Москва
Yaroslavsky Station Ярославский вокзал Most Trans-Siberian trains depart from Moscow's Yaroslavsky station, on pl Komsomol (metro: Komsomolskaya). Yaroslavsky station is very distinctive, built in 1902 as a stylized reproduction of an old Russian *terem* (fort), its walls decorated with coloured tiles.

Note that a few services to Siberian destinations via Yekaterinburg – including the No 16 Yekaterinburg, No 32 Novokuznetsk, No 36 Barnaul, No 38 Tomsk, No 60 Tyumen, No 76 Tynda, No 118 Novokuznetsk, No 122 Ulan Ude and No 908 via Novosibirsk to Irkutsk – depart from adjacent **Kazansky Station**, also on pl Komsomol.

Get to the station early as trains invariably leave on time. Carriages have destination plates fixed to their sides but any railway official will point you in the right direction if you show them your ticket. If you're arriving in Moscow from Siberia and leaving again by train the same day, you may need to take the metro or a taxi to one of the city's nine other stations.

Km13: Los Лось Just after this station, the train crosses over the Moscow Ring Road. This road marks the city's metropolitan border and in order to stop the lavatories being used in urban areas loo doors remain bolted until this point.

Km15: Taininskaya Таининская A post-Soviet monument here, dedicated to Russia's last tsar, Nicholas II, says, 'To Tsar Nikolai II from the Russian people with repentance'.

Km18: Mytishchi Мытищи (pop: 156,000) is famous for three factories. The railway carriage factory, **Metrovagonmash**, manufactured all the Soviet Union's metro cars and now builds the N5 carriages to be seen in Moscow's

metro. There is a museum at the factory, although the best metro museum is in Moscow (see p163).

The **Mytishchinsky monument factory**, the source of many of those ponderous Lenin statues that once littered the country, has at last been forced to develop a new line. It now churns out the kind of 'art' banned in the Soviet era: religious statues, memorials to the victims of Stalin's purges and busts of mafia bosses. Some of its earlier achievements displayed in Moscow include the giant Lenin in front of Oktyabrskaya metro station, an equestrian statue of Moscow's founder, Yuri Dolgoruky, on pl Tverskaya, and the Karl Marx across from the Bolshoi Theatre.

Production has also slowed at the **armoured vehicle factory**, one of Russia's three major tank works, the others being in the Siberian cities of Kurgan and Omsk.

The smoking factories and suburban blocks of flats are now left behind and you roll through forests of pine, birch and oak. Amongst the trees there are picturesque wooden *dachas* where many of Moscow's residents spend their weekends. You pass through little stations with long, white-washed picket fences.

Km54: Fryazevo Фрязево This is the junction with the line to Moscow's Kursky station. Although km posts here say 54km you're actually 73km from Moscow's Yaroslavsky station: see the box on kilometre posts, opposite. (Turn to p416 if you're travelling via Yaroslavl).

Km68: Pavlovsky Posad Павловский Посад This ancient town is a centre of textile manufacturing. The local museum is famous for its large collection of scarves and handkerchiefs but unless you have a very special interest in such items it's probably not worth getting off the train.

Dacha
A dacha is much more than a country cottage or holiday home: it provides its city-dwelling owners with somewhere to grow vegetables, a base for mushroom and wild berry collecting operations as well as providing a place to relax away from the urban environment. Growing fruit and vegetables and collecting mushrooms and berries are not just pastimes for Russians but provide a means of survival during lean years and a supplement to their winter diet during better times. People also pick mushrooms and berries to sell in street markets in the cities. Russians are generally very knowledgeable about preserving techniques, food value and homeopathic remedies.

As one approaches a city on the train, the dacha colonies become larger and more frequent. Each privately-owned house will be set on a large wood-fenced lot. The design of the house is very eclectic: small greenhouses abound and many properties have a sauna building. The earth closet of classic design is at the foot of the garden. Electricity is supplied and there is water from a community well or tap. There may be chickens; other livestock such as a goat or milk cow would belong to permanent residents. Some of the outlying villages contain a mix of small farmsteads and old houses that have been rehabilitated into dachas.

Nancy J Scarth (Canada)

❏ **Important note on km posts – Moscow–Vyatka**
The km posts on this 900km section of the route, between Moscow and Kotelnich (near Vyatka), were originally calibrated from Kursky station. Now that most Trans-Siberian services no longer run on the line via Yaroslavl but via Vladimir and Nizhny Novgorod, there's a chance that the posts may be updated and repainted with the distance from Yaroslavsky station, 19km further away than Kursky. When that happens you'll need to increase all kilometre readings from Fryazevo (Km54) up to the station before Kotelnich. At Kotelnich (Km870) you rejoin the old route.

Km90: Orekhovo Орехово   The town, at the junction with the line to Aleksandrov, is the centre of an important textile region. It gained its pre-revolutionary credentials in 1885 with the Morozov strike, the largest workers' demonstration in Russia up to that time.

Km106: Pokrov Покров   It was in the nearby village of Novoselovo that Yuri Gagarin, the world's first astronaut, died in a plane crash in 1968. He was piloting a small aircraft when another plane flew too close. The resulting turbulence forced his aircraft into a downward spin which he was unable to correct.

Km126: Petushki Петушки   If you ever see a communist-era film with bears in it, chances are it was shot in the countryside around Petushki. The town's most famous attraction is the nearby zoo, source of many animals used in Russian movies. Petushki sits on the left bank of the Klyazma River.

Km135: Kosterevo Костерево   The 19th-century painter Isaak Levitan lived near here. His house has been moved into Kosterevo and opened as a museum.

Km161: Undol Ундол   The station is named after Russian bibliographer VM Undolsky, who was born near here. The town is known as Lakinsk after MI Lakin, a revolutionary killed here in 1905. But the area is probably best known for its brewery, a Soviet-era Czechoslovak joint venture. Lakinsk beer, very popular in the 1990s, is now under strong competition from Western brands.

Approaching Vladimir you can see the domes of the Ascension Cathedral, built in 1160, rising above the city.

Km191: Vladimir Владимир (●●●)   [see p196]
Vladimir was founded in 1108. In 1157 it became capital of the principality of Vladimir-Suzdal and therefore politically the most important city in Russia. It's worth visiting for its great Ascension Cathedral, and as a stepping-stone to the more interesting town of Suzdal, 35km away, and the wonderful Church of the Intercession on the Nerl, 10km from Vladimir.

Km202: Bogolyubovo Боголюбово   [see p199]
Visible from the train (**N**) about 1.5km east of Bogolyubovo is the **Church of the Intercession on the Nerl**, one of Russia's loveliest and most famous

---

The Golden Ring

You are now passing through Russia's most famous historical region, ancient birthplace of the mighty Russian state. Major Golden Ring towns on or near the current Trans-Siberian route are Vladimir, Suzdal and Nizhny Novgorod (formerly Gorky). Along the older route via Yaroslavl are Sergiev Posad (73km from Moscow; see p179), Rostov-Yaroslavski (224km) and Yaroslavl (284km).

Following the collapse of Kievan Rus, the first feudal state in Eastern Europe, its capital was shifted in 1169 from Kiev to Vladimir. At that time Vladimir and the other Golden Ring towns were little more than villages but over the next two centuries all of them grew rapidly into political, religious and commercial centres.

The typical Golden Ring town of the 11th to 18th centuries consisted of *kremlin*, *posad* and *sloboda*. The kremlin (fortress), usually in an elevated position, was ringed by earth embankments topped with wooden walls. Watch-towers were positioned strategically along the walls. Over time the earth and wooden walls were replaced by stone and brick. Inside the kremlin were the prince's residence, plus religious and administrative buildings. Outside the kremlin was the undefended posad, which was the merchants' and artisans' quarter. Often next to the posad was a sloboda, a tax-exempt settlement established to attract a new workforce.

After the Tatar-Mongol invasion in 1236 Moscow (Muscovy) became the invaders' centre for tax collection and its prince was granted the title of Grand Prince. Gradually Moscow's influence eclipsed that of the Golden Ring principalities and they were soon annexed, their economic and military power used to expand Moscow's own domination. By the end of the 16th century Moscow was on its way to becoming the capital of Russia. While several Golden Ring towns retained their commercial importance due to their locations on major trading routes, their golden era was over.

---

churches. Built in 1165, the single-domed church sits in the middle of a field at the junction of the Nerl and Klyazma rivers. It was constructed in a single summer on the orders of Andrei Bogolyubsky, in memory of his son who died in battle against the Volga Bulgars. It was built on this prominent spot to impress visiting ambassadors. To symbolize Vladimir's inheritance of religious authority from Byzantium and Kiev the church was consecrated and a holiday declared without permission being sought.

Km240: Novki Новки This large town at the junction of the line to Ivanovo boasts one of Russia's ugliest stations. The original building is about a century old. In the 1980s, in an attempt to make it appear contemporary, it was encased in pink and fawn tiles. The result is a monumental eyesore.

About 13km eastward the train crosses the wide Klyazma River. The original bridge, built in the 1890s, was washed away in a flood. To avoid the problems of extending a new bridge across the river, engineers came up with a clever alternative. They built a bridge on dry land, on the inside of a bend in the river 1km to the west, then dug a canal beneath the bridge, detoured the river through it and filled in the old river bed. As you pass by you can see the old river course on each side of the bridge's eastern embankment.

Km255: Kovrov Ковров This ancient town gets its name from *kovyor*, the Russian word for 'carpet'. During the Mongol Tatar's reign in the 14th century, the local tax collector accepted carpets as one of the tributes.

The town's most famous son was engineer Vasili Alekseyevich Degtyarev (1879-1949), father of the Soviet machine-gun. The **Degtyarev factory**, founded here in 1916, now manufactures motorcycles, scooter engines and small arms. In the town centre there is a monument to Degtyarev, holding an engineering micrometer rather than a gun. His grave is nearby and his house at ul Degtyareva 4 has been turned into a museum.

Kovrov is also famous for its excavator **factory** founded in the mid-19th century to build and maintain railway rolling stock. Its claims to fame include the world's first steam-heated passenger carriage (1866) and Russia's first hospital carriage (1877). The factory's importance is illustrated by large, colourful murals of digging machinery on the sides of Kovrov's nine-storey accommodation blocks. There's a **museum** devoted to this factory at ul Bortsov 1.

Km295: Mstera Мстера The village of the same name, 14km from the station, is famous for its folk handicrafts and has lent its name to particular styles of miniature painting and embroidery. Mstera miniatures, notable for their deep black background and warm, soft colours, usually depict scenes from folklore, history, literature and everyday life. They are painted in tempera (from pigments ground in water and mixed with egg yolk) onto papier-mâché boxes and lacquered to a high sheen. Mstera embroidery is characterized by two types of stitch, called white satin stitch and Vladimir stitch. A large range of products is on display and for sale at the little museum in the village.

Km315: Vyazniki Вязники The name means 'little elms', after the trees on the banks of the Klyazma River among which this ancient village's first huts were sited. The town got on the map when pilgrims started flocking here after 1622 to see the miracle-working Kazan Mother of God icon. Vyazniki became famous for its icon painters, with two local masters invited in the mid-17th century to paint cathedral icons in Moscow's kremlin.

Km363: Gorokhovets Гороховец One of the smallest of the Golden Ring towns, Gorokhovets (about 10km from the station) is worth visiting as it gives a different perspective on these ancient towns while allowing you to observe

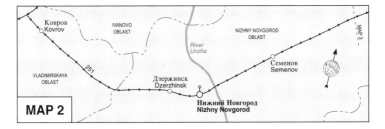

life in what is now a quiet Russian village. Gorokhovets was first mentioned in 1239 when it was burned down by the Tatar-Mongols. A fortress was built on top of the hill overlooking the town but this was destroyed in 1619 by marauding Ukrainian Cossacks under Polish command.

Architectural highlights include the Purification of the Virgin Monastery (1698) and the St Nicholas Monastery (1681-6), both of which have high, open stairways, pilasters at the corners and intricate window frames. There are also several unusual two-storey stone houses from the second half of the 17th century which were designed to imitate traditional Russian wooden mansions. Also of interest is the former *ostrog* complex, used as a stopping-point for prisoners on their way to Siberia.

Km442: Nizhny Novgorod/Gorky Нижний Новгород/ Горький (●●●)
[see p206] With a population of about 1.9 million, Nizhny Novgorod (still called Gorky on train timetables) is Russia's fourth-largest city after Moscow, St Petersburg and Novosibirsk. It was closed to foreigners until 1991 but tourists have now returned to this attractive Golden Ring city.

East of Nizhny Novgorod the train crosses the mighty **Volga River**, which is about 1km wide at this point. In times gone by Russians held this river in such esteem that train passengers would stand and take off their hats to Mother Volga as the train rattled onto the first spans of the long bridge. Rising in the Valdai hills, Europe's longest river meanders 3700km down to the Caspian Sea. It is to Russia what the Nile is to Egypt: a source of life and a thoroughfare.

Km509: Semyonov Семёнов Settled in the 18th century by Old Believers (see p62), Semyonov still boasts many buildings from that period, identified by the five or six windows on each façade, walls covered with intricate carvings, high surrounding fences, wicket gates and large prayer rooms. In the 19th century the town became famous for rosary beads and other products of its woodworkers. It was later known for a particular form of *khokhloma* painting – fine golden patterns of flowers on a red or black background. A khokhloma school was founded here in 1925.

Km531: Ozero Озеро To the left of the station (whose name means 'lake') is shallow Svetloyar Lake, at the bottom of which, according to legend, is the invisible village of Kitezh.

Km623: Uren Урен The town was founded deep in the forests by Old Believers fleeing from persecution in the 18th century. Little remains from this period and the town's major industry is a (struggling) factory producing work clothes.

Km682: Shakhunya Шахунья This town near the Shakhunya River derives its name from the Russian word *shag* ('step') as the river was so narrow here that it could be crossed in one jump. The town grew in the 1930s when the railway line between Nizhny Novgorod and Vyatka was built. Most buildings are two- and five-storey apartment blocks from the 1950s, but 1930s wooden workers' barracks can still be seen.

Km701: Tonshayevo Тоншаево Confusingly, the town around the station is called Shaigino while the town of Tonshayevo is 10km to the south-east.

Km743: Sherstki Шерстки This station, on the border between Nizhny Novgorodskaya and Kirovskaya oblasts, also marks the first step away from Moscow time.

──────────── **Km 743-1266 TIME ZONE MT + 1** ────────────

Km870: Kotelnich Котельнич (pop: 30,700) This station sits at the junction of the Trans-Siberian (Moscow–Vladimir–Nizhny Novgorod–Vyatka) line and the Moscow–Yaroslavl–Vyatka line. For Yaroslavl this is not the place to change lines; instead go 87km east to the major city of Vyatka (Kirov) where tickets are much easier to get.

Kotelnich is an ancient commercial centre on the right bank of the Vyatka River, a major trading route between Arkhangelsk and the Volga region. Finding your way around the town is not easy as it lies in three ravines with only the town centre laid out in an orderly fashion. Here the major thoroughfare is ul Moskovskaya and along part of it are a number of buildings built in Vyatka Provincial Style from 1850 to 1880. Sights include the John the Baptist (Predtichi) Monastery and the Presentation of the Virgin (Vvedenski) Nunnery. The town has a museum.

After leaving the station, the train crosses over the **Vyatka River**. This is the 10th longest river in European Russia, meandering for 1367km, and the Trans-Siberian crosses over it several times. When the train reaches the Vyatka River basin a few kilometres to the west of Kotelnich there is a noticeable change in the landscape as forests give way to fields and more frequent villages.

Km890: Maradykovski Марадыковский It's probably sensible not to break your journey here. The nearby air force base has in the past been used for storage of chemical weapons agents (mustard gas, lewisite, hydrocyanic acid and phosgene). Destruction of these chemicals was begun in 1995 but will not be completed until 2005. Ironically, the name of the settlement around the station is Mirny (Мирный) which means 'peaceful'.

Km957: Vyatka/Kirov Вятка/Киров (●●●) (pop: 463,000) [See p210]

Vyatka, formerly known as Kirov (and still called this on train timetables), was founded on the banks of the Vyatka River in 1181, as Klynov.

A branch line runs north to the Kotlas area, setting for Alexander Solzhenitsyn's *A Day in the Life of Ivan Denisovitch,* describing 24 hours in the life of a Siberian convict.

Km975: Pozdino Поздино

The town around the station is called Novovyatsk and boasts one of Russia's largest ski factories. During Soviet times the factory produced 20% of the nation's skis.

Km995: Bum-Kombinat Бум-Комбинат

This unfortunately-named town gets its name from its principal employer, a paper complex.

Km1052: Zuyevka Зуевка (pop: 15,700)

Zuyevka was founded in 1895 during construction of the railway; during WWII hundreds of Leningraders settled here, and today their descendants manufacture swings and see-saws.

Km1127: Yar Яр

About 20km before this station you leave Kirovskaya Oblast and cross the administrative frontier into the heavily industrialized **Udmurtia Republic**. Yar is the first town here and has a number of Udmurt speakers. It sits on a steep river bank (*yar*). There has been a metallurgical plant here for over two centuries, but nothing else of note.

Between Yar and Balyezino there are many market gardens set in rolling, open countryside. You pass vast fields of grey-green cabbages, and rows of greenhouses covered in plastic sheeting line the track in some places. There are tiny villages of log cabins with brightly painted front doors.

Km1136: Balyshur Балышур

Just before arriving at the station, you pass a steam train storage depot.

Km1165: Glazov Глазов (●, *Rossiya* only) (pop: 105,900)

Originally an Udmurt village, Glazov soon became infamous as a desolate and impoverished place of exile. All this was to change with the arrival of the railway and by 1900 there were over a hundred enterprises. Within a few more years the town grew

---

The Udmurt Homeland

The Udmurtia Republic is one of 16 republics of indigenous peoples within the Russian Federation. The population of Udmurtia is about 1.6 million, only one third of them Udmurts. They are descendants of Finno-Ugric peoples who in turn were descended from Neolithic and Bronze Age people living in the area. Udmurts started cultivation and stock raising in the 9th century AD, and from 1236 to 1552 were dominated by the Golden Horde and the Kazan khans. In 1558 Russia incorporated the entire Udmurt area and it was only in 1932 that the indigenous inhabitants were acknowledged with the declaration of an Udmurt Autonomous Oblast. Today the Udmurts are the largest Finno-Ugric language group in Russia.

into the region's largest flax, oats and oakum trading centre (oakum is a fibre used for caulking the seams of ships).

There are still a few Udmurt log huts remaining. Known as *korkas*, they are positioned along an open paved courtyard. The courtyard had a massive gate which, like the hut, was often decorated with carved geometrical and plant designs. Glazov has a history museum.

Km1194: Balyezino Балезино (●●●) A change of locomotive gives you a chance to stock up from the traders on the platform.

Km1223: Cheptsa Чепца About 2km west of this station the line crosses the Cheptsa River (Km1221) which the route has been following for the last 250km. The train begins to wind its way up into the Urals. Between Cheptsa and Vereshchagino is the frontier between the Udmurt Republic and **Permskaya Oblast**. Permskaya's 160,600 sq km are, like those of Kirovskaya Oblast, lost to the swampy forests of the taiga. But Permskaya has greater prizes than its millions of pine and birch trees, for the region includes the mineral-rich Ural Mountains. The main industries include mining, logging and paper-making. Agriculture is confined to market gardening.

────────── **Km 1267-2496 TIME ZONE MT + 2** ──────────

Km1310 (S): Vereshchagino Верещагино (pop: 25,000) Vereshchagino was founded at the end of the 19th century as a railway depot, and its main industry is still railways. There is a preserved FD21 steam locomotive on a plinth about 1km west of the station near the main rail depot. The town is named after Russia's greatest battlefield painter, VV Vereshchagin, who stopped here on his way to the Russo-Japanese War front in 1905. It was his final and fatal commission.

There are some good views, a few kilometres after Vereshchagino.

Km1340: Mendeleevo Менделеево The town is named after the chemist Dmitri Mendeleev (1834-1907), who developed the Periodic Table. He often visited this town during his inspections of the region's metallurgical plants. There is a Mendeleev museum in nearby Tobolsk.

Km1387: Chaykovskaya Чайковская This station is named after the composer Pyotr Ilich Tchaikovsky (1840-1893), who was born 180km south-

east of here at a factory settlement around the Kamsko-Votkinsk industrial plant. Until recently it was believed that Tchaikovsky died of cholera but historians have now concluded that he was blackmailed into taking poison to prevent his liaison with the nephew of a St Petersburg noble being made public.

The nearby town (a construction settlement for the hydroelectric dam) is called Maiski.

From here to Perm there are excellent opportunities to get photos of the train as it snakes along the winding railway.

Km1410: Overyata Оверята An 11km branch line leads south to the dirty industrial town of Krasnokamsk, which was founded in the 1930s and has a large cellulose mill. Surprisingly near the town is the popular Ust-Kachka health resort, with medicinal mud baths.

Km1429: Perm freight yard Пермь-Сортировочная This is one of Russia's largest freight yards, handling up to 135 trains simultaneously.

Km1432: Kama River Река Кама Just before the train reaches Perm, you cross over the Kama River. From the 900m bridge which was built in 1899 you can see Perm stretching away to the left. The mighty Kama River, flowing over 2000km from the Urals to the Volga, is one of Russia's great waterways. Near the bridge the river banks are lined with cranes and warehouses.

A short distance west of Perm station (N) there's a turntable and beside it an ancient green 'O' Class locomotive (OB 14). Engines of this type were hauling Trans-Siberian trains at the end of the 19th century.

Km1436: Perm 2 Пермь 2 (●●●)   [see p212]
Perm, now a city of just under a million inhabitants, was founded in 1723 when copper smelting works were established here. Because of its important position on the Kama River, the Great Siberian Post Road and later the Trans-Siberian Railway, Perm quickly grew into a major trading and industrial centre.

In the days before the railway reached Perm most travellers would arrive by steamer from Nizhny Novgorod and Kazan. RL Jefferson (see p103) cycled here from London in 1896 on his Siberian bike ride and was entertained by a Mr Kuznetsoff, 60-year-old president of the Perm Cycling Club, and 50 enthusiasts.

On 20 July 1907 the cyclists came out to escort an equally sensational visitor, the Italian Prince Borghese, who had just driven across Siberia from Peking in his Itala and was on his way to Paris, to win the Peking to Paris motor rally. One of the wheels of the car was damaged and after the Prince's chauffeur had replaced some of its wooden spokes he declared that the wheel must be soaked to make the wood expand before the repair could be completed. A local official suggested sending it to one of the bathing establishments along the Kama River. A bathing-machine (of the type used by Victorian swimmers at English seaside resorts) was hired and the wheel spent the night taking the waters.

Unfortunately, the centre of Old Perm is out of sight, 5km away from Perm 2 station where the Trans-Siberian train stops. This is a pity as the approaches and area around Perm 2 are dominated by dilapidated industrial enterprises.

Shortly after leaving the station the train crosses a small bridge over a busy street. This street was once part of the Siberian *Trakt* (Great Post Road) which passed through Perm from 1863.

After Perm the landscape changes abruptly and forests give way to meadows and fields.

Km1452: Ferma Ферма The attractive, green-domed church (S) might make a good photograph.

Km1460-1777 The train winds its way up to the highest point in the Urals. One would expect the mountains dividing Europe from Asia to be rather more impressive than these hills but they rise up not much more than 500m (1640ft) above sea level here. Colin Thubron (*In Siberia*) describes them as 'a faint upheaval of pine-darkened slopes'.

RL Jefferson wrote in 1896: 'The Urals certainly are not so high or majestic as the Alps or the Balkans but their wild picturesqueness is something to be seen to be appreciated.' Their wild picturesqueness is somewhat marred today by open-cast mines at Km1507 (N) and Km1509 (N). There is a large timber mill at Km1523 (N).

Km1534: Kungur Кунгур Just outside the town is a fascinating and almost unknown tourist attraction, the **Kungur Ice Caves** (see p213). The stockade town of Kungur was founded in 1648, 17km from its present site. By the 18th century the town was one of the largest centres in the Urals as it was a transit point on the Siberian Trakt. It had three big markets a year, numerous factories and the first technical college in the Urals, which opened in 1877. Today the town is much less important, though it is still well known in Russia for its guitar factory.

Soon after leaving Kungur you see the steep banks of the Sylva River which mark the start of the Kungur Forest Steppe. This area is characterized by rolling hills which reach 180-230m (600-750ft), a landscape pitted with troughs and sinkholes, and copses of birch, linden, oak and pine interspersed with farmland.

Km1537 (N) A picturesque church stands alone on a hill across the Sylva River. The railway line follows this river up the valley to Km1556 where it cuts across a wide plain. The trees close in again from about Km1584 but there are occasional clearings with villages and timber mills at about Km1650 (N).

Km1672 Shalya Шаля (pop: 26,900) Shalya is a forestry town of no special interest. Fifty kilometres to the west you enter **Sverdlovskaya Oblast**, covering 194,300 sq km, taking in parts of the Urals and extending east onto the Siberian plain. Like most of the other oblasts you have passed through, this one is composed almost entirely of taiga forest. From rich deposits in the Urals are mined iron ore, copper, platinum, gold, tungsten, cobalt, asbestos and bauxite as well as many varieties of gemstones. The soil is poor so there is very little agriculture in the region.

Km1729: Kuzino Кузино East of the large marshalling yard here the line rises once more, passing a little town built around a freshly whitewashed church with a green dome. After about 10km the train reaches one of the Urals' most attractive rivers, the Chusavya. The line follows the course of the river for some 30km.

Km1748: Krylosovo Крылосово A large factory with rows of workers' apartment blocks looks a little out of place amongst the forests up here in the Urals. From Km1764 east the area becomes quite built up.

Km1770: Pervouralsk Первоуральск (pop: 135,500) The city's name translates as First Ural as it was here in 1727 that the Urals' first factory was opened. Following the success of its cast iron works dozens of other factories sprang up and today the city is home to numerous heavy engineering complexes including one of Russia's largest pipeline factories. In the current economic climate many are either facing closure or have already closed.

You can see Pervouralsk's main tourist attraction, the **Europe-Asia border obelisk** from the train so there's no reason to get off. If you do, about the only place to stay in the city is *Hotel Pervouralsk* at prospekt Ilicha 28 (bus No 10 from the station). The hotel has a good restaurant; the other recommended choice is *Restaurant Talaktuka* at ul Trubnikov 52. The city boasts a **Museum of Folklore**, at ul Lenina 65.

Km1777 (S): Europe–Asia Border Obelisk People begin collecting in the corridor long before you reach the white stone obelisk which marks the continental division at this point in the Urals. The obelisk is about 15m to the east of the small Vershina (Вершина) railway platform.

When RL Jefferson reached the point near here where the road crosses the Urals (also marked with an obelisk) he wrote enthusiastically of the view: 'Hills piled upon hills, shaggy mountains and gaunt fir trees, and beyond them dwindling away into the mist of the horizon the great steppe lands of Siberia.' George Kennan wrote in 1887: 'The scenery of the Urals where the railroad crosses the range resembles in general outline that of West Virginia where the Baltimore and Ohio railroad crosses the Alleghenies; but it differs somewhat from the latter in colouring, owing to the greater preponderance in the Urals of evergreen trees'. Unfortunately you won't get much of a view from the train today.

The U2 Affair: USSR 1, USA 0

The U2 affair represented an unprecedented Cold War embarrassment for the West. On 1 May 1960, an American U2 spyplane was shot down from a height of 20,700m (68,000ft), some 45km south of Sverdlovsk (as Yekaterinburg was then known). Its pilot, Gary Powers, baled out without activating the plane's self-destruct mechanism for fear that he would blow himself up (criticisms were later raised in Congress that he had not killed himself, either by destroying the aircraft or by pricking himself with the poisoned needle so thoughtfully provided by the CIA). He was picked up shortly after reaching the ground.

Four days later the USA announced that a U2 'meteorological aircraft' had 'gone missing' just north of Turkey after its pilot had reported problems with his oxygen mask. In a detailed press announcement it was speculated that he had fallen unconscious while the plane, automatic pilot engaged, might possibly have flown itself over Soviet territory. Shortly after this announcement, Khrushchev told the Supreme Soviet that a U2 'spyplane' had been shot down over Sverdlovsk. US presidential spokesman Lincoln White commented that 'this might be the same plane', and did his best to cool the situation by explaining the oxygen supply theory again. He concluded: 'there was absolutely no deliberate attempt to violate Soviet airspace and never has been', and he grounded all other U2s to 'check their oxygen systems'.

On 7 May Khrushchev addressed the Supreme Soviet again: 'I must tell you a secret. When I made my first report I deliberately did not say that the pilot was alive and well ... and now just look how many silly things they (the Americans) have said'. Khrushchev exploited his position, revelling in the details of the American cover-up: he was in possession of the pilot ('alive and kicking'), the 'plane, the camera, and had even had the photographs developed. He also had Powers' survival pack, including 7500 roubles, other currencies and gold rings and gifts for women. 'Why was all this necessary?' he asked, 'Maybe the pilot was to have flown still higher to Mars and was going to lead the Martian ladies astray?' He laughed at the US report that the U2 had a maximum height of 16,700m (55,000ft): 'It was hit by the rocket at 20,000m. And if they fly any higher we will also hit them'.

The U2 Affair brought the 1960 Paris Summit to a grinding halt. Following the arrival of the first U2s in England in August 1962, Moscow remarked that they ought to be 'kept far away from us'. In the USSR, Powers was sentenced to ten years but released in exchange for Rudolph Abel, a KGB spy, in 1962. The Soviet press maintained that Powers had been sent home as an 'act of clemency'. No mention was made of the exchange. The wreckage of the plane is now on display in Yekaterinburg.

Dominic Streatfeild-James (UK)

Km1816: Yekaterinburg/Sverdlovsk Екатеринбург/Свердловск
(●●●+; ●●● for **Trans-Mongolian, Trans-Manchurian**)   [see p214]
As soon as you reach the suburbs of Yekaterinburg (pop: 1,256,600) you see a large lake on the right (Km1807-9) which feeds the Iset River running through the city. There's a **locomotive depot** west of the station. The train halts here in the largest city in the Urals, for a change of engine.

After the train leaves the station, on the right along the Iset River a mass of chimney stacks pollutes the horizon. This is Yekaterinburg's main industrial region.

For about 70km east of Yekaterinburg the train winds down and out of the Urals to the West Siberian plain. You are now in Asia (not quite in Siberia yet) but the scenery and houses look no different from those on the European flank of the mountains.

Km1912: Bogdanovich Богданович There is nothing of interest in this town unless you want to pick up some of the fireproof bricks which are its biggest product. Clay quarries and other factories make this town and region very ugly.

About 16km from Bogdanovich are the **Kurinsk mineral springs**. The *1900 Guide to the Great Siberian Railway* states, 'They are efficacious for rheumatism, paralysis, scrofula and anaemia. Furnished houses and an hotel with good rooms are situated near the baths. There is a garden and a promenade with band; theatricals and concerts take place in the casino'. Such frivolous jollities are hard to imagine in this rather gloomy region today. There's still a hotel, however.

Km1955: Kamyshlov Камышлов The town was founded in 1668 as a fortress and is one of oldest settlements in the Urals. The original buildings have all gone and today the architecture of the town is predominantly late 19th and early 20th century. There is a museum here dedicated to the locally-born poet SP Shchepachev and the writer PP Bazhov, who lived here on and off from 1914 to 1923.

About 6km to the west of the town, on the banks of the Pyshma River, is the Obukhov sulphur and chalybeate mineral water sanatorium, which has been famous since 1871.

Km2033: Talitsa Талица (pop: 20,100) The town is famous for its Mayan (Маян) brand of bottled mineral water, believed to be good for stomach disorders. The town, which is 3km south of the station, is also known for another drink which is less beneficial: watered-down industrial alcohol which is sold as rough vodka.

Km2064: Yushala Юшала The sailors from the battleship *Potemkin* were shot here and buried at nearby Kamyshlov station.

Km2102: Siberia (Сибирь) begins here (ends here, for those going west). The border between Sverdlovskaya and Tyumenskaya oblasts is the frontier between the Urals and Siberia. **Tyumenskaya Oblast** comprises 1.44 million sq km of flat land, tundra in the north, taiga in the south. Until oil was discovered in the region 20 years ago, inhabitants were engaged in reindeer herding in the north and farming in the south. Many people have been brought into the oblast in recent years to work in the petroleum and construction industries.

South of the railway line, the point where the Great Post Road crossed Siberia's frontier was marked by 'a square pillar ten or twelve feet in height, of stuccoed or plastered brick', wrote George Kennan (on his way to research *Siberia and the Exile System* in 1887). He added: 'No other spot between St Petersburg and the Pacific is more full of painful suggestions, and none has for the traveller a more melancholy interest than the little opening in the forest where stands this grief-consecrated pillar. Here hundreds of thousands of exiled human beings – men, women and children; princes, nobles and peasants – have bidden good-by (sic) forever to friends, country, and home ... The Russian peasant even when a criminal is deeply attached to his native land; and heart-rending scenes have been witnessed around the boundary pillar ... Some gave way to unrestrained grief; some comforted the weeping; some knelt and pressed their faces to the loved soil of their native country and collected a little earth to take with them into exile ... Until recently the Siberian boundary post was covered with brief inscriptions, good-byes and the names of exiles ... In one place, in a man's hand, had been written the words "Prashchai Marya" (Goodbye Mary!) Who the writer was, who Mary was, there is nothing now left to show ...' (see p94).

Km2144: Tyumen Тюмень (●●●) (pop: 509,000)   [see p223]

Tyumen is Siberia's oldest town, founded in 1586. It was built on the banks of the Tura River, site of the former Tatar town of Chingi Tura, said to date back to the 14th century. The Russian settlement was named by Tsar Feodor Ivanovich after Tyumen Khan, who once ruled this region. It grew quickly as a trading centre, with goods arriving and being shipped on from the large port on the Tura River.

At least one million of the people who passed through this town before 1900 were convicts and exiles. Many were lodged, under the most appalling conditions, in the Tyumen Forwarding Prison. When George Kennan visited the prison in 1887, he was horrified by the overcrowded cells, the dirt and the terrible smell. He wrote: 'The air in the corridors and cells.....was laden with fever germs from the unventilated hospital wards, fetid odors from diseased human bodies and the stench arising from unemptied excrement buckets.....' After a miserable two-week stay here, convicts were sent on prison barges to Tomsk. Conditions were not much better for the 500,000 emigrants who flooded through the town between 1883 and 1900, but they at least had their freedom. When the new railway reached Tyumen in 1888 prisoners from Russia were no longer herded over the Urals in marching parties but travelled in relative luxury in box-cars used also for the transport of cattle and horses.

Tyumen is becoming increasingly important because of oil and gas discoveries in the oblast. Other industries include shipbuilding and timber processing.

Km2222: Yalutorovsk Ялуторовск (pop: 37,900) The town sits on the bank of the wide, 1591km-long Tobol River. In 1639 it was the most easterly fortress of the Tsar's expanding empire. It later became one of the places of exile for Decembrists, who opened the first Siberian school for girls here. The school is now a museum and is next to the Decembrist museum, the latter in the house of an early and well-known exile, Sergei Muravyev-Apostol.

After crossing over the Tobol River, you will see dozens of small, mostly salt lakes on both sides of the railway.

Km2431: Ishim Ишим (●●) (pop: 62,500) The town sits on the left bank of the Ishim River which was a major trading route before the arrival of the Trans-Siberian. The town's strategic location made it a natural site for one of Western Siberia's largest trading fairs. The Nikolsk Fair was held every December and attracted more than 2000 traders, some from as far away as China. The town, founded in 1670 as Korkina, became Ishim in 1782.

North of Ishim, up the Ishim and Irtysh Rivers, lies the city of **Tobolsk**, one of Siberia's oldest settlements. Yermak (see p90) reached the area in 1581 and established a fort here. The Tsar hoped to develop the region by encouraging colonization but to the Russian peasant, Siberia was as far away as the moon and no voluntary mass migration over the Urals occurred. A policy of forced migration was rather more successful.

The first exiles arriving in Tobolsk were former inhabitants of the town of Uglich who had been witnesses to the murder of Tsarevich Dmitry. With them came the **Uglich church bell** which rang the signal for the insurrection that fol-

---

A German spy in Ishim

George Kennan recounts an amusing incident that occurred in Ishim in 1829, when Baron von Humboldt was conducting a geological survey for the Tsar. The famous explorer (who gave his name to the Humboldt Current off the west coast of South America) was growing more than a little annoyed by the petty Siberian officials who kept him from his work. He must have been rather short with the police prefect in this little town for the man took great offence and despatched an urgent letter to his governor-general in which he wrote 'A few days ago there arrived here a German of shortish stature, insignificant appearance, fussy and bearing a letter of introduction from your Excellency to me. I accordingly received him politely; but I must say I find him suspicious and even dangerous. I disliked him from the first. He talks too much .... despises my hospitality .... and associates with Poles and other political criminals .... On one occasion he proceeded with them to a hill overlooking the town. They took a box with them and got out of it a long tube which we all took for a gun. After fastening it to three feet they pointed it down on the town .... This was evidently a great danger for the town which is built entirely of wood; so I sent a detachment of troops with loaded rifles to watch the German on the hill. If the treacherous machinations of this man justify my suspicions, we shall be ready to give our lives for the Tsar and Holy Russia.' Kennan adds: 'The civilized world is to be thanked that the brilliant career of the great von Humboldt was not cut short by a Cossack bullet .... while he was taking sights with a theodolite in that little Siberian town of Ishim.'

lowed the assassination. The bell was reconsecrated in Tobolsk church but in the 1880s the Uglich Town Council decided it would like it back. Tobolsk Council refused and the case eventually went to court. The judge ruled that as the bell had been exiled for life and it was still calling the people to prayer, it had not yet completed its sentence and must therefore remain in Tobolsk.

Km2497   This is the administrative frontier between Tyumenskaya and Omskaya oblasts. **Omskaya Oblast**, on a plain in the Irtysh River basin, occupies 139,700 sq km. Thick taiga forests cover the northern part of the oblast. In the south there is considerable agricultural development, the main crops being spring wheat, flax and sunflowers. As well as sheep and cattle farms, there are numerous dairy farms. This has been an important butter-producing region since the 19th century, when butter was exported to as far away as Turkey and Germany. It is said that butter-making was introduced to the region by the English wife of a Russian landowner. There are many swamps and lakes in the oblast which provide habitat for a multitude of water birds including duck, coot, grey goose, swan and crane.

—————————— **Km 2497-3478 TIME ZONE MT + 3** ——————————

Km2565: Nazyvayevskaya Называевская (pop: 14,400) Founded in 1910 with the arrival of the railway Nazyvayevskaya grew rapidly with the influx of new agricultural workers during Khrushchev's Virgin Lands campaign. The plan was conceived following years of chronic grain shortages after WWII and involved the cultivation of 25 million hectares of land in southwestern Siberia and northern Kazakhstan.

To put the size of this massive undertaking into perspective, the total surface area of the United Kingdom is only 13 million hectares. By the 1960s overintensive farming had reduced five million of these hectares to desert. The Trans-Siberian runs through the northern part of the area; this, unlike the more fragile south, is still fertile.

The area is famous as much for its insects as for its agriculture. In 1887 Kennan found travelling through this marshy region a singularly unpleasant experience. He wrote: 'We were so tormented by huge gray mosquitoes that we were obliged to put on thick gloves, cover our heads with calico hoods and horse hair netting and defend ourselves constantly with leafy branches.' You, however, should be quite safe in your compartment.

MAP 7

Km2706: **Irtysh River** Речка Иртыш   The Irtysh rises in China and flows almost 3000km into the Ob River. It's joined here by the Om. The 650m long bridge is built on pillars of granite from the Urals which had to be brought 1000km by river to the construction site.

Km2712: Omsk Омск (●●●) (pop: 1,132,300)   [see p226]
Omsk is Siberia's second largest city, and a great deal of effort has gone into making it the greenest. The 2500 hectares of parks and gardens cannot, however, disguise the fact that Omsk is essentially an industrial city.

Just before reaching the suburbs of Omsk, you see the airport on the left. The first suburban station you pass is Karbyshevo (Карбышево) and this is where the railway from Chelyabinsk joins the Trans-Siberian railway. The train then crosses the 500m wide Irtysh River which gives a view of Omsk to the left. The old centre of Omsk is on the right bank (eastern side). After the bridge, the train makes a left turn and on the right passes an old brick water tower, built for steam engines in the early 20th century. This has been preserved as an architectural monument.

The line between Omsk and Novosibirsk has the greatest freight traffic density of any railway line in the world.

For the next 600km the train runs through the inhospitable **Baraba Steppe**. This vast expanse of greenish plains is dotted with shallow lakes and ponds, and coarse reeds and sedge grass conceal swamps, peat bogs and rare patches of firm ground. From the train it appears as if there is a continuous forest in the distance. However, if you walk towards it, you will never get there as what you

---

The Kyrgyz
South of Omsk and the Baraba Steppe region lie the **Kyrgyz Steppes**, the true home of the Kyrgyz people. The area extends from the Urals in the west to the mineral-rich Altai Mountains in the south. The Kyrgyz are direct descendants of the Turkic-Mongol hordes that joined Ghengis Khan's armies and invaded Europe in the 13th century. When SS Hill paid them a visit in 1854 they were nomadic herders who professed a mixture of Shamanism and Islam and survived on a diet of boiled mutton and *koumiss* (fermented mare's milk). They lived in *kibitkas* (felt tents or yurts), the doors of which were arranged to face in the direction of Mecca. Fortunately this alignment also kept out the southern winds that blew across the steppe. Of these people Hill wrote: 'The Kirgeeze have the high cheek bones.....of the Mongol Tatars, with an expression of countenance that seemed at least to us the very reverse of agreeable.' However he warmed to his 'new half-wild friends' when they shared their 'brave mess of *stchee*' (soup) with him.

George Kennan found them equally hospitable in 1887. Inside the tent he was offered a container filled with about a litre and a half of koumiss. For fear of causing offence he swallowed the lot and to his horror, his host quickly refilled the container. Kennan wrote 'When I suggested that he reserve the second bowlful for my comrade, Mr Frost, he looked so pained and grieved that in order to restore his serenity I had to go to the *tarantas*, get my banjo and sing "There is a Tavern in the Town"'. This did not have quite the desired effect and they left shortly afterwards.

are seeing are clumps of birches and aspen trees spaced several kilometres or more apart. The lack of landmarks in this area has claimed hundreds of lives.

In spring this place is hell as the air is grey with clouds of gnats and mosquitoes. The Baraba Steppe is also a vast breeding ground for ducks and geese and every year hunters bag about five million birds from this area. Below the steppe is an enormous natural reservoir of hot water, a potential geothermal energy supply currently being investigated.

Km2760 (S): There is a locomotive storage depot here (mostly electric) and 3km east of it is the station of Kormilovka (Кормиловка).

Km2795: Kalachinsk Калачинск (pop: 24,800) One of the more attractive towns in Omsk Oblast, this town was founded in 1792 by Russian peasants who were distinct from other settlers because of their unusual dialect – *kalachon* means 'a sharp bend in a river'; *kalach* in modern Russian means 'a small padlock-shaped white bread loaf'. There's a useful bit of information.

Km2840 This is the administrative frontier between Omskaya and Novosibirskaya oblasts. The 178,200 sq km of **Novosibirskaya Oblast** extend across the Baraba Steppe region of swamps and lakes. Some of the land has been drained and is now extremely fertile. Crops include spring wheat, flax, rye, barley and sunflowers, with dairy farming in many parts of the Baraba region. You might see cowherds rounding up their stock on horseback.

Km2885: Tatarskaya Татарская (●, *Rossiya* only**)** (pop: 30,000) A rather uninteresting small town of apartment blocks and log cabins. The *1900 Guide to the Great Siberian Railway* was not enthusiastic about the place:

'The country is swampy and infested with fever. The water is bad, supplied by a pond formed by spring and bog water.' There was a church, a centre for emigrants, a school and 'the butter manufactures of Mariupolsky, Padin, Soshovsky, Popel and Weiss, producing annually about 15,000 *puds* (250,000 kg) of cream butter'.

Km2888 (N) An attractive group of colourful log cabins. About 50km south of the line between Chany and Binsk lies Lake Chany, the centre of a local fishing industry. Catches are smaller now but in the 19th century the lake was famous for its abundant stock of large pike (weighing up to 14kg/30lbs) and carp.

> **The West Siberian Railway (Km2716-3343)**
> The original line started in Chelyabinsk, south of Yekaterinburg, and ran
> through Kurgan and Petropavlovsk (both south of the modern route) to Omsk. Work
> began in July 1892 under the direction of chief civil engineer Mikhailovsky. He was
> beset by problems that were also to be experienced along other sections of the line: a
> shortage of labour and animals, a complete lack of suitable trees for sleepers, and
> inhospitable working conditions (eg swamps that swarmed with insects). But in 1894
> the first section from Chelyabinsk to Omsk was completed, and the Omsk to Novo-
> Nikolayevsk (now Novosibirsk) section opened in October 1895. The total cost of the
> line was 46 million roubles, a million roubles less than the original estimate.

Km3040: Barabinsk Барабинск (●●●) (pop: 36,100) Founded at the end
of the 19th century during the construction of the Trans-Siberian. About 12km
northwards is the bigger and older town of Kuybyshev (Kainsk-Barabinski).

Km3212: Chulymskaya Чулымская A large railway junction.

Km3322: Ob Обь On the left, just before reaching this station, you can see
Tolmachevo airport which is one of two airports serving Novosibirsk. The city
of Novosibirsk is visible to the north-east.

Km3332: The Great Ob River Bridge After nearly a century of operation,
many of the steel bridges of the early Trans-Siberian are still in use today.
Known as hog-backed bridges because of the hump in the middle of each span,
they are supported by massive stone piers, each with a thick buttress that slants
upstream to deflect the huge ice chunks that float down the river in the spring
thaw. The 870m-long Ob Bridge is a classic hog-backed bridge made up of
seven spans.

   The writers of the *1900 Guide to the Great Siberian Railway* were clearly
impressed by the Ob Bridge, which at the time had only just been completed.
They devote almost a whole page to it, beginning: 'At the 1,328 *verst*, the line
crosses the Ob by a bridge 327.50 *sazhens* long, having seven spans, the I and
VII openings are 46.325 *sazhens*, the II, IV and VI, 53.65 *sazhens*, and III and
V, 53.15 *sazhens*. The upper girders of the bridge are on the Herber's system.'

For those unfamiliar with Russian Imperial measurement, a *verst* is 1.06km or 3500ft and a *sazhen* is 2.1m or 7ft.

Work on the bridge started in 1893 with construction of wooden falsework which supported sections of the permanent steel structure until they could be riveted together. Bridge-building proceeded year-round and was an extremely hazardous occupation in winter. Gangs were perched 30m or more above the frozen river, bolting and riveting without safety lines or protective hoardings. More than a few dropped to their death below.

The Ob River is one of the world's longest, flowing more than 4000km north across Siberia from the Altai Mountains to the Gulf of Ob below the Arctic Ocean.

As you are crossing over the Ob River, you can see Novosibirsk city centre on the left and Oktyabrsky port on the right. The passenger river station is a further 800m upstream from the port. On reaching the right bank the train turns northwards, passing the city's long-distance bus station. About 800m onwards on the right you pass a **steam locomotive** on a plinth.

Km3335: Novosibirsk Новосибирск (●●●) (pop: 1,395,500)   [see p230]
Novosibirsk is the capital of Western Siberia. Most trains stop long enough for you to get a good look at Siberia's largest station, an impressive glass-vaulted building that took from 1929 to 1941 to complete.

Travelling east you pass through a flat land of fields and swamps with the dachas of Novosibirskians in little groups amongst the trees. Some are particularly photogenic (eg, at Km3409 (S)). The line traverses an area of thin taiga to Oyash (Km3424).

Km3463: Bolotnaya Болотная The town was founded in 1805 as a stop on the Siberian Trakt, at the junction with a 250km road south to Barnaul. The town's name means 'swampy', which is certainly appropriate for this area.

———————— **Km 3479-4473 TIME ZONE MT + 4** ————————

Km3479: The **administrative frontier** between Novosibirskaya and Kemerovskaya oblasts.

Km3491: Yurga 1 Юрга 1 (pop: 84,200) The station of Yurga 2 is 7km to the south of Yurga 1. A few kilometres to the east the train crosses the Tom River,

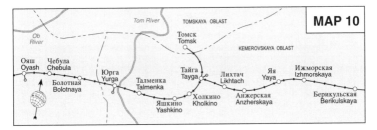

flowing an unimpressive (by Siberian standards) 700km (or twice the length of the Thames) from the Kuznetsk Basin into the Ob River.

Km3570: Tayga Тайга (●●●; ● for Trans-Mongolian, Trans-Manchurian)

(pop: 25,600) This town once stood in the midst of dense taiga forest. Nowadays the closest taiga is far to the east.

RL Jefferson was here in 1897 and wrote later: 'This little station was bang in the midst of the most impenetrable forest I had ever set eyes on....in the centre of a pit it seemed, for the great black trunks of pines went up all around and left only a circular space of blue sky visible.' Annette Meakin wrote a few years later that she 'thought Taiga one of the prettiest stations in Siberia. It is only a few years old, built something after the style of a Swiss chalet.' Unfortunately it has since been replaced by a building that is rather more substantial but aesthetically less pleasing.

The station sits at the junction of a 79km branch line to the ancient city of **Tomsk**, and in retrospect the site of the junction was badly chosen. The basic problem is that there are no rivers or large reservoirs near Taiga so water had to be carted in to feed the steam engines. Tomsk was once the most important place in Siberia. It was founded in 1604 on the Tom River and developed into a large administrative, trading and gold-smelting centre on the Great Siberian Post Road. When it was originally bypassed by the railway, Tomsk began to lose out to the stations along the main line. It is still, however, a sizeable city of half a million people, the administrative capital of Tomskaya Oblast and a large centre of industrial engineering.

The Mid-Siberian Railway (Km3343-5191)

Work began on the Mid-Siberian Railway starting at the Ob River in the summer of 1893. Since Tomsk was to be bypassed, part of the route had to be hacked through the thick forests of the taiga regions around the station, which was aptly named Taiga. It would have been far easier to have followed the route of the Great Siberian Post Road through Tomsk but some of that city's administrators wanted nothing to do with the railway, since it would break their trade monopolies and bring down prices, damaging the economy as far as they were concerned. By the time they realized that the effect was quite the opposite it was too late to change the route. Besides, the engineers had discovered that the bypass would save 90km. The tiny village of Novo-Nikolayevsk (now Novosibirsk), situated where the railway crosses the Ob, grew quickly and soon eclipsed Tomsk as an industrial and cultural centre.

This was difficult territory to build a railway across. The swampy taiga is frozen until mid-July, so the building season was barely three months long. There was the usual labour shortage and 1500 convicts had to be brought in to help. In 1895 a branch line from Tayga reached Tomsk. Although only about 80km long, it had taken a year to build, owing to the virtually impenetrable taiga and the terrible swamps. In 1896 the line reached Krasnoyarsk and work began on the eastern section to Irkutsk. Numerous bridges were needed in this hilly country but by the beginning of 1898 the mid-Siberian was complete and the first trains rolled into Irkutsk. Total cost was about 110 million roubles.

Tomsk was visited by almost every 19th-century traveller to Siberia. The city was an important exile centre and had a large forwarding prison. Having almost succumbed to the stench from the overcrowded cells in 1887, Kennan wrote: 'If you visit the prison my advice to you is to breakfast heartily before starting, and to keep out of the hospital wards.' By the time Annette Meakin visited Tomsk 14 years later the railway had removed the need for forwarding prisons and she could write: 'It was not unlike a group of alms houses. We found very few prisoners.' Tomsk achieved international notoriety when at nearby Tomsk-7 on 6 April 1993 a radioactive waste reprocessing plant blew up, contaminating an area of 120 square km.

Near the station is a **steam engine**, P-360192, built in 1956.

Km3602: Anzherskaya Анжерскаяа (pop: 92,700)

This ugly coal-mining town is at the northern extremity of the giant Kuzbass (Kuznetsk Basin) coal field which contains a massive 600 billion tons of high quality, low sulphur coal. The town, formerly called Anzhero-Sudzhensk (Анжеро-Судженск), was founded in 1897 during the construction of the Trans-Siberian and in the early days of coal mining here. From the late 19th to early 20th centuries, 98% of all coal from the Kuzbass came through Anzherskaya. Most of the original miners were Tsarist prisoners, whose short and brutal lives are documented in the town's Museum of Local Studies.

A railway branch line leads south from here to **Novokuznetsk** which is the heart of the Kuzbass. In the early 1900s a plan had been put forward to link these coal fields with the Ural region where iron-ore was mined and coal was needed for the blast furnaces. The plan was not put into action until the 1930s when the so-called Ural-Kuzbass Kombinat was developed. Trains bring iron ore to Kuzbass furnaces and return with coal for the foundries of the Urals. You will have met (or will meet if you're going west) a good deal of this traffic on the line between Novosibirsk and the Urals.

Km3613-3623:

Several long views south across the fields. The line climbs slowly through birch forests and small fields to Mariinsk.

Km3715: Mariinsk Мариинск (●●●) (pop: 39,100)

Founded as Kisskoye in 1698, this place was nothing more than a way-station for postal riders who carried messages on the Moscow–Irkutsk postal road. In 1826, however, news of a

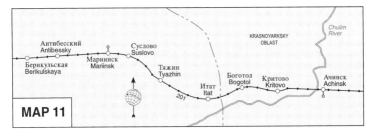

MAP 11

massive gold find brought tens of thousands of fortune seekers. The gold rush lasted for decades and between 1828 and 1917 more than 50 tons of gold were extracted from the region. The town was renamed Mariinsk in 1857 after Maria Alexandrovna, the German wife of Tsar Alexander II.

Just west of the station there are large **engine repair yards** (S). Two kilometres east of the town you cross the Kiya River, a tributary of the Chulim. East of the river the line rises to cross the watershed at Km3760, where there are good views south. The line descends through the market town of **Tiazhin** (Km3779) to the river of the same name and then climbs over the next watershed, descending to **Itat**, another agricultural town.

Km3820: This is the administrative frontier between Kemerovskaya Oblast and Krasnoyarsky Kray. A *kray* is a large oblast, usually established in less developed areas of Siberia. This is also the border between Western and Eastern Siberia. **Krasnoyarsky Kray** covers 2.34 million sq km (an area the size of Saudi Arabia) between the Arctic Ocean and the Sayan Mountains in the south. Most of it is covered with taiga, although there is tundra in the region within the Arctic Circle and some agricultural land in the south. The economy is based on timber processing but there are also important mineral reserves.

Km3849: Bogotol Боготол (●●; ● for **Trans-Mongolian**, **Trans-Manchurian**) This railway town has a **museum** in its locomotive depot which is 1km to the west of the station. There are also several **steam locos** here. The town was founded in 1893 as a station on the Trans-Siberian although there is a much older village of the same name 8km away.

Near Bogotol are lignite (brown coal) deposits. Open cut mines can be seen from the train, scarring the landscape.

About 30km eastwards the line begins to descend, crossing the **Chulim River** at Km3917. RL Jefferson arrived here in the winter of 1897, describing the river as 'rather a small stream when compared to the Obi, Tom or Irtish but still broad enough to make two of the Thames River at London Bridge'. At the time the bridge was unfinished but engineers had the brilliant idea of freezing the rails to the thick ice, thus allowing the train to cross the river.

Km3917: Achinsk 1 Ачинск 1 (●) (214m/700ft) Achinsk was founded in 1642 as a stockaded outpost on the banks of the Chulim. It was burnt down by the Kyrgyz 40 years later but soon rebuilt. In the 18th and 19th centuries this was an important trading centre, linked by the Chulim to Tyumen and Tomsk. Tea arrived by caravan from China and was forwarded in barges. To the north, in the valleys around the Chulim basin, lay gold mines. The most valuable mines today, however, are those producing lignite. There's also a giant aluminium complex, visible from the train.

Km3932-33 (S): This is the halfway point on the line from Moscow to Beijing (via Mongolia). There's a **white obelisk** to mark it on the south side of the line but it is difficult to see. The line continues through hilly taiga, winding round sharp curves (Km4006-12) and past picturesque groups of log cabins (Km4016).

There are occasional good views, at Km4058 (N) and at Km4078 (N) after the village of Minino (Km4072).

Km3960: Chernorechenskaya Чернореченская The name of the town around the station is Novochernorechenskaya (Новочернореченская) meaning New Black River.

Km4098: Krasnoyarsk Красноярск (●●●) (pop: 867,300)   [see p239]
This major industrial city was founded in 1628 beside the Yenisey River. (*Yenisey* is also the name of the Moscow–Krasnoyarsk Express which you may see standing in the station). The original fort was named Krasny Yar. As an important trading centre on the Great Siberian Post Road and the Yenisey waterway, the town grew fast in the 18th century.

The railway reached Krasnoyarsk in 1896, some of the rails for this section having been brought from England by ship via the Kara Sea (within the Arctic Circle) and the Yenisey. Murray would not now recognize the town he described in the 1865 edition of his *Handbook for Russia, Poland and Finland* as 'pleasantly situated and sheltered by hills of moderate elevation'.

A former governor of Krasnoyarsk was the late hardline General Alexander Lebed, who stood against Boris Yeltsin in the 1996 presidential elections but finally stood down and supported Yeltsin. Yeltsin no doubt had something to do with Lebed's successful election campaign in Krasnoyarsk.

Km4100-2: Yenisey River Река Енисей Good views (N) and (S). Leaving Krasnoyarsk to the east the train crosses the great river that bisects Siberia. The Yenisey (meaning 'wide water' in the language of the local Evenki people) rises in Mongolia and flows into the Arctic Ocean, 5200km north of its source.

The river is crossed on a bridge opened only in 1999. The old bridge, almost 1km in length, dated from the 1890s and had to be built on heavy granite piers to withstand the huge icebergs which steamroller their way down the river for a few weeks each year. The cement was shipped from St Petersburg, the steel bearings from Warsaw. It took 94,000 workers three years to build it. The old bridge was awarded a gold medal at the World Fair in Paris in 1900 (the other engineering feat to win a gold medal in that year was the Eiffel Tower).

The Yenisey is the traditional border between Western and Eastern Siberia. For several kilometres after you've crossed it, lumber mills and factories blight

MAP 12

> **Evenki National Okrug**
> About 900km due north of here lies the town of Tura, capital of the
> **Evenki National Okrug**, 745,000 sq km of permanently frozen land, specially
> reserved for the indigenous population. The **Evenkis** belong to the Tungus group of
> people (the names are often used interchangeably), who were originally nomadic
> herders and hunters. After the Buryats and the Yakuts they form the largest ethnic
> group in Siberia but they are scattered in small groups right across the northern
> regions. They once lived in wigwams or tents and survived off berries and reindeer-
> meat (a great delicacy being the raw marrow sucked straight from the bone, prefer-
> ably while it was still warm). They discovered that Christianity fitted in well with
> their own Shamanistic religion and worshipped St Nicholas as deputy to the Master
> Spirit of the Underworld. After the Revolution they were organized into collective
> farms and although most of the population is now settled, there are still some rein-
> deer-herders in the extreme north of the region.

the countryside. Opencast mining has created ugly gashes in the hills around
Km4128 (N).

Km4117: Bazaikha Базаиха There is a branch line northwards from here to
the closed city of Krasnoyarsk-26, a nuclear waste reprocessing facility. The
line goes through Sotsgorod station and terminates at the Gorknokhimichesky
Chemical complex. Neither this line nor the city appeared on Soviet-era maps.

Between Krasnoyarsk and Nizhneudinsk the line crosses picturesque hilly countryside, with the train climbing in and out of successive valleys. There are numerous bridges on this section. There are good places for photographs along the train
as it curves round bends at Km4165-4167 and Km4176-4177; then the land
becomes flatter.

Km4227: Uyar Уяр At the western end of the station is a strategic reserve of
working **steam locos** and also a dump of about 10 engines rusting away
amongst the weeds. This town's full name is something of a tongue-twister: try
saying 'Uyarspasopreobrazhenskoye' after a few glasses of vodka. In 1897 the
name was changed to Olgino in honour of grand duchess Olga Nikolayevna,
and in 1906 to Klyukvenaya, after the railway engineer who built this section of
the line. In 1973 it again became Uyar.

Km4262: Zaozyornaya Заозёрная (●; no stop for Trans-Mongolian) (pop:
15,600) A branch line runs northwards to the once-secret city of Krasnoyarsk-45
(also known as Zelenogorsk) where there's a space centre. East of the station are
are huge opencast coal mines beside the track.

**Km4343: Kansk-Yeniseysky Канск-Енисейский (●; no stop for Trans-
Mongolian)** (pop: 105,300) This big town, usually called Kansk, had an inglo-
rious start. Its original wooden fortress was built in 1628, 43km from the present site. The location was badly chosen and in 1640 the fortress was moved. It
was almost immediately burnt down by local Buryats, and after being rebuilt it

was burnt down again in 1677. Over the following two centuries the town became a major transit point for peasants settling in Siberia. Russian author Anton Chekhov wasn't very impressed, writing that Kansk belonged among the impoverished, stagnant little towns famed only for an abundance of taverns. It's unlikely he'd change his view if he visited today.

Km4375: Ilanskaya Иланская (●●●; ●●●+ for Trans-Mongolian, Trans-Manchurian) (pop: 18,000) The site of the town was selected in 1734 by the Danish-born Russian naval explorer Vitus Bering (after whom the Bering Straits are named) during the Second Kamchatsky Expedition to explore the coast of America. It may seem strange that Bering was surveying central Siberia but he was under orders to make himself useful as he crossed to the Russian Far East. There is a **museum** of the town's history at the locomotive depot.

Between here and Tayshet there are large deposits of brown coal. Our provodnitsa, well aware of this bit of information, issued four of us with buckets to collect coal for the carriage boiler, from the piles lying about the platform.

Km4453: Reshoty Решоты (●, *Rossiya* only) This is the junction for the line south to Abakan, an industrial centre in the foothills of the Sayan Mountains.

Km4473: Uralo-Klyuchy Урало-Ключи This small station's name translates as 'Key to the Urals'. It sits near the administrative frontier between Irkutsk and Krasnoyarsk oblasts.

─────────── **Km 4474-5780 TIME ZONE MT + 5** ───────────

Local time is now Moscow Time + 5 hours. The line gradually swings round to the south-east as it heads towards Irkutsk. For the next 600km you will pass through one of Russia's biggest logging areas. Many of the rivers are used to transport the logs and you can often see log packs being towed down the river or piles of loose logs washed up on the banks. This section of the line is very impressive, the train constantly climbing and descending as it crosses numerous rivers and deep ravines.

Km4501-02: The river here conveniently marks the **halfway point** for the Moscow to Beijing (via Manchuria) run.

Km4516: Tayshet Тайшет (●) This town is at the junction of the Trans-Siberian and BAM (Baikal Amur Mainline) railways. The 3400km BAM line (see p127) traverses Siberia from Lake Baikal to the Pacific Ocean, and is the gateway to a rarely visited region known as the BAM Zone. The single-track line is about 600km to 1000km north of the Trans-Siberian Railway, running parallel to it through pristine taiga, mountain tundra and wide river valley meadows.

Before the 1970s the BAM Zone was virtually uninhabited taiga, dotted with indigenous villages. Today it has a population of about 300,000 involved in extracting natural resources from the region's enormous reserves. Only about 100 Westerners visit the region each year.

Tayshet was founded when the Trans-Siberian arrived in 1897. There is nothing to see in the town, although it is famous in Soviet 'gulag' literature. Tayshet was a transit camp for Stalin-era prisoners heading east or west, and was a major camp of Ozerlag, the gulag complex whose prisoners built the Tayshet–Bratsk section of the BAM. Construction of this section started in earnest after WWII. At the height of the work there were over 300 camps dotted along the line's 350km, with a total population of 100,000 prisoners. In *The Gulag Archipelago*, Alexander Solzhenitsyn writes that Tayshet had a factory for creosoting railroad ties (railway sleepers) 'where, they say, creosote penetrates the skin and bones and its vapours fill the lungs – and that is death'. The factory which makes the ties still operates.

Km4555 (S): Razgon Разгон A small, poor-looking community of log cabins. About 1km east of here the line rises and there are views across the taiga at Km4563 (S), Km4569 (N) and Km4570.

Km4631: Kamyshet Камышет It was here that George Kennan stopped in 1887 for repairs to his tarantass. While the wheel was being replaced he watched the amazing spectacle of a Siberian blacksmith shoeing a horse. 'The poor beast had been hoisted by means of two broad belly-bands and suspended from a stout frame so that he could not touch the ground', he wrote. Three of the horse's legs had been secured to the frame and 'the daring blacksmith was fearlessly putting a shoe on the only hoof that the wretched and humiliated animal could move'.

Km4640-4680: The train snakes its way through the foothills of the Eastern Sayan Mountains. The Sayan Range forms a natural frontier between Siberia and Mongolia.

At Km4648-9 you are at the **half-way point** between Moscow and Vladivostok. There are some good views and several chances for photographs of the whole train as it winds around the valleys. The best spots are around Km4657 (S), Km4660 (S), Km4662-5 and Km4667.

Km4680: Nizhneudinsk Нижнеудинск (●●●) (pop: 42,000) The area is best known for sawmills, swamps and insects. Of the mosquitoes, Kennan complained, 'I found myself blotted from head to foot as if I were suffering from some eruptive disease.'

> ### The Tunguska Event
> About 800km due north of here, on 30 June 1908, one of the largest (pre-atomic era) explosions in human history took place, in the Tunguska River region. Some 2000 sq km of forest were instantly destroyed in what came to be known as the Tunguska Event. The sound of the explosion was heard up to 350km away, the shock waves were registered on seismic equipment right around the world, and the light from the blast was seen throughout Europe.
>
> Newspapers of the time proposed all kinds of theories to explain it, from the testing of new explosives to crash-landing Martian spaceships. Scientists now believe that it was caused by a fragment of Encke's Comet, which disintegrated as it entered the Earth's atmosphere, creating a vast fireball.
>
> In September 2002 it was reported that a meteorite hit a forest area north of Lake Baikal. On a Siberian scale this was a blip compared to the Tunguska Event but it still managed to destroy an area of 65 sq km.

Near Nizhneudinsk is a famous Siberian beauty spot, the **Ukovsky Waterfall**, 18km upstream along the Ude River which flows through Nizhneudinsk. About 75km further upstream, the **Nizhneudinsky Caves** contain ancient paintings.

Siberia's smallest indigenous group, numbering less than 500, is the Tofalar (Tofy), living in and around the isolated settlement of Tofalaria, 200km from Nizhneudinsk. There are no roads to this village and its only regular link with the rest of the world is a helicopter service from Nizhneudinsk.

Between Nizhneudinsk and Irkutsk the country becomes flatter and the taiga thins out. The train passes through numerous timber-yards.

Km4789 (S): There is a large **graveyard** with a blue fence around it, standing close to the line. Some of the graves are topped with red stars, some with red crosses. Kennan wrote in 1887: 'The graveyards belonging to the Siberian settlements sometimes seemed to me much more remarkable and noteworthy than the settlements themselves.....Many graves (are) marked by three-armed wooden crosses and covered with narrow A-shaped roofs.'

Km4794: Tulun Тулун (●, *Rossiya* only) (pop: 52,600) Tulun sits at the junction of the M55 Moscow–Irkutsk Highway and the main road to the city of Bratst, 225km to the north. The town's centre, near the station, still consists mainly of wooden houses. Tulun has a **Decembrists museum**.

How the post was sent to Siberia

The building of the Trans-Siberian Railway revolutionized postal services across the vast Siberian steppes. By 1902 a letter could be carried from St Petersburg to Vladivostok in less than two weeks instead of several months as previously.

The first Siberian letter on record was carried to Moscow in 1582 by Yermak's Cossacks, and informed Tsar Ivan the Terrible that Siberia was now his. A regular postal system had been established in Siberia by 1600, Russian peasants being encouraged to emigrate to Siberia to work as Post House keepers and post-riders or *yamshchiki* (see p101). The post always had priority when it came to horses and to right-of-way on the new post roads. Each Post House keeper had to keep some horses permanently in reserve in case the post should arrive, and on the road a blast of the courier's horn was enough to make other road users pull over and allow the post to pass. Indeed the yamshchiki were not averse to using their whip on the drivers of carts which were slow to move out of the way.

In April 1829 the German writer Adolph Erman, travelling down the still-frozen Lena River from Irkutsk to Yakutsk, wrote that he had 'the good luck of meeting the postman from Yakutsk and Kamchatka. At my desire he waited until the frozen ink which I carried with me had time to thaw, and a few lines to friends in Berlin were written and committed to his care. The courier, or paid overseer who attended the mail from Yakutsk to Irkutsk carried, as a mark of his rank and office, a sword and a loaded pistol, hanging by a chain from his neck. In winter he obtains from the peasants the requisite supply of sledges and horses; and when the ice-road is broken up he takes boats, sometimes, to ascend the Lena' (*Travels in Siberia*).

By the time Annette Meakin travelled along the Trans-Siberian Railway in 1900 she was able to send letters home speedily by train, but she had evidently heard about dishonest postal officials and took pains to register all her letters. In *A Ribbon of Iron* she wrote 'If you do not register in Siberia there is every chance that the stamps will be taken and the letter destroyed long before it reaches the border. You cannot register after 2pm, in which case it is advisable to use a black-edged envelope. Superstition will then prevent its being tampered with'. Black-edged envelopes were used during a period of mourning.

Much of the mail still travels by train, and passenger trains in Siberia often include a travelling post office coach in which mail is sorted. These have an aperture at platform level, through which letters and cards can be posted.

Philip Robinson (UK)

Philatelists may be interested to know that Philip Robinson is the author of *Russian Postmarks* and *Siberia – Postmarks and Postal History of the Russian Empire Period*. He has since published a collection of railway postcards, *The Trans-Siberian Railway on Early Postcards*. Many of these postcards date from the 1890s and show scenes of railway construction and tunnel building.

Enquiries to the address on p2 concerning these books will be forwarded to Philip Robinson.

The line follows the river, crossing it at Km4800 and passing a large saw-mill at Km4804 (S) which might make a good photo with the town behind it. For once there are no wires to get in the way. At Km4809 (S) there is a large opencast mine. You pass through an area of large cultivated fields.

Km4875: Kuytun Куйтун The town's name means 'cold' in the language of the Buryat people (see p362). There are cold springs in the area.

Km4940: Zima Зима (●●●) (460m/1500ft, pop: 35,900) Zima means 'winter' and at the beginning of the 19th century this was a place of exile for members of the Sectarian sect. When the Tsarevich Nicholas visited Zima on 8 July 1891 the Buryats presented him with a model yurt cast in silver.

About 3km to the east of the town the railway crosses the 790km-long Oka River. The river runs brown as it cuts through seams of coal and copperas (ferrous sulphate). The mineral-rich water and earth have their benefits as the water was used to blacken tanned animal skins and, during epidemics of cholera, the copperas earth was used as a disinfectant. But it also causes goitre, which many locals suffer from today. Down the Oka near the riverside village of Burluksk are 1000-year-old petroglylphs of cattle, horses and riders.

As the line crosses the watershed you get several reasonable views: Km4958 (S), Km4972 (N), Km4977 (S) and Km4990 (S).

Km5000-40 You pass through the Ust-Ordinsky Autonomous Okrug. There's another graveyard close to the track at Km5010 (S).

Km5027: Kutulik Кутулик This station is the biggest railway town in the **Ust-Orda Buryat Nationality District**. The Ust-Orda Buryats are related to the Buryats to the east of Lake Baikal and to Mongolians but have a different language and culture. The best time to be here is during the harvest festival of Surkharban when there are races, archery competitions and the Ust-Orda's peculiar brand of wrestling. Kutulik has a museum which contains information on the Ust-Orda Buryats.

Km5061: Cheremkhovo Черемхово (●, _Rossiya_ only) (pop: 68,300) The town revolves around the Cheremkhovo coal deposit, and various mining and industrial complexes are dotted along 10km of the railway. The first mine can be seen from the railway about 20km east of the station.

Thirty-one km to the south is **Belsk (Бельск)** where a blackened watchtower is all that remains of a wooden Cossack fortress built in 1691.

Km5087: Polovina Половина The station, whose name means 'half', was once the halfway point on the Trans-Siberian between Moscow and Vladivostok. Today Moscow is 5090km away and Vladivostok 4212km. The reason for this discrepancy is that the station was named at a time when the Trans-Siberian ran to Moscow via Chelyabinsk and not Yekaterinburg, and to Vladivostok through Manchuria, rather than along the banks of the Amur.

Km5100: Malta Мальта It was in a house in Malta, in February 1928, that farmer Platon Brilin was helping a comrade to build a cellar. As he was digging his spade struck a white object which turned out to be a mammoth tusk carved into a female form. Excavations revealed dwellings with walls made from mammoth bones and roofs of antlers. He had discovered the remains of an ancient settlement, dating from the 13th millennium BC. A grave yielded the body of a child, still wearing a necklace and headband of bones. The child may have been a young shaman (see p248) for the gods were thought to select their earthly representatives by branding them with some kind of deformity: the boy has two sets of teeth. Numerous figurines made of ivory have been found at Malta and also at a site in Buret, 8km from here. Many of the excavated artefacts may be seen in museums in Irkutsk. The oldest settlement so far discovered in Russia (1-2½ million years old) is at Dering Yuryakh in northern Siberia, near Yakutsk.

Km5124: Usolye-Sibirskoye Усолье-Сибирское (●, *Rossiya* only) (pop: 102,100) This city on the left bank (western side) of the Angara River is the salt capital of Siberia. Don't, however, expect to find Siberian salt mines here. Until 1956 all salt was produced by pumping salty water from shallow wells into pans and leaving it to evaporate. These can still be seen on the left bank of the Angara River and on Varnichnoe Island. Nowadays the salt is produced at a **salt factory**, the biggest in Russia and source of the Extra brand of table salt, common throughout the country. The town's other big industrial plant is a 150-year-old **match factory**. Nearby, the **Usolye Health Resort** offers salt, sulphur and mud baths to cure afflictions of the limbs.

Across the river is the nearly abandoned village of **Alekandrovskoye** which was renowned for the particularly brutal conditions of its Tsarist prison founded in 1873. In 1902 a failed revolt led by Felix Dzerzhinsky broke out here. Many of the participants in the failed 1905 Revolution were imprisoned here.

Km5130 (N) There is a large oil refinery here.

Km5133: Telma Тельма Siberia's first textile mill opened here in 1731 and it still operates today, producing work clothing.

Km5160: Angarsk Ангарск (●) (pop: 262,700) Although primarily an industrial city, Angarsk is well planned and very attractive as its industrial and civic parts are separated by a wide green belt. From the station the industrial part is to the north-east (left side if you're heading away from Moscow) and the civic area on the south-west. Angarsk's major industry is oil refining and oil is pumped here by pipeline from the West Siberian, Tatarstan and Baskir oil fields. This pipeline can occasionally be spotted alongside the railway.

The city has a river port and from here hydrofoils travel downstream to Bratsk. Ferries also run between Irkutsk and Angarsk, and coming here from Irkutsk makes a pleasant day trip.

Km5170: Meget Мегет Just north of Meget there's a strategic reserve (N) of L and Ye 2-10-0s **steam engines**.

Km5178: Irkutsk Sortirovka Иркутск Сортировка (●●; **no stop for Trans-Manchurian**) This marshalling yard was once a small station called

Innokentievskaya, in honour of St Innocent, Archbishop of Irkutsk, said to be Siberia's first miracle-worker. The nearby **St Innocent Monastery of the Ascension** was founded in 1672.

The Tsar stopped here on his tour of Siberia in 1891 and the visit was thus described: 'After having listened to the singing, the Tsarevich (sic) knelt at the shrine of the Siberian Saint, kissed the relics and received the image of Innocent, presented to him by Agathangelius, Vicar of Irkutsk. At the same time a deputation from the Shaman Buryats expressed the desire of 250 men to adopt the orthodox religion and to receive the name of Nicholas in commemoration of the Tsarevich's visit to Siberia, which was thus to be preserved in the memory of their descendants. The Imperial traveller graciously acceded to this request.'

Km5182: Irkutsk Most Иркутск Мост Just east of this little station the railway crosses a bridge over the River Irkut, from which Irkutsk takes its name.

Km5185: Irkutsk Иркутск (●●●) (440m/1450ft, pop: 594,400)   **[see p245]** Once known as the 'Paris of Siberia,' Irkutsk is still a fascinating place and just 65km away is beautiful Lake Baikal. From the railway you cannot see much of central Irkutsk, located on the other side of the Angara River. In the distance, however, you can see the large Church of the Elevation of the Cross.

Km5214: Goncharovo Гончарово The town around the station is named Shelekhov (Шелехов, pop: 53,600) after a Russian merchant who led several trading expeditions to North America in the 1780s. He was made governor of the Russian settlement in America and become one of Siberia's richest merchants, with an empire based in Irkutsk.

Passing through Goncharovo you can see the town's main industry, the giant Irkutsk Aluminium Complex, founded in 1956.

The train soon begins climbing into the Primorsky Mountains. Winding through valleys of cedar and pine and crossing numerous small streams, it passes **Kultuk**, junction for the old railway line from Port Baikal. At Km5228 (N) a giant etching of Lenin waves nonchalantly from a hill. The line climbs steeply to Km5254 and then snakes downwards, giving you your first glimpse of **Lake Baikal** from Km5274-8.

After a tunnel at Km5290 there is a splendid view over the lake at Km5292 (N).

Km5297-8: Through another tunnel the line curves sharply round the valley and descends to the water's edge. After a junction and goods yard at **Slyudyanka 2** (Km5305) the train crawls along a part of the line that is prone to flooding from the lake.

Km5312: Slyudyanka 1 Слюдянка 1 (●●) (pop: 20,700) The station is only about 500m from the lake. The train used to stop here for 15 minutes, just enough time to run between the log cabins down to the water and dip your hand in for good luck (see p258). It now stops for just 10 minutes so only speedy sprinters should try this, and only if the carriage attendant confirms that the train is stopping for the usual time. Some people have been left behind doing this! ('The provodnitsas were horrified at your suggestion that it is possible to run down to Lake Baikal from Slyudyanka 1.' Howard Dymock, UK).

The station building was constructed of marble in 1904 to commemorate the building of the Circumbaikal Railway. There are usually interesting things to buy on the platform – sometimes even Baikal's own *omul* fish and boiled potatoes, or raspberries and bags of *orekha* (nuts, here meaning cedar nuts, the classic Siberian snack).

There are some photogenic log cabins near the station but Slyudyanka is otherwise a rather unattractive mining town. It does have a basic hotel should you miss your train. Slyudyanka is the starting point for hikers and rafters travelling into the Khamar-Daban Mountains to the south. Fur-trappers hunt sable and ermine in the forests here. From Slyudyanka the 94km **Circumbaikal Railway** (see p361) branch line runs along the shore of Lake Baikal to Port Baikal.

The train passes through a short tunnel and runs within sight of the water's edge for the next 180km. Some of the best views on the whole trip are along this section of the line.

Km5358: Baikalsk Байкальск (pop: 16,700) The skiing here is said to be among the best in the country. There are two hotels in town, one near the ski base and the other in the town centre opposite the sports centre; the latter also has a restaurant. The town also makes a good base for walks and rafting in the Khamar-Daban Mountains.

About 3km past the town on the left is the **Baikalsk Cellulose and Paper Combine**, source of an strong cellulose used in aircraft tyres. Until recently its chlorine-contaminated waste water was dumped directly into the lake, causing the number of crustacean species within a 50km radius to drop from 57 to 5. Not surprisingly the factory was the brainchild of that environmental vandal Khrushchev, who wanted to 'put Baikal to work'. This was by far Lake Baikal's biggest environmental problem, and because of the enormous cost of upgrading the plant and fitting filters, it continued its destructive operations well into the 1990s. Despite a recent upgrade, rumours persist of leaks of waste material into the lake.

Km5390: Vydrino Выдрино The river just before the station marks the border of the **Buryat Republic**. This region, which is also known as Buryatia, comprises an area of about 351,300 sq km (about the size of Italy). It was originally set aside for the Buryats (see p362), an indigenous ethnic group once

The Circumbaikal Line

The original line from Irkutsk did not follow the route of the present railway but ran to Port Baikal. Until 1904 passengers crossed Lake Baikal on ferries which took them from Port Baikal to Mysovaya. In 1893 it had been decided that it would be impossibly expensive to build the short section of railway along the mountainous southern shore of the lake, and the idea was shelved in favour of a ferry link. From the English company Armstrong and Mitchell a specially designed combined ice-breaker and train-ferry was ordered. The 4200-ton ship, christened the *Baikal*, had three pairs of rails laid across her decks for the carriages and could smash through ice up to four feet thick. A sister ship, the *Angara*, was soon brought into service. The *Angara* has now been converted into a museum and is moored in Irkutsk (see p249).

The ferry system was not a great success, however. In mid-winter the ships were unable to break through the ice and in summer the wild storms for which the lake is notorious often delayed them. Since they could not accommodate more than 300 people between them, many passengers were subjected to long waits beside the lake. The Trans-Siberian Committee realized that, however expensive it might prove, a line had to be built to bridge the 260km gap between the Mid-Siberian and Transbaikal railways. Further surveys were ordered in 1898 and in 1901 ten thousand labourers started work on the line.

This was the most difficult section to build on the entire railway. The terrain between Port Baikal and Kultuk (near Slyudyanka) was virtually one long cliff. Thirty-three tunnels and more than 200 bridges and trestles were constructed, the task made all the more difficult by the fact that in many places labourers could only reach the route by boat. Work went forward simultaneously on the Tankhoy to Mysovaya section.

The labour gangs hacked out embankments and excavated 7km of tunnels but the line was not ready at the time it was most needed. On 8 February 1904 Japan attacked the Russian Navy as it lay at anchor in Port Arthur on the Pacific. Troops were rushed by rail from European Russia but when they arrived at Port Baikal, they found the *Baikal* and *Angara* ice-bound in the severe weather. The only way across the lake was a 17-hour march over the ice. It was then that the Minister of Ways of Communication, Prince Khilkov, put into action a plan which had been successful on several of Siberia's rivers: rails were laid across the ice. The first train to set off across the frozen lake did not get far along the 45km track before the ice gave way with a crack like a cannon-shot and the locomotive sank into the icy water. From then on engines were stripped and their parts put on flatcars pulled over the ice by gangs of men and horses.

Working as fast as possible, in all weathers, labourers completed the Circumbaikal Line in September 1904 at a cost of about 70 million roubles. The first passengers found this section of the line particularly terrifying, not on account of the frequent derailments but because of the tunnels: there were none in European Russia at that time.

In the 1950s a short-cut was opened between Irkutsk and Slyudyanka, which is the route followed by the train today. The line between Irkutsk and Port Baikal is now partly flooded and no longer used. The Port Baikal to Kultuk section, however, is still operational and makes an entertaining side-trip. See p260.

nomadic but now adapted to an agricultural or urban life. Their republic is composed of mountainous taiga, and the economy is based on fur-farming, stock-raising, food and timber-processing and the mining of gold, aluminium, manganese, iron, coal, asbestos and mica.

The Buryats

The largest ethnic minority group in Siberia, Buryats are of Mongolian descent. When Russian colonists first arrived at Lake Baikal the Buryats were nomads who spent their time herding their flocks between the southern shores of the lake and what is now northern Mongolia, in search of pastureland. They lived in felt-covered yurts and practised a mixture of Buddhism and Shamanism.

The Buryats lived on lake fish, bear meat and berries, although their favourite food was said to be *urme*, the thick dried layer of scum skimmed from the top of boiled milk. They hunted the Baikal seal for its fur and in winter, when the lake was frozen, they would track these animals on the ice, wearing white clothing and pushing a white sledge as a hide.

Back in their yurts the Buryats were not the tidiest of tribes, lacking even the most basic hygiene as the Soviet anthropologists Levin and Potapov point out in *The Peoples of Siberia*. Describing an after-dinner scene, they wrote: 'The vessels were not washed, as the spoons and cups were licked clean. An unwashed vessel was often passed from one member of the family to another as was the smoking pipe. Customs of this kind promoted the spread of various diseases.' It seems likely, however, that most of these diseases were brought by Russian colonists.

Although at first hostile to the Russians, the Buryats became involved in the fur trade with the Europeans and a certain amount of inter-marriage occurred. Some gave up their nomadic life and their yurts in favour of log cabins in Verkhneudinsk (now Ulan Ude) or Irkutsk. The Buryats, who now number about 350,000, have their own **Buryat Republic** around the southern part of Lake Baikal. Its capital, Ulan Ude (see p266), was opened to tourists in 1990 and is certainly worth a visit.

Km5421 (N): The lonely collection of ramshackle buildings by the water's edge here might make a good photograph.

Km5426: Tankhoy Танхой (pop: 3000) Tankhoy sits in the middle of the 263,300-hectare **Baikalsky Nature Reserve** which was created to preserve the Siberian taiga. Occasional ferries travel from here to Listvyanka and Port Baikal.

When Prince Borghese and his team were motoring through this area in 1907 on the Peking to Paris Rally they found that since the building of the railway, the Great Siberian Post Road had fallen into disrepair. Most of the post-stations were deserted and many road bridges were rotten and dangerous. The Italians were given special permission by the governor-general to drive across the railway bridges. In fact they covered a considerable part of the journey here by driving along the railway line.

Their 40-horsepower Itala was not the only unorthodox vehicle to take to the rails. On his cycling tour through south Siberia in 1896 RL Jefferson found it rather easier to pedal his Imperial Rover along the tracks than on the muddy roads.

Km5477: Mysovaya Мысовая (pop: 7200) This was the port where the *Baikal* and *Angara* (see p249) delivered their passengers (and their trains).

When Annette Meakin and her mother disembarked from the *Baikal* in 1900 they were horrified to discover that the awaiting train was composed entirely of fourth class carriages. The brave ladies commandeered seats in the corner of one compartment but were soon hemmed in by emigrating peasants. When 'two dirty moujiks' climbed into the luggage rack above them, the ladies decided it might be better to wait at Mysovaya, and got out. But the station-master allowed them to travel in an empty luggage-van, which gave them privacy if not comfort.

The village surrounding the town is known as Babushkin (Бабушкин) in honour of Lenin's friend and Irkutsk revolutionary. Ivan Babushkin was executed by Tsarist forces at this railway depot in 1906 and an obelisk marks the spot. While Mysovaya is still a major Baikal port, over 70% of the village's population works for the railways.

Between Mysovaya and Petrovsky Zavod the line skirts the lower reaches of the Khamar-Daban Mountains. Around Km5536 the line enters the wide valley of the Selenga River, which it follows as far as Ulan Ude (Km5642).

Km5504: Boyarsky Боярский The hills on the right of the station are all that remain of the ancient volcanoes of the Khamar-Daban foothills. East of the station the line leaves Lake Baikal.

Km5530: Posolskaya Посольская About 500m west of this station the train crosses over a narrow, shallow river with the odd name of Bolshaya Rechka (Big Little Stream). About 10km downstream from here the river flows

---

American soldiers die defending communists

During the Russian Civil War, American, Canadian and Japanese troops occupied parts of Eastern Siberia and the Russian Far East, helping White Russian forces battling the communists. The undisciplined White Russians were often little more than bandits and murderers, and allied forces were often put in the awkward position of simultaneously supporting White Army soldiers and protecting the Russian population from them. An incident at Posolskaya station in January 1920 was just one of many unpleasant events that eventually undermined the allies' faith in the White Army.

White Army General Nicholas Bogomolets arrested the station master at Ulan Ude and announced that he would execute him for Bolshevist activities. The American Colonel Morrow, based in Ulan Ude, threatened to call out 2500 soldiers under his command unless the innocent man was released. Bogomolets retreated with the railway official to Posolskaya in his armoured train, where he opened fire in the middle of the night on the boxcar barracks of a small American garrison comprising one officer and 38 enlisted men. These soldiers swarmed out of their quarters, dropped into a skirmish line and blazed away. Sergeant Carl Robbins disabled the train's locomotive with a hand grenade before being killed. At the cost of two dead and one wounded on their side, the Americans captured the train, the general, six other officers and 48 men.

Bogomolets was released for political reasons and emigrated to Hollywood before being deported to Latvia. Sergeant Robbins and Second Lieutenant Paul Kendall posthumously received the Distinguished Service Cross.

into Lake Baikal at the site of the ancient village of Posolskoye. In earlier days Russian ambassadors travelling overland to Asian capitals would rest here; the rough village got a mention in the papers of Ambassador Fyodor Baikov when he passed through in 1656. In 1681 an abbot and a monk built a walled monastery here but it has long since disappeared. Today Bolshaya Rechka hosts the Baikalsky Priboy (Baikal Surf) Holiday Camp.

Km5562: Selenginsk Селенгинск The town was founded in the 17th century as a stockaded outpost on the Selenga River. Unfortunately its wood-pulping factories are rather more in evidence today than the 16th century monastery built for missionaries attempting the conversion of the Buryats. The factories here and in Ulan Ude are notorious for the industrial waste they dump into the Selenga River, which flows into Lake Baikal. Pollution from the Selenga and from the once notorious cellulose mill at Baikalsk has affected over 60% of the lake, and even if the pollution were to stop tomorrow it would take 400 years for the waste to be flushed out.

Km5596: Lesovozny Лесовозный The town around the station is called Ilyinka (Ильинка). About 28km east of the station the train crosses over the Selenga River, providing an excellent photo opportunity. At Km5633-4 (N) there's an army camp with some abandoned tanks.

The train approaches Ulan Ude along the right bank (northern side) of the Selenga River. About 1km before the station (N) is a monument to five railway workers executed by Tsarist forces in 1906 for revolutionary activities.

Km5642: Ulan Ude Улан Уде (●●●; ●●●+ for Trans-Mongolian) (544m/1785ft, pop: 370,900) [see p266] Ulan Ude is the capital of the Buryat Republic. Stretch your legs on the platform where there is a **steam loco** (Class Su) preserved outside the locomotive workshop (N) at the western end of the station. Turn to p385 for the **Trans-Mongolian route to Beijing**.

Two km east of the station you cross over the Uda River. After a further 500m you can see the Palace of Culture (N) and a WWII memorial.

Km5655: Zaudinsky Заудинский The line to Mongolia branches off from the Trans-Siberian here.

Km5675 (N): Onokhoy Онохой There is a large number of **steam locos** at

the west end of the station. From Onokhoy the train follows the valley of the River Brian. From Zaigrayevo (Km5696), the line begins to climb to Ilka, on the river of the same name. It continues to ascend the Zagon Dar range, reaching the highest point (882m/2892ft) at Kizha.

Km5734: Novoilyinsky Новоильинский About 20km past this station the train crosses the administrative frontier between the Buryat Republic and **Chitinskaya Oblast**. Chitinskaya's 431,500 sq km comprise a series of mountain ranges interspersed with wide valleys. The dominant range is the Yablonovy (highest peak: Sokhondo, 2510m/8200ft) which is crossed by the Trans-Siberian near Amazar (Km7010). The mountains are covered in a vast forest of conifers and the climate is dry. The economy is based on mining (gold, tungsten, tin, lead, zinc, molybdenum, lithium, lignite), timber-processing and fur-farming.

––––––––––––––– **Km 5781-8183 TIME ZONE MT + 6** –––––––––––––––

Km5784: Petrovsky Zavod Петровский Завод (●) (pop 28,300) Local time is now Moscow Time + 6 hours. The name of the station means 'Peter's Factory', after the foundry established here in 1789 to supply iron for the region's gold mines, and still going strong today. The factory was rebuilt in 1939 next to the railway and from the train you can see the flames from its open-hearth furnaces.

To its workers in 1830 were added Decembrists brought from nearby Chita and housed in the factory prison. A **memorial** to them can be seen on the station's platform. There is also a **Decembrist museum** in the former house of Yekaterina Trubetskaya. Princess Trubetskaya (1800-54) was the first wife of a Decembrist to voluntarily follow her husband into exile. In doing so she renounced her civil rights and noble privileges. Her name is immortalized in *Russian Women*, a poem by Nikolai Nekrasov.

The Transbaikal Railway (Km5483-6532)

In 1895 work was begun to connect Mysovaya (the port on Lake Baikal) with Sretensk, on the Shilka River near Kuenga (see p369), where passengers boarded steamers for the voyage on to Khabarovsk. Construction materials were shipped to Vladivostok and thence by boat along the Ussuri, Amur and Shilka Rivers. There was a shortage of labour, for it proved impossible to get the local Buryats to work on the line. Gangs of reluctant convicts were brought in, although they became more interested in the operation after it was decided that they should receive 50 kopecks a day in return for their labour.

The terrain is mountainous and the line meanders up several valleys and over the Yablonovy Range. Owing to the dry climate, work could continue throughout the winter, although water was in short supply during these months. Workers were also faced with the problem of permafrost which necessitated the building of bonfires to thaw the ground, or dynamite to break it up.

A terrible setback occurred in July 1897 when over 300km of track and several bridges were damaged or swept away in a freak flood. The line was completed in early 1900 by which time it had cost over 60 million roubles.

Stretching along the railway in the narrow river valley between mountain ridges, Petrovsky Zavod makes a worthy day-trip from Chita.

East of Petrovsky Zavod the line turns north-east into the wide, picturesque valley of the Khilok River, which it follows for almost 300km to Sokhondo, crossing the Yablonovy Range between Mogzon and Chita.

Km5883: Look out for the large graveyard of old steam locomotives.

Km5884: Bada Aeroport Бада Аэропорт The little town is clearly a product of the aerodrome and not vice versa: it's built around a large Soviet monument, a MiG fighter plane facing skyward. The runway (N) is interesting for the large number of old aircraft there. These might make an interesting photograph but discretion is advised.

Km5899 (S): Here is a good place for a photo along the train as it travels on higher ground beside the river. Another is at Km5908 (S), where the train winds slowly along the water's edge.

Km5932: Khilok Хилок (●, **Trans-Manchurian only**) (805m/2640ft, pop: 13,700) East of this small industrial town you continue to climb gently up the valley beside the Khilok River. There are pleasant views over the wide plain all along the river. North of the line are the Khogoy and Shentoy mountains, part of the Tsagan Khuntei range. Near the station a granite monument topped with a star commemorates 11 communists slain here during the Civil War.

The train now crosses the Yablonovy Mountains. The eastern escarpment is steeper than the western side and heavy freight trains travelling westwards invariably require extra engines.

Km6053: Mogzon Могзон (●●●) (907m/2975ft) There's a steam locomotive dump in this dismal town, and heavily guarded prisons for several kilometres around, including one at Km6055 (N).

Km6093: Sokhondo Сохондо (944m/3095ft) This station is named after the highest peak (2510m/8230ft) in the Yablonovy Range. The line leaves the river valley and starts its climb into the range. There is a long view at Km6097 (N). In the 1914 edition of *Russia with Teheran, Port Arthur and Peking*, Karl Baedeker drew his readers' attention to the '93 yard tunnel inscribed at its west-

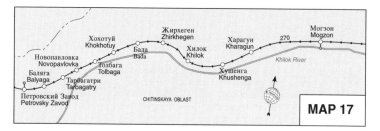

MAP 17

ern entrance "To the Great Ocean" and at its eastern entrance "To the Atlantic Ocean" in Russian', here. The line has now been re-routed up onto a huge grassy plain. It then descends steeply through Yablonovaya, with several good views (Km6107-9).

Km6116 (S): There was a graveyard of **steam locomotives** here but now most of the engines have been dismantled. West of the town of **Ingoda** the train enters the narrow winding valley of the Ingoda River, which it follows eastwards for the next 250km. The line passes through **Chernovskaya**, where lignite is mined.

Km6125: Yablonovaya (Яблоновая) At 1040m/3412ft this is the **highest point on the line**.

Km6131 (S): The line crosses a picturesque meadow with a stream meandering across it, good for a photograph when the flowers are out in May and June.

Km6197: (N) About 2km west of Chita is 16 sq km Kenon Lake. Only 6m deep, the lake is warmed by the nearby power station and at its eastern end there's a popular beach beside the railway line.

Further on the train crosses the small Chita River, and about 1km before the main station you pass through Chita 1 station where a railway factory is located.

Km6199: Chita Чита (●●●) (655m/2150ft, pop: 304,600)   [see p272]
Founded in 1655, the capital of Chitinskaya Oblast stands beside the Chita and Ingoda rivers, surrounded by low hills. A stockaded fort was built here by Cossacks at the end of the 17th century and the town became an important centre on the Chinese trade route.

In 1827 a large group of exiled Decembrists arrived here and spent the first few months building the prison that was to be their home for the following three years. Many stayed on after they had served their sentence and the town's development in the 19th century into an industrial and cultural centre was largely due to their efforts.

East of the city of Chita the train continues to follow the left bank of the Ingoda River downhill for the next 250km. The line passes through **Novaya**, whose original community and dwellings were wiped out in the great flood of 1897 (see p108). At Km6225 (S) there's a collection of log cabins (some of them

MAP 18

quite photogenic) which looks rather vulnerable, being built on the edge of the river flood plain.

Km6265: Darasun Дарасун (●, *Rossiya* **only**) Darasun is renowned for its carbonic mineral springs and the water from them has been exported to China and Korea for years. Near the station is a sanatorium where various cardiovascular and intestinal ailments are treated.

About 1km east of the station there's a good view as the train snakes along the river.

Km6270: Here you can see an army supply base surrounded by a wooden stockade.

Km6293: Karymskaya Карымская (●●●) (605m/1985ft) This small industrial town was first settled by Buryats.

Km6312: Tarskaya Тарская Formerly known as Kaidalovo, this is the junction for the **railway to Beijing via Manchuria (see p395)**. A whitewashed church stands on a hill (S) above the village. You can catch good views along the river at Km6316 (S) and across the wide plains for the next 100km, especially around Km6332 (S) and Km6369 (S). The best views are all to the south, across to Mongolia.

Km6417: Onon Онон (515m/1690ft) A few kilometres east of here the clear waters of the Ingoda River are joined by those of the muddy Onon, on whose banks the great Mongol leader, Genghis Khan, was born in 1162. The Onon and Ingoda together form the Shilka River, a tributary of the mighty Amur. The railway follows the picturesque valley of the Shilka for the next 120km.

Km6446: Shilka Шилка (●) (505m/1655ft, pop: 18,200) The adjacent village of Shilka, on the Shilka River, was founded in 1897 just to serve the railway. Two years later it became a popular tourist destination with the opening of the Shivanda Health Resort (*shivanda* means royal drink in the indigenous language). Mineral water is still used to treat digestive and respiratory system disorders here. A few years later the discovery of gold nearby brought more visitors. In 1954 fluoric spar, a mineral essential in chemistry and metallurgy, was discovered in the area.

There are several interesting-looking wooden buildings near the platform.

Crossing the Kiya River, the train continues over a great wide plain, grazing land for cattle that you may see being rounded up on horseback.

Km6496: Priiskovaya Приисковая (●) *Priisk* means mine, referring to the gold-mining town of **Nerchinsk** (Нерчинск), 10km down a branch line from here. This is where the 1689 Treaty of Nerchinsk was signed, which was to give the Manchurian emperor control over the Russian Far East and deprive the Russians of the valuable Amur region for the next 170 years.

Nerchinsk was the centre of a rich silver, lead and gold mining district in Tsarist times, although the deposits were known to the Buryats long before the

Russians arrived in the 17th century. In 1700 a Greek mining engineer founded the Nerchinsky Zavod works, and the first convict gangs arrived in 1722. George Kennan visited the mine in 1887 and was shown around by one of the convict labourers. Not all the mines were the property of the Tsar, and some private owners became immensely wealthy. In one mansion he visited in Nerchinsk, Kennan could hardly believe that such opulence (tapestries, chandeliers, Oriental rugs, silk curtains and a vast ballroom) was to be found in one of the wildest parts of Siberia. From 1826 to 1917 the mines of Nerchinsk were a major Tsarist labour camp.

Today Nerchinsk has 17,000 inhabitants and some worthwhile sights. These include the early 19th century Resurrection Cathedral and a house built in the 1860s in Moorish style by a rich merchant named Butin. Next door is the Hotel Dauriya (now closed), where Chekhov stayed in 1890. Nerchinsk has a museum and a basic hotel.

On the south side of Priiskovaya station is the small village of **Kalinino**. The Russian explorer Yerofei Pavlovich Khabarov is buried under the walls of the old church. It is believed, however, that the corpse in the grave is actually that of his brother, Nikifor, the last resting place of Yerofei remaining unknown.

Km6511-2 (S): Standing just across the river is a large deserted church and another building beside it. In the middle of nowhere and with a thick conifer forest rising behind them, these two lonely buildings make an eminently photogenic scene.

Km6532: Kuenga Куэнга (●) This is the junction for a line which runs 52km eastwards to **Sretensk** (Сретенск), which was the eastern end of the Transbaikal Railway. Sretensk sits on the northern bank of the Shilka River, a tributary of the mighty Amur. The Amur forms the Chinese-Russian border for hundreds of kilometres before passing through Khabarovsk on its way northeast to the Pacific.

It was this river route that put Sretensk on Russian maps. It was a thriving river-port (considerably larger than Chita) in the 19th and early 20th centuries before the Amur Railway was opened. Passengers transferred here to ships of the Amur Steamship and Trade Company. Most of the 40 steamers that plied between Sretensk and Khabarovsk were made either in Belgium or the Glasgow yards of Armstrong and Co. Waiting here with her mother in 1900 Annette

Meakin caught sight of some Chinese men with traditional pig-tails. She was not impressed and wrote, 'To me their appearance was quite girlish.'

Sretensk (pop: 10,300) is spread over both banks of the river with the centre on the eastern bank and the railway station on the high western bank. The two were joined by a bridge across the river only in 1986. There is a museum and a basic hotel in Sretensk, although it's not as interesting to visit as Nerchinsk. In 1916 the Amur Railway was completed and Sretensk, bypassed, became a backwater.

The line leaves the Shilka River here, turns northwards, crosses a plain and climbs towards the eastern end of the Yablonovy Range.

Km6593:Chernyshevsk Zabaikalsky Чернышевск Забайкальский (●●●) Nikolai Chernyshevsky (1828-89) was a revolutionary who toiled for years at hard-labour camps in the region.

Km6629: Bushuley Бушулей This is not the easiest area in which to build a railway, as Trans-Siberian engineers discovered. In winter it was bitterly cold and in the hot summers all surface water dried up. For most of the year the ground had to be thawed out with gigantic bonfires before track could be laid. The complex around the station is a molybdenum ore enrichment plant. The

---

The Amur Railway (Km6532-8531)

The building of the Amur Railway was proposed in the early 1890s but surveys showed that it would prove expensive, on account of the difficult terrain. More than 100 bridges and many kilometres of embankments would be needed. Furthermore much of the region was locked in permafrost. In 1894, when the government signed the treaty with China which allowed Russian rails to be laid across Manchuria from Chita to Vladivostok, the Amur project was abandoned in favour of this considerably shorter route. The change of plan proved to be false economy, for the East Chinese line, despite a considerable saving in distance, was ultimately to cost more than the whole of the rest of the Trans-Siberian Railway.

Russia's embarrassing defeat by Japan in the 1904-5 War revealed the vulnerability of the East Chinese line. Japan was as keen as Russia to gain control of the rich lands of Manchuria and if they did decide to invade, the Russian naval base of Vladivostok would be deprived of a rail link with European Russia. A line within Russian lands was needed. The Amur project was reconsidered and, in 1907, approved.

Construction began in 1908 at Kuenga. For most of its 2000km the line would follow a route about 100km north of the Amur River, out of range of Manchuria on the southern bank of the river. Winters are particularly harsh in this region and consequently track-laying could only take place over the four warmer months; even in mid-summer considerable amounts of dynamite were needed to blast through the permafrost. There were the usual problems with insects and disease but as the rest of the railway was operating it was comparatively easy to transport workers in from west of the Urals. By 1916 the long bridge over the Amur at Khabarovsk had been completed and the railway was opened. Ironically the Japanese, as allies of the White Russians, in 1918 took over the running of the Amur Railway during the Civil War.

mineral is added to steel to make it suitable for high-speed cutting tools. Scattered along the line are molybdenum and gold mines.

Km6670: Zilovo Зилово (●) The adjacent town is called Aksenovo-Zilovskoye (Аксеново-Зиловское). Southwards were the gold mines of the Kara region, also visited by Kennan, who found 2500 convicts working under appalling conditions. These mines were the property of the Tsar and from them and other Imperial mines in Eastern Siberia he could expect an average of 1630kg (3600 lb) of pure gold each year.

Km6789: Ksenyevskaya Ксеньевская (●) From here the line continues across the forested southern slopes of the Eastern Yablonovy Range for 200km with occasional good views over the trees.

Km6906: Mogocha Могоча (●●●) (pop: 17,500) This ugly railway settlement in the Bolshoy Amazar River Valley is probably one of the harshest places on the Trans-Siberian route to live because of permafrost and summer sun. In winter the top 10cm of earth that thawed over the summer freeze again to as low as -60°C (-87°F), killing all but the hardiest plants, while the intense summer sun singes most young shoots. The town was founded in 1910 when this section of the Trans-Siberian was being built, and later became the base for geological research expeditions seeking gold in the hills.

The town of **Olekminsk** lies on the Lena River about 700km due north of here (this being no more than a short hike for a Siberian, for, as Russian guides never tire of saying, 'In Siberia a thousand kilometres is nothing to travel and a litre of vodka is nothing to drink', although these days they rarely add the rest of the aphorism, 'and a hundred roubles is nothing to spend'). Olekminsk holds the world record for the widest annual temperature range, from minus 60°C (minus 87°F) to plus 45°C (113°F).

This was also the place of exile in the 18th century for a bizarre Christian sect whose followers were known as the Skoptsy. They saw their salvation in abstinence and castrated themselves to be sure of a place in heaven. They lived in mixed communities which they referred to as 'ships', each having a 'helmsman' and 'crew'. They avoided drink and tobacco and were excellent farmers. Since Olekminsk is experiencing something of a baby-boom at present it must be assumed that the more unconventional practices of the Skoptsy have been abandoned.

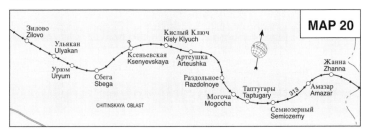

Km7010: Amazar Амазар **(●●●)**   The remains of a large strategic reserve of steam engines can be seen here. About 100km southwards the Shilka flows into the Amur (Heiling Chu to the Chinese). The Amur rises in Mongolia and flows 2800km along the frontier with China into the Pacific at the Sea of Okhotsk. The river is exceptionally rich in fish and navigable for six months of the year. Russians explored the Amur region in the 17th century, but the 1689 Treaty of Nerchinsk with the Chinese was to lock them out for 150 years. Colonization began in the mid-19th century with Cossack garrisons along the river. By 1860 the Amur Basin had 60 villages with a population of 11,000. The Amur is still a vital communications link in the area.

Km7075:   The administrative frontier between Chitinskaya and Amurskaya oblasts also marks the border between Siberia and the Far Eastern Territories. **Amurskaya Oblast** covers 363,700 sq km in the middle part of the Amur basin and extends to the Stanovoy Range in the north. The southern region of the oblast is a fertile plain where wheat, soya-beans, flax and sunflowers are grown. Most of the area in the north is under thick forest.

Km7119: Yerofei-Pavlovich Ерофей-Павлович **(●●●)**   The town is named in honour of the brutal explorer Yerofei Pavlovich Khabarov (see p91). At the eastern end of the station (N) is a **steam locomotive** (Em726-88) on a plinth.

   The river through the town is the Urka, down which Khabarov travelled with his mercenaries in 1649 to reach the Amur. The river route opened up a shortcut to the Russian Far East from Yakutsk.

   This area is particularly inhospitable, with frosts lasting from mid-October to early April, and an average January temperature of -33°C. Patches of snow persist on shaded mountainsides as late as July.

The Yakuts

Yakuts, numbering about 300,000, form the largest ethnic group in the Far Eastern Territories. They were originally semi-nomadic herders who roamed around the lands beside the Lena River. What seems to have struck 19th century travellers most about the Yakuts was their rather squalid lifestyle. They never washed or changed their clothes, they shared their huts with their reindeer and they preferred their meat and fish once it had begun to rot. They drank a form of *koumiss* (fermented mare's milk) which they froze, sometimes into huge boulders. To give the Yakuts their due, they were considerably more advanced than many other Siberian tribes. Although they were ignorant of the wheel (hardly much use in such a cold climate) they used iron for weapons and tools. Most Yakut clans had a blacksmith who was usually also a shaman, since metal-working was considered a gift from the gods. The Yakuts were unique among Siberian tribes in that they made pottery. Russian colonists treated them badly and demanded fur tributes for the Tsar. Yakuts have now almost completely adopted Russian culture, and although some are still involved in reindeer-herding, most work in mining and the timber industry.

Km7211: Urusha Уруша (●) Running mostly downhill for the next 100km the line passes through an area of taiga interspersed with uncultivated plains, most of it locked in permafrost.

Km7266: Takhtamygda Тахтамыгда A small settlement with a view (N) across the river valley (good views to the north continue for the next 150km). About half a kilometre east of the village (N) stands a prison, surrounded with barbed wire and patrolled by uniformed guards.

Km7273: Bamovskaya Бамовская This is a junction with the Little BAM, the line which runs north to join the Baikal-Amur Mainline (see p127). It is not advisable to get off the train here without knowing when your connecting train up the Little BAM will arrive as only a few head north each day; change at Skovorodino instead. Bamovskaya has no hotel.

East of the junction there are good views (S) between Km7295 and Km7300.

Km7306: Skovorodino Сковородино (●) (pop: 14,100) Named after a revolutionary leader killed here in 1920 during the Russian Civil War, Skovorodino is the first stop on the Trans-Siberian line for trains travelling down the Little BAM from Tynda to Khabarovsk. If you are getting off the Trans-Siberian to go up the Little BAM, Skovorodino is the place to do it. There's also a railway depot, forestry mills and a permafrost research station.

You can see a lime-green P36-0091 **steam locomotive** by the station platform.

Km7323: Bolshoy Never Большой Невер On the left (N) side of the railway is the 800km long Amur Yakutsk Highway ('highway' being something of a misnomer). This terminates in **Yakutsk** (see p264), capital of the Republic of Sakha, formerly known as Yakutia. This must be one of the most dismal places on the planet, for the region, which is about 13 times the size of Britain, is entirely covered with permafrost. Even in mid-summer the soil in Yakutsk is frozen solid to a depth of over 100m.

To the east the scenery becomes more appealing. There are good views at Km7318-25 (N) and around Km7335 (N). After the tunnel (Km7343-5) there's

a long view (S) down a valley towards China, with more views (S) at Km7387 and Km7426-28.

Km7501: Magdagachi Магдагачи (●●●) The train descends gently through Magdagachi, out of the taiga and onto a wide plain.

Km7566: Tygda Тыгда (●) There is usually a short stop here.

Km7602: Ushumun Ушумун The border with China is no more than 40km south-west of here. The train turns south-eastwards again, soon crossing an obvious climatic boundary and a not-so-obvious one marking the southern border of permafrost. From here on the larches grow much taller, reaching 35m, and birches and oaks spring up. These oaks are different from European oaks as they do not lose their leaves in winter but retain them even though they are stiff and brown. The train continues across flat lands with small clumps of trees.

Km7723: Shimanovskaya Шимановская (●) (pop: 25,000) Named after a revolutionary hero, this town played an important part in the development of both the Trans-Siberian and BAM railways. There's a small museum in Shimanovskaya. To the south the land becomes more fertile and parts of the wide plain are under cultivation.

Km7772: Ledinaya Лединая Hidden away in the trees just to the north of this station is the once-secret Svobodny-18 cosmodrome. One of the advantages of this facility over over the northern Russian Plesetsk cosmodrome is said to be its lower latitude (meaning smaller rockets for the same payload). Those interested in visiting the site may not get much further than the station!

Km7815: Svobodny Свободный (●) (pop: 70,600) An attractive town on the right bank of the Zeya River, Svobodny has a proud history associated with the railways. It was founded in 1912 as Alekseyevsk, in honour of the Tsar's haemophiliac son Alexei. It expanded rapidly into a major railway town, with factories building carriages, plus a hospital, schools and an orphanage all sponsored by the railways. By the mid 1930s it was headquarters for both the Amur section of the Trans-Siberian and the new BAM project. There's a **railway museum** here.

Beyond the town the line crosses the Zeya River, the Amur's largest Russian

MAP 22

Blagoveshchensk – the New York of Siberia

Blagoveshchensk, administrative capital of Amurskaya Oblast, is a large industrial centre of 200,000 people on the left bank of the Amur River. The name means 'Good News', for it was here in 1858 that Count Muravyev-Amursky announced the signing of the treaty under which China granted Russia the Amur region. The city became a centre of colonization, growing fast in the second half of the 19th century. Locals called it 'the New York of Siberia' because its streets were laid out in a grid pattern, American-style. It became the major port on the voyage between Sretensk and Khabarovsk in the days before the Amur Railway.

In July 1900 Blagoveshchensk witnessed the cold-blooded massacre of its entire Chinese population (several thousand people) by Cossack forces, in retaliation for the murders of Europeans in China during the Boxer Rebellion. Annette Meakin wrote: 'The Cossacks, who were little better than savages, threw themselves on the helpless Chinese ... and drove them down to the water's edge. Those who could not get across on rafts were either brutally massacred on the banks or pushed into the water and drowned. The scene which followed was horrible beyond description, and the river was black with dead bodies for weeks afterwards. I have this from no less than five eye-witnesses.'

Good relations between the people of Blagoveshchensk and their Chinese neighbours across the river in the city of Heihe have been cemented in recent years with a rise in cross-border trade. Siberian lumber and machinery is ferried across the Amur to be exchanged for Chinese consumer goods. Heihe is connected by rail to Harbin, with onward links to Beijing. There is no bridge but ferries cross the river six times a day.

This border crossing has recently been opened to foreign visitors, and while there are few amenities on the Chinese side, for the moment this is quite probably the cheapest permitted land route from Moscow to Beijing. Blagoveshchensk has enough of interest to occupy a couple of days. The best accommodation is at *Hotel Zeya* (☎ 41622-21100), ul Kalinina 8. Travel agents who can help organize the river crossing and rail tickets on the other side include Intourist (☎ 416 22-45772), ul Lenina 108/2, and Amurturist (☎ 416 22-27798, 90377, 23122, 🖹 27798, 23122), ul Kuznechnaya 1.

tributary. In the rainy season the water level may rise as fast as 30cm per hour and 10m floods have been recorded.

The area beyond the river, called the Zeysko-Bureinskaya Plain, is the main granary for the Russian Far East. This is the most highly populated area of the Amur region with villages every 10-20km separated by fields of barley, soya beans and melons. Climate and landscape are similar to parts of Ukraine and attracted many Ukrainians in the 19th century. Today over half the locals are of Ukrainian descent. You can easily spot their white-washed houses (*khatas*). The solid log constructions with overlapping log ends are Russian.

Km7873: Belogorsk (●●●+) Белогорск (pop: 74,100)

Some older folk among the 70,000 inhabitants of this agricultural centre must find it difficult to remember the name of their city as it has been changed so many times. It was founded in 1860 as Aleksandrovka, which stuck until 1935 when the local council decided it should be changed to the rather more impressive Kuybyshevkavostochnaya. Just when everyone had got used to this exotic mouthful it changed again, to boring Belogorsk.

There's a branch line from Belogorsk to **Blagoveshchensk** (see p375). In Belogorsk you can stay at the basic *Hotel Zarya* (☎ 24101-23750), ul Partizanskaya 23.

You can see a P36-0091 **steam locomotive** as you leave the station.

Km7992: Zavitaya Завитая (●) (pop: 22,300) This town is famous for soya bean oil and soya flour. There is a 90km branch line to the south which terminates at Poyarkovo on the Chinese–Russian border. Only Chinese and Russian passport holders can cross there.

Km8037: Bureya Бурея (●) On the river of the same name, this town was once the centre of a large gold mining region. It now produces tools for the coal mining industry.

The area was once inhabited by several different tribes, most of whom were Shamanists. The **Manegres** were a nomadic people whose trade-mark was their shaven heads, save for one long pig-tail. The **Birars** lived in hive-shaped huts beside the Bureya and grew vegetables and fruit. North of here lived the **Tungus** (Evenki), who were hunters, and the **Orochen**, who herded reindeer.

To the east were the **Goldi**, described thus in the *1900 Guide to the Great Siberian Railway*: 'They are below average stature, and have a broad and flat face with a snub nose, thick lips, eyes shaped after the Mongolian fashion and prominent cheek-bones ... The women adorn themselves with earrings and pendants. Some of them, as a mark of particular elegance, introduce one or several small rings into the partition of the nose. The people of this tribe are characterized by great honesty, frankness and good will ... Their costume is very various and of all colours; they may at different times be seen wearing a Russian overcoat, a fish-skin suit or the Chinese dress.'

Km8088: Arkhara Архара (●) A stop at the station here is usual, with women selling snacks and fruit on the platform.

Km8118: Uril Урил On the right (S) side of the line from here to the next station, Kundur, is the Khingan Nature Reserve. The sanctuary consists of swampy lowlands dotted with Amur velvet trees and Korean cedar pine woods with a thick undergrowth of hazel trees, wild grapes and wild pepper which is related to ginseng. The sanctuary is rich in Mongol and Siberian animals seldom encountered elsewhere, including a raccoon-like dog.

Km8150-8198: There are good photo opportunities on this stretch as the train winds around the valleys.

Km8167: A second tunnel under construction here should now be complete.

Km8184: This is the administrative frontier between Amurskaya Oblast and Khabarovsky Kray. Khabarovsky Kray is, like much of Russia east of the Urals, composed almost entirely of swampy taiga. In the far south, however, there is an area of deciduous trees. Although the kray is extremely rich in minerals, its economy is heavily based on wood-processing, fishing and the petroleum industry.

—————————— **Km8184-9289 TIME ZONE MT + 7** ——————————

Local time is now Moscow Time + 7 hours. East of this frontier you enter an autonomous oblast within Khabarovsky Kray. Some stations between Obluchye and Priamurskaya are signposted in Yiddish as well as Russian, for this is part of the Yevreyskaya (Jewish) Autonomous Oblast, otherwise known as **Birobidzhan**, after its capital.

This remote region was set aside for Jewish emigration in 1928 (and the oblast established in 1934), though it never proved popular. The oblast's Jewish population today stands at about 6000 – 3% of the approximately 200,000 inhabitants of this 36,000 sq km territory.

A glossy coffee-table book about Birobidzhan (written in Russian, Yiddish and English) used to be sold in the bookshops of Khabarovsk. After pages of smiling cement-factory workers, beaming miners and happy-looking milk-maids, the book ends with the following statement: 'The flourishing of the economy and culture of the Jewish Autonomous Region, the happiness of the people of labour of various nationalities inhabiting the Region, their equality, friendship and co-operation lay bare the hypocrisy (sic) of the propaganda cam-paign launched by the ringleaders of Israel and international Zionism, about the "disastrous situation" of Jews in the Soviet Union, about the "oppression and persecution" they are supposedly being subjected to. The working people of Jewish nationality wrathfully condemn the predatory policy of the ruling circles of Israel and give a resolute rebuff to the Zionist provocateurs.' What the book doesn't tell you is that in Stalin's anti-Jewish purges Birobidzhan's synagogue was closed and the speaking of Yiddish outlawed even here.

Km8198: Obluchye Облучье (●●●) (pop: 11,700) The town is just inside the border of the Jewish Autonomous Oblast. The tunnel just east of Obluchye was the first in the world to be bored through permafrost.

Km8234: Izvestkovaya Известковая The name means 'limestone' and there are large quarries in the area. The town sits at the junction of the Trans-Siberian and a 360km branch line to Novy Urgal on the BAM railway. Much of this branch line was built by Japanese POWs until their repatriation in 1949, and Japanese graves litter the area. Izvestkovaya is a typical small town with a can-teen, post office, dairy farm and market but little else. The old part of town, with its rustic wooden buildings and household garden plots, is hidden in the trees to the west.

Km8306: Bira Бира The obelisk on the platform commemorates the good works of local philanthropist Nikolai Trofemovich and his wife. The railway runs beside the Bira River for about 100km and passes through hills rich with the ingredients of cement.

Km8351: Birobidzhan Биробиджан (●) (pop: 77,000) [see p276]
Originally known as Tikhonkaya, the capital of the 'Jewish' region was founded in 1928 on the Bira River. Once famous for the bright-red, self-propelled combine harvesters made at the Dalselmash factory and exported to Cuba, Mexico, Iraq and China, the town has been hard hit by the economic downturn. The few remaining Jewish people are leaving as fast as they can get their papers organized.

Just east of Birobidzhan on the left (N) you pass the huge **Iyuan-Koran Memorial** which commemorates a fierce Russian Civil War battle on this site in 1922. Near the memorial are the mass graves of fallen Red Guards.

Km8480: Volochayevka 1 Волочаевка 1 This small station is just a junction for the Trans-Siberian and the 344km railway to Komsomolsk-na-Amur. Volochayevka is famous as the scene of a major battle during the Russian Civil War, which took place in temperatures as low as -35°C (there is a panoramic painting of the battle in Khabarovsk's Museum of Local History). The town itself is 9km from the station.

Km8512: Priamurskaya Приамурская This small town is just on the border of the Jewish Autonomous Region.

After crossing 3km of swamp and small streams you reach the 2.6km **bridge across the Amur River**, the longest bridge on the Trans-Siberian and completed in 1998. It's a combined rail and road bridge, with trains running beneath the road. Before it opened cars had to cross the Amur by ferry and trains used an old bridge, completed in 1916 and now dismantled. There is also a 7km tunnel under the Amur, built in 1937-42 for 'strategic reasons', and westbound trains sometimes use this. Khabarovsk stretches along the eastern bank of the river and the beaches here are packed with sunbathers on summer weekends. The main fishing port is 2.5km upstream.

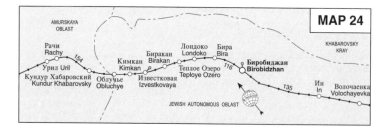

Km8521: Khabarovsk Хабаровск (●●●) (pop: 604,300) [see p278]

Khabarovsk was founded in 1858 as a military outpost against the Chinese. Today it is the most pleasant of all Russian Far East cities.

The train normally stops here for at least 20 minutes. Souvenirs and maps are sold in the Intourist Hall at the station. Outside the station there's an impressive statue of Yerofei Pavlovich Khabarov, the city's founder.

From Khabarovsk the line runs south to Vladivostok following the Ussuri River and the border with China. This region is a mixture of hilly country and wide flat valleys. Some 200km east of the line lies the Sikhote Alin Mountain Range, where most of the rivers you will cross have their source. In the south, firs and pines give way to a wide range of deciduous trees. There are good views across the plains to China.

Km8597:
Here is the longest bridge on the Ussuri Railway. It crosses the Khor River, one of the Ussuri's widest tributaries, whose turbulent waters made its construction in 1897 extremely difficult.

Km8598: Pereyaslavka Переяславка
The town around the station is called Verino (Верино) and was the site of a fierce Civil War battle. In front of the station there is a war memorial. There's a museum in Verino.

Km8621: Khor Хор
The train crosses the Khor River again. The river here marks the southern boundary of the 46,000 hectare **Bolshoy-Khekhzirzky Sanctuary**.

The indigenous Udegeytsy people have a legend to explain why plants from both north and south Siberia are found here. Once two birds flying in opposite directions collided in thick fog and dropped their loads. They'd been sent by the Good Spirit of the South and Good Spirit of the North to throw seeds on the desert plains and mountains respectively. Since then, southern wild grapevines wind around northern pine trees and the northern berry *klukva* grows side by side with the southern spiky palm *aralia,* with its metre-long leaves.

The vegetation changes considerably with elevation. At the foot of the mountains broadleaf species dominate. On the slopes are cedar, Amur velvet ash (cork is produced from the black bark) and Manchurian nut trees while on higher slopes angular pine and fir trees dominate.

The Ussuri Railway (Km8531-9441)
The first plans for the Ussuri Line, as the section between Khabarovsk and Vladivostok is called, were made in 1875 and the foundation stone for the whole of the Trans-Siberian Railway was laid in Vladivostok by Tsarevich Nicholas in 1891. Priority was given to the Ussuri line as it was seen as vital for ensuring that the strategic port of Vladivostok was not cut off by the Chinese. This was difficult territory for railway building. There was a severe shortage of labour. The local Goldi tribe, who at the time were happily existing in the Stone Age, were of no help, unable to grasp the concept of paid labour nor to understand the point of the work, never having seen a train. Prisoners recruited from the jails of Sakhalin Island were not as co-operative as convicts used on other sections of the Trans-Siberian, preferring an evening of robbery and murder in Vladivostok to the railway camps. The men here were plagued not only by vicious mosquitoes, like their fellow-workers on other sections of the line, but also by the man-eating tigers which roamed the thick forests beside the line. Siberian anthrax decimated the already small population of pack animals, and rails and equipment had to be shipped from Europe, taking up to two months to reach Vladivostok.
    In spite of these difficulties the line was opened in 1897, 43 million roubles having been spent on its construction. It was double tracked in the 1930s and the branch line to Nakhodka was built after the Second World War.

Km8642: Vyazemskaya Вяземская (●●●)   (pop: 18,200) This railway town was founded in 1895 and during the Russian Civil War there was fierce fighting around it. There are several memorials and a museum. To the west of the station is a plinthed **Ea series locomotive**. Some 20km to the south the countryside changes dramatically with forests of maple, alder, willow and elm.

Km8756: Bikin Бикин (●)   According to the *1900 Guide to the Great Siberian Railway* the line crossed the river here and followed it south for 30km. The book states that 'this is one of the most picturesque parts of the line offering an alpine scenery. The cuttings made in basalt rocks seem to be protected by columns of cyclopean construction. Wide expanses lying amidst the cliffs are covered with a most various vegetation, shading numerous Chinese huts. The river is enlivened by the small boats of the Golds and other natives, moving swiftly on the water's surface.' Unfortunately the line does not follow exactly the same route now, instead traversing rolling hills and marshy land strewn with telegraph poles keeling over at drunken angles.
    The railway crosses the Bikin River. About 200km upstream is Krasny Yar, the largest village of the indigenous **Udeghe**. Known as the Forest People for their lifestyle of fishing, hunting and gathering in the taiga, the Udeghe are facing the end of their way of life because of the voracious logging industry.

Between Bikin and Zvenyevoy is the administrative border between Khabarovsky Kray and Primorsky Kray. **Primorsky Kray** has a population of over two million people.

Km8839: Guberovo Губерово (●●●)   There is a leisurely stop here.

Decline of the Amur Tiger

Once the scourge of railway construction workers, the largest member of the cat family is now just another zoological statistic dwindling towards extinction. The tigers' habitat once stretched as far west as Lake Baikal and to Beijing in the south but now only 250-350 cats remain in an area from Vladivostok north into the Sikhote Alin Range.

Large-scale forest clearance for timber sold to Japan and Korea forces tigers out of their territory. A male tiger can weigh up to 380kg (840lbs), almost twice the size of a lion, and requires about 400 sq km of hunting ground. A decline in their food source (deer and wild boar) has also reduced the population and forced remaining tigers to roam ever larger areas for prey.

In 1987 a train just outside Nakhodka was held up by a tiger that had strayed onto the tracks. An Amur tiger can be worth as much as US$10,000 in China, Korea and Taiwan for the medicinal value that parts of its body are believed to have, and for its skin. Poachers now slip across Russian borders that are no longer tightly patrolled.

The animals are found in and around several nature reserves in this area: Kedrovaya Pad (near Vladivostok), Lazo and Sikhote Alin, but your chances of seeing a live Amur tiger here are close to zero. There are in fact about twice as many of them in zoos around the world as in the wild.

Km8890: Dalnerechensk Дальнереченск (●) (pop: 32,200) Founded by Cossacks in 1895, this town quickly became a timber centre thanks to the region's large pine and red cedar forests. A factory here is one of the few in Russia which still produces wooden barrels for salted fish and seal blubber.

The town has a museum and a memorial to the guards killed in the 1969 border conflict with the Chinese over Damansky Island in the Ussuri River. There were several skirmishes and each country claimed the communist high ground as being the true Marxist revolutionary state. As both began preparing for nuclear confrontation a political solution was reached when Soviet premier Alexei Kosygin stopped in Beijing on his way home from the funeral of Ho Chi Minh. Although progress has been made the border demarcation has not yet been finalized.

Km8900: Muravyevo-Amurskaya / Lazo Муравьево-Амурская / Лазо
This station is named after the explorer and governor of Eastern Siberian, Count Nikolai Muravyev-Amursky. It was formerly known as Lazo in honour of the communist revolutionary SG Lazo (1894-1920), who was captured in 1920 by the Japanese when they invaded the Russian Far East, and executed at the station, allegedly by being thrown alive into a steam engine firebox. Two other revolutionaries, Lutsky and Sibirtsev, met a similar fate and a monument to all three stands in front of the station.

Km8941: Ruzhino Ружино (●●) A long stop for the *Rossiya* here.

Km8991: Shmakovka Шмаковка About 29km from the station is the mostly derelict Shmakovsky Trinity-St Nicholas Monastery, with a very curious history. Its land is now being fought over by two groups, both claiming to be its original owners. The Russian Orthodox Church maintains they built the monastery; the Russian military accept its religious past but claim that they constructed the monastery as a front for an espionage academy. It does seem more than a little coincidental that ex-army officer and Father-Superior Aleksei, who was commissioned to build the monastery, selected a site next to the remote Tikhmenevo telegraph station. This was no ordinary relay station but was classified a 'top secret military object' connected to Khabarovsk by an underground cable. And the monastery was certainly well equipped: there was even a printing press and photo lab. The military sanatorium here still operates today and the monastery is also home to 10 monks who are slowly rebuilding it.

Km9050: Spassk-Dalny Спасск-Дальний (●●●) (pop: 54,800) Alexander Solzhenitsyn was imprisoned in this town, where he helped build the large cement works that still operates here.

About 40km west is Lake Khanka which has a surface area of 4000 sq km but is nowhere more than 4m deep The lake is famous for the lotus flower *eurea* which has giant buds and 2m wide leaves.

Km9092: Muchnaya Мучная (●) Usually a short stop here.

Km9109: Sibirtsevo Сибирцево (●) This area is the centre of an extremely fertile region where wheat, oats, soya beans and rice are grown. Because of labour shortages these are aerially sown and fertilized. The climate of the southern part of the Russian Far East makes most areas ideal for agriculture as the warm summer rains create a hothouse atmosphere.

A branch line runs from here through dairy-farming countryside to Lake Khanka. From Sibirtsevo south, the line winds down to Ussurisk.

Km9177: Ussurisk Уссурийск (●●●) (pop: 154,500) The fertile area around Ussurisk has been inhabited for over 1000 years, first as the legendary kingdom of Bokhai and then by the Manchus. In the mid-19th century European emigrants began to settle here. At that time the town was called Nikolskoye, in honour of the Tsar. The town stands at the junction of the Ussuri and Chinese Eastern railways. When Tsarevich Nicholas visited in 1891 there were three wooden churches, a half-built stone cathedral and a population of 8000, many

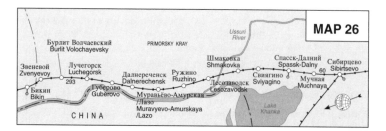

of them Chinese. Ussurisk is a now an agricultural and engineering centre, home of the Okean brand of refrigerator.

From Ussurisk there are branch lines to Harbin in China via the East Chinese Railway and to Pyongyang in North Korea. The scenery is very different from the Siberian taiga. The train winds through the hills in misty forests of deciduous trees (oak, elm, alder and maple) and across European-looking meadows filled with Friesian cows and willow trees.

Km9221: Amursky Zaliv Амурский Залив A branch line runs from here to the port of **Nakhodka**. Since most passenger ships now leave from Vladivostok there's little reason for visiting. For information on the line to Nakhodka, see p384.

Km9246: If you're heading east keep a lookout on the right (S) for your first glimpse of the Pacific Ocean.

Km9255: Uglovaya Угловая (●) The town here, called Trudovoye (Трудовое), sits at the northern edge of Uglovy Zaliv (Uglovy Bay). Pleasant beaches and clean water make it a popular swimming spot for Vladivostok's day trippers.

East of the station the railway travels down a peninsula named in honour of the famous Russian explorer, Count Nikolai Muravyev-Amursky.

Km9262: Sadgorod Садгород Near Sadgorod (which means 'garden city') was a station called Khilkovo, named in honour of Prince MI Khilkov, Minister of Ways of Communication in the Tsarist government and one of the main supporters of the Trans-Siberian. Khilkovo station has long since disappeared.

The accepted date for the start of construction of the Trans-Siberian Railway is 19 May 1891, although by that time an 18km section had already been laid from Vladivostok to Sadgorod. The Tsar's son Nicholas travelled up this line and formally inaugurated the project by tipping a barrow of ballast onto the embankment at Sadgorod, then returned by train to unveil a commemorative plaque at Vladivostok.

Km9269: Sanatornaya Санаторная The hotels that rate as Vladivostok's best are located here but only local trains will make a stop.

> **The Vladivostok–Nakhodka Railway**
> Few travellers visit Nakhodka since the Japanese ferry which connects
> with Trans-Siberian trains now docks at Vladivostok, which is also the location of the
> only airport in the region. The journey of some 216km from Vladivostok to
> Tikhookeanskaya (Тихоокеанская), the port just south-west of Nakhodka, runs
> through Uglovaya (Угловая) at Km34, the mining and industrial city of Artem-
> Primorski (Артем-Приморский) at Km43, Novonezhino (Новонежино) at Km91,
> Partizansk (Партизанск) at Km170, past the vineyards of the Suchan River Valley
> to Nakhodka (Находка) at Km206, and on to the terminus at Tikhookeanskaya.

Km9281: Vtoraya Rechka Вторая Речка Vladivostok's main long-distance bus station is here (including buses for the airport).

Km9284: Pervaya Rechka Первая Речка According to the original 1880s
plan for the Trans-Siberian this was to have been the railway's terminus, with a
small branch line extending to Vladivostok. Despite the difficulties of building
a multi-track railway along the steep shore, it was decided in the 1890s to
extend the Trans-Siberian through to Vladivostok. Near Pervaya Rechka was a
small settlement called Convicts' Hamlet, inhabited by exiled settlers who had
completed their sentences.

Km9289: Vladivostok Владивосток (pop: 592,100)   [see p287]
The beginning or the end of your journey.

Trans-Mongolian Route

The branch line to Mongolia and China leaves the main Trans-Siberian route at Zaudinsky, east of Ulan Ude. From there it takes $5^1/_2$ hours to cover the 250km to the Russia–Mongolia border. Between Ulan Ude and the border the train travels through the heart of Buryatia, the Buryat Republic.

Note that the line turns predominantly southwards after Zaudinsky. For the entire Trans-Mongolian line we shall use (E) and (W) to show which side of the train points of interest are located. Thus if you're coming from Moscow (E) means the left side of the train and (W) the right.

Km5642: Ulan Ude Улан Удэ (pop: 371,000) [see p266]
The suburbs of Ulan Ude extend for several kilometres and there are good views back to the city at Km5659 (W) as the train climbs high above the east bank of the Selenga River. The line follows the valley of the Selenga all the way to the Mongolian border. The scenery changes remarkably quickly to the rolling green hills which make excellent pasture for the area's many cattle. Passing through the little station of **Sayatun** (Km5677) the line crosses to the west bank of the river at Km5689-90 and continues to climb through **Ubukun** (Km5732).

Km5769: Zagustay Загустай The station sits in the shadow of an ugly factory belching out thick smoke. About 6km from here is the mining town of **Gusinoozyorsk** (Гусиноозёрск), which grew from nothing to today's population of some 29,000 following the 1939 discovery of a huge coal basin.

The Trans-Mongolian Line
This route to China is an ancient one, followed for centuries by tea-caravans between Peking and Moscow. Travelling non-stop, foreigners and imperial messengers could manage the journey in 40 days of acute discomfort. This was the route of the 1907 Peking to Paris Rally, the great motor race that was won by the Italian Prince Borghese and journalist Luigi Barzini in their 40-horsepower Itala. Until the middle of the 20th century a rough track across the steppelands of northern Mongolia and the Gobi Desert in the south was the only route through this desolate country.

In 1940 a branch line was built between Ulan Ude and the Mongolian border. After the Second World War work started on a line south from Naushki, and in 1949 this reached the Mongolian capital, Ulan Bator. The line between Ulan Bator and Beijing was begun in 1953 with a workforce of Russians, Mongolians and Chinese. By early 1956 it was completed and a regular rail service began between Ulan Ude and Beijing.

Km5771-99: Goose Lake

The line passes along the western shore of Gusinoye Ozero (Goose Lake). Until the Revolution the most important Buddhist *datsan* (lamasery) north of Ulan Bator was at **Selenginsk**, 20km to the south-east and overlooking the lake.

In 1887 George Kennan, while researching his book on Siberian prisons, arrived in Selenginsk and visited the datsan. 'We were tired of prisons and the exile system and had enough misery,' he wrote. Nevertheless he found Selenginsk 'a wretched little Buriat town'. At the datsan Kennan and his companions were entertained by the Khamba Lama, the chief lama, who claimed through an interpreter that they were the first foreigners ever to visit his lamasery. They were treated to dinner and a special dance performance. The Khamba Lama had never heard of America, Kennan's native land; and, unaware that the earth was anything but flat, was nonplussed when Kennan explained that 'it lies nearly under our feet; and if we could go directly through the earth, this would be the shortest way to reach it'.

Today Selenginsk datsan is operating again.

Km5780: Gusinoye Ozero Гусиное Озеро (●)

The line leaves the lake after this station and continues to climb from one valley to another, passing though **Selenduma** (Km5827) and still following the river.

The old border town of Kyakhta

The border post for the railway is at the modern town of Naushki, but for the tea-caravans of old the crossing was near the large town of **Kyakhta**, 20km east of Naushki. In the 18th and 19th centuries this town, together with **Maimachen** on the Mongolian side of the border, formed one of the world's most important trading centres, based almost entirely on the tea trade. Great camel caravans brought the precious leaves here from Peking, across the Gobi Desert. Kyakhta was a bustling town of wealthy traders and tea-barons until the Trans-Siberian provided a cheaper way to move tea from China to European Russia. Maimachen is now called Altan Bulak.

On 24 June 1907 Prince Borghese and his team roared into town in their Itala and were entertained royally by local dignitaries. The morale of the tea-merchants had sunk with the recent decline in trade but was greatly boosted by the arrival of the car and they began making plans for their own motor-caravans.

An earlier visitor to these border towns was George Kennan, who attended a banquet in Maimachen where he was served dog-meat dumplings, cocks' heads in vinegar and fried lichen from birch trees, washed down by several bottles of French champagne. He was sick for the next two weeks.

In January 1920 Kyakhta witnessed a particularly appalling atrocity when the sadistic White Army General Semenov despatched 800 people suspected of being communists, using a different method of execution each day.

Today Kyakhta has a population of 18,000 and a large border-post garrison nearby. It's an interesting place to visit, however, with many crumbling old buildings and several vast churches hinting at prosperous times past. There's an impressive regional museum, and basic accommodation at the *Hotel Druzhba*.

Km5852 (W): Dzhida Джида **(●)** There is what appears to be a small air-base here, with hangars dug into hummocks in the ground.

Km5895: Naushki Наушки **(●●●++)** At this **Russian border post** the train stops for at least two hours, usually for considerably longer. Customs officials collect passports, visas and currency declaration forms (see Scam, p64), returning them (often to the carriage attendant) after about half an hour. It would be unwise to get off the train before you've got your passport back since guards may not let you back on the train without it.

It's worth noting that the station tends to be crowded with black marketeers and some may get on the train and start selling roubles to travellers heading west; don't buy too many as the rate is unlikely to be favourable – and **watch your valuables** when these traders are around. There's a **bank** on the platform, signposted in English, but the exchange rate is poor (about 5% below the standard rate). The bank is a long way down the platform, in the Mongolia direction. East-bound travellers should exchange any unspent roubles here as it's difficult to exchange them outside Russia.

It's worth noting that the toilets on the train remain locked until you leave the border post. The station lavatories would not win any hygiene awards but are located in the building to the left of the station building. Have your insect repellent to hand as the air can be thick with mosquitoes in summer.

Km5900: Russia–Mongolia border (●) The border, called Dozorny (Дозорный, meaning 'patrolled') on timetables, is marked by a menacing-looking electrified fence. The train pauses here, but don't even think about getting out! The landscape is actually rather attractive, with the impressive Selenga River (prone to flooding in late summer) to the south and hills rising to the north.

MONGOLIA

Kilometre numbers below are based upon Mongolian kilometre posts. For approximate cumulative distances from Moscow see the timetables (p423).

Km21: Sühbaatar Сухбаатар **(●●●++)** (pop: 23,700) The customs and immigration process at this **Mongolian border town** used to be a fairly nervewracking affair. Whole compartments would be rigorously searched, mag-

Mongolia

Mongolia is one of those countries, like Guyana or Chad, that rarely makes headlines unless there's a dramatic change of leadership or policy. With just 2,700,000 people (a third of them below the age of 14) in an area the size of Western Europe or Alaska, it's a sparsely populated place. Mongolia is changing fast but the capital, Ulan Bator, is changing even faster. Nearly half the population lives in the capital, and it's estimated that over a third live below the poverty line.

Mongolia contains a surprising variety of terrain: a vast undulating plain in the east, the Gobi Desert to the south, and snow-capped mountains and extensive forests in the west. Most of the eastern plain is at an elevation of 1500m and the sun shines here for around 250 days of the year.

For many centuries the deserts and grasslands of Mongolia have been inhabited by nomadic herders living in felt tents (*yurts* or *ghers*). At certain times in world history they have come together under a powerful leader, the most famous being Genghis Khan and his grandson Kublai Khan in the 13th century. Kublai Khan introduced Tibetan Buddhism to the country although it was not until the early 17th century that most Mongolians were converted and Buddhism gained a strong grip on the country.

By the late 17th century control of Mongolia and its trade routes was in the hands of the Manchus. In 1911 the country became an independent monarchy, in effect a theocratic state since power lay with the 'Living Buddha', the chief representative of Buddhism in Mongolia, at Urga (now Ulan Bator). In 1921 a communist government took power and, with considerable help from the Soviet Union, set out to modernize a country that was technologically in the Dark Ages.

In 1990 the constitution was amended to legalize opposition parties, although the first democratic elections were won by the communist Mongolian People's Revolutionary Party (MPRP). The 1996 presidential election was won by the MPRP's Natsagiin Bagabandi, but parliamentary elections the same year saw the formation of Mongolia's first non-communist government under the Democratic Union Coalition (DUC). After the DUC's pledge to introduce market reforms was stalled by former communists, the MPRC won the 2000 parliamentary election by a landslide, with Bagabandi re-elected the following year. The next parliamentary elections are due in 2004, and presidential elections in 2005.

The country is divided into 18 *aimaks* (districts). The railway line passes through three of these (Selenga, Tov and Dornogov).

azines confiscated and film ripped out of cameras. It's all rather tame now for foreigners, although the baggage of local travellers is thoroughly inspected. During the procedures a diesel engine is attached. The Mongolian dining-car, however, is not added until Ulan Bator.

Some travellers have managed to get Mongolian visas on arrival here (at a cost of US$50) but others have been refused: the situation is subject to changing regulations and to the whims of border officials. Being turned back here is decidedly not worth the hassle, so don't count on getting a visa here.

The station building is an excellent example of whimsical Mongolian railway architecture. It's an incredible mélange of architectural styles: mock Gothic, Moghul and Modern topped with crenellations and painted what looks like lime green in the artificial light. Strawberry pink is the other popular colour for Mongolian station buildings.

Situated at the confluence of the Selenga and Orhon Rivers, Sühbaatar was founded in 1940 and named after the Mongolian revolutionary leader Damdinii Sühbaatar (Sukhe Bator). It grew quickly, superseding the border town on the caravan route, Maimachen (now called Altan Bulak). Sühbaatar is now Mongolia's third largest industrial centre (although in a country so sparsely populated and industrially primitive this is not a breathtaking statistic). Matches, liquor and flour are produced here by some of the 20,000 inhabitants.

Km123: Darhan (Darkhan) Дархан **(●●●)** It takes about eight hours to cover the 380km between Sühbaatar and Ulan Bator. The train passes through the town of **Darhan**, capital of Selenga *Aimak* (district). Darhan was founded in 1961 and is now the second most important industrial centre in Mongolia after Ulan Bator. It's a show town of planned urbanization, and its population has increased from 1500 to over 69,000 since 1961. The main sources of employment are opencast mining, food production, construction and the production of leather and sheepskin coats. The town is an important junction with a branch line that runs westwards to a big mining complex at **Erdenet**, and the port serves many villages along the Selenga and Orkhon Rivers.

About 120km west of Darhan in the foothills of Mt Burenkhan is **Amarbayasgalant Monastery**. This vast 18th-century temple complex, which once housed 10,000 monks and drew pilgrims from many parts of Asia, was desecrated during an anti-religious movement in the 1930s but is now being restored with grants from the Mongolian government and UNESCO. Darhan is the closest train station to Amarbayasgalant. However, anyone interested in visiting the monastery would need a guide and their own vehicle, which can only be easily arranged from Ulan Bator.

Genghis Khan
For many decades the name of this famous Mongolian conqueror has been taboo in his home country. The Russians saw Genghis Khan as a brutal invader to be erased from the history books but with their influence rapidly fading there has been a sudden rise in Mongolian nationalism. Genghis Khan, founder of the 13th century Mongolian Empire, is a hero once more, lending his name to the most luxurious hotel in town and also to a brand of vodka.

Along with his rehabilitation have come a number of interesting characters each claiming to be his legitimate descendant. One of the best publicized was Ganjuurijin Dschero Khan, who claimed to have been smuggled out of the country to escape the Communists when he was four years old. Mongolians were intrigued to meet him, although they didn't quite know what to make of his appearance. He arrived in a military tunic, decked out with medals inscribed 'Bazooka', 'Carbine', 'Paratroopers' and 'Special Forces', which he claimed to have won in Korea and Vietnam. Support for him waned after it became apparent that he didn't speak Mongolian.

If you'd been doing this part of the journey in the not too distant past before the railway was built, you would now be swaying back and forth in the saddle of a camel, one of many in the caravan you would have joined in Kyakhta. In the 1865 edition of his *Handbook for Russia, Poland and Finland*, Murray gives the following advice: 'It is customary for caravans to travel sixteen hours a day and they come to a halt for cooking, eating and sleeping ... The Mongols are most trustworthy in their transactions, and the traveller may feel in perfect safety throughout the journey.' He also gives the following useful tips concerning local currency: 'The use of money is as yet almost unknown in this part of the country, brick-tea cut up into slices being the token of value most recognized; but small brass buttons are highly prized.'

Km232: Zuunhara (Dzhunchara) Дзунхара (●●●)   There is a long stop at this tiny station, though the town's only claim to fame is its alcohol factory.

Km381: Crossing wide open grasslands with only the occasional yurt to break the monotony, the line begins to descend into the valley where Ulan Bator is situated. Looking south you catch the first glimpse (Km386) of ugly factories on the outskirts of the city (Km396).

Km404: Ulan Bator Улаанбаатар (●●●+) (pop: 804,000)   [see p297]
(1350m/4430ft) The train spends half an hour at the Mongolian capital, giving you a chance to stretch your legs. Outside the locomotive shed on the east side of the line is a collection of **steam and diesel engines** including 2-6-2 S-116, T31-011 and T32-508 diesels, a 750mm gauge 0-8-0 469, and a 2-10-0 Ye-0266. They are beside the public road and fenced off but quite accessible. In the station building postcards (and weird Mongolian stamps which leave little room for a message on a card) can be purchased at the bar. Black marketeers may approach you to change money. Don't change too much until you're sure of the rate.

The Gobi Desert

This vast wilderness extends for 1000km north to south and 2400km west to east. Most of the part crossed by the railway is not desert of the sandy Saharan type but rolling grassy steppes. It is impressive for its emptiness: very few towns and just the occasional collection of yurts, herds of stocky Mongolian horses and small groups of camels or gazelles.

While it may not appear so, the Gobi is rich in wildlife although numbers of some species are rapidly dwindling. This is mainly the result of poaching and the destruction of habitat. There are large reserves of coal, copper, molybdenum, gold, uranium and other valuable exports. It's estimated that up to 10 billion tons of coal exist beneath the Gobi, and Japanese and Western companies are negotiating with Mongolia to extract it using strip mining techniques, which could seriously affect the delicate environmental balance. An American conservation group, Wildlife Conservation International, is helping the Mongolian Association for Conservation of Nature and Environment (MACNE) to monitor species at risk in the area. Among these are the 500 remaining wild Bactrian camels, the Gobi bear, the *kulan* (Asian wild ass) and Przewalski's wild horse (the last recorded sighting was in 1962).

The dining-car is attached here if you're en route to Beijing, and usually removed if you're Moscow-bound. For meals and souvenirs sold in the dining-car both Mongolian currency and US$ are accepted although staff seem to make up dollar prices as they go along.

Km409: Ulan Bator extends this far west. At around Km425 the line starts to climb and for the next 50km, to Km470, snakes around giving good opportunities for photos along the train. There are good views over the rolling hills on both sides of the train.

Km507: Bagakangay Багакангай Here you can see an airfield (W) with camouflaged bunkers.

Km521: Manit Манит The blue station with its tower and weather-vane looks rather like a church.

Km560: Camels are occasionally to be seen roaming across the wide, rolling plain.

Km649: Choyr Чоыр (●●●) (pop: 9300) Just behind this pink and white wedding-cake of a station is a statue of the first Mongolian cosmonaut, VVT Ertvuntz. He's had the all-over silver paint treatment but still looks impressive. The Soviet airbase here has now closed.

Km733 (W): The pond here often attracts groups of camels and antelope.

Km751: Airag Аираг The train doesn't usually stop at this small station, which is in the middle of nowhere and surrounded by scrap metal.

Km875 (E): There's a collection of old **steam locos** on display just to the west of Saynshand station.

Km876: Saynshand Саыншанд (●●●) (pop: 28,700) This is the largest town between the capital and Zamiin Uud on the southern border. Main industries include food-processing and coal-mining.

Km1113: Zamiin Uud (Dzamyn Ude) Дзамын Уде (●●●++) The station in this Mongolian border town looks like a supermarket at Christmas, with all its festive lights. There's a bank and a restaurant, both usually closed in the evening. Customs and immigration forms are collected. Customs officers

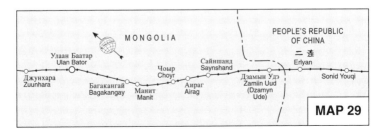

inspect the luggage of Chinese and Mongolian travellers but don't seem too interested in others. This process may take an hour and a half. If it's dark you can try to spot the soldiers standing half concealed in the undergrowth by the tracks.

THE PEOPLE'S REPUBLIC OF CHINA

The kilometre numbers below show the distance to Beijing.

Km842: Erlyan (Erenhot/Ereen) (●●●++) Chinese officials are obviously trying to outdo the evening show their Mongolian counterparts put on across the border, with a full-blown son-et-lumière. The *Vienna Waltz* blares from speakers to welcome the train and the station is decked out in red neon and fairy lights.

Chinese customs officials come on board here. If you're travelling to Beijing you must fill in health and baggage/currency declaration forms. Passports are collected.

Bogie-changing The train spends about 20 minutes at the platform and is then shunted off to the bogie-changing shed. When you get off take something warm with you as it will be several hours before you're allowed on board again.

It may be possible to stay on the train until it gets to the shed and then get off before they lock the doors (for safety reasons while raising the carriages), and watch some of the bogie-changing operations.

The Chinese railway system operates on standard gauge (as do Europe and North America), which is $3^1/_2$ inches narrower than the five-foot gauge in the former Soviet Union and Mongolia. Giant hydraulic lifts raise the carriages and the bogies are rolled out and replaced. Photography is now permitted but take care not to get in the way or the authorities may decide to restore the old ban on photography!

> ❏ **Track and markers**
> Chinese trains ride on the left side of twin tracks (unlike right-hand-drive Russia). Kilometre markers come in a variety of sizes, usually like little gravestones down at trackside, and there is some disagreement between them and the official kilometre locations on timetables etc. The book follows these markers where possible but for the last 70km of the journey they are not reliable, jumping at one point by 25km.

You can walk back to the station building but you should be careful at night as the path is not well lit. There are usually cycle-rickshaw drivers hanging round to take you, but bargain hard and be clear whether you are paying in yuan or dollars to avoid arguments at the other end.

Back in the station you can change money at the bank (passport not necessary but you do need to know your passport number), or visit the Friendship Store (Chinese vodka, Chinese champagne, beer, tea, Ritz crackers and other snacks) and bar/restaurant (if open). The loos, however, are usually in a terrible state. Upstairs is a foreigners' waiting room where fictitious literature (eg *Human Rights in China*) is available free of charge. The platform is crowded with traders, and food and drink are also sold here.

The Age of the Steam Train has not yet passed in China and it is likely that the train will be shunted back to the platform by a puffing Class 2-10-2 locomotive built in Datong (see below). Passports are returned and you depart shortly thereafter, the whole operation having taken anything from three to six hours.

Passing through towns with Mongolian names like **Sonid Youqi** and **Qahar Youyi Houqi**, you reach Jining in about five hours.

Km498: Jining (●) The bulky white modernist station building is topped by a red flag. Beside it is an extensive goods yard full of working steam engines.

Travelling due south from Jining the train leaves the province of Inner Mongolia and enters Shanxi Province. This mountainous area was a great cultural and political centre over 1000 years ago. There are hills running parallel to the west and wide fields either side of the line. The train follows the course of a river which leads it into a valley and more rugged countryside after Fenezhen.

Km415: Fenezhen Between this drab town and Datong you cross the line of the **Great Wall of China** for the first time. Occasional glimpses are all you get until the spectacular crossing at Km82.

Km371: Datong (●●) (pop: 1,276,000) This sprawling city, founded as a military outpost by Han armies, stands in the centre of the coal-rich Datong Basin. Its major tourist attraction is the **Yungang Grottoes**, a group of Buddhist cave temples in the foothills of Wuzhou Mountain (16km west of the city). These caves, dating back to 460 AD, are richly decorated and renowned as one of China's three most impressive Buddhist complexes, the others being at Luoyang and Dunhuang.

If you're stopping off here, a visit to the **Datong Locomotive Works** is an interesting and educational experience. This was one of the last places in the world where steam trains were made. In the 1980s they were turning them out at the rate of 240 locos per year, but the manufacture of the Class QJ 8WT/12WT 2-10-2 engine (133 tonnes; max speed 80kph) ceased in 1986 and the Class JS 2-8-2 (104 tonnes; max speed 85kph) in 1989; both are used for

freight haulage and shunting work. The factory now produces parts for steam and diesel locomotives and has customers in many parts of the world. Tours are conducted twice a week and must be arranged through the Datong office of China International Travel Service (CITS).

At Datong the line swings eastwards to run parallel to the Great Wall, about 20km south of it as far as Zhangjiakou. About 100km west of Zhangjiakou you leave Shanxi and enter Hebei province. Between Km295 and Km272 (E) the Great Wall can be seen parallel to the line, on the hillside to the east. The best view is at Km284 (E).

Km193: Zhangjiakou (●) (pop: 385,400)   Founded 2000 years ago, this city used to be known by its Mongolian name, Kalgan (meaning gate or frontier). It stands at the point where the old caravan route between Peking and Russia crossed the Great Wall. Luigi Barzini described it as being like one of those 'cities one sees pictured upon Fu-kien tapestries: varied and picturesque, spreading over the bank of a wide snowy river'. He would not recognize it now; it has grown into an industrial city of over a million people. Yet he might recall the stink he'd noticed as he drove into town on 14 June 1907, for tanning and leatherwork are still major industries here. About 15km south of the city a large factory pollutes the air with orange smoke.

From around Km175 the scenery becomes hilly and more appealing as the line climbs the mountains north of Beijing. There are small valleys full of sunflowers, poplar groves and even apple orchards. At Km99 you cross the San Gan River, above which (E) can be seen a small isolated section of the Wall.

Km82: Kanzhuang (●) The train stops for a banking engine to be attached before a steep ascent past the Great Wall.

Km73: Badaling The first of the stations for the **Great Wall** itself. To the east is a 2km tunnel beneath the Wall. Look up (E) to the east as you come out for a good view and be ready to get off for the short stop at Qinglongqiao ^{1}/$_2$km further on.

Km70: Qinglongqiao There are good views of the Great Wall high above this attractive station. From here the train reverses downhill through a spectacular series of tunnels alongside the road. Progress is very slow because of the tortuous bends and the need for heavy braking, which gives some people time to jump off the train and gather the wild marijuana plants which flourish near the tracks in this area. You pass a Tourist Reception Centre at Km68.

Km63: Juyongguan (●) Continuous application of the brake blocks makes them very hot necessitating a brief rest here.

Km53: Nankou (●) The name means 'Southern Pass'. After a short stop to detach the rear engine the train speeds off across the fertile plain to Beijing.

Something strange happens to the kilometre markers in this area, with 30km suddenly added at around Km35.

Km0: Beijing Turn to p315 for more information.

Trans-Manchurian Route

For the entire Trans-Manchurian line we use (E) and (W) to show which side of the train points of interest are located. Thus if you're coming from Moscow (E) means the left side of the train, (W) the right.

Km6199: Chita Чита (●●●)   This is the last major Trans-Siberian station before Trans-Manchurian trains branch off to China. Detailed information on Chita is on p272.

Km6293: Karymskaya Карымская (●●●)   The branch line to Beijing via Manchuria leaves the main Trans-Siberian route at Tarskaya (formerly Kaidalovo), 12km east of Karymskaya. Leaving Tarskaya you cross the Ingoda River and head through open steppeland.

Some 20km further south you enter the Buryat Republic (Buryatia). The train makes brief stops at **Adrianovka** (Адриановка, Km6314), **Sedlovaya** (Седловая, Km6329) and **Mogoytuy** (Могойтуй, Km6370).

Km6444: Olovyannaya Оловянная (●)   The 120-flat apartment block by the station was constructed by Chinese labourers using Chinese materials. It was one of many barter deals between the Zabaikalsk (Russia) and Harbin (China) railways. Since 1988, when the first barter contract was signed, most deals have involved Russia swapping fertilizers, old rails and railway wheel sets for Chinese food, clothes and shoes. As confidence has grown Harbin Railways has provided specialist services such as doctors of traditional Chinese medicine for railway staff at nearby Karpovka, uniforms for Zabaikalsk workers, and reconstruction specialists for Chita 2 and Petrovsky Zavod stations.

Leaving this picturesque town you cross the Onon River, which flows north of the main Trans-Siberian line, joining the Ingoda to form the Shilka. Genghis Khan (see p389) was born on the banks of the muddy Onon in 1162. It might be wise to avoid taking photographs out the windows here, as there were once said to be ballistic missile facilities in the town's outskirts.

MAP 31

Between Olovyannaya and Borzya you cross the Adun Chelon mountain range, passing through **Yasnaya** (Km6464) and **Byrka** (Km6477).

Km6486: Mirnaya Мирная At the western end of the station there are two small tanks whose guns appear to be aimed at the train.

Km6509: Khadabulak Хадабулак This small village is below a large hill-top telecommunications tower. There are long views northwards across the plains to the surrounding hills.

Km6543: Borzya Борзя (●●●) This town was founded in the 18th century and with the arrival of the railway became the transport hub for the south-east Zabaikalsk region. A branch line runs westwards all the way to the Mongolian city of Choibalsan. Black marketeers come aboard (if you're coming from Beijing) to tempt you with army uniforms, military watches and rabbit-fur hats. **Watch your valuables**.

There are several opportunities for photographs along the train as it snakes around the curves between Km6554 and Km6570, and especially Km6564-5 (W).

Km6590: Kharanor Харанор There is a branch line from here to the east which runs to the military towns of Krasnokamensk and Priargunsk.

Km6609: Dauriya Даурия (●) This small village is surrounded by a marsh of red weeds.

Km6661: Zabaikalsk Забайкальск (●●●++) This town is within 1km of the border. Customs declarations and passports are checked on the train. If you are leaving Russia you may still be required to produce your currency declaration form (see Scam, p64). Although the rule no longer seems to be uniformly enforced, any remaining roubles are subject to confiscation so don't admit to having them if you want some as souvenirs. The guards don't seem bothered about tourists but might check the Chinese traders.

The train is shunted into the **bogie-changing sheds** at the south end of the station. You can either stay at the station, remain in the carriage or get out and watch the bogie-changing. Taking photos in the sheds was once strictly prohibited but is now permitted. You'll have to stay at the station for two to six hours.

The station has a **restaurant** which just about serves hot borshch and warm goulash to Russians or anybody with Russians, but is shy of serving anyone else. There is a **bank** upstairs with predictably poor rates. Black marketeers will catch you on your way in and this is probably the only time that it's worth using them. The **lavatories** are bearable if you hold your breath. In the building opposite the station and across the line there is a **shop** selling vodka, champagne and *palekh* boxes. There's a small department store next door.

THE PEOPLE'S REPUBLIC OF CHINA

Note that kilometre markers between the border and Harbin show the distance to Harbin, while those further on show the distance to Beijing.

Km935 (Bei:2323): Manzhouli (●●●++) (651m/2135ft, pop: 53,000) At this Chinese border town (once known as Manchuria Station) you must fill out currency and health declarations if you're arriving in China or, if you're leaving, fill out a departure card and present your currency declaration form. The train spends one to three hours here so you can visit the **bank** and the **Friendship Store** (tins of good quality peanuts, Chinese vodka, beer and fake sports clothes); postcards and stamps are also available. Puffing steam locomotives shunt carriages around the yard, a particularly impressive sight if you arrive in the early hours of a freezing winter morning. The toilets stink, less so in winter.

Leaving the station you pass **Lake Dalai Nor** and roll across empty steppeland. You may see mounted herders, as did Michael Myres Shoemaker in 1902 when he passed through on his journey to Peking. Of the first Chinese person he saw, he wrote (in *The Great Siberian Railway from St Petersburg to Pekin*) 'these northern Celestials appear on the whole friendly, and are flying around in all directions swathed in furs, and mounted on shaggy horses.' European newspapers of the time had been filled with reports of atrocities committed by the xenophobic Boxer sect in Manchuria, hence his surprise at the apparent friendliness of the local population.

Km749 (Bei:2137): Hailar (●●) (619m/2030ft) Rolling steppes continue from here to Haiman. If you'd been travelling in 1914 you would have the latest edition of Baedeker's *Russia with Teheran, Port Arthur and Peking* with you and would therefore be looking out for 'the fortified station buildings (sometimes adorned with apes, dragons and other Chinese ornaments), the Chinese carts with their two high wheels and the camels at pasture'. Modern Hailar is an unexotic city of 170,200 people, the economic centre of the region. Local architecture is a blend of Russian and Mongolian, including log cabins, some with yurt-style roofs. The average temperature in this area in January is a cool minus 27°C.

THE EAST CHINESE RAILWAY 1897-1901
The route

The original plans for the Great Siberian Railway had not included the laying of track across territories outside the Russian Empire. But when surveyors returned from the Shilka and Amur valleys in 1894 with the news that the Sretensk to Khabarovsk section of the line would prove extremely costly owing to the difficult terrain, the Siberian Railway Committee were obliged to consider an alternative. Their greedy eyes turned to the rich Chinese territory of Manchuria and they noted that a line straight across this province to Vladivostok would cut 513 *versts* (544km) off the journey to the port. Since the Chinese would obviously not be happy to have Russian railway lines extending into their territory, the Committee had to think up a scheme to win Peking over to the idea.

The Manchurian Deal

It did not take wily Russian diplomats long to work out a deal the Chinese were forced to accept. After the 1894 Sino-Japanese war the victorious Japanese concocted a peace treaty that included the payment of a heavy indemnity by the Chinese. Knowing that China was unable to pay, the Russians offered them a generous loan in exchange for the right to build and operate a railway across Manchuria. They were granted an 80-year lease on a thin strip of land 1400km long and the project was to be disguised as a Chinese enterprise financed through the Russo-Chinese Bank. The rest of the world suspected Russia of flagrant imperialism, and Russia proved them right in 1897 by annexing Port Arthur.

Work begins

Construction began in 1897 but it soon became obvious that the project faced greater problems than any that had arisen during the building of other sections. There were difficult conditions (the Greater Khingan Mountains had to be crossed); there were not enough labourers; interpreters were needed to translate the orders of Russian foremen for Chinese coolies; and the area through which the route passed was thick with *hunghutzes* (bandits). It was necessary to bring in a force of 5000 policemen to protect the workers. After the Boxer (anti-foreigner) riots began in the late 1890s it became necessary to protect the rails too, for when they were not murdering missionaries the Boxers tore up track and derailed trains.

Set-backs

After the annexation of Port Arthur another Manchurian line was begun – from Harbin south through Mukden (now Shenyang) to Dalni (now Dalian) and Port Arthur (now Lushun). Work was disrupted in 1899 by the outbreak of bubonic plague, although despite Chinese refusal to co-operate with quarantine procedures, only 1400 people died out of the total work-force of 200,000. In May 1900 Boxers destroyed 200km of track and besieged Harbin. The Russians sent in a peace-keeping force of 200,000 men but by the time the rebellion had been put down, one third of the railway had been destroyed.

Despite these setbacks the line was completed in 1901. It would have been far more economical to build the Amur line from Sretensk to Khabarovsk, for in the end the East Chinese Railway cost the government more than the total spent on the entire Trans-Siberian track on Russian soil.

Km674 (Bei:2062): Haiman   Also known as Yakoshih, this town stands near the foot of the Great Khingan Range which extends from the Russian border southwards into Inner Mongolia. The line begins to rise into the foothills of the range.

Km634 (Bei:2022): Mianduhe   The train continues to climb the gently rising gradient.

Km564 (Bei:1952): Xinganling/Khingan (958m/3140ft) This station stands at the **highest point on the Trans-Manchurian line**. The 3km tunnel built here in 1901-2 was a considerable engineering achievement since most of the drilling was done during the winter, with shift workers labouring day and night.

Km539 (Bei:1927): Boketu (●●)   The line winds down partly-wooded slopes to the town of **Balin/Barim** (Bei: 1866) and continues over the plains, leaving Inner Mongolia and crossing into Heilongjiang Province.

Km270 (Bei:1658): Angangxi (●●●) (pop: 67,900) About 40km southwards is the ancient city of **Qiqihar** (Tsitsikar). By the time he reached this point Michael Myres Shoemaker had become bored with watching 'Celestials' from the windows of the train and was tired and hungry. He writes 'In Tsitsikar, at a wretched little mud hut, we find some hot soup and a chop, also some coffee, all of which, after our days in lunch baskets, taste very pleasant.'

Over lunch they may well have discussed the nearby **Field of Death** for which the city was notorious. In this open area on the edge of Qiqihar public executions were regularly performed. Most of the criminals decapitated before the crowds were *hunghutzes* (bandits). Since the Chinese believed that entry to Heaven was denied to mortals who were missing parts of their bodies, their heads had to be sewn back in place before a decent burial could take place. However, so as not to lower the moral tone of Paradise, the government ordered that the heads be sewn on backwards.

Some 20km east of Angangxi is a large area of marshland, part of which has been designated a nature reserve. The marsh attracts a wide variety of waterfowl since it is on migration routes from the Arctic and Siberia down to southern Asia. The **Zhalong Nature Reserve**, 20km north of here, is best known for

its cranes. Several of these (including the Siberian Crane) are now listed as endangered species.

Km159 (Bei:1547): Daqing (●●) At the centre of one of the largest oilfields in China, Daqing is a model industrial town producing plastics and gas as well as oil. Higher wages attract model workers from all over the country. But apart from the thousands of oil wells in this swampy district there's very little to see.

Km96 (Bei:1484): Song This small station is in an island of cultivation amongst the swamps.

Km0 (Bei:1388): Harbin (●●●) (152m/500ft, pop: 2,904,900)   [see p311]
Crossing the wide Sungari (Songhua) River, a 1840km-long tributary of the Amur to the north, the line reaches Harbin, industrial centre of Heilongjiang Province. It was a small fishing village until the mid 1890s when the Russians made it the headquarters of their railway building operations in Manchuria.

After Michael Myres Shoemaker visited the town in 1902 he wrote: 'The state of society seems even worse at this military post of Harbin than in Irkutsk. There were seven throats cut last night, and now, as a member of the Russo-Chinese Bank expressed it, the town hopes for a quiet season.' The *Imperial Japanese Railways Guide to East Asia* (1913) recommended 'the excellent bread and butter, which are indeed the pride of Harbin' and warned travellers away from the numerous opium dens.

After the Revolution, White Russian refugees poured into the town and Russian influence on the place continued. There are few onion-domes or spires to be seen in what is today just another Chinese city: the Russian population is now small.

The city's main tourist attraction is its **Ice Lantern Festival**, which takes place from January to early February. Winters here are particularly cold and during the festival the parks are filled with ice-sculptures: life-size elephants, dragons and horses as well as small buildings and bridges. Electric lights are frozen into these sculptures and when they are illuminated at night, the effect is spectacular.

At the station you can get good views along the track of the numerous steam locos, from the bridges between the platforms.

Between Harbin and Changchun you cross an immense cultivated plain, leaving Heilongjiang and entering Jilin Province.

Km1260: The line crosses a wide tributary of the Songhua River. There are numerous small lakes in the area.

Km1146: Changchun (●●) (230m/760ft, pop:1,959,200) Changchun is the provincial capital. The station is worth a stroll, with white concrete sculptures of 'The Graces' and lots to buy from snack sellers on the platform.

Back in 1913 the *Imperial Japanese Government Railways Guide to East Asia* was reminding its readers (all of whom would have had to change at this large junction) about 'the need of adjusting their watches – the Russian railway-time being 23 minutes earlier than the Japanese'. From 1933 to 1945 Changchun was the centre of the Japanese puppet-state of Manchukuo.

It has now grown into an industrial metropolis of more than a million people. Local industries include a car factory where Red Flag limousines are assembled (guided tours possible), a rail-carriage factory and film studios. If you do get off here, local delicacies include antler broth, hedgehog hydnum stewed with orchid, and a north-eastern speciality, *qimian*, which is the nose of a moose.

But Changchun is probably more popular with rail enthusiasts than with epicureans. RM Pacifics and QJ 2-10-2s are to be seen here and on the Changchun–Jilin line.

Km1030: Siping (●●●+) This unattractive town does have lots of working steam locos in the station. About 10km further south the train crosses the provincial border into Liaoning Province.

Km841: Shenyang (●●●) (50m/160ft, pop: 3,574,100) An industrial giant founded 2000 years ago during the Western Han dynasty (206BC–AD24). At different times during its long history the city has been controlled by Manchus (who named it Mukden), Russians, Japanese and the Kuomintang, until it was finally taken over by Chinese communists in 1948. Shenyang is now one of the largest industrial centres in the People's Republic, but between the factories there are several interesting places to visit, including a small version of Beijing's **Imperial Palace**. There is also a **railway museum** beside the Sujiatun shed. The station has a green dome and the square outside it is dominated by a tank on a pedestal.

Km599: Jinzhou (●) From here the line runs down almost to the coast, which it follows south-west for the next 300km, crossing into Hebei Province. Beijing is just under eight hours from here.

Km415: Shanhaiguan (●●) As you approach the town from the north, you pass through the **Great Wall** – at its most eastern point. This end of the Wanlichangcheng (Ten Thousand Li Long Wall) has been partially done up for the tourists. Although the views here are not as spectacular as at Badaling (70km north of Beijing, see p317), the restoration at Shanhaiguan has been carried out more sympathetically – it is restoration rather than reconstruction. The large double-roofed tower houses an interesting museum.

Km262: Tangshan (●) (pop: 812,500) This was the epicentre of an earthquake which demolished this industrial town on 28 July 1976. The official death toll stands at 150,000 but may have been as high as 750,000. Many of the factories have been rebuilt and the town is once again producing consumer goods. Locomotives are built here at the Tangshan Works, which until 1991 produced the SY class 2-8-2 steam engine.

Km133: Tianjin/Tientsin (●●) (pop: 4,333,900) This is one of China's largest ports. In the mid-19th century the British and French marched on the capital and 'negotiated' the Treaty of Peking which opened Tianjin to foreign trade. Concessions were granted to foreign powers just as they were in Shanghai. Britain, France, Austria, Germany, Italy, Belgium, Russia, Japan and the United States each controlled different parts of the city, which accounts for the amazing variety of architectural styles to be found here.

Chinese resentment at the foreign presence boiled over in 1870 in an incident that came to be known as the **Tientsin Massacre**, during which ten nuns, two priests and a French official were murdered. To save female babies from being killed by their parents (the Chinese have always considered it far more important to have sons than daughters) the nuns had been giving money for them. This had led more gullible members of the community to believe rumours that the nuns were eating the children or grinding up their bones for patent medicines.

One of several ferry services between China and Japan (see p36) terminates at Tianjin.

Km0: Beijing The beginning or the end? You are now 9001km from Moscow. See p315 for information on the city.

This section contains basic information for those spending a few days in Tokyo, Hong Kong, Helsinki, Berlin, Budapest, Prague, Warsaw, Minsk, Tallinn, Riga or Vilnius at the end or beginning of the trip. Details of how to arrange tickets in these cities for the rail journey across Siberia are given in Part 1.

JAPAN: TOKYO

General information

● **Visas** Visas are not necessary for passport holders from the UK, other Western European countries, North America and most Commonwealth countries.

● **Money/costs** The unit of currency is the yen (¥). Japan is thought of as an expensive destination but it does not need to be. However, you should allow about £50/US$75 per day for basic accommodation and cheap meals.

● **Climate** Japan has four clearly-defined seasons: winter being cold and snowy, summer being hot and humid, and spring and autumn being warm.

● **Language** Since English is taught in the schools and the people are very keen to make contact with foreigners, you will almost always be able to find someone to help you.

Tourist information

A wealth of useful maps and tourist brochures is provided free of charge at branches of the Japan National Tourist Organization (JNTO). JNTO has a website at 🖳 www.jnto.go.jp and some of their offices are at:

● **USA**: (☎ 212-757-5640), Suite 1250, 1 Rockefeller Plaza, New York, NY 10020 (offices also in San Francisco and Los Angeles)

● **Canada**: (☎ 416-366-7140), 165 University Ave, Toronto, Ontario, M5H 3B8

● **Australia**: (☎ 02-9232 4522), Lvl 33, Chifley Tower, Chifley Square, Sydney, NSW 2000

JNTO's UK office closed in October 2003; information is now available by email (🖳 info@jnto.co.uk) or fax (🖹 020-7734 4290) or from 🖳 www.see japan.co.uk).

In Tokyo, go to **Tokyo Tourist Information Centre** (☎ 03-3201 3331), 10th Floor, Tokyo Kotsu Kaikan Bldg, 2-10-1 Yurakucho, Chiyoda-ku, Tokyo 100-0006, open 9:00-17:00 weekdays, 9:00-12:00 Saturday.

Arrival and departure

Travel is expensive in Japan so try to ensure you have booked internal flights or bought a rail pass (see below) before arrival.

● **By air** Transport to the city centre is expensive since **Narita Airport** is 60km outside the capital. The cheapest way to get in if you don't have a rail pass is to take the Keisei Limited Express train from the airport to Keisei Ueno Station in

Tokyo. Alternatively, if you already have a hotel reservation consider taking one of the limousine buses that go between the main hotels and the airport.

● **By train** If you plan to spend some time touring the country, you should purchase a Japan Rail Pass – ¥28,300 (US$244/£150) for 7 days, ¥45,100 (US$389/£240) for 14 days, or ¥57,700 (US$497/£306) for 21 days. You must buy the pass before arriving in Japan. *Japan by Rail* by Ramsey Zarifeh (Trailblazer) is a comprehensive guide to travel by train in Japan. All railway stations have signs above the platforms in both Japanese and Roman letters.

● **By ferry** For details of ferry services to China and Russia (as well as information about arranging **Trans-Siberian** tickets) see Part 1.

Where to stay

This can be expensive: a bed in a youth hostel will set you back US$22/£15. A basic *minshuku* (including supper and breakfast) or business hotel (no meals) will cost about US$43/£30, and a *ryokan* (Japanese-style hotel including supper and breakfast)/upmarket Western-style hotel about US$135/£93.

The best way to find somewhere to sleep is to visit the TIC (see above) in Tokyo where there is a Welcome Inn Reservation Center (🖥 www.itcj.or.jp, open Mon-Fri 09:15-11:30 and 13:00-16:45). Reservations can be made here free of charge. Alternatively collect an accommodation list and a map and do it yourself by phoning the hotel/youth hostel (phone calls are reasonably cheap). Check prices and availability and then ask for directions.

Some places to try for cheap accommodation in Tokyo are:

● *Tokyo International Youth Hostel* (☎ 03-3235 1107; Iidabashi station), 18F Central Plaza Building, 1-1 Kagurakashi, Shinjuku-ku 162-0823.

● *Asia Center of Japan* (☎ 03-3233 0111; Akasaka station), 5-5 Saragakucho 2-chome, Chiyoda-ku.

● *Taito Ryokan* (☎ 03-3843 2822, 🖥 www.libertyhouse.gr.jp; Asakusa station), Nishi-Asakusa 2-1-4, Taito-ku, 111-0035.

● *Hotel Skycourt Narita* (☎ 0478-736211) has reasonably-priced accommodation and offers a discount for YH members as well as a free shuttle bus to/from Narita airport.

HONG KONG

General information

Hong Kong is a Special Administrative Region of China.

● **Visas** British citizens can stay for six months, with no automatic right of employment, though may need to show proof of onward travel. Most other nationalities can stay for three months.

Visas for China are easy to get in Hong Kong. Either use a travel agent or do it yourself at the Visa Office (☎ 3413 2424) of the People's Republic of China, 6-7th floor, Lower Block, China Resources Building, 26 Harbour Rd, Wanchai. Remember that you will be without a passport while processing the visa, so if you need to cash travellers' cheques do this first.

● **Money** The currency is the Hong Kong dollar (HK$).

● **Climate** Mild with fairly hot and humid summers and cool winters.
● **Language** Cantonese and English.

Tourist information

The Hong Kong Tourist Board (HKTB) has branches in many countries. Details are available on the HKTB website (🖳 www.Discoverhongkong.com/eng/index.jsp).

In Hong Kong there are well-stocked and helpful tourist information centres at the airport (open 07:00-23:00 daily; brochures available 24 hours), Star Ferry Terminal (Kowloon; open 08:00-18:00 daily) and on the Ground Floor, The Center, 99 Queen's Road Central, Hong Kong Island (open 08:00-18:00 daily). There is also a telephone information service with multi-lingual operators (☎ 2508 1234; open 08:00-18:00 daily).

Arrival and departure

● **By air** The huge new **Chek Lap Kok Airport** is on the north side of Lantau Island. There is a very helpful tourist information desk and accommodation can be booked at the HK Hotels Association desk. As in all airports, the rates the money-changers offer are bad so change only a little or use an ATM.

It's easy to get to Kowloon or Hong Kong Island from the airport; either catch the Airport Express Link (AEL), a high-speed rail link that takes 19 minutes to Kowloon and 23 minutes to Hong Kong Island, or take the airport bus.

● **By rail** The Beijing–Hong Kong and Shanghai–Hong Kong trains take around 28 hours and run on alternate days of the week.

To get to Guangzhou (Canton) you can take the $2^1/_2$-hour, direct express train which runs from Kowloon (Hung Hom Station). From China it is cheaper, however, to take local trains from Canton to Shenzhen; there is also a bus service on this route. You walk across the border into Hong Kong and then take a local train from Lo Wu station to Hung Hom.

For **Trans-Siberian** tickets, see pp40-1.

● **Hydrofoil/jetcat to/from Guangzhou (Canton)** Hydrofoils and jetcats between Guangzhou and Hong Kong arrive and depart from the China Ferry Terminal in Kowloon. Book tickets from the China Ferry Terminal or through travel agents in Hong Kong. Journey time is under two hours. The overnight boats no longer run.

Local transport

Most famous is the Star Ferry service which operates between Kowloon and Hong Kong Island. Ask at any of the HKTB information offices for details of ferries to outlying islands. There is also a fast and efficient subway system and the old trams still operate on Hong Kong Island. Taxis are cheap too.

Where to stay

A list of government licensed hotels and guesthouses is available at 🖳 www.info.gov.hk/had_la/english.

For a cheap place to sleep, **Chungking Mansions**, Nathan Rd, is the best. In these blocks in Kowloon, near the harbour and a stone's throw from the famous Peninsula Hotel, there's a large number of small hotels with tiny rooms and low prices. Have a look at a few before you decide as the rooms vary in size, cleanliness and price. The ***Travellers' Hostel*** (☎ 2368 7710) on the top floor of Block A is a popular meeting place for backpackers and has cheap dormitory accommodation and a restaurant as well as a travel agency that can organize visas for China.

 Salisbury YMCA (☎ 2268 7000, 🗎 2739 9315, 🖳 room@ymc ahk.org.hk) is next door to the Peninsula Hotel.

FINLAND: HELSINKI
General information
● **Visas** Visas are not necessary for stays of 90 days or less for passport holders from most countries including the EU, UK, USA, Canada, Australia and New Zealand. South African citizens are required to have a visa.
● **Money/costs** The unit of currency is the euro. As in most Scandinavian countries, prices are higher than in many European countries.
● **Climate** Pleasantly warm in summer but winters are long and severe.
● **Language** There are two official languages – Finnish and Swedish (the Swedish name for Helsinki is Helsingfors). Most people also speak English.

Tourist information
There are Finnish tourist offices in the **UK**: (☎ 020-7365 2512), PO Box 33213, London W6 8JX and **USA/Canada**: (☎ 212-885-9700, ☎ 800-FIN-INFO). For general information about Finland visit 🖳 www.finlandtravelguide.com.

 In Helsinki your first stop should be **Helsinki City Tourist & Convention Bureau** (☎ 9-169 3757, 🖳 tourist.info@hel.fi, www.hel.fi), at Pohjoisesplanadi 19 on the Esplanadia (the park next to the water-side market square). It is open 09:00-18:00 weekdays, 10:00-16:00 weekends (longer in summer) and provides an accommodation list.

Arrival and departure
● **By sea** A number of companies offer routes to/from Stockholm (Sweden), Tallinn (Estonia) and Rostock (Germany); most operate year-round. The agencies listed below accept bookings online and have agents in several countries.

 Viking Line (🖳 www.vikingline.fi) services from Stockholm and Tallinn dock at Katajanokka Terminal in Helsinki. **Silja Line** (🖳 www.silja.com) ships from Stockholm and Rostock dock at Olympia Terminal. The Superseacat service to Tallinn operates several times daily from the Olympic Terminal (though some services from Tallinn arrive at Makasiini Terminal). Silja Line's Finnjet service to Tallinn operates in winter only and goes from Katajanokka Terminal.

 The terminals are a 15-20 minute walk from the city centre.
● **By air** Helsinki-Vantaa Airport is situated 20km north of the city centre. There is a regular bus service (local bus No 615, 40 mins, €3, or Finnair bus, 30 mins, €4.90) to the railway station.

● **By rail** The railway station is six blocks west of the harbour and two blocks north. There are daily services to St Petersburg and Moscow.

For booking the **Trans-Siberian** in Helsinki see p27.

● **By bus** Matkahuolto (☎ 9-6136 8433, 🖳 matkapalvelut.helsinki@matkahuol to.fi, www.matkahuolto.fi/english) has four departures daily to St Petersburg. Seat reservations are compulsory. Tickets are sold at travel agencies or by Matkapyörä at the main bus station.

Sovavto (🖳 www.pohjolanliikenne.fi) and Finnord Bus Agency (☎ 060 7718) also operate services to St Petersburg; tickets are sold at travel agencies or at the main bus station.

Where to stay

You can get information about, and book, accommodation at the tourist office (see above) or the **Hotel Booking Centre** (Hotellikeskus; ☎ 9-2288 1400, 🗎 9-2288 1499, 🖳 hotel@helsinkiexpert.fi) at the main railway station. The office is open weekdays only from 1 Sept to 31 May, daily in summer.

For information about youth hostels in Finland see 🖳 www.srmnet.org.

GERMANY: BERLIN

General information

● **Visas** Not necessary for most nationalities.

● **Money/costs** The unit of currency is the euro. Living and travelling costs can be high.

● **Language** It's useful to be able to speak a little German. Most Berliners study English at school and many speak it fluently.

Tourist information

Berlin Tourist Office (☎ 030-250025) in the Europa Center, Budapester Strasse 45 (the building with the Mercedes star on the top of it) is a ten-minute walk from Zoo Bahnhof (Zoo railway station) and is open 10:00-19:00 Monday to Saturday (10:00-18:30 on Sunday), longer between 1 April and 31 October.

There is also an information centre at Brandenburg Gate (open daily 10:00-18:00, longer in summer). The friendly staff will supply you with maps and brochures and book accommodation.

The EurAide desk (main hall, Zoo Bahnhof) provides train (including rail passes) and tourist information. The office is open daily (8:00-12 noon, 13:00-18:00) June to October and weekdays only (8:00-12 noon, 13:00-16:45) the rest of the year.

Information is available online at 🖳 www.btm.de/english.

Arrival and departure

● **By air** Flights to/from Western Europe generally use Tegel Airport (8km from the city centre). Most of the flights to eastern Europe and Asia are handled by Schönefeld (18km from the city centre). There are regular bus/train services between these airports and the city centre. For cheap flights buy a copy of the weekly magazine *Zitty*, which has several pages of travel deals.

● **By car** A system of car-sharing can be arranged through *mitfahrzentrale* agencies (⌨ www.mitfahrzentrale.de; German only); you pay the agency a fee to find you a ride in a private car to other European cities and pay the driver a contribution towards petrol costs. There is a branch in Zoo Bahnhof.

● **By train** Zoo Bahnhof (Zoo Railway Station; train info (☎ 01805-996633) is the main station for trains to/from Western Europe. There are left-luggage lockers and a bureau de change. International services also operate from Ostbahnhof station. To make a booking on the **Trans-Siberian**, see pp28-9.

Fare and timetable information is available online at ⌨ www.bahn.de.

● **By bus** Services to many parts of Europe depart from the Zentraler Omnibusbahnhof (Central Bus Station; ☎ 301 8028). For further details see ⌨ www.btm.de/english.

Where to stay

The cheapest places to stay are the youth hostels which are luxurious by international YHA (HI) standards but comparatively expensive (dorm beds start from €15) and popular so book in advance.

● *Jugendherberge Berlin International* (☎ 030-261 1097; ⌨ www.hostel.de), Kluckstrasse 3, D-10785

● *Wannsee Jugendgastehaus* (☎ 030-803 2034; ⌨ www.hostel.de), Badeweg 1, D-14129

● *Ernst Reuter Youth Hostel* (☎ 030-404 1610; ⌨ www.hostel.de), Hermsdorfer Damm 48, D-13467

● *Jugendgastehaus am Zoo* (☎ 030-312 9410, ⌨ www.sportjugend.org), Hardenberg Strasse 9a, Charlottenburg. It is located near Zoo Railway Station.

HUNGARY: BUDAPEST

General information

● **Visas** Visas for stays of 90 days or less are not necessary for passport holders from the USA, UK (six months), Canada, New Zealand, or most European countries. Australian and South African passport holders need a visa. For further information visit ⌨ www.kum.hu.

● **Money** The currency is the Forint (Ft). ATMs are easy to find and credit cards are increasingly accepted.

● **Language** Magyar is one of the world's more difficult languages for foreigners to learn. Most people connected with tourism speak a little English though knowledge of German is more widespread.

Tourist information

Information can be obtained from the Hungarian National Tourist Office's website (⌨ www.hungarytourism.hu) or **Tourinform** (☎ 1-438 8080, ⌨ hungary@tourinform.hu, www.tourinform.hu), V Viugado utca 6 (open 24 hours) or Suto utca 2 (near Deak ter metro station; open 08:00-20:00 daily).

The **information office** (☎ 302 8580) in the main hall in Nyugati (Western) Railway Station is open daily 10:00-18:00 (longer in summer).

There are also touch-information terminals at all the main railway stations. Online information is also available from 🖳 www.budapestinfo.hu.

Arrival and departure
There are train, plane and bus services to most destinations in Europe.
● **By rail**   Most international services come into Keleti Station (East); Nyugati Station (West) is used for some train services to/from Germany. Both have metro stations.

   For **Trans-Siberian** bookings see Part 1.
● **By air**   Ferihegy International Airport is 28km south-east of the city centre. There are shuttle buses every 30 minutes to the city; the journey takes 45 minutes.
● **By bus**   International services use Népliget Bus Station on the Pest side of Budapest. Eurolines (☎ 219 8080, 🖳 ticketoffice@eurolines.hu) has an office here.

Where to stay
Budapest has a range of accommodation for all budgets. At the top end there is the *Hilton*, which blends well with the ancient walls of the castle tower it incorporates and stands on the hill above the city.

   Information about accommodation can be obtained from Tourinform (see above). Hotel/youth hostel accommodation can be booked at the Express Travel office (open 24 hours) at Keleti Station. Alternatively check out 🖳 www.hostels.hu.

CZECH REPUBLIC: PRAGUE

General information
● **Visas**   Visas are not necessary for passport holders from the UK (180 days), USA, New Zealand, Japan or EU countries for stays of 90 days or less. Canadian, Australian, and South African citizens need a visa. For further information check 🖳 www.czechembassy.org.
● **Money/costs**   The unit of currency is the koruna (crown).
● **Language**   Many Czech people involved in tourism now speak English. German and Russian are also spoken.

Tourist information
General information about the Czech Republic is available on www.czech.cz.

   In Prague, **Prague Information Service** (☎ 544 444, 🖳 tourinfo@pis.cz, www.prague-info.cz) has branches at 20 Na Prikope, Starometske namesti (Old Town Hall), and at the main railway station. They are open 8:30-19:00 weekdays and 9:00-17:00 weekends. Information in English is also available Monday to Friday 20:00-07:00 by phoning ☎ 12 444.

Arrival and departure
● **By rail**   There are four railway stations: Hlavní Nádrazí (the main station, also called Wilsonovo Station), Holesovice to the north, Masarykovo Nadrazi near the centre, and Smíchovoske nadrazi to the south (mainly for local trains). For

24-hr information on railway schedules in English or German phone ☎ 2-2461 4030. For **Trans-Siberian** bookings, see Part 1.

● **By air** The international airport is 10km from the city centre. There is a frequent bus service between the airport and the city centre.

● **By bus** For information about bus services in Europe visit 🖳 www.eurolines.cz/English. Other operators from Britain include: **Capital Express** (UK ☎ 020-7243 0488, 🖳 www.capitalexpress.cz), 57 Princedale Rd, Holland Park, London W11 4NP, charges £42/63 single/return and the service runs daily (in Prague tickets can be bought at Capital's office, ☎ 2-2087 0368, in Florenc bus station and buses depart from there), and **Kingscourt Express** (☎ 020-8673 7500; 🖳 www.kce.cz), 15 Balham High Rd, London SW12, charges from £45 (you can get tickets in Prague at Havelska 8 (☎ 2-2423 4583).

Where to stay

There's a good range of accommodation but in the summer it's best to book in advance or start looking for a place to stay early in the day.

Details about accommodation are available from 🖳 www.travelguide.cz, or from the Prague Information Service office or website (see above). Hostel information is available at 🖳 kmc@kmc.cz, www.kmc.cz.

Pragotur (☎ 2-2171 4130, 🖳 pis.pragotur@mbox.vol.cz), 186 50 Praha 8, Za Poricskou branou 7, has a booking service for accommodation. It's near Powder Gate and Metro Náměstí Republiky and is open 10:00-17:00.

POLAND: WARSAW

General information

● **Visas** (for stays of up to 90 days) for US, UK and EU passport holders are obtainable on arrival; Canadian, Australian, New Zealand and South African citizens need to arrange a visa before departing.

● **Money** The zloty is the unit of currency. Banking hours are 07:30 to 17:00 but cash can also be obtained from the many ATMs around the city. Travellers' cheques can be difficult to exchange. Credit cards are accepted in most hotels, restaurants and shops.

● **Language** Polish is the national language. Most people connected with tourism speak English, German or Russian.

Tourist information

● **UK**: The Polish National Tourist Office (☎ 020-7580 8811 brochure, ☎ 020-7580 6688 general information, 🖳 www.pnto.dial.pipex.com), 1st Fl, 310-12 Regent St, London WIR 5AJ, is open 10:00-17:00 Monday to Friday.

● **USA**: PNTO (☎ 201-420-9910, 🖳 pntony@polandtour.org, www.polandtour.org), 5 Marine View Plaza, Hoboken, NJ 07030

Warsaw Tourism Information Centre (☎ 022 9431 (English), 🖳 www.explorewarsaw.com) has branches on Plac Zamkowy 1/13 (Castle Square), in Warszawa Centralna railway station, at the airport and at Warsaw West Coach Station. The Castle Square office is open weekdays 08:00-18:00 and weekends 09:00-15:00 (longer in summer).

Arrival and departure

International train and bus tickets can be bought at major travel agencies or at the train/bus station. ICIS student card-holders should ask about discounted fares.

● **By rail** Warsaw is a major stopping point between Berlin and Russia. International trains depart from Warszawa Centralna Station. Tickets can be booked at the station or through Orbis travel offices.

● **By air** Many airlines fly to Warsaw and the national carrier, Lot Polish Airlines, has services to dozens of places.

● **By bus** Buses leave regularly for most European cities and are cheaper than trains. Services depart from Warszawa Dworzec Zachodnia (central) bus station. Operators providing international services include Pekaes (PKS, 🖥 www.pekaesbus.com.pl/english) and Eurolines (🖥 www.eurolinespolska.pl).

Where to stay

Warsaw has a vast range of accommodation. For details go to the tourist information office or their website (see above). Central and close to the station is the expensive *Novotel Centrum Hotel* (☎ 22-210270, 📠 22-625 0476) on ulica Nowogrodzka 24/26; singles start from US$100. *Hotel Metropol* (☎ 22-6294 001, 📠 22-625 3014) on ulica Marszalkowska 99a charges from US$30 a room including breakfast. *Hotel Saski* (☎ 22-204611) on Plac Bankowy 1 has rooms from US$20.

For a list of hostels visit 🖥 warsaw-travel.com or contact the Polish Association of Youth Hostels (🖥 hostellingpol@pro.onet.pl). The most centrally-located *youth hostel* is at ulica Smolna 30 (☎ 22-827 8952). It is, however, often full during the summer.

BELARUS: MINSK

General information

● **Visas** Visas are necessary for virtually all passport holders. If you're crossing the country before or after a Trans-Siberian trip you need a Belarusian transit visa. The only place you can get a visa on arrival is at Minsk-2 Airport; this could be quite time consuming so it is best to get one in advance. For information about getting a visa, as well as an application form, visit 🖥 www.mfa.gov.by/eng.

● **Money** The Belarusian ruble, nicknamed the *zaichiki* (rabbit), is the official currency. In January 2000 a new currency (minus three zeros) was introduced; check you are given the correct notes.

The most widely-accepted foreign currencies are US$ and Euros. Make sure the notes are in perfect condition otherwise changing them may be difficult. In Minsk, you can cash travellers' cheques and receive cash advances on your credit card but it may be expensive and is not easy. There are now a good number of ATMs in Minsk but they do not accept all cards; MasterCard is the most likely to be accepted. Food and entertainment are cheap.

● **Language** Belarusian is an Eastern Slavonic language related to Ukrainian and Russian. However, Russian is still spoken by the majority of people.

Tourist information

There are no tourist information offices in Belarus, only service bureaus and excursion offices within hotels. However, general information about Belarus can be obtained from 🖳 www.mybelarus.info.

● **Belintourist** (Belarus' version of Intourist; ☎ 17-226 9840, 🖹 17-223 1143, 🖳 request@belintourist.by, www.belintourist.by), at praspekt Masherava 19, open daily 08:00-20:00.

● **Hotel Minsk** (☎ 17-220 0132), praspekt Skaryny 11. This place has the best service bureau and the staff speak English.

Arrival and departure

● **By rail** Minsk's international train station is south of the city centre. There are direct services to Vilnius, Warsaw, Moscow and St Petersburg. At the station is the metro station Ploshcha Nezalezhnastsi (formerly Lenin Square).

You can get **international train tickets** on the upper floor of the main railway station. A less stressful place to buy them is at the Belintourist office (see above). Another ticket office, at praspekt Skaryny 18, between vulitsa Lenina and Kamsamolskaya, is also open daily.

● **By air** Minsk-2 airport, which is 40km east of the city, is used for most international flights. There is an hourly bus service to the city. Minsk-1 airport is nearer the city and is used for short-distance international flights.

The state-owned Belavia (Belarusian airlines; ☎ 17-229 2838, 🖳 www.belavia.by) has an office at 14 vulitsa Nemiga.

● **By bus** The central long-distance bus station is at vulitsa Babrujskaja 12. There are three buses a day to Bialystok in Poland, and daily buses to Brest, Kaliningrad, Riga, Kaunas, Klaipeda and Vilnius. Vostochny bus station, about 3km south-east of the city centre, services Homel, Vitsebsk, Pinsk, Polatsk and Warsaw. Bus No 8 and trolleybus No 13 travel between these two bus stations.

Where to stay

Both Belintourist's office and website (see above) have some information about accommodation in Minsk.

Hotel Minsk (☎ 17-220 0132), praspekt Skaryny 11, has small but clean rooms starting from US$42 for a single. *Hotel Svislach* (☎ 17-220 9783) on vulitsa Kirava 13 has rooms for as little as US$15 for a single. *Hotel Druzhba* (☎ 17-266 2481), vulitsa Tolbukhina 3, has very basic rooms for US$5 a night. One of the nicest hotels is *Hotel Kastrychnitskaja* (☎ 17-222 3289), vulitsa Enhelsa 13, where a single room with all amenities costs from US$70. *Hotel Jubileynaja* (☎ 17-226 9002), praspekt Masherava 19, charges US$55 a single as does *Hotel Planeta* (☎ 17-226 7855), praspekt Masherava 31.

ESTONIA: TALLINN

General information

● **Visas** These are not necessary for passport holders from Australia, Canada, Japan, New Zealand, the UK, USA or most European countries. If you do need

a visa, you can obtain one on arrival but it's much cheaper if bought in advance. For further information visit the Estonian Ministry of Foreign Affairs' website 🖥 www.vm.ee/eng.
● **Money** The unit of currency, the kroon (EEK), is pegged to the euro. There are exchange offices at the airport and the central railway station.
● **Language** The official language is Estonian. However, most Estonians speak some Russian and/or English.

Tourist information
General information is available online from the Estonian Tourist Board's website (🖥 www.visitestonia.com).

In Tallinn, the **Tourist Information Centre** (☎ 645 7777, 🖹 645 7778, 🖥 turismiinfo@tallinnlv.ee, www.tourism.tallinn.ee), at Niguliste 2/Kullassepa 4, is open 09:00-17:00 weekdays and 10:00-15:00 weekends (longer in summer; closed on Sunday in winter). The centre has a wide range of information, maps and guides and the staff will book accommodation.

Arrival and departure
● **By air** Tallinn has air links with many cities. The airport is 4km from the city centre and the No 2 bus goes regularly between the airport, port and city centre.
● **By sea** There are daily ferries/hydrofoils/catamarans between Tallinn and Helsinki; see Helsinki p406 for further information. Tallink (🖥 www.tallink.ee) operates a daily ferry service between Tallinn and Stockholm.
● **By bus** Buses between Tallinn Autobussijaam (the central bus station) and St Petersburg are cheap and operate daily. Services are also frequent between Tallinn and many cities in Germany and in the other Baltic State countries. Information and tickets for all services are available from the central bus station or online from 🖥 www.eurolines.ee.
● **By rail** Tallinn has direct services to Moscow, St Petersburg and Warsaw. Trains depart daily from Balti Jaam (Baltic Station). Tickets can be bought from window No 26 at the back of the main long-distance booking hall beside the platform (open 08:00 to 13:00 and 14:00 to 20:00 every day).

Where to stay
Tallinn has a variety of accommodation to suit all budgets. For details check 🖥 www.visitestonia.com or go to the tourist information centre (see above).

Vana Tom Hostel (☎ 631 3252, 🖥 www.hostel.ee/eng), Vaike-Karje 1, in the Old Town, charges from €15 for a dorm bed.

Further information about youth hostels is available from the Estonian Youth Hostels Association (🖥 eyha@online.ee, www.baltichostels.net).

LATVIA: RIGA

General information
● **Visas** Visas are not necessary for passport holders from the UK, USA, Australia, New Zealand, or most EU countries. Further information is available from 🖥 www.mfa.gov.lv/en.

● **Money** The unit of currency is the lati. There are exchange offices at Riga airport and throughout Riga. Most major banks will cash travellers' cheques and credit cards are increasingly accepted. ATMS are widespread.

● **Language** Latvian is the national language. English is spoken by most people living in the cities.

Arrival and departure

● **By air** Riga has air links with many cities including St Petersburg and Moscow. The airport is 8km south-west of the city centre. The information office on the first floor of the departure hall is open 09:00-21:00.

● **By rail** Riga Station is at Stacijas laukums. There are rail connections from Riga to St Petersburg and Moscow, and to Berlin via Warsaw but not to countries in Western Europe.

● **By bus** The bus terminal (🖥 www.autoosta.lv) is a few hundred metres from the train station. Eurolines (☎ 721 4080, 🖥 info@eurolines.lv, www.eurolines.lv) operates services from Riga to many European cities. Their office is in the international bus station, 1 Pragas St.

Tourist information

General information on Latvia is available from 🖥 www.latviatourism.lv.

For assistance with travel and accommodation in Riga contact **Riga Information Centre** (☎ 704 4377, 📄 704 4378) at Ratslaukums 6, LV-1050. The office is open 10:00-19:00 daily.

Where to stay

There are hostels all over Riga and information on them can be obtained from the tourist office. However, the only hostel in Riga that accepts the Hostelling International card is *Placis* (☎ 755 1824, 🖥 placis@delfi.lv) at Laimdotas 2a. Other places to try include: *Viesnica Aurora* (☎ 722 4479) on Marijas iela 5, conveniently located opposite the station; upmarket *Hotel Riga* (☎ 704 4222, 📄 704 4223, 🖥 info@hotelriga.lv) on the outskirts of Old Riga at Aspazijas bulvaris 22.

For all kinds of accommodation contact **Patricia Ltd** (☎ 728 4868, 📄 728 6650, 🖥 www.rigalatvia.net), Elizabetes 22-6. The office is a short walk from the train station and staff can also reserve air, train and bus tickets.

LITHUANIA: VILNIUS

General information

● **Visa** Visas are not necessary for passport holders from the EU, UK, USA, Canada, Australia and New Zealand. Check 🖥 www.urm.lt for details about the situation regarding other countries.

● **Money** The unit of currency, the litas, is pegged to the euro. Money can be exchanged at the airport and the railway station. Banks and special currency exchange booths are also located all around town. Credit cards are accepted in places which cater for tourists.

● **Language** Lithuanian is the national language but many people in the cities speak Russian and some speak English.

The Baltic States
Estonia, Latvia and Lithuania lie within easy reach of Moscow and St Petersburg, and any of them makes an interesting staging post for entering or leaving Russia. For in-depth information on the Baltic States useful guides are Bradt's *Baltic Capitals* and *Estonia, Latvia, Lithuania*; Lonely Planet's *Estonia, Latvia & Lithuania* and Insight's *Baltic States Guide*.

Arrival and departure
● **By air** Vilnius has air links with many cities in Europe. The airport is 4km south of the centre in the suburb of Kirtimai. Bus No 1 runs from the railway station to the airport. For general flight information phone ☎ 2-630201.
● **By rail** Vilnius is connected by rail to Kaliningrad, St Petersburg, Moscow, Riga and Warsaw. There is also a service to Tallinn via Kaunas. The station is situated at Gelezinkelio 16, at the southern end of the Old Town. For further information visit 🖳 www.litrail.lt.
● **By bus** Eurolines Baltic International (☎ 2-251377, 🖳 www.eurolines.lt) operates services to most Western European cities. Services also link Vilnius with Estonia, Latvia, Minsk, Berlin and Warsaw. The long-distance bus station is at Sodu gatve 22, next to the railway station. Tickets can be bought in the main ticket hall of the bus station.

Tourist information
The **Visit Lithuania TIC** (☎ 5-262 5241, 🖳 tic@visitlithuania.net, www.visitlithuania.net) is at Liejuklos gatve 8/26.
   Vilnius Tourist Information Centre (☎ 5-262 9660, 🖳 tic@vilnius.lt, www.turizmas.vilnius.lt) at Vilniaus Str 22 provides information, sells maps and books accommodation. There is also a branch at Didzioji Str 31 (☎ 5-262 6470, 🖳 turizm.info@vilnius.lt), open 09:00-19:00 weekdays, 10:00-16:00 weekends.

Where to stay
For B&B accommodation, contact **Litinterp** (☎ 5-212 3850, 🖳 vilnius@litinterp.lt, www.litinterp.lt), Bernardinu Str 7-2.
   The centrally-located *Hotel Astorija* (☎ 2-220110, 🖹 2-221762, www.sasradisson.com), at Didzioji gatve 35/2, has doubles from US$150. *Ars Viva* (☎/🖹 2-752495, 🖳 www2.omnitel.net/arsviva), Liubarto 17, is a small guest-house with rooms from US$53.
   The **Lithuanian Youth Hostels Association** (🖳 www.lithuanianhostels.org) has two hostels in Vilnius: *Old Town Hostel* (☎ 5-262 5357, 🖳 oldtownhostels@delfi.net), Ausros Vartu Str, 300 metres from the railway and bus stations, and *Filaretai Hostel* (☎ 5-225 4627, 🖳 filaretai@post.omnitel.net), Filaretu gatve 17.

APPENDIX A: ALTERNATIVE ROUTE

For travellers visiting Sergiev Posad, Rostov-Yaroslavski and Yaroslavl, the more northern rail route avoiding Nizhny Novgorod is included here. The routes follow the same track as far as Fryazevo (Km54). After Yaroslavl this route joins the main Trans-Siberian route at Kotelnich (Km870).

Km0: Moscow Москва   **Yaroslavsky Station** Ярославский вокзал
See pp327 for the route as far as Fryazevo (Km54).

Km57: Abramtsevo Абрамцево   About 3km from the station is the Abramtsevo Estate, one of the most important centres of Russian culture in the second half of the 19th century. Today the Abramtsevo estate is a museum and well worth a day trip from Moscow (see p165).

Km59: Khotkovo Хотьково   This town (pop: 22,000) has a well preserved historic section on the high bank of the Pazha River which flows through its centre.

Km73 (N): Sergiev Posad Сергиев Посад   [See p179]
Have your camera ready for the stunning blue and gold domes of the cathedrals of Sergiev Posad (pop: 110,000), known as **Zagorsk** between 1930 and 1993.

Km112: Aleksandrov Александров   This little-known town was, for nearly two decades in the 16th century, the real capital of Russia. From 1564 to 1581 Ivan the Terrible lived here and directly ruled the half of the country which he called the *oprichnina,* having abandoned the rest to the authority of the *boyars* (nobles) and monasteries. The oprichnina was policed by *oprichniki,* mostly low class thugs, mercenaries and foreign adventurers. Ivan the Terrible certainly deserved his soubriquet. In his dungeons here he devised and supervised some of the cruellest tortures imaginable.
    In the yard just east of the station (N) are six old **steam locomotives**.

Km145: Berendeyevo Берендеево   There is a 21km branch line to the west from here to the Golden Ring town of Pereslavl-Zalesski.

Km200: Petrovsk Петровск   About 15km east of Petrovsk you will see **Lake Nero** on the right. Rostov-Yaroslavski sits on the western shore.

Km224: Rostov-Yaroslavski Ростов-Ярославский (pop: 34,800)   [See p184]
Attractively located by Lake Nero, this is one of the most interesting Golden Ring cities.

Km240 (N): Amidst the fields and quite close to the track is a sadly neglected but **picturesque church** with five dilapidated domes and a tower.

Km284: Yaroslavl Ярославль (●●) (pop: 608,600)   [See p189]
Yaroslavl was founded in 1010 by the Christian king Yaroslavl the Wise. It grew quickly into an important trading centre on the Volga shipping route. Many of the ancient cathedrals still stand in spite of the heavy fighting that went on here during the Civil War.

MAP 2a

About five minutes after entering Yaroslavl's outskirts you pass the suburban station of **Kotorosl** (Которосль) and on the left you can see the **Church of St Peter and St Paul** with a 58m bell-tower beside it.

Km289: Volga River About five minutes after leaving the station, the train changes direction from north to east and crosses the mighty Volga River, which is about 1km wide here. In times gone by Russians held this river in such esteem that passengers would stand and take off their hats to Mother Volga as the train rattled onto the first spans of the long bridge. Rising in the Valdai hills, Europe's longest river meanders 3700km down to the Caspian Sea.

Km356: Danilov Данилов (●●●) (pop: 19,000) A change of locomotive allows time for buying provisions from the traders on the platform.

Km394: Lyubim Любим Lyubim's population is decreasing – down at least 10% since 1980 to about 6000 – typical of the Russia-wide migration trend from villages to large cities.

───────── **Km 420-1266 TIME ZONE MT + 1** ─────────

Km450: Buy Буй (●●) (pop: 28,700) There is nothing of interest in this industrial town specializing in cheese, flax and mineral fertilizers. Rotting silt (sapropel) is extracted from the lake and dried to be used as fuel or made into fertilizer.

Km501: Galich Галич After the station, on the right (S) you pass **Paisiev Monastery**.

Km651: Manturovo Мантурово (pop: 21,100) After leaving this industrial and forestry town the train crosses the Unzha River (Km654).

Km698: Sharya Шарья (●●) (pop: 26,400) Some steam locos are stored here (L and Er classes) but numbers are dwindling. This is the region's biggest timber centre.

Km818: Svetcha Светча Roughly mid-way between Sharya and Svetcha you enter **Kirovskaya Oblast**. Most of this region's 120,800 sq km are within the basin of the Vyatka River. The greater part of the oblast is taiga and the main industry here is logging.

Km870: Kotelnich Котельнич (pop: 30,700) See p333.

MAP 3a

APPENDIX B: TIMETABLES

Timetables for the most popular trains on the Trans-Siberian, Trans-Mongolian, and Trans-Manchurian routes are given below. Unless otherwise indicated, departure times are shown; for arrival times simply subtract the number of minutes shown as the stopping time.

Another useful source of information is the *Thomas Cook Overseas Timetable*, updated every two months, with single issues available from Thomas Cook Publishing (☎ 01733-416477, 🖳 www.thomascooktimetables.com, PO Box 227, Peterborough PE3 8XX, UK) for £9.50 online or £11/13/14.50 from the UK/Europe/elsewhere.

On the Internet you can find Russian train timetables searchable by town at 🖳 parovoz.com/spravka/timetables.html, which also has an English version. For others, follow the 'timetables' link at 🖳 parovoz.com/cgi-bin/rrr.cgi (Railway Ring). Another option is 🖳 www.poezda.net/train.htm, with timetables searchable by station, train number or end points (though you must use specific and sometimes curious transliterations for town names, e.g., Moskva, Pekin, Habarovsk, Blagovescen, Ulan-bator). See p13 for more on these and other useful websites.

But timetables change all the time, so you should not take any of these as the last word; the only truly reliable timetable will be the one posted in the corridor of your carriage!

Table 1 Trans-Siberian: Moscow–Vladivostok (Train Nos 1 & 2: *Rossiya*)

Departures are every other day in each direction, usually eastbound on odd dates and westbound on even dates. Times shown are departure times – subtract stop for arrival time.

MT = Moscow Time; **LT** = Local Time; **–** = no stop

Station		Km from Mos	Stop (mins, E/W)	Eastbound No 2 MT	LT	Westbound No 1 MT	LT	Time Zone MT+
Moscow (Yaroslavsky)	Москва (Ярославский)	0		Day 1 17:16	17.16	16:42	16:42	0
Vladimir	Владимир	191	23/23	20:38	20:38	13:35	13:35	0
Nizhny Novgorod (Gorky)	Нижний Новгород (Горький)	442	15/15	23:50	23:50	09:59	09:59	0
Vyatka (Kirov)	Вятка (Киров)	957	20/20	Day 2 05:45	05:45	03:45	03:45	0
Glazov	Глазов	1165	2/2	08:31	08:31	00:40	00:40	0
Balyezino	Балезино	1194	23/23	09:22	09:22	00:14	00:14	0
Perm 2	Пермь 2	1436	20/20	13:11	15:11	Day 7 20:15	22:15	2
Yekaterinburg	Екатеринбург	1816	41/41	19:34	21:34	14:17	16:17	2
Tyumen	Тюмень	2144	20/20	Day 3 00:08	02:08	09:17	11:17	2

❑ Kilometre-post discrepancies

Distances on official timetables do not always match those indicated by kilometre posts beside the track. Close to Moscow you may notice discrepancies of 10km or more. Beyond Kotelnich (Km870), the junction of the Trans-Siberian and Moscow–Yaroslavl–Vyatka lines, differences grow to 30-40km, largely because until a few years ago most Trans-Siberian traffic used the (longer) line via Yaroslavl.

Table 1 Trans-Siberian: Moscow–Vladivostok (Train Nos 1 & 2: *Rossiya*) cont'd

Station		Km from Mos	Stop (mins, E/W)	Eastbound No 2 MT	LT	Westbound No 1 MT	LT	Time Zone MT+
Ishim	Ишим	2431	12/12	03:46	05:46	05:29	07:29	2
Omsk	Омск	2712	25/25	07:43	10:43	01:53	04:53	3
						Day 6		
Tatarskaya	Татарская	2881	2/-	09:39	12:39	–	–	3
Barabinsk	Барабинск	3040	17/15	11:40	14:40	21:44	00:44	3
Novosibirsk	Новосибирск	3335	21/27	15:40	18:40	17:55	20:55	3
Tayga	Тайга	3570	25/25	19:18	23:18	14:18	18:18	4
Mariinsk	Мариинск	3715	20/20	21:42	01:42	11:56	15:56	4
Bogotol	Боготол	3849	8/3	23:46	03:46	09:30	13:30	4
				Day 4				
Achinsk 1	Ачинск 1	3917	2/2	00:45	04:45	08:24	12:24	4
Krasnoyarsk	Красноярск	4098	20/20	04:04	08:04	05:15	09:15	4
Zaozyornaya	Заозёрная	4262	2/2	06:44	10:44	02:04	06:04	4
Kansk-Yeniseysky	Канск-Енисейский	4343	2/5	07:56	11:56	00:50	04:50	4
Ilanskaya	Иланская	4375	20/20	08:48	12:48	00:12	04:12	4
						Day 5		
Reshoty	Решоты	4453	2/2	10:04	14:04	22:41	02:41	4
Tayshet	Тайшет	4516	5/5	11:10	16:10	21:41	02:41	5
Nizhneudinsk	Нижнеудинск	4680	23/23	14:09	19:09	19:10	00:10	5
Tulun	Тулун	4794	2/2	15:44	20:44	17:11	22:11	5
Zima	Зима	4940	25/25	18:04	23:04	15:14	20:14	5
Cheremkhovo	Черемхово	5061	2/2	19:50	00:50	13:08	18:08	5
Usolye-Sibirskoye	Усолье-Сибирское	5124	2/2	20:43	01:43	12:11	17:11	5
Angarsk	Ангарск	5160	2/2	21:14	02:14	11:42	16:42	5
Irkutsk Sortirovka	Иркутск Сортировка	5178	12/12	22:00	03:00	11:06	16:06	5
Irkutsk	Иркутск	5185	23/23	22:36	03:36	10:39	15:39	5
				Day 5				
Slyudyanka 1	Слюдянка 1	5312	10/10	00:53	05:53	08:13	13:13	5
Ulan Ude	Улан Уде	5642	23/23	05:57	10:57	03:23	08:23	5
Petrovsky Zavod	Петровский Завод	5784	2/3	08:02	14:02	01:02	07:02	6
						Day 4		
Khilok	Хилок	5932	3/4	10:31	16:31	21:33	03:33	6
Mogzon	Могзон	6053	19/15	12:38	18:38	20:43	02:43	6
Chita	Чита	6199	21/21	15:30	21:30	18:02	00:02	6
Darasun	Дарасун	6265	2/2	16:49	22:49	16:28	22:28	6
Karymskaya	Карымская	6293	20/20	17:46	23:46	15:50	21:50	6
Shilka	Шилка	6446	3/3	20:16	02:16	13:00	19:00	6
Priiskovaya	Приисковая	6496	2/2	21:02	03:02	12:10	18:10	6
Kuenga	Куэнга	6532	2/2	21:47	03:47	11:29	17:29	6
Chernyshevsk-Zabaikalsky	Чернышевск-Забайкальский	6593	25/25	23:17	05:17	10:25	16:25	6
						Day 6		
Zilovo	Зилово	6670	2/2	00:45	06:45	08:36	14:36	6
Ksenyevskaya	Ксеньевская	6789	2/2	02:51	08:51	06:17	12:17	6
Mogocha	Могоча	6906	15/15	05:05	11:05	04:27	10:27	6

Table 1 Trans-Siberian: Moscow–Vladivostok (Train Nos 1 & 2: *Rossiya*) cont'd

Station		Km from Mos	Stop (mins, E/W)	Eastbound No 2 MT	LT	Westbound No 1 MT	LT	Time Zone MT+
Amazar	Амазар	7010	20/20	06:57	12:57	02:32	08:32	6
Yerofei--Pavlovich	Ерофей-Павлович	7119	21/21	09:25	15:25	00:19 Day 3	06:19	6
Urusha	Уруша	7211	2/2	11:08	17:08	22:14	04:14	6
Skovorodino	Сковородино	7306	3/3	13:00	19:00	20:21	02:21	6
Magdagachi	Магдагачи	7501	15/15	16:14	22:14	17:13	23:13	6
Tygda	Тыгда		2/2	17:15	23:15	15:55	21:55	6
Shimanovskaya	Шимановская	7723	2/2	19:31	01:31	13:41	19:41	6
Svobodny	Свободный	7815	5/5	20:44	02:44	12:26	18:26	6
Belogorsk	Белогорск	7873	30/30	22:06	04:06	11:28	17:28	6
Zavitaya	Завитая	7992	5/2	23:56 Day 7	05:56	09:16	15:16	6
Bureya	Бурея	8037	5/2	00:38	06:38	08:34	14:34	6
Arkhara	Архара	8088	2/2	01:34	07:34	07:40	13:40	6
Obluchye	Облучье	8198	15/15	03:45	10:45	05:46	12:46	7
Birobidzhan	Биробиджан	8351	5/5	06:37	13:37	02:54	09:54	7
Khabarovsk	Хабаровск	8521	23/23	09:15	16:15	00:32 Day 2	07:32	7
Vyazemskaya	Вяземская	8642	16/16	11:20	18:20	22:15	05:15	7
Bikin	Бикин	8756	1/1	12:47	19:47	20:28	03:28	7
Guberovo	Губерово	8839	20/20	14:20	21:20	19:20	02:20	7
Dalnerechensk	Дальнереченск	8890	1/1	14:58	21:58	18:21	01:21	7
Ruzhino	Ружино	8941	12/12	16:05	23:05	17:29	00:29	7
Spassk-Dalny	Спасск-Дальний	9050	20/20	18:05	01:05	15:37	22:37	7
Muchnaya	Мучная	9092	1/1	18:44	01:44	14:37	21:37	7
Sibirtsevo	Сибирцево	9109	2/2	19:09	02:09	14:12	21:12	7
Ussurisk	Уссурийск	9177	18/18	20:31	03:31	13:06	20:06	7
Ugolnaya	Угольная	9255	2/2	21:54	04:54	11:32	18:32	7
Vladivostok	Владивосток	9289		22:35	05:35	10:50 Day 1	17:50	7

Table 2 Irkutsk–Ulan Bator (Train Nos 263 & 264: *Angara*)

Departures are daily, although at the time of writing there were plans to reduce the service to every other day. Times shown are departure times – subtract stop for arrival time.

MT = Moscow Time; **LT** = Local Time; **–** = no stop

1hr+ = 1 hour minimum stopping time but invariably much longer

Station		Km from Mos	Stop (mins, E/W)	Eastbound No 264 MT	LT	Westbound No 263 MT	LT	Time Zone MT+
Irkutsk	Иркутск	5185		15:27 Day 1	20:27	03:27	08:27	5
Kaia	Кая	5192	2/2	15:42	20:42	03:16	08:16	5
Goncharovo	Гончарово	5214	2/3	16:01	21:01	03:00	08:00	5
Bolshoy Lug	Большой Луг	5223	2/2	16:21	21:21	02:39	07:39	5
Khanchin	Ханчин	5227	1/1	16:29	21:29	02:32	07:32	5
Podkamennaya	Подкаменная	5249	2/2	16:54	21:54	02:06	07:06	5

Table 2 Irkutsk–Ulan Bator (Train Nos 263 & 264: *Angara*) cont'd

Station		Km from Mos	Stop (mins, E/W)	Eastbound No 264 MT	LT	Westbound No 263 MT	LT	Time Zone MT+
Glubokaya	Глубокая	5262	2/2	17:11	22:11	01:48	06:48	5
Andrianovskaya	Андриановская	5274	2/2	17:27	22:27	01:32	06:32	5
Angasolka	Ангасолка	5285	2/2	17:43	22:43	01:15	06:15	5
Slyudyanka	Слюдянка	5307	2/2	18:11	23:11	00:47	05:47	5
Slyudyanka 1	Слюдянка 1	5312	10/16	18:34	23:34	00:33	05:33	5
						Day 3		
Utulik	Утулик	5340	1/1	19:07	00:07	23:43	04:43	5
Baikal Pass.	Байкал Пасс	5351	1/1	19:17	00:17	23:33	04:33	5
Baikalsk	Байкальск	5358	2/2	19:26	00:26	23:28	04:28	5
Murino	Мурино	5362	1/1	19:40	00:40	23:04	04:04	5
Vydrino	Выдрино	5390	2/2	20:01	01:01	22:50	03:50	5
Kedrovaya-Sibirskaya	Кедровая-Сибирская	5412	2/2	20:23	01:23	22:27	03:27	5
Tankhoy	Танхой	5426	2/2	20:41	01:41	22:08	03:08	5
Pereyemnaya	Переемная	5437	2/2	20:56	01:56	21:54	02:54	5
Mishikha	Мишиха	5456	2/2	21:21	02:21	21:29	02:29	5
Klyuyevka	Клюевка	5467	2/2	21:35	02:35	21:15	02:15	5
Mysovaya	Мысовая	5477	2/2	21:50	02:50	21:01	02:01	5
Boyarsky	Боярский	5504	2/2	22:20	03:20	20:33	01:33	5
Kultushnaya	Култушная	5512	1/1	22:30	03:30	20:23	01:23	5
Posolskaya	Посольская	5530	2/2	22:46	03:46	20:08	01:08	5
Timlyuy	Тимлюй	5549	2/2	23:06	04:06	19:48	00:48	5
Selenginsk	Селенгинск	5562	2/2	23:26	04:26	19:29	00:29	5
Talovka	Таловка	5585	2/2	23:46	04:46	19:10	00:10	5
Lesovozny	Лесовозный	5596	2/2	23:57	04:57	18:59	23:59	5
				Day 2				
Tataurovo	Татаурово	5609	2/2	00:10	05:10	18:45	23:45	5
Mostovoy	Мостовой	5625	2/2	00:30	05:30	18:25	23:25	5
Divizionnaya	Дивизионная	5637	2/2	00:51	05:51	18:04	23:04	5
Ulan Ude	Улан Уде	5642	42/40	01:43	06:43	17:50	22:50	5
Zaudinsky	Заудинский	5655	2/2	02:00	07:00	16:53	21:53	5
Komushka	Комушка	5661	1/1	02:10	07:10	16:35	21:35	5
Medvedchikovo	Медведчиково	5666	2/2	02:25	07:25	16:26	21:26	5
Sayantuy	Саянтуй	5680	2/2	02:46	07:46	16:04	21:04	5
Shaluty	Шалуты	5694	1/1	03:02	08:02	15:46	20:46	5
Omulevka	Омулевка	5702	1/1	03:12	08:12	15:22	20:22	5
Ganzurino	Ганзурино	5710	2/2	03:38	08:38	15:14	20:14	5
Orongoy	Оронгой	5723	2/2	03:57	08:57	14:56	19:56	5
Ubukun	Убукун	5732	2/2	04:19	09:19	14:37	19:37	5
Telman	Тельман	5745	1/1	04:27	09:27	14:16	19:16	5
Sulfat	Сульфат	5757	3/2	05:05	10:05	14:04	19:04	5
Zagustay	Загустай	5769	2/5	05:22	10:22	13:45	18:45	5
Baraty	Бараты	5782	2/2	05:38	10:38	13:25	18:25	5
Murtoy	Муртой	5792	1/1	05:49	10:49	13:10	18:10	5
Gusinoye Ozero	Гусино Озеро	5800	3/2	06:03	11:03	13:00	18:00	5
Temnik	Темник	5813	1/1	06:15	11:15	12:42	17:42	5

Table 2 Irkutsk–Ulan Bator (Train Nos 263 & 264: *Angara*) cont'd

Station		Km from Mos	Stop (mins, E/W)	Eastbound No 264 MT	LT	Westbound No 263 MT	LT	Time Zone MT+
Selenduma	Селендума	5827	2/6	06:39	11:39	12:25	17:25	5
Butikha	Бутиха	5842	1/1	06:50	11:50	11:58	16:58	5
Dzhida	Джида	5852	2/5	07:09	12:09	11.50	16:50	5
Khuzhir	Хужир	5866	1/1	07:32	12:32	11:27	16:27	5
Kharankhoy	Харанхой	5880	2/2	07:51	12:51	11:10	16:10	5
Naushki	Наушки	5895	1hr+	12:50	27:50	10:40	15:40	5
MONGOLIA						**RUSSIA**		
Sühbaatar	Сухбаатар	5925	1hr+	21:05 UB time		09:45		
Darhan	Дархан	6023	57/10	00:25		02:48 Day 2		
Zuunhara	Дзунхара	6132	20/__	__		__		
Ulan Bator	Улаанбаатар	6304		06:20*		20:45 Day 1		

* often up to two hours late into Ulan Bator.

Table 3 Moscow–Irkutsk (Train Nos 9 & 10 *Baikal*)

Departures are every other day in each direction, eastbound on odd dates and westbound on even dates. Times shown are departure times – subtract stop for arrival time.

MT = Moscow Time; **LT** = Local Time; – = no stop

Station		Km from Mos	Stop (min, E/W)	Eastbound No 10 MT	LT	Westbound No 9 MT	LT	Time Zone MT+
Moscow (Yaroslavky)	Москва (Ярославский)	0		Day 1 23:30	23:30	16:52	16:52	0
Vladimir	Владимир	191	23/23	Day 2 02:50	02:50	13:45	13:45	0
Nizhny Novgorod (Gorky)	Нижний Новгород (Горький)	442	15/15	06:09	06:09	10:09	10:09	0
Kotelnich 1	Котельнич	870	2/2	10:42	10:42	05:10	05:10	0
Vyatka (Kirov)	Вятка (Киров)	957	20/20	12:19	12:19	03:55	03:55	0
Glazov	Глазов	1165	2/2	15:17	15:17	00:50	00:50	0
Balyezino	Балезино	1194	23/23	16:08	16:08	00:24 Day 4	00:24	0
Perm 2	Пермь 2	1436	20/20	19:59	21:59	20:27	22:27	2
Yekaterinburg (Sverdlovsk)	Екатеринбург (Свердловск)	1816	24/23	Day 3 02:02	04:02	14:31	16:31	2
Tyumen	Тюмень	2144	20/20	06:35	08:35	09:50	11:50	2
Ishim	Ишим	2431	12/12	10:14	12:14	06:01	08:01	2
Nazyvayevskaya	Называевская	2565	2/2	11:59	14:59	04:12	07:12	3
Omsk	Омск	2712	15/15	13:53	16:53	02:22	05:22	3
Tatarskaya	Татарская	2881	2/2	15:54	18:54	00:05 Day 3	03:05	3
Ozero Karachinskoye	Озеро Карачиское	2945	2/2	16:40	19:40	23:18	02:18	3

Table 3 Moscow–Irkutsk (Train Nos 9 & 10 *Baikal*) cont'd

Station		Km from Mos	Stop (min, E/W)	Eastbound No 10 MT	LT	Westbound No 9 MT	LT	Time Zone MT+
Barabinsk	Барабинск	3040	15/15	17:58	20:58	22:10	01:10	3
Novosibirsk	Новосибирск	3335	20/16	21:55 **Day 4**	00:55	18:23	21:23	3
Tayga	Тайга	3570	5/10	01:11	05:11	14:55	18:55	4
Mariinsk	Мариинск	3715	20/20	03:26	07:26	12:47	16:47	4
Bogotol	Боготол	3849	3/3	05:25	09:25	10:21	14:21	4
Achinsk 1	Ачинск 1	3917	2/2	06:24	10:24	09:15	13:15	4
Krasnoyarsk	Красноярск	4098	20/20	09:43	13:43	06:08	10:08	4
Zaozyornaya	Заозёрная	4262	2/2	12:22	16:22	02:57	06:57	4
Kansk--Yeniseysky	Канск-Енисейский	4343	2/2	13:34	17:34	01:44	05:44	4
Ilanskaya	Иланская	4375	20/23	14:26	18:26	01:09 **Day 2**	05:09	4
Tayshet	Тайшет	4516	24/5	17:03	22:03	22:41	03:41	5
Nizhneudinsk	Нижнеудинск	4680	23/23	20:02	01:02	20:10	01:10	5
Tulun	Тулун	4794	2/2	21:37	02:37	18:11	23:11	5
Kuytun	Куйтун	4875	2/2	22:44 **Day 5**	03:44	17:05	22:05	5
Zima	Зима	4940	25/25	00:01	05:01	16:08	21:08	5
Zalari	Залари	4995	2/2	00:57	05:57	14:52	19:52	5
Cheremkhovo	Черемхово	5061	2/2	01:53	06:53	13:57	18:57	5
Usolye-Sibirskoye	Усолье-Сибирское	5124	2/2	02:46	07:46	13:00	18:00	5
Angarsk	Ангарск	5160	2/2	03:17	08:17	12:31	17:31	5
Irkutsk Sortirovka	Иркутск Сортировка	5178	2/3	03:53	08:53	11:55	16:55	5
Irkutsk	Иркутск	5185		04:06	09:06	11:35 **Day 1**	16:35	5

Table 4 Trans-Mongolian: Moscow–Beijing (Train Nos 3 & 4)

One per week in each direction: currently ex-Moscow on Tues, ex-Beijing on Wed. Times shown are departure times – subtract stop for arrival time.

MT = Moscow Time; **LT** = Local Time; **–** = no stop

1hr+ = 1 hour minimum stopping time but invariably much longer

Station		Km from Mos	Stop (min, E/W)	Eastbound No 4 MT	LT	Westbound No 3 MT	LT	Time Zone MT+
Moscow (Yaroslavsky)	Москва (Ярославский)	0		**Day 1** 22:03	22:03	14:19	14:19 **Day 2**	0
Vladimir	Владимир	191	23/23	01:26	01:26	11:02	11:02	0
Nizhny Novgorod (Gorky)	Нижний Новгород (Горький)	442	15/15	04:37	04:37	07:13	07:13	0
Vyatka (Kirov)	Вятка (Киров)	957	25/20	10:42	10:42	01:05	01:05	0

Table 4 Trans-Mongolian: Moscow–Beijing (Train Nos 3 & 4) cont'd

Station		Km from Mos	Stop (min, E/W)	Eastbound No 4 MT	LT	Westbound No 3 MT	LT	Time Zone MT+
						Day 6		
Balyezino	Балезино	1194	23/23	14:31	14:31	21:39	21:39	0
Perm 2	Пермь 2	1436	20/20	18:20	20:20	17:42	19:42	2
				Day 3				
Yekaterinburg (Sverdlovsk)	Екатеринбург (Свердловск)	1816	23/23	00:18	02:18	11:52	13:52	2
Tyumen	Тюмень	2144	20/20	04:47	06:47	07:12	09:12	2
Ishim	Ишим	2431	12/12	08:25	10:25	03:24	05:24	2
						Day 5		
Omsk	Омск	2712	15/15	12:00	15:00	23:54	02:54	3
Barabinsk	Барабинск	3040	15/15	15:56	18:56	20:00	23:00	3
Novosibirsk	Новосибирск	3335	15/28	19:50	22:50	16:13	19:13	3
Tayga	Тайга	3570	5/3	23:08	03:08	12:29	16:29	4
				Day 4				
Mariinsk	Мариинск	3715	20/20	01:23	05:23	10:32	14:32	4
Bogotol	Боготол	3849	3/3	03:22	07:22	08:06	12:06	4
Achinsk 1	Ачинск 1	3917	2/2	04:21	08:21	07:00	11:00	4
Krasnoyarsk	Красноярск	4098	20/20	07:40	11:40	03:52	07:52	4
						Day 4		
Ilanskaya	Иланская	4375	23/20	12:21	16:21	23:00	03:00	4
Tayshet	Тайшет	4516	2/2	14:39	19:39	20:35	01:35	5
Nizhneudinsk	Нижнеудинск	4680	23/23	17:38	22:38	18:07	23:07	5
Zima	Зима	4940	20/25	21:24	02:24	14:05	19:05	5
				Day 5				
Angarsk	Ангарск	5160	2/2	00:25	05:25	10:42	15:42	5
Irkutsk Sortirovka	Иркутск Сортировка	5178	10/12	01:09	06:09	10:06	15:06	5
Irkutsk	Иркутск	5185	23/23	01:45	06:45	09:39	14:39	5
Slyudyanka 1	Слюдянка 1	5312	10/10	04:02	09:02	07:13	12:13	5
Ulan Ude	Улан Уде	5642	31/23	09:14	14:14	02:23	07:23	5
						Day 3		
Gusinoye Ozero	Гусино Озеро	5800	2/2	11:58	16:58	23:19	04:19	5
Dzhida	Джида	5852	2/2	12:50	17:50	22:31	03:31	5
Naushki	Наушки	5895	1hr+	16:40	21:40	21:40	02:40	5
Dozorny	Дозорный	5900	3/30	16:54	21:54	17:43	22:43	5
MONGOLIA				**Day 6**		**RUSSIA**		
Sühbaatar	Сухбаатар	5925	1hr+	00:20 UB time		22:05		
Darhan	Дархан	6023	20/10	02:13		19:20		
Zuunhara	Дзунхара	6132	25/21	04:33		17:05		
Ulan Bator	Улаанбаатар	6304	30/35	07:50		13:50		
Choyr	Чойр	6551	15/20	12:29		09:05		
Saynshand	Сайншанд	7778	20/25	16:03		05:15		
Zamiin Uud	Дзамын Уд	7013	1hr+	21:35		01:20		
CHINA						**MONGOLIA**		
				Day 7		**Day 2**		
Erlyan		7023	1hr+	01:55 Bei time		23:16		

Table 4 Trans-Mongolian: Moscow–Beijing (Train Nos 3 & 4) cont'd

Station	Km from Mos	Stop (min, E/W)	Eastbound No 4 MT	LT	Westbound No 3 MT	LT	Time Zone MT+
Jining	7356	13/10	06:41		16:23		
Datong	7483	8/16	08:35		14:26		
Zhangjiakou	7661	6/5	11:04		11:42		
Beijing	7865		15:33		07:40 Day 1		

Table 5 Trans-Manchurian: Moscow–Beijing (Train Nos 19 & 20: *Vostok*)

One per week in each direction; currently ex-Moscow on Fri, ex-Beijing on Sat. Times shown are departure times – subtract stop for arrival time.

MT = Moscow Time; **LT** = Local Time; **–** = no stop

1hr+ = 1 hour minimum stopping time but invariably much longer

Station		Km from Mos	Stop (min, E/W)	Eastbound No 20 MT	LT	Westbound No 19 MT	LT	Time Zone MT+
Moscow (Yaroslavsky)	Москва (Ярославский)	0		Day 1 23:58 Day 2	23:58	17:55	17:55	0
Vladimir	Владимир	191	23/23	03:23	03:23	14:44	14:44	0
Nizhny Novgorod (Gorky)	Нижний Новгород (Горький)	442	15/15	06:45	06:45	11:03	11:03	0
Vyatka (Kirov)	Вятка (Киров)	957	20/20	12:49	12:49	04:40	04:40	0
Balyezino	Балезино	1194	23/23	16:16	16:16	01:14 Day 7	01:14	0
Perm 2	Пермь 2	1436	20/20	20:08	22:08	21:18	23:18	2
Yekaterinburg (Sverdlovsk)	Екатеринбург (Свердловск)	1816	23/23	Day 3 02:09	04:09	15:27	17:27	2
Tyumen	Тюмень	2144	20/20	06:45	08:45	10:47	12:47	2
Ishim	Ишим	2431	12/12	10:24	12:24	06:59	08:59	2
Omsk	Омск	2712	15/15	14:13	17:13	03:30 Day 6	06:30	3
Barabinsk	Барабинск	3040	15/17	18:07	21:07	23:34	02:34	3
Novosibirsk	Новосибирск	3335	25/26	22:10 Day 4	01:10	19:40	22:40	3
Tayga	Тайга	3570	3/4	01:26	05:26	15:58	19:58	4
Mariinsk	Мариинск	3715	20/20	03:39	07:39	13:59	17:59	4
Bogotol	Боготол	3849	3/3	05:38	09:38	11:33	15:33	4
Achinsk 1	Ачинск 1	3917	2/2	06:37	10:37	10:27	14:27	4
Krasnoyarsk	Красноярск	4098	20/20	09:56	13:56	07:20	11:20	4
Zaozyornaya	Заозёрная	4262	2/2	12:35	16:35	04:09	08:09	4
Kansk-- Yeniseysky	Канск- Енисейский	4343	2/2	13:47	17:47	02:57	06:57	4
Ilanskaya	Иланская	4375	22/20	14:39	18:39	02:24 Day 5	06:24	4
Tayshet	Тайшет	4516	2/2	16:54	21:54	23:59	04:59	5
Nizhneudinsk	Нижнеудинск	4680	23/23	19:53	00:53	21:31	02:31	5

Table 5 Trans-Manchurian: Moscow–Beijing (Train Nos 19 & 20: *Vostok*) cont'd

Station		Km from Mos	Stop (min, E/W)	Eastbound No 20 MT	LT	Westbound No 19 MT	LT	Time Zone MT+
Zima	Зима	4940	25/25	23:44	04:44	17:39	22:39	5
				Day 5				
Angarsk	Ангарск	5160	2/2	02:45	07:45	14:16	19:16	5
Irkutsk	Иркутск	5185	23/23	03:54	08:54	13:26	18:26	5
Slyudyanka 1	Слюдянка 1	5312	10/10	06:11	11:11	11:00	16:00	5
Ulan Ude	Улан Уде	5642	23/23	11:15	16:15	06:10	11:10	5
Petrovsky Zavod	Петровский Завод	5784	2/3	13:20	19:20	03:50	09:50	6
Khilok	Хилок	5932	3/3	15:49	21:49	01:19	07:19	6
						Day 4		
Mogzon	Могзон	6053	19/15	17:56	23:56	23:28	05:28	6
Chita	Чита	6199	21/20	20:48	02:48	20:47	02:47	6
Karymskaya	Карымская	6293	25/25	23:05	05:05	18:40	00:40	6
Adrianovka	Адриановка	6314	3/–	23:36	05:36	–	–	6
Sedlovaya	Седловая	6329	–/2	–	–	17:19	23:19	6
				Day 6				
Mogoytuy	Могойтуй	6370	2/2	01:09	07:09	16:19	22:19	6
Olovyannaya	Оловянная	6444	2/2	02:57	08:57	14:21	20:21	6
Borzya	Борзя	6543	19/25	05:50	11:50	11:49	17:49	6
Dauriya	Даурия	6609	1/2	07:43	13:43	09:33	15:33	6
Zabaikalsk	Забайкальск	6661	1hr+	14:06	20:06	08:25	14:25	6
CHINA						**RUSSIA**		
Manzhouli		6678	1hr+	23:10 Bei time		07:01		
				Day 7				
Hailar		6864	14/8	01:57		02:15		
						Day 3		
Boketu		7074	11/8	05:36		22:35		
Angangxi		7343	18/10	09:29		18:45		
Daqing		7454	8/4	10:47		17:22		
Harbin		7613	15/15	12:45		15:38		
Changchun		7855	8/8	15:34		12:40		
Siping		7971	30/3	16:55		11:14		
Shenyang		8160	15/15	19:20		09:02		
Jinzhou		8402	3/3	21:52		06:12		
				Day 8				
Shanhaiguan		8586	8/8	00:01		04:16		
Tangshan		8739	3/3	02:11		02:01		
Tianjin		8868	8/8	03:49		00:28		
						Day 2		
Beijing		9001		05:20		22:50		
						Day 1		

APPENDIX C: LIST OF SIBERIAN FAUNA

There are extensive displays of local animals in the natural history museums of Novosibirsk, Irkutsk and Khabarovsk but the labelling is in Russian and Latin. The following translation is given for non-Russian-speaking readers whose Latin is rusty or non-existent. In the list below the letters given beside the animal's English name indicate its natural habitat. NS = Northern Siberia/Arctic Circle; SP = Siberian Plain; AS = Altai-Sayan Plateau/Mongolia; BI = Lake Baikal/Transbaikal region; FE = Far Eastern Territories. Where a Latin name is similar to the English (eg *Vipera* = Viper) these names have been omitted.

Accipiter gentilis goshawk (AS/SP/NS/BI/FE)

Aegoceras montanus mountain ram (AS)

Aegoceras sibiricus Siberian goat (BI)

Aegolius funereus boreal/Tengmalm's owl (BI/FE)

Aegypius monachus black vulture (AS)

Aethia cristatella crested auklet (NS/FE)

Alces alces elk/moose (AS/SP/BI/FE)

Allactaga jaculus five-toed jerboa (SP/BI)

Alopex lagopus arctic fox (NS)

Anas acuta pintail (BI)

Anas clypeata shoveler (SP/BI/FE)

Anas crecca teal (BI/SP/FE)

Anas falcata falcated teal (SP/BI/FE)

Anas formosa Baikal teal (BI)

Anas platyrhynchos mallard (AS/SP/BI/FE)

Anas poecilorhyncha spotbill duck (AS/BI)

Anser anser greylag goose (SP/BI)

Anser erythropus white-fronted goose (AS/SP/BI/FE)

Antelope gutturosa/crispa antelope (FE)

Arctomis bobac marmot (AS/SP)

Ardea cinerea grey heron (AS/SP/BI)

Aquila clanga greater spotted eagle (SP)

Botaurus stellaris bittern (SP/BI/FE)

Bubo bubo eagle owl (BI/FE)

Buteo lagopus rough legged buzzard (NS/SP/FE)

Butorides striatus striated/green heron (FE)

Canis alpinus mountain wolf (AS/FE)

Canis corsac korsak/steppe fox (BI/FE)

Canis lagopus arctic fox (NS)

Canis lupus wolf (SP/BI/FE)

Canis procyonoides Amur racoon (FE)

Capra sibirica Siberian mountain goat/ibex (AS/BI)

Capreolus capreolus roe deer (SP/BI/FE)

Castor fiber beaver (SP/BI/FE)

Certhia familiaris common treecreeper (AS/BI/FE)

Cervus alces elk (AS/BI/FE)

Cervus capreolus roe-buck (BI/FE)

Cervus elephas maral deer (AS/BI/FE)

Cervus nippon sika/Japanese deer (FE)

Cervus tarandus reindeer (NS/FE)

Circus aeruginosus marsh harrier (SP/BI)

Citellus undulatus arctic ground squirrel/Siberian souslik (NS/BI/FE)

Cricetus cricetus common hamster (AS/SP/BI/FE)

Cygnus cygnus whooper swan (SP/BI)

Dicrostonyx torquatus arctic lemming (NS)

Dryocopus martius black woodpecker (SP/BI/FE)

Enhyra lutris Kamchatka beaver (FE)

Equus hemionus kulan/Asian wild ass (FE)

Eumentopias Stelleri sea-lion (NS/FE)

Eutamias sibiricus Siberian chipmunk (AS/SP/BI/FE)

Ealco columbarius merlin (NS/SP/BI/FE)

Falco peregrinus peregrine (NS/SP/BI/FE)

Falco tinnunculus kestrel (SP)

Falco vesperinus hawk (SP)

Felis irbis irbis/panther (FE)

Felis lynx lynx (SP/BI/FE)

Felis manul wild cat (AS/BI/FE)

Felis tigris altaica Amur tiger (FE)

Foetorius altaicus ermine (SP/BI)

Foetorius altaicus sibiricus polecat (SP/BI)

Foetorius vulgaris weasel (SP/BI)

Fulica atra coot (SP/BI/FE)

Gallinago gallinago common snipe (SP/BI/FE)

Gavia arctica black-throated diver/loon (BI)

Gavia stellata red-throated diver/loon (SP/BI)

Gazella subgutturosa goitred gazelle (AS)

Grus cinerea grey crane (SP)

Grus grus common crane (SP/BI/FE)

Grus leucogeranus Siberian white crane (NS/SP/FE)

Gulo gulo wolverine/glutton (SP/BI/FE)

Gypaetus barbatus L. lammergeyer (AS)

Haematopus ostralegus oystercatcher (SP/BI/FE)

Lagomis alpinus rat hare (FE)

Lagopus lagopus willow grouse/ptarmigan (NS/SP/FE)

Larus argentatus herring gull (BI/FE)

Larus canus common gull (BI/FE)

Larus ridibundus black-headed gull (BI/FE)

Lemmus obensis Siberian lemming (NS/SP)

Lepus timidus arctic hare (NS/BI/FE)

Lepus variabilis polar hare (NS)

Lutra vulgaris otter (BI/FE)

Marmota camtschatica Kamchatka marmot (FE)

Marmota sibirica Siberian marmot (AS/SP/BI)

Martes zibellina sable (SP/BI/FE)

Melanitta deglandi American black scoter (BI)

Melanocorypha mongolica Mongolian lark (BI/FE)

Meles meles Eurasian badger (AS/BI/FE)

Microtus hyperboreus sub-arctic vole (NS/SP/FE)

Moschus moschiferus musk deer (AS/BI/FE)

Mustela erminea ermine (NS/AS/SP/ BI/FE)

Mustela eversmanni steppe polecat (AS/SP/BI/FE)

Mustela nivalis common weasel (NS/SP/BI/FE)

Mustela sibirica kolonok (FE)

Myodes torquatus/obensis Ob lemming (NS)

Nucifraga caryocatactes nutcracker (AS/SP/BI/FE)

Nyctea scandiaca snowy owl (NS)

Ochotona alpina Altai pika (AS)

Oenanthe isabellina Isabelline wheatear (AS/SP/BI)

Omul baikalensis omul (BI)

Otaria ursina sea bear (NS/FE)

Otis tarda bustard (SP/BI)

Ovis ammon argalis (sheep) (AS)

Ovis argali arkhar (AS)

Ovis nivicola Siberian bighorn/snow sheep (FE)

Panthera pardus orientalis Amur leopard (FE)

Panthera tigris altaica Siberian/Amur tiger (FE)

Panthera uncia snow leopard (AS)

Perdix perdix grey partridge (AS/SP/BI/FE)

Perisoreus infaustus Siberian jay (BI/FE)

Phalacrocorax carbo great cormorant (BI/FE)

Phoca barbata groenlandica seal (NS/FE)

Phoca baicalensis Baikal seal (BI)

Phocaena orca dolphin (NS/FE)

Picoides tridactylus three-toed woodpecker (SP/BI/FE)

Plectophenax nivalis snow bunting (NS)

Podiceps auritus Slavonian/horned grebe (AS/BI)

Podiceps cristatus great crested grebe (AS/SP/BI)

Procapra gutturosa Mongolian gazelle (FE)

Pteromys volans Siberian flying squirrel (SP/BI/FE)

Rangifer tarandus reindeer/caribou (NS/BI/FE)

Ranodon sibiricus five-toed triton (AS/SP)

Rufibrenta ruficollis red-breasted goose (NS)

Salpingotus crassicauda pygmy jerboa (SP/AS)

Sciurus vulgaris red squirrel (SP/BI/AS/FE)

Spermophilus eversmanni Siberian marmot (BI)

Spermophilus undulatus arctic ground squirrel (FE)

Sterna hirundo common tern (BI/FE)

Strix nebulosa great grey owl (SP/BI/FE)

Surnia ulula hawk owl (SP/BI/FE)

Sus scrofa wild boar (AS/BI/FE)

Tadorna ferruginea ruddy shelduck (SP/BI/FE)

Tamias striatus striped squirrel (BI)

Tetrao urogallus capercaillie (SP/BI/FE)

Tetrao parvirostris black-billed capercaillie (BI/FE)

Tetraogallus himalayanensis Himalayan snowcock (AS)

Tetraogallus altaicus Altai snowcock (AS)

Tetrastes bonasia hazel grouse (SP/BI/FE)

Turdus sibiricus Siberian thrush (SP/BI/FE)

Uria aalge guillemot (NS/FE)

Ursus arctus bear (SP/FE)

Ursus maritimus polar bear (NS)

Ursus tibetanus Tibet bear (FE)

Vulpes vulpes red fox (AS/SP/BI/FE)

APPENDIX D: BIBLIOGRAPHY

Baedeker, Karl *Russia with Teheran, Port Arthur and Peking* (Leipzig 1914)
Barzini, Luigi *Peking to Paris. A Journey across Two Continents* (London 1907)
Byron, Robert *First Russia Then Tibet* (London 1933)
Collins, Perry McDonough *A Voyage down the Amoor* (New York 1860)
De Windt, Harry *Siberia as it is* (London 1892)
Des Cars J and Caracalla, JP *Le Transsiberien* (1986)
Dmitriev-Mamonov, AI and Zdziarski, AF *Guide to the Great Siberian
    Railway 1900* (St Petersburg 1900)
Fleming, HM and Price JH *Russian Steam Locomotives* (London 1960)
Gowing, LF *Five Thousand Miles in a Sledge* (London 1889)
Heywood AJ & Button IDC *Soviet Locomotive Types* (London/Malmo 1994)
Hill, SS *Travels in Siberia* (London 1854)
Hollingsworth, JB *The Atlas of Train Travel* (London 1980)
An Official Guide to Eastern Asia Vol 1: Manchuria & Chosen (Tokyo 1913)
Jefferson, RL *Awheel to Moscow and Back* (London 1895)
Jefferson, RL *Roughing it in Siberia* (London 1897)
Jefferson, RL *A New Ride to Khiva* (London 1899)
Johnson, Henry *The Life of Kate Marsden* (London 1895)
Kennan, George *Siberia and the Exile System* (London 1891)
Lansdell, Henry *Through Siberia* (London 1883)
Levin, MG and Potapov, LP *The Peoples of Siberia* (Chicago 1964)
Macaulay, Lord *History of England from the Accession of James II*
Manley, Deborah *The Trans-Siberian Railway* (London 1988)
Marsden, Kate *On Sledge and Horseback to Outcast Siberian Lepers* (London 1895)
Meakin, Annette *A Ribbon of Iron* (London 1901)
Massie, RK *Nicholas and Alexandra* (London 1967)
Murray *Handbook for Russia, Poland and Finland* (London 1865)
Newby, Eric *The Big Red Train Ride* (London 1978)
Pifferi, Enzo *Le Transsiberien*
Poulsen, J and Kuranow, W *Die Transsibirische Eisenbahn* (Malmo 1986)
St George, George *Siberia: the New Frontier* (London 1969)
Shoemaker, MM *The Great Siberian Railway – St Petersburg to Peking* (London 1903)
Theroux, Paul *The Great Railway Bazaar* (London 1975)
Thubron, Colin *In Siberia* (Penguin 2000)
Tupper, Harmon *To the Great Ocean* (London 1965)

APPENDIX E: PHRASE LISTS

English-speaking travellers are unforgivably lazy when it comes to learning other people's languages. As with virtually every country in the world, it's possible to just about get by in Russia, Mongolia and China on a combination of English and sign language. English is spoken by tourist guides and some hotel staff but most of the local people you meet on the train will be eager to communicate with you and unable to speak English. Unless you enjoy charades it's well worth learning a few basic phrases in advance. Not only will this make communication easier but it will also earn you the respect of local people. You might even consider evening classes before you go, or teaching yourself with books and cassettes from your local library.

The sections here highlight only a few useful words. It's well worth also taking along phrasebooks: Lonely Planet's pocket-sized phrasebooks in Russian, Mongolian and Chinese are recommended.

Russian

CYRILLIC ALPHABET AND PRONUNCIATION GUIDE

It is vital to spend the few hours it takes to master the Cyrillic alphabet before you go, otherwise you'll have trouble deciphering the names of streets, metro stations and, most important, the names of stations along the Trans-Siberian and Trans-Mongolian routes (Mongolian also uses a modified Cyrillic script).

The Cyrillic alphabet is derived from the Greek. It was introduced in Russia in the 10th century via a translation of the Bible made by two Greek bishops, Cyril (who gave his name to the new alphabet) and Methodius.

Cyrillic letter	Roman equiv	Pronunciation*	Cyrillic letter	Roman equiv	Pronunciation*
А а	a	father	П п	p	Peter
Б б	b	bet	Р р	r	Russia
В в	v	vodka	С с	s	Samarkand
Г г	g	get	Т т	t	time
Д д	d	dog	У у	u, oo	fool
Е е	ye	yet (unstressed: year)	Ф ф	f, ph	fast
Ё ё	yo	yoghurt	Х х	kh	loch
Ж ж	zh	treasure	Ц ц	ts	lots
З з	z	zebra	Ч ч	ch	chilly
И и	i, ee	seek, year	Ш ш	sh	show
Й й	y	boy	Щ щ	shch	fresh chips
К к	k	kit	Ы ы	y, i	did
Л л	l	last	ь	(softens preceding letter)	
М м	m	Moscow	Э э	e	let
Н н	n	never	Ю ю	yu	union
О о	o	tore (unstressed: top)	Я я	ya	yard (unstressed: yearn)

* pronunciation shown by underlined letter/s

KEY PHRASES

The following phrases in Cyrillic script may be useful to point to if you're having problems communicating:

Please write it down for me Запишите это для меня, пожалуйста

Help me, please Помогите мне, пожалуйста

I need an interpreter Мне нужен переводчик с английского

CONVERSATIONAL RUSSIAN

Run the hyphenated syllables together as you speak and roll your 'R's:

General
Hello	*Zdrahz-tvooy-tyeh*
Good morning	*Doh-broyeh-ootro*
Good afternoon/evening	*Doh-bree-dyen/vyecher*
Please	*Pa-zhal-sta*
Do you speak English?	*Gava-ree-tyeh lee vy pa-an-glee-skee?*
No/Yes	*Nyet/da*
Thank you	*Spa-see-ba*
Excuse me (sorry)	*Eez-vee-nee-tyeh*
good/bad	*ha-ra-shaw/pla-hoy*
cheap/expensive	*de-sho-vee/da-ra-goy*
Wait a minute!	*Ad-noo mee-noo-too!*
Please call a doctor	*Vy za-vee-tyeh, pa-zhal-sta, vra-cha*
Goodbye	*Das-vee-dah-nya*

Directions
map	*kar-ta/skhe-ma*
Where is ...?	*G'dyeh...?*
hotel	*ga-stee-nee-tsa*
airport	*a-eh-ro-port/a-eh-ro-drom*
bus station	*stant-si-ya ahf-toh-boosa*
metro/taxi	*mi-tro/tak-see*
tram/trolley-bus	*tram-vai/tro-ley-boos*
restaurant/café	*r-sta-rahn/ka-fyeh*
museum/shop	*moo-zyey/ma-ga-zyeen*
bakery/grocer's	*boo-lotch-naya/gas-tra-nohm*
box office (theatre)	*te-ah-trahl-naya kassa*
lavatory (ladies/gents)	*too-a-lyet (zhen-ski/moozh-skoy)*
open/closed	*aht-kri-ta/za-kri-ta*
left/right	*na-prah-va/na-lyeh-va*

Numerals
1 *adeen*; 2 *dvah*; 3 *tree*; 4 *chetiri*; 5 *pyaht*; 6 *shest*; 7 *syem*; 8 *vosyem*; 9 *dyeh-vyet*; 10 *dyeh-syet*; 11 *adeenatsat*; 12 *dvenatsat*; 13 *treenatsat*; 14 *chetirnatsat*; 15 *pyatnatsat*; 16 *shest-natsat*; 17 *semnatsat*; 18 *vasemnatsat*; 19 *dyevyet-natsat*; 20 *dvadsat*; 30 *treedsat*; 40 *sorok*; 50 *pidisyat*; 60 *shizdisyat*; 70 *syem-deset*; 80 *vosyem-deset*; 90 *devya-nosta*; 100 *sto*; 200 *dveh-stee*; 300 *tree-sta*; 400 *chetiri-sta*; 500 *pyatsot*; 600 *shestsot*; 700 *semsot*; 800 *vosemsot*; 900 *devetsot*; 1000 *teesacha*.

How much/many?	*skolka?*
rouble/roubles	*roobl (1), rooblyah (2-4), rooblyey (5+)*
Please write down the price	*Na-pee-shee-tyeh, pa-zhal-sta, tseh-noo*

ticket	*beel-yet*
1st/2nd/3rd Class	*perviy/ftoroy/treh*tyi class
express	*ekspres*
What time is it?	*katori chas?*
hours/minutes	*chasof/meenoot*
today	*sevodnya*
yesterday/tomorrow	*fcherah/zahftra*
Monday/Tuesday	*pa-ni-dyel-nik/ftor-nik*
Wednesday/Thursday	*sri-da/chit-vehrk*
Friday/Saturday	*pyat-nit-sah/soo-boh-ta*
Sunday	*vas-kreh-sen-ya*

Food and drink

menu	*min-yoo*
mineral water	*mee-nee-rahl-naya va-da*
fruit juice	*sok*
vodka/whisky	*vodka/veeskee*
beer	*peeva*
wine/cognac	*veenoh/kan-yahk*
champagne	*sham-pahn-ska-yeh*
Cheers!	*Zah vah-sheh zda-ro-vyeh!*
caviare	*eek-ry*
salmon/sturgeon	*syom-ga/ah-syo-tra*
chicken/duck	*tsy-plyon-ka/oot-ka*
steak/roast beef	*bifshteks/rostbif*
pork	*sveeneena*
veal	*telyahtina*
ham/sausage	*vichinah/kalbahsa*
bread/potatoes	*khlyep/kartoshka*
butter/cheese	*masla/syr*
eggs/omelette	*ya-eet-sa/ahmlet*
salt/pepper	*sol/perets*
tea/coffee	*chai/kohfyeh*
milk/sugar	*malako/sakhar*
bill	*shchot*

Questions and answers

What's your name?	*Kahk vahs zavoot?*
My name is....	*Minyah zavoot....*
I'm from	*Yah preeyekhal eez....*
Britain/USA	*Anglee/Sa-Sha-Ah*
Canada/Australia	*Kanady/Avstralee*
New Zealand/Japan	*Novoy Zelandee/Yaponee*
Sweden/Finland	*Shvetsee/Finlandee*
Norway/Denmark	*Narvegee/Danee*
Germany/Austria	*Germanee/Avstree*
France/Netherlands	*Frantsee/Gollandee*

Opposite: Mongolia – see pp297-310. **Top:** On excursions from Ulan Bator accommodation is often in gers (yurts). **Bottom left:** Mongolians have long been famous for their riding skills. Riding holidays for visitors are easy to organize; bring a hard hat if you're worried about falling off. **Bottom right:** A tour guide models traditional Halkh Mongolian clothing at the Elstei Ger Camp. (Photos © Nick Hill).

Where are you going?	*Kudah viy idyotyeh?*
I'm going to...	*Yah eedoo...*
Are you married?	*Viy zhenahty* (m)/*zamoozhnyaya* (f)?
Have you any children?	*Yest-li oo vas dyeh-ti?*
boy/girl	*mahlcheek/dyehvushka*
How old are you?	*Skolka vahm lyet?*
What do you do?	*Shto viy dyelayetyeh?*
student	*studyent* (m), *studyentka* (f)
teacher	*ucheetyel* (m), *ucheetyelneetsa* (f)
doctor/nurse	*vrach/myed-sistra*
actor/artist	*aktyor/khudozhneek*
engineer/lawyer	*eenzhenyehr/advokaht*
office worker	*slu-zhash-chi*
Where do you live?	*Gdyeh viy zhivyotyeh?*

RAILWAY DICTIONARY (Словарь железнодорожных терминов)

Ticket window
for tickets after 24 hours	касса
	предварительная касса
for tickets within 24 hours	в день отправления касса
	текущая продажа билетов
working from 08.00 to 20.00	часы работы с 8 до 20
open 24 hours	круглосуточная касса
break from 13.00 to 14.00	перерыв 13 до 14
technical break from 10.15 to 10.45	технический перерыв 10.15 до 10.45

Timetable
	расписание
even days (ie 2, 4, 6, ... of May)	Чет. (четным числам)
odd days (ie 1, 3, 5, ... of May)	Неч. (по нечетным числам)
weekends and public holidays	вых (по выходным)
weekdays	раб (по рабочим дням)
departure	От. (отправление)
arrival	Пр. (прибытие)
platform	Пл. (платформа)
station of destination	станция назначения

Train
	поезд
fast train	скорый поезд
transit train	транзитный поезд
passenger train	пассажирский поезд
suburban train	пригородный поезд
deluxe express train	фирменный поезд
train is late	поезд опаздывает
train does not stop	поезд не останавливается
train does not stop at the station	поезд не заходит на станцию

Station
	вокзал, станция
station master	начальник вокзала
station attendant	дежурный по станции
information	справка

Opposite Top: Tiananmen Gate, Beijing (see p316), the main entrance to the Forbidden City. (Photo © Nick Hill). **Bottom:** The Moscow-Beijing railway line passes under the Great Wall at Badaling.

Carriage
SV (1st/soft), 2-berth compartments

kupé (coupé/2nd/hard), 4-berth
open sleeping carriage
open sitting carriage
wagon which separates and joins
  another train part way through
  the journey

вагон
СВ (спальный вагон)
  (or) мягкий вагон
    купейный вагон
плацкартный вагон
общий вагон
безпересадочный вагон
  (or) отцепной вагон

Ticket
one way
return
adult (full) fare
child fare
berth number
upper berth
lower berth
pass such as a monthly pass
discount ticket (pensioners, students etc)
price zones

билет
туда
туда и обратно
полный
детский
место
верхнее место
нижнее место
проездной билет
льготный билет
зона

Time
Moscow time
local time

время
московское время
местное время

On the train
Train Captain (head conductor)

conductor
emergency stop handle
baggage rack
blankets
sheets
rolled-up mattress and pillow

на поезде
начальник поезда, начальник
  бригады проводников
проводник, проводница
стоп-кран
багажная полка
одеяло
белье
постельные принадлежности

Useful railway expressions
Here is my ticket
Please show me my place
Please wake me at ....
Please wake me an hour before
  we arrive at ....
Where is the restaurant car or
  buffet car?
Where is the toilet?
May I smoke here?
Please bring me a (another) blanket

What is the next station?
How many minutes will the
  train stop here?
I am late for the train

Полезные железнодорожные выражения
Вот мой билет
Покажите, пожалуйста, мое место
Разбудите меня в ...... часов
Разбудите меня, пожалуйста, за
  час до прибытия в ....
Где находится вагон-ресторан
  или буфет?
Где находится туалет?
Здесь можно курить?
Принесите, пожалуйста, (еще одно)
  одеяло
Какая следующая станция?
Сколько минут стоянка поезда?

Я опоздал на поезд

Mongolian

Westerners tend to have difficulty mastering the tricky pronunciation of the national language of Mongolia. Until very recently, Mongolian was written in the same script as Russian (see p430), with two additional characters: θ (pronounced 'o') and Y ('u'). When Mongolian is transliterated into Roman script, stress is indicated by doubling the vowels. You will see Ulan Bator written as 'Ulaanbaatar' to show that the first 'a' in each word is stressed.

Hello	*Sayn bayna uu*
Thank you	*Bayar-lalaar*
Yes/No	*Teem/Ugu-i*
Sorry	*Ooch-laarai*
I don't understand	*Bi oilgokh-gu-i bayna*
What's your name?	*Tani ner khen beh?*
Where do you live?	*Th khaana ami-dardag beh?*
Goodbye	*Bayar-tai*
Where is ...?	*Khaana bayna veh....?*
hotel/airport	*zochid buudal/nisyeh ongotsni buudal*
railway station/bus station	*galt teregniy buudal/avtobusni zogsool*
temple/museum	*sum/moosei*
lavatory	*zhorlon*
left	*zuun*
right	*baruun*
soup	*shol*
egg	*ondog*
mutton	*honini makh*
rice	*budaar*
noodles	*goimon*
bread	*talh*
cheese	*byaslag*
potato	*toms*
tomato	*ulaan lool*
tea	*tsai*
coffee	*kofee*
beer	*peevo*
fermented mare's milk	*airag*
How much?	*Khed?*
cheap	*khyamd*
expensive	*kheterhiy unetiy yum*

1 *neg*; 2 *khoyor*; 3 *gurav*; 4 *doroy*; 5 *tav;* 6 *zurgaar*; 7 *doloo*; 8 *naym*; 9 *ee-us*; 10 *arav*; 11 *arvan neg*; 12 *arvan khoyor*; 13 *arvan gurav*; 14 *arvan dorov*; 15 *arvan tav*; 20 *khori*; 21 *khori neg*; 30 *guchin*; 31 *guchin neg*; 40 *doch*; 50 *tavi*; 60 *zhar*; 70 *dal*; 80 *naya*; 90 *er*; 100 *zuu*; 200 *khoyor zuu*; 1000 *neg myanga*.

Chinese

The phrases below aim to give some assistance but a phrase book really is a necessity. Better still, if you have some time in hand before you depart for China, try to learn a little Chinese, either through lessons or a language tape. At least you will have a starting point, and the effort you have made, even to learn to say 'hello', will be appreciated.

The problem with Chinese is one of pronunciation – so much depends on your tone and emphasis that if you do not get the sound exactly right you will not be understood at all. The country's main dialect is Mandarin, spoken by about three quarters of the population. Mandarin has four tones: high tone (–), rising (/) where the voice starts low and rises to the same level as the high tone, falling-rising (ˇ) where the voice starts with a middle tone, falls and then rises to just below a high tone; and falling (\) which starts at the high tone and falls to a low one.

READING PINYIN CHINESE

Pinyin is the system of transliterating Chinese into the Roman alphabet. Pronunciation is indicated by the underlined letters below:

Vowels

a as in f<u>ar</u>
e as in w<u>e</u>re
i as in tr<u>ee</u> or as in
  w<u>e</u>re after c,r,s,z,ch,sh,zh

o as in <u>or</u>
u as in p<u>oo</u>h
ü as in c<u>ue</u>

Consonants

c as in ea<u>ts</u>
q as in <u>ch</u>eap
r as in t<u>r</u>ill
x as in <u>sh</u>eep

h as in lo<u>ch</u> or the <u>kh</u> in an Arabic word,
  with the sound from the back of the throat
z as in plo<u>ds</u>
zh as in <u>j</u>aw

KEY PHRASES

The following phrases in Chinese characters may be useful to point to if you're having problems communicating:

Please write it down for me	请 为 我 写 下 来
Help me please	请 帮 帮 我
Please call a doctor	请 叫 个 医 生 来

USEFUL WORDS AND PHRASES
General

Hello	*Ni hao*	你 好
Goodbye	*Zai jian*	再 见
Please	*Qing*	请
Do you speak English?	*Ni hui shuo ying yu ma?*	你 会 说 英 语 吗?
Yes/no	*Dui/Bu dui* (literally correct/incorrect)	对 / 不 对

No/Sorry, but no	*Mei you*	没 有
Thank you	*Xie xie*	谢 谢
Excuse me (sorry)	*Dui bu qi*	对 不 起
Excuse me (may I have your attention?)	*Qing wen*	请 问
Good/bad	*Hao/bu hao*	好 / 不 好
I understand/do not understand	*Wo dong le/wo bu dong*	我 懂 了 / 我 不 懂
UK/USA	Ying guo/Mei guo	英 国 / 美 国
Canada/Australia	Jia na da/Ao da lia	加 拿 大 / 澳 大 利 亚
France/Netherlands/Germany	Fa guo/He lan/De guo	法 国 / 荷 兰 / 德 国
China	Zhongguo	中 国
Foreigner	Wai guo ren/Guilo	外 国 人 / 鬼 佬
Translator	Fan yi	翻 译

Directions

Where is...?	Zai nar...?	在 哪 儿 ?
Toilet (ladies/gents)	ce suo (nu/nan)	厕 所
Telephone	dian hua	电 话
Airport	ji chang	机 场
Bus station	che zhan	长 途 汽 车 站
Train	huoche	火 车
Railway station	huo che zhan	火 车 站
Taxi	chu zu qi che	出 租 汽 车
Museum	bo wu guan	博 物 馆
Hotel/restaurant	fan dian	饭 店
Guesthouse	binguan	宾 馆
Post office	you ju	邮 局
PSB/CAAC office	Gong an ju/Zhong hang gongsi	公 安 局 / 中 航 公 司
What time will we arrive at...?	Lie che shenme shi jian dao...?	列 车 什 么 时 候 到 ?
What station is this?	Zhe shi na yi zhan?	这 是 哪 一 站 ?
North	Bei	北
South	Nan	南
East	Dong	东
West	Xi	西

Street names

Many of the street names throughout China are similar. In most of the cities you visit, for example, you will find a Renmin Lu (People's St) and Jiefang Lu (Liberation St). You will also discover that streets are named (usually) according to a system which divides them into sections: north, centre, south etc. Thus if the thoroughfare of the city is Renmin Lu, and it runs from east to west, it may well have three (or more) separate names: Renmin Rd West – Renmin Xilu, Renmin Rd Centre – Renmin Zhonglu, Renmin Rd East – Renmin Donglu. By way of an indication, the designation that is given to a particular avenue also indicates its size. Roughly the following equate to English terminology:

Street	Lu	路	Road	Jie, Dajie	街 , 大 街	Lane	Qiang	巷

Numbers

1	一	*yi*	18	十八	*shi ba*
2	二	*er*	19	十九	*shi jiu*
3	三	*san*	20	二十	*er shi*
4	四	*si*	21	二十一	*er shi yi*
5	五	*wu*	30	三十	*san shi*
6	六	*liu*	40	四十	*si shi*
7	七	*qi*	50	五十	*wu shi*
8	八	*ba*	100	一百	*yi bai*
9	九	*jiu*	101	一百零一	*yi bai ling yi*
10	十	*shi*	110	一百一十	*yi bai yi shi*
11	十一	*shi yi*	150	一百五十	*yi bai wu shi*
12	十二	*shi er*	200	二百	*er bai*
13	十三	*shi san*	500	五百	*wu bai*
14	十四	*shi si*	1000	一千	*yi qian*
15	十五	*shi wu*	10,000	一万	*yi wan*
16	十六	*shi liu*	100,000	十万	*shi wan*
17	十七	*shi qi*	1 million	一百万	*yi bai wan*

How much?	*Duo shao qian?*	多少钱
That's too expensive	*Tai gui le*	太贵了

Time

One o'clock,two o'clock...	*Yi dian, er dian...*	一点，二点
Ten past one (1.10)	*Yi dian shi fen*	一点十分
Quarter to two (1.45)	*Yi dian si shi wu fen*	一点四十五分
Two thirty (2.30)	*Er dian ban*	二点半
Monday/Tuesday/Wednesday	*Xing qi...yi/er/san*	星期一/星期二/星期三
Thursday/Friday/Saturday	*Xing qi...si/wu/liu*	星期四/星期五/星期六
Sunday	*Xing qi ri*	星期日
Yesterday/tomorrow/today	*zuo tian/ming tian/jin tian*	昨天/明天/今天

Transport

ticket	*piao*	票
Hard seat/Soft seat	*Ying Zuo/Luan Zuo*	硬座/软座
Hard sleeper/soft sleeper	*Ying Wo/Luan Wo*	硬卧/软卧
Please may I upgrade this ticket...	*Qing ni huan gao yi ji de piao*	请你换高一级的票

Food and drink

menu	*cai dan*	菜单
Mineral water/tea/beer	*kuang quan shui/cha/pi jiu*	矿泉水/茶/啤酒
noodles/noodle soup	*mian/tang mian*	面/汤面
bread/egg	*mian bao/ji dian*	面包/鸡蛋
pork/beef/lamb	*zhu rou/niu rou/yang rou*	猪肉/牛肉/羊肉
chicken/duck/fish	*ji/ya/yu*	鸡/鸭/鱼
vegetables	*shu cai*	蔬菜

Do you have any vegetarian dishes?	*Ni zher you su-cai ma?*	你这儿有蔬菜吗?
steamed rice	*mi fan*	米饭
fujian fried rice	*fu jian chao fan*	福建炒饭
fried rice	*ji chao fan*	鸡蛋炒饭
pork in Sichuan-style sauce	*yu xiang rou si*	鱼香肉丝
sweet & sour pork	*gu lao zhu rou*	咕老(猪)肉
pork and onion in soy sauce	*hui guo rou*	回锅肉
pork in sweet thick sauce	*tang cu liji*	糖醋里脊
beef chow mien	*niu rou chao mian*	牛肉炒面
spicy beef soup with veg	*shui zhu niu rou*	水煮牛肉
chicken in Sichuan sauce	*yu xian ba kuai ji*	鱼香八块鸡
chicken chow mien	*ji rou chao mian*	鸡肉炒面
chicken with cashew nuts	*yao guo ji ding*	腰果鸡丁
fried tofu with meat and veg	*jia chang doufu*	家常豆腐
green beanshoots	*dou miao*	豆苗
vegetable chow mien	*su chao mian*	素炒面
hot and sour soup	*suan la tang*	酸辣汤
Delicious	*Hao chi*	好吃
Cheers!	*Gang bei!*	干杯!

INDEX

UPDATE – 2004

Thanks to the numerous readers who have written with updated information, in particular: Olga Belnik (Russia), Jim Gill (Australia), Julia Fitzgerald, Andy Jones (China). Please note that the information reproduced here has not been verified by me. To contact me with further updates, comments or recommendations please write to Bryn Thomas c/o Trailblazer (address on p2) or email me at bryn@trailblazer-guides.com. If we can use your information you'll be sent a free copy of the next edition.

Page 13 – Internet resources
A useful website for visa information and general travel to Russia is **www.waytorussia.net** although it is a commercial site. For a list of Russian embassies around the world try **www.russianembassy.net**.

Page 25 – Making a booking: private trip by Great Rail Journeys
A luxurious Trans-Siberian journey is planned by Great Rail Journeys Ltd (☎ 01904-521920, 🖳 www.greatrail.com), Saviour House, 9 St Saviourgate, York YO1 8NL. This excellent rail-holiday specialist is organizing a 21-day trip on a specially-chartered private train for departure on 11 May 2005 from London Waterloo crossing Europe and Russia to Vladivostok, a journey of almost 8000 miles. The cost will be approximately £4500; contact Great Rail Journeys for more information.

Page 33 – Making a booking from Australia
Note change of tel/fax numbers for The Travel Directors: ☎ 08-9242 4200; 🖹 08-9242 5366.

Page 38 – Monkey Business (Beijing)
Given the development that is taking place in the area near the Monkey Business Infocenter there is a chance that the office may have to be relocated. Although the bars and school across the road have been knocked down, the Hidden Bar has escaped and the Infocenter should still be operating from here until the end of the summer at least – and it may not even have to move. If you're travelling with Monkey Business, check the latest situation on their website: 🖳 **www.monkeyshrine.com**.

For 2004 Monkey Business have introduced packages to Ulan Ude and Lake Baikal homestays at the village of Bolshoe Goloustnoe rather than the increasingly touristy Listvyanka. They also have day trips to Ust Orda and camping trips to Olkhon Island, a national park island in Lake Baikal.

Prices for their most popular packages are currently quoted in euros on their website: €335 (€555 deluxe class) for the Trans-Mongolian Beijing–Moscow or €390 (€630 deluxe class) for Moscow–Beijing; €380 (€600 deluxe class) for the Trans-Manchurian Beijing–Moscow or €440 (€680 deluxe class) for Moscow–Beijing. In Moscow they now also use *Hotel Zarya* (tel 482 2458; ulitsa Gostinichnaya 4/9) in the north of the city; nearest metro is Petrovsko-Razumovskaya.

Page 38 – Russian Embassy (Beijing): important tourist visa change
As from 12 April 2004, the Russian embassy in Beijing has changed the visa regulations for the issuing of tourist visas. From now on they will issue Russian tourist visas only to residents of China. To qualify as a resident you must have a Chinese green card (resident permit). It is not enough to have either a Chinese tourist or business visa.

Thus the rule that used to affect only German passport holders has been extended to all foreigners. They introduced a new and much longer application form for foreigners the week before and seemingly didn't like the extra work-load. No idea how long it will last as they must be getting sick of the peeved travellers turning up at their door, although they don't seem to care about the loss of revenue at all. As far as we can tell the regulation has not been extended to other Russian embassies in Asia. (Andy Jones, China).

Page 39 – Mongolian visa prices in Beijing
From 6th May 2004 only Chinese RMB are acceptable for payment for a visa. Surprisingly, the prices have actually gone down:

Single Entry / Exit Visa (Tourist visa for maximum 30 days)
¥250 Normal service (4 working days)
¥475 Express service (24 hours)

Transit visa for 48 hours transit
¥160 Normal service (4 working days)
¥295 Express service (24 hours)

Page 75 – Money
Exchange rates have not altered significantly. Current rates are now:

US$1	R29.08
UK£1	R51.05
Euro €1	R34.39
Aus $1	R19.98
Can $1	R20.86
China Y10	R35.11
Japan ¥100	R25.38
Mong T1000	R24.98
NZ$	R17.48
Sing$	R16.84

To get the latest rates of exchange visit www.oanda.com/convert/classic.

Page 169 – Intourist in Moscow
New address and phone number for Intourist Central Office:
13/1, Milyutinsky per., Moscow, 101990
Open: Monday to Friday from 9:30 am to 5:30 pm.
☎ 7 (095)923-5089
☎/🖷 7 (095) 923-8575
🖷 7 (095) 956-42-02
🖳 www.intourist.ru

Page 303 – Ulan Bator – Telephone cards
You can make international calls from the post office using a phonecard. To use a phonecard, however, is not quite as straightforward as it might seem. Scratch off the silver layer to reveal a code – don't let anyone see the code or they could use it before you do. Call the number on the card and you'll be asked (in English) for the code. Key it in and you'll be asked for another code but this is, in fact, just the last four digits of the original code. Key in the last four digits of the code again and then you can dial your international number.

Page 305 – Ulan Bator – Where to stay
I recommend the *LG Guesthouse* Bayangol district 3 th Khoroo, Teeverchdiin St (Lundaa Ganzaga) ☎ 976-11-328572. 🖳 LG@mbox.mn. It is about 5 minutes from the train station, 2 minutes from the huge food market and 10 minutes from the Gandan Monastery on foot.

There is email, laundry, phone, cheap excursions to Teralj, observatory etc and help with any problems (ie train tickets). It's $3 in a dorm and $5 for a double room. A woman called Bimba speaks perfect English and loves to help in any way. She helped make our time in Ulan Bator a magical one. (Julia Fitzgerald)

Page 418 – Timetables
The timetables are currently still reasonably accurate +/- half an hour in some cases. Train No 1 now leaves Vladivostok at 10:35 and arrives in Moscow at 16:43; Train No 2 leaves Moscow at 17:06 and reaches Vladivostok at 22:05. Train No 3 leaves Moscow at 21:57 and reaches Beijing at 14:31. Train No 10 now leaves Moscow at 23:24. Train No 20 now leaves Moscow at 23:53. Times for Train Nos 4, 9, 19, 263 and 264 are unchanged.

On the Internet, currently difficult to access are the Russian train timetables searchable by town at 🖳 parovoz.com/spravka/timetables.html, which also has an English version. A better option seems to be 🖳 www.poezda.net/train.htm, with timetables searchable by station, train number or end points (though you must use specific and sometimes curious transliterations for town names, e.g., Moskva, Pekin, Habarovsk, Blagovescen, Ulanbator).

❑ OTHER GUIDES FROM TRAILBLAZER

Adventure Cycling Handbook	1st mid 2005
Adventure Motorcycling Handbook	4th edn out now
Australia by Rail	4th edn out now
Azerbaijan	3rd edn June 2004
The Blues Highway – New Orleans to Chicago	2nd edn out now
China by Rail	2nd edn Sep 2004
Good Honeymoon Guide	2nd edn out now
Inca Trail, Cusco & Machu Picchu	2nd edn out now
Japan by Rail	1st edn out now
Kilimanjaro – a trekking guide	1st edn out now
The Med Guide	1st edn mid 2004
Nepal Mountaineering Guide	1st edn Sep 2004
New Zealand – Great Walks	1st edn out now
Norway's Arctic Highway	1st edn out now
Siberian BAM Guide – rail, rivers & road	2nd edn out now
The Silk Roads – a route and planning guide	1st end out now
Sahara Overland – a route and planning guide	2nd edn Sep 2004
Sahara Abenteuerhandbuch (German edition)	1st edn out now
South-East Asia – The Graphic Guide	1st edn out now
Tibet Overland – mountain biking & jeep touring	1st edn out now
Trans-Canada Rail Guide	3rd edn out now
Trans-Siberian Handbook	6th edn out now
Trekking in the Annapurna Region	4th edn Sep 2004
Trekking in the Everest Region	4th edn out now
Trekking in Corsica	1st edn out now
Trekking in the Dolomites	1st edn out now
Trekking in Ladakh	3rd edn July 2004
Trekking in the Moroccan Atlas	1st edn out now
Trekking in the Pyrenees	2nd edn out now
Tuva and Southern Siberia	1st edn mid 2005

UK Walking Guides – new 7-title series inc Coast to Coast, Cornwall Coast Path, Offa's Dyke, Pembrokeshire Coast Path, Pennine Way, South Downs Way, West Highland Way

For local stockists, guidebook updates or for credit card mail order sales (post-free) visit:
www.trailblazer-guides.com

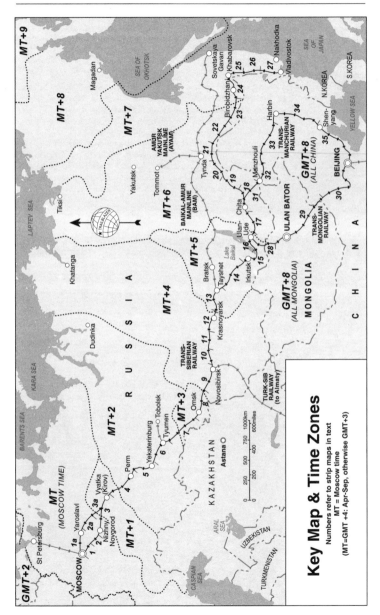

Key Map & Time Zones

Numbers refer to strip maps in text
MT = Moscow time
(MT=GMT +4: Apr-Sep, otherwise GMT+3)

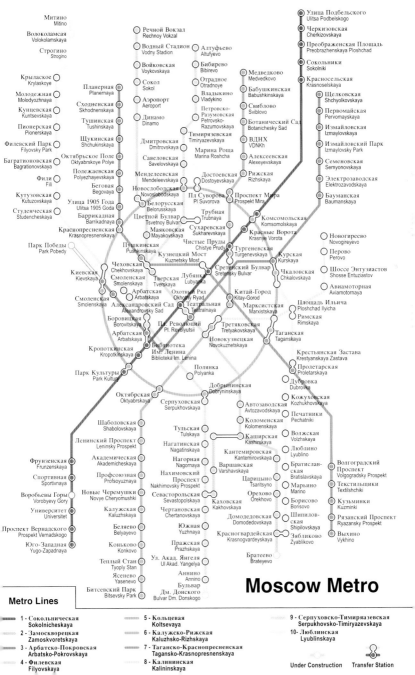

Moscow Metro

Митино
Mitino

Волоколамсая
Volokolamskaya

Строгино
Strogino

Крылаское
Krylaskoye

Молодежная
Molodyozhnaya

Кунцевская
Kuntsevskaya

Пионерская
Pionerskaya

Филевский Парк
Filyovsky Park

Багратионовская
Bagrationovskaya

Фили
Fili

Кутузовская
Kutuzovskaya

Студенческая
Studencheskaya

Планерная
Planernaya

Сходненская
Skhodnenskaya

Тушинская
Tushinskaya

Щукинская
Shchukinskaya

Октябрьское Поле
Oktyabrskoye Polye

Полежаевская
Polyezhayevskaya

Беговая
Begovaya

Улица 1905 Года
Ulitsa 1905 Goda

Баррикадная
Barrikadnaya

Краснопресненская
Krasnopresnenskaya

Парк Победы
Park Pobedy

Киевская
Kievskaya

Чеховская
Chekhovskaya

Смоленская
Smolenskaya

Арбатская
Arbatskaya

Смоленская
Smolenskaya

Боровицкая
Borovitskaya

Арбатская
Arbatskaya

Кропоткинская
Kropotkinskaya

Парк Культуры
Park Kultury

Фрунзенская
Frunzenskaya

Спортивная
Sportivnaya

Воробьевы Горы
Vorobyevy Gory

Университет
Universitet

Проспект Вернадского
Prospekt Vernadskogo

Юго-Западная
Yugo-Zapadnaya

Речной Вокзал
Rechnoy Vokzal

Водный Стадион
Vodny Stadion

Войковская
Voykovskaya

Сокол
Sokol

Аэропорт
Aeroport

Динамо
Dinamo

Дмитровская
Dmitrovskaya

Савеловская
Savelovskaya

Менделеевская
Mendeleevskaya

Новослободская
Novoslobodskaya

Белорусская
Belorusskaya

Цветной Бульвар
Tsvetnoy Bulvar

Маяковская
Mayakovskaya

Пушкинская
Pushkinskaya

Кузнецкий Мост
Kuznetsky Most

Тверская
Tverskaya

Охотный Ряд
Okhotny Ryad

Александровский Сад
Aleksandrovsky Sad

Театральная
Teatralnaya

Пл. Революции
Pl. Revolyutsii

Библиотека
Им. Ленина
Biblioteka Im. Lenina

Полянка
Polyanka

Октябрьская
Oktyabrskaya

Серпуховская
Serpukhovskaya

Шаболовская
Shabolovskaya

Ленинский Проспект
Leninsky Prospekt

Академическая
Akademicheskaya

Профсоюзная
Profsoyuznaya

Новые Черемушки
Novye Cheryomushki

Калужская
Kaluzhskaya

Беляево
Belyayevo

Коньково
Konkovo

Теплый Стан
Tyoply Stan

Ясенево
Yasenevo

Битцевский Парк
Bitsevsky Park

Алтуфьево
Altufyevo

Бибирево
Bibirevo

Отрадное
Otradnoye

Владыкино
Vladykino

Петровско-
Разумовская
Petrovsko-
Razumovskaya

Тимирязевская
Timiryazevskaya

Марина Роща
Marina Roshcha

Достоевская
Dostoyevskaya

Пл Суворова
Pl Suvorova

Трубная
Trubnaya

Сухаревская
Sukharevskaya

Чистые Пруды
Chistye Prudy

Тургеневская
Turgenevskaya

Сретенский Бульвар
Sretensky Bulvar

Лубянка
Lubyanka

Китай-Город
Kitay-Gorod

Марксистская
Marksistskaya

Третьяковская
Tretyakovskaya

Новокузнецкая
Novokuznetskaya

Таганская
Taganskaya

Добрынинская
Dobryninskaya

Тульская
Tulskaya

Нагатинская
Nagatinskaya

Нагорная
Nagornaya

Нахимовский
Проспект
Nakhimovsky Prospekt

Севастопольская
Sevastopolskaya

Чертановская
Chertanovskaya

Южная
Yuzhnaya

Пражская
Prazhskaya

Ул. Акад. Янгеля
Ul Akad. Yangelya

Аннино
Annino

Бульвар
Дм. Донского
Bulvar Dm. Donskogo

Медведково
Medvedkovo

Бабушкинская
Babushkinskaya

Свиблово
Sviblovo

Ботанический Сад
Botanichesky Sad

ВДНХ
VDNKh

Алексеевская
Alexeyevskaya

Рижская
Rizhskaya

Проспект Мира
Prospekt Mira

Комсомольская
Komsomolskaya

Красные Ворота
Krasnye Vorota

Курская
Kurskaya

Чкаловская
Chkalovskaya

Площадь Ильича
Ploshchad Ilyicha

Римская
Rimskaya

Крестьянская Застава
Krestyanskaya Zastava

Пролетарская
Proletarskaya

Дубровка
Dubrovka

Кожуховская
Kozhukhovskaya

Печатники
Pechatniki

Волжская
Volzhskaya

Люблино
Lyublino

Братислав-
ская
Bratislavskaya

Марьино
Marino

Борисово
Borisovo

Шипилов-
ская
Shipilovskaya

Зябликово
Zyablikovo

Автозаводская
Avtozavodskaya

Коломенская
Kolomenskaya

Каширская
Kashirskaya

Кантемировская
Kantemirovskaya

Варшавская
Varshavskaya

Царицыно
Tsaritsyno

Орехово
Orekhovo

Каховская
Kakhovskaya

Домодедовская
Domodedovskaya

Красногвардейская
Krasnogvardeyskaya

Братеево
Brateyevo

Улица Подбельского
Ulitsa Podbelskogo

Черкизовская
Cherkizovskaya

Преображенская Площадь
Preobrazhenskaya Ploshchad

Сокольники
Sokolniki

Красносельская
Krasnoselskaya

Щелковская
Shchyolkovskaya

Первомайская
Pervomayskaya

Измайловская
Izmaylovskaya

Измайловский Парк
Izmaylovsky Park

Семеновская
Semyonovskaya

Электрозаводская
Elektrozavodskaya

Бауманская
Baumanskaya

Новогиреево
Novogireyevo

Перово
Perovo

Шоссе Энтузиастов
Shosse Entuziastov

Авиамоторная
Aviamotornaya

Волгоградский
Проспект
Volgogradsky Prospekt

Текстильщики
Tekstilshchiki

Кузьминки
Kuzminki

Рязанский Проспект
Ryazansky Prospekt

Выхино
Vykhino

Metro Lines

1 - Сокольническая
Sokolnicheskaya

2 - Замоскворецкая
Zamoskvoretskaya

3 - Арбатско-Покровская
Arbatsko-Pokrovskaya

4 - Филевская
Filyovskaya

5 - Кольцевая
Koltsevaya

6 - Калужско-Рижская
Kaluzhsko-Rizhskaya

7 - Таганско-Краснопресненская
Tagansko-Krasnopresnenskaya

8 - Калининская
Kalininskaya

9 - Серпуховско-Тимиряязевская
Serpukhovsko-Timiryazevskaya

10- Люблинская
Lyublinskaya

Under Construction   Transfer Station

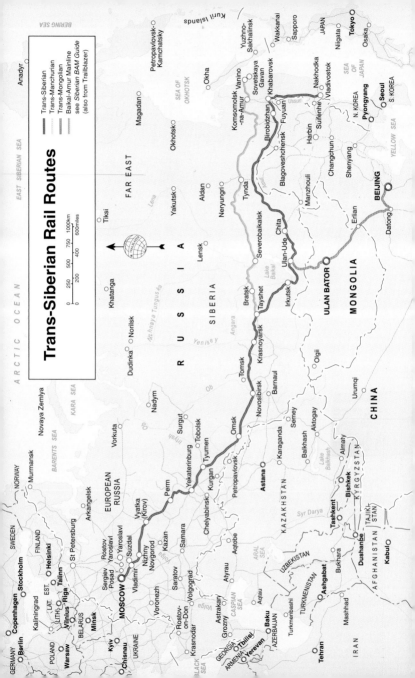